Baseball

Baseball

The Turbulent Midcentury Years

Steven P. Gietschier

UNIVERSITY OF NEBRASKA PRESS · *Lincoln*

Manufactured in the United States of America.

The University of Nebraska Press is part of a land-grant institution with campuses and programs on the past, present, and future homelands of the Pawnee, Ponca, Otoe-Missouria, Omaha, Dakota, Lakota, Kaw, Cheyenne, and Arapaho Peoples, as well as those of the relocated Ho-Chunk, Sac and Fox, and Iowa Peoples.

∞

Library of Congress Cataloging-in-Publication Data
Names: Gietschier, Steven Philip, 1948– author.
Title: Baseball: the turbulent midcentury years / Steven P. Gietschier.
Description: Lincoln: University of Nebraska Press, [2023] | Includes bibliographical references and index.
Identifiers: LCCN 2022034428
ISBN 9781496235374 (hardback)
ISBN 9781496236050 (epub)
ISBN 9781496236067 (pdf)
Subjects: LCSH: Baseball—United States—History—20th century. | Baseball—Social aspects—United States—History—20th century. | Baseball players—United States—Biography.
Classification: LCC GV863.A1 G53 2023 |
DDC 796.357—dc23/eng/20220811
LC record available at https://lccn.loc.gov/2022034428

Set in Quadraat by A. Shahan.

To my picked nine:
Donna, Katie, Sarah,
Jason, Justin,
Andy, Patrick, Joey, and Max

I prefer turbulent progress
rather than quiet stagnation.

—**Branch Rickey**,
BBWAA Diamond Dinner,
Milwaukee, January 24, 1960

Contents

Introduction · xi

Prologue: "A Grim Harvest" · 1

1. "The Ball Player Is a Fortunate Man" · 31
2. "So You're the Goddamned Prohibitionist" · 60
3. "A Tyro in the Intricacies of Organized Baseball" · 89
4. "The Yankees Need Building Up" · 122
5. "Keen Competition throughout the Closing Month" · 155
6. "They Could Never Say He Wasn't a 'Real Jew'" · 190
7. "It Would Be Best for the Country to Keep Baseball Going" · 221
8. "A Great Display of Tingling Patriotism" · 253
9. "The Smiling Young Man with the $1,000,000 Check Book" · 282
10. "Bright Colored Paper and Red Ribbons" · 314
11. "Il A Gagné Ses Épaulettes" · 345
12. "A Sound If Not Spectacular Choice" · 376
13. "I Have Long Desired to See California" · 407
14. "Henry, Don't Go Out There" · 434

Acknowledgments · 467

Notes · 469

Bibliography · 513

Index · 543

Introduction

This book is a scholarly work exploring the history of organized baseball during the middle of the twentieth century. It examines the sport on and off the field and places its development as both sport and business within the broader contours of American history. Combining narrative and analysis, the book pays attention to most of the seasons across more than three decades while simultaneously exploring the sport's politics and economics, including, for example, the ways in which organized baseball's entrepreneurs controlled their labor supply—that is, the players—and how the business of baseball interacted with the federal government. More broadly this work is set against the great tumults of the twentieth century—the Great War, the Great Depression, World War II, and the postwar transformations that defined the decade of the 1950s.

Credit for the first scholarly histories of baseball belongs to Harold Seymour, who earned his doctorate from Cornell University in 1956, and his wife, Dorothy, his partner in research, writing, and editing. Working together, they revised his dissertation and published *Baseball: The Early Years* in 1960. Eleven years later, they continued their effort with *Baseball: The Golden Age*, and in 1990 they published *Baseball: The People's Game*. Since the appearance of these pioneering works, a resilient coterie of academic historians—individuals trained in graduate school and committed to earning their livelihoods by doing history—has struggled to have the study of baseball accepted as a legitimate subject for scholarly inquiry. Even within the wider field of sport history, itself embattled and bruised within the academy, those dedicated to baseball history have found the going quite tough. Nevertheless, these scholars have produced substantial books and journal articles that should have earned their chosen discipline the respect they have sought. Simultaneously, baseball scholars in other disciplines—literature, philosophy, sociology, statistics, economics, communications, labor relations, marketing, law, and some of the sciences—have fought their own battles and developed their own bodies of work that have made our understanding of baseball enormously robust.

In addition, other authors, writing for a wider or popular audience, have generated their own noteworthy books, many of which have become essential parts of any baseball library. These include statistical encyclopedias and biographical dictionaries, team histories, anthologies, studies of eras and particular seasons, memoirs, biographies, anthologies, and an extraordinary collection of large-format books that have made baseball's photographic and artistic history a pleasure to peruse.

Finally, an enthusiastic band of aficionados, most of whom practice history as an avocation and aim at a narrow audience, has added a diverse collection of monographs, statistical studies, and specialized publications to baseball's bibliography. Many of these authors belong to the Society for American Baseball Research (SABR), an organization established in 1971 and now with more than seven thousand members. SABR's sixteen founders outlined several objectives, including fostering "the study of baseball as a significant American social and athletic institution" and establishing "an accurate account of baseball through the years." Some work produced by SABR members bypasses the standards demanded of academic history and the readability for which popular historians strive, but much of it is enriched by a stalwart commitment to painstaking research at the most detailed level. Indeed no question about baseball's past seems too daunting to attract the interest of at least one enterprising SABR member and usually many more than that.

To give just a few examples of this dedication, SABR's Biographical Research Committee has verified birth and death data and other vital statistics for more than twenty thousand players and managers who have appeared in the Major Leagues since 1871. The Biography Project Committee produces BioProject, an ongoing effort to publish a comprehensive biographical article on every person who has played or managed in the Major Leagues, as well as other persons who have touched baseball in significant ways. The Pictorial History Committee's Player Image Index has as its goal locating at least one photograph of everyone who has played in the Majors. The Baseball Index Project Committee manages The Baseball Index (TBI), SABR's digital card catalog, "an electronic index to baseball literature encompassing books, pamphlets, magazine and feature newspaper articles" that now includes more than 250,000 entries.

This sustained outburst of writing about baseball in its variegated forms has taken us far beyond the Seymours' beachhead. We know so much more now about baseball and all its elements as a sport, a business, and a cultural institution. Before digitization, baseball researchers relied upon such books as *The Baseball Encyclopedia*, *Total Baseball*, *The Sports Encyclopedia: Baseball*, and the *Complete Baseball Record Book*. Other publications close at hand included specialized reference works on the Major Leagues during the nineteenth century, the Negro Leagues, and a host of Minor Leagues. Researchers could consult a baseball dictionary, a cultural encyclopedia, a home run encyclopedia, a book dedicated to uniforms, another dedicated to uniform numbers, and many encyclopedias devoted to specific teams. In addition there were shelves of monographs covering every aspect of the game from its origins to the effects of work stoppages.

Nor did biography lag behind. Before BioProject, researchers had at their disposal general works such as *The Ballplayers*, *Baseball: The Biographical Encyclopedia*, and several volumes of the *Biographical Dictionary of American Sports* devoted to baseball. There were collective biographies based on teams and themes, collections of oral interviews patterned on *The Glory of Their Times*, and individual biographies nearly too numerous to count. Finally, those looking for summary works could turn to sociologist David Quentin Voigt's three-volume *American Baseball* and single volumes by historians Charles C. Alexander and Benjamin G. Rader and journalists Leonard Koppett and George Vecsey.

Taking advantage of all this work that has followed the Seymours and is, in some ways, inspired by them, the time has come for a new summing up. *Baseball: The Turbulent Midcentury Years*, encouraged by the late Dorothy Seymour Mills, is an attempt to digest the enormous amount of baseball literature produced since the Seymours were active. *Baseball: The Golden Age*, a study of professional baseball exclusively, ends around 1930, and *The People's Game*, devoted entirely to the "House of Baseball," the game beyond the professional ranks, comes to rest at the start of World War II. The goal herein is to produce a new synthesis based not only on secondary sources, but also on primary research grounded, in part, in the notes the Seymours compiled for books they never wrote and deposited in the Harold and Dorothy Seymour Collection in the Carl A. Kroch Library at Cornell.

Baseball: The Turbulent Midcentury Years covers the history of organized baseball from the depths of the Great Depression to the uncertainties of World War II to the following decade and a half of postwar recovery. It looks at how the Depression affected the sport and how baseball responded at both the Major League and Minor League levels. It also considers a new group of owners who took control of teams during these years and surveys the great teams of the era and some of the outstanding players often regarded as heroes of the game. It then examines how the sport confronted, and barely survived, the conditions imposed upon the United States by the country's entrance into World War II. Finally, it analyzes how organized baseball reacted to the return to peacetime; studies the end of the sport's segregation; and explores how baseball reacted to the emergence of television, the threat of government intervention in its labor relations, and the pressure to move franchises and expand to new markets.

This book includes a prologue and fourteen chapters. None are biographical sketches, but each is built around a particular figure in baseball's past, some forgotten or overlooked and some still prominent in the sport's collective consciousness.

The prologue, centered on Ernest Barnard, second president of the American League, sets the stage by surveying how the business of baseball developed in the late nineteenth and early twentieth centuries, including the evolving relationship between the Major Leagues and the Minor Leagues and the decision by Major League owners to replace organized baseball's first governing structure, the three-man National Commission, with a single commissioner. Chapter 1 focuses on Connie Mack, player, manager, and club owner, and how the Major Leagues tried to deal with the Great Depression, including tinkering with the rules and broadcasting baseball on the radio. Chapter 2 highlights the career of Branch Rickey, player, manager, executive, and innovator, and dissects his development of the farm system and its effects on the St. Louis Cardinals. Chapter 3 concentrates on Kenesaw Mountain Landis, baseball's first commissioner, and studies how the Minor Leagues tried to cope with the financial stringencies of the Depression.

Chapter 4 looks at Ed Barrow, manager and executive; reviews the careers of Babe Ruth and some of his teammates; and shows how Barrow built the New York Yankees into baseball's most successful franchise. Chapter 5 covers the career of Larry MacPhail, the tempestuous, headstrong impresario who ran several Minor League and Major League teams and brought night baseball to the Major Leagues. Chapter 6 explores the career of Hank Greenberg, ethnicity in baseball, the development of the All-Star Game, and baseball's evolving relationship with radio. Chapter 7 considers the plight of Don Barnes, owner of the hapless St. Louis Browns as World War II began, and studies how baseball acted and reacted during the first three wartime seasons.

Chapter 8 centers on Yogi Berra and the last years of the war, including the All-American Girls Professional Base Ball League, the election of Happy Chandler as commissioner to succeed Landis, and the difficulties organized baseball experienced as players who served in the armed forces returned to civilian life. Chapter 9 examines the life of Boston Red Sox owner Tom Yawkey and analyzes the disruptions caused by the American Baseball Guild and the Mexican League. Chapter 10 focuses on iconoclastic owner Bill Veeck and looks at the sport's attempts to control the salaries of prospective players and the campaign of the Pacific Coast League to become a third Major League.

Chapter 11 reviews the career of broadcaster Red Barber and probes the desegregation of both the Major Leagues and the Minor Leagues and the attempt by Congress to investigate the sport's antitrust status. Chapter 12 highlights Ford Frick, sportswriter, league president, and commissioner, and studies several lawsuits filed by players against organized baseball, as well as the sport's first encounters with television. Chapter 13 focuses on Henry Aaron and on the decisions of five Major League clubs to move to new locations. Chapter 14 assesses the efforts of New York attorney Bill Shea to return Major League baseball to that city, the unsuccessful plan to establish the Continental League as a third Major League, and the hesitancy of the two Major Leagues as they fumbled their way to expanding from eight teams each to ten.

To be a baseball fan is, in a certain sense, to be a student of baseball history. Hardly a day goes by during any baseball season or any off-season that fans do not reflect upon what happened yesterday, last week, last year, or "way back when" and why. But a historian striving to write with some degree of objectivity must attempt to keep the passion of the fan in check or even dismiss it. My first history professor, Carroll Quigley, told his Georgetown University freshmen that the historian's job is twofold: to see things as they really were and to see that they could have been different. If this work approaches these two targets, it will have accomplished much.

Prologue

"A Grim Harvest"

His friends—and they were many—called him Barney, but his stern countenance belied the affability of that nickname. Photographs of Ernest Sargent Barnard portrayed him as a man who meant business, his lips pursed, his eyes peering straight ahead, his graying hair combed straight back. He favored a well-pressed suit and a starched collar, and he secured his tie with a tack just an inch or so beneath the knot. Altogether dignified and restrained, he wore round, tinted eyeglasses and often carried a cigar in his left hand. He must have taken the last job he held, president of the American League, quite seriously. Thorough, dedicated, and judicious, he was above all completely devoid of the bombast that had consumed his predecessor. His colleagues, who this day came to mourn and lay him to rest, agreed that he had been the perfect man for the position to which he had been elected less than four years before. "A real baseball man," said Emil Fuchs, president of the National League's Boston Braves, "who knew the game in every detail, a fine sportsman, and a perfect gentleman at all times." Those who gathered at Cleveland's Masonic Hall on March 31, 1931, to pay their respects knew Barnard to be a fine executive and someone who, in his earlier years, had been a passionate sports fan and a bit of an athlete besides.[1]

The tributes the sport's leaders bestowed upon Barnard after his sudden death rose above the mundane. They were genuine and heartfelt, frank expressions of shock mixed with gratitude. Clark Griffith, president of the American League's Washington club, had spent the previous weekend with Barnard. He gave voice to his distress. "I had known Mr. Barnard since he came into the league in 1903," he said. "We were the very closest of friends. When I heard of his death, I could hardly believe it." An editorial in the *Sporting News*, the unofficial newspaper of the baseball establishment, was more expansive. "At the very moment in which he was most happy in his surroundings, and looking forward with confidence to the future," it read, "an affliction of which he may have had little real personal knowledge, as regarded its seriousness, deprived him of his life." Barnard's friends tried to convey their own sense of personal and professional loss. Frank Navin, president of the Detroit Tigers and the new acting league president, praised Barnard's honesty; John Heydler, president of the National League, commended his constructive approach to the game; and Kenesaw Landis, the commissioner of baseball, extolled him as "a fine combination of integrity, intelligence, and industry." He added, "It was a common saying that 'you don't have to have it on paper with Barney.' His word was always good."[2]

Barnard was born in West Columbia, a blip of a village on the West Virginia side of the Ohio River, just a bend north of Gallipolis, Ohio, in 1874. His father, Elias, was an itinerant minister in the United Brethren, and West Columbia was just one stop on a long road that meandered through several other towns before ending in Westerville, Ohio, northeast of Columbus. Young E.S., as he signed his name, enrolled at Otterbein, a private school founded in 1847, spending three years in the academy, a prep school of sorts, and then four years in the college. Undone as a student by Greek, Barnard found a home in sports. "The first football game I ever saw," he remembered, "I was called upon to umpire. I continued to umpire football games for six years. I was also umpire at baseball games for the same length of time." While still in the academy, he organized Otterbein's first football team, played halfback, and fashioned himself into a coach at the age of sixteen. After graduating in 1895, he became the school's paid football coach, leading his team to victory over Ohio State University, a school of nearly five thousand students but not yet an athletic power.[3]

Single and living with his parents, Barnard took a position as secretary of the Columbus Builders' Exchange and, on a freelance basis, contributed articles on football to one of the city's daily newspapers, the *Columbus Dispatch*. One evening the telephone rang at home, and the newspaper's owner offered him the job of sports editor. Protesting his utter lack of experience, Barnard was won over by an expression of confidence in his inherent abilities and a promise that no one would interfere with his work for six months. But no one helped much either. His interim predecessor bolted for covering police court as soon as Barnard walked through the door, and the press room jumped all over him when he laid out his first days' stories without writing headlines. "The proofreaders took pity on me and gave me helpful hints," he said. "I don't recall I got them from anyone else." Making just $18 a week, Barnard soon regretted his commitment to journalism, but before he could act on his misgivings, baseball intervened.[4]

Columbus, Ohio's capital, played third fiddle to its neighbors to the north and south, Cleveland and Cincinnati. As the nineteenth century turned into the twentieth, the capital had but 125,560 inhabitants, compared to Cleveland's 381,768 and Cincinnati's 325,902. In baseball, too, Columbus lagged behind. Cleveland hosted its first Major League team, the Forest Citys, in 1871. Cincinnati was home to baseball's first openly professional club, the Red Stockings of 1869 and 1870. Columbus, by contrast, was a Minor League city, and its teams tended toward the peripatetic, bouncing from one Minor League to another. In 1899, for example, Columbus was home to two teams. The Senators, playing in the Western League, could not complete the season despite the presence on their roster of Rube Waddell, a pitcher so outstanding that he later led the American League in strikeouts for six consecutive seasons and earned election to the Hall of Fame. The team moved to Grand Rapids, Michigan, on July 17 and became the Furnituremakers. Three days later Grand Rapids' team in the Interstate League came south to become the new Senators, but ten days later, they left for Springfield, Ohio.[5]

One year later this Springfield club returned to the capital, there to be managed by a stocky, energetic young man and native son named Bob Quinn. He had played catcher for a tough amateur team called the Shamrocks when he was only sixteen and later for several Minor League clubs. Early on he and Barnard had become partners in a typical collegiate baseball scam. "Barnard was the athletic director at Otterbein," Quinn told sportswriter Fred Lieb years later. "When Otterbein played some stiffer opponents, they needed a little outside help. It was Barnard's custom to dig up a hired battery for their big games. So he used to drive in from Westerville in a horse and buggy to Columbus, a distance of fifteen miles, and take me back with him. As I recall," he said, "I made several hits in the pinches which won for dear old Otterbein." Decades later, the college's athletic association recognized Quinn in a team photograph and voted him an overdue "O" that he rightly declined. "I was never nearer the college than its ball field," he admitted.[6]

After the 1900 season several Interstate League club owners tried to turn their business into something larger. They sought to form a new league, dropping smaller cities in favor of Louisville, Kentucky; Marion and Indianapolis, Indiana; and Grand Rapids. To keep professional baseball in Columbus, Quinn and Barnard joined with Jack Ryder, a young sportswriter who had coached the Ohio State football team that Barnard's Otterbein squad had defeated. They were determined to secure a franchise in this new league, the Western Association, and thought it would be quite easy to raise $2,500, the purchase price. Quinn figured that they would find one person willing to invest the total amount. Not so. "The business men of Columbus had little faith in baseball," he recalled. Nobody wanted to own the entire club or even a significant part of it. The enterprising triumvirate decided to sell shares of stock at $25 per share. "The biggest plunger I met," said Quinn, "took five shares. Most of the stockholders took one and two." Nearing their goal, the trio held a meeting of their investors. They needed to sell just one final share. "Down in the audience," Quinn said, "a man in overalls stalked up to the front, dug his hands into his jeans, pulled out some bills and peeled off twenty-five dollars." With the deal done Quinn returned to his off-season job selling baseball gloves. He thought he would be playing and managing in Anderson, Indiana, in 1901, but just before the start of the season, the Anderson club was thrown out of its league. Barnard, still at the *Dispatch*, called Quinn back to Columbus to run their new version of the Senators. Quinn signed players, sold tickets, groomed the field, and more than once stepped in to replace fired managers. All this, and the Senators finished next to last.[7]

The Western Association proved none too stable, but the league's close pennant race in 1901, its only season, propelled Barnard to baseball prominence. Three franchises switched cities, and the league's president, William Myer, was forced to resign when he could not account for all the league's funds. Editor Barnard challenged not only Myer's fiscal integrity, but also his ability to calculate the league's standings accurately. Myer's habit was to issue official standings once a month, but near the end of the season Barnard realized that his own records did not agree with Myer's tally. Newspapers in other league cities scoffed at Barnard, who nevertheless was sure that his figures were correct. When the season ended on September 22, Myer declared that Louisville/Grand Rapids had won the pennant. Barnard disagreed and awarded the honor in the pages of the *Dispatch* to the Dayton Old Soldiers. After Barnard published the complete records of both teams, Myer conceded his error. This attention to detail, coupled with Myer's financial difficulties, granted Barnard his wish. He got to leave the newspaper business. League owners elected him president in Myer's place, but even before that, they picked him to represent them in New York at the second meeting of the National Association of Professional Base Ball Leagues, the organization recently established to take charge of Minor League baseball.[8]

In the nineteenth century professional baseball developed haphazardly, absent any grand plan. When the National League played its inaugural season in 1876, it stood alone. There was no hint of any hierarchy to come. Other leagues arrived and disappeared with bewildering rapidity, and some league names were recycled frequently, adding to the confusion. Entrepreneurs outside the National League did not intend to relegate their clubs to a permanently inferior or "Minor League" status, nor were the players they employed categorically second rate to those who toiled in the National League. Harold Seymour, baseball's first academic historian, identified about fifty other professional teams in 1877 that were good enough to play National League teams and beat them. Over the next few years, though, the National League created a structure designed to define itself as a Major League and place other leagues in subordinate positions. The first National Agreement, negotiated in 1883 by the National League, the American Association, and the Northwestern League, did just that. Implicit in the agreement, known as the Tripartite Pact, was the understanding that the National League and the American Association would be Major Leagues, the Northwestern League would be a junior partner of the other two, and each league would possess certain territorial rights. This treaty, Seymour asserted, marked the beginning of the business known as organized baseball. It was an orderly arrangement so long as all new leagues consented to its terms.[9]

The National Agreement also codified the leagues' control of the labor supply. It stipulated that at the end of every season, each club in leagues adhering to the agreement could reserve up to eleven players for the following season. Reserving a player meant that no other club within the agreement could legally offer him a contract for the upcoming season. This "reserve clause," written into players' contracts, gave club owners ruthless control over reserved players, effectively prohibiting the movement of players from one club to another except by the clubs' decision. Leagues that agreed to reserve players were limiting competition against one another and intensifying competition against outsiders. Independent leagues, therefore, were encouraged by this restricted market to sign onto the agreement, and the Eastern League did so the very next year. The number of players a club could reserve increased to twelve in 1886 and to fourteen a year later, thereby including almost every player on most rosters. This protection fostered the steady, if haphazard, growth of additional Minor Leagues within the terms of the National Agreement. Six such leagues played in 1884, ten in 1888, and seven in 1892.[10]

Beyond the advantages of the reserve system, owners of Major League clubs chafed at their inability to procure the contracts of Minor League players except by purchasing them at prices negotiated with Minor League club owners. In 1887 the two Major Leagues acted. They rewrote the National Agreement as a two-party compact and appended to it a separate document called the "Articles of Qualified Admission to the National Agreement of Professional Base Ball Associations." The former included reserve rights, but the latter did not. Instead the Major Leagues decreed that Minor League clubs now could protect only those players who had already signed contracts for the following season. Since most players did not sign contracts until near the start of spring training, Minor League players became fair game for Major League clubs during each off-season. Francis Richter, editor of *Sporting Life*, a weekly newspaper, argued that the Minors should regain the right to reserve players, but this did not happen until the demise of the American Association after the 1891 season. Then the National League and the Minor Leagues amended the National Agreement to restore the Minors' reservation rights and include a Minor League player draft, a formalized procedure by which Major League teams could acquire the contracts of Minor League players, even reserved players, for fixed, minimal sums. As announced on March 1, 1892, the amended agreement divided the Minors into "A" leagues and "B" leagues and allowed Major League teams to draft players each off-season from "A" Minor League teams for $1,000 each. Teams in "A" leagues could reserve players, and they could also draft players each off-season from "B" teams for $500. "B" league teams had neither reservation rights nor drafting rights. As simple as this scheme seemed, it still left plenty of room for disagreement over the number of players that teams could reserve, the number they could draft or lose by draft, and the proper price.[11]

The allegation that National League teams could now acquire Minor League players by drafting them at prices far below their market value was one of the grievances that led to the unraveling of the amended National Agreement less than a decade later. But this didn't happen until an aggressive Minor League president, Ban Johnson, decided to act. The legend is that on a day in 1893 Johnson and Charles Comiskey, player-manager of the Cincinnati Reds, were having a drink or two at the Ten-Minute Club, a Cincinnati establishment so called because the house rules demanded that someone at each table order a round of drinks every ten minutes. As the tale goes, the two were well acquainted and united by their zeal. They conspired to resuscitate the recently defunct Western League, move its teams to larger cities, and elevate it to Major League status to compete with the National League. Johnson was sports editor of the *Cincinnati Commercial-Gazette*. From this position he developed a deep knowledge of baseball, displayed in his reportage. He favored colorful prose, in the style of the day, when writing about the game on the field and more measured phrases when he covered league meetings and administrative matters. In particular, he formed the opinion that the National League lacked respectability. The game's image was being tarnished, he believed, by unruly play, rowdy behavior, intemperance, and utter disrespect for umpires by players and fans alike. The Reds, who gave no quarter on the field and expected none in return, frequently drew his scorn.[12]

Apocryphal though the Ten-Minute Club story might be, Comiskey had become Johnson's friend after he moved to Cincinnati in 1892 to become the Reds' player-manager. Following the 1893 season, he traveled south to recruit players for the next year. On his journey he met two Minor League club owners who were contemplating resurrecting the Western League for 1894. He encouraged them and suggested that Johnson be league president. This was accomplished at a November 20–21, 1893, reorganization meeting in Indianapolis. With teams in Detroit, Grand Rapids, Indianapolis, Kansas City, Milwaukee, Minneapolis, Sioux City (IA), and Toledo, the Western League began play in 1894. Over the next few seasons Johnson, who was now president, secretary, and treasurer, labored to weed out weak franchises and move clubs to bigger, stronger cities. But he was frustrated. He could not combat the debilitating effects of the draft, and the practice called "farming" was even worse. John Brush, who owned the Indianapolis Hoosiers in Johnson's league in addition to the Reds, was expert at both. He would draft players from other Western League clubs ostensibly to play for Cincinnati but then "farm" them out—that is, transfer their contracts to the Hoosiers. Johnson resented the destabilizing effect of this strategy, but his threats to combat Brush's tactics got nowhere.[13]

Johnson petitioned National League owners several times without success to make the draft less onerous. He was particularly upset when the Minneapolis Millers, Western League champions for 1896, were decimated so badly by Brush that they finished fifty-six and a half games out of first place the next year. When the National League eliminated four of its twelve teams after the 1899 season, Johnson saw his opening. He changed the name of the Western League to the American League and negotiated carefully to move two teams into National League territory. The Grand Rapids Furnituremakers became the Cleveland Blues, and the St. Paul Saints, owned by Comiskey after he left the Reds, became the Chicago White Stockings (later the White Sox). Later that year Johnson refused to renew his league's adherence to the National Agreement, in essence throwing down the gauntlet. American League clubs began to sign National League players to contracts, and war between the one established Major League and its new competitor was on. Late in 1900 Johnson strengthened his hand even more by giving up on four more western cities—Buffalo, Indianapolis, Kansas City, and Minneapolis—and moving these franchises to Baltimore, Boston, Philadelphia, and Washington.[14]

The American League that Johnson got was pretty much the American League that Johnson wanted. Eugene C. Murdock noted in his biography that the *Sporting News* once approvingly called Johnson "a benevolent autocrat," but an image more frequently employed in the contemporary press was to describe him as the "Theodore Roosevelt of baseball"—not Roosevelt the trust buster but Roosevelt the progressive chief executive. Although the league constitution stipulated that the president be elected, Johnson's intimate involvement in club affairs, including holding a financial stake in some of them, ensured his continuation in office for better than two decades. National League owners frequently fought among themselves, but the American League, at least in its formative years, spoke with one voice. Johnson determined who would own his league's franchises, where they would play, and (in any number of cases) who would play for them. Most particularly he understood that baseball's reputation as a rowdy sport—for that is what it was in the late nineteenth century—could be corrected only if the game on the field could be put in the hands of competent umpires whose authority and discipline the league would back without hesitation. It took Johnson about five years to assemble the staff of umpires he needed, but from the beginning he supported them absolutely. This strategy, coupled with many successful player raids, worked. Umpires eliminated most of the shenanigans that had plagued the sport. American League games were expert, crisp, and entertaining. The National League took note, but fans flocked to the new league. In 1902 attendance at American League games exceeded National League attendance by more than half a million.[15]

Late in the fall of 1901 Ernest Barnard journeyed to New York along with representatives from several other Minor Leagues to deal with chaos. Responding to Ban Johnson's salvos as he declared his American League to be a Major League and refused to renew the National Agreement, the National League had announced its intention to abrogate the agreement, thereby ripping organized baseball apart. In response seven Minor Leagues came together in Chicago to establish the National Association for their mutual protection and in particular to combat the threat of wholesale player raids. Their action was so popular that four more leagues applied for membership as the Chicago group elected Patrick Powers of the Eastern League president and John Farrell of the New

York State League secretary. Six weeks later in New York, the Minors adopted their own National Agreement, a ten-year pact that restored the reserve clause and the draft among themselves. The agreement assigned leagues to one of four classifications (Classes A, B, C, and D), established salary limits and club territorial limits, and set up a board to arbitrate disputes among its members. Barnard made his mark at this meeting by successfully opposing a resolution to adopt a particular manufacturer's brand of baseball as the official National Association ball for a period of twenty-five years. His victory proved bittersweet. The losers retaliated by sabotaging a subsequent effort by Barnard and others to create a new Minor League incorporating some cities abandoned by Johnson's Western League and some from Barnard's Western Association, including Columbus. The disgruntled worked their will. The new league, called the American Association, came to life, but it had to play its first season, 1902, as an outlaw league without the blessing of the National Association. As the Western Association died, Barnard resigned his presidency and returned to the *Dispatch*, his baseball career seemingly put on the shelf.[16]

From his desk in Columbus, Barnard became a baseball crusader, producing the same kind of exhortatory journalism as Johnson had in Cincinnati. What concerned him, though, was the legal status of the new league he had helped to found. Sportswriter F. C. Lane called Barnard "a militant press agent for the American Association" who wrote "columns of invective" directed at the National Association's efforts to weaken the new league and entice its players to jump their contracts. Barnard's work was reprinted in newspapers throughout the league, which upset prognostications by finishing its schedule intact. The American Association's first pennant race was not decided until the season's final day. The Senators, Barnard's home team, finished fifth in the eight-team league, eight games below .500. Afterward the National Association gave up the fight and admitted the American Association to its ranks for 1903. Barnard, however, did not stick around to enjoy this triumph. The Cleveland club in the American League needed a new secretary, someone to handle the business affairs of the franchise, and manager Bill Armour recommended Barnard to the team's owners. Armour had owned and managed the Dayton club in the 1901 Western Association, and it was his team that had benefited from Barnard's careful recordkeeping. The two renewed their friendship during the season when the Cleveland club, barred from playing on Sundays at home, often journeyed to Columbus or Dayton for exhibition games that Barnard covered. His interview went well, and he moved to Cleveland in the spring of 1903, kissing journalism goodbye forever.[17]

Cleveland's history in professional baseball was already star-crossed. The Forest Citys started as amateurs in the 1860s and played as professionals in the National Association of Professional Base Ball Players in 1871 and 1872, finishing seventh both years. The city's first National League team, christened the Forest Citys, became the Blues in 1882, when the league assigned each team specific uniform colors. They played six seasons but finished as high as third only once before going out of business after an ignominious 1884 season. The American Association Blues (1887–88) and the Players League Infants (1890) fared no better, but it was Cleveland's second National League team, the Spiders, that compiled the worst season's record in Major League history. After several successful years, the Spiders won only 20 games in 1899 and lost an astounding 134, playing before an average home crowd of 145 people. The reason for their ineptitude was fairly simple: under the rules of the day team owners could hold more than one club simultaneously, and brothers Frank and Stanley Robison favored the Perfectos, the National League team in St. Louis they also owned, over the Spiders. They bought the St. Louis club at the tail end of a multifaceted bankruptcy sale in March 1899 and commenced to devastate the Cleveland franchise by transferring all its best players, including Cy Young, already an outstanding pitcher, to St. Louis. In essence, they made one National League club the farm team of another. The Perfectos finished a disappointing fifth, and the decimated Spiders started poorly and limped to the finish line. They won two in a row only once and lost seventy-seven of their final eighty-six games. The Robisons were unable to find a buyer for what was left of the Spiders, and when the National League contracted following the season from a dozen teams to eight, the Cleveland franchise was dropped. The owners, rewarded for their perfidy, received $25,000.[18]

After Johnson moved his league's Grand Rapids team to Cleveland to fill the void left by the demise of the Spiders, his search for stable local ownership led him to banker Davis Hawley. He begged off, but he directed Johnson to two younger men, John Kilfoyl and Charles Somers. They accepted the challenge. Kilfoyl became president and treasurer of the club, and Somers, the thirty-two-year-old heir to his family's coal and shipping business, became vice president. His father admonished him to avoid "such a foolish and unprofitable thing as baseball," but Somers admitted years later that he "had always been a baseball enthusiast." Soon he began to play a dominant role. "My partners knew little about the game," he told sportswriter Val J. Flanagan in 1932, "and I was forced to take an active part to protect our investment." Moreover, he bankrolled not only the Cleveland team but also the American League franchises in Boston, Philadelphia, and Chicago. Eugene C. Murdock estimated that Somers's total investment might have reached $5 million. "Ban Johnson built the American League, but Charles Somers paid the bills," he wrote. It was Somers who hired Barnard, listening both to Armour and Johnson, who had appreciated Barnard's journalism. The position offered and accepted was at first a temporary one, but Somers quickly realized Barnard's worth and gave him a full-time job called variously "traveling secretary" or "business manager." Barnard took on this assignment with his usual vigor. When the team was on the road, he would return to Cleveland a day early to get things ready for the next home stand. For years he stayed so busy behind the scenes that he never saw a game being played. On the last Friday of the 1908 season, for example, Addie Joss pitched a perfect game, allowing not a single base runner. In the middle of this contest, a park employee yelled, "Barney, come down. Old Addie is making history." "Can't do it," replied Barnard. "There's work to be done."[19]

While Johnson controlled the affairs of his league single-handedly, governance in the National League rested with its individual owners, including a young German immigrant, Bernhardt Dreyfuss. Isaac and Bernhard Bernheim had come to America shortly after the Civil War not to brew German beer but to make Kentucky whiskey, and their seventeen-year-old cousin, Bernhardt, soon joined them from Germany. Within a few years the brothers gave him part of the business. Barney, as he was called, was on his way to becoming rich, but he was short and frail, and he came to baseball on doctor's orders. He organized a semipro team and played second base. In 1884 this club went to Memphis and won a game, 22–2, but Dreyfuss remembered the business side of things. "The score was bigger than the gate receipts," he recalled, "so I fed it to the squirrels in the public square in Memphis." The Bernheims moved their operation to Louisville in 1888 and took Dreyfuss along as credit manager. He made a small investment in the Colonels, the city's team in the Major League American Association, and soon became the club's treasurer. When the association collapsed, Louisville was one of four teams absorbed into the National League. Dreyfuss increased his stake in the club and was elected to the board of directors. "I knew that baseball was a game of the people," he said. "It thrilled me, an immigrant from Germany. I decided to go on with the game." Just a few years later, when the National League announced its intention to drop four teams, including Louisville, Dreyfuss acted fast. He engineered a massive trade that sent eleven players to the Pittsburgh Pirates. He then persuaded the Pirates' principal owners to sell him what the *Sporting*

News called "a nice block of stock" in their club and to elect him president. The trade cemented Dreyfuss's reputation as a fine judge of baseball talent. He read the baseball press religiously, friends across the country sent him additional tips, and he took notes in what he called his "dope book." More immediately, the ex-Colonels transformed the Pirates from cellar dwellers to a contending ball club. They finished second in the National League in 1900 and won the pennant in 1901, 1902, and 1903.[20]

Pittsburgh's success on the field pleased Dreyfuss, but he also knew that a protracted war between his league and the upstart American League would threaten his investment. Early on Johnson too had hoped to minimize antagonism, but his quest for equal status was rebuffed at nearly every turn. Over the next two years the leagues raided each other for players, filed lawsuits, and fought openly in the pages of the sporting press. The American League won most of these clashes, but the costs to each league, including rising salaries, propelled them to a truce. By happenstance Frank Robison, on his way to New York in December 1902 for the winter meetings of National League owners, found himself on the same train with Somers and Kilfoyl on their way to a special meeting of American League owners. Convinced by the Clevelanders that Johnson was ready to move the American League's Baltimore team to New York, Robison told his colleagues when he arrived that it was time to seek peace. Within little more than a month the leagues signed a treaty that led to a new National Agreement and to a 1903 season played with relative tranquility. Still resentment remained until Dreyfuss intervened. With his Pirates about to win their third straight pennant, he wrote to Henry Killilea, owner of the Boston team soon to capture the American League pennant, and suggested that the two clubs play a best-out-of-nine World Series as a gesture of interleague cooperation. Killilea sought Johnson's advice, and the league president gave his consent.[21]

When the two Major Leagues ended their war, the Minor Leagues rolled their own agreement into a larger accord with the Majors called the Major–Minor League Agreement. In his history of the Minor Leagues, political scientist Neil Sullivan scolded the founders of the National Association for scurrying back to a cozy arrangement that promised security but delivered subservience. The Minors, he wrote, could "have fought for autonomy or for equality with the American and National Leagues," but "they meekly accepted a secondary role in the game." Francis Richter concurred. In 1901 he had praised the founders of the National Association for throwing off "the fetters long imposed upon them by selfish and arrogant power" and for creating an organization free of "any entangling alliance with either of the grasping, selfish major leagues." Two years later he complained that "the minor leaguers yielded every important proposition they had formulated and accepted what little the majors chose to give them." The Major–Minor League Agreement reasserted the right of Minor League clubs to reserve players and gave each team the exclusive right to operate within a certain territory, but it also reinvigorated the draft. Clubs would pay $750 to select the contract of a player from Class A, $500 to draft a player from Class B, $300 from Class C, and $200 from Class D. Major League teams could draft an unlimited number of players except that no more than two players could be drafted from any single Class A club each year.[22]

For a decade or so the Minor Leagues prospered under the rules of 1903, at least somewhat. Leagues that had been operating outside the previous National Agreement joined the fold, and new leagues sprang up across the country. In 1902 eighteen Minor Leagues had begun play, fifteen within the National Association and three outside its jurisdiction. Across the country and in Canada, leagues overlapped each other geographically, and club owners used colorful team nicknames to attract fans. The Jersey City Skeeters and Newark Sailors played in the Eastern League, the Peoria Distillers in the Western League, and the Binghamton Bingoes and Utica Pent-Ups in the New York State League. The Southern Association had the Memphis Egyptians; the Three-I League, the Terre Haute Hottentots; the Western League, the Des Moines Midgets; and the Cotton States League, the Baton Rouge Cajuns. There were teams named for animals (Bisons, Bronchos, Bulls, Colts, Grizzlies, Panthers, Ponies, Rabbits, and Tigers), birds (Blackbirds, Canaries, Mud Hens, Pelicans, and Red Birds), colors (Blues, Browns, Maroons, and Reds), and occupations (Brewers, Clamdiggers, Cowboys, Electricians, Farmers, Firemen, Hustlers, Marines, Millers, Smoke Eaters, Truckers, and Whalers). There were Colonels in Louisville, Commodores in Decatur, Millionaires in Colorado Springs, Orators in Bridgeport, Senators in Columbus and Lansing, and Volunteers in Nashville. There were Convicts and Crooks, Saints and Apostles, Lunatics, Cotton Pickers, Hill Climbers, Gold Bugs, and Gasbags. And that was just the beginning. Twenty-one leagues opened play in 1903, thirty-four in 1905, and forty in 1908. By end of the decade fifty-two leagues started the season, a total that would not be surpassed until the late 1940s.[23]

Based roughly on the populations of the cities in them, four leagues qualified for Class A status in 1903: the Eastern League, the Western League, the American Association, and the Pacific National League (PNL). Of these the

Eastern League was the oldest, tracing its lineage directly back to 1892 and less clearly to a pair of leagues that had begun play several years before. In 1903 the Eastern League played in eight cities: Baltimore, Buffalo, Jersey City, Newark, Providence, Rochester, Toronto, and Worcester (MA), a club that moved to Montreal in July. In 1912 club owners acknowledged the presence of the two Canadian clubs within their midst by renaming their league the International League. The second Class A league was a new Western League, formed in 1900 after Ban Johnson's Western League became the American League. This league played its inaugural season with clubs in Denver, Des Moines, Omaha, Pueblo (CO), St. Joseph (MO), and Sioux City (IA). The American Association, the third Class A league, had been born an outlaw, but it proved more stable than any other Minor League over the first half of the twentieth century. In 1903 its clubs played in Columbus, Indianapolis, Kansas City, Louisville, Milwaukee, Minneapolis, Toledo, and St. Paul. As sturdy as the American Association proved to be, the PNL was just the opposite. Established in 1892, it joined the National Association in 1902 as a Class B league, rose to Class A in 1903, and reverted to Class B in 1904, its final season. West Coast fans preferred the Pacific Coast League (PCL), an independent league that challenged the PNL and won. Enticed by two sweeteners—exemption from the draft and a guaranteed place in the Minors' highest classification—the PCL took the PNL's spot as the fourth Class A league and prospered. Taking advantage of the West Coast climate, teams played extraordinarily long seasons—220 games in 1904 was the longest, but 200 was common—and even survived the San Francisco earthquake in 1906 by moving games scheduled there to Oakland.[24]

Pursuant to the National Agreement of 1903, organized baseball was governed by the National Commission, an unwieldy arrangement consisting of the presidents of the two Major Leagues and a third person elected annually by the other two, but no one from the Minor Leagues. Johnson sat on the commission for its entire life, but the office of the National League presidency had a revolving door. At the time the two leagues ended their war, the National League president was Harry Pulliam, former president and secretary of the Louisville club and Barney Dreyfuss's partner. Caught more than once in the middle of raging disputes between Dreyfuss and John McGraw, the tempestuous manager of the New York Giants, Pulliam could not cope with the vicious New York press that habitually backed McGraw. Late in 1908, after deciding against the Giants in the famous Merkle boner play that eventually cost them the pennant, Pulliam took a six-month leave of absence, came back to work, and a month later took his own life. Secretary-Treasurer John Heydler filled out the balance of Pulliam's term and became one of three candidates to succeed him, but when the owners deadlocked, the dark horse who emerged was former umpire Thomas Lynch, a compromise choice. Each year at the league's winter meetings, a faction plotted to deny him another year in office, and in 1913 they succeeded. His replacement was John Tener, a former pitcher and the governor of Pennsylvania. Tener held both jobs, governor and league president, for two years and served an additional year as league president beyond his term. But in August 1918 he resigned in protest when the owners refused to support his position in a dispute with the American League over a player's contract. Finally, it was Heydler's time. He had been an umpire and a sportswriter before joining the league as a statistician, Pulliam's secretary, and then the league's secretary-treasurer. There he waited until taking over Tener's duties and then getting elected in his own right that winter.[25]

The only man to hold the job as the third member of the commission was Garry Herrmann, president of the Reds. He was born August Herrmann in Cincinnati in 1859 and apprenticed to a printer who liked to give his employees nicknames. "Bismarck" was already assigned, so the boss picked "Garibaldi," soon shortened to "Garry." Herrmann learned his trade, but he made his career in Republican politics. In 1902 political boss George Cox joined forces with the Fleischmann brothers, of gin and yeast fame, and Herrmann to force John Brush to sell the Reds to them. Herrmann bought only a small stake in the team, but he was elected president. A year later he found himself holding the commission's swing vote. As a National League executive, he was acceptable to that league's owners, and as a Cincinnatian more than slightly familiar with the city's watering holes, he was just as suitable to Johnson, his buddy. Criticized as favoring his own league when he voted with Pulliam and condemned as "Ban's boy" when he voted the other way, Herrmann nevertheless exhibited good judgment and maintained his good humor throughout his tenure. As he traveled by train from one league city to the next and to each season's World Series, he transported sausages, sauerkraut, pigs' feet, cheeses, beer, and assorted other German treats with him wherever he went. Baseball historian Lee Allen called him "a walking delicatessen," and newspapers often parodied his heavily accented speech by recording his quips phonetically. When McGraw's Giants won the 1904 National League pennant and refused to play the American League's champions, Boston again, Herrmann, mustachioed and with his hair parted properly down the middle, helped fashion the deal that made a World Series an annual event starting the next year.[26]

Within a few years after 1903 the number of Minor Leagues doubled, and the structure of organized baseball grew more complex. When the Southern Association argued in 1905 that its cities had populations large enough to merit Class A status, the American Association and the Eastern League objected but without success. These two leagues wanted to maintain a certain amount of separation from the Southern Association, and they suggested the creation of a new classification, Class Double-A, just for them. Their argument revolved around population too, but the real issue was the draft. The American Association and the Eastern League proposed that Class Double-A league—that is, themselves—be exempt from drafting by the Majors but still have the right to draft players from Class A leagues. When this tactic failed, they introduced a resolution at the National Association's October 1907 meetings to demote the other three Class A leagues to Class B. In January 1908 the National Commission rejected this scheme, but the idea did not die, and a compromise emerged. The American Association and the Eastern League were granted Class Double-A status, but they would not be exempt from the draft. The Pacific Coast League, under terms of its entrance into the National Association several years previously, also earned promotion to Class Double-A while the Southern Association and the Western League remained in Class A. In January 1912 a new National Agreement, completed pursuant to population figures compiled in the 1910 census, cemented this arrangement and simultaneously revised the draft's procedures and prices. Major League clubs could draft players from Class Double-A for $2,500, but each Class Double-A club could lose only one player. Each Minor League class could in turn draft players from every class beneath it at the following rates: $1,500 for players from Class A, $1,200 for Class B, $750 for Class C, and $500 for Class D.[27]

If the architects of these 1912 revisions thought they were crafting an agreement to create stability for the long term, they were mistaken. Nearly before the ink was dry, two groups of businessmen tried to form new Major Leagues outside the structure of organized baseball. The Columbian League died before a single game was played, and the United States League did only slightly better, playing just a few games in 1912. Despite these failures, some of the people involved persevered. They formed the Federal League, six teams that played a 120-game schedule in 1913 as an independent league and were successful. The Feds, as they were called, added two teams for 1914 and placed themselves in direct geographic competition with clubs in the American League, the National League, the American Association, and the International League. The challenge the Feds provided affected the Minors at least as much as the

Majors. In Baltimore, for example, the 1914 Terrapins drew 30,000 fans to their Federal League opener in a new ballpark, while across the street the International League's Orioles attracted only 1,500 to an exhibition game against the National League champions, the Giants. More generally, the Feds wounded Minor League teams by signing their players to lucrative contracts and granting them more rights than did organized baseball. The Feds ignored the reserve clause, but they pledged at first to sign only players not under contract for the coming season. Later the upstart league widened its reach and approached players already signed to American or National League contracts. Harold Seymour calculated that 221 players left organized baseball to play in the Federal League, writing that "18 players jumped major league contracts; 25 broke minor league contracts; 63 disregarded reserve claims of major league clubs; and 115 ignored the minor league reserve."[28]

The effects of the Federal League's player raids trickled down throughout the Minors. As owners complained, the draft remained in force, snatching even more players at bargain prices. Even though the Feds played only three seasons before going out of business, the fallout was devastating and not short-lived. More than forty Minor Leagues began play in 1914, but two years later, that number dwindled to twenty-six. There were factors external to baseball at work too. In the fall of 1913 the American economy had entered a recession that grew much worse by the following spring. Ticket sales to baseball games suffered as a result. In 1914, following the assassination of Archduke Franz Ferdinand in June, Europe plunged into the first horrific months of the Great War. The United States maintained a strict neutrality until April 1917, when President Woodrow Wilson asked Congress for a declaration of war against Germany. As the country began to mobilize, the Minors continued their downward trend. Twenty-one Minor Leagues began the 1917 season, but only eleven played a complete schedule. Leagues in the higher classifications managed to survive, but their attendance plummeted. Buffalo's Bisons, for example, drew only 116,000 fans after attracting almost 275,000 the year before. Both Class C leagues quit early: the Virginia League disbanded on May 15, and the South Atlantic League (also known as the SALLY) concluded its season on the Fourth of July. Just three of the eight leagues in Class D completed their schedules. Two stopped in May, one in June, and two more on July 4, hoping, no doubt, that holiday crowds would give the revenue side of the ledger one final boost.[29]

Like other segments of American society, organized baseball jumped to support the emergency created by the Great War so long as the core of its business was not adversely affected. At Ban Johnson's insistence, American

League players performed close-order military drills with bats instead of rifles. Some teams tried to schedule exhibition games on Sundays with profits intended for military families, but laws prohibiting Sunday baseball won out. Clark Griffith, both manager and minority owner in Washington, established a "ball and bat" fund to send equipment overseas. When the first military draft under the Selective Service Act of 1917 occurred on July 20, few players were summoned, and teams played out the season to its normal conclusion. But attendance at Major League games fell 20 percent, and over the winter club owners began to see the war effort as an intrusion. Johnson suggested that the government exempt eighteen players on each team from military service, but even National League president John Tener rebuked him for this foolish proposal. Owners also objected when Provost Marshal Enoch Crowder announced his "work-or-fight" order in May 1918 and classified baseball as a nonessential occupation. After Senators catcher Eddie Ainsmith's draft board told him he was immediately eligible for induction, Griffith lodged an appeal with the War Department, but Secretary of War Newton Baker rejected it. Dozens of ballplayers rushed to enlist, and both Major Leagues feared that they would have to shut down. Instead they appealed to Baker again, and he granted a reprieve until September 1. The leagues fumbled their way to the end of a season truncated to 140 games, reducing players' salaries for games not played. Major League attendance tumbled again, but the Minors fared even worse. Only ten leagues began play in April, and only one, the International League, completed its schedule. It was, in Francis Richter's words, "the most unsatisfactory, harassing and unprofitable campaign in the 47 years' history of Organized Baseball."[30]

On November 12, 1918, the day after the armistice brought quiet to the Western Front, the National Association passed a resolution protesting continuance of the draft. The Minor League presidents who assembled for their winter meetings in December were not certain they would be able to play a season in 1919, but they were sure that the Minors' relationship with the Major Leagues had to change. A. R. Tearney, president of the Three-I League, made the case succinctly. "We shall demand the right to dispose of our youngsters to whom we see fit . . . ," he said, adding, "It is the minor leagues that develop these stars for the majors and the smaller leagues should reap the financial reward." In January the presidents met again, and they voted to withdraw from the National Agreement if their demand was not met. To no one's surprise, the Major Leagues refused to abolish the draft, but just as astonishingly, they let the Minors pull out. "The radical elements were in ascendancy," wrote

Richter, and he predicted that this separation "will be universally resented by the players, and perhaps also by the public." Richter argued that the draft was good for players, allowing the best of them to advance systematically, and that its abolition would permit Minor League owners to retain players at inferior salaries and dissuade clubs from selling players except at exorbitant prices. "This will have a disastrous effect on the minor league quality of ball," he said. As peacetime returned, players "will prefer taking chances in the many semi-professional clubs scattered all over the country."[31]

Baseball recovered quickly following the Great War. The cautious Major Leagues played a second season abbreviated to 140 games, only to find their timidity shortsighted. Attendance more than doubled to over 6.5 million, and fans were rewarded with exciting seasons in both leagues. The Minors also fared very well. Fifteen leagues began the season, and only two quit early. The *Reach Guide* reported that prosperity came "from every quarter of the land." Six of eight teams in the International League made money, and all eight clubs in the Southern League finished in the black. The Pacific Coast League expanded from six teams to eight and was a great success despite the costs involved in adding Portland and Seattle to the league's California base. Still, when the Minors gathered in convention in Springfield, Massachusetts, in November 1919, they resolved to forsake independence and reestablish a relationship with the Major Leagues. Negotiating the details of a new National Agreement required an additional season, in part because the Major Leagues were busy replacing the three-man National Commission with a single commissioner. The National Association accepted the new commissioner as baseball's ultimate authority and received in exchange voice and vote on the new Advisory Council, composed of the presidents of the two Major Leagues, when the matter being considered affected the Minors. Similarly, the Minors agreed to reinstate the Major League draft, albeit with higher draft prices, adding the stipulation that any league could opt out of the draft if it agreed not to draft players from lower leagues. The new agreement had a seven-year term and set the Minors toward new heights of prosperity.[32]

During all this turmoil Ernest Barnard worked quietly and efficiently behind the scenes in Cleveland. Midway through the 1902 season the club had acquired Nap Lajoie, the second baseman generally regarded as the best player in the American League in its first decade. Lajoie became the team's star, its captain, and then its manager. With Lajoie at the helm the Naps nearly won the pennant in 1908. Addie Joss, the Naps' best pitcher, got credit for twenty-eight wins, including his perfect game. The tension of the pennant race adversely affected John Kilfoyl's health, and he resigned as team president after the season. Charles Somers replaced him and promoted Barnard to vice president. Their sad duty in 1911 was to arrange an exhibition game to benefit Joss's family after the pitcher died at thirty-one of tubercular meningitis. Barnard began acting as the club's general manager, a term not yet in use, and he acquired limited control over several Minor League teams, an arrangement that would later be called a farm system. Within a couple of years, though, Somers's other investments pushed him $2 million in debt, and he decided to discharge Barnard to cut costs. Johnson rushed to the rescue. He urged Somers to reconsider and even offered to pay Barnard's salary out of his own pocket. Barnard survived this threat and remained on the payroll through the sale of the club in 1916 from Somers to a group headed by James Dunn, a partner in a railroad construction firm. This time Johnson turned his back on his protégé. He recommended that the new owner hire Robert McRoy, once Johnson's private secretary, as "executive manager." When reporters asked Dunn about Barnard, he said curtly, "Barnard is out." Johnson, it seems, had heard rumors that his own position as league president might be in jeopardy, and he acted to remove someone who might be his rival.[33]

The American League had its offices on the twelfth floor of the aging Fisher Building in downtown Chicago, but a good deal of its unofficial business was conducted in the J.V.B. Club, a bar on the building's ground floor. It was in this bar that Johnson had anointed Dunn, a man with no baseball experience, as the next owner of the Cleveland team. Johnson blackballed Barnard, but the two leading baseball writers in Cleveland came vigorously to his defense. Dunn gave in and rehired him for a minor office job, and when McRoy died in December 1917, Barnard regained his old position. "I've been silly about this thing," admitted Dunn. "You're the general manager around here from now on." Barnard's immediate task was to make a good team better. Lajoie's contract had been sold in 1915, but the Indians, as the team was now called, soon began to improve. McRoy had engineered a trade with the Boston Red Sox to obtain Tris Speaker, an outstanding center fielder, before the 1916 season. Cleveland finished sixth that year but rose to third in 1917. After Barnard took over, he continued to fine-tune the roster. The Indians finished second in 1918 and 1919 and won their first pennant in 1920. These were tumultuous times for the American League. The White Sox became the Black Sox after they consorted with gamblers before the 1919 Series, but the eight accused players were not suspended until September 28, 1920, five days before the end of the season. Six weeks before, the Indians had watched helplessly as their shortstop, Ray Chapman, was felled by a pitched ball to the head and died the following morning. Barnard, working closely with Dunn and Speaker, now the manager, helped the team recover by acquiring two Minor League players, Duster Mails and Joe Sewell, who played key roles down the stretch. The deals worked, and the Indians topped off their season by defeating Brooklyn in the World Series, five games to three. Yet Dunn's triumph was short-lived. The Indians finished second in 1921, and their owner fell ill just before the start of the 1922 season. When he died in June, the club passed into his wife's hands, and Barnard became president.[34]

The consensus enabling the National Commission to govern with some degree of effectiveness broke apart, not over the Black Sox scandal, as is commonly believed, but rather over reasons more complicated and structural. The system was inherently unstable and given to controversy. In most disputes Garry Herrmann held the swing vote, but he was also a National League owner and Ban Johnson's pal whose every decision was decried as biased by the losing side. National League presidents were caught in a similar quandary, charged with governing their league and its eight owners while one of those owners simultaneously held a superior position. The whole contraption came crashing down starting in 1919, when an argument erupted over the suspension of Carl Mays, an ill-tempered pitcher for the Red Sox who stomped off the mound after the second inning on July 13. After his outburst Mays asked to be traded, and Boston agreed, sending him to the New York Yankees on July 29 for two pitchers and $40,000. Boston's decision to entertain trade offers for Mays enraged Johnson, who had a terrible relationship with Red Sox owner Harry Frazee. Johnson announced that Boston had to discipline the pitcher for leaving a game in progress before any transaction could transpire. Mays, Johnson feared, was simply looking for an easy way to move from an also-ran to a pennant contender, an act of defiance the league simply could not allow. Frazee disagreed and traded him anyway, so Johnson took it upon himself to suspend Mays before he could pitch for the Yankees. New York's co-owner, Jacob Ruppert, a wealthy brewer, objected strenuously, saying that Johnson could not interfere in a club's internal affairs. The Yankees went to court and won a temporary injunction to restrain Johnson from enforcing the suspension. This move caused American League owners to divide into two camps: Boston, Chicago, and New York as the "Insurrectionists" opposed to Johnson's heavy hand, and Cleveland, Detroit, Philadelphia, St. Louis, and Washington as the "Loyal Five."[35]

The Mays case was actually the fourth serious dispute over a player's contract to affect adversely the stability of organized baseball's governing structure. The first clash had involved George Sisler, an exciting young prospect from Manchester, Ohio. In 1911, while underage, Sisler signed a Minor League contract that was subsequently purchased by the Pirates. By the time the contract came to light, Sisler had spent a year at the University of Michigan, where the baseball coach, Branch Rickey, couldn't wait for Sisler to start playing varsity baseball as a sophomore. Aware that a binding contract would ruin Sisler's college eligibility, Rickey asked the National Commission to void the contract. Commission members recognized that the law was on Sisler's side, but they also felt some moral obligation to Pirates owner Barney Dreyfuss, who had purchased the contract in good faith. But when the commission set the young player free in January 1915, Dreyfuss lost. After Sisler graduated, Dreyfuss found his new offer topped by the St. Louis Browns, whose manager was now none other than Rickey. Dreyfuss cried foul. He swore vengeance against the commission and particularly against Herrmann.[36]

The second squabble concerned pitcher Scott Perry, whose contract the Boston Braves purchased from the Atlanta Minor League club in June 1918 on a conditional basis, $500 down with $2,000 more due if the Braves kept him. Before the end of Perry's thirty-day trial, he jumped the club and signed with an independent team. The commission ruled that Boston had an equity stake in the player. If he were to return to organized baseball, the Braves could have him by paying the $2,000. The next year Perry rejoined the Atlanta team, only to be sold to the Philadelphia Athletics, clearly in violation of the previous season's transaction. Boston exercised its prior claim, and the commission upheld the Braves on a split vote over the objections of Athletics owner Connie Mack.[37]

In the third dispute the commission sided with the Yankees in 1919 over the White Sox in the matter of Jack Quinn, thereby alienating Charles Comiskey. Quinn had pitched for the Yankees and the Red Sox before jumping to the Federal League in 1914. Four seasons later he was pitching for the Vernon Tigers in the Pacific Coast League when that league ended its season prematurely because of the Great War. Quinn joined the White Sox as a free agent with the commission's permission and won five games for Chicago, but the Yankees, ignoring these facts, purchased his contract from Vernon and claimed him too. Each of these decisions alienated one owner or another, with the Quinn decision driving a wedge between Comiskey and Johnson and severing the friendship that had been in large measure responsible for the development of the American League.[38]

Owners sharply divided when Johnson announced his decision in the Mays case. Partial resolution came only with the establishment of an arbitration committee empowered to review all Johnson's future rulings. Curtailing the power of the league's founder in this way played into the hands of those who had for a while been urging that the third person on the National Commission be a neutral outsider, someone not directly connected with baseball. This movement's leader was Albert Lasker, a prominent Chicago advertising executive, a power broker in national Republican politics, and a stockholder in the Chicago Cubs. Reacting to the Mays case, Lasker proposed that the sport transfer its governance to a new three-man body composed entirely of outsiders, eminent individuals without any financial ties to the game. The Lasker Plan made little headway, but the dysfunctionality of the existing system persisted. Ruppert attempted to call a league meeting to resolve the Mays situation but failed to attract a quorum. He then summoned the league's board of directors, controlled by the Insurrectionists. Meeting without Johnson and James Dunn, one of the Loyal Five, the board reinstated Mays. The Tigers' Frank Navin, another loyalist, retaliated. The 1919 season had ended with the Yankees in third place and the Tigers in fourth. Revenues from the World Series were normally distributed among each league's top three finishers, and under this arrangement the Yankees were due a total of $13,000. Navin argued that games New York had won with Mays on its roster should be thrown out and that the Tigers deserved third-place money. The commission could not decide how to handle this complaint, but the Yankees forged on. They filed a petition for a permanent injunction in the Mays matter, and during the proceedings New York suggested strongly that Johnson had opposed the Mays trade because of his financial interest in the Cleveland club, still contending for the American League pennant when Mays had walked off the mound in Chicago. Victory went to the Yankees when New York State Supreme Court justice Robert Wagner granted their petition. Ruppert and his co-owner, Til Huston, issued a triumphant statement: "Our fight has not been for Mays alone, but to safeguard the vested and property rights of the individual club owner against the continual encroachments on club rights by the president, who has never been clothed with the powers that he has taken unto himself."[39]

In December 1919, when owners in both leagues usually met in the same city to facilitate transacting joint business, the American League was still rent asunder. The Insurrectionists agreed to meet in New York simultaneously with the National League, but Johnson and the Loyal Five gathered in Chicago and were persuaded to journey east only through Navin's intercession. Never intending to make peace, the loyalists proceeded to oust their opponents from the board of directors and reaffirm their intention to honor the contract Johnson had signed in 1910 to continue as president for twenty years at an annual salary of $30,000. The Insurrectionists, defeated on one parliamentary motion after another, sought recourse in the courts. They filed a series of legal actions designed to stifle Johnson, capped by the Yankees' $500,000 suit accusing him of attempting to drive Ruppert and Huston out of baseball. Rumors flew that the Insurrectionists were planning to join National League owners, equally frustrated from watching Herrmann, one of their own, side so often with Johnson, to form a new twelve-team league. The Loyal Five took this threat seriously. Moreover, they decided that protracted legal action would simply bleed their treasuries dry. So when Navin once more brought the warring sides together in February, the loyalists were forced to yield. Mays was reinstated, the Yankees got their third-place money, and authority to decide important league matters passed from Johnson to a two-man board of review. In exchange the Insurrectionists agreed to withdraw all their lawsuits and not to secede. This accord effectively marked the end of the National Commission, but the future remained unclear. A few weeks before, National League owners had instructed their new president, John Heydler, not to vote for Herrmann's reelection as chairman. Herrmann resigned, and when the league meetings adjourned, baseball was essentially without leadership.[40]

Lasker's plan bubbled up again, but before the owners could consider it anew, the smell of corruption distracted them. Players who for decades had resented the reserve clause and their concomitant paltry salaries had sometimes thrown their lot in with gamblers to supplement their incomes and thumb their noses at their employers. Talk of such dishonesty had been in the air during the 1919 World Series, won by the Reds over the White Sox in eight games, yet when sportswriter Hugh Fullerton went public that fall in the *New York World* with his suspicions that the Series had not been played square, the baseball press lambasted him. Another reporter, James Crusinberry of the *Chicago Tribune*, uncovered hard evidence of a fix in July 1920, but his editor refused to publish a story that might invite libel suits from those Crusinberry fingered. Nothing perhaps might have come of these accusations had not another Chicago newspaper, the *Herald-Examiner*, run a story on September 4, 1920, with the headline "$50,000 Bet on the Cubs and Phillies Sure-Thing Game," a contest played four days before in Chicago. Bill Veeck Sr., president of the Cubs, revealed that he had received inside information that this game had been fixed, and he invited the Chicago chapter of the Baseball Writers'

Association of America (BBWAA) to pursue an investigation. Within days Cook County judge Charles McDonald urged State's Attorney Maclay Hoyne to convene a grand jury to look into this game and the broader question of gambling in baseball generally. As the pressure mounted, eight members of the White Sox were implicated in a conspiracy to throw the 1919 Series. After Eddie Cicotte, Joe Jackson, and Lefty Williams confessed their involvement to the grand jury, Comiskey suspended the seven still playing during the final week of the 1920 season, and the grand jury handed down indictments on October 29.[41]

Had the Black Sox scandal not erupted, the National Commission might have endured, but its structure would surely have changed. Even before Garry Herrmann resigned, owners had asked Ban Johnson and John Heydler to find his successor, but Johnson, hanging on to every last ounce of his power, sabotaged this effort. His intransigence caused a small group of owners to begin plotting a new course. They met in the offices of Alfred Austrian, attorney for both the Cubs and the White Sox, and the basis for their discussions was the Lasker Plan. By the end of September 1920 all eight National League clubs along with the three insurrectionist American League clubs had assented to the idea that three outsiders should govern baseball. Among the names floated as a potential chairman for this board were Generals John J. Pershing and Leonard Wood, Senator Hiram Johnson (R-CA), former secretary of the treasury William Gibbs McAdoo, and Kenesaw Mountain Landis, a federal district court judge in Chicago. Johnson and his Loyal Five disagreed, and they refused to attend an owners' meeting called for October 18. It didn't matter. The reformers approved a plan to establish a three-man board with a chairman to be paid $25,000 annually and two associates to be paid $10,000 each. In addition they put the Loyal Five on notice: either commit to the new order or risk being excluded from a new twelve-team league. Johnson still did not give in. He advanced his own candidate for chairman, Judge Charles McDonald, but simultaneously he worked with the loyalists to kill the entire scheme. Three weeks of backroom politicking ensued, but no compromise resulted. Proponents of the Lasker Plan focused on Landis as their candidate for chairman, and they were prepared to increase the salary for the position to $50,000 in order to entice him from the federal bench. On November 8 eleven clubs met to carry out their ultimatum. They elected Landis chairman for a seven-year term. Then the eight National League clubs dissolved their league, and the three insurrectionist American League clubs withdrew from theirs. They agreed to form a new league with the twelfth franchise going to the first loyalist willing to break with Johnson. A six-man committee called on Landis and beseeched him to accept the job. Judiciously and perhaps with a sense of the moment, he said he would think about it.[42]

The six executives who hopped out of taxicabs and trudged through the doors of the Federal Building and into Landis's chambers were searching for a new order. Besides Austrian, Herrmann, Jacob Ruppert, and Bill Veeck Sr., the group included William Baker, owner of the Philadelphia Phillies, and Brooklyn's owner Charles Ebbets. Baseball was in a crisis, they believed, that could well have been linked in their minds to more worrisome uncertainties already present throughout postwar American society. The war in Europe had unleashed disruptive forces that the return to peace had not abated: rapid industrialization; declining farm prices; the migration of thousands of workers, both white and Black, to urban areas; labor unrest; racial tension; and fear of radicalism, especially Bolshevism. More quickly than millions wanted, American culture was debunking its agrarian, moralistic, isolationist roots and adopting a new ethos that was urban, liberal, and cosmopolitan. Many embraced these changes and would smoke, drink, and dance their way through the 1920s, but many others faced the new decade with trepidation. In May 1920 Republican presidential candidate Warren Harding urged the country to return to "normalcy," a neologism that captured the fears of millions and propelled him to office. Veeck and his colleagues knew they could not repair the system that had governed their sport for nearly two decades, and they believed they were entrusting their business to a strong leader who would rule, they hoped, with prewar common sense. They took solace perhaps in the opinion of Landis rendered by the *Sporting News*: "His program since 1905 has been to apply horse sense to human troubles." The judge took four days to make up his mind, and in the interim the Loyal Five gave up the fight, with St. Louis owner Phil Ball being the last to consent. Meeting on November 12, all sixteen clubs confirmed Landis's election, and after some coy conversation during which the judge professed his love for the bench, he accepted. The owners decided that he could be both a federal judge and baseball's commissioner, a title he selected, and they ceremoniously reduced his compensation by $7,500, the amount of his federal salary. They agreed, too, to dispense with Albert Lasker's idea for a three-man board and to vest all powers in Landis alone. There would be no associate commissioners, and each of the league presidents would be reduced to the role of a "special pleader . . . only in the cases in which their leagues and clubs are involved."[43]

For reasons long-standing and convoluted, Johnson resigned as president and treasurer of the American League but not until October 1927. Although his declining health was given as the proximate cause, he never came to terms with playing a supporting role to Landis. Moreover, many owners nursed grievances that just could not be ameliorated by anything short of his removal. Barney Dreyfuss, for example, resented Johnson's decision in the George Sisler case. Charles Comiskey had begun to fall out with his old friend even before the Jack Quinn case, over practical jokes perpetrated during a pair of hunting trips, and their disagreements over the Black Sox scandal made the rupture permanent. More substantively, Johnson's refusal to adjust to life as a subordinate eventually grew tiresome. Ernest Barnard remained above these political machinations. As president of the Indians, he ran the team for James Dunn's widow and worked with Cleveland's civic leaders to plan construction of an enormous new ballpark on the lakefront. In 1927 he arranged the sale of the club to a syndicate headed by real estate developer Alva Bradley for the seemingly outrageous price of $1 million. Barnard then resigned as president, but the American League's owners had already offered him Johnson's job for a term of three years, and he accepted. Said Tom Shibe, president of the Athletics, "We have figured on Barnard for the last two years as the ultimate successor to Ban Johnson. In fact, there never has been anyone else."[44]

As if to distance himself from his predecessor, Barnard moved the league's headquarters from the Fisher Building on Van Buren Street to new quarters at 310 South Michigan Avenue, with his own office overlooking Lake Michigan. He promoted Will Harridge from secretary to the president to secretary of the league and hired an office girl, a bookkeeper, a publicity man, and a stenographer. Just a few months after Barnard's election the *Reach Guide* called him "a man of character, reliable, and sane," who already "has proved his fitness for the position." Barnard ran the league with quiet efficiency. In his annual report to the owners on December 12, 1928, he took pride that his instructions to the league's umpires had markedly shortened the length of games. In December 1930 the owners rewarded him with a five-year term of office and a $40,000 salary, tributes, said the *Reach Guide*, to his "executive ability, poise, tact, and untiring energy." The guide's editor, sportswriter James C. Isaminger, lauded him as "a tireless worker, . . . a frequent visitor at all parks," and "a contact man, never a bureaucrat." After Johnson left office, he spent twenty-four weeks in a St. Louis hospital and then traveled west to California and Mexico before settling into a house he and his wife had purchased in her hometown, Spencer, Indiana. His weight dropped precipitously, his eyesight began to fail, and the effects of diabetes and arteriosclerosis weakened him considerably. In October 1930, looking drawn and haggard, he entered St. John's Hospital in St. Louis for treatment on his eyes when he developed an infection in his right foot. After doctors did surgery and mandated a recuperative stay at Hot Springs, Arkansas, the infection recurred, and his general health declined even more. He returned to St. John's, rejecting the doctors' advice that his right leg be amputated.[45]

Nary a year goes by that baseball does not endure the passing of some number of its greats, and 1931 was no exception. In that year the sport lost George Washington Bradley, who pitched the first no-hitter in National League history; Jack Chesbro, the pitcher who won forty-one games in 1904 for the New York Highlanders (later the Yankees) but lost the American League pennant by throwing a wild pitch on the last day of the season; Jimmy McAleer, who played outfield for the Spiders, managed several teams, and briefly owned the Red Sox with Robert McRoy; Charles Murphy, who bought the Cubs in 1905 and sold them in 1913 for a huge profit; and Bonesetter Reese, an idiosyncratic physical therapist whose skills helped pitchers recover from sore arms. Former pitcher Albert Spalding saw his brother, James, an executive in the family sporting goods firm, die, and Dreyfuss buried his son and heir apparent, Sam, who succumbed at thirty-five to pneumonia. But that was not all. Just before the year began, on December 9, 1930, came word of the death of Rube Foster, the founder of the Negro National League, the first stable league for players excluded from organized baseball for race. Later that same month Barnard suffered an influenza attack at the league's annual meeting in New York. He retreated to Florida to recuperate and then commenced visiting each team's spring training site. That tour was interrupted when he complained of what he thought was indigestion and journeyed by train to the Mayo Clinic in Rochester, Minnesota. There the doctors diagnosed him with advanced heart disease, and his condition deteriorated rapidly. On Friday afternoon, March 27, Barnard, thoughtful to the end, ordered flowers to be sent to Johnson, still in the hospital, and then, while talking to his wife, suffered a fatal heart attack. He was fifty-six.[46]

Sixteen hours later Johnson, too, died, and baseball braced itself for a pair of funerals on successive days. Barnard's body was transported back to Cleveland to lie in repose at the George Sharer Son & Parish, Inc. Funeral Home. On Tuesday, March 31, the Allenby Commandery No. 73 of the Knights Templar accompanied the body to Masonic Hall, an imposing brown brick building on Euclid Avenue, where more than forty of baseball's leaders, led by Landis and members of the Indians team, mourned. All sixteen Major League teams sent flowers, and Dr. Miles Krumbine, pastor of Plymouth Church in Shaker Heights, a Cleveland suburb, and a friend of Barnard's, presided. Burial followed in Knollwood Cemetery, after which many of the dignitaries boarded a train for Indiana. Ball, one of Johnson's staunchest defenders during his last years as president, had arranged a wake at the Marshall Funeral Home in St. Louis, and then Johnson's body had been transported to Spencer, where his wife had remained during his last illness. There, on Wednesday, April 1, Rev. Wiley Hastings and Rev. John Henry officiated at the funeral service at the Christian Church. Hastings eulogized Johnson in an address that concluded with Tennyson's "Crossing the Bar." The founder of the American League was then laid to rest in a mausoleum in Riverside Cemetery.[47]

Lee Allen later wrote that this pair of deaths reminded him of the passing of Presidents John Adams and Thomas Jefferson, both of whom died on July 4, 1826, as the nation was celebrating the fiftieth anniversary of the Declaration of Independence. That reaction, while understandable, seems hyperbolic, but when the editor of the *Spalding Guide* for 1932 titled its necrology section "A Grim Harvest," he was right on the mark. For the deaths of Barnard and Johnson were only the beginning. Before the year was out, Herrmann and Comiskey were also dead, and Dreyfuss followed them early the next year. The 1932 *Reach Guide* noted that only two of the American League's pioneers were still in charge of their teams. One was Clark Griffith, a native of Missouri who began pitching in the Major Leagues in 1891, managed the White Sox to the first American League pennant, and became principal owner of the Senators in 1920. The second was Connie Mack, the son of Irish immigrants who began playing professional baseball in 1884, helped Johnson establish the American League as a Major League as manager and co-owner of the Athletics, and won nine pennants in the league's first three decades. These two would both endure and help the league celebrate its fiftieth anniversary, but for them and for others, 1931, this year of the "grim harvest," marked a real transition, a time to reflect on what had been and to consider the opportunities and challenges ahead.[48]

One

"The Ball Player Is a Fortunate Man"

The 1931 Major League baseball season opened on Tuesday, April 14, with a full schedule of eight games. In the American League, starting its thirty-first year of play, the Philadelphia Athletics began defense of their second straight World Series championship in Washington before a crowd of 32,000 that included President Herbert Hoover. Opening Day was also Pan-American Day. After the members of the presidential party took their seats, Secretary of War Henry Stimson led a procession that included the U.S. Army band, the two teams in new uniforms, and a group of Boy Scouts. The flags of twenty-one North and South American republics were run up along a horizontal cable, each one accompanied by the band playing its national anthem, and field artillery pieces fired in celebration. Washington manager Walter Johnson handed a ball to Hoover, who tossed it gracefully toward starting pitcher Lloyd Brown, but coach and team comedian Nick Altrock grabbed the ball instead. The president and Mrs. Hoover laughed. Looking on from his place in the Philadelphia dugout was a tall, thin, elderly man wearing a business suit, not a uniform, and clutching a scorecard. He was the co-owner of the A's and the team's manager, Cornelius McGillicuddy, a distinguished and even revered man known throughout the baseball world and beyond as Connie Mack. Following Hoover's ceremonial first pitch, the A's defeated the Senators, 5–3, in eleven innings. Lefty Grove pitched three innings in relief of Rube Walberg to earn the win. In New York, 70,000 fans watched the Yankees beat the Boston Red Sox, 6–3, with the great slugger Babe Ruth hitting the 566th home run of his career. The Cleveland Indians got fourteen hits and defeated the Chicago White Sox, 5–4, and the St. Louis Browns beat Detroit, 7–3, as pitcher Lefty Stewart held the Tigers to six hits while getting a triple and two singles himself. The National League began its fifty-sixth season with its champion, the St. Louis Cardinals, opening on the road in Cincinnati and defeating the Reds, 7–3. The New York Giants overpowered the Philadelphia Phillies, 9–5, despite two home runs from Phillies center fielder Chuck Klein. The Boston Braves came from behind to beat Brooklyn (then called the Robins), 7–4, and Charlie Root held Pittsburgh to four hits as the Cubs beat the

Pirates, 6–2, before a record crowd of 45,000 at Chicago's Wrigley Field. All in all, 245,000 fans saw the eight games, breaking the record for Opening Day attendance set in 1925.[1]

The *Sporting News*, the weekly newspaper that covered organized baseball to the exclusion of all other sports and virtually ignored its segregation, waxed lyrically about the start of the season, calling this Opening Day "the most eventful in the history of baseball." Crediting "clear skies and balmy breezes in some cities" and the expectation that both Major Leagues would feature close pennant races, the editorial noted that the crowds at all eight ballparks "were almost all of them record-breaking for an opening day." Yankee Stadium officials had expected about forty thousand fans, but many more showed up, some of them to watch new manager Joe McCarthy show off the changes he had wrought in a team that had won six pennants in the preceding ten years but none in the last two. "The crowd saw a team of hustlers," wrote Joe Vila in the weekly, "taking advantage of every point, playing heads up ball and looking for all the world like winners." The *New York Herald Tribune*'s Rud Rennie agreed. "The Yankees made eleven hits and had a happy faculty of grouping them to make runs," he wrote. In St. Louis, the Major Leagues' westernmost city, Opening Day was considerably less flashy. Only six thousand patrons showed up at Sportsman's Park, but this was not a bad crowd for the Browns, who had averaged less than two thousand fans per game the year before. With no American League pennants to its credit, St. Louis fielded a team stocked with newcomers and promised its supporters "flash and fighting spirit," baseball metaphor for mediocrity. The roster of the visiting Tigers, by comparison, was so weak and unsettled that manager Bucky Harris started the season platooning six outfielders, three left-handed batters playing against right-handed pitchers and three right-handed batters going against lefties.[2]

In Cincinnati the Cardinals gave notice that they had no intention of surrendering the National League pennant willingly. Their starting pitcher was Flint Rhem, a tall right-hander for whose behavior the adjective "colorful" was not colorful enough. Rhem had finished the previous season with eight straight victories, and on Opening Day he extended that streak. He yielded a two-run homer to Joe Stripp in the sixth inning, but his teammates scored six runs in the final three innings to secure the victory. The Associated Press (AP) called the Cubs' win over Pittsburgh "the most auspicious opening ever played at Wrigley Field," adding that "Root mowed the Pirates down with monotonous skill," suggesting that the team might cure its pitching ills and return to the top. In Boston the Robins, a team expected to do well, got "all the ego knocked out of them" by the Braves. The Brooklyn club, with a reputation for zaniness, had rookie Al Cohen single while batting out of turn, but the Boston dugout did not notice. The Giants and Phillies displayed so much offense at Baker Bowl—twenty-three hits between them—that the *Herald Tribune*'s Harry Cross felt compelled to comment on the new baseball being introduced by the National League. "If the new horsehide is deader than it was last year, then a cow can jump over the moon," he wrote. Watching the game and the ceremonies that preceded it was the commissioner of baseball, Kenesaw Mountain Landis, sporting a new pearl gray hat and seated in a box decorated with bunting. The Phillies wore new cream-colored uniforms and black armbands in memory of their deceased owner, William Baker, who had died in December. National League president John Heydler, Giants president Charles Stoneham, and Philadelphia's mayor, Harry Mackey, accompanied Landis, who characteristically spent much of the game resting his chin and his folded arms on the railing in front of him. His entourage was impressive but not so notable as the party of VIPs that surrounded the president in Washington. Hoover was there along with his wife, their son Allan, their daughter-in-law, and the entire Cabinet except for Attorney General William Mitchell. Treasury Secretary Andrew Mellon, much the fan, had arrived forty-five minutes early to watch batting practice.[3]

Hoover's interest in baseball almost certainly preceded his student days as a member of the first class at Stanford University. During his freshman year he tried out for the baseball team. He played shortstop for a while but switched to business manager, either because he injured a finger or because he just wasn't good enough. "My colleagues decided that I would be a better manager than shortstop," he wrote in his memoirs. While Hoover was running for president in 1928 as a Republican, a newspaper reported that Ruth was in his camp. The Babe, a celebrity with more star power than any other American, excluding perhaps Charles Lindbergh, denied it. He was for Al Smith, he said, the governor of New York and the Democratic candidate. Ruth even posed for a photograph wearing a Smith placard. Hoover showed up at Yankee Stadium a few days later, but Ruth refused to meet him except to shake his hand beneath the stands. Newspapers had a field day with this snub, but Ruth's agent and publicity man, Christy Walsh, smoothed things over and got a picture of the two of them after all. Hoover survived this brouhaha and won the election. The following autumn, the new president traveled by train to Philadelphia to watch the fifth game of the 1929 World Series, with the Athletics ahead of the Cubs, three games to one. The Cubs took a 2–0 lead into the bottom of the ninth inning, but a two-run homer by Mule Haas and a double by Bing Miller that scored Jimmie Foxx gave the A's the championship. Ten days later, a day known as Black Thursday, the stock market crashed. A record 12.9 million shares changed hands amid catastrophically tumbling prices, and Hoover had a lot more to worry about than the plight of the Cubs.[4]

Several writers have identified this World Series game as the occasion when raucous Philadelphia fans, upset over Prohibition, yelled at Hoover, "Beer! Beer! We want beer!"[5] Not so. Researchers David Jordan and Norman Macht wrote that when the president and Mrs. Hoover walked across the field at Shibe Park with Mayor Mackey to their box, fans roared their approval. The fans' "shocking manifestation of bad manners and lack of respect," as sportswriter Joe Williams characterized it, did not occur for another two years, during the third game of the 1931 World Series, also in Philadelphia. On Sunday, October 4, the day before Game Three, the president met with banking and insurance leaders until past midnight to discuss worsening economic conditions at home and abroad. Yet the executives conferring with the president had offered no real solution to the nation's financial problems. Hoover was in no mood to attend a World Series game the next day. He wrote in his memoirs, "I kept this engagement only because I felt that my presence at a sporting event might be a gesture of reassurance to a country suffering from a severe attack of 'jitters.'" When he and Mrs. Hoover entered the field, the game's starting pitchers, Grove for the A's and Burleigh Grimes for the Cardinals, stopped warming up. The president waved to the crowd and drew light applause. Then a few boos rang out, and they quickly became a cascade, but the protest concerned alcoholic beverages, not economics. After the eighth inning the Hoovers left the ballpark, and the Shibe Park public address announcer pleaded for silence, but the boos and the chanting returned. Concluded Williams, "This must be the first time a president ever has been booed in public, and at a ball game, of all places."[6]

Having become a professional ballplayer in 1884, Connie Mack was, in 1931, the sport's most venerable citizen. Just a year before, the city of Philadelphia had given him the Bok Award, a prestigious $10,000 prize usually given to scientists or statesmen. Mack's family name was McGillicuddy, but he told Fred Lieb in the 1940s that "except when we voted, our people always called themselves Mack." Those people included his mother, Mary McKillop McGillicuddy, who gave birth to two children before Cornelius was born on December 22, 1862, and four after, and his father, Michael, a native of Ireland's County

Kerry who enlisted in the Fifty-First Massachusetts Volunteer Infantry in August 1862 and was dispatched to New Bern, North Carolina. After being mustered out in July 1863, Mack worked sporadically in the cotton mills in and around East Brookfield, Massachusetts. Young Connie worked with him during his summers and then quit school at sixteen to work first at Stoddard's farm and market and then in the Green and Twitchell Shoe Factory. His parents objected to their son's growing fondness for baseball, fearful that it would divert his attention from earning a living. Mack stood more than 6 feet tall at age fifteen, and he soon became the regular catcher for East Brookfield's best amateur team. In April 1882 the Worcester (MA) Ruby Legs of the National League came to town for an exhibition game in which Mack got three hits. Later that summer the best team in the country, the National League's Chicago White Stockings, paid a visit. Mack played again. When the formidable Cap Anson came to bat, he allegedly turned toward the tall youngster behind the plate and said, "I've looked at a lot of catchers, but I don't think I ever saw one built as high as you." Connie was gangly but strong, and he was a good hitter. He excelled when the four Brookfield towns joined others to organize the Central Massachusetts Amateur League in 1883 and decided soon thereafter to test his skills as a professional.[7]

The new Connecticut State League placed teams in six nearby towns, but Mack failed to elicit any interest when he made inquiries with clubs in New Britain, Hartford, and Willimantic. Luck intervened in the person of pitcher Willie Hogan. He had signed to play for the Meriden club and persuaded the team's management to offer Mack a tryout in a game against the Yale University freshman team. Mack handled the catching flawlessly and secured a contract for $90 a month. He played well enough during the 1884 season to merit a gold watch and chain from the team's fans, and he also courted Hogan's sister, Margaret, although they did not get married until November 1887. Mack played the next two seasons at Hartford with significant raises in pay and hooked up with another pitcher, Frank Gilmore, as skinny as he. Together they were known as the "Bones Battery," skilled on the field and fan favorites as well. Toward the end of the 1886 season Walter Hewett, son of the owner of the Washington club of the National League, bought the contracts of five Hartford players, including Gilmore and Mack, for $3,500, a hefty sum. The "Bones Battery" made its Major League debut when Washington played Philadelphia on September 11, 1886. Mack batted .361 in ten games and convinced Hewett that he could play in the Major Leagues. The owner paid him $800 for his September work and signed him to a $2,250 contract for 1887.[8]

Over the next ten seasons Mack proved to be a competent defensive catcher but never much of a hitter. "If they kept the ball low on me, I couldn't hit for sour apples," he recalled years later. Convinced that his offensive prowess was not sufficient to keep him in the Majors, Mack became an astute handler of pitchers and a crafty defensive player. Trickery was an important part of his game. He would signal his pitcher with his foot that a runner was taking too big a lead and could be picked off. When the rules said that any caught foul was an out, he learned that clicking his tongue against the roof of his mouth might convince the umpire that the batter had fouled off a pitch that Mack had caught. After catchers began positioning themselves immediately behind the plate instead of several paces further back, he became expert at tipping bats, thereby throwing off hitters' swings. Before the 1888 season began, Gilmore suffered an arm injury that the liniments and snake oils of the day could not cure, and the club wound up finishing last. The following year, 1889, Washington was last again, but Mack had become a very popular player. Young John Heydler, then a government printer who dreamed of a career in baseball, recalled that Mack would visit a butcher shop before each game to buy a small steak, not to eat, but to insert into his flimsy glove for added protection. "We younger fellows also would buy steaks to put into our gloves," said Heydler, "and the butcher could never understand why Connie's daily steak didn't put more flesh on his bones."[9]

The shocking news in baseball in 1889 happened after the season was over. The Brotherhood of Professional Base Ball Players, the sport's first trade union, decided to form a league of its own starting in 1890. Nearly all the Washington players, Mack included, jumped to the Buffalo team in the Players League. "I was younger then," Mack told Lieb years later, "and things looked different to me. It seemed to me that we had a good cause." But the Players League lasted only one season. Mack returned to the National League in 1891 and had his contract assigned to Pittsburgh, where he played six seasons. The Pirates, as they came to be called, had a fine year in 1893, but Mack played only thirty-seven games, breaking his ankle in a collision at home plate. "I was never the same player after that," he said. "I was slower on the bases and couldn't stoop as well behind the plate." It hardly mattered, though. By the end of the following season, Mack was the Pirates' manager, and his diminished playing skills were incidental to his unfolding career. Mack made his managerial debut on September 3, 1894, and the Pirates' players responded to their new boss by winning, 22–1. "The scoreboard almost ran out of numbers," he said.[10]

Thus began a managerial career that would stretch more than fifty-six years, until October 1950, but only two full seasons in Pittsburgh. Mack's 1895 Pirates flirted with first place for much of the season, but they tumbled at the end, finishing seventh in a twelve-team league. The following year Pittsburgh finished fifth, and Mack's frequent clashes with co-owner William Kerr spelled the end of Mack's tenure. When the Pirates lost a game on the road and Kerr fired off a wire asking Mack why he had done this and not that, Mack wired back intemperately. The two agreed to a parting of the ways at the end of the season, but watching Mack trying to do his job under these less than ideal conditions was Ban Johnson, then the ambitious president of the Western League. He contacted Mack immediately and invited him to come to Chicago for a chat, the result of which had Mack taking control of the Milwaukee Creams in 1897 as manager and part owner. Johnson changed the name of his enterprise to the American League after the 1899 season, and a year later he chose Mack to head a new franchise in Philadelphia in direct competition with the National League's Phillies. "They know you in Pennsylvania, and I think the fans will be receptive," said Johnson, according to Lieb, adding, "Of course, we'll revive the name of the old Philadelphia American Association team—the Athletics."[11]

Connie Mack was both the field manager in Philadelphia and one of the team's owners, but financing the Athletics by himself was well beyond his means. Ban Johnson's plan called for Mack to receive 25 percent of the club's 1,500 shares for an investment estimated to be $2,500. Charles Somers, the Cleveland entrepreneur who owned half of the American League club in that city and chunks of the teams in Boston, Chicago, and Philadelphia, took the other 75 percent until additional local ownership could be located. Mack contacted Sam Jones, baseball writer for the Associated Press, and Frank Hough, sports editor of the *Philadelphia Inquirer*. Together they agreed to invest and located a site for a ballpark, a vacant lot in a section of the city called Brewerytown. They hired builder James Foster to erect a grandstand and named it Columbia Park. Jones and Hough also introduced Mack to Ben Shibe, a partner in A. J. Reach & Co., manufacturers of sporting goods. Mack tempted Shibe by telling him that the Reach baseball might be named the official ball of the American League. Shibe hesitated, but Reach urged him to take a 50 percent interest (750 shares), leaving Jones and Hough with 25 percent, and that's what Shibe did. He was present when Somers signed the lease for the Columbia Park grounds, and in March 1901 he was elected president of the club.[12]

Over the next three decades Mack refined a personal demeanor and managerial style that gave him honored status throughout baseball, win or lose. He was "Mr. Mack" to almost everyone, respected by his own players and his opponents alike and quite nearly canonized by fans. Out of respect for his players he early on abandoned wearing a uniform in favor of street clothes. One day in Milwaukee, he told Fred Lieb, he had been so angry with his team after a loss that he did not dare enter the clubhouse until all the players had dressed and left. Henceforth he avoided entering the clubhouse at all and saw no reason to change out of a business suit into a baseball uniform. The esteem Mack earned for his conduct and appearance was redoubled because he was also an excellent manager. His strength was identifying skilled young players, acquiring them at low prices, and getting them to play to their potential. In addition to scouring the Minor Leagues, Mack turned regularly to colleges and universities as sources for players. He found pitcher Eddie Plank at Gettysburg College, second baseman Eddie Collins at Columbia, and catcher Mickey Cochrane at Boston University, to name just a few. All of them became stars. Mack's other strength was tactical. He was a pioneer in figuring out how to pitch to particular batters and how to position his fielders accordingly. He was, in the common parlance of the game, the "Tall Tactician."[13]

Shibe and Mack simply did not have the cash to win a bidding war for players. Shibe poured most of the money he made during the team's first decade into constructing the ballpark that bore his name, and Mack's personal finances resembled a salaried employee's, even after Shibe arranged a complicated financial deal that included giving Mack a loan to buy out Jones and Hough and making him an equal partner. Mack, as historian Bruce Kuklick showed, was learning how complex baseball economics could be, but he still chose to define the team's annual bottom line by comparing gate receipts to the cost of acquiring and paying players. After winning the pennant in 1910, 1911, 1913, and 1914, his stated goal was not to destroy his team but to reduce his payroll by selling off high-priced stars and using the revenues to acquire scrappy young players who would attract fans, allow the team to make a profit, and, in time, win again. It didn't work. The 1915 Athletics sank rather quickly to last place with a final record of 43-109. Moreover, attendance plummeted further to just 146,223, barely over 2,000 per game. Mack was a manager, not a Midas, and he went through fifty-six players trying to find enough with competitive skills. He used sixteen different men at third base and twenty-seven pitchers. But saving one's way to prosperity was a tough business strategy in baseball, and Mack could not pull it off. Discovering unheralded young players capable of performing at the Major League level took skill; doing it on the cheap required a miracle. The 1915 A's were a terrible team, and the 1916 A's were even worse. Their last-place finish was the team's second of seven in a row. As Kuklick pointed out, even the fictional Jack Keefe, created by sportswriter and humorist Ring Lardner in *You Know Me, Al*, finished his rather inglorious career with the Athletics.[14]

Shibe's death in January 1922 was a sign that things were about to change. Control of his half of the club passed to his four children, but only his two sons took an active role. Tom, named president, performed mostly ceremonial duties. Jack, vice president and secretary, helped Mack remodel and expand Shibe Park in 1925. Even more important, the co-owners decided to forsake signing untested players and let Mack spend borrowed money to acquire established Minor League talent. He began by buying the contract of first baseman Joe Hauser from the American Association Milwaukee Brewers. He hit seventeen home runs for the A's in 1923 and twenty-seven in 1924 before injuries hampered him. Outfielder Bing Miller came from the Red Sox in a trade, and pitcher Eddie Rommel, who arrived from the Baltimore Orioles in the International League, won twenty-seven games for Mack in 1922. Not every purchase from the Minor Leagues worked out. Paul Strand, who cost Mack $40,000, had hit .394 in the rarified air of Salt Lake City in the Pacific Coast League and only .228 with Philadelphia. But second baseman Max Bishop, bought from Baltimore, and Rube Walberg, a pitcher picked up on waivers from the Giants, proved more than capable. When Mack purchased Al Simmons from Milwaukee, the outfielder used a very unorthodox batting stance to commence a Hall of Fame career. The Athletics got better slowly, finishing in seventh place in 1922, sixth in 1923, and fifth in 1924. Over the following winter Mack acquired a trio of players that would turn out to be among his greatest. He paid the Orioles $100,600, spread out over ten years, for Lefty Grove, an outstanding pitcher. On a tip he signed Jimmie Foxx, a young catcher, and later converted him to a first baseman. Finally, Mack purchased an interest in the Portland team in the Pacific Coast League to ensure that he could then purchase Mickey Cochrane for $50,000.[15]

But for the Yankees, who had initiated their long dominance of the American League by winning their first pennant in 1921 and then repeating that triumph in 1922, 1923, 1926, 1927, and 1928, the Athletics of the late 1920s might have won a slew of championships. As it was, they finished second in 1925, third in 1926, and second again in 1927 and 1928 before finally rising to the top. The roster of the 1927 Philadelphia team glittered with seven future members of the Hall of Fame: Ty Cobb, Cochrane, Collins, Foxx, Grove, Simmons, and Zack Wheat. The Yankees' Murderers' Row, as their slugging lineup was called, buried this team by nineteen games, and New York eked out another pennant in 1928, but a year later everything came together for the Athletics. Combining excellent hitting with outstanding pitching, Philadelphia ran away with the 1929 pennant. The Tigers led the league in several key offensive categories, but the A's finished second in batting average, slugging average, and runs scored, and the team's pitchers led the league in earned run average (ERA), strikeouts, and fewest hits allowed. Simmons batted .365, second in the league, and led in runs batted in (RBIs) with 157. George Earnshaw led the league in wins with twenty-four, and Grove added twenty with a league-best winning percentage of .769. The A's led the Yankees by twelve games in the middle of August and finished eighteen games ahead. They won the World Series too, defeating the Cubs, four games to one. For the Mackmen, as they were called, 1929 was their sixth American League pennant and fourth World Series championship.[16]

In September, while the Athletics were salting away the pennant by winning fourteen games against only six losses, the great stock market boom of the 1920s shuddered. Economist John Kenneth Galbraith wrote that stock prices had begun to rise in the second half of 1924 but that the boom took off in 1927. By the end of 1928, according to Galbraith, "The market began to rise, not by slow, steady steps, but by great vaulting leaps." More important, domestic consumption of manufactured goods had slowed markedly as wage increases simply did not keep pace with production. Many individuals had bought into the market, it is true, though not as many as is commonly supposed, but corporations and banks were involved to a much greater extent. Large companies, seeing inventories beginning to stockpile, invested cash reserves in the market instead of in new plants and machinery. Banks, not being asked for loans to expand commercial activity, lent money to fuel both stock market and real estate speculation. On September 3, as the A's were pounding the Yankees, 10–2, "the great bull market of the nineteen-twenties," in Galbraith's words, "came to an end." Stock prices wavered, broke downward two days later, and then remained ragged for several weeks until the great crash came at the end of October.[17]

Although most people did not recognize it at the time, the United States was tumbling into the abyss of international economic chaos. The popular perception of Herbert Hoover that has trickled down through the decades is of an unfeeling president who refused to take action to counteract the effects of the

Great Crash and who, therefore, hastened the arrival of the Great Depression. Historians have developed an alternative view in which Hoover is seen as more of a progressive and a pragmatist but still unequal to the task at hand. In June 1929, only three months after being inaugurated, he attacked the agricultural crisis by signing into law the Agricultural Marketing Act, designed to control surpluses and promote orderly markets. But dealing with the collapse of the industrial side of the economy was a matter that proved to be beyond his and everyone else's ken. As business conditions deteriorated, Americans could not know how long the downturn would last or how severe it would be. As a recent point of reference, the recession of 1921, severe but brief, suggested that the current crisis might be no more than an exaggerated swing in the business cycle that would shortly correct itself. Even after banks began to fail at an alarmingly accelerating rate late in 1930, many Americans simply denied the depth of the problem. "Of this fact I am very positive," wrote a Maryland building contractor to the president in 1931, "that there is not five percent of the poverty, distress, and general unemployment that many of your enemies would have us believe." Some residents of Cincinnati wore buttons that read, "I'm sold on America. I won't talk depression." Yet as historian David M. Kennedy wrote, "What was still in 1931 called the depression was about to become the unprecedented calamity known to history as the Great Depression."[18]

The success the A's enjoyed as the 1920s collapsed into the 1930s unfolded against an unprecedented offensive explosion. Baseball shorthand dictates that the period before 1920 be called the "Deadball Era" and the period starting with 1920 the "Lively Ball Era." Indeed there is evidence that baseballs produced for the 1920 season were made with better yarn and wound tighter than in years before, making them more resilient. Statistics seem to back this up. Batting average, slugging average, home runs, and runs scored all jumped in 1920. More important, these increases continued throughout the decade. Still, factors other than the way baseballs were being manufactured were also at work. A new rule adopted for 1920 prohibited pitchers from doctoring the ball, outlawing the spitball, the emery ball, and a host of other tricks. The death of Cleveland shortstop Ray Chapman, hit in the head by a pitched ball in August 1920, led quickly to umpires' throwing baseballs out of play before they became too dirty. And then there was the emergence of the mighty Babe Ruth, a hitter unlike any ever seen before. In 1919 he hit 29 home runs while no one else hit more than a dozen. The following year he hit 54 homers, more than every other American League team. Old-time players tried to denigrate

Ruth's slugging talent as unschooled muscle, but fans embraced him and the changes in the game he wrought. Major League attendance passed the nine million mark for the first time in 1920, and new records were set in 1924, 1926, and 1927. But all of this was mere prelude to 1930.[19]

If Major League owners had intended to react to the growing economic crisis by doing something to jack up offense, a doubtful proposition, their decision to introduce a new, still livelier baseball in 1930 was just the trick. The result was a stunning offensive season that baseball researcher Bill James called "a hitter's bacchanalia" and record attendance that kept the wolf from the owners' doors. Again statistics tell the tale. Batters hit .303 in the National League and .288 in the American League. The Giants' Bill Terry won the National League batting championship by hitting .401, beating out Brooklyn's Babe Herman, who batted .393, and Chuck Klein and Lefty O'Doul of the Phillies. The Giants hit .319 as a team, led the league, and finished third; the Phillies hit .315 and finished last, forty games out of first place. Forty-three National League batters hit over .300, and homers in the National League increased 18 percent. Hack Wilson's 56 homers, 13 more than the previous league record, set a standard not surpassed until 1998. National League games saw an average of 11.4 runs scored, and the fans loved it. In the American League Al Simmons won the batting title, hitting .381 and besting the Yankees' Lou Gehrig, who hit .379. American League batters hit 673 home runs, up 13 percent over 1929, and thirty-three players batted .300 or better. Total attendance hit 10.1 million, and owners cleared $1.5 million in profits, a healthy 16.4 percent over their expenses. Perhaps because of these offensive fireworks, the effects of the Depression did not yet reach baseball, but some of the players knew bad times were coming. Speaking during the 1930 World Series, Cardinals pitcher Burleigh Grimes said, "The ball player of this year is a fortunate man. In other occupations," he added, "there has been shrinkage in salaries and lack of employment. The ball player, under the terms of his contract, has gone on daily and been paid in full."[20]

The leading hitters for the Athletics in 1930, as they repeated as World Series champions, were Simmons, Mickey Cochrane, and Jimmie Foxx, and their best pitcher was Lefty Grove. Besides winning the batting championship, Simmons hit 36 home runs and drove in 165 runs, second only to Gehrig. Cochrane batted .357, fifth highest in the league, and Foxx drove in 156 runs, third in the league. They were a formidable trio. Simmons signed a professional contract in 1922 and played only two years in the Minor Leagues before Connie Mack bought his services for a reported $50,000. He quickly became a star. He batted .387 in 1925 and got 253 hits, just 4 short of George Sisler's Major League record. The BBWAA voted him to the *Sporting News* Major League All-Star team in 1927 and 1929, and the *Sporting News* named him the Most Valuable Player (MVP) in the American League in 1929. Simmons's nickname was "Bucketfoot Al." A right-handed hitter, he stood at the plate with his left foot pointing down the third-base line instead of toward the pitcher. This open stance, with his foot in the "bucket"—that is, aimed toward the water bucket in the dugout—harmed him not at all. "The rest of me," he argued, "from the belt up, especially my wrists, arms, and shoulders, was swinging in a proper line over the plate." Mack agreed. "Let that young man alone," he warned. Simmons was also a fine outfielder. He possessed speed, good hands, and a strong throwing arm. In the 1930 World Series Simmons batted .364 and hit home runs in the first game and the last.[21]

Cochrane's family called him by his given name, Gordon, but to everyone else he was "Kid." One of Mack's college boys, he played baseball, basketball, and football; ran track; and boxed at Boston University before signing his first professional contract in 1923 with Dover (DE) in the Eastern Shore League. Cochrane wanted to play the outfield, but the only vacancy was at catcher, and so behind the plate he went. After batting .322, he attracted the attention of Tom Turner, a scout for the Portland Beavers. Turner gave him a $1,000 bonus to sign a contract for 1924 and a new nickname. Overlooking the Cochrane family's Irish Protestant roots, Turner declared, "You're a Boston Irishman named Mickey Cochrane." After Cochrane spent one season on the West Coast, Turner bought the Beavers. Mack or maybe the Shibe family helped him by acquiring part of the club for about $132,000 and then purchasing Cochrane's contract for an additional $50,000. Cochrane went to spring training with the Athletics in 1925, and it quickly became apparent that his defensive skills were sorely inadequate. Mack turned him over to veteran catcher Cy Perkins, who worked him long hours every day in the Florida sun with great success. "Cochrane was a misfit in February," Mack said, "but a star in April." No one could question the catcher's durability, his skill as a batter, or his speed, and after Perkins's tutelage, he quickly became an outstanding handler of pitchers. Even though the Yankees won the American League pennant in 1928, Cochrane won the Most Valuable Player Award. He hit .331 in 1929 and .357, his career high, in 1930. In the 1930 World Series against the Cardinals, he too hit a pair of home runs.[22]

After John "Home Run" Baker, one of Mack's earlier stars, stopped playing, he retired to his Maryland farm but returned to baseball to manage the Easton

(MD) team in the Eastern Shore League. There in 1924, he tried out Foxx, a sixteen-year-old high-schooler, and offered him a contract as a catcher. Foxx was even more of a scholastic star than Cochrane, excelling at basketball, soccer, and track, and he joined the Easton team after finishing his junior year. He caught seventy-six games, batted .296, and hit 10 home runs, impressing Baker so much that he journeyed to New York to try to interest either the Yankees or the visiting Athletics in his protégé. The Yankees passed, but Mack agreed to send a scout south, bought Foxx's contract for $2,000, and had him come to Philadelphia after the Eastern Shore League's season was over. Not good enough to supplant Cochrane behind the plate, Foxx, save for a short trip to the Minors, spent most of the next three seasons on the A's bench. Mack called him "the easiest boy on the team to handle," but clearly Foxx needed a permanent position. In 1929, still only twenty-one, he replaced the injured Joe Hauser at first base and rewarded Mack's confidence by batting .354, driving in 118 runs and hitting 33 home runs. His next year was just as good, if not better: .335, 37 homers, and 156 runs batted in. As he grew, Foxx earned a reputation for his strength and his ability to hit long and hard home runs. His nickname was "The Beast," and some of his homers were described in the press as "Ruthian." In the 1930 World Series, he was the sole player on either team to hit safely in all six games, and he won Game Five with a two-run home run off Grimes in the top of the ninth inning.[23]

In contrast to these hitters who came to the Athletics relatively unproven, Grove was an established pitcher, albeit in the Minor Leagues, when Mack bought his contract late in 1924. Although he was only twenty-four, Grove was the best pitcher on one of the best teams in the Minors. Baltimore won seven straight pennants (1919–25), and Grove was 109-36 in just four seasons. Grove had one pitch to call his own, his fastball, but he used it to great advantage, leading the International League in strikeouts four times, and he complemented it by being plenty wild and plenty mean. "Never bothered me who was up there with the bat," he told baseball historian Donald Honig years later. "I'd hit 'em in the middle of the back or hit 'em in the foot. It didn't make any difference to me." He started slowly with Philadelphia, but in 1927 he began a string of seven straight seasons with twenty or more victories. He won twenty-four games in 1928 and twenty-eight in 1930, led the league in strikeouts from 1925 through 1931, and had the lowest earned run average four times in the same period. In an offensive era, he was the supreme defensive force. In 1929 Ruth ruefully admitted, "When that guy is right, there isn't a team, and never has been a team, that could lick him." The A's won the pennant in 1930 by eight games over the Senators with the Yankees fading to third, and they beat the Cardinals in a six-game World Series. Grove started and won Game One, 5–2, started and lost Game Four, 3–2, and then relieved George Earnshaw the next day, working two innings to earn the win. Two days later, back at home, Earnshaw shut down the Cardinals, 7–1, to win the championship. Still, attendance at Shibe Park fell 14 percent in 1930. Mack saw this decline, Depression or not, as evidence that Philadelphia fans just would not support a winner.[24]

By the time the A's won their second consecutive championship, baseball fans were accustomed to listening to the World Series on the radio. The sport's involvement with this new technology dated from radio's very beginning. Media historian James R. Walker called Pittsburgh radio station KDKA's broadcast of the 1920 presidential election returns "the birth of commercial broadcasting in the United States," and just a few months later, on August 5, 1921, the same station broadcast a game from Forbes Field between the Pirates and the Phillies. The broadcaster on this occasion was a twenty-six-year-old named Harold Arlin. During the day, he worked for Westinghouse, which built, owned, and ran KDKA, and at night, he was a studio announcer. Arlin regularly reported baseball scores, and his plans included broadcasting a tennis match and a college football game. "Since I'd already done these things, or was planning to do them," he recalled, "the Pirates were a natural." Arlin sat in a box seat behind home plate with his equipment right next to him. No one at the station thought baseball on the radio would last, and this first effort had its deficiencies. "Sometimes the transmitter worked and sometimes it didn't," Arlin remembered. "No one had the foggiest *idea*, the slightest hint of an *inkling*, that what we started would take off like it did [emphasis in original]." Yet, just a few weeks later, another station, WJZ in Newark, New Jersey, inaugurated its operations by broadcasting Game One of the World Series between the Giants and the Yankees on October 5. For this game, no broadcaster was in the Polo Grounds. Instead, a sportswriter for the *Newark Call*, which owned WJZ, sent pitch-by-pitch information by telegraph from the ballpark to Sandy Hunt, his editor in Newark. Hunt used a telephone to relay what he learned to Tommy Cowan, positioned in a make-shift studio on the roof, and from there Cowan informed his listeners what had transpired on the ball field.[25]

In 1922 Westinghouse linked three stations, WJZ, WGY in Schenectady, New York, and WBZ in Springfield, Massachusetts, to create a network transmitting broadcasts of the second consecutive Series between the two New York teams.

Sportswriter Grantland Rice, hired by the stations while also working for the *New York Tribune*, positioned himself near home plate, like Arlin, and quickly learned that broadcasting required intense focus. He told *Wireless Age* magazine that his job was "as simple as talking to one man," but later admitted that "once was enough for me for all my life." Not too many people owned radios, so fans within the stations' limited reach gathered in stores selling them to hear the games. Others, especially in New York, clustered around publicly located speakers in such numbers to demonstrate that baseball on the radio had a future. In 1923 Rice ceded his place to his *Tribune* colleague, W. O. McGeehan, but in the fourth inning of Game Three, McGeehan simply gave up and turned over the microphone to a young man named Graham McNamee, who thus began broadcasting the first of nine straight World Series. McNamee had come to New York from Washington, hoping to become a professional singer. In May 1923 he walked into the offices of station WEAF on a lark, asked for a tour, did an audition, and wound up with a job as an announcer. He handled a boxing match in August well enough to be assigned to the Series, and he soon became America's most recognized voice. McNamee was not a sports fan, but he took quick measure of the tool at his disposal. "You must make each of your listeners," he said, "though miles away from the spot, feel that he or she, too, is there with you in the press stand."[26]

For the 1924 Series, matching the Giants against the Senators, coverage originated with WEAF and was transmitted to Washington and at least five other stations in Boston, Pittsburgh, Providence, Schenectady, and South Dartmouth, Massachusetts. Other stations not part of this group used studio announcers to relay information to their listeners from wire-service play-by-play accounts. In 1925 the Senators won the American League pennant again and played the Pirates in the Series. AT&T, which owned the long-distance telephone lines essential to linking stations together, produced the broadcasts for an even larger number of cities. In September 1926 RCA (the Radio Corporation of America) created NBC (the National Broadcasting Company) and assumed control of the AT&T network that reached an audience estimated at fifteen million when the Yankees returned to the Series to play the Cardinals. In 1927 CBS (the Columbia Broadcast System) challenged NBC. Much smaller than its competitor, CBS used Andrew White, the editor of *Wireless Age*, as its announcer for two Series, but in 1929 it replaced him with Ted Husing, a young man eager to make a name for himself in radio. Husing's baseball knowledge was more than sufficient, and his on-air personality rivaled McNamee's. The pair went head-to-head for three years (1929–31) before they were both eased aside into a role later called "color commentator." By 1931 broadcasts of the Series were so popular, according to the *Sporting News*, that two stations, WRH in Carlstadt, New Jersey, and KUP in San Francisco, broadcast the play-by-play to fans on ocean liners with assistance from the American Radio News Corporation and the International News Service.[27]

During the 1927 Series between the Yankees and the Pirates, the first to be broadcast coast-to-coast, Ring Lardner sat in a press box seat close enough to hear McNamee at work. "Here I was watching a World Series ballgame," Lardner wrote, "and listening to the broadcast of it at one and the same time. You might almost say I attended a doubleheader, the game Mac was describing and the one I was watching." Lardner's wisecrack was one salvo, albeit gentle, in the battle pitting newspapers' coverage of ball games against the immediacy of play-by-play on the radio. Many newspapers believed early on that radio might prove to be an effective way to promote their own product. The *Chicago Tribune* for example, began its foray into radio by providing news for KYW, the city's first station. In 1924 the *Tribune*, having learned that Chicagoans had bought more than one hundred thousand radios, took control of WJAZ and renamed it WGN (for "World's Greatest Newspaper"). Radio was slow to build its own news operations, but sportswriters saw the threat to their craft. In May 1923 the BBWAA, founded in 1908 to advocate for the sport's growing press corps, wired the commissioner and the two league presidents to protest an apparent agreement to allow "a wireless corporation to broadcast results of games at [the] Polo Grounds and other parks throughout the country, giving detailed results play by play." The wire continued, "If this is permitted, it will kill circulation of afternoon papers and in the end will result in curtailment of baseball publicity." This protest went nowhere. Afternoon newspapers did not collapse. They pushed back their deadlines, allowing them to publish as many final scores as possible. Radio had already proved that it was on the scene to stay, and newspapers adjusted and profited from the new medium's ability to create and nurture new fans.[28]

Major League owners also regarded the emergence of radio with apprehension, fearing that fans who could hear games on the radio might be less inclined to buy tickets. Walker noted that Midwest teams were more accepting of the new medium than East Coast teams. The Cubs allowed WMAQ, owned by the *Chicago Daily News*, to broadcast every home game in 1925, and WGN did the same starting two years later. Owner William Wrigley Jr., whose family business sold chewing gum, and club president Bill Veeck Sr. saw radio as a vehicle to promote their product, ball games, for two hours or more every day. Their view proved prescient. The Cubs' attendance rose after they began broadcasting, and Veeck insisted that radio was "the very best possible advertisement." Other clubs agreed, including the Reds and the Cardinals, who began broadcasting in 1927, but only for a few seasons. In December 1929 two executives from the National Association of Broadcasters spoke at baseball's winter meetings, lauding radio's potential for baseball and calling broadcasting a gift that is "yours without charge . . . something that we must carry on to satisfy the great interest that the American people have in baseball." National League owners seemed to agree. They passed a resolution declaring that "it is the sense of the National League that radio broadcasting is an individual club matter." American League owners, once under orders from founder Ban Johnson to prohibit any radio, were less sanguine. Browns owner Phil Ball said he believed that broadcasting cut into attendance while league president Ernest Barnard objected to radio because "broadcasters are reaping a golden harvest from the major league clubs without any financial return to the clubs which provide the entertainment." Two years later, league owners adopted a resolution forbidding clubs from contracting for radio rights after the 1932 season when the owners would again discuss the question.[29]

Over the next several years, baseball argued about radio's proper place in the game. Owners ceded control over broadcasting the World Series to the commissioner, but policy for the regular season was a club matter. Veeck never retreated from his pro-radio position, but Sam Breadon, owner of the Cardinals, did. He claimed that his attendance was adversely affected by Chicago's high-powered radio stations, and he doubled back on the concern that radio threatened newspapers. In 1932 the Cardinals permitted no broadcasts on Sundays or holidays. Breadon introduced a resolution at the joint Major League meetings in December calling for the elimination of all broadcasting of Major League games. Veeck objected, as did the White Sox and both Boston teams. Still, the resolution was not defeated until the Giants' representative, speaking for his anti-radio club, rose to oppose it as an intrusion into club matters. "If we start to regulate the other man's business with radio, no one knows where that will finish," said Leo Bondy. Left to make their own decision, the Cardinals dropped radio entirely in 1934, but those opposed to broadcasting were on the retreat. Perhaps they were influenced by the idea Barnard had once raised, that stations should be required to pay clubs rights fees to broadcast games, fees that could be supported by advertising. Thus, in December 1934, when L. C. McEvoy, vice president of the Browns, introduced an anti-radio resolution at the American League's winter meetings, it garnered only four votes, leaving each club free to carve out its own radio policy. Yankees owner Jacob Ruppert continued to insist that radio would hurt attendance, but Connie Mack announced that the A's would begin broadcasting in 1936. There was no consensus except in New York where the anti-radio strategy led to an agreement between the Yankees, Giants, and Dodgers in 1934 not to broadcast any games for the next five seasons.[30]

What smoothed the relationship between baseball and radio was the advent of rights fees and sponsorships. Many of the first radio stations had been public service endeavors, and most programming, including sporting events, was unsponsored. Commercializing broadcasts came slowly, spurred in part by the development of regional and national networks that required substantial resources to produce programs that would attract wide audiences. Radio stations had argued that broadcasting games gave clubs free publicity, but some club owners wanted more. They began to charge rights fees and demand other considerations to compensate for what they perceived might be lost ticket revenue. Early in 1934, the Reds said that stations would have to pay to broadcast their games, and the Cubs announced that stations broadcasting from Wrigley Field would have to promote each day's game at five-minute intervals between 10 a.m. and 2:30 p.m. Later that year, Walgreens, the drugstore chain, paid WGN $45,000, and Prima beer paid WBBM, another Chicago station, $40,000 to sponsor broadcasts. Nationally, cereal maker General Mills recognized that baseball could help sell Wheaties, "the Breakfast of Champions," to young fans and their mothers, sponsoring both Major League and Minor League broadcasts. General Mills also worked with teams to organize events to draw fans into ballparks, and a corporate ad crowed that "every Wheaties announcer knows that his job depends in part on how many listeners he turns into *customers* [emphasis in original]." In June 1936, when General Mills commissioned the Market Research Corporation to ask Philadelphians about the effect of A's broadcasts on their ticket-buying habits, the results were predictable. Co-owner Jack Shibe reacted profanely, but other companies, including Kellogg's, Procter & Gamble, Coca-Cola, Goodrich, and two gasoline companies, Atlantic Refining and Socony-Vacuum, also decided that baseball was good for business. By 1938 General Mills was spending $1 million a year to sponsor broadcasts, and the marriage between baseball and radio was nearly complete. Listeners heard commercials at the end of each half-inning, and broadcasters also dropped references to sponsors' products into their play-by-play. Red Barber, whose Dodgers broadcasts were sometimes farmed out from Wheaties to Ivory Soap, would say that the bases are "Ivory clean" and that a pitcher being removed from the game would be heading for an "Ivory shower."[31]

A few weeks before Ban Johnson died in March 1931, he gave one of his final interviews to Edgar G. Brands, editor of the *Sporting News*, from his St. Louis hospital bed. Johnson allowed himself to be photographed. The published image showed him worn and unkempt, but Brands wrote that the former league president's voice was strong and his mind sharp and that he was fully capable of giving the "New Year's message" that Brands had sought. Johnson spoke at some length about several matters confronting organized baseball, including changes in the draft rules, the growing determination of some Major League clubs to create farm systems, night baseball, and the increase in offense that had defined the game during the previous few seasons. On this last point he was most emphatic, saying, "Unless the rubber is reduced and the lively ball deadened, there will continue to be a lot of meaningless home runs, which will not only hurt the infield and outfield play, but the attendance as well, for the public does not like long-drawn out ball games." Johnson expressed his belief that the baseball used in Major League play after the Great War was different from the one used before the war. "There was some excuse for the ball used shortly after the war, because it was impossible to obtain the right materials," Brands quoted Johnson, "but after that contingency passed, more rubber was inserted in the core." Johnson recalled that he had cut up several balls while he was president to see what was inside and argued many times with George Reach, who asserted that the Reach ball had not changed, but the former president said he remained unconvinced.[32]

When Johnson disparaged "meaningless home runs" and claimed they hurt attendance, he was forgetting that complaints about boring, dull ball games devoid of scoring had been lodged during the Deadball Era and that a significant change in the ball had been made in 1910 as a countermeasure. The National League bottomed out with 9,566 hits in 1907 and 4,139 runs (6.65 per game for both teams) in 1908. The American League followed suit: 9,702 hits in 1908 and 4,264 runs (6.88 per game) in 1909. National Leaguers hit only 126 home runs in 1906, and American Leaguers hit even fewer, 104, a year later. In 1905 just three American League batters reached the .300 mark, and in 1907, only four National League hitters did so. Among the proposals advanced but rejected to swing the pendulum back the other way and to inject more offensive excitement into the game, some were reasonable, like reducing the size of the strike zone, and some preposterous, like allowing runners left on base to return the next inning, but the one that was adopted was simple and expedient: use a livelier baseball.[33]

Although it was standard practice for the Reach company to deny ever making changes in the way baseballs were manufactured so as to alter their performance, Reach admitted years later that his company had done exactly that. "We used our newly-patented cork center ball for the first time in the 1910 World Series," he confessed to sportswriter Dick Cresap in 1949, "and nobody knew about it except a few people in our factory." He continued, "The next year, 1911, the ball was the liveliest it ever has been. In fact, we had to tone it down." Reach explained that it really wasn't the cork center that enlivened the ball. It was the way the wool was wound around the core that counted. Wind the wool tighter, he explained, and the ball would be more resilient and travel further. Reach also debunked another ball-making myth. He countered the notion that there was any difference between the official National League ball manufactured by Spalding and the official American League ball manufactured by Reach. "That was so much rubbish," Reach told Cresap. As early as 1880, Spalding had given Reach a contract to manufacture balls stamped with the Spalding name, and in 1892, a massive reorganization of the entire sporting goods industry made Reach and several other companies part of the Spalding enterprise. Thus, unbeknownst to all but a few, the official balls for both Major Leagues had been for years manufactured to identical standards in Reach's Philadelphia factory. All that distinguished one from the other was the ink stamped on them. "There was absolutely no difference in the ball until the late Twenties when the cover on the National League ball was a little thicker and had extra stitches. The balls for both leagues were made on the same machines and wound exactly the same way."[34]

Twenty years before Reach's admission, Tom Shibe, a Reach executive as well as president of the Athletics, had insistently toed the company line. He told Ed Burns of the *Chicago Tribune* that the balls his company had made for the 1929 season were identical to those made for the 1911 season. "Absolutely no change," he declared as he showed Burns the manufacturing process. In fact Shibe asserted that the Major Leagues did not pay his company enough to enliven the ball. "We make baseballs on contract, and the leagues never have kept pace with the rise in cost of materials," he explained. "The ball could be made more lively, I suppose, but you can see for yourself what an expensive outlay would be involved in changing machinery and materials." However much Shibe was dissembling, the evidence suggests that the baseballs used just a season later, in 1930, were livelier. Moreover, the owners decided, quite openly, to tone things down for 1931. Meeting in New York in early February, American League owners decided to approve a ball sewn with heavier stitching, thereby giving pitchers a better grip. Simultaneously, National League owners went a step further, approving heavier stitching plus a cover thicker by .012 of an inch. American League president Ernest Barnard admitted that the stitching had been altered a few years before, sinking it a bit, because the threads kept breaking. He explained that the new raised seam would enable pitchers "to increase the spin of the ball and give it a better curve or break. The raised seam also will increase wind and air resistance, thus making it seem reasonable that the new ball will not travel far when hit." But Barnard also conceded that the 1931 ball would be an experiment, the results of which were yet unknown. National League president John Heydler took a different tack. He argued that games had gotten longer in recent seasons and that "one of the delaying factors was the necessity of bringing in relief pitchers. If the new ball is as helpful to pitchers as we hope, more of them may be able to pitch complete games."[35]

Contemporary observers disagreed about the effects these changed specifications would have. John B. Foster, editor of the *Spalding Guide*, was a dissenter. He argued that the increased number of home runs could be blamed on ballparks with outfield fences too close to home plate. "The normal distance of a batted home run hit, which really should be never less than 360 feet, had been brought down as low as 225 feet," he wrote. Pitchers Eppa Rixey and Red Faber, both future members of the Hall of Fame, supported the change to a new ball in 1931, but Bill Veeck Sr. did not. "They've been making it too tough for pitchers. This new ball will give us a break," Faber said. Countered Veeck, "The new ball will make no difference to our bunch of hammersmiths. Good hitters can wallop any kind of a ball and any kind of pitching." Babe Ruth agreed with Veeck, saying, "The ball will go if it's hit." Sportswriter Dan Daniel took a different approach, seeing the economic implications of the new ball. "The men who pay the salaries hope the new ball will cut batting averages and reduce the holdouts by 50 per cent," he said. "However, there may be a flea in the butter. That 1931 ball is going to make the pitchers a lot more effective and a holdout hurler isn't easier to handle than a holdout hitter." Editorializing, the *Sporting News* proceeded cautiously, saying that "such a fine shade has been made in favor of the pitcher that it requires sharpshooting guesswork to try to imagine what may happen."[36]

To suggest that the owners deadened the ball in 1931 solely to contain upward pressure on players' salaries is to ignore the general prosperity owners were experiencing at the time of their decision as well as the imbalanced system that determined salaries. If fans were tiring of offensive baseball, the number of tickets they continued to buy did not reflect their discontent. Total attendance for both leagues surpassed nine million every season from 1924 through 1929 and jumped to over ten million in 1930. Net income for all clubs combined (after taxes and before distribution of dividends) peaked at better than $2.3 million in 1926 but remained strong, growing in 1929 and 1930. Profit margins, again for all clubs combined, stayed comfortably in double figures throughout the 1920s and rose from 11.3 percent in 1929 to 16.4 percent in 1930. Connie Mack complained that his attendance dropped, but only two of the Majors' sixteen clubs, the Reds and the Browns, failed to show a profit in 1930. Three others wound up in the black after several years in the red.[37]

Baseball's playing rules committee, including owners and league officials but no players, met in December 1930 to enact a thoroughgoing revision of the rules. Designed mainly to eliminate inconsistencies and correct slight omissions, the new code contained three changes directly relevant to home run hitters and the way their statistics were calculated. Two of these were incorporated into new Rule 41, "Balls Batted Outside the Playing Field." Previously, according to old Rule 48, when a batter hit a ball "outside the ground or into a stand," the umpires had to call it fair or foul "according to where it disappears from the umpire's view." Thus, if a batter hit a long fly ball that left the playing field in fair territory and then curved foul before landing, the umpire might call "foul ball" if he could follow its flight all the way. New Rule 41 changed this and required the umpire to declare such a ball fair or foul "according to where it leaves the playing field." A note in the rule book called this "a change of great justice to the player." Old Rule 48 also decreed that "a fair batted ball that goes over the fence or into a stand shall entitle the batsman to a home run," even if the ball made it over the fence or into the stand after hitting the ground. New Rule 41 eliminated the bounce home run: "A fair hit ball that bounds into a stand or over a fence shall be a two-base hit." Thus, as the first of these changes served to augment batters' home run totals, this second provision, creating what has so often been called the ground rule double, took home runs away.[38]

A third significant alteration in the rules wiped sacrifice flies off the books. This change concerned not how the game was played but how it was scored, that is, how a particular play was to be recorded statistically. Starting in 1908, a batter who made out by hitting a fly ball that allowed a runner to score from third base after the catch was credited with a sacrifice and not charged with a time at bat. Sacrifice bunts or, as they are called in the official statistics, sacrifice hits had been part of the scoring rules for more than a decade, and now sacrifice flies were lumped in with them. Since neither out was counted as an at bat, neither adversely affected a player's batting average. In 1926 the definition of a sacrifice fly was expanded to include any fly ball out that allowed a runner to advance from one base to the next. This rule held force through the 1930 season, but in the new rule book, sacrifice flies were eliminated entirely. Both John B. Foster in the *Spalding Guide* and James C. Isaminger, editor of the *Reach Guide*, applauded the rescission. Foster wrote that "the Rules Committee wisely concluded that a sacrifice meant something more than swinging for a home run and knocking a fly long enough to permit a runner to score from third." Isaminger agreed, saying, "The man hitting the sacrifice fly, however, was making a sheer effort to hit the ball as far and hard as possible and deserved no such boon from the scorers."[39]

Players could request or even demand salary increases for outstanding performances, and they did so regularly in good times, but the reserve clause ensured that contract negotiations would nearly always be resolved to the owners' satisfaction. Trumpeted to maintain stability and foster competition and defended as absolutely necessary for the game's survival, the reserve clause in fact gave players no say about which team would employ them and at what salary. Typically, clubs would mail their players contracts for the coming season shortly after January 1. A player who did not accept the salary offered by his club could ask for a raise and could, if the contract remained unsigned beyond the start of spring training, be designated a "holdout." But disagreements of this sort were negotiations in name only. Owners might worry that a disgruntled player might not have a productive season, but owners generally risked taking the hard line. A player had only one real alternative to accepting the owner's proffered salary, and that was to seek employment in another line of work. When a spate of holdouts followed the offensive surge of 1920, the commissioner gave owners an additional weapon. He warned players who did not report to spring training on time that they could be fined, and those who remained recalcitrant could be declared ineligible to play. Under these rules, players generally joined the flock meekly, if unhappily, and often made light of their own powerlessness. Brooklyn's Zack Wheat, a holdout in 1921, demanded at $7,000 raise but settled for a meager $800 increase that he later derided as a joke. Given the inequities inherent in this system, perhaps sportswriter H. G. Salsinger was correct when he concluded, "the object in introducing a new ball is to cut down the superfluous hitting, particularly to reduce the extra-base walloping."[40]

In January 1930 pollsters had asked the members of the National Economic League, an organization composed of what journalist Frederick Lewis Allen called "substantial and well-informed citizens," to list the paramount problems facing the United States in the coming year. "Administration of Justice" finished first, "Prohibition" was second, and "Unemployment" was far down in eighteenth place. A year later, "Prohibition" was first, "Administration of Justice" second, and "Unemployment, Economic Stabilization" had risen all the way to fourth. The Depression had arrived, to be sure, but the worst of its extreme dislocations was still in the future. Baseball, too, realized that the prosperity it had experienced in the previous decade might not be sustained. The *Sporting News* reminded players in a February 1931 editorial how lucky they were to have played the previous season with their contracts intact, with "no half time nor curtailment of wages." Similarly, the weekly said, "the salaries of 1931 are very substantial," and they will be paid in full "no matter what the conditions may be on October 1, 1931." Many players agreed and signed their contracts with no fuss. The Reds announced early in the year that they had received signed contracts from more than a dozen players, including their best pitcher, Red Lucas, and their leading hitter, Harry Heilmann, who would nevertheless miss the entire season because of arthritic wrists. Reds owner Sidney Weil reminded his players that a contract with no increase in salary counted as a raise since a dollar in 1931 was worth more than a dollar in 1930. Most of the Athletics also came to terms with no incident although Mickey Cochrane and Jimmie Foxx were enticed by three-year deals, and Lefty Grove had his base salary augmented with a bonus for every win he might accumulate over twenty. Press reports about Al Simmons said that he had received Connie Mack's permission to skip spring training and get into shape on his own in Hot Springs, Arkansas. When Simmons did join the A's just before Opening Day, he signed a three-year contract for a total of $100,000.[41]

Other players were not so compliant. Hack Wilson got a nice raise from the Cubs, up to $35,000 from $22,500 in 1930, but his original demand was for $40,000. By comparison, Babe Ruth played for the Yankees in 1931 under the second year of a two-year contract at $80,000 per year. Lou Gehrig reportedly asked for a three-year contract at $30,000 per year and settled for one year at $25,000. Five members of the Indians, including pitcher Wes Ferrell, first baseman Eddie Morgan, and outfielder Earl Averill, declined to return signed contracts. Brooklyn's holdouts were two stars, Babe Herman and pitcher

Dazzy Vance, who wanted $25,000. Chick Hafey refused to sign his Cardinals contract, and Chuck Klein said he would retire if the Phillies did not pay him $14,500. St. Louis put Hafey on the trading block and offered him to the Phillies for Klein, but the deal was not consummated before Klein signed. All the Indians agreed to their team's terms. Ferrell had been threatened with a trade, and Morgan did not like the alternative career he faced, working in a factory manufacturing boxes. Herman signed for the Robins' original offer, and Vance wrangled a raise to $24,000. Hafey did not surrender until late April and did not report to the Cardinals until May 3. Bill Terry and the Giants could not agree on terms, either. Terry's initial demand was for a three-year contract at $30,000 per year. Giants president Charles Stoneham countered by offering the batting champion one year at $18,000, the same salary he had made in 1930. Terry balked, and the team raised its offer to $22,500. When Terry relented and asked for only one year at $25,000, the Giants announced that they would trade or sell him, their best player, if the proper deal could be reached. With no further recourse, Terry gave in and signed for $22,500, the team's figure. Owners like Stoneham—and he was typical and not unique—had little need for deadening the baseball or changing the scoring rules to enforce the salary structure they wanted. The reserve clause was all the ammunition they needed.[42]

Not long into the 1931 season, the A's made it clear that they would live up to their own expectations as two-time defending World Series champions and dispel any doubts that they might not be up to the task. Connie Mack told Philadelphia sportswriter Bill Dooly in March, "I think we have an excellent chance of finishing on top again," and Lefty Grove proclaimed, "With the new American League ball and nothing to worry about, I feel I can win thirty games this season." John B. Foster, in his annual preseason predictions, picked the A's with reservations. "The Athletics may win the championship again," he wrote in the *Sporting News*, "but they will know that they have been in a ball game." Fred Lieb also hesitated, writing, "The Mackmen are not as strong as they were. This year, I do not think the club will do much better than 95 victories, which should be enough to win." As it turned out, 95 wins would have been enough to win, but Philadelphia won 107 games, obliterating its competition. The A's started a bit slowly, losing six of eleven games in April, but then they went 23-4 in May, including a seventeen-game winning streak. They built a five-game lead over Washington on June 11 by which time Grove already had ten victories. Another thirteen-game winning streak in July virtually salted the pennant away. After occupying first place steadily from May 12, they clinched the flag on September 15 and finished thirteen and a half games ahead of the Yankees. It was a dominating performance. The *Reach Guide* would call this team Mack's best and point out that Philadelphia was the first team in American League history to win one hundred or more games in three consecutive seasons.[43]

In late June National League owners declared the new, less resilient ball a success. Batting averages were lower, and games were closer, more competitive, more interesting. John Heydler said, "We have enjoyed excellent attendance despite the nation-wide depression and feel that the improved play has had something to do with it." In the league's first 212 games, 1,954 runs scored compared to 2,495 in the same number of games the year before. The owners ignored an earlier warning from the *Sporting News* cautioning against any premature judgments. Perhaps they were buoyed when Dr. R. W. Wood, a physics professor at Johns Hopkins University, announced that he had tested new balls versus old balls and that the old ones had bounced higher. Giants manager John McGraw, too, was pleased. Long opposed to offense based on slugging, he told Joe Vila he was happy with the new ball and the tight games it engendered. Final statistics at the end of the season showed a marked decrease in offense. Hits and runs fell just a bit in the American League, but home runs declined more than 14 percent. In the National League, the drop-off was more pronounced: hits down 10 percent, runs down 21 percent to less than five per game, and home runs down an astounding 45 percent. Batting averages also decreased although some of this could be attributed to the change in the sacrifice fly rule. American League batters hit .278 (down from .288), and National League batters hit .277 (down from .303).[44]

President Herbert Hoover's meeting with the nation's banking tycoons on October 4, the day before he attended the World Series and got booed, led to the creation of the National Credit Association, a pool of $500 million volunteered by strong banks to prop up failing ones. It proved inadequate to the task and impelled Hoover toward broader government involvement in the economy. Over the next few months he proposed a series of measures that some historians have characterized as his "second program," a fundamental adjustment to the role of government and a precursor to Franklin Roosevelt's New Deal. But nothing the government had done in 1931 or would do in 1932 could stem the tide of what had become a worldwide depression, especially when European financial institutions felt the withdrawal of American dollars. In September the U.S. Steel Company cut wages by 10 percent, a move quickly imitated by other large corporations, and the economic wheels that had powered the boom of the 1920s ground to a halt. Unemployment loomed very large as the country's most visible economic problem. By early 1932 nearly ten million people, a fifth of the labor force, were out of work. Officials in eastern cities reported alarming cases of hunger and malnutrition while in the agricultural Midwest and West crops rotted and wasted away. Private relief simply could not cope with the anomaly of these dislocations that some experts feared might be permanent.[45]

A small economic upturn in the spring of 1931 perhaps gave baseball executives some ray of optimism, but end-of-season accounting exposed the unreality of this dream. Total Major League attendance fell more than 16 percent to 8,467,107 with only two teams, the Braves and the Cardinals, showing an increase. Pittsburgh's attendance, 260,392, was the lowest in the National League, and the Browns drew only 179,126 fans, less than 2,500 per game, the lowest total in the American League. Even the seventh game of the World Series drew only 20,805 to Sportsman's Park in St. Louis. Net income for all teams combined fell from nearly $2 million in 1930 to just over $200,000, and profit margin dropped to just over 2 percent. Only two American League clubs and three National League clubs showed a profit. Mack's financial gamble, signing his stars to multiyear contracts, paid off with the A's third straight pennant, but Philadelphia's attendance nose-dived by nearly a hundred thousand, thereby supporting Mack's contention that great teams could breed complacency among fans. The A's reported a profit of $102,123, off 37 percent from the year before. Moreover, when Philadelphia got to the World Series, the Cardinals, a team guided by a second-year manager and featuring a twenty-seven-year-old rookie, defeated them, four games to three. Mack got his comeuppance from a club assembled by a wily executive whose revolutionary schemes were making Mack's way of doing business obsolete.[46]

In the face of these economic difficulties, Mack acted deliberately following his club's defeat in 1931. His lineup for the following season was virtually the same as the year before, and the team won 94 games, good for second place behind the Yankees, who won an astounding 107. Jimmie Foxx batted .364 and led the league in runs batted in with 169. Moreover, he hit 58 home runs, barely falling short of Babe Ruth's mark of 60, set in 1927. Lefty Grove won 24 games against only 7 losses. Still, sometime in midseason, Mack consulted with the Shibes, and they agreed to pare the league's highest payroll. On the morning of the first game of the 1932 World Series, the A's shipped Al Simmons, with one year to go on his contract, and two other players to the

White Sox for $100,000. In 1933 the club's hitting remained strong, but the pitching, save for Grove, collapsed. Foxx won the Triple Crown, an unofficial award for leading the league in batting average (.356), home runs (48), and RBIs (163), but no pitcher besides Grove won more than 13 games. Philadelphia dropped one more place in the standings, finishing behind Washington and New York. The A's won 79 games, their lowest total since 1924, and on December 12, Mack bid goodbye to both Mickey Cochrane and Grove. Detroit wanted Cochrane to be a player-manager, so Mack traded him for a reserve catcher and $100,000. Grove went to the Red Sox, with two other players, for two players and $125,000.[47]

Only Foxx remained from the dynasty years, but he, along with a host of newcomers, could not prevent the team from sliding into fifth place in 1934 and last in 1935. Mack's pre-eminent skill, identifying young players who could play successfully for low salaries, was diminished, and he now had little cash to spend on Minor Leaguers. The A's won only fifty-eight games in 1935 and finished thirty-four games behind Cochrane's pennant-winning Tigers, and the worst was yet to come. After the season, Mack dealt his last star, trading Foxx along with pitcher Johnny Marcum to the Red Sox for two bit players and $150,000. Mack insisted that these transactions were absolutely necessary. "We had incurred obligations of between $700,000 and $800,000 in renovating our park," he told Lieb, and "our payroll was terrific. We didn't have a man under $10,000 on the club." Mack noted, too, that Philadelphia was an industrial city hit hard by the Depression. Indeed the club's attendance bottomed out at 233,173 in 1935 and did not rise over half a million until 1941. In that season, the A's finished eighth for the second time in a row and the fifth time in seven years. They finished last five more times and never higher than fourth before Mack retired as manager after the 1950 season. He was just short of his eighty-eighth birthday. One measure of how the team's quality declined was how poorly its players fared competing for the sport's annual awards. Foxx was named the American League's Most Valuable Player in 1932 and 1933, but no other Athletic won this award until Bobby Shantz in 1952, and from 1937 through 1950, the annual All-Star teams selected by the *Sporting News* included not one player from the A's.[48]

Two

"So You're the Goddamned Prohibitionist"

The handiwork behind the rosters that propelled the St. Louis Cardinals to their first pennants in 1926, 1928, 1930, and 1931 belonged to Branch Rickey, a baseball visionary and the club's vice president. He had been a player, a manager, and an executive with the St. Louis Browns and an executive with the Cardinals before the Great War, but it was after the Armistice that he began a revolution in how successful baseball teams could be assembled. Rickey's mother's family, the Browns, had journeyed from Scotland to New England in 1646 and then on to New York. Except for his adventurous great-grandfather, David, the Browns were devout Methodists. David's boisterous behavior scandalized the family of his intended, Sallie Hubbard, and when she married him anyway, her family disowned her. Right after the War of 1812, the two of them made their way from Buffalo to a village in southern Ohio named Sciotoville. There they farmed, and Sallie bore eleven children, including a girl named Emily, instilling in them her profound religious faith. Making much the same journey was Rickey's paternal family. They were Baptists and included in their number a couple of lay preachers. Ephraim Rickey brought his family west on the Ohio River, and his son, called Frank, married Emily Brown in 1873. The young couple burned with religious fervor. Frank, a vegetable farmer, helped organize a number of churches, and Emily taught her children hymns and told them Bible stories they remembered all their lives. They named their first son Orla and their second son, born on December 20, 1881, Wesley Branch, but the boy dropped his first name when he was twelve to avoid confusion with two cousins.[1]

Before Branch turned two, his father bought just over a hundred acres of land in Duck Run, a speck of a farming village near Lucasville, Ohio. Here the Rickey children, including youngest brother Frank, began school and learned to read, not only the Bible, but also a host of books and newspapers when they were available. The Rickeys' religious convictions were firm, but they never forbade their sons from secular reading, even on the Sabbath. Rickey's biographer, Murray Polner, wrote that father Frank once heard about a fire sale at a bookstore in Portsmouth and drove his wagon ten miles each way, a total of six hours, to buy a dozen books for $2.25. In 1892 the family moved to a rented house in Lucasville so Branch could attend a bigger and better school where two students from Ohio Wesleyan University in Delaware, Ohio, were teachers. He finished this school, missed out on appointments to West Point and Annapolis, and quit a job selling books door to door when he realized that most folks had no money to spare. Encouraged by his teachers, he spent two years as a teacher in a pretty rough school and also indulged himself by taking an interest in baseball, forming a pretty good battery on the town team with Orla as the pitcher. Then after overcoming the objections of his father, who reasoned that any college would corrupt his son, he enrolled at Ohio Wesleyan's prep school, hoping to gain admission to the college itself.[2]

To say that Rickey was on the threshold of a most unpredictable life would be an understatement. When he left home in March 1901, he had no way of knowing what the next two decades would hold in store for him. Like many students, he had a tough time adjusting to the academics, economics, and social imperatives of college life, but helpful professors lent a hand. In the fall the school's athletic director recruited him to play football, and in the spring he caught for the baseball team, on which his cousin, Eph Rickey, played first base. Home for the summer after his first year of studies, he played baseball for the semipro Portsmouth Navvies at $25 a week without realizing that he was surrendering his college eligibility. Back at school but disqualified from college football, he played instead for the Shelby Steel Tube Company's team, earning $50 each autumn Saturday. When baseball season came around again, Ohio Wesleyan found itself without a coach. The school's president offered Rickey the job, and he accepted. The team's first baseman was an African American named Charles Thomas. When the University of Kentucky varsity, set to play Rickey's team, objected to Thomas's presence, Rickey stood firm, and the Kentucky coach relented. That summer Rickey played professional baseball for the first time with two Minor League teams in Terre Haute, Indiana, and LeMars, Iowa, and in the fall it was semipro football again, plus school, of course. In the spring of 1904 Rickey and his team traveled to South Bend, Indiana, to play Notre Dame. The clerk at the Oliver Hotel refused to admit Thomas because of his race. Rickey negotiated a compromise. Thomas would stay in the coach's room until the team could rent a room for him in a local YMCA. But once Thomas was upstairs, Rickey reneged on the deal and refused to let his player leave. In an episode that became legendary, Thomas then broke down and bemoaned his dark skin. Rickey recalled years later,

"Whatever mark that incident left on the Black boy, it was no more indelible than the impressions made on me."[3]

Rickey graduated in 1904 with a BLitt degree. Having completed prep school and most of the college curriculum in three and a half years, he lacked only some mathematics courses to qualify for the more comprehensive BA degree. Unsure of what to do next, he jumped at a chance to play Minor League ball again, with the Dallas Giants in the Texas League for $175 a month, and he was glad to finish the season in the dugout of the Cincinnati Reds. He did not get into any Major League games, but he still enraged his manager, Joe Kelley, by announcing his intention to leave the team each Saturday to observe the Sabbath with his family in Lucasville. Reds president Garry Herrmann intervened and sided with Rickey, but Kelley refused to play him any day of the week. Cincinnati released him back to Dallas, who sold his contract to the Chicago White Sox, but Rickey made other plans. At first he thought about returning to school to complete his BA degree, but friends secured him a position at Allegheny College in Meadville, Pennsylvania, coaching baseball and football and teaching as well. During the winter the White Sox traded him to the Browns, who wanted Rickey to report for spring training. Again Rickey demurred. He wanted it all: to play ball, to coach, to teach, to observe the Sabbath, and also to marry his sweetheart, Jane Moulton, the daughter of the prosperous owner of Lucasville's general store. The Browns' owner, Robert Hedges, gave in. Rickey would play only between June 15 and September 15 and never on Sundays, but after he got into just one game in 1905, St. Louis returned his contract to Dallas. Rickey went back to Allegheny after the season and decided to read for the law, but the Browns promoted him again in 1906. He played in sixty-five games, batting .284. His baseball salary earned him permission from Jane's father to marry her in June, and in the fall he returned to Delaware, ready to coach and study for the BA, which he earned before Christmas. That winter the Browns sold his contract to the New York Highlanders, (later the Yankees), but he had to tell manager Clark Griffith that he had hurt his arm. Even a stay at a spa in Hot Springs, Arkansas, did not help. Nevertheless, the New Yorkers needed him on occasion. On June 28 Rickey was behind the plate, and the Washington club took advantage, stealing thirteen bases, still an American League record. At the end of season Rickey's playing career was over.[4]

Returning to Ohio Wesleyan, Rickey taught and coached, picked up a part-time job as a YMCA administrator, and took a few night classes at the Ohio State University Law School. He started giving temperance talks for the

Anti-Saloon League and campaigned for Republican William Howard Taft, an Ohioan running for president in 1908. Shortly thereafter he got sick, and doctors diagnosed tuberculosis, then a deadly disease. He and Jane journeyed to Saranac Lake, New York, so he could check into the Trudeau Adirondack Care Sanatorium, where a high-calorie diet, dry air, and complete bed rest sometimes allowed patients to recover. Gradually Rickey began feeling better. He and Jane were able to venture out to local restaurants, where he drank beer against his will and convictions but on doctors' orders. By the end of the summer he was strong enough to be discharged. He moved to Ann Arbor to enroll at the University of Michigan Law School and with his customary gusto set out to complete the three-year curriculum in two. "I know how to study," he told a friend, and he proved it, graduating in 1911, even though he had picked up the extra burden of coaching Michigan's baseball team. Looking for a dry climate, the Rickeys decided to move to Boise, Idaho, but the legal work they anticipated there never materialized, and back to Ann Arbor they came. Once again he coached the baseball team, including several future Major League players. As Rickey wavered between the sport he loved and the profession at which he thought he was sure to succeed, Hedges asked him to run a Minor League team in Kansas City. Rickey said no, but he agreed to take a summer-long trip to the West Coast to do some scouting. During this summer Hedges met Rickey in Utah and offered him a job with the Browns in St. Louis. Rickey said he was committed to coaching the Michigan baseball team in 1913, so Hedges adjusted his proposal: fulfill the obligation in Ann Arbor and then come to St. Louis to be the team's number two executive at an annual salary of $7,500.[5]

Rickey moved into his office in Sportsman's Park in June 1913 and served as Hedges's assistant, a prototypical general manager. Before the season was over, though, the owner fired manager George Stovall and put Rickey in the dugout. The following spring gave him his first opportunity to try out with Major League players the training techniques he had developed as a college coach. Rickey believed firmly that proficiency in baseball could be taught to anyone with a reasonable amount of natural athletic ability. He began each spring training day with a lecture, the contents of which sometimes started with baseball technique and then meandered to family life, history, and morality. Afterward Rickey's players used handball courts, sliding pits, batting cages, and a variety of other gizmos to hone their baseball skills. The Browns advanced from eighth place in 1913 to fifth in 1914 and then back to sixth in 1915. More important, Rickey acquired the services of George Sisler, one of his stars at Michigan. The National Commission had voided the contract Sisler had signed while he was underage, and Rickey got Hedges to sign him. After the season Hedges, ill, tired of losing, and upset by the financial bath he took competing for players against the insurgent Federal League, sold the team to Phil Ball, who had made millions selling ice machines to meat-packing plants and breweries. Ball had owned the St. Louis Terriers in the Federal League, but he was Hedges's opposite in demeanor: loud and gruff and not much taken with his manager.[6]

Ball and Rickey clashed immediately. Right after purchasing the team, the new owner walked into the Browns' offices and accosted Rickey with the gruff greeting, "So you're the goddamned prohibitionist." He informed Rickey that Fielder Jones from the Terriers would be the new manager and told him to get back to work. Rickey rebelled and soon met with James C. Jones, an attorney trying to buy the Cardinals. Within a short time Ball agreed to let Rickey leave, but American League president Ban Johnson intervened, not pleased that Rickey might be moving to the National League. Even as Rickey was signing a contract with Jones and the Cardinals, Ball, under pressure from Johnson, was regretting his willingness to let him go. Ball quarreled with Rickey and went to court for an injunction, knowing the facts were against him. The parties agreed to a face-saving decree that enjoined Rickey from moving but only for twenty-four hours. Rickey moved into his new office on April 6, the same day on which the United States declared war on Germany. Jones and his partners bought the Cardinals from Helene Britton for $375,000, paying half in cash and taking a loan from her for the rest. They hatched a plan to raise the money through a public offering of stock at $25 a share. Moreover, they declared that everyone who bought stock would receive an additional benefit: one season's pass for a boy for every share purchased. This was the birth of the "Knothole Gang," a success once Rickey convinced a substantial number of shareholders to assign their passes back to the club so that he could distribute them to youth organizations throughout the city. Rickey had promised to buy two hundred shares himself with money he did not have, and he was gratified when his parents mortgaged their farm to give him the cash he needed.[7]

The best player on the Cardinals as Branch Rickey took command was shortstop Rogers Hornsby. In 1917, his second full season, he led the league in slugging average (.484), tied for first in on-base percentage (.385), and was second in batting average (.327). He hit 8 home runs and led the league with 17 triples. Hornsby was born in 1896 in Winters, Texas, a small village on the windy plains south of Abilene, and raised in Fort Worth. While his older brothers found jobs in the city's meat-packing plants, young Rogers—his first name was his mother's maiden name—dropped out of high school and signed his first professional contract in 1914, when he was eighteen. He played for teams in Hugo, Oklahoma, and Denison, Texas, batting .277 in 1915 but committing 58 errors. Despite this defensive deficiency, Denison was able to sell his contract to the Cardinals. Helene Britton did not have the resources to acquire many Minor League players, but her only scout, Bob Connery, had watched Hornsby play a three-game exhibition series in the spring against a team of St. Louis reserves. "The more I looked at the kid, the better I liked him," Connery recalled. Hornsby got into eighteen games for the Cardinals in 1915 and batted .246. Manager Miller Huggins expected that the youngster would spend 1916 in the Minors, but Hornsby altered his batting stance in spring training and began hitting line drives consistently. His defensive problems aside, he won the job as the Cardinals' starting shortstop. Hornsby bounced around the infield, playing more games at third base than anywhere else, and batted .313 for the season. The *Sporting News* called him the best youngster in the league, and the Cardinals turned down offers from two other clubs to buy his contract. Even after Britton announced her intention to sell the team, she declared that every St. Louis player was on the market except Hornsby.[8]

Rickey may not have agreed completely with this dour assessment of the Cardinals' roster, but he did make enough changes to propel the team upward in the standings. Gene Paulette arrived from the Browns to start at first base. Dots Miller moved from first to second, Hornsby moved back to shortstop, and Doug Baird came in a trade from the Pittsburgh Pirates to play third. Hornsby was not just the best player on the team; he was also quickly developing a very high opinion of himself. After playing for $2,000 in 1916, he demanded double that during spring training before settling for $3,000. The next winter he wanted $7,000, but after Rickey visited him in Fort Worth, he signed a two-year contract for $4,000 per season. The 1918 Cardinals, though, fell back into last place. Huggins had departed for New York, and his successor, Jack Hendricks, made the poor choice to tangle with his star player, who struggled all year and hit only .281. Rickey inserted more young players into the lineup, including pitcher Bill Sherdel and outfielder Austin McHenry, but the season was a disaster. When Hornsby's draft board overlooked the fact that he was the sole support of his mother and sister and put him in Class 1, subject to induction, the youngster announced that he would seek war-related employment in a shipyard. Other players departed too, and after the season ended,

James C. Jones declared that the franchise had lost more than $30,000 for the year and would have a tough time making its payments on the debt to Britton.[9]

Before the season was over, Rickey decided to join some of his players by enlisting to serve his country. Thirty-seven years old, married, and the father of four, he saw a simple storefront sign in downtown St. Louis that read, "Closing up after six months in business. I am going to war." Soon after, at the suggestion of his acquaintance Percy Haughton, former Harvard football coach and president of the Boston Braves, and over the strenuous objections of his wife, he accepted a commission as a major in the First Gas Regiment of the Chemical Warfare Service. Rickey boarded a troop ship in the summer of 1918, survived a bout with pneumonia, and landed in France. The Chemical Warfare Service was brand new, and Rickey's job—to instruct soldiers how to use mustard gas—brought him very close to the horrors of the front, albeit for a short time. He led missions during the day and could socialize a bit at night, spending some time with two other officers in his unit, Captains Ty Cobb and Christy Mathewson. Rickey's special charge was to school twenty noncommissioned officers, wounded and shocked by severe fighting, and help them earn their commissions. These men all made the grade, and after the Armistice they hosted a dinner in Rickey's honor. He sailed home in December and resumed his peacetime job early in 1919.[10]

Branch Rickey learned at a January board of directors meeting that the Cardinals were nearly bankrupt. The team still owed Helene Britton almost half the purchase price, and several key stockholders were beginning to put financial concerns ahead of civic pride. Jack Hendricks had been fired, and Rickey agreed to become field manager, in addition to his duties as president, as a way to cut costs. He continued to acquire new players at bargain basement prices, including former Browns outfielder Burt Shotton, who would serve as field manager on Sundays since Rickey still declined to come to the ballpark on the Sabbath. Still, he had the audacity to refuse the New York Giants' offer to buy Hornsby's contract for $175,000, a sum roughly equal to his club's entire debt. The Cardinals were so poor that instead of going south for spring training, they worked out at Washington University in St. Louis, wearing stitched-up uniforms from the previous season and hoarding baseballs as if they were five-dollar bills. One of the stockholders who viewed these developments not just as a crisis but also as an opportunity was Sam Breadon, whose initial stake in the club had been only $200. Breadon, the son of poor immigrants from Northern Ireland, was born in New York's Greenwich Village. His formal education ended when he finished the fourth grade at Ninth Ward Grade School, but by the time he was twenty-three, he had a good job as a bank clerk, making $125 a month. Breadon's friends, the Halsey brothers, moved to St. Louis to jump into its burgeoning automobile business, and Breadon joined them at a salary of $75 a month. "I didn't know a thing about automobiles," he confessed to sportswriter Martin J. Haley in 1943, "but most all of the others were in the same boat. The automobile was a new contraption. However, the customers who came to the Halseys looked upon me as the expert from New York."[11]

Breadon's long suit was ambition, not discretion, and when the Halseys overheard him talk about opening his own car agency, they fired him. Out of work and soon nearly out of money, he finagled enough credit to buy thirty cases of Honey Boy popcorn and hired a dozen boys to sell it along the route of the giant parade St. Louis staged to dedicate the 1904 World's Fair. With his $35 in profits, he bought himself a steak dinner and soon thereafter entered into a partnership with Marion Lambert, whose family fortune came from pharmaceuticals. Breadon had tended to Lambert's car while working for the Halseys, and now they opened the Western Automobile Company. Lambert supplied the capital and Breadon the labor, and the pair made $20,000 in one year selling Fords. Two years later Breadon bought out his partner and began selling luxurious Pierce-Arrows. At about the same time a friend convinced him to invest in the Cardinals. He bought eight shares in the offering that James C. Jones and Rickey organized to buy the team, and when Jones threw a celebratory dinner party for his stockholders at the Mercantile Club, Breadon, fascinated by the chance to meet ballplayers in person, anted up another $1,800. As the club fell on hard times, he lent it another $18,000 and was rewarded with a seat on the board of directors. And then in December 1919 Jones asked him to assume the club presidency. "I agreed," Breadon recalled, "if the number of directors was reduced to five. There were more than twenty directors at the time. Naturally, with so many, there was little direct action." The board compromised at seven directors, and Breadon became president. Rickey remained manager but was demoted to vice president.[12]

The two could not have been less alike. Rickey was a country boy and a college graduate, an evangelical Protestant who read the Bible, abstained from tobacco and alcohol, and voted Republican. Breadon was city-born and street tough, a school dropout, a Catholic, and a Democrat. Rickey loved to spend time with his family but rarely declined an invitation to orate before any audience. Breadon loved socializing and singing in barbershop quartets but was content to have Rickey be the club's public face. Rickey projected an image of moral righteousness but savored sharp business deals. Breadon sold automobiles but was lauded as "a man of his word" and, except to his players, was generous to a fault. Their only common ground was baseball. "Rickey was the dreamer, Breadon the hard, sound businessman," according to sportswriter Bob Burnes. The two rarely spoke to one another outside the office, but each respected the other's strengths. Breadon's first key decision was to abandon rickety Cardinal Field and rent the use of the Browns' Sportsman's Park, a scheme made possible because the teams' home schedules did not conflict. Phil Ball was not receptive to Breadon's proposal at first, but when the Cardinals suggested that they might build a new ballpark instead, Ball gave in, accepting annual payments exceeding $20,000. Breadon demolished the old grandstand and sold part of the property to the city's board of education for $200,000 and the remainder to the Public Service Corporation, the city's transit company, for another $75,000. "It was the most important move I ever made on the Cardinals," he recalled in 1949. "It gave us money to clean up our debts [to Mrs. Britton], and something more to work with. Without it, we never could have purchased the minor league clubs, which were the beginning of our farm system."[13]

Rickey matched Breadon's innovation by transforming the way Major League clubs built their rosters by developing a nexus of practices that came to be called the farm system. In the 1890s John Brush had turned one of the clubs he owned, the Indianapolis Hoosiers in Ban Johnson's Western League, into a de facto farm team for his National League club, the Reds. Two decades later Ernest Barnard assembled a modest farm system for the Cleveland Indians. Robert Hedges had much the same idea when he recruited Rickey to operate a team in Kansas City that Hedges intended to buy. These efforts, though, were tentative and piecemeal. Major League clubs—and Minor League ones too—could retain any players on their rosters using the reserve clause. Major League clubs could also acquire new players by drafting them or purchasing their contracts. But when Major League clubs sought to farm players while maintaining the right to recall them, owners had to deal with confusing rules intertwined with a tradition of informal agreements muddled by the self-interests of Minor League clubs. Rickey and Hedges tested the strength of these practices and found them wanting. The Browns drafted many more players than they could use at the Major League level, but they found it difficult to place their surplus with Minor League clubs safely. In 1913 Hedges made arrangements with a quintet of Minor League teams scattered around the country, but he could not depend on their owners to respect the sanctity of informal arrangements. The

Browns could protect some players more formally by optioning them—that is, selling them to Minor League clubs with the right to repurchase them at a later date for a predetermined price—but when they optioned more players than the rules allowed, they jeopardized their claims to recall them.[14]

Rickey's brainstorm was to change all that, to create a new order out of chaos. The impetus for his scheme may well have been his request that Breadon purchase the contract of an undistinguished pitcher named Jesse Haines in February 1920 for $10,000. Breadon borrowed the money to acquire him with reluctance, and Rickey knew that similar purchases would be difficult. He invested some of the club's limited capital in several Minor League teams, hoping to cultivate informal partnerships that would facilitate movement of promising players toward St. Louis, but the resultant relationships were haphazard at best. Sources differ on the exact sequence of these acquisitions, but the first four involved the Ft. Smith (AR) Twins in the Western Association, the Houston Buffaloes in the Texas League, the Sioux City (IA) Cardinals in the Tri-State League, and the Syracuse Stars in the International League. Breadon recalled for sportswriter Hugh Bradley in 1934 that the Cardinals began by taking minority positions in these clubs and eventually increased their stake, in some cases to full ownership. Rickey explained that he was content at first to develop "working agreements" with Minor League clubs, but he soon realized that these could be ineffective. St. Louis bought 50 percent of the Syracuse club in February 1921 for $20,000, with owner E. C. Landgraf remaining president of the club. Midway through the 1922 season Rickey wanted to acquire Syracuse first baseman Jim Bottomley, whom the Cardinals had originally signed, but Landgraf balked because other clubs craved this prospect too. When Landgraf threatened to hold an auction for Bottomley's services, Rickey hurried to Syracuse and worked out an accommodation involving, Rickey later said, persuasion, logic, and money. Bottomley came to St. Louis, and Breadon soon bought the other half of the Stars. Reflecting on this developing strategy, Rickey told the editor of the *Sporting News* in 1932 that he did not think that "the farming system we have established is the result of any inventive genius—it is the result of stark necessity. We did it to meet a question of supply and demand of young ballplayers. We learned long before that partnership operation of minor clubs was not feasible; that there were too many clashing influences."[15]

Newcomers Haines and Bottomley, who remained with the Cardinals for eighteen and eleven seasons respectively, personified the transformation of the St. Louis franchise from a team of pathetic also-rans to perennial contenders for the National League pennant. Haines signed a professional contract in 1913 with the Dayton Veterans in the Central League and began a fairly typical sojourn through the Minors. He started the 1914 season with Fort Wayne (IN) in the Central League but spent the bulk of the year and the first half of 1915 with Saginaw in the Southern Michigan Association. This league disbanded on July 1, and Haines found himself sitting on the bench, but not pitching, for the Detroit Tigers. He spent 1916 and 1917 back in the Central League with the Springfield (OH) Reapers and 1918 in the Western League with the Topeka (KS) Kawnees, who moved in June to become the Hutchinson (KS) Salt Packers. Before the season was over, the Reds bought his contract, but manager Christy Mathewson let him pitch only once. Along the way Haines developed into a fine pitcher with a lively fastball that he could control. Nevertheless, Cincinnati sold him to Tulsa back in the Western League, and the Oilers traded him in June 1919 to the Kansas City Blues in the American Association for, as Haines said, "a song and a silk handkerchief." There he went 21-5 while walking only two batters per nine innings. That command of the strike zone is what attracted Rickey, who persuaded Breadon to buy Haines's contract. Although no one could know it at the time, the club would not purchase another player until the mid-1940s.[16]

Bottomley's career, in contrast, served as a precursor of modern player development. He signed a contract with a Major League organization, not a Minor League team, and despite a rocky start that saw him released once, he remained the property of that organization as he advanced through the Minors to the parent club. Bottomley grew up in Nokomis, Illinois, a coal mining community about seventy miles northeast of St. Louis, and he played baseball for his high school team and for a semipro team in neighboring Witt. A St. Louis police officer saw a game in which Bottomley hit three triples and two home runs, and he alerted Charley Barrett, Rickey's scout, who signed Bottomley to a contract in 1920. The youngster spent that season in South Dakota, six games at Sioux City in the Western League and ninety-seven games at Mitchell in the South Dakota League, where he hit .312. The Cardinals sent him to Houston in 1921 and then to Syracuse in 1922. There he batted .348, and following Rickey's negotiations with Landgraf, he came to St. Louis in August. Rickey had begun to sour on first baseman Jack Fournier, and Bottomley began his audition on August 18, getting a hit and handling seventeen chances in the field without an error. "I never got any help while I was in the minors," Bottomley told sportswriter Harry T. Brundidge of the *St. Louis Star*, but when Rickey questioned his easy manner, he said, "I can hit. I always could hit. I can hit all kinds of pitching. If I'm not good enough to get in there as a regular, I'd rather quit now." In thirty-seven games he hit .325, more than good enough, and the club traded Fournier to the Brooklyn Dodgers before the start of the next season. With Rickey at the helm the Cardinals' lineup began to improve, but erratically so. There was no immediate success.[17]

Starting in 1920, Rogers Hornsby put together the most remarkable string of six offensive seasons the National League had ever seen. He led all hitters in batting average, on-base percentage, and slugging average all six years, in hits and doubles five times, and in triples and home runs twice. Hornsby batted consecutively .370, .397, .401, .384, .424, and .403. Over these six seasons, in short, he came to the plate 3,770 times and got on base over 1,700 times. This reign of excellence began in the same season that the Major Leagues boosted offense by introducing a new, livelier ball and outlawing the use of the spitball and other trick pitches. While all the league's batters over these six years averaged .285, .340 in on-base percentage, and .393 in slugging, Hornsby outpaced everyone else by averaging .397, .467, and .666 respectively. Early in 1920 he hit two triples to defeat Chicago Cubs pitcher Grover Cleveland Alexander, after which the future Hall of Fame member said, "Hornsby is the greatest hitter I've ever had to face. . . . Personally I don't think a more skillful man ever stepped up to the plate." After the 1924 season, when the National League reestablished an award for its most valuable player, asking members of the Baseball Writers' Association of America to rank ten players, Hornsby finished second to Brooklyn pitcher Dazzy Vance only because one voter left the Cardinal off his ballot entirely. Hornsby's private life was a mess. During this period he became a father, got involved in an extramarital affair that drew considerable press attention, got divorced, got married again, and became a father again. Yet he remained completely dedicated to his craft, eschewing smoking, drinking, and going to the movies lest he damage his eyesight. "People ask me what I do in winter when there's no baseball," he said in an oft-quoted remark. "I'll tell you what I do. I stare out the window and wait for spring."[18]

Like many star players who wrangled with their management, Hornsby disagreed, often testily and at length, with Sam Breadon over what his salary should be and with Branch Rickey over how the team should be handled. After the 1920 season he asked the club for a three-year contract at $18,000 per year and settled for a one-year contract paying $11,000. The following winter he upped his demand to three years at $25,000 annually and signed for three years at $18,500 each. After this deal expired, he signed another three-year contract for a total of $100,000, making him the highest-paid player in the league. Hornsby's rapport with Breadon waxed and waned, and his relationship with Rickey was also rocky. Player and manager came to blows in the clubhouse after a game in August 1923, prompting new rumors that the Cardinals would trade their star, but when Breadon suggested early in 1925 that Hornsby replace Rickey as manager, the infielder demurred. In May, though, Breadon, fed up with the team's slow start, made this very change. Rickey had not wanted to be the Cardinals' manager, but seven years into his tenure, his pride did not allow him to surrender the job willingly. He sold his stock in the club to Hornsby and remained vice president with an annual salary of $25,000. The player-manager guided his team to a fourth-place finish, one game below .500 and eighteen games behind the pennant-winning Pirates.[19]

Hornsby lasted only a year and a half as manager, but in 1926 he brought St. Louis its first pennant since the Browns won the American Association flag in 1888. Rickey made a midseason trade with the Giants for outfielder Billy Southworth and acquired Alexander from the Cubs on waivers, and both moves paid dividends. Southworth batted .317 in ninety-nine games, and Alexander contributed one of the most memorable strikeouts in baseball history. In Game Seven of the World Series against the Yankees, it was the aged Alexander, "bowed by the weight of his 39 years and nursing a crick in his venerable back," wrote sportswriter Damon Runyon, who struck out second baseman Tony Lazzeri in the seventh inning to preserve the Cardinals' 3–2 lead. Hornsby's triumph, though, was short-lived. On Labor Day he had quarreled in the clubhouse with Breadon when the owner insisted that the team play a pair of exhibition games en route from Pittsburgh to Boston. Hornsby protested and kept his starters out of these contests, and then over the winter he locked horns with Breadon again over his contract and his chief recreation, going to the racetrack. The owner had had enough. With Rickey's approval he traded Hornsby to the Giants in December for Frank Frisch and pitcher Jimmy Ring. Catcher Bob O'Farrell, the league's Most Valuable Player in 1926, became the team's new player-manager.[20]

The Cardinals won two more pennants in 1928 and 1930, but they were defeated in the World Series each time. Breadon changed managers frequently: O'Farrell in 1927, Bill McKechnie in 1928, Southworth and McKechnie again in 1929, and former catcher Gabby Street in 1930. Rickey made some trades along the way, but the basis of the club's continuing success was the productivity of its farm system. The 1926 team that had begun auspiciously by winning twenty-two of twenty-four exhibition games included fifteen homegrown players on its twenty-five-player roster. Bottomley played first base and led the league in runs batted in, and Hornsby played second. Hampered by injuries, he batted only .317. Les Bell and Tommy Thevenow, both signed by Charley Barrett, had outstanding seasons at third base and shortstop respectively. Farmhands also manned two of the three outfield spots. Taylor Douthit played center field, and Ray Blades played left field until he was injured. Chick Hafey took Blades's place, but he suffered severe vision problems. Hafey donned eyeglasses, but his sight varied so much from day to day that he switched among three different pairs as needed. He hit only .271 in seventy-eight games and .185 in the World Series, but in 1927 he blossomed into one of the league's best-hitting outfielders. Other farmhands followed as the Cardinals finished second in 1927, losing the pennant to the Pirates by a game and a half, and first in 1928. This time the Yankees swept St. Louis in four games, with Babe Ruth hitting three home runs and Lou Gehrig four. After falling back to fourth place in 1929, the Cardinals won the pennant again in 1930, aided by the maturation of a left-handed pitcher nicknamed "Wild Bill" Hallahan. Cardinals fans hoped that their underdog team would upset the defending champion Philadelphia Athletics in the Series, but it was not to be. After the clubs split the first four games, veteran Burleigh Grimes pitched a five-hitter in Game Five, only to be victimized by Jimmie Foxx's two-run home run in the ninth inning. After a day of rest the Cardinals managed only five hits as right-hander George Earnshaw captured the sixth and deciding game.[21]

Pepper Martin sat in the St. Louis dugout during the 1930 Series and did not play in a single inning. He had gotten into thirty-nine Major League games in 1928 and six in 1930, but he was far from a regular. Still, his slow rise through the Minor Leagues showed exactly how Branch Rickey's farm system was designed to work. Years later, well after young Johnny Martin had been nicknamed "Pepper," he explained. "I liked baseball," he said, "and had ambitions to be a professional player, and Babe Ruth and Dutch Leonard, then pitchers on the Boston Red Sox, were my heroes." In the summer of 1922 Martin sold concessions at the Oklahoma City ballpark, pitched batting practice, shagged flies, and won the job as batboy. His enthusiasm got him a contract to play with a team sponsored by the Brooks Hardware Company, and from there he moved to several other semipro outfits. Finally, in 1924 a friend arranged for Martin to become a professional ballplayer with the Guthrie (OK) club in the Oklahoma State League. "I certainly made up my mind that I wasn't going to flim the folks in Guthrie," Martin told the *Philadelphia Inquirer* several years later, but the club could not return the favor. It moved twice within a few weeks, and then the entire league disbanded. Somehow in the confusion the Greenville (TX) Hunters of the East Texas League purchased Martin's contract. In 1925 he played for Greenville again. He hit .340 in ninety-eight games and stole 38 bases, but he made 33 errors. "I was not satisfied with my playing, and I didn't think I was getting along so good," he confessed. So it came as quite a shock to Martin when the Cardinals organization purchased his contract in July. Reporting to the team in Ft. Smith, Martin discovered that his reputation for hustling had preceded him, and he found himself with a new nickname.[22]

The man responsible for this bit of pizzazz was Blake Harper, president of the Ft. Smith Twins and a man with a flair for promotion. Once, for example, he held a "penny day," offering two tickets for a dollar, the usual price of one. When the Twins acquired Martin, Harper knew he had a player to attract fans, so he persuaded the local newspaper to announce the imminent arrival of "Pepper" Martin. Playing second base and batting leadoff in his first game for Ft. Smith, Martin got a single and a double, and he relayed one throw from his right fielder into the Okmulgee (OK) Drillers' dugout. He impressed the local newspaper with his "peppery" play, but his defensive lapses tarnished his offensive prowess for the rest of the season. In forty-five games for the Twins he batted .344 and made 21 errors. These statistics earned him a promotion to Syracuse for 1926, but the pattern continued: lots of hits tempered by many errors, augmented by the occasional boneheaded play. At Syracuse he hit .300 and led the International League by committing 45 errors. The following season saw him demoted to Houston, where manager Joe Mathes transformed him, perhaps out of desperation, into an outfielder. The change worked; he made only 9 errors in the outfield while batting .306, good enough to be invited to spring training with the Cardinals in 1928. Rickey liked Martin's potential, but manager Bill McKechnie did not share his boss's optimism. Martin remained with the Cardinals the entire season, but he came to bat just thirteen times. In 1929 he was sent back to Houston to improve his defense, and in 1930 he was again invited to spring training with the Cardinals, only to be sent down yet again. The Syracuse Stars were now the Rochester Red Wings, and the Red Wings were a great team. Martin contributed mightily to their first-place finish. He batted .363, drove in 114 runs, and picked up a new nickname for his flamboyant base running, the "Wild Horse of the Osage." In the Junior World Series, pitting Rochester against the Louisville Colonels, champions of the American Association, he got 10 hits, scored 8 runs, and stole 4 bases. He was an All-Star and a champion, but he badly wanted to be a Major Leaguer.[23]

In 1931 St. Louis won the National League pennant by 13 games over the Giants. In first place almost all year long, the Cardinals won 101 games, more than any other National League team since New York in 1913. Rickey's farm system had produced both players and revenues as fans turned out to watch this excellent club. On July 12 a doubleheader with the Cubs drew 45,715, a Sportsman's Park record, and attendance for the season jumped nearly 20 percent to more than 608,000. Chick Hafey hit .349 to win the batting title, edging out Jim Bottomley and the Giants' Bill Terry, and Wild Bill Hallahan tied for the league lead in pitching wins with 19. Rookie Paul Derringer, a teammate of Martin at Rochester the year before, added 18 victories and led the league in winning percentage. Bottomley was frequently injured, and his replacement, Ripper Collins, another Red Wing alumnus, hit .301. When Hafey sat out the first month of the season in a contract dispute, one rumor had Martin replacing him in left field, but Opening Day saw Ernie Orsatti, another former farmhand, starting in Hafey's place. Martin complained to Rickey that he was "tired of chasing up and down these minor leagues" and demanded to play every day. Rickey agreed but on his own schedule and only after he unloaded Taylor Douthit's $14,000 salary on the Reds. The trade occurred on June 15, and Martin took over in center. In 123 games he hit .300 and drove in 75 runs. Even more impressive, he led the team's outfielders in putouts and earned a $500 bonus in August to supplement his $4,000 salary. The 1931 Cardinals "were the happiest, merriest ball club I ever played with," recalled Frank Frisch, the club's leader on the field. "The Old Sargeant [Gabby Street], as he liked to be called, said early in the season that the ball club was a team of destiny. He insisted day by day that we were going to win the pennant and the World Series."[24]

In September Mickey Cochrane, star catcher for the two-time defending World Series champion Athletics, was confident enough in his teammates to tell guests at a Philadelphia Rotary Club luncheon, "I don't see how the St. Louis Cardinals can knock us out of another world championship." What Cochrane could not include in his calculation, of course, was the impact that Martin would have in the World Series. In seven games he got a dozen hits, including four doubles and a home run; scored five runs; stole five bases; and fielded flawlessly. Lee Allen wrote that "not since [Christy] Mathewson in 1905 did any player ever dominate a World Series as did Pepper Martin in 1931," and the statistics affirm this judgment. Martin's twelve hits tied the record for most hits in a seven-game series, set in 1925 by Sam Rice, and not until 1964 did anyone surpass it. His five stolen bases were the most since Honus Wagner stole six in 1909, and not until 1967 did anyone steal more. Martin was not only the star of the Series; he was Cochrane's personal nemesis. The "Wild Horse of the Osage" left his mark on every game but one, and the catcher's throwing arm was held responsible, so much so that for years fans remembered Cochrane as the "goat" of the Series. In the opening contest at Sportsman's Park, Lefty Grove, fresh from his thirty-one-win season, bedeviled St. Louis and Derringer, 6–2, despite surrendering a dozen hits. Martin got three of these, including a double that drove in the Cardinals' second run, and he stole a base. In the second game Hallahan pitched a three-hitter to beat George Earnshaw, 2–0. Martin got two hits, scored both runs, and stole two more bases, flashing the head-first slide that Frisch had taught him.[25]

When the Series shifted to Shibe Park for Game Three, Martin kept up his offensive heroics. This was the day fans booed President Herbert Hoover, both before the game and after the eighth inning, when he and his party left. Martin was appalled. "They cheered me, a rookie from Oklahoma who could run a little, and booed the President of the United States," he later told sportswriter John P. Carmichael. "It just didn't seem right, and I sure felt sorry for Mr. Hoover." But not for the Athletics. Martin got two more hits in the game and scored two more runs as the Cards beat Grove, 5–2. In Game Four Earnshaw held St. Louis to two hits and won, 3–0, to even the Series. Martin got both hits and stole his fourth base, and Frisch stole a base too. Sportswriters, who had now watched the Cardinals steal six bases, defended Cochrane. John Kieran, writing in the *New York Times*, blamed Grove and Earnshaw for not holding runners close, and he also suggested that Cochrane was playing with an injured leg. Regardless, Martin continued to shine. In Game Five he drove in four runs on three hits as Hallahan beat the A's, 5–1, and when the Series returned to St. Louis for its climax, Martin was already its star. Newspapers across the country had been lauding his performance for days, with James C. Isaminger of the *Philadelphia Inquirer* calling him "a whole team in himself on the attack." When the A's defeated Derringer in Game Six to even the Series again, Grove held Martin hitless, and that made news. The headline in one newspaper read "Grove Stops Pepper Martin." But not for long. In Game Seven Martin did not get a hit, but his walk and stolen base led to an errant throw by Cochrane that allowed the Cards to score a key run. They won the game, 4–2, and Martin recorded the last out by catching a fly ball hit by Max Bishop. "The ball," he said afterward, "looked like $1,500 dropping in my hands."[26]

Players on the winning and losing teams in the World Series received compensation based on gate receipts for the first four games, and Martin's share for helping the Cardinals win in 1931 amounted not to $1,500 but rather $4,467.59. He invested a good chunk of this by purchasing eighty acres west of Oklahoma City and spent most of the winter in the outdoors. Just before spring training he developed a serious skin rash, probably from insect bites, and the resulting infection lingered. As the Cardinals tried to defend their championship, Martin was little help, playing in only eighty-three games and batting a mere .238. Frisch, who had been the National League's Most Valuable Player in 1931, saw his offensive numbers fall off too, perhaps because he had toured the Orient after the season with a team of All-Stars and did not return until just before spring training. Rickey, ever mindful of the bottom line on the club's financial statement, had made two key off-season trades, but neither brought much to the team except cash. He shipped the thirty-eight-year-old Burleigh Grimes, who had won Games Three and Seven in the Series, to the Cubs and sent Hafey, who once again groused about his salary, to Cincinnati. Rickey continued to invest in the farm system, but none of the young players inserted into the lineup could prevent the team's collapse into a tie for sixth place with a dismal record of 72-82. Rickey had Street start Collins at first base fairly often, but this move just alienated Bottomley. With Martin under par and Hafey gone, the outfield was a mess. The club's attendance plummeted to just under 280,000, a drop of more than 350,000 from the season before. Rickey's pay fell from a high of $95,000 in 1928 to below $35,000. Cardinals fans were undoubtedly dissatisfied with their team's performance, but the worsening effects of the Great Depression hit hard, too, and not just in St. Louis. Total Major League attendance declined more than 1.5 million, and even the commissioner agreed to take a pay cut.[27]

About the only bright spot on the 1932 roster was a preternaturally talented and outrageously self-confident rookie pitcher named Dizzy Dean. Born to Arkansas sharecroppers in 1910 and incongruously named Jay Hanna for robber baron Jay Gould and political boss Mark Hanna, Dean grew up in extreme rural poverty. His mother died when he was eight, and what schooling he endured was minimal after third grade. Ab Dean moved with his three sons about forty-five miles east of their birthplace and eked out a living on a farm owned by a man named Gibbs Coffey. The boys helped in the fields and played baseball using bats whittled from sticks and balls made from rocks wound tightly with yarn or string. After seven years or so the family moved again, this time to near Holdenville, Oklahoma, where the boys got another touch of school, not really to learn, but just to be able to play ball on an organized team. Paul, the youngest brother, played shortstop, and Jay pitched with spectacular results. One day when he was sixteen, the team played a tripleheader in a tournament, and Jay won all three games, striking out a total of forty-nine batters. School was a mere pretense, and picking cotton held no thrill, so in November 1926 Dean enlisted in the army. "You got your shoes free and all the grub you wanted and the pay was $19 a month," he said, "and that was more money than I'd ever seen or was gonna make on a farm somewhere." Stationed at Fort Sam Houston near San Antonio, he displayed an extraordinary disregard for army discipline and military precision, but he did get to pitch very effectively for several teams on the post and a couple more nearby semipro teams. After Dean was assigned to work in the kitchen, one of his managers, James Brought, caught him practicing by throwing peeled potatoes at trash can lids. Brought called him "you dizzy son of a bitch," and the nickname stuck. Local newspapers soon were reporting the exploits of Dizzy Dean.[28]

According to Dean's biographer, Robert Gregory, Brought knew Dean showed promise, and he worked with him to improve his control, turning him, as the phrase goes, from a thrower into a pitcher. Shortly after Dizzy got out of the army in March 1929, Don Curtis, a scout for the Cardinals, watched him pitch and agreed with Brought's assessment. He signed Dean to a contract with the Houston Buffaloes in the Texas League, but he allowed him to play the 1929 season with the San Antonio Public Service Utilities team. They won the state amateur championship, and the following spring Dean reported to Houston. Right or wrong, the Buffaloes decided he was not ready for the Texas League and sent him to St. Joseph, Missouri, in the Western League. Dean arrived in town filthy, perhaps from hitching a ride on a freight train, and without a suitcase or a change of clothes. Completely oblivious to the social niceties, Dizzy lived up to his nickname. He spent money he didn't have, tooled around town in a series of rented cars that he abandoned at will, returned from road trips with no more than the clothes on his back, and dated nearly every girl he could find. But he won seventeen games for this last-place club and was named to the league's All-Star team. More than once Dizzy suggested he be called "the Great Dean," and when Branch Rickey came to town to watch him pitch, Dean greeted the dignified team vice president with a cheeky, "Hello, Branch." When the Saints finished their season, the Cardinals promoted him to Houston, where he went 8-2, and then in late September they called him up to St. Louis. One Texas writer lauded the skills Dean took to the Majors: a baffling windup, a blazing fastball, a sweeping curve, a change of pace, and perfect control. With the pennant already secured, manager Gabby Street let him start the last game of the 1930 season. Dizzy beat the Pirates, 3–1, giving up only three hits and three walks and striking out five. When Dean, who was not eligible for the Series, went back to St. Joseph, he bragged to his friends, "Show me another pitcher in the majors who has never been defeated."[29]

Over the winter Dean assured Rickey that given the chance, he would certainly win three games in the 1931 Series. He signed a contract for $2,400, but before spring training in Bradenton, Florida, had barely begun, the expenses he charged to the Cardinals had wiped out his entire salary and then some. Boasting frequently of his pitching prowess and openly disdainful of the club's rules and practice regimen, Dean made it easy for Street to keep him on the bench as the season began. Even without his pitching a single inning, Dean's loud mouth alienated his teammates, and a few weeks later Rickey decided to ship him back to Houston, hoping that regular work might settle him down. Not quite. In May he got involved in an on-field brawl that required five police officers to untangle. In June he married a woman who had been married twice before. On the Buffaloes' next road trip he returned to the team's hotel at 3:00 a.m. and ran into Fred Ankenman, the club president. "Don't you worry none," said Dean, "I won't tell nobody." On the mound Dizzy was as good as he advertised himself to be. He won twenty-six games, including eleven shutouts, lost ten, struck out 303 batters, and compiled an earned run average of 1.53. The Buffaloes won the pennant, and Dean was named the league's Most Valuable Player. Houston set a club attendance record, with crowds when Dean pitched far exceeding those when he didn't, both at home and on the road. So popular was he that a national newspaper syndicate contracted with him during the season to publish—with a ghostwriter's assistance—a ten-part autobiography, "They Call Me Dizzy."[30]

Dean attracted large crowds throughout the league, and when the Buffaloes played the Birmingham Barons, champions of the Southern Association, in the annual postseason Dixie Series, standing room only was the order of the day. Yet according to Gregory, when the Houston fans voted for their most popular player, Dean finished a disappointing fifth, far behind the winner, right fielder Homer Peel. Just as surprising, one spot behind Dean in this popularity contest was another outstanding prospect, center fielder Joe Medwick. He had attracted a faithful following of female fans, one of whom suggested in a letter to the sports editor of the *Houston Post-Dispatch* that her favorite player should be nicknamed "Ducky" because of the way he walked.

More than just an athlete as a youth, Medwick ran nearly everywhere he went and displayed considerable skill in several sports. He played baseball, football, and basketball on organized teams at an early age and vanquished all comers in handball and ping-pong. He was the best diver anyone had ever seen, and when his elementary school principal put a golf club in Medwick's hands for the first time, he outdrove the principal after two swings. The son of immigrants, Medwick spoke both English and Hungarian, but he was very quiet, his social skills not nearly as developed as his athletic abilities. In the summer after his sophomore year of high school, he played for several ball clubs simultaneously: a local semipro team called the Young Cardinals, an American Legion team, and the American Cyanamid factory team, plus games with other pickup teams. He was an all-state football player too, so good that several Notre Dame alumni suggested that Medwick would fit in well playing in South Bend for Knute Rockne and the Fighting Irish.[31]

Medwick failed to impress Ira Thomas, a scout for Connie Mack, and when he tried out for the Newark Bears of the International League in September 1929, manager Tris Speaker told the seventeen-year-old to finish high school. He completed his senior year one credit short of graduation and entertained a suggestion from Notre Dame that he attend LaSalle Prep in Chicago. But the Cardinals intervened. Pop Kelchner, one of Rickey's scouts, watched him get four doubles in one game and offered him a contract on the spot. Medwick and his parents and friends negotiated for three days, even causing Rickey himself to come to town. The result was a \$500 bonus, a contract for \$200 a month, and a railroad ticket to Scottdale, Pennsylvania, home of the Scotties in the Middle Atlantic League. Medwick signed using an alias, Mickey King, hoping to preserve his amateur standing just in case baseball did not work out. He played seventy-five games for Scottdale and hit an astounding .419, with 22 home runs and 100 runs batted in, thereby earning a quick promotion to the Danville (IL) Veterans as they prepared to play in the Little World Series, the championship of the Three-I League. In 1931 Medwick joined Dean in Houston. After a slow start he began to hit as the Cardinals hoped he would, finishing at .305 while leading the league in home runs and runs batted in. In the final game of the Dixie Series, with the teams having won three games apiece and Houston trailing by a run, Medwick came to bat in the eighth inning and slammed a ball that some thought cleared the left-field fence. The umpire, though, ruled that the ball had landed in temporary bleachers and was a ground-rule double. Houston did not score, and the Barons went on to win, 6–3. Medwick left for home with an extra \$600 in his pocket thanks to record gate receipts for the series supplemented with money contributed by the Buffaloes' owners. Moreover, he abandoned any inclination to play college football and with it his alias. Even though he despised the nickname suggested by that Houston fan, he would be Ducky Medwick thereafter.[32]

Not yet twenty years old, the outfielder wondered as he reported to Houston's spring training camp in 1932 when he would advance to the Major Leagues. The Cardinals' outfield appeared to be in turmoil, but Rickey chose not to make a place for the youngster. Medwick opened the season as a member of the Buffaloes, and by the end of June, he was hitting .377. Critics noted that Medwick was a bad ball hitter—that is, he swung at a lot of pitches that were not strikes—and that, like Al Simmons, he put his front foot "in the bucket," but neither of these flaws seemed to matter. George Sisler, manager of another Texas League team, the Tyler Sports, said, "He's smart, and he'll hit any kind of pitching." Moreover, he was so popular that when he endorsed a locally produced candy bar, the Duckie-Wuckie Bar, it sold extremely well at Buffalo Stadium and in candy stores throughout the city. At the end of August, the Cardinals paid Houston about $50,000 for Medwick's contract, and he joined the parent club in Chicago. Serious and professional in his manner, he took umbrage at the standard hazing directed at a rookie, and he particularly resented those who called him "Ducky." Before his Major League career was a week old, he upbraided an older player for making a baserunning mistake on a Medwick single, and a group of veterans turned against him. Medwick bristled, but manager Street persuaded him to let his playing ability speak for him. Quiet by nature, the youngster did so. He got into twenty-six games and got 37 hits, including a dozen doubles. His batting average for this abbreviated season was .349 with an on-base percentage of .367 and a slugging average of .567.[33]

After the season, Branch Rickey endured two setbacks. On November 8 American voters went to the polls and expressed their preference that Franklin Roosevelt replace Herbert Hoover as president. The election was a landslide, but for Rickey, the prospect that a New York Democrat and an advocate for repealing Prohibition would gain the White House was disturbing. Hoover had professed compassion for the unemployed, but his faith in local government and private institutions as a source for remedy had proved insufficient. In New York City, for example, charitable giving to the poor rose from $4.5 million in 1930 to $21 million in 1932, and municipal relief expenditures jumped from $9 million to $58 million during the same period. Yet this total of $79 million represented less than a month's wages for those no longer working. Roosevelt's plan for ameliorating the plight of the unemployed was vague, but he did pledge relief using public funds. Hoover carried only six states. No Republican, except in 1912, when the party split, had ever run so poorly, and the American political landscape was transformed. Just before Thanksgiving Rickey received more bad news. Charlie Gelbert, the Cardinals' starting shortstop since 1929, accidentally shot himself in the leg while hunting and would be out indefinitely. Rickey knew that his farm system had no one ready to replace Gelbert, who was only twenty-six. The club tried several options early in 1933 without success, including bringing back Rogers Hornsby, then thirty-seven, to play second base, with Frank Frisch moving to shortstop. Fairly desperate, Rickey called Sidney Weil, owner of the Reds, looking for help. Taylor Douthit and Chick Hafey had played well since being traded from St. Louis to Cincinnati, and Weil was not averse to trading his shortstop, Leo Durocher, and two pitchers to St. Louis. The price, however, was steep, and it included the outstanding young pitcher, Paul Derringer. He had won 11 games for the Cardinals in 1932, his second big league season, and would go on to win 194 more for the Reds.[34]

Rickey agreed to part with Derringer because he believed his club had enough pitching. Besides, the left-hander had been a salary holdout, and he lived an active social life that appalled the Cardinals' vice president. But Durocher had his own baggage too. Born in West Springfield, Massachusetts, and signed by the Yankees, he came to the Major Leagues cocky, aggressive, loud, and profane. Durocher was a pool shark, a gambler, and a ladies' man. A sharp dresser, he often changed clothes several times a day, and he relished living the New York high life, drinking, dating, and spending money while paying scarce heed to his meager salary. Not popular with his Yankees teammates, he even offended Babe Ruth, who labeled him the "All-American Out" and reportedly accused him of stealing his wristwatch. Durocher's feisty play pleased manager Miller Huggins, but after Huggins died suddenly near the end of the 1929 season, the Yankees placed Durocher on waivers, and the Reds claimed him. Seemingly exiled to the Midwest to toil on a tail-end ball club, he soon learned, as he said, "It is possible to spend money anywhere in the world if you put your mind to it." He married a show girl shortly after arriving in Cincinnati, but when she became pregnant and involved with a concessionaire at the ballpark, divorce ensued rapidly. Weil shared all this information with Rickey, his friend, and the trade was consummated over Durocher's objection. In their first meeting the Cardinals executive used his considerable oratorical skills to convince the shortstop that playing in St. Louis might give him a chance to win a pennant or two.[35]

But not in 1933, a year that began with Major League owners tightening their belts considerably. Attendance the season before had fallen nearly 18 percent, and owners resolved to cut salaries by about $50,000 per team. Even Ruth, who had batted .341 and hit 41 home runs, was sent a contract from the Yankees calling for a reduction from $75,000 to $50,000. Dizzy Dean signed his Cardinals contract for the same $3,000 he had earned in 1932, and when one of Joe Medwick's New Jersey pals attempted to act as his agent in salary negotiations with Rickey, the result was an ultimatum to sign at the proffered figure, also $3,000, or risk spending the season in Rochester. Medwick, of course, gave in. He had no choice, but once the team settled into its spring training regimen in Bradenton, he learned he would be the starting left fielder. The season, though, opened inauspiciously for the Cardinals, and save for a temporary improvement immediately after Durocher's arrival, it ended just as glumly. Even Sam Breadon's decision to replace Gabby Street with Frisch as manager in late July did not have enough positive effect. The Cardinals finished in fifth place, nine and a half games behind the pennant-winning Giants. Moreover, they dropped their final two games and lost their chance for the World Series bonus money that went to teams finishing in the first division. Martin hit .316 and led the league in stolen bases, and Medwick hit .306, but the pitching staff, absent Derringer, simply did not produce as Rickey had hoped. Dean won twenty games, but only two other pitchers won more than nine. One day during the season stood out. On July 2 the Cardinals were in New York to play a doubleheader against the Giants. The first game went eighteen innings, with the Giants winning, 1–0, as Carl Hubbell pitched a complete game for the victory. In the nightcap Dean faced Roy Parmelee and lost by the same 1–0 score.[36]

Rickey did not despair after two straight second-division finishes, figuring that his young team, which had led the league in runs scored, would improve in 1934. Thus he made just a few roster changes during the offseason, including promoting Dizzy Dean's brother Paul, a pitcher, from the Cardinals' farm team in Columbus. Even more significant, he declined to trade Frisch to the Braves for catcher Al Spohrer, deciding instead to split the job between veteran Spud Davis and rookie Bill Delancey. All these moves paid off, especially giving the younger Dean a chance. He won nineteen games and combined with Dizzy, who won thirty, pulled the pitching staff out of the doldrums. On September 21, with the pennant still very much up for grabs, the Deans pitched a doubleheader in Brooklyn. Dizzy threw a three-hitter in the opener, and Paul followed with a no-hitter in the second game, a feat lauded by his brother, who nevertheless joshed that he would have held the Dodgers hitless if he had known his brother was going to do so. The Deans' fraternal solidarity had its downside, though. They had both held out in spring training before signing the contracts offered by Rickey, and in May Dizzy had threatened to strike over what he called Paul's inadequate compensation. On a more serious note, when the brothers skipped an August exhibition game to attend a barbecue, Frisch fined and suspended them both. Paul soon got reinstated, but Dizzy took his case to Commissioner Kenesaw Landis, who ruled in favor of the club. Dizzy said, "I got a raw deal," but he was placated by the team's offer to reduce the fine and the length of the suspension so that he could get back on the mound. Hardly had this commotion settled when Durocher implored Rickey to speak on his behalf to Grace Dozier, a divorced mother whom the shortstop desperately wanted to marry. Rickey believed that ballplayers should be married, but a wedding during the season surely could be disruptive. Even Dozier thought so. Nevertheless, Rickey telephoned and assured her that a quick ceremony would allow Durocher to concentrate on baseball, and the two were married that day in a civil ceremony.[37]

The 1934 Cardinals, who survived all this turmoil to win the pennant, have been memorialized as the "Gas House Gang," based on their scrappy, intense style of play and frequently unkempt appearance. However apt, the nickname was not generally used until May 14, 1935, when a column by sportswriter Tom Meany in the *New York World-Telegram* was accompanied by a Willard Mullin cartoon depicting the team as a tough bunch, carrying oversized bats and determined to take on all comers. Frisch worked his team hard with two practices a day in spring training, lots of emphasis on proper fundamentals, and a dedication to "win today's game." After a slow start the team found themselves in a three-way race with the Giants and the Cubs, and at midseason, St. Louis was in third place. Injuries and fatigue set in, but the suspensions meted out to the Deans lit a spark under their teammates, who won seven games in a row. Still, with a week to go in the season, the team sat in second place, trailing the Giants by two games. The Cardinals closed with a rush, winning five of their last six, while the Giants dropped their final five. This turnaround gave St. Louis its fifth pennant in nine seasons, snared with twenty wins in the team's final twenty-five games. Besides the Deans' heroics—including four wins during the last week—the rest of the Gas House Gang produced an outstanding offensive season. The team led the league in hits, runs, stolen bases, slugging average, and on-base percentage. Pepper Martin led the league in stolen bases with 23. He batted .289, Medwick hit .319, and the catching duo of Davis and Delancey hit over .300. Even Frisch, thirty-five years old, hit. 305. As the Cards hustled into their clubhouse anticipating the World Series, Collins began crooning one of the hit songs of the Depression, "We're in the Money."[38]

Not quite. Standing between St. Louis and a big Series check were the Tigers, winners of their first pennant since 1909. The Detroit club had acquired Mickey Cochrane during the winter and installed him as their player-manager. He inherited a young ball club that had finished fifth the year before, and by the force of his personality and leadership, he convinced his players that they were good enough to win the pennant. Elden Auker, a twenty-three-year-old right-handed pitcher, later called Cochrane "the perfect player and the perfect manager in the perfect situation." His roster included three future members of the Hall of Fame besides himself: first baseman Hank Greenberg, who hit .339 and drove in 139 runs; second baseman Charlie Gehringer, who hit .356 and drove in 127 runs; and left fielder Goose Goslin, who hit .305 and drove in 100 runs. Detroit led the American League in batting average, on-base percentage, runs scored, doubles, and stolen bases, and the club's pitching staff did nearly as well. Schoolboy Rowe won 24 games, and Tommy Bridges won 22. Auker and Firpo Marberry added 15 each, while the veteran Alvin Crowder, obtained in August from Washington, won 5 games down the stretch. The Tigers led the league in shutouts and were second in earned run average. Winners of 101 games, they appeared to be more than a match for St. Louis. Connie Mack had surprised the Cardinals by starting seldom-used Howard Ehmke in Game One of the 1929 Series, and Cochrane tried much the same thing by giving the ball to Crowder. He had started a pair of games in the 1933 Series for Washington but won neither, and he suffered a similar fate against the Cardinals, who beat him, 8–3. Medwick got four hits, including a home run, and Dizzy Dean, who got a double himself, earned the win by giving up eight hits and striking out six. Detroit bounced back to win Game Two, 3–2. Rowe pitched a seven-hitter over twelve innings, surrendering only a run in the second and another in the third. When Medwick tried to score another run in the third, a strong throw from Goslin to Cochrane cut him down, but not before the feisty Medwick slid hard into the catcher with his spikes high. The Tigers tied the score in the ninth, aided by a muffed foul ball the Cardinals should have caught, and won the game in the twelfth when a single by Goslin scored Gehringer.[39]

After a twelve-hour overnight train to St. Louis, the teams played Game Three in Sportsman's Park the next afternoon. Now it was Paul Dean's turn. He gave up eight hits pitching a complete game and won, 4–1. Martin, the A's nemesis in 1931, opened the first inning with a triple and the fifth inning with a double and scored both times, but Cochrane threw him out when he attempted to steal third base in the seventh. The following day young Auker, a submariner—that is, a pitcher who threw nearly underhand—helped Detroit even the Series at two games each. He gave up ten hits and four runs while his teammates tallied ten times. This game is remembered for what Auker called "the stupidest move ever made by a manager." In the bottom of the fourth inning, with runners on first and third and none out, Dizzy Dean jumped out of the dugout when Frisch called for a pinch runner at first. Martin grounded to Gehringer, who tossed the ball to shortstop Billy Rogell to force Dean. Rogell rifled the ball to first, but Dean forgot to slide, and the ball hit him in the head. He took a few steps and collapsed. Teammates carried Dean off the field, and he went to a hospital for X-rays, but he was soon released. Legend has it that one newspaper's headline the next day read "X-Rays of Dean's Head Show Nothing," but the pitcher's biographer searched in vain for this attempt at humor. It is remarkable that Dean was fit enough to pitch Game Five, but this time Bridges beat him, 3–1. Back in Detroit the next day Paul Dean got the start again. He faced Rowe, knowing that the Cardinals had to win consecutive road games to capture the Series. St. Louis scored first on Medwick's single, but Detroit tied the game in the third on an infield hit by Cochrane. The Cardinals added two more runs in the fifth, and the Tigers countered again with two of their own in the sixth. With one out in the top of the seventh, Durocher doubled, and Dean singled him home with what proved to be the winning run. The Series was tied at three games each.[40]

Game Seven, the first since 1931, was nearly anticlimactic. Dizzy Dean faced Auker, and the Cardinals settled things early by scoring seven runs in the third inning on their way to an 11–0 triumph. In the top of the sixth inning Medwick hit a line drive off the center-field wall to score Martin with the eighth run. As Medwick rounded second, he saw third base coach Mike Gonzalez waving him on. It had been a rough Series. There had been collisions and close pitches and lots of shouting back and forth, so Medwick's hard slide into Marv Owen was not out of character for him, his team, or this Series. Medwick went in with his spikes high. The pair got tangled, Medwick kicked at Owen, and the two nearly came to blows. Umpire Bill Klem separated them, and the game went on. In the bottom half of the inning Medwick took his position in left field.

When someone in the stands threw an apple at him, he tossed it aside, but within seconds other irate fans tossed lots of fruit and bottles onto the field. The umpires ordered the grounds crew to clean up, and Medwick retreated to the infield. When he returned to his position, a second barrage ensued, and Medwick moved out of range again. The four umpires gathered to discuss a possible forfeit, but the crowd could not hear the public address announcer's warning over its own din. Nor could Cochrane quiet the boos and jeers. Home plate umpire Harry Geisel suggested that Frisch take Medwick out of the game, but the manager refused. Everyone involved gathered in front of the commissioner's box along the third base line for a prolonged discussion, after which Landis ordered Frisch to remove Medwick from the game. Frisch was furious. His player had done no wrong, he argued, and was no more culpable than Owen, who was allowed to stay in the game. Frisch suggested moving Medwick to right field, where there were no bleachers, but Landis would not budge. Medwick stomped into the dugout and flung his glove down. He later needed a police escort to leave the dugout and make his way to the clubhouse, and when the victorious Cardinals left the ballpark for their hotel and then the train station, police protection was again required.[41]

Landis's action was unprecedented. Never before in the World Series had the commissioner removed a player from a game, even in the face of an unruly crowd. Landis apparently argued that a forfeit was simply an unacceptable way to end a World Series game and that such a decision would have inflamed the fans even more. In addition the commissioner seemed to suggest that Klem should have ejected Medwick immediately after the altercation at third. Moreover, Landis later admitted that he probably would not have forced Medwick out of the game had the score been closer. Sportswriter Paul Gallico said that "Landis did the sane and reasonably thing," and the *Sporting News* said that he had "acted wisely." Curiously, Rickey did not object either, even after the fact. He knew that the commissioner admired some of the Cardinals' players and their grit, especially Martin. Rickey had quarreled with Landis before, and he would do so again. Landis certainly did not care for the way in which Rickey had built this winning club. He had opposed the idea of the farm system ever since Rickey had initiated it. The two had sparred several times during the 1920s, with the commissioner arguing that Minor League teams must remain totally independent. A Rickey speech in 1929 had exacerbated their differences and turned them personal. Landis was a genuine fan, but he ruled baseball as an autocrat, and in this instance, with the Cardinals on the verge of winning the World Series, he brooked no dissent.[42]

The victorious Cardinals returned home to a massive parade during which fans littered the streets with toilet tissue or "Depression ticker tape," some said. Despite home attendance of only 325,056, the club had made a profit. Sam Breadon declared a dividend of $10 per share and pocketed $80,000. Yet he worried that the poor national economy and competition from the Browns would jeopardize the continued success of his investment. Breadon considered selling the club to Lewis Wentz, an Oklahoma oilman and Rickey's friend, but Wentz would not agree to Breadon's asking price. Rickey perhaps anticipated having a larger budget with which to work had Wentz bought the club, but the lack of a sale did not dampen his enthusiasm for the future of the Gas House Gang. More pennants, rivaling the Cardinals' run between 1926 and 1931, certainly seemed within reach. Dizzy Dean was only twenty-five when the 1935 season began, the rest of the lineup remained powerful, and the farm system was sure to continue producing a stream of Major League talent. Yet the Cardinals did not win another pennant until 1942. Each season brought its own travails. In 1935 St. Louis fell victim to the onrushing Cubs, who won twenty-one games in a row late in September and nipped the Cardinals by four games. In 1936 Paul Dean hurt his arm and won only five games. The next year Dizzy Dean injured his arm when he tried to come back too soon after breaking the big toe on his left foot in the All-Star Game. Despite the debuts during these years of an outstanding outfielder, Terry Moore; a fine shortstop, Marty Marion; and two players, Johnny Mize and Enos Slaughter, who were eventually inducted into the Hall of Fame, thin pitching proved to be the team's undoing. Breadon and Rickey contributed to this downward slide by showing no reluctance to improve the bottom line by selling players. Then in 1938 Landis interfered with the Cardinals' way of doing business. He had never liked the convoluted way in which Rickey had constructed the organization's farm system, and now he was prepared to act.[43]

Three

"A Tyro in the Intricacies of Organized Baseball"

The image of Kenesaw Mountain Landis that abides in baseball's collective memory shows the judge sitting in the front row at the ballpark. He is hunched over the railing separating the field from the stands, his fist is clenched, and his gaze is fixed upon the action unfolding before him. The particular game is unimportant. It could be Opening Day or a regular season encounter or a World Series contest. It doesn't matter. As he watches, he is motionless, deep in concentration, and his lower jaw juts forward single-mindedly. He wears a high, starched collar and a three-piece suit adorned with a gold watch fastened across his waistcoat, sometimes obscured by an overcoat. His undisciplined mane of white hair, befitting a jurist, is a bit long. Parted on the right, it flops across his forehead down toward his left eye. Other spectators in nearby seats might be eating, drinking, keeping score, or conversing. The judge does not partake. He is watching the game. Landis is a fan. He played baseball as a boy in Logansport, Indiana, and attended many Major League games while he sat as a federal judge. But his box seat is a place of business as well as pleasure. He is the commissioner of baseball, the czar, the lord over all he sees. The ballpark, the players, the owners, the fans, the very game itself—they are all his domain.[1]

The Landis family tree had its roots in Switzerland, where one ancestor, a Mennonite, had been executed for his faith in 1614. About the time of the American Revolution, eight brothers left Europe and settled in farming country near Lancaster, Pennsylvania. Phillip Landis, the son of one of these eight, and his wife, Elizabeth Hoch, moved to Butler County, Ohio, just northwest of Cincinnati, where their son, Abraham, was born in 1821. He studied at the Ohio Medical College in Cincinnati and married Mary Kumler in 1850. Her family, strong evangelicals, included two bishops in the United Brethren of Christ and several missionaries who worked in Africa. Abraham and Mary had five children—two daughters and three sons—before a fourth son was born on November 20, 1866. They named him Kenesaw Mountain after the Civil War battle during which a spent cannonball ricocheted off a tree and shattered Abraham's left leg. After the family moved to northern Indiana in

1875, the boys took to journalism and Republican politics, but young Ken seemed uninterested in either of those career paths. He dropped out of school, clerked at a general store, worked as an errand boy for the Vandalia Railroad, and set his sights on becoming a brakeman. Turned down because he was too small—only 5 feet 6 inches—he resigned himself to covering the Cass County courthouse for the *Logansport Journal*, where his brother, Charles, worked. In his spare time he played baseball, rode a bicycle competitively, and ran a roller skating rink. He helped elect a friend secretary of state and used the subsequent patronage job to gain admission to the state bar without sitting for an examination. Suffering from a dearth of clients, he decided to get a legal education. Without even a high school diploma, he enrolled first at Cincinnati's YMCA Law School and finished at the Union Law School in Chicago.[2]

Landis began practicing law anew and got involved in politics. He was a Republican like his father and brothers, and his patron was Walter Gresham, his father's commander in the Union Army and a federal district court judge. Gresham was a Republican too, but he was also the political rival of fellow Hoosier Benjamin Harrison, elected president in 1888. Moreover, while the Republican Party supported a high protective tariff on imported goods, a minority, including Gresham, doubted the wisdom of this position. The Populist Party, a third party favoring a lower tariff, approached Gresham about running against Harrison in 1892, but the judge declined, instead campaigning for Democrat Grover Cleveland, who won. The grateful New Yorker appointed Gresham secretary of state, and Gresham took Landis with him to Washington as his secretary, a powerful post. Landis risked his own political future by accepting this offer, but he and Gresham were friends, and they shared a personal warmth. Gresham died suddenly in 1895, the same year that Landis married Winifred Reed, and the man wondered about his future. The president then asked him to become minister to Venezuela, but the new husband decided instead to resume practicing law.[3]

The young couple moved to Chicago, and Landis moved back to Republican politics. He pursued a career in corporate law for nearly a decade, but he was drawn to the progressive wing of the Republican Party, and when Theodore Roosevelt ascended to the White House in 1901, Landis realized that he fit right in. Biographer David Pietrusza noted that Landis possessed several traits that many progressives shared. He was young, middle-class, born of what was called "old American stock," and educated in the law. Pietrusza might have added that most progressives were also white, male, and insensitive to racial injustice. Progressives courted strong leaders, men who believed that government should be, in political theorist Walter Lippmann's words, society's "benevolent guardian." Landis idolized Roosevelt, and he jumped to support Roosevelt's ally, Frank Lowden, a candidate for the Republican nomination for governor of Illinois in 1904. Lowden lost out at the state convention, but after Roosevelt rolled to an easy reelection victory that fall, Lowden was able to have the president appoint Landis to the U.S. District Court for Northern Illinois. Landis set up shop in the new Chicago Federal Building, a magnificent structure designed by Henry Ives Cobb and occupying the full city block. A profile of the judge in the *Saturday Evening Post* noted that the courtroom was appointed in marble, brass, and mahogany, with a mural of King John signing Magna Carta on one wall and a depiction of Moses about to destroy the Ten Commandments tablets on the other.[4]

Much has been made of Landis's demeanor on the bench and of the sentences he imposed in a number of high-profile cases, particularly *United States v. Standard Oil Company of Indiana*, announced on August 3, 1907. Sociologist David Quentin Voigt called him a "showman who ran a lively courtroom" and noted that he "combined tantrums and whimsical humor in badgering witnesses, lawyers, and reporters." Fred Lieb called him "totally honest, but he was vain, egotistical, domineering, and a show-off." Journalist John Helyar described him as "an utterly unpredictable jurist," and legal historian G. Edward White depicted him as "a man entirely comfortable with exercising power arbitrarily, in accordance with his intuitions." Harold Seymour criticized Landis's "flare for showmanship" and wrote that "his spare frame housed a narrow, arbitrary, and vindictive nature." He argued that "visceral response and caprice often swayed his decisions" and quoted newspaperman Heywood Broun's pointed characterization: "His career typifies the heights to which dramatic talent may carry a man in America if only he has the foresight not to go on the stage." Pietrusza painted a more nuanced portrait, asserting that the judge mixed harsh sentences with leniency and tempered his vitriol with a populist demeanor that earned him admiration from defendants and the public alike. Landis was a lightning rod for cases that garnered publicity, and even in more mundane actions he could make news. He was, wrote contemporaneous journalist Henry Pringle, "a plain man whose lack of ostentation was ostentatious."[5]

The Standard Oil case put Landis on the judicial map. As part of Roosevelt's initiative to break up the country's largest monopolies, the Department of Justice filed suits against John D. Rockefeller's enormous company in several states. The case Landis heard in Illinois alleged that the company had knowingly shipped its oil by rail at far below the published rate, in effect by exacting a rebate from the Chicago and Alton Railroad. Testimony in the trial lasted more than a month, and the jury returned a guilty verdict on all counts after deliberating just three hours. The size of the fine to be imposed was up to Landis, and he decided, while compiling the financial data he needed, that Rockefeller himself must appear as a fact witness. His appearance in the courtroom caused quite a stir, but his routine answers to the judge's nineteen questions proved far less dramatic than the fine itself: a whopping $29.4 million, the largest judgment rendered in an American court to that date. Standard Oil appealed, of course, but the weight of popular opinion was with the judge, suddenly a figure of national prominence. After the Seventh Circuit Court of Appeals overturned the verdict and ordered a new trial, Roosevelt branded this reversal a "gross miscarriage of justice," and some newspapers groaned that large corporations remained above the law. Landis's judgment has been criticized for its extravagance, but the appeals court's decision was itself controversial, and in its wake a pair of law review articles supported Landis's decision.[6]

A decade later several cases surrounding American participation in the Great War raised the judge's profile even higher. In 1917 his son, Reed, became a pilot, but all the judge could do was use his seat on the bench to do his patriotic duty. In July he sentenced 117 draft protesters who had destroyed a jail in Rockford, Illinois, to a year and a day in prison and ordered thirty-seven others deported. In another case he sentenced a pacifist minister who had spoken against the sale of Liberty Bonds to ten years in the federal penitentiary in Leavenworth, Kansas. The following spring the judge presided as 113 members of the Industrial Workers of the World (IWW), a militant labor union sometimes called the Wobblies, were tried on five counts of illegal antiwar activities. The trial, which lasted five months, attracted enormous publicity and a plethora of visitors culled from America's radical subculture, including socialist leader Eugene V. Debs and young John Reed, just returned to the United States from reporting on the Russian Revolution. Landis handled the trial with such scrupulous fairness and sympathy for the personal needs of the defendants that even they praised his conduct, and after the jury returned guilty verdicts, he handed out sentences that differentiated between rank-and-file IWW members and the leadership. Still, the jail terms and fines he imposed were severe. Thirteen union leaders each received twenty years in prison and $30,000 fines, with the total of all the sentences exceeding 807 years in jail and $2.3 million in fines.[7]

Throughout his judicial career Kenesaw Landis remained passionate about baseball. One associate recalled that the only three things the judge cared about were baseball, his son, and fishing. Big Bill Haywood, the IWW leader who later fled the United States rather than go to prison and died in the Soviet Union, noticed during the Wobblies' trial that Landis was so busy that he could not attend as many ball games as was his custom. A Chicago Cubs fan to the core, the judge would dash off whenever he could to watch his team or perhaps the White Sox, always, as an officer of the court, refusing offers of free admission. For three seasons beginning in 1913, he could enjoy the games of a third home team, Chicago's entry in the Federal League, called the Chifeds and then the Whales. John T. Powers started the Federal League as an independent league outside organized baseball, with teams in Chicago, Cincinnati (playing in Covington, Kentucky, and then moving to Kansas City), Cleveland, Indianapolis, Pittsburgh, and St. Louis. Powers was a timid executive, and the Feds declined at first to sign any Major League players. Before the 1913 season was over, though, club owners replaced him with James A. Gilmore, a wealthy Chicago industrialist who pursued a much more aggressive path, hoping to turn the Feds into a third Major League. He enticed several other very wealthy men to invest in the league as owners, dropped Cleveland as a franchise, and added teams in Baltimore, Brooklyn, and Buffalo. Moreover, the Feds began to go after established Major Leaguers. At first they approached only players who had not signed contracts for the upcoming season, even though they were legally bound by the reserve clause, but after several months the battle for players widened, and no one was considered out of bounds.[8]

Not surprisingly, disputes between the Feds and the two established Major Leagues over players' contracts wound up in court. The first such case concerned Philadelphia Phillies catcher Bill Killefer. He played in 1913 for $3,200, and after the season, agreed verbally to accept a raise for 1914. Instead, he signed a three-year contract with the Whales for a total of $17,500, and then, when the Phillies enticed him by offering $2,000 more, he signed a contract with them, too. A federal district court in Michigan denied Whales owner Charles Weeghman's claim for an injunction to force Killefer to play for his club, and an appeals court upheld this ruling. This opened the litigation dam. Federal League owners reasoned that they need not respect Organized Baseball's contracts if National and American League teams would not respect theirs. The Federal League declared itself to be a Major League, and the 1914 season played out against a backdrop of constant legal wrangling. In January 1915 the Federal League itself brought a lawsuit. It named as defendants the three members of the National Commission, along with all sixteen Major League teams and charged them with actions "in contravention of the anti-trust and anti-monopoly statutes of the United States of America." Because the Feds expected a trust-busting judge to treat them equitably, they filed the suit in Landis's court.[9]

Testimony in the trial lasted four days, and spectators eager to see ballplayers up close packed the courtroom. They were not disappointed. National League president John Tener attended the proceedings, as did Washington Senators star pitcher Walter Johnson, who had jumped to the Federal League and then jumped back before playing a game. The plaintiffs presented a deposition from one of the judge's favorite players, former Cubs pitcher Mordecai Brown, nicknamed "Three Finger" because of two farm injuries, and Whales manager Joe Tinker, also a former Cub, testified in person. The Feds' attorneys argued that the contract organized baseball forced players to sign, including the reserve clause, was so one-sided as to be unfair. Brown's deposition recalled an instance when a team traded a player for a bulldog, and Tinker criticized the clause that allowed a club to release a player upon only ten days' notice. Otto Knabe, a former second baseman then managing the Feds' Baltimore Terrapins, asserted that players were not even allowed to suggest amendments to the printed contracts presented to them. Landis listened to all of this, but at the end of the fourth day he wondered exactly what the Feds hoped their suit would accomplish. "Do you realize," he cautioned, "that a decision in this case may tear down the very foundations of this game, so loved by thousands, and do you realize that the decision must also seriously affect both parties?" The Feds responded that their initial goal was a temporary injunction to prohibit the two established leagues from seeking an endless series of injunctions designed to hamstring Federal League clubs and the players who wanted to play for them, tampering with their players, and continually disparaging the league and its chances for survival.[10]

To the surprise of those who expected Landis to render a decision before players reported for spring training, the judge stalled. He knew that if he ruled for the defendants, he might be reversed on appeal. One other judge, at least, had already declared the standard player contract to be "peonage" that forced players to submit to "the dominion of a benevolent despotism." Landis could also foresee that a judgment for the plaintiffs would turn the baseball world he loved so much topsy-turvy. He delayed issuing a ruling, hoping that the parties would come to an accommodation by themselves, and this they did. Organized baseball's continuing legal parries did not put the Feds out of business, and the 1915 season was played to a conclusion, albeit with considerable financial losses on both sides. During the World Series Gilmore and two Federal League owners, Harry Sinclair and Phil Ball, met with the National Commission and began to discuss terms for a peaceful resolution. Prior to their winter meetings in New York, National League owners met with Gilmore and Sinclair over dinner at the Republican Club and came to a tentative agreement. Pittsburgh Pirates owner Barney Dreyfuss, on good terms with the American League, got its owners to assent as well. All that remained was the lawsuit itself, and Landis complied with the parties' wishes by dismissing it on February 7, 1916. At that time he defended his delaying tactic as follows: "The court's expert knowledge of baseball obtained by more than 30 years as a spectator, convinced me that if an order had been entered, it would have been, if not destructive, at least vitally injurious to the game of baseball." The terms of the settlement were complicated. They began with the Feds agreeing to cease operations. Organized baseball paid $600,000 in compensation to several Federal League owners. Ball received $50,000 to help him purchase the St. Louis Browns, and Weeghman bought the Cubs. The Terrapins' stockholders, however, rejected an offer of $50,000 to disband their Federal League franchise and filed their own lawsuit against organized baseball. That suit, *Federal Baseball Club of Baltimore v. National League of Professional Baseball Clubs*, eventually reached the Supreme Court, where the decision cemented baseball's labor relations and the reserve clause for decades.[11]

With the demise of the Whales after three seasons, Judge Landis was left to watch the home games of Chicago's two other teams. The Cubs' history predated the birth of the National League in 1876, while the White Sox reveled in their role as one of Ban Johnson's successful American League upstarts. In 1869 fifty or so city fathers formed the Chicago Base Ball Club, declaring it to be "a nine which should play ball and nothing else, a nine which should beat the world." Club officers had no need to recruit players for their venture because many of the best from around the country jumped at the chance to play in Chicago. The club made its debut in 1870, wearing white flannel uniforms, blue caps, shoes made of white goatskin, and "stockings of pure white British thread" that gave a sportswriter the chance to call the team the White Stockings. The following spring the Chicago club joined the nascent National Association of Professional Base Ball Players, and five years later the White Stockings joined an entirely new league, the National League of Professional Base Ball Clubs, its organizational structure aimed at its owners' desire for financial stability and competent governance. Rejecting a suggestion that clubs from the east be excluded, William Hulbert, the Chicago businessman who established the new league, extended invitations to the largest cities, including Boston, New York, and Philadelphia.[12]

Over the first half century of National League history, the Chicago club was the league's most successful team. Through the 1925 season Chicago had won more games, gotten more hits, scored more runs, and hit more home runs than any of its competitors. Only the Boston club had matched Chicago by playing in every National League season, and only the New York Giants, led by their masterful manager, John McGraw, had captured more pennants. In addition the Chicago club won three postseason championships, the "World Championship Series" in 1885 against the St. Louis Browns of the American Association and the World Series in 1907 and 1908, both over the Detroit Tigers of the American League. The club retained the nickname White Stockings for a while, but when manager Cap Anson inserted several youngsters in the lineup in 1890, fans began referring to their team as the Colts, the Babies, or the Cubs. Thus when newspaperman Franklin P. Adams penned eight lines of doggerel in 1910 immortalizing the team's double play combination—shortstop Joe Tinker, second baseman Johnny Evers, and first baseman Frank Chance—he called them a "Trio of bear cubs, fleeter than birds." These Cubs played their games at West Side Grounds, but after the Federal League went out of business, Whales owner Charles Weeghman purchased the Cubs and moved them to his own ballpark, Weeghman Park (later Wrigley Field), located on the city's near north side. In 1918 William Wrigley Jr., whose family made its fortune manufacturing soap, baking powder, and chewing gum, bought the club and did something unusual: he hired a sportswriter habitually critical of the team to become its president. That man, Bill Veeck Sr., struggled in his new position, but he was among the group of owners and executives who invited Landis to become commissioner of baseball, a one-man chief executive to replace the three-man National Commission.[13]

The White Sox, at whose ballpark Landis also spent the occasional afternoon, were the product of one man, Charles Comiskey, who settled in Chicago when his St. Paul Saints moved to the Windy City in 1900 and became the White Stockings, the nickname the Colts had ceased using several years before. Chicago won the American League pennant in 1900 and 1901, but it was the 1906 White Sox, the "Hitless Wonders," that captured the fans' imagination. This team's batting average was only .230 and its slugging average a mere .286, both last in the league, but its defense was superb and its pitching outstanding. In fifth place on July 1, the club won nineteen games in a row in August, won the pennant, and beat the Cubs in the first World Series between teams in the same city. After 1906 the White Sox did not return to the World Series for more than a decade, but when they did, they triumphed again with a club far superior to the Hitless Wonders. In the interim there was little to celebrate until 1917, when they won one hundred games, more than any other White Sox team in the twentieth century, and beat the Giants in the World Series, four games to two. Inherent in this club, as good as it was, was a sharp division between two cliques, one that formed around Eddie Collins, Red Faber, Ray Schalk, Shano Collins, and Nemo Leibold and another that found leaders in Eddie Cicotte and Chick Gandil and followers in Hap Felsch, Swede Risberg, Buck Weaver, and Fred McMullin. Eddie Collins's high salary and the fact that he had graduated from college were sources of resentment, as perhaps was the perception, not borne out in fact, that Comiskey was much more tight-fisted than other Major League owners.[14]

The 1918 White Sox plunged to sixth place, but dissension was only partly to blame. Once the United States declared war on Germany, several players left the team to do defense work, and others joined the armed forces. Comiskey blamed manager Clarence Rowland, known as "Pants," for the team's dismal finish and fired him after the season, hiring in his place Kid Gleason, a former pitcher and coach who had squabbled with the owner more than once. In contrast to Rowland, Gleason was a disciplinarian with a wry demeanor that bound the players to him with loyalty and affection. The 1919 White Sox were beset by pitching woes, and Gleason turned to veteran Grover Loudermilk and rookie Dickie Kerr for stability. Offensively the Sox were a machine. Joe Jackson hit .351, and the team led the league in runs scored. They hustled on the base paths, played outstanding defense, and held off Cleveland for the pennant with ease. Still, sometime near the end of the season Gandil renewed his acquaintanceship with Boston gambler Sport Sullivan, and somehow a plot, convoluted and inchoate, was hatched to fix the World Series. The White Sox anticipated meeting the Giants again, but when the Cincinnati Reds won the National League pennant instead, it mattered little. The White Sox were heavy favorites to repeat their triumph of two years previous, and gamblers, including perhaps kingpin Arnold Rothstein, sensed a huge opportunity if Chicago could somehow lose. How exactly the corrupted Series was supposed to unfold was never clarified, and who exactly was involved and to what extent remained unclear. But when a Chicago grand jury, impaneled in September 1920 to investigate other allegations of thrown games, began to examine the

Series, the result saw eight members of the White Sox indicted: Cicotte, Felsch, Gandil, Jackson, McMullin (who was tried separately), Risberg, Weaver, and Lefty Williams, a group that collectively became known as the Black Sox.[15]

The trial came to an end on August 2, 1921, when a jury found the defendants, seven players and four gamblers, not guilty after deliberating less than three hours. The courtroom audience roared its approval, and Judge Hugo Friend commended the jury for its service, after which jurors and the defendants found themselves in the same Italian restaurant for an unintended party that lasted well into the wee hours. Come the very next morning, Landis was ready with his own brand of justice, a white-haired, steel-jawed, down-from-on-high thunderbolt that the Black Sox, all eight of them, were out, banned from organized baseball for life. The commissioner had earlier banned Gene Paulette for his failure to explain his associating with known gamblers, but it was the Black Sox decision that cemented the commissioner's place at the pinnacle of baseball's hierarchy and laid the groundwork for a crusade against gambling in baseball. Landis investigated numerous other allegations involving fixed games. Bill James wrote that these charges implicated thirty-four players and that in addition to the Black Sox, eleven active players and four already retired were banned permanently. According to David Pietrusza, the commissioner did not act indiscriminately or with a heavy judicial hand. He heard each case on its own merits and did only what was necessary, fully aware that those who bought tickets to see games might well abandon baseball if they came to believe the sport to be widely corrupt.[16]

Major League owners offered Judge Landis the job of commissioner in November 1920, and he accepted, but if organized baseball were to become a unified confederation again, the Minor Leagues would need to come back into the fold. The National Association of Professional Base Ball Leagues, the Minors' governing body, had withdrawn from the National Agreement in January 1919, severing its ties with the Majors, but agreed ten months later to attempt to fashion a new relationship. Working out the details took a long time, and when the various parties gathered in Chicago on January 10, 1921, the draft for a new National Agreement was still unacceptable to the Minors. The eight-man committee empowered to speak for the National Association objected after the fact that the Minors had been left out of the process that chose Landis and were being excluded from the new Advisory Council, composed solely of the two Major League presidents. Additional negotiations produced a quick resolution. The Minor Leagues agreed to accept the commissioner as the new head of organized baseball. They signed onto the National Agreement for seven years, co-incident with Landis's term, and they accepted two seats on the Advisory Council, places to be given to the National Association's president and secretary-treasurer.[17]

The Major Leagues made additional concessions by agreeing to raise the prices for drafting players considerably and allowing individual Minor Leagues to opt out of the draft system. The escalating scale remained: players selected from teams in Class D, the Minors' lowest classification, now cost $1,000, and those drafted from Class Double-A teams cost $5,000. Leagues that thought these higher prices insufficient could opt out entirely, surrendering the right to select players from lower classifications in exchange for being immune from having their own players plucked from above. In essence owners in these leagues decided to acquire players from other clubs only by purchase and to transfer them only by sale at prices they were free to negotiate. The 1921 agreement also expanded the right of Major League clubs to option players to the Minors. Optioning had begun informally in the nineteenth century and had been incorporated into the 1903 National Agreement. Beginning in 1921 Major League clubs could option eight players for up to two years each, while Minor League clubs could option fewer players to teams in lower classifications. In summarizing the anticipated effect of these new provisions, the editor of the *Reach Guide* rejoiced hyperbolically that "the two great divisions of the base ball family are once more bound together, to the great and lasting benefit of the National Game, whose cause they all must, and do, serve!" Club owners, though, were more restrained in their assessment as events of the next few years proved.[18]

Landis wanted the Minors back within organized baseball, but he did not agree with draft exemption. On the contrary, he saw an unrestricted or universal draft as a necessary corrective to the reserve clause, itself of dubious legality, and he was more than willing to dress his opinion in patriotic garb. At one point early in his tenure, he said, "A situation where a group of ball players can be boxed into a minor league and can advance higher only at the whim of their employer is intolerable and un-American. So long as I am on this job, I will fight for the full restoration of the draft." The National Agreement of 1921 hardly met this standard. Under its terms all three Class Double-A leagues (the American Association, the International League, and the Pacific Coast League) plus the Western League (Class A) and the Three-I League (Class B) declared themselves exempt. Clubs in these leagues would therefore be able to sell players for more than the draft price, but they would pay more to buy players too. Major League owners chafed at exemption; optioning, which in effect gave them the chance to control several players not on their rosters was not enough to mollify them. Nor were these new arrangements close to satisfactory to Landis. When the National Association held its annual meeting in Buffalo in December 1921, he criticized draft exemption, saying, "It cannot be a good thing for something calling itself a sport that it is within the power of any individual in that sport to place a stone wall in the path of the advancement of a ball player."[19]

Allowing leagues to withdraw from the draft decelerated player advancement. In 1921 Major League clubs spent only $26,500 to draft thirteen players, and Minor League clubs drafted just seven players at a cost of $5,100, figures that were not much exceeded in the next few seasons. Yet as Minor League historian Bob Hoie wrote, clubs spent skyrocketing sums for players from draft-exempt leagues, sometimes with indifferent results. In December 1921, for example, the Giants paid the San Francisco Seals of the Pacific Coast League $75,000 for Jimmy O'Connell, an outfielder who played only two Major League seasons before being implicated in a scheme to throw a game. Just a few months later the White Sox paid San Francisco $100,000 for third baseman Willie Kamm, who batted only .281 over thirteen seasons. "If a club either refuses to sell at all," wrote Francis Richter in the 1922 *Reach Guide*, "or places a prohibitive price upon a player, the latter is hopelessly bound to the minor league club to life, or as long as the minor league club chooses to hold him in the absence of the draft." Looking for a way to eliminate exemption, the Majors proposed raising the draft price from Class Double-A to $7,500, but this idea drew scorn from the Minors. Similarly, a threat to declare all optioned players by Minor League clubs subject to draft also went nowhere. So in December 1922 the Major Leagues, meeting at New York's Hotel Commodore, unilaterally and with Landis's approval, raised the number of players that could be optioned from eight to fifteen and decreed that optioned players would be sent only to those leagues willing to have them subject to the draft. Minor League owners could continue to accrue significant revenues if they developed players on their own and sold them for high prices, but clubs that resisted the draft now risked not having enough good players to field competitive teams. The International League's Baltimore Orioles stood out as the team that played this dangerous game most successfully, but other clubs developed holes on their rosters that only optioned players could patch.[20]

Richter editorialized in the 1923 *Reach Guide* against draft exemption as "a gross injustice to players, who were thereby prevented from advancing in their profession." Once the Major Leagues had allowed Minor League clubs to reserve players, a draft was necessary, he explained, "as compensation to the players for surrender of their free agency rights." Richter added that both Major League presidents held the view that the draft was a matter of basic fairness and that Landis, albeit "a tyro in the intricacies of Organized Ball," agreed. In December 1923 the warring parties reached a compromise. The Majors consented to start optioning players to exempt leagues if these leagues agreed in turn to allow certain players to be drafted. This became known as the "modified draft plan," and the Western League and the Three-I League accepted it immediately, each of them glad to have players with Major League potential on their clubs' rosters. Draft exemption had turned many Class Double-A teams into stagnant clubs of, in Richter's words, "old and decaying players." Pacific Coast League president William H. McCarthy complained that the Minors had been "humbugged, deluded, deceived and cheated by the two major leagues." Yet his league and the American Association soon acquiesced to the modified draft, and after the 1924 season the International League gave in too. The Orioles had won their sixth straight pennant that season by nineteen games, and other clubs decided they could not compete without optioned players. The leagues agreed to a draft price of $5,000 and to having no more than one player from each team selected. Clubs could still sell players, and they did. Baltimore sold pitcher Lefty Grove to the Philadelphia Athletics for more than $100,000 in 1924, and Louisville in the American Association sold pitcher Wayland Dean to the Giants for $72,000. At least three Class Double-A teams put together package deals that brought them $100,000 in exchange for two or more players.[21]

When the 1921 National Agreement expired in 1927, the draft remained an issue. Absent a new agreement, the modified draft continued in place, and many Class Double-A teams prospered. In 1929 New York Yankees owner Jacob Ruppert complained that the Minors still had the upper hand and that few other Major League clubs could afford to purchase the contracts of the best Minor League players. He suggested, too, that Major League teams might find it more economical, as the St. Louis Cardinals already had, to own Minor League teams outright. The Majors continued to push for a universal draft by suggesting higher draft prices, but the Minors still said no. Finally, after the 1930 season, the Majors forced a compromise by threatening to sever all relations with the Minors. A deal followed soon. The Minors accepted a compulsory universal draft with higher prices: $7,500 for a Class Double-A player down to $2,000 for one in Class D, and they allowed Major League clubs to option up to fifteen players. The Majors agreed not to draft any Class Double-A players who did not have at least four years' playing experience and not to take more than one player from a single club. In addition the Majors retained their right to sign collegiate players, but they left high school and sandlot players to the Minors. Approval of the agreement came league by league. The Pacific Coast League gave its tentative assent first, subject to several reservations, but gave in after American League president Ernest Barnard announced that the Majors would not accept any concessions. The American Association voted in favor by mail ballot, and the International League voted yes by a telegraphic poll. In the *Sporting News* John B. Foster, editor of the *Spalding Guide*, claimed that it restored the basic principle that organized baseball had established in 1892. "There is," he wrote, "more equity in this arrangement than there ever has been in regulations arranged to provide for the transfer of players to and from major leagues to minor organizations." The first draft under the new rules was held before the first game of the 1931 World Series, but Major League clubs paid the new price for only fifteen Class Double-A players, a disappointing total. Over the next few years, as the effects of the Depression began to hit baseball harder, this price, once deemed too low by Minor League club owners, became more attractive, but the draft failed as a tool to advance the careers of many players. Major League clubs gradually emulated the Cardinals' approach, and they worked to restrict the number of players eligible for the draft. By 1939 clubs could reserve forty players on their winter rosters, and only thirteen Class Double-A players were selected in the draft. The *Sporting News* concluded editorially that the draft had become "a mere sideshow."[22]

Shortly after the 1921 World Series, the first over which Kenesaw Landis presided as commissioner, players billing themselves as the "Babe Ruth All-Stars" boarded a train in New York bound for Buffalo to start a barnstorming tour that would take them through New York, Pennsylvania, and west to Oklahoma. The Series had been the first one played in just one city since 1906, and Commissioner Landis had come east from his office in Chicago, moving into the Hotel Commodore for the occasion. It was also the last Series contested as a best-five-of-nine affair and the first broadcast on the radio. The Giants, having won their first National League pennant since 1917, defeated the Yankees, making their inaugural Series appearance, five games to three. Ruth scraped his arm sliding into third base in Game Two, and the wound became infected. He played in the next three games against doctors' orders but thereafter managed only one appearance as a pinch hitter in Game Eight. Nevertheless, when the barnstormers' train got ready to pull out of the station, Ruth, who had batted .378 during the regular season and hit an astounding 59 home runs, was on it. He had contracted with vaudeville promoter E. F. Albee to play a series of games for $1,000 each and then to perform on the stage for $3,000 a week. That Landis had specifically forbade Ruth from undertaking this venture by invoking a rule against barnstorming by World Series players hardly mattered. "I'm notifying you," Ruth told the commissioner, "that I am going to violate the rule, and I don't care what you do about it."[23]

Barnstorming—that is, traveling from town to town to play a series of exhibition games, sometimes against local talent—went back to baseball's earliest days as an amateur sport. By the 1880s barnstorming was rather common, both before each season as teams traveled north from their spring training sites and after each season as a way for players to supplement their incomes before settling into more mundane and less lucrative winter jobs. Small towns without professional teams of their own attracted barnstormers, and Cuba became their most popular foreign destination. In 1891 the All-Americans, a group of Major Leaguers headlined by John McGraw, began what came to be called the American Series or the American Season, a string of nearly annual visits to the tropical island by one team or another that continued for decades. Barnstorming was also an essential part of Black baseball, not only during the off-season but also during the summer. No African American had appeared in the Major Leagues since 1884, when Moses Fleetwood Walker and his brother, Welday, played briefly for Toledo in the American Association, and by the mid-1890s Jim Crow had driven Black players from organized baseball. Barnstorming became the norm for Black teams. They would play each other as well as local semipro teams, both Black and white. Then in the autumn they would get to test their skills against barnstorming aggregates of Major Leaguers. Cuba was an attractive destination for players who had competed in the World Series. Major League executives reacted frostily to these and other warm-weather excursions and to barnstorming in general. Some of this was racially based. "We want no makeshift club calling themselves the Athletics to go to Cuba to be beaten by colored teams," Ban Johnson said. But there were other reasons too. Owners worried that their players might be injured. They were concerned that successful tours might take some of the luster off the World Series, especially if barnstorming paychecks got too large. In 1910 clubs considered signing their players to twelve-month contracts. A year later they forbade barnstorming by anyone who had played in the World Series, and in 1914 they attempted to ban the practice entirely.[24]

Players objected strenuously to this prohibition, and none did so more blatantly than Ruth. On the Sunday after Boston won the 1916 World Series, he joined most of his Red Sox teammates for an exhibition game in New Haven. It was only one game, and the players claimed that Boston's owner had given them his blessing, but the National Commission adjudged them guilty. After threatening to withhold the players' Series checks as punishment, the commission decided instead to deprive them of their World Series emblems, miniature gold baseballs studded with diamonds and worth about $100 each. The following year's Series teams, the White Sox and Giants, thumbed their noses at the ban, too, but then canceled their planned exhibition tour when the commission announced it would hold back $1,000 from every player's Series share until they agreed to abandon their scheme. Boston won the Series again in 1918, and four Red Sox, not including Ruth, incurred the commission's wrath for some post-Series barnstorming. A year later, when the Red Sox announced that they had sold Ruth's contract to the Yankees late in December 1919, the Babe was playing ball in southern California. In one exhibition he faced a string of pitchers for a full hour and knocked 125 balls over the fence, but neither this feat nor his entire trip brought any disciplinary action at all from on high.[25]

The season Ruth put together in 1920 was the greatest slugging performance baseball had ever seen by far. He smashed his previous record of 29 home runs on July 19 and finished the year with 54, more than any other entire team in the American League. Moreover, he led the league in runs scored, runs batted in, and on-base percentage, and his slugging average, .847, was not exceeded until Barry Bonds did so in 2001. Ruth slashed at the ball with a vicious, hell-bent uppercut, a revolutionary batting style that had its detractors, but fans poured into ballparks to see him, both at home and on the road. Even when he swung and missed, the drama was thrilling. Even though New York did not win the pennant in 1920, Ruth still wanted to cash in on his box office appeal after the season. Two Cubans tried to sign Ruth for a postseason visit, but McGraw, who had traveled to Cuba many times, pushed them aside. Just as the United States was on the verge of Prohibition, McGraw's dream was that wealthy American tourists would visit his Havana casino to drink, dance, gamble, and watch baseball, and he wanted Ruth as his star attraction. The Babe played a few postseason games in the United States and then joined McGraw's squad for a month-long tour that paid him $1,000 a game. He grossed about $40,000 for a few weeks' work but spent most of it, including losing a whopping $25,000 on a horse race fixed by hustlers eager to separate the great American star from his money. Playing in large ballparks, Ruth hit only one home run, and he spoke degradingly of Cuban ballplayers, most of whom appeared Black to him. Back in the United States Ruth had another monstrous season at the plate in 1921. Besides his .378 batting average and 59 home runs, another record, he scored 177 runs, drove in 171, and slugged .846. Soured perhaps on Cuba as a postseason destination, Ruth displayed no hesitation in accepting Albee's offer to barnstorm domestically after the season. Despite sitting out part of the Series hurt, the Babe was raring to go. "I heal quick," he said, and the money Albee was offering was irresistible.[26]

The day after the World Series ended, Ruth, outfielder Bob Meusel, and two young pitchers left New York for Buffalo, where they played their first game. Landis, traveling back to Chicago on the Twentieth Century Limited, was outraged, but Ruth figured that even a fine as large as his Series share would be easy to recoup. The tour moved on to Elmira and Jamestown, New York, but the crowds were small, and the weather was terrible. Ruth was set on fulfilling his obligations, but the Yankees' co-owners were more worried than he about what punishment Landis might mete out. Colonel Til Huston, Jacob Ruppert's partner until 1923, intercepted Ruth in Scranton and persuaded him to give up the baseball portion of his deal. Huston paid off the tour's local promoters, but Ruth rebuffed his advice to apologize to Landis in person. The commissioner took his time administering justice. He reminded reporters that he had no liberty to disregard the rule against barnstorming by World Series players. It had been written into the 1921 National Agreement, and Ruth had refused to ask for an exemption. On December 5 Landis announced that the guilty players would not only forfeit their Series checks, but they would also be suspended without pay for the first thirty-nine days of the 1922 season. Landis had made his point. The players eventually got their Series money but not their lost pay. They had to apply for reinstatement too, and Landis approved their return effective on May 20. The Yankees lost to the Browns that day, 8–2, but all the box and reserved seats at the Polo Grounds had been sold two days before, and the team needed city police by mid-morning to manage the crowd bent on seeing Ruth's delayed debut.[27]

Ruth was baseball's premier gate attraction by far, and everyone suffered during the weeks he was idle. The Babe lost money, his suspended teammates lost money, the Yankees lost money, and other teams on New York's schedule lost money. Landis had called the barnstorming tour a "mutinous" act when he announced the suspensions, but even he waffled on the rule's fairness.

Before leaving New York to return to Chicago, he had admitted to reporters, "Whether or not the rule is fair or unfair to the player is not the question. It was adopted for good reasons, I presume, and was in the code before I came to baseball. My duty concerns its enforcement or penalizing its violation." Leslie O'Connor, Landis's assistant, suggested that the commissioner would have interpreted the rule less strictly if Ruth had not been so defiant. The Yankees opened their 1922 spring training in New Orleans. Landis allowed Ruth to play in exhibition games, but he did not succumb to New York's plea that the suspensions punished the entire team unreasonably. Ruth and Meusel formally applied for reinstatement by meeting with the commissioner at his hotel room. The judge lectured them for two hours, after which the Babe commented, "He sure can talk." But the suspensions stuck. After the season opened, Ruth and the others were allowed to practice in the morning, but they had to be out of uniform by the time the gates opened. In August Landis loosened the rules against barnstorming by World Series participants. He allowed games through the end of October, with written consent, so long as no more than three players from the Series took the field in any one game. The Yankees won the pennant in 1922, and both Ruth and Meusel barnstormed again, this time within the rules and without penalty.[28]

The German word for death is *tod*, so perhaps it is appropriate that Phil Todt, future Major League ballplayer, was born in a cemetery. A native of St. Louis, he first saw the light of day on August 9, 1901, in the Saints Peter and Paul Cemetery, where his father was superintendent. While still in high school, Todt showed promise as a pitcher, and he signed a contract with the Cardinals that his father refused to co-sign. Branch Rickey released him with the understanding that his contract would be picked up by the Sherman (TX) club in the Western Association, and then, after this league did not play in 1918 and 1919, by the Houston club in the Texas League. Todt, though, signed no contract with either team, nor did he play even one Minor League game. Thinking he was a free agent, he signed with the Browns in the middle of the 1920 season, a development that Rickey protested vigorously, arguing that the Cardinals still had some claim on Todt's services. Rickey appealed to the National Commission, but by this time Garry Herrmann had resigned, and the two league presidents held the case over until the new commissioner could handle it as his very first decision. Kenesaw Landis ruled against the Cardinals, declaring, "Todt was a free agent when signed by the St. Louis American League club in whom clear title was invested." Rickey resigned himself to the decision.

"Legally Judge Landis is correct," he said, while adding his belief that his club still had a right to Todt on moral grounds.[29]

The specifics of the Todt case aside, Rickey's assertion that his club and others should be able to "cover up" players not yet good enough to play in the Majors required that National Commission rules be circumvented or at least stretched. No one was willing to argue that baseball could survive without the reserve clause, but everyone knew that binding players to clubs in perpetuity trampled on players' rights. Since 1903 the commission had endeavored to mitigate that injustice in a variety of ways. In theory the commission affirmed that players should be able to advance from one league to another based only on their abilities. In practice, of course, the commission could not ignore the desire of Major League clubs to control as many players as possible. The conglomeration of rules about farming, working agreements, optional assignments, drafting, and outright ownership of Minor League clubs constituted an elaborate dance to balance these two competing interests while simultaneously striving to sustain competitive balance between those Major League clubs with substantial resources and those without. The National Agreement of 1903 had banned the kind of farming that John Brush had done in the 1890s, so in 1905 the Giants, a rich club, responded by developing what was called a working agreement, a deal that allowed them to send surplus players to a Minor League club and recall them at season's end. Other clubs refined this practice, and the commission countered with elaborate rules to restrict it. Pursuing a new tack, two clubs, Brooklyn and Cleveland, bought one Minor League team each. The commission reacted again, first by putting a limit on the total number of players a Major League club could control under any guise, and then, in 1913, by attempting to outlaw outright ownership of Minor League clubs. Throughout this period, clubs often simply ignored the rules, almost without peril, sending players to the Minors with a "gentlemen's agreement" that they could be returned at some time in the future. This was the basis of Rickey's appeal to morality in the Todt case.[30]

The 1921 National Agreement refined the rule against farming. Article II of the agreement contained this language: "All right or claim of a major league club to a player . . . shall cease when such player becomes a member of a minor league club, and no arrangement between clubs for the loan or return of a player other than by an approved optional agreement shall be binding." Landis took this provision seriously. Soon after his installation, he discovered that three Major League clubs had sent four players to the Minors extra-legally—that is, using only "gentlemen's agreements"—and he set them free, allowing them to sign new contracts with any club. But the commissioner was powerless to oppose Rickey's nascent effort to construct a farm system because the 1921 agreement removed the prohibition on outright ownership. Why this was so is puzzling. Most club owners believed that Minor League teams should be healthy, independent businesses operated by local owners and that Minor League rosters should be relatively stable throughout a season. Rickey would counter in time that a farm system would provide its own stability: better coaching and better facilities and better baseball played by teams less dependent upon the vagaries of local entrepreneurship. But in 1921 his view was novel and untested. Historian Robert Burk suggested three reasons why Landis did not move quickly against outright ownership. One was that owners Frank Navin of the Tigers and Barney Dreyfuss of the Pirates may have persuaded him that Rickey's scheme would ultimately prove to be economically untenable. A second possibility was that Landis hesitated because William Wrigley Jr., owner of his favorite team, the Cubs, had already purchased the Los Angeles Angels in the Pacific Coast League. Or perhaps the commissioner tacitly accepted farm clubs—that is, rosters full of Major League prospects that might overwhelm clubs with no prospects—as a way to pressure reluctant Class Double-A leagues to strengthen their rosters by surrendering on the issue of draft exemption.[31]

To affirm his position that farm systems could ensnare players unfairly, Landis continued to liberate a few every so often, but he had no weapon other than moral suasion to use against a rule he was powerless to change. Even when the American Association amended its constitution in 1927 to forbid Major League clubs from owning any of its teams, a move that ultimately proved futile, Landis could offer little more than verbal support. "I'm agin it," he said, according to *Sporting News* publisher Taylor Spink. The trouble was that owners other than Rickey were taking to the idea that a farm system might be worth the considerable cost. Major League owners came to understand that they could store players safely on the farm, and Minor League owners began to value the assistance, financial and otherwise, Major League clubs could provide. At the 1928 Major League winter meetings Landis had Leslie O'Connor poll each club to find out how many farm teams existed. National League clubs held twelve, and American League clubs, six. Just one year later, when the Majors and the Minors met together in Chattanooga, the floodgates were open. Minor League owners filled the hotel, seeking deals with Major League clubs. Landis continued to protect the rights of individual players he thought the system had wronged, but when one of his actions led to a court case decided in his favor, Major League owners reacted. At the 1931 winter meetings they voted to strip him of the authority to supervise the optioning process. Moreover, they gave themselves the power to negotiate working agreements with any Minor League club. Simply by paying a one-time fee, a Major League club could assign as many players to the Minors as it wished without having them count against reserve limits. Landis was stymied. The *Sporting News* reported that he did little more at these meetings than play golf, sometimes thirty-six holes a day. American League owners wanted to go farther. They passed a resolution barring the commissioner from stopping any transaction between farm teams owned by the same Major League club. At this Landis threatened to resign, and National League owners backed off, but only for an additional year. In 1932 the leagues united behind the American League's position, and Landis was left to fume.[32]

The changes wrought in the relationship between the Majors and the Minors during Landis's first decade in office were no mere adjustments. The universal draft was a victory for the commissioner and his desire for player movement based solely on ability, but the rules permitting outright ownership of Minor League clubs and unrestricted working agreements gave the Majors a counterweight, something they had not even envisioned before Landis took the job: a secure system for investing in large numbers of players by signing them, developing their skills, and promoting them without fear that other clubs would snatch them away. Early critics of Rickey's scheme derided the farm system as "chain store baseball" and bewailed the Minors' resulting loss of autonomy. A Minor League owner signing a working agreement surrendered control of his roster, and a club becoming part of a farm system was no longer an independent business. In truth, though, as national economic conditions worsened, baseball was not immune, and many Minor League owners could not continue to go it alone. The third winter of the Depression etched its ferocity into the life story of nearly every American. In the nation's cities unemployment skyrocketed to nearly 50 percent of the workforce. General Motors laid off 100,000 of its 260,000 Detroit employees, and Chicago's unemployed exceeded 600,000. Ethnic Americans were particularly hard hit. Black workers were 8 percent of Pittsburgh's population but 40 percent of its unemployed. The various fraternal and religious organizations that might have ordinarily provided succor were overwhelmed. In smaller cities and in rural America where Minor League teams played, the situation was at least as desperate. Families deprived of steady income lost their gas and electricity and then their homes. Mothers repaired tattered clothes and inserted cardboard into worn-out shoes. Fathers scrounged for food, often in garbage cans and city dumps, and sometimes, robbed of their dignity, they left home forever. In many cities the homeless cobbled together ramshackle shelters made from boxes, scrap metal, lumber, and cloth, and they mocked President Herbert Hoover by calling these camps "Hoovervilles." The spring of 1932 brought to Washington DC, the "Bonus Expeditionary Force," thousands of unemployed veterans of the Great War who petitioned Congress to pay out early the war bonuses not due them until 1945. After the Senate refused to act, city officials attempted to remove the veterans from vacant buildings they had occupied along Pennsylvania Avenue. A riot ensued, and the president intervened by summoning the army. Chief of Staff Douglas MacArthur led a column of tanks and cavalry armed with sabers and bayonets into downtown Washington. They attacked the bonus marchers and then proceeded to the Anacostia Flats southeast of the Capitol and put the veterans' settlement to the torch, scattering men, women, and children.[33]

Major League attendance had rebounded from the effects of the Great War in 1919, and it remained strong throughout the 1920s while Minor League attendance peaked in 1923 and then declined. The Minor League game thrived in some leagues and cities, but in the lower classifications instability was more common. On the plus side, the International League's Orioles grossed almost $1 million from player sales during the decade. J. Cal Ewing, owner of the Oakland Oaks in the Pacific Coast League, was twice blessed. He received $140,000 in compensation in 1926 for allowing the Vernon Tigers in Los Angeles County to relocate to neighboring San Francisco, where they became the Mission Bells. Three years later he sold his team, reportedly for more than $500,000. One of the most prosperous clubs, the Los Angeles Angels, was valued at $2 million in the late 1920s. William Wrigley Jr. paid $150,000 for the Angels in 1921, and he hired Zachary Taylor Davis to design a new ballpark. Davis had been the architect for Comiskey Park and Weeghman Park, and he made this new facility a near replica of the Cubs' home in Chicago. Built at an estimated cost of $1.3 million and opened in September 1925, the park, also called Wrigley Field, was dedicated to the memory of those who died in the Great War. PCL president Harry Williams called it "the latest in stadium architecture." The ballpark was home to two PCL clubs, the Angels and the Hollywood Stars, and in the off-season the park brought in more revenue by hosting the California Winter League and a wide variety of games featuring barnstorming teams.[34]

The drop in Minor League attendance, slight for a while, became precipitous as the Depression took hold. Entrepreneurs operating clubs in Class C and Class D leagues, in particular, took considerable risk trying to stay in business. Bob Hoie argued that a number of leagues failed, even before the Great Crash of 1929, because the towns in them were too close together and too small to support professional baseball. During the 1924 season, for example, three leagues did not complete their schedules. The Tri-State League, with four teams in Nebraska and one each in Iowa and South Dakota, went out of business on July 17. The Florida State League, with six teams clustered across the center of the state, lost two franchises on August 1 and quit entirely a week later. The Oklahoma State League, with eight teams clustered in one state, died a more elaborate death. The Guthrie team moved to McAlester on May 24 and to Wewoka on June 8. The Ardmore Bearcats became the Pawhuska Huskies on that same date, the Duncan Oilers disbanded on July 6, and the whole league followed suit two days later. How much volatility the Minors endured varied from season to season, but as the Depression tightened its grip across the nation, both individual clubs and entire leagues found it impossible to escape its effects. Twenty-six leagues started the 1929 season, and all but two completed it. Twenty-three leagues opened in 1930, but two more went out of business. In each of the next two seasons only nineteen leagues began play. Three folded in 1931 and six in 1932. The low point came in 1933, when just fourteen played, including just two in Class C and two in Class D, the lowest overall total since 1918.[35]

Eight leagues—four Class B, one Class C, and three Class D—completed the 1930 season but then retrenched by deciding not to play in 1931. Two of these eight had their clubs located in medium-sized southeastern cities, and they surrendered to the Depression reluctantly. President Cliff Green of the Southeastern League threw in the towel in early February and gave his clubs permission to seek berths in other leagues. The South Atlantic Association soon also suspended operations. A proposal surfaced late in February to take cities from both leagues and create a new one, the Dixie Association. Organizers thought for a while about establishing a twelve-team league, and they even agreed on a salary limit of $3,200 per club, but the venture simply could not get off the ground. The Central League also did not play in 1931. Even though the league informed its six clubs in March that they were free to release their players, the Erie (PA) Sailors kept theirs and applied for admission to the New York–Pennsylvania League. They were denied. The Blue Ridge League billed itself as the oldest Class D league, but it did not operate during 1931 either.

President J. Vincent Jamison admitted that the league had failed to solicit sufficient financial support from clubs in the Majors and high Minors in order to keep going. Blue Ridge teams had garnered help worth about $75,000 in 1929, mainly through working agreements, but only four clubs had such deals in 1930, and only three were promised aid for 1931. That was not enough to keep going. Moving in the other direction, somewhat incongruously, the Piedmont League added two teams in 1931, and four leagues bucked economic conditions to play their inaugural seasons. These four were all in Class D, and three of them—the East Texas League, the Palmetto League, and the Rio Grande Valley League—disbanded before the end of July. The fourth, the Arizona-Texas League, was propped up by monthly payments of $750 made by the El Paso club to its five competitors, but they all fell on harder times when the First National Bank of El Paso, holding the team's accounts, failed. The league finished the season and started play again in 1932 only to disband on July 24.[36]

Some leagues with salary limits already in place tightened them, and others introduced them for 1932. The Texas League adopted a strict salary limit and reduced the roster size of each team from eighteen to seventeen. The Three-I League cut its monthly salary limit from $3,750 per club to $3,500, and the league told clubs that players carried above the roster limit would be declared free agents. The International League brought its salary limit into conformity with other Class Double-A leagues, lowering it to a reported $12,000 per month. When several leagues, including the Texas League, attempted to impose limits on individual player salaries, Commissioner Landis stepped in to remind them that such a policy would violate federal law. The Minors, said the commissioner, have shown "careless disregard for the rights of the individual," and he called such limits "an affront to the social relations between men." Despite these economies, 1932 proved to be a worse season than the one before. Besides the six leagues that did not survive the year, two others went out of business after the season. The Southeastern League tried to come back after not playing in 1931 but made it only to July. The Central League also got a restart but barely limped to the end of its schedule. The Western Association started with six clubs and ended with four. Two teams in this league spent time in Joplin, Missouri; two in Hutchinson, Kansas; and two in Muskogee, Oklahoma. One team started the season in Independence, Missouri, moved to Joplin and back to Independence, and then to Hutchinson. Perhaps the most startling collapse was the demise of the Eastern League on July 17. Three of its eight teams were farms of the three New York Major League clubs, but the league collapsed when the Dodgers withdrew support from the Hartford (CT)

Senators and the Giants gave up on the Bridgeport (CT) Bears. In the fall the American Association slashed its monthly salary limit to $6,500. The three Class Double-A leagues considered acting in concert to control salaries, but the PCL declined to go along with the other two. In December the National Association decided that each Class Double-A league should fix its own salary maximum. Yet despite all these restrictions, many clubs found it difficult to meet their salary obligations to their players. By the end of 1932, 309 players throughout the Minors had claims for salary arrears totaling $106,513.34, nearly $350 per player.[37]

To confront the effects of these hard economic times, the National Association turned to a new leader, William Bramham. A lawyer, a Minor League president, and a man who, like Kenesaw Landis, was called "Judge," Bramham was described in the caption for a *Sporting News* cartoon at the time of his election as "a noble orator, a great joiner, and a man of multiple activities." Born in Hopkinsville, Kentucky, on July 13, 1874, Bramham, the son of two teachers, was a sandlot baseball player with but a modicum of athletic ability. Married in 1897 to Ninnon Marie Umstead and the father of one son, he studied the law under several private tutors before moving to Durham, North Carolina, in 1900 to become secretary to Brodie Duke of the American Tobacco Company. North Carolina cities hosted professional baseball teams in the 1890s, and the North Carolina League, with clubs in six cities, played its only season in 1901. Bramham served on the league's executive committee and for a time managed the Durham Bulls, the first team to be named for the Bull Durham brand of tobacco manufactured by one of Duke's competitors. The league went out of business in July, and Bramham shortly thereafter enrolled in the North Carolina School of Law, earning his degree in 1905.[38]

Bramham parted his hair near the middle, favored three-piece suits, and ate so heartily that he once earned a certificate for consuming a massive quantity of chitlins and cornbread, one of his favorite dishes. After graduation he established what became a very lucrative corporate practice in Durham, and he was active in Republican politics. Distinguished in manner and given to rhetorical flourishes, he had earned his nickname, "Judge," from younger law school classmates, but he never came closer to the bench than considering a run for a district judgeship. Moreover, he participated in civic and political organizations with a zeal that would have made the fictional George Babbitt proud. At one time his resume listed memberships in the Presbyterian Church; the Durham Chamber of Commerce; the American, North Carolina, and Durham Bar Associations; the YMCA; the North Carolina Sons of the American Revolution; the Masons; the Elks; the Kiwanis; the Knights of Pythias; the Woodmen of the World; and six country clubs. He was president of Knitwell Hosiery Mills, president of the Commonwealth Bond and Mortgage Company, chairman of the First National Bank of Durham, and director of the North Carolina State Fair Association. He was a member of the Republican State Executive Committee, Republican state chairman, and a delegate to the 1924 and 1928 Republican national conventions. In 1924 he was part of the group whose duty it was to inform Calvin Coolidge that he had won the party's nomination for president.[39]

Bramham helped organize the North Carolina State League in 1913. He ran its Durham club and became league president after the 1915 season, but in May 1917 the league went out of business. After the Great War several cities from the defunct league joined with others to form the Piedmont League, and Bramham headed that too. At roughly the same time he became a member of the National Board of Arbitration, the body that adjudicated serious disputes within the membership of the National Association. So esteemed was he as an administrator that he became president of three other Minor Leagues, the South Atlantic League, the Eastern Carolina League, and the Virginia League, for a time holding all these offices simultaneously. When Ban Johnson resigned as president of the American League in 1927, owners considered Bramham as his replacement. Like Johnson, Bramham was a steadfast supporter of his leagues' umpires, protecting them against abuse. Like Ernest Barnard, the man who got Johnson's job, he regularly worked long hours, a practice he regretted later in life. Like Landis, he vigorously opposed gambling and other taints on the game. When the National Association met in December 1931, various league presidents concluded that new leadership for the Minors was in order. The *Reach Guide* reported "a demand from the owners for a new regime with forward-looking policies, embracing complete rehabilitation of the game, the strengthening of existing leagues, the organization of new circuits, and concentrative and collective efforts for the betterment of baseball in general." Michael Sexton, president of the association since 1909, remained in that office, but administrative power passed to an executive committee. Bramham chaired this committee, whose other members were Warren Giles, president of the Rochester club in the International League; Ross Harriott, president of the Terre Haute club in the Three-I League; J. Alvin Gardner, president of the Texas League; and Joseph F. Carr, president of the Columbus club in the American Association.[40]

The executive committee established a promotional department in Columbus, designed to assist clubs and leagues in distress, and a press bureau in Auburn, New York, where the association's secretary, John Farrell, had his office. Two years later the bureau's director, L. H. Addington, reported sending out 41,507 pieces of news copy. In December 1932 Bramham and his committee presented a report on how the association should be reformed. Members debated its provisions from early morning until late at night over several days before voting their approval. The document they endorsed created a stronger presidency with enhanced enforcement powers over the association's membership and a streamlined administrative system intended to save money. The National Board of Arbitration, deemed unwieldy, gave way to a three-man Executive Committee composed of one representative from Class Double-A, one from Class A, and one representing Classes B, C, and D. Its primary job would be to hear appeals from decisions of the president. New rules also limited rosters and salaries: Class Double-A clubs, eighteen players and with salary maximums to be set by each league individually; Class A, sixteen players and a $4,250 per month salary limit; Class B, fifteen players and $2,000; Class C, fifteen players and $1,800; and Class D, fourteen players and $1,000. The association also agreed to set aside $2,500 to foster the creation of new Class D leagues, hoping that the Major Leagues would match this "missionary money." Sexton and Farrell both retired with severance pay, and Bramham, who had at first declined to serve, was elected president for one year at a salary of $6,000. He announced that he would move the association's headquarters to the First National Bank Building in Durham, and he urged all leagues and clubs to desist from "high hatting," trying to outdo one another with expensive ballparks and other luxuries. Bramham and his committee predicted that the new organizational structure would save between $15,000 and $20,000 a year. A *Sporting News* editorial lauded the Minors for "getting back to sound business principles" and for "the accomplishment of more constructive work and the creation of a greater spirit of mutual helpfulness than has been witnessed in many years."[41]

Debts both personal and professional confronted Bramham as he assumed his new position. Despite his many business involvements, or maybe because of them, he had been forced to file for personal bankruptcy in April 1932, listing assets of $78,593 against liabilities of $138,900. He hoped to continue practicing law during his presidency, but the workload of his new job soon made that impossible. Addington, whom Bramham appointed secretary, recalled his saying, "This job does not permit one to spend his afternoons on the golf links, and it deprives one of many enjoyable visits out among our people. I knew what I was going into when I took the presidency. I took over a job and it's going to get my full time." The association's members were in dire financial straits too. Bramham believed that many leagues might disband if they did not reduce operating expenses. Collectively the Minors were $375,000 in debt and on the verge of collapse since as few as five leagues appeared able to start play in 1933. That fourteen leagues began the season and completed it with no defections points to Bramham's springing into action immediately. He had testified before the U.S. Senate Finance Committee in 1932 against proposed legislation to levy a 10 percent tax on tickets sold to amusements, including ball games, but this effort was not successful. Bramham also moved forcefully against club owners with limited assets, so-called shoestring operators who often limped through the first part of the season only to disband their teams after a lucrative Fourth of July doubleheader. Bramham demanded that each owner provide a guaranty deposit equal to one-half the club's monthly payroll. He stipulated, too, that leagues stop ignoring their own salary limits, enunciating the simple truth that "no business can continue to operate when it continues to spend more than it takes in." Rather quickly overall conditions in the Minors improved. Bramham's policies not only drove unscrupulous owners out of the game; they also attracted new capital advanced by investors who saw value in stability and the potential for steady growth. Progress was such that Bramham was reelected in December 1933 to a five-year term and given a $2,500 per year raise.[42]

Over the eight seasons starting in 1933, the number of Minor Leagues commencing play in the spring rose from fourteen to forty-four. Individual clubs experienced financial troubles here and there, but only the Central League in 1934 and the Arkansas-Missouri League in 1940 disbanded while play was underway. In 1932 there had been two leagues in Class D; in 1940 there were twenty-three. Bramham reported in December 1937 that the Minors' collective indebtedness had been cut to $25,000, and he said after the 1939 season that Minor League attendance that year had hit an all-time high, over eighteen million, three million more than in 1938. One year later Bramham noted that many cities had constructed new ballparks over the preceding seven seasons, including twenty-five in Class B, forty-three in Class C, and thirty-five in Class D. Teaching club owners how to promote their teams as well as baseball in general was also part of Bramham's agenda. The program for the Minors' 1935 winter meetings included the first annual School of Instruction, led by George Trautman, who had followed Carr in Columbus. Designed to tutor club officials in matters of publicity, promotion, and business administration, the school featured oral presentations and poster exhibits from clubs that were succeeding despite the Depression. Some teams had run successful promotions even during the early years of the decade, and more did so as economic conditions improved. Clubs offered discounted or free admission to women, Boy Scouts, priests and ministers, and other groups. They distributed tickets through local businesses and community organizations. They shot off fireworks and gave away merchandise, including cars. They honored players present and past with "days," heaping them with gifts, and they presented awards to outstanding players. The *Sporting News* inaugurated its own Minor League awards for player, manager, and executive of the year in 1936, and when outfielder Lou Novikoff won the Player of the Year Award for 1939, the ceremony in Los Angeles included a Russian orchestra, the Los Angeles Civic Chorus, and Novikoff himself singing the popular old song "My Wild Irish Rose." Several pairs of leagues teamed up to stage postseason competitions modeled on the World Series. Precedent for such events went back to 1903, when the champion of the New England League met the champion of the Connecticut League in the New England Championship. The two series with the longest pedigree were the Junior World Series, which began in 1904, and the Dixie Series, commencing in 1920. Under Bramham's tenure Minor League fans got to enjoy the Midwest Series, the Little Dixie Series, the International Border Series, the Mississippi-Louisiana Series, and the Northern Championship, among others.[43]

Like the Empire State Building, opened in 1931 and at once the most prominent feature of the New York City skyline, Kenesaw Landis and William Bramham stood as tall as skyscrapers on the landscape of organized baseball. Both earned the nickname "Czar," applied apparently without irony. Close friends had liberty to call them "Ken" and "Bill" respectively, but "Judge" fit each much better. Charged with the responsibility to supervise and, if necessary, discipline the men who hired them and paid their salaries, both Landis and Bramham defined baseball as a public trust with themselves as its guardians. They were more than administrators and adjudicators; they were lord protectors who felt no compunction about taking their case, in any particular matter, directly to the people—that is, the fans—and they could, if the stakes were high enough, threaten to cause a scandal by resigning. Given how delicate their power bases were, it is remarkable that each held office so long. Landis's first term stretched to 1927, but a year before it would have expired, he was reelected for seven years and given a raise from $50,000 to $65,000 a year. In December 1932, as the two Major Leagues were cutting costs to deal with the Depression, Landis accepted a $25,000 pay cut that remained in effect for five years. The following winter, again with a year to go in his term, he was reelected for seven additional years. That would have extended his tenure to 1941, but the year before that he was granted a fourth term, this time for five years. Bramham was also rewarded with regular raises. In 1936, three years into his five-year term, he received a $4,000 raise to $12,500. At the Minors' winter meetings in December 1937, his salary was increased to $20,000, and two years later it went to $25,000. It was money well earned. In 1939 the National Association headquarters handled $3 million, mainly from player transaction fees, and employed a staff of nine.[44]

However similar Landis and Bramham were in some respects, they disagreed over whether Major League clubs should be allowed to continue to develop farm systems. After his defeat on this issue in 1932, Landis continued to fight a rear-guard action, hoping that his pesky, sporadic interference would cause Rickey and those who had adopted the Cardinals' ways to abandon them. Bramham, on the other hand, accepted farm systems as a necessary part of the Minors' recovery from the Depression and their drive toward prosperity. In 1936 Bramham told Taylor Spink that while "the ideal situation, no doubt, calls for a club to be owned by citizens of the town in which it is located, . . . I must say that during our dark years in 1932 and 1933 it [the farm system] saved minor league baseball. . . . Big league money went to the rescue of many of these clubs. Had they been dependent entirely on local backing, believe me when I say they could not have survived." Two years later he told Edgar G. Brands that he continued to view both outright ownership and working agreements with equanimity. Some communities, he added, desired baseball but lacked men with either the means or the knowledge to run a club successfully. In such cases big league clubs could contribute capital, players, and executives, to everyone's advantage. The Minor Leagues, adopting Bramham's pragmatism, had already begun an attempt to amend the rules governing their relations with the Majors, changes that would make farming easier.[45]

Landis seemed to be standing alone in this fight without any allies. All he could do was harass clubs for technical violations of the complicated regulations governing the movement of players upward through the Minor Leagues. His most famous decision, promulgated on December 10, 1936, concerned the rule that Major League clubs could not sign high school or sandlot players. Somewhat surprisingly, though, Landis's judgment in this case was directly contrary to what was expected. In 1935 Bob Feller, a sixteen-year-old high school student in Van Meter, Iowa, was pitching for three teams: his high school team; the Oakviews, an amateur team that played on a field Feller's father had carved out of a grove of oak trees near their home; and the Farmers Union semipro team in Des Moines. Farmers Union qualified for the national amateur tournament in Dayton, Ohio, where Feller showed off his remarkable fastball before an array of Major League scouts. Some dangled contract offers, but Feller declined. He was already under contract, albeit secretly. Indians scout Cy Slapnicka had already persuaded Feller and his father, since the son was underage, to sign a contract with the Fargo-Moorhead (ND) Twins of the Northern League. This move was a subterfuge. The Twins had a working agreement with Cleveland, and Slapnicka had no intention of sending Feller to North Dakota. This was an example of "covering up," trying to hide a prospect in the Minors. It was a practice Landis despised and a clear subversion of the rules.[46]

Over the winter of 1935–36 Slapnicka arranged for Fargo-Moorhead to transfer Feller's contract to a Cleveland farm team, the New Orleans Pelicans of the Southern Association. New Orleans put Feller on the "voluntarily retired" list so he could finish high school, after which Slapnicka brought him to Cleveland. Feller pitched one game for a semipro team, the Rosenblums, and then took the mound for the Indians in an exhibition game against the Cardinals, striking out eight batters in three innings. The Indians announced that they would purchase Feller's contract from New Orleans, making him a Major Leaguer at age seventeen. Feller got into fourteen games in 1936, winning five. He pitched sixty-two innings with 76 strikeouts and 47 walks. At some point Landis received a complaint about Feller's contract status from Lee Keyser, the owner of the Des Moines Demons in the Western League. Keyser argued that he had attempted to sign Feller to a contract but had been thwarted by Cleveland's illegal conduct. Landis met with Feller after the season and took the case under advisement. Cleveland had clearly snubbed the rules, and Landis could well have declared Feller a free agent, able to sign with any other team. The trouble was that Feller wanted to remain with the Indians, and he was willing to turn his back on whatever huge contract offers other teams might tender. Moreover, Feller's father told Landis that his son would sue if the commissioner prevented his playing with Cleveland. Landis announced his decision at the National Association's winter meetings in Montreal. In it he declared that the Indians had been duplicitous, but he also acknowledged that Feller was not a player whose rights were being trampled. He ordered the Indians to pay $7,500 in damages to Des Moines and declared that Feller would remain Cleveland's property.[47]

The Feller case was not Landis's first run-in with the Indians, nor was it his last. The following spring, 1937, the commissioner acted on a complaint by Minor League outfielder Tommy Henrich and declared him a free agent. Cleveland scout Bill Bradley had signed Henrich and promised him a spot on the Indians roster within three years. Henrich played for two teams in the lower Minors before being transferred in 1936 to New Orleans, where he hit .346. The Pelicans then assigned him to another Cleveland farm, the Milwaukee Brewers in the American Association, at which point Henrich asked Landis to decide who owned his contract, Milwaukee or Cleveland. The judge determined that Cleveland was covering up Henrich and preventing him from advancing to the Majors. Once Landis set Henrich free, he signed with the Yankees for a $20,000 bonus and a $5,000 salary. He played just seven games with Newark in the International League before advancing to New York. In 1938 the commissioner struck at Cleveland once more, freeing players Charles Stanceu and Myron McCormick on much the same grounds. Months before, he had explained in a letter to Cleveland owner Alva Bradley exactly why he opposed farm systems. "A very real objection to the whole thing," he wrote, "is the hypocrisy that characterizes the operation. The Major League gentlemen not only are raping the Minor League organization, but during the actual process, they talk about ethics and ideals and morals and how they are 'saving' the Minors; whereas, the truth is, that down to this blessed minute, not one of them has let go of a thin dime to any Minor League interest without extorting from the victim a mortgage on his past, present and future baseball assets."[48]

Throughout this long struggle over the proper relationship between the Major Leagues and the Minors, Landis stuck to the romantic view that every Minor League team should remain a small-town enterprise owned and operated by members of the local community. Rickey's more rational vision, born of the peculiar circumstances in which the Cardinals found themselves after the Great War, held that a Major League club could profit economically by vertically integrating its labor supply, and Bramham was realistic enough to recognize that Major League money could sustain the Minors. Landis's friends among the owners, including Barney Dreyfuss and Frank Navin, bolstered his opinion that no Major League club was rich enough to finance a farm system and survive. But Rickey, even with limited resources, proved Landis wrong. He and Landis continued to be antagonists. Rickey fulminated, and the commissioner refused to budge. The most telling blow, though, in the evolution of farm systems came when affluent clubs realized that they, too, would have to engage in "chain store baseball" to stay competitive. The Yankees were baseball's richest team in the late 1920s. They won six American League pennants in that decade and three World Series, but by 1930 they were nevertheless on their way to creating their own farm system. Nine seasons later Dan Daniel noted that the Yankees had put together another spectacular decade on the field, relying on only one player acquired in a trade. More than Rickey's eloquence or his business acumen, the Yankees' decision to create a farm system made Landis's defeat on this crucial issue inevitable.[49]

Four

"The Yankees Need Building Up"

Had Ed Barrow waited just a few more days, he could have made true what was often said about him in later life—namely, that he had been born in a covered wagon. Not quite. His father, John, was a native of Chillicothe, Ohio, about fifty miles south of Columbus, and a farmer. After serving in the Civil War, John returned home in poor health and with his hearing impaired, and he met Effie Ann Vinson-Heller. She was from Hillsboro, southwest of Chillicothe, and after a short courtship, they married in July 1867. As war veterans, Barrow and his three brothers had earned the right to land grants of 160 acres each in Nebraska, and soon after the wedding the Barrow party set out: John and Effie with his mother, his brothers, and his sisters. As Ed Barrow recalled years later, "They were intrigued by the tremendous promise and allure of the Golden West." The trip took nearly two years. The family got only as far as Springfield, Illinois, before the first winter, which they spent at a hemp farm owned by relatives. There, on May 10, 1868, shortly before the party set out again, John and Effie's first son was born. They named him Edward and gave him a middle name to honor General Ulysses Grant. After another summer's trek and a second winter spent in Holden, Missouri, the family reached Nebraska City, Nebraska, in the spring of 1869 and took title to their land. It was, as Ed Barrow wrote in his memoirs, "desolate country."[1]

Battling the perils of the prairie—including grasshoppers, fires, floods, and hostile Native Americans—John and Effie farmed their land for six exhausting years before selling out to one of his brothers and moving to a second farm outside Des Moines. There they stayed for three more years until John's health deteriorated. Into the city the family went. Young Ed attended the Third Ward School, where he learned how to box and play baseball. He pitched for his high school team and for the YMCA but quit after injuring his arm in a cold rain. Barrow was broad and robust, and his boxing skills helped define his personality. An early job at a roller skating rink ended when he got too physical with some unruly customers. He then went to work in the business side of the newspaper business, including circulation and advertising manager for the *Des Moines Leader*. But baseball was creeping back into his life. "No matter what job I held on the *Leader*," he wrote, "I always reported the news of the ball games and the theaters." Along the way he managed the Stars, an amateur baseball team whose roster included future Hall of Fame member Fred Clarke. Fairly comfortable with his newspaper salary, $30 a week, Barrow nevertheless found himself enthralled with his brother Frank's wanderlust. They tried without success to sell advertising in Chicago and then a newly invented carpet cleaner in western Pennsylvania. Full of enthusiasm for a highly speculative venture, the brothers took their family's savings, some $3,000, and committed to buy one freight car load of H&H soap every month. Four months later they owned lots of carpet cleaner but were otherwise broke. Frank took a job as a night clerk at the Staley Hotel in Pittsburgh, staying just long enough to earn enough money to return to Des Moines. Ed, determined not to go home until he could repay his family, replaced Frank at the Staley. He met Harry M. Stevens, a caterer who lived at the Schlosser Hotel next door and whose growing business including selling concessions at several theaters and at Exposition Park, the Pirates' home field. Stevens became his friend and offered him a partnership that Barrow accepted.[2]

Within a year young Ed had moved from registering hotel guests to selling peanuts and scorecards to running his own Minor League ball club, the Wheeling (WV) franchise in the new Interstate League. The league did not survive the 1895 season, but as Barrow said, "I was lost in baseball. It had got into my blood." In 1896 Stevens moved to New York to take over the concessions business at the Polo Grounds, home ballpark of the Giants. He proposed that Barrow accompany him to New York, but Barrow said no. "I have made three big mistakes, financially, in my career," he reminisced in 1950, and turning down Stevens was the first and biggest. Instead Barrow partnered with Charles I. McKee, a Pittsburgh restaurateur, to acquire the Paterson (NJ) Silk Weavers in another new league, the Atlantic League, for $800. Paterson, called the "Silk City," was the nation's fifteenth largest city when Barrow moved there. Some workers toiled in cotton mills, others built locomotives, and better than seventeen thousand worked in over a hundred silk mills, producing more silk products than any other American city. Barrow fit in well. A photo from this time shows him with hair parted down the middle, a walrus mustache, and a resolute jaw. He met Garrett A. Hobart, president of Paterson's streetcar company and soon to be William McKinley's first vice president. Hobart agreed to build a ballpark for the Silk Weavers along one of his trolley lines, and Barrow began to assemble a roster. He picked up several players who would eventually reach the Majors but none who had prospects brighter than

Honus Wagner. Barrow had seen this awkward, bowlegged athlete play the year before, and "all I could think of," he recalled as he went back to Pittsburgh to sign him to a contract, "was his tremendous strength and power." Wagner stayed in Paterson for a season and a half, and the impression he left on Barrow was indelible. "Wagner was the greatest all-around ballplayer who ever lived," he wrote.[3]

As owner of the Paterson club and later president of the league, Barrow noted, "[I] used every device I could think of to hold the players, encourage the club owners, and bring out the fans. . . . I did many things I never would have done in later years, or, for that matter, been allowed to do after baseball became well organized and regulated." On the Fourth of July, Paterson played one of the earliest night games on record in Wilmington, Delaware, as the third part of a morning-afternoon-evening tripleheader. The night game was a laughable exhibition played with special white baseballs under sorely inadequate lights. Players lost the ball many times, and the game ended prematurely when Wagner came to bat and hit a pitch that exploded because the pitcher had replaced the ball with a firecracker. Barrow claimed in his memoirs that his other tricks included hiring a woman pitcher named Lizzie Arlington to barnstorm around the league, but records indicate she made only a single professional appearance for the Reading (PA) Coal Heavers, pitching the ninth inning against Allentown on July 5, 1898, and giving up one walk, two hits, and no runs. Barrow used his boxing connections to recruit other celebrities to visit the ballpark. Former heavyweight champion John L. Sullivan umpired a few games, and Gentleman Jim Corbett, who had defeated Sullivan in 1892, played first base on occasion. James J. Jeffries umpired a Paterson game right after he won the heavyweight championship in 1899, but none of these stunts did very much to boost attendance at Silk Weavers games. Minor League baseball suffered at the gate during the Spanish-American War, and the Atlantic League limped through the 1899 season. Two clubs disbanded in July, and the rest of the league stopped playing in August. Barrow, perhaps disheartened, declined to calculate the league's final statistics.[4]

After the league expired, Barrow tried his hand at vaudeville, not as a performer but as a theater owner. He had done a variety of things to earn money during previous off-seasons, and now he hooked up with the owner of the Atlantic League team in Richmond, Jacob Wells, who persuaded Barrow to join him in buying and refurbishing Richmond's Ford Theater. Snow delayed the theater's opening, and as Barrow wrote, "Our vaudeville business didn't take Richmond as Grant did." As the debts piled up, Barrow was relieved to have McKee agree to buy him out. This was Barrow's second big financial mistake. Within three years Wells and McKee were making a fortune as owners of twenty-one theaters and eight amusement parks throughout the South. Barrow's attention, meanwhile, had turned north at the suggestion of former Major League shortstop Arthur Irwin, whose brother had managed in the Atlantic League. Arthur had managed the Toronto Maple Leafs in the Eastern League in 1898 and owned a quarter of the team, and when he decided to move to Syracuse, he offered Barrow his share. Barrow became manager and part owner of the Maple Leafs, but he lacked sufficient operating capital to have a real impact on the roster. Moreover, the Leafs played their games at Hanlan's Point, a park on an island in the Don River. Fans had to ride a ferry to attend games, and a mediocre team did not provide much incentive for them to do so. After a sixth-place finish in 1900, Barrow and another quarter-owner bought out the Toronto Ferry Company (which owned the other half of the team), sold stock to the public to raise $10,000, and built Diamond Park on the mainland. The Leafs jumped to second place behind the Rochester Bronchos, and they won the pennant in 1902. The best player on that club was Lou Bruce, a Mohawk who started the season at shortstop, moved to the outfield because he had a strong throwing arm, and then tried pitching. Astonishingly, he won eighteen games, including both ends of a doubleheader on September 2 in Rochester, against only two losses.[5]

Barrow was suddenly famous. Despite a temper that more than once got him embroiled in violent arguments with umpires, he found himself in demand. The Eastern League was a prominent organization with clubs in some cities that had hosted Major League teams, and Major League club owners took notice. Barrow's success in Toronto brought him one offer to manage the Philadelphia Phillies, which he declined, and another to manage the Detroit Tigers, which he accepted. The Tigers' new owner, Samuel Angus, whose money was in railroads and insurance, signed Barrow's contract, but the power behind the throne soon became a young bookkeeper named Frank Navin, "a cold, uncommunicative man," in Barrow's words, "with a poker face." Navin freely counseled both Angus and William H. Yawkey, who took control from Angus in 1904, but as Barrow wrote, "He interfered with my handling of the ball club." And Barrow still sometimes let his temper get the better of him. Navin's meddling had not helped the club much in 1903, and when he altered a trade Barrow had worked out with the Chicago White Sox midway through the 1904 season, the manager got steamed and resigned. He finished the year back in the Eastern League, managing the Montreal Royals to twenty wins in their last twenty-one games. He then signed a two-year contract to manage the American Association's Indianapolis Indians, but his Detroit experience had soured him on his chosen profession. After the Indians finished sixth in 1905, he asked the club owner to let him resign. Barrow returned to Toronto, ostensibly to manage the Maple Leafs again, but really to be close to Frances Taylor, the young woman whom he would marry in 1912. Weeks before the cash-strapped Leafs finished last in 1906, he resigned and got back into the hotel business.[6]

Barrow purchased the Windsor Hotel in downtown Toronto, but he did not abandon baseball entirely. He wrote at least one story for the *Sporting News* about Wagner, and players boarded at his hotel for a dollar a day. Still, "Those three years out of baseball," Barrow told the *Sporting News*, "were the most agonizing of my life." Somewhere along the way, he made his third great financial blunder, turning down an opportunity from the Dodge Company to sell its cars throughout Canada. But more than this, he realized he missed baseball. Barrow found himself going to lots of games and offering suggestions to his former partner, still running the Maple Leafs. When the Montreal club came looking for a manager for the 1910 season, "I leapt at the offer, and I was never out of baseball again," he wrote. In fact, by the end of that year, he found himself elected Eastern League president. This was an important position within the baseball establishment. The Eastern League was the oldest surviving Minor League and the strongest. Patrick Powers had been league president since 1892, but discontent with his service had been growing for several years. In December club owners met in New York and elected Barrow to replace him. He proved to be a diligent and attentive president, and a rumor emerged that the Eastern League would soon seek Major League status. This didn't happen, but in December 1911 Barrow did persuade the league to re-assume its old name, the International League, to acknowledge the clubs in Toronto and Montreal and its robust prosperity. The owners rewarded him with a five-year contract and agreed to pick up the salary and expenses of his secretary.[7]

Barrow guided his league through seven years of what he called "strife, toil, and anxiety." Upon assuming office, he reconciled Powers's critics with his defenders among the league's owners, and he worked to eliminate rowdyism on the field by completely revamping the umpiring staff. He also claimed to have persuaded American League president Ban Johnson to vote in favor of a proposal elevating Barrow's league, along with the American Association and the Pacific Coast League, from Class A status to Class Double-A by giving

Johnson a twelve-gauge over-and-under shotgun with a grained walnut stock. Lauded by the editor of the *Reach Guide* as "a capable and popular official," Barrow found his abilities severely tested twice, first when the Federal League challenged organized baseball and then again when Canada and the United States entered the Great War. The Feds put teams in three International League cities: Buffalo and Baltimore in 1914 and Newark, New Jersey, the following year. Each did substantial damage to Barrow's clubs. The Buffalo club survived, but competition forced the Baltimore Orioles to relocate to Richmond and the Newark Indians to become the Harrisburg (PA) Senators. Barrow fought back. He vowed that no player who jumped to the Federal League would ever play in the International League again and that no Federal League owner would ever get any rights in International League territory. His pledge stuck, and both exiled teams were able to return to their original cities in 1916 after the Feds went out of business, but the cost of this victory was substantial. Orioles owner Jack Dunn objected when Barrow charged him $15,000 to recoup some of the league's legal fees, and Dunn began a campaign to remove the president.[8]

Once the Great War erupted, league owners got nervous. They agreed to close the 1917 season on August 4 and sought to cap the summer with an interleague schedule against the American Association, but when the latter refused to go along, Barrow's league fell into disarray. Owners quickly restored forty-four games to their schedule, and at a December meeting they acted on their anxieties. Unconvinced that Barrow's blustery style would lead them through this crisis, they voted to reduce his salary from $7,500 to $2,500. "Gentlemen," Barrow said, "if this is a challenge to resign, I accept your challenge. I quit." Buffalo owner Joseph Lannin, one of Barrow's critics, yelled, "Good riddance." Barrow lunged for him, was restrained, and stormed out of the meeting. In Barrow's memoir he embellished the melodrama of the moment by recalling that he immediately ran into his friend, Harry Frazee, a theatrical producer and owner of the Boston Red Sox, in the hotel lobby. Barrow wrote that Frazee offered him a job as his team's manager on the spot and that he jumped at the chance. Robert Creamer, in his biography of Babe Ruth, painted a less dramatic picture. He agreed that Barrow and Frazee were already acquainted but that Frazee was in Chicago during the International League's tumultuous meeting. Moreover, Barrow did not resign on the spot. He waited until February, when his league's owners met again, and then he became manager of the Red Sox for 1918. In the interim he gave Frazee advice on roster moves, including a pair of transactions with the Philadelphia Athletics that brought to Boston players who would help propel the club back to first place.[9]

The team that Ed Barrow inherited had won three pennants and three World Series in the past six seasons, but its roster had been depleted by the United States' entry into the war. Barrow got his job, in fact, because player-manager Jack Barry had enlisted in the navy. Only two everyday players and two starting pitchers from 1917 were regulars in 1918, but this quartet included veteran right fielder Harry Hooper and Babe Ruth, still exclusively a pitcher. Born in Baltimore in 1895, Ruth was not an orphan, but from an early age he roamed the streets, avoided school, and tested his parents' meager efforts to control his conduct. Blissfully lacking any sense of right and wrong, he pinched money from his father's cash register and may have skirted the law in more serious ways. When he was eight, his parents gave up and sent him to St. Mary's Industrial School for Boys, an institution for orphans, the poor, and the recalcitrant. Run by the Xaverian Brothers, a Catholic order, St. Mary's provided education, training in manual trades, and a healthy dose of discipline to its eight hundred residents. Most prominent in the life of these boys was Brother Matthias, the prefect of discipline, standing 6 feet 6 inches tall and weighing at least 250 pounds. His very presence commanded respect, so he never resorted to corporal punishment. To Ruth, who was in and out of the school several times over the next dozen years, as well to many other boys, Brother Matthias was the father figure their lives so desperately needed. Said Ruth in later life about the person to whom he owed so much, "Brother Matthias was the greatest man I ever knew."[10]

Ruth got the equivalent of a high school education at St. Mary's, and the trade he learned was shirt making. The Xaverians' other strength was their commitment to athletics, especially their baseball teams. While Ruth was there, the program fielded forty-four ball teams classified by age and ability. Brother Matthias, who could awe the student body by hitting prodigious fungoes one-handed across the schoolyard, coached a team called the Red Sox, and he took on Ruth as his special project. That the youngster possessed athletic talent was manifest. "I could hit the first time I picked up a bat," Ruth recalled, "but Brother Matthias made me a fielder." Within a few years Ruth was playing with boys several years older than he was. He played catcher most of the time, despite being left-handed, and then, when challenged by Brother Matthias, he tried pitching. The results were spectacular. The teams from St. Mary's played in their own intramural leagues and against teams from other schools. Ruth also got permission from the brothers to leave the campus on weekends to play with local amateur and semipro teams. In 1913 the Xaverians arranged a special game, matching the best St. Mary's team against the varsity from Mount St. Joseph's College in Baltimore. Ruth pitched that day, and he notched more than a few strikeouts. One of the spectators at this game may have been Jack Dunn. He had signed other local schoolboys to contracts, and at some point he learned about Ruth and his stunning ability. Ruth's biographers admit that the exact sequence of events is hard to unravel, but what is certain is that in February 1914 Dunn signed Ruth, just nineteen, to a professional contract with the Orioles.[11]

Ruth left St. Mary's and joined his new teammates as they prepared to leave for spring training. The Federal League had placed a team in direct competition with the Orioles, and Dunn knew that Baltimore's fans had fallen in love with the very idea of the Terrapins, considering them a Major League enterprise. Within a couple of weeks Dunn discovered that Ruth would be a substantial asset in his battle to keep his business afloat. A story in the *Baltimore Sun* quoted Dunn, a former Major League pitcher and infielder, saying of the youngster, "He has all the earmarks of a great ballplayer," and in a letter to Brother Gilbert, athletic director at Mount St. Joseph's, he wrote, "He's the most promising young ballplayer I've ever had." Dunn was also Ruth's guardian, and older players on the team began to call his charge "Dunnie's babe." The nickname stuck, and even before the International League season began, Babe Ruth began to make a name for himself. He played in several exhibition games against Major League teams, and after Opening Day, he was impressive both on the mound and at the plate. His contract called for a salary of $600 for the season, but Dunn gave him two raises, to $1,200 and then to $1,800. Like many rookies, Ruth's performance at bat was not consistent, but when he was on, he was spectacular. Eschewing the conventional wisdom that batters should swing conservatively, strive not to miss the ball, and be satisfied with singles, Ruth swung from the heels and cared not if he missed. He aimed to hit the ball a long way. Robert Creamer debunked the notion that the model for Ruth's batting style was Shoeless Joe Jackson, noting that Ruth had never seen Jackson play. The Babe's huge uppercut swing was, if anything, reminiscent of the one-handed cuts that Brother Matthias took in the St. Mary's schoolyard. Dunn's intention was to compete with the Terrapins by fielding a contending team, but the fans stayed away in droves. Dunn threatened to sell the club to a group in Richmond, and he complained that the National Commission should protect his investment by amending the draft rules. He got no relief, and his only alternative was to sell his best players for cash. One went to the New York Yankees for $8,000, two went to the Cincinnati Reds for $15,000, and on July 9 pitcher Ernie Shore, catcher Ben Egan, and Ruth went to the Red Sox for at least $20,000.[12]

Ruth grew quickly from an untested rookie to one of the game's premier pitchers. In his first three seasons (1914–16), he started 80 games, winning 43 against 21 losses. In 1916 he won 23 games while leading the league with 9 shutouts and a 1.75 earned run average. Ruth did not pitch in the 1915 World Series, but the following fall he took the mound in Game Two against the Brooklyn Dodgers. It remains one of the best games in World Series history. Ruth yielded an inside-the-park home run in the first inning—center fielder Tilly Walker tripped starting after the ball—and then pitched thirteen scoreless innings before the Red Sox pushed across a run in the bottom of the fourteenth to win, 2–1. When Barrow arrived in 1918 with little Major League experience, Hooper, a college graduate and an intelligent veteran, became Barrow's de facto deputy, advising his manager "on every aspect of the business, from lineup selection to game strategy." Most important, Hooper suggested that Ruth, already one of the game's top pitchers, switch positions so that he could play—and bat—every day. Even in 1916, when Ruth was still a pitcher, he showed explosive power at bat, hitting only three home runs, but doing so in three straight games, an astounding feat. He played first base in May 1918, his first game at a position other than pitcher, and his first game in the outfield later that month. His hitting simply amazed those who watched him. He swung hard and twisted his body completely around when he missed, and his long drives, even though they came not as frequently as they would later, made him a new kind of star. Creamer quoted a sportswriter who said of this attraction, "When Ruth misses a swipe at a ball, the stands quiver." Years later Hooper recalled how surprising this all was. "I still can't believe what I saw: this nineteen-year-old kid, crude, poorly educated, only lightly brushed by the social veneer we call civilization, gradually transformed into the idol of American youth and the symbol of baseball the world over—a man loved by more people and with an intensity of feeling that perhaps has never been equaled before or since."[13]

Once this move to the outfield proved its worth, Barrow did not shy from taking credit for it, but the change came slowly. In 1918 Ruth started 13 games at first base, 12 in center field, and 47 in left field. He batted .300, getting 95 hits, 18 doubles, and 11 triples, and hitting 11 home runs, tying Walker for the league lead. He also continued to pitch, starting 19 games and winning 13. Boston was in first place from July 6 on and won the pennant by two and a half games over the Cleveland Indians. In a World Series that saw a total of only 19 runs scored, the Red Sox defeated the Chicago Cubs, four games to two. Ruth extended his streak of consecutive scoreless innings to twenty-two in Game One and to twenty-nine in Game Four, breaking the record of twenty-eight set by Christy Mathewson in 1905 and setting a standard that would not be broken until 1961. The next season, 1919, was tumultuous in Boston, and the Red Sox sank to sixth place. As the club's war veterans returned from military service, Harry Frazee felt comfortable disposing of surplus talent, sometimes for players but more often for cash. When the players he acquired failed to perform to expectations, fans and members of the Boston press, whom Frazee had never courted, began to attack the owner. That most of the players leaving the Red Sox did not excel with their new teams did not matter. Frazee was branded as a man in financial difficulties who sold players to pay debts he had incurred as a theatrical entrepreneur. Ruth played in 130 games, but he pitched in only 17. Off the field Ruth, increasingly obstreperous and demanding, tangled with Barrow more than once. In one memorable encounter, the pair stood toe to toe in the clubhouse the afternoon following one of Ruth's frequent late-night escapades. Instead of a fistfight, Barrow suspended Ruth, but the two reached an accommodation shortly thereafter.[14]

Frazee's most infamous deal was, of course, his sale of Ruth to the Yankees, announced in early January 1920. Ruth had batted .322 and hit a whopping 29 home runs in 1919, but four American League teams drew more fans than the Red Sox. Barrow opposed the transaction, but since Frazee was determined, the manager insisted that the deal be for cash only and not players. In his memoirs Barrow recalled telling Frazee, "Listen, losing Ruth is bad enough, but don't make it tougher for me by making me show off a lot of ten-cent ballplayers that we got in exchange for him." He concluded, "There is nobody on that ball club [the Yankees] that I want." The sale brought Frazee more than $100,000—$25,000 in cash plus three $25,000 notes at 6 percent paid annually over the next three years. Ruth was a hit in New York as soon as he joined the home team. Long fly balls that were outs in spacious Fenway Park were home runs when he hit them down the line in the oddly shaped Polo Grounds, where the Yankees were the Giants' tenants. New Yorkers even appreciated the force of his strikeouts, and his personal life, however scandalous in Boston, was more easily forgiven and forgotten in the city where celebrity was king. Within a short while after his arrival, Yankees fans adopted Ruth as their own, and Italian Americans rechristened him the "Bambino." Ruth got off to a slow start, but when he hit his first home run on May 1, it was a spectacular drive over the right-field roof. He hit 12 homers in May and another 12 in June and broke his own record on July 19. His total for the year, 54, was more than every other team in the league except the St. Louis Browns and 39 more than the National League leader, Cy Williams of the Phillies. Ruth also proved to be more than a slugger. He put together a twenty-nine-game hitting streak, and his batting average rose steadily throughout the summer, peaking at .391 and finishing fourth best in the league.[15]

Ruth's purchase by the Yankees was part of a process. When Til Huston and Jacob Ruppert bought the club in 1915, they set out to revolutionize the business of baseball ownership. Huston had made his money as a civil engineer and contractor, and Ruppert was fabulously wealthy from his family's brewery. Writer Henry D. Fetter contrasted them, able to spend money on their club without disturbing their wealth, with most other owners whose primary business was baseball and who had to reap a steady return to keep going. Ruppert's affluence overwhelmed his fellow owners, and the industry in which it had been earned made baseball look puny. Fetter wrote that when Ruppert was elected president of the U.S. Brewers' Association in 1911, Major League baseball's combined income was about $3–4 million, while sales in the alcoholic beverage industry approached $2 billion. Given their wherewithal, Huston and Ruppert did not live off their club's profits. They reinvested those profits to make their team better. Moreover, they began their tenure by firing nearly every club employee and installing a management style with strictly delineated responsibilities. At the start, the owners had to take a role in player acquisitions, but after a time Ruppert insisted that Huston and he refrain from interfering with baseball operations, and he differed with his partner when Huston refused to stop second-guessing the team's manager. To run the front office as business manager, the owners first turned to Harry Sparrow, one of John McGraw's associates on the Giants. As manager, they took Ban Johnson's advice and hired handsome, personable "Wild Bill" Donovan, a former pitcher who had apprenticed in the Minor Leagues. The owners and the business manager tended to their own jobs. The Yankees' clubhouse, the dugout, and the playing field were the manager's inviolate bailiwick.[16]

Ruppert and Huston went about acquiring players just as other teams did. They purchased them, abetted initially by the entire league's desire to see its New York franchise get stronger. "The Yankees need building up," said Donovan when he took the job as manager, and no one disagreed. Johnson helped New York acquire first baseman Wally Pipp and outfielder Hugh High from Detroit before the 1915 season, and in June the Yankees paid $3,000 to acquire pitcher Bob Shawkey from the Athletics. After the season they grabbed outfielder Lee Magee as the Federal League went out of business, and in February 1916 Ruppert and Huston paid the A's $37,500 for third baseman Home Run Baker. He was a legitimate star whom the Yankees had to pay $24,000 over three seasons after he'd sat out 1915 in a salary dispute. New York also set its sights on Tris Speaker, the game's best center fielder, who was refusing to accept a salary cut from the Red Sox. Ruppert and Huston wanted to bid for his services, and they were more than miffed when Johnson engineered Speaker's sale to the Cleveland Indians. None of these deals transformed the team. The Yankees finished fifth in 1915 and fourth in 1916, and when the United States declared war on Germany in April 1917, Huston enlisted, eventually becoming a lieutenant colonel, and Ruppert assumed sole command of the team. He was not satisfied with Donovan's discipline over the club or with the team's plunge to sixth place, twenty-eight and a half games behind the first-place White Sox. After the season he dismissed the manager with approval from Huston via mail from France and hired the diminutive Miller Huggins.[17]

After the armistice in November 1918 Huston returned from Europe and began to harass Huggins, whose performance did not satisfy him. He also expressed his dissatisfaction with the team's fourth-place finish. Ruppert had attempted to bolster the roster in December by acquiring Dutch Leonard, Duffy Lewis, and Shore from the Red Sox. Lewis had a fine season in 1919, but Shore won only five games, and after Leonard refused to report, the Yankees sold him to Detroit. Huggins brought his club home in third place in 1919, but it was the legal dispute over Johnson's suspension of pitcher Carl Mays that occupied most of the owners' time as the season progressed. When Frazee traded Mays to New York and Johnson ordered his umpires not to allow Mays to play for the Yankees, Ruppert and Huston, seeing their chance for a successful season and maybe even a pennant slipping away, retaliated. They retained a prominent New York law firm and petitioned the New York State Supreme Court for relief to void the suspension. Justice Robert F. Wagner Sr. issued a temporary injunction permitting Mays to pitch, and when Johnson sought to use league monies to fund his case, Wagner ruled against him again. This was personal as well as business. The judge made the injunction permanent in October, after which Johnson petulantly maneuvered to deny the Yankees their share of World Series revenues for finishing third. Ruppert and Huston paid their players out of their own pockets and in December got this decision overturned too. Less than a month later Frazee cemented his insurgents' alliance with the Yankees' owners by selling Ruth to New York. A year later Barrow joined him.[18]

The Yankees that Babe Ruth joined in 1920 were already a "Murderers' Row." A cartoonist for the *New York World* had used this phrase to describe the 1919 lineup, which featured Baker, Ping Bodie, Lewis, Del Pratt, and Pipp, the league's home run champion in 1916 and 1917. The team had swatted 45 home runs in 1919 to lead the league for the fourth time in five seasons, had stayed in the pennant race most of the summer, and had drawn 619,164 fans, their highest total yet, to the Polo Grounds. In 1920 they more than doubled this total as 1,289,422 showed up to watch Ruth and his teammates hit 115 homers. Despite Ruth's heroics at the plate, the team's first pennant proved elusive. As the Bambino surged in late May, so did the Yankees, battling head to head with the White Sox and Indians for several weeks. Injuries took their usual toll, and the club was devastated on August 16, when Mays, a submarine pitcher, hit Cleveland shortstop Ray Chapman in the head and fractured his skull. Chapman died the next morning, and Mays, whose teammates could not be sure if he had thrown at the batter deliberately, lost what few friends he had. The Yankees lost five of their next seven games and settled in third place. Without Ruth the 1920 Red Sox won six more games than they had the season before, but the team tumbled in the standings, winding up in fifth place. Barrow was unable to make trades, stifled by Johnson's heavy hand and his dislike of Frazee, but once the season ended, Barrow's luck changed. Frazee called him and indicated that Huston wanted to speak to him on behalf of the Yankees about becoming New York's business manager, a position later called general manager. Barrow accepted, left Boston, and moved into the Yankees' front office on October 29, 1920. "It was not a hard decision to make," he admitted in his memoirs.[19]

Once Ed Barrow took charge as the Yankees' business manager, his first important decision, according to biographer Daniel R. Levitt, was relocating spring training camp from Jacksonville, Florida, where the nightlife had proven too attractive, to Shreveport, Louisiana. His second move was hiring scout Paul Krichell, a former backup catcher who would later sign five future Hall of Fame members to Yankee contracts. Perhaps more significant, he forged an alliance with Miller Huggins, whose job security hung in the balance as Til Huston and Jacob Ruppert argued about him. "You're the manager," Barrow told him, "and you're going to get no interference or second-guessing from me. You tell me what you need, and I'll make the deals—and I'll take full responsibility for every deal I make." Under these terms the first trade came quickly. Barrow shipped Del Pratt, Muddy Ruel, outfielder Sammy Vick, and pitcher Hank Thormhalen to Boston for catcher Wally Schang, infielder Mike McNally and pitchers Harry Harper and Waite Hoyt. On paper this looked like a trade that favored Boston. Pratt, Ruel, and Vick were regulars, and Thormhalen was a young left-hander, and while Schang was a regular, McNally was a utility player, and Harper and Hoyt were untested youngsters. Yet over time it was the Yankees that got the better of the deal. Schang was an adequate replacement for Ruel, and Hoyt blossomed into one of the league's finest pitchers, winning 145 games over his first eight seasons in New York. Barrow had seen Hoyt pitch for an independent team and signed him to a contract. Once Barrow was in New York, he remembered that Hoyt had won the first three games he pitched for the Red Sox, and he also knew that young pitchers often had trouble adjusting to the quirky confines of Fenway Park. Barrow reasoned that Hoyt would mature and fare better in the Polo Grounds as long as he could keep batters from hitting the ball down the lines, and that is what happened. He won nineteen games each in 1921 and 1922, as the Yankees won their first two pennants, and seventeen in 1923 as they captured the World Series for the first time.[20]

Hoyt was one of several good pitchers on these Yankees teams, but their real star was Ruth. As excellent as his 1920 season had been, 1921 was even better. Besides batting .378 and slugging .846, he got more hits (204), scored more runs (177), hit more homers (59), and got more RBIs (171) than the year before. In peak physical condition, he also hit 16 triples and stole 17 bases. When pitchers walked him—which they did a league-leading 144 times—Bob Meusel was there to clean up, hitting 24 homers and driving in 135 runs. As a team, the Yankees led the league in runs, home runs, slugging average, and strikeouts. Huggins was smart enough not to complain about the strikeouts since his team's home run total, 134, was 52 more than runner-up Philadelphia. When the Yankees reached the World Series for the first time, sitting in the other dugout were the Giants. In fact, tenant and landlord were meeting for the first of three straight Series, and Henry D. Fetter argued that when they were concluded, the balance of power in New York baseball had shifted. The Giants, darlings of the city's sporting scene for two decades, gave way to the upstart Yankees. John McGraw's team had won the Series in 1905 and lost four others before confronting the Yankees. After beating the American Leaguers in 1921 and the following year, the Giants did not defeat the Yankees again. The Yankees, on the other hand, began a run of excellence in 1923 unequaled in American professional sports history, winning the World Series twenty-six times through the 2000 season and then again in 2009. The Giants did not collapse. They captured the National League pennant in 1924 and the pennant and the Series in 1933, but well before McGraw retired midway through the 1932 season, New York had become the Yankees' town. In only three seasons after 1919 did the Giants lead the Yankees in attendance. Both clubs remained profitable, but the Yankees' profits exceeded the Giants' by 65 percent in the first half of the decade (1920–24) and by 94 percent in the second half (1925–29).[21]

Following the 1922 Series, which the Giants won in five games, Ruppert said that he had endured enough second-guessing from the bickering Huston and that he would attempt to buy him out. Negotiations took several months, but in May 1923 the deal was consummated for $1.25 million. Barrow said in his memoirs that he borrowed $350,000 from his old friend Harry M. Stevens to acquire 10 percent of the club, but the more important news was contained in a telegram Ruppert sent to his team, then playing in Chicago: "I am now the sole owner of the Yankees. Miller Huggins is my manager." Hoyt recalled for historian Eugene C. Murdock that Ruppert maintained his office at his brewery. It was on the fourth floor, Hoyt remembered, and one reached it by walking down a long marble hallway. "All the woodwork was rosewood and paneled, and the brewery was immaculate. You could eat off the floor." The office was "a sumptuous place," Hoyt said. "[Ruppert] was a king. . . . One of the best-dressed men of his time. . . . His Rolls Royce always looked brand new when it was ten years old. He was that way about everything." Ruppert was just as fastidious about how his team would look and how it would be run. He arranged for the purchase of two additional sets of uniforms, eschewing the convention that uniforms were supposed to look dirty. Similarly, he continued to stipulate that the club operate with the lines of authority among Huggins, Barrow, and himself clearly drawn. Even before Huston had left the scene, Ruppert insisted that Huggins and Barrow, and not the owners, would make personnel decisions. Early in 1922, when Huggins and Barrow agreed that the team needed an everyday center fielder, Ruppert supplied the cash to purchase Whitey Witt from the Athletics. In July Barrow worked a trade with Boston, with Ruppert adding $40,000 or perhaps $50,000 to cement the deal. So great were the complaints from other teams that the Yankees were trying to buy the pennant that baseball soon changed its rules, prohibiting trades between teams in the same league after June 15 unless the players involved had first cleared waivers—that is, unless all other teams in the league had waived the chance to claim the players in the proposed trade.[22]

The 1923 World Series, in which the Yankees rallied from a two-games-to-one deficit to crush the Giants by scores of 8–4, 8–1, and 6–4, was the first one played in Yankee Stadium. Egged on by McGraw, who was jealous of Ruth's growing popularity and resentful, as were many others, of his style of play, Giants owner Charles Stoneham briefly ignored how much money he was making from having the Yankees as tenants and told them to get out of the Polo Grounds. He got over this fit of pique, but it was too late. Ruppert and Huston, before their split, cast about for a site upon which to build their own ballpark. They considered and rejected several plans before settling on ten acres owned by the estate of William Waldorf Astor, at one time the richest man in America. The parcel of land the Yankees bought for a reported $600,000 was in the Bronx, just across the Harlem River from the Polo Grounds. It was close to two mass transit train lines and had a soft granite bed, quite suitable for construction. The Osborn Engineering Company of Cleveland handled the design, heeding Ruppert's directive to make it big, and the White Construction Company built the park in 284 days for a flat fee of $2.5 million. Even though construction delays forced the original design to be scaled back, the result was still truly spectacular, far larger than any previous ballpark and a real showplace besides, highlighted by an ornate copper frieze that hung from the roof of the upper grandstand. The stadium was the first ballpark to feature three decks, the first to accommodate more than sixty thousand seats, and the first to feature a huge electronic scoreboard that displayed an unprecedented amount of information. When the stadium opened on April 18, 1923, Fred Lieb called it "The House That Ruth Built," but years later, Ruppert recalled, "The Yankee Stadium is a mistake, not mine, but the Giants."[23]

Undergirding the Giants' determination to dislodge their tenants was a prolonged struggle among the city's three teams to seize lucrative Sunday dates for home games. In 1919 New York's governor, Al Smith, signed legislation allowing local governments in the state to overturn a long-standing prohibition against professional sporting events on Sunday. Within a week the New York City Board of Aldermen exercised its local option, and Mayor John Hylan signed the ordinance. The Brooklyn Dodgers and the Giants played their first lawful Sunday games on May 4. Each drew their largest crowds ever, and the Yankees followed suit a week later. Sunday baseball proved immediately and enduringly popular, and the three clubs scrambled to reconfigure the rest of their 1919 schedules to take advantage of these opportunities, often moving Monday games back to the preceding Sunday. The Dodgers and Yankees benefited most in the short run. Each got to host a dozen Sunday games that season, compared to the Giants' ten. When the clubs designed their schedules for 1920, the Dodgers retained the upper hand. They managed to play twenty Sunday home games while the Giants and the Yankees, sharing the same ballpark, had to divide these lucrative dates between them. Pennsylvania and Massachusetts still outlawed Sunday ball, so both leagues rigged their schedules to maximize Sunday play where it was allowed. More than once, one of the two Philadelphia clubs and one of the two Boston clubs would play at home on Saturday, dash into Brooklyn or New York to play on Sunday, and then leave Monday for games elsewhere. This arrangement also worked to the Giants' detriment. In 1920 all four of their Sunday games against the Dodgers were played in Ebbets Field, and twice in 1921 the Giants and Dodgers moved from the Polo Grounds on Saturday to Ebbets Field on Sunday so the Yankees could play at home against the Athletics or the Red Sox. Since 40 percent of the Giants' attendance came from their Sunday dates, sharing Sundays with the Yankees became a liability. The *Sporting News* estimated that six or seven additional Sunday home games might net the Giants $100,000, quite substantially more than the $60,000 the Yankees were paying in rent.[24]

Ed Barrow had proven to be a fine judge of baseball talent, but trading for Major League players, even young ones with promise, or purchasing their contracts was expensive. The Yankees, perhaps a bit complacent after winning three straight pennants and their first World Series, slipped to second place in 1924 and then plummeted to seventh in 1925, finishing twenty-eight and a half games behind the Washington Senators. The starting lineup had remained intact for the three pennant-winning seasons, and Barrow did not see quickly enough that his regulars were getting old. He had begun to acquire youngsters, but they were not quite ready for starring roles. The first to arrive was Earle Combs, a center fielder. A multisport star at Eastern Kentucky State Normal School, Combs had intended to become a teacher until he discovered he could make more money playing professional baseball. Combs rose to stardom in Louisville, where his manager was Joe McCarthy, and the Yankees bought his contract after the 1923 season, sending Elmer Smith and yet another $50,000 to Louisville. Combs was a speed demon, but before he could test himself adequately against Major League competition, he broke his ankle after just twenty-four games in 1924 and was out for the year. More important, he lived an exemplary personal life that did not require discipline from Miller Huggins. Starting in 1925, Combs held down center field for the Yankees for nine seasons until he suffered a near-fatal accident in Sportsman's Park, St. Louis. Chasing a fly ball on July 23, 1934, he crashed into the concrete outfield wall, fracturing his skull and severely injuring his shoulder. He was in a coma for hours and on the critical list for weeks, but the Cardinals' team physician, Dr. Robert F. Hyland, pulled him through, and eventually he returned to the New York lineup. While he was a starter, Combs was a steady .300 hitter, leading the league in hits in 1927 with 231 and in triples three times.[25]

As Barrow continued to search for other players good enough to join the Yankees, he relied more often on a small coterie of scouts. For a time he could depend upon Bob Connery, who had scouted first for the Cardinals and discovered Rogers Hornsby. Connery had come to the Yankees with Huggins, but in 1925, he left to head a group that purchased the St. Paul Saints of the American Association. He pledged to maintain an informal relationship with the Yankees and to help develop players for them. Barrow recalled that his scouting staff then numbered four: Bob Gilks, who had been a Minor League manager; Joe Kelley, who had played with the Baltimore Orioles in the 1890s; Ed Holly, one of Barrow's players in Montreal; and Paul Krichell. A native of New York City, Krichell played two seasons with the Browns, batting .222 in just eighty-seven games. Memorably, he once was behind the plate for a game against Detroit when Ty Cobb stole second base, third, and home in the same inning. Barrow hired Krichell as a coach for the Red Sox and brought him to the Yankees. Most scouts traveled thousands of miles a year and watched dozens of insignificant games, all done to unearth one diamond among so many pieces of coal. Krichell was lucky. He did travel, but his territory also included New York City and the greater metropolitan area. Every spring Krichell would accompany the Yankees to spring training, just to recall what Major League baseball was like, and then he would head north to beat the bushes in search of talent. On April 26, 1923, he boarded a morning train to New Brunswick, New Jersey, there to watch Rutgers University play Columbia. That's when he first saw Lou Gehrig.[26]

Born on June 19, 1903, Gehrig was the son of German immigrants. His father, Wilhelm Heinrich, was an ornamental metal worker who lacked most of the drive to succeed often associated with first-generation Americans; his mother, Anna Christina, was a tall, robust, and stern woman who was only nineteen when she married Heinrich in 1901. The Gehrigs lived in the Yorkville section of Manhattan, a neighborhood inhabited by many other German American families, and later moved to Washington Heights, further uptown and not far from Hilltop Park. Lou attended Public School 132, learned to play baseball with his schoolmates, and rooted for the Giants. At the High School of Commerce, Gehrig, incredibly withdrawn, declined to try out for any teams in his freshman year, but thereafter he played football, soccer, and baseball. Clumsy in the field but enormously powerful, he pitched and played first base. On the mound he threw hard but lacked control; at bat he learned how to hit the ball a long way. Commerce, the best team in the city in 1920, earned a trip to Chicago to play the Windy City's best team, Lane Technical High School, and Gehrig hit a home run in the ninth inning of that game. After graduating but lacking enough credits to be accepted immediately at Columbia, where he had been offered an athletic scholarship, he enrolled in the university's extension program, failed to impress John McGraw during a tryout with the Giants, and risked his college eligibility by playing a few Minor League games in Hartford, Connecticut, under assumed names. In his sophomore year he was Columbia's best pitcher, and on April 18, 1923, the same day Yankee Stadium opened, Gehrig got two hits and struck out seventeen Williams College batters in a game Columbia lost, 5–1. Sometime that spring Columbia coach Andy Coakley, a former Major League pitcher, took his star to Yankee Stadium for the first time. Years later Gehrig recalled seeing Babe Ruth and being impressed with the "perfect rhythm and timing" of his swing.[27]

Krichell was impressed too. In the game against Rutgers, Gehrig played right field awkwardly, but he hit two home runs, and the scout told Barrow on the telephone that he had found the next Ruth. Barrow sensed some exaggeration, but after Gehrig shone again in Columbia's next game against New York University, the Yankees brought him to the ballpark and offered him a contract: a $1,500 bonus plus $400 a month in salary. Gehrig left school with no regrets. On June 15 he got into a game for the first time, replacing Wally Pipp at first base for the ninth inning against the Browns. Three days later he got his first at bat, pinch hitting for Aaron Ward and striking out. Finally, on July 7 he got another pinch-hitting opportunity and lined a long single off the right-field wall for his first Major League hit. Huggins sent Gehrig back to Hartford on August 1 and recalled him in late September. Pipp sprained his ankle stepping off the train in Boston, and Gehrig took his place in the lineup. In the spring of 1924 Huggins thought Gehrig needed one more season in the Minors, but Barrow had a tough time getting him through waivers. After other teams that might have claimed him were placated, Gehrig was off to Hartford again. He hit .369 in 134 games with 37 homers, and in September he came back to New York to stay. Still, Pipp was the regular first baseman and Gehrig his backup for the rest of the season and the beginning of the next. On June 1, 1925, Huggins used Gehrig as a pinch hitter, and the next day he inserted him into the starting lineup. An oft-told story has Pipp complaining of a headache and asking Huggins for the day off, but Gehrig's biographer doubted this was the case. More likely, the manager was trying to shake up a club that had gotten off to a very poor start by benching not only his first baseman, but two other regulars as well. Whatever the reason, Gehrig played that game and the next 2,128 in succession.[28]

Jacob Ruppert's position as one of baseball's wealthiest owners gave him certain influence within the game's inner circle. He had moved to the forefront of American League governance early in his tenure, both to protect his investment and to serve as a moderating influence. In December 1915 he was one of five owners who, together with president Ban Johnson, formed the league's delegation to arrange peace with the Federal League. Later he and partner Til Huston advised Charles Comiskey while the Cook County grand jury was investigating allegations surrounding the 1919 World Series, and they both were involved in modifying Albert Lasker's plan to replace the National Commission. Lasker had doubts that Ruppert would stomach a prolonged legal battle against Johnson and the owners still loyal to him, but he was mistaken, and when a contingent of owners approached Judge Kenesaw Landis in November to ask him to become commissioner, Ruppert was part of the group. In December 1926, when renewing Landis's contract was on the agenda at the Major League owners' winter meetings, Ruppert introduced the motion granting him a second seven-year term and accepted a friendly amendment from Cubs president Bill Veeck Sr. raising the judge's salary by $15,000 to $65,000. Ruppert had a hand in Johnson's departure too. As the league president's behavior became erratic, Ruppert led a delegation from a special league owners' meeting in 1927 that persuaded Johnson to resign.[29]

Even during Prohibition, when breweries forbidden from producing beer switched to non-alcoholic concoctions, Ruppert's income from his family's business remained handsome. As a result, when the Yankees earned more than $3.5 million in profits during the 1920s, the club paid no dividends and dedicated that entire sum to improving the team. To this end Ed Barrow acquired three other players to help the Yankees rebound from their seventh-place finish in 1925. The first of these, who actually arrived near the end of the 1925 season, was shortstop Mark Koenig. Miller Huggins and Paul Krichell had both seen him play in the Minors before Barrow bought his contract from Bob Connery's St. Paul club for $50,000 and six players. Koenig was only twenty-three when he made his debut on September 8, and his skills needed to mature. In 1926 he hit .271, but he led the league's shortstops in errors with 52. Barrow's second acquisition was Tony Lazzeri. Raised in San Francisco, he boxed and played semipro baseball and in 1922 signed a contract with the Pacific Coast League's Salt Lake City Bees. In 1925 he played the full PCL season (197 games) in Salt Lake City. He batted .355, got 252 hits, drove in 222 runs, scored 202 runs, and hit 60 home runs, more than any other professional ballplayer ever had and more than enough to impress future Yankees scout Bill Essick. Lazzeri was an epileptic, but everyone agreed that his talent was genuine and that all his seizures occurred off the field. After the season Barrow worked out a trade: Lazzeri to the Yankees in exchange for five players and $50,000 or perhaps as much as $65,000. At age twenty-two Lazzeri came east for the first time in the spring of 1926, signed a contract for $5,000, and heard Huggins tell him that he would move from shortstop to second base. The new position fazed him not at all. Lazzeri played the entire season, hitting .275 with 162 hits, 18 home runs (third in the league), and 114 runs batted in (tied for second in the league). Barrow later called Lazzeri's acquisition his "greatest bargain," but still he was not satisfied. He sent Bob Gilks to scout a twenty-eight-year-old pitcher named Wilcy Moore, on his way to a 30–4 season with Greenville (SC) in the South Atlantic Association. Gilks doubted that the balding Moore was only twenty-eight, but Barrow bought his contract anyway, this time spending only $3,500.[30]

New York maintained a substantial lead over the second-place Indians for a while, but when the Yankees arrived in Cleveland to start a six-game series beginning on September 15, the lead was down to five and a half games. The Indians won four of the games to cut two games off the lead, but neither team finished strong, and the Yankees won the pennant by three games. Thus the 1926 World Series featured the American League champions, a team built primarily by trades and purchases, against the St. Louis Cardinals, a team beginning to show the positive effects of Branch Rickey's commitment to the farm system. The Series opened in New York, and the Yankees won the first game, 2–1. Herb Pennock pitched a three-hitter, and Lou Gehrig singled home Babe Ruth with what proved to be the winning run in the sixth inning. St. Louis rebounded to take Game Two, 6–2, with Cardinals outfielder Billy Southworth hitting a three-run home run in the seventh inning. The teams traveled to St. Louis, and the Cardinals won Game Three, 4–0, but in Game Four the Yankees slugged their way to a 10–5 win, led by Ruth, who did the unprecedented: he hit three homers, the first player to do so in a Series game, with the third one landing in the center-field bleachers and then bouncing out into the street. Game Five was crucial, and the Yankees won it, 3–2 in ten innings, with Pennock pitching a seven-hit complete game and Lazzeri driving in the winning run on a sacrifice fly. Back in New York Grover Cleveland Alexander pitched Game Six, and the Cardinals won easily, 10–2. That set the stage for the third Game Seven in three years, with Jesse Haines pitching for the Cardinals and Waite Hoyt for the Yankees. New York got single runs in the third and sixth, sandwiched around three St. Louis tallies in the fourth. The Yankees loaded the bases with two out in the seventh, and manager Hornsby summoned Alexander from the bullpen. He struck out Lazzeri to end the inning and closed out the Series for the Cardinals with the final out coming as Ruth was thrown out trying to steal second base.[31]

The Yankees got their revenge not just in 1927, when they swept the Pirates in the Series, outscoring them, 23–10, but also in 1928, when they won their third straight pennant for the second time and then swept the Cardinals in the Series. The 1927 season was the Yankees' greatest. They won 110 games and finished 19 games ahead of second-place Philadelphia as Ruth rewrote the home run record again: he hit 60, a mark that stood until 1961. Gehrig, moved by Huggins to the fourth spot in the batting order, added 47 homers and drove in 173 runs. Ruth out-homered every other American League team, and Gehrig out-homered four of them. Together, their 107 home runs nearly doubled the Athletics' total, 56. The only significant change to New York's roster was Moore, a right-handed pitcher not quite good enough to crack the team's starting rotation. Determined to use him anyway, Huggins brought him into games when the starter got in trouble. Victimized by a broken arm in 1925, Moore threw a peculiar sinker that baffled batters. He pitched in fifty games but started only twelve and averaged more than three innings per relief appearance. The press called him "Doc" because he cured ailing games, but the role he filled got the name "fireman." Firpo Marberry had been doing much the same thing for Washington since 1925, but Moore got more publicity because he pitched for a pennant-winning team in New York. The Yankees' lineup was much the same in 1928 as it had been the season before. Again the Athletics finished second, but this time the margin was only two and a half games. The Cardinals offered scant resistance in the Series. Like the Pirates in 1927, they scored only 10 runs while Ruth put on a show. He batted .625, got 10 hits, and hit 3 home runs, all in the same game. Gehrig meanwhile hit 4 home runs and drove in 9 runs, a Series record. Many sportswriters had followed Grantland Rice's lead in 1927 and called the Yankees of that year one of the best clubs of all time. The team's performance a year later seemed to confirm that judgment.[32]

Philadelphia owner Connie Mack perhaps matched Barrow as a keen evaluator of talent, and over the next three seasons his Athletics more than matched the Yankees' performance. They won three straight pennants, besting New York, in turn, by eighteen games, sixteen games, and thirteen and a half games, and captured two World Series. In 1930, in fact, the Yankees dropped to third place, their worst finish since 1925. Mack had reconstructed his club in much the same way that Ruppert and Barrow had built the Yankees, mostly through trades and purchases. But there was a difference in how the two clubs handled their finances. From 1925 through 1931 the Athletics earned nearly $1.1 million, a total surpassed only by the Yankees, Giants, and Cubs, but Mack did not reinvest this money in his club or save it to maintain an even keel during difficult times. The A's paid out $400,000 in dividends during these years, a good portion of this to Mack himself. In 1931, as Mack was already contemplating breaking up his champions, the dividend paid was $250,000. Then, as operating revenue fell, from $967,000 in 1929 to $311,000 in 1933, he had no alternative but to sell off his star players. In 1933 he netted $250,000 from player sales but still closed his books with a $21,000 loss. The club never paid a dividend again. By 1935 the A's were in last place, and by the end of the decade Mack had to use his stock in the club as security for $85,000 in loans from the league.[33]

Ed Barrow continued to make changes in his club's roster, and he continued to use Jacob Ruppert's money to do so when necessary. More than a decade removed from the Minor Leagues, Barrow had to rely on his scouts increasingly, and their recommendations did not always pan out. Leo Durocher, whose contract had cost $6,000 in 1925, was a case in point. He was a fine fielder, but his zest for the high life cut his tenure in New York short. An exorbitant hotel bill caused him to ask Barrow for a $1,000 raise for 1930, payable in advance. Barrow refused, Durocher cursed him, and the next day the shortstop was a member of the Reds, sold for the waiver price. His job went to Lyn Lary. Together with second baseman Jimmy Reese, he had come from Oakland in the Pacific Coast League for more than $100,000. Lary started for only two seasons, and Reese was never more than a reserve. Catcher Bill Dickey came from Little Rock in the Southern Association for $12,500, and the Yankees paid $45,000 for outfielder Myril Hoag and another $45,000 for pitcher Lefty Gomez. The club's stability was further rocked when, in the closing days of the 1929 season, Miller Huggins developed erysipelas, an aggressive skin disease, under his left eye. He entered the hospital, where the wound became infected, and without antibiotics he succumbed to blood poisoning on September 25. Coach Art Fletcher finished the season as interim manager, and during the winter Barrow turned to former pitcher Bob Shawkey to run the team on the field.[34]

Sometime after Ruppert realized that the Yankees' investment in Lary and Reese would not pan out, he counseled Barrow: "We cannot make another mistake like this." Historian Glenn Stout suggested that Ruppert's wallet was wearing a little thin. There were reasons why this might have been so. Building Yankee Stadium had been expensive, and after several years of robust crowds, attendance dropped below a million per year in 1931 and remained flat until after the end of World War II. Ruppert lost out on additional revenue when his club swept two straight World Series in 1927 and 1928. The refund for tickets sold for the unplayed fifth game in 1927 totaled $217,000. The Yankees also had baseball's fattest payroll—$350,000 in 1927—with Ruth, who made $70,000 in 1927, 1928, and 1929, signing for $80,000 for each of the next two seasons. There is evidence that Ruppert's expenses rose as well. When Prohibition ended in 1933, he invested substantially to return to the business of brewing beer. He also underwrote Admiral Richard Byrd's expedition to the South Pole with a grant of a quarter of a million dollars, and he sank a great deal of money into several real estate ventures that failed to develop. Still, Ruppert did not complain about his personal finances, at least in public, and he certainly was not being pinched in 1929, when he spoke out at a meeting of Major League owners, declaring that no ball club, not even the Yankees, could continue to pay the high prices being demanded by the owners of Minor League clubs. Without relief from the arcane rules that made it difficult for a Major League team to develop Minor Leaguers and retain them, he asserted that his club was "going to be forced into owning minor league clubs, and so is every other major league owner in this room."[35]

Other owners besides Ruppert had been impressed with the innovative farm system pioneered by the Cardinals. Taking over a team that was near bankruptcy, Branch Rickey had assembled a hierarchy of Minor League teams that had begun to produce a steady stream of Major League–caliber players. Rickey's competitors followed his lead, but they did so slowly. The Dodgers, for one, cut an early deal with the Macon (GA) Peaches, and when the South Atlantic League ceased operations after the 1930 season, they shifted their relationship to Hartford (CT) in the Eastern League. The Giants purchased the Bridgeport (CT) Bears in the same league in 1929, and the Yankees bought the Chambersburg (MD) Maroons in the Blue Ridge League and renamed them the Young Yanks. But one team did hardly a farm system make, and the compromises forced in the way players could be drafted after the 1930 season eased the Majors' player acquisitions costs somewhat. Thus when Barrow and others met with Ruppert in the fall of 1931 to discuss the concept of a farm system, Barrow believed they talked their owner out of it. Yet two weeks later Ruppert's attorney, Max Steuer, walked into the owner's office to inform him that Paul Block, owner of the Newark Bears, wanted to sell his club. Block was a newspaper publisher who, like many Minor League owners, had entered baseball with a great deal of enthusiasm. He had even hired Walter Johnson, the great retired pitcher, as his manager. The Bears, though, played in the International League, and its dominant team was the Rochester Red Wings, a Cardinals farm team stocked with promising players. Block decided to sell after finding it difficult to obtain players good enough to compete with Rickey's chain store operation, as it was called. Ruppert turned down the Block offer, but after fifteen minutes Steuer persuaded him to change his mind. In a move the *Sporting News* called a "bombshell," Ruppert bought the Bears for $250,000. Barrow was astonished at this turn of events, but the *Sporting News* explained it nicely: "A few years ago there was a great hue and cry against the Cardinal 'monopoly,' but the baseball men of the country are realizing it is the only way to consistent prosperity."[36]

By 1932 the New York farm system, albeit less than half as extensive as the Cardinals' operation, included five clubs: the Newark Bears in the International League, the Springfield (MA) Rifles in the Eastern League, the Erie (PA) Sailors in the Central League, the Binghamton (NY) Triplets in the New York–Pennsylvania League, and (replacing Chambersburg) the Cumberland (MD) Colts in the Middle Atlantic League. The Yankees desired to opt for quality over Rickey's preference for quantity, but they still needed someone to direct the club's Minor League operations. Barrow's choice was Bob Connery, who expressed his willingness to sell his interest in the St. Paul club, but Ruppert would have none of it. He had spent nearly $300,000 buying players from Connery, but only Koenig had panned out. So the owner turned instead to George Weiss, thirty-seven years old, who had become general manager of the Orioles after owner Jack Dunn died of a heart attack in 1928. Weiss was born in 1894 in New Haven. He played baseball for a while at Hillhouse High School, but like Herbert Hoover, his athletic ability dictated that he become the team's manager instead of one of its infielders. Hillhouse won the state championship with a pair of future Major Leaguers on its roster, and after graduation in 1911, Weiss kept the boys together as a semipro team called the Colonials. "I approached the guys," he said, according to biographers Burton A. Boxerman and Benita W. Boxerman, "and suggested that we play some semipro ball. I told them that if they played, I'd make the dates." The team was quite successful and reunited during several subsequent summers. Weiss spent only one semester at Yale, having to leave to run the family grocery store after his father's death. That gave him the chance to turn the Colonials into a lucrative business.[37]

New Haven had a team in the Eastern League, but its meager success paled in comparison to that of the Colonials. With Sunday baseball banned within the city limits, Weiss secured a lease to play at Lighthouse Point Park, an amusement park just over the city line. He also augmented his lineup with famous college players and in April 1916 arranged to have the Colonials play the Yankees at the Polo Grounds. The Yankees won, 5–0, and what Weiss did not pocket from the game—his share of the receipts was only $10.42—he picked up in prestige. He set up games against Major Leaguers who were then prohibited from playing on Sundays in New York and Boston, and after the 1916 World Series it was he who booked the entire Red Sox squad, fresh from winning the championship, to play in New Haven. That game, a 3–3 tie, with Babe Ruth pitching for Boston and Ty Cobb playing first base for the Colonials, earned the wrath of baseball officials and led to a rule prohibiting more than three members of a World Series championship team from playing in the same barnstorming game. As the Colonials became known as one of the most popular semipro teams ever, the Eastern League Murlins were mired in red ink. After the 1918 season the league asked Weiss to buy the struggling franchise for $5,000, and he consented. The Murlins became the Weissmen and then the Indians and then the Profs, and they became winners too, finishing first in 1920, 1922, and 1928, Weiss's last year in New Haven.[38]

After Dunn died in 1928, administrative control of the Orioles, one of the best Minor League clubs in the 1920s, passed to attorney Charles Knapp, no baseball expert but a man smart enough to call Weiss. While in New Haven, Weiss had, by his own testimony, "managed to sell more players to the majors and higher classifications than the rest of the league combined," grossing by one account an estimated $300,000. He was well connected, and Knapp was sharp enough to hire him. But Weiss's career and his life nearly came to a tragic end on the night of December 9, 1923. He and Wild Bill Donovan, New Haven's manager, were traveling on the 20th Century Limited, a train going from New York to Chicago, for baseball's winter meetings. The pair finished their evening meal, and Donovan went to the club car to smoke a cigar. Weiss retreated to the compartment the two shared, poured himself a drink, and climbed into the upper berth, leaving the lower for his manager. As the train approached a crossing at Forsyth, New York (about twenty-five miles east of Erie, Pennsylvania), a spectacular wreck occurred. Eight people, all those occupying lower berths in the last car, including Donovan, were killed, and only four people in upper berths survived. Weiss was lucky, but he spent the next four months in the hospital. After finally moving to Baltimore, he guided the Orioles to second place once and third place twice. After the 1931 season he journeyed to West Baden, Indiana, for that year's winter meetings. That's where he met Ruppert, making such an impression that a job offer came within a few weeks. Knapp let him go. "George," he said, "I will not stand in your way. But don't fall for that big league glamour. You stay here and you will own the Baltimore club. You will be your own boss and in time develop a rich property. This is a great baseball city, and you can't miss." Weiss considered this advice for several weeks, but on February 11, 1932, he signed with the Yankees.[39]

After winning 107 games in 1932, the Yankees returned to the World Series for the first time since 1928. The starting lineup was hardly different from the season before, but new manager Joe McCarthy had a year of New York experience under his belt, and the A's, his chief rivals, had passed their peak. Hiring McCarthy after the 1930 Series was perhaps the best executive decision of Ed Barrow's career, but it probably would not have happened if Bill Veeck Sr. and the Cubs had not first plucked McCarthy from the Minor League ranks in October 1925. McCarthy took over a Chicago team that had finished last and advanced them to the World Series in just four seasons. But the Cubs lost the 1929 Series to the A's, and Chicago's owner, William Wrigley Jr., took the defeat hard. With four games to go in the 1930 season and the Cubs a mere three games out of first place, Wrigley flinched and fired his manager. Barrow jumped to sign McCarthy in late October. The Yankees finished second in 1931, and in 1932 they put the pennant away early, beating up on the American League's western teams in the first half of the season. McCarthy had a powerful lineup and a strong pitching staff. Moreover, he also fully embraced the Ruppert-Barrow style of doing business by instilling in his players a code of behavior that became known as the "Yankee way." Players were to wear coats and ties on the road and to eat breakfast at 8:30. In the clubhouse there were no radios, no smoking, no shaving, and no card playing. Baseball was a business, and its governing code was McCarthy's Ten Commandments, rules whose theme of professionalism was embodied in Number Six: "Do not alibi on bad hops. Anybody can field the good ones."[40]

The 1932 World Series has lived on in baseball legend because of a memorable incident that occurred during Game Three in Chicago. The Yankees won that day, 7–5, on their way to a four-game sweep, but the enduring story concerned Babe Ruth's antics when he walked to the plate in the top of the fifth inning with the score tied, 4–4. As Ruth came to bat in Wrigley Field, Cubs players and fans alike razzed him unmercifully. They were retaliating for comments Ruth had made when the Series had opened in New York, excoriating the Cubs' players for their lack of generosity toward former Yankee Mark Koenig when they voted him only half a World Series share. Chicago's pitcher was Charlie Root, a right-hander who had won fifteen games that year. He threw the first pitch for a called strike, and Ruth looked at the Cubs' dugout and held up his right index finger, seemingly indicating "strike one." Two balls followed and then a second called strike. Ruth raised his right hand again, either to signify "strike two" or perhaps to point to the center-field stands. He turned to catcher Gabby Hartnett and said, "It only takes one to hit it," and then perhaps he pointed to the Cubs' dugout again and to Root. The next pitch was off-speed, low and outside. Ruth swung and hit the ball deep into the center-field bleachers. As he rounded the bases, Ruth laughed, chattered, and gestured toward the Cubs. He clasped his hands over his head like a victorious boxer and scurried into the New York dugout. Democratic presidential candidate Franklin Roosevelt, attending the game during his campaign, laughed and watched him all the way. Joe Williams, sports editor for the Scripps-Howard newspaper chain, wrote in his story published in the afternoon papers right after the game, "In the fifth, with the Cubs riding him unmercifully from the bench, Ruth pointed to center and punched a screaming liner to a spot where no ball had ever been hit before."[41]

Starting in the days immediately after the game and continuing for decades, those who were in Wrigley Field that day began debating exactly what they had witnessed, and many others not present debated what exactly they had missed. Did Ruth, as Williams had written, call his shot like a billiards player? Did he, with the count at 2-2, point to center field and then deposit the next pitch where he had pointed? Or was his gesturing merely part of his response to the Cubs' taunts? No one knows for sure. John Drebinger, writing right after the game for the *New York Times*, described the incident as Williams had and in detail, but within a couple of days other sportswriters began to refer to the "called shot" as if it had certainly happened—even though they had not written as much right after the game. Root disagreed vociferously at the time and stuck to his story: "If he had made a gesture like that, well, anybody who knows me knows that Ruth would have ended up on his ass." Years later, when Root was offered the chance to play himself in a movie based on Ruth's autobiography, he replied, "Not if you're going to have him pointing." And so the controversy, clothed in the romance of the game and the spectacular aura of the Babe, endured. Even two snippets of 16mm movie film, shot by fans in the stands and discovered years later, left the mystery unsolved. In 1995 retired sportswriter Stan Isaacs, just a youngster in 1932, investigated the "called shot" anew. His conclusion was that one or more radio broadcasters, reporting the game live, had announced that Ruth had called his shot and that in the days after the game, sportswriters, believing that they had missed something, amended their accounts. Ruth himself played it coy to the end of his days. "It's all right there in the papers," he said.[42]

The Yankees' Series triumph set them on course to become the dominant team in the Majors for the next three decades. Starting with the 1936 season, the New Yorkers won twenty-two of the American League's next twenty-nine pennants and took the World Series sixteen times, an unparalleled skein of success. Twice they won five consecutive pennants, and once they won five consecutive World Series. But at no time during this extended run were they more overpowering than from 1936 through 1939. During these seasons the Yankees captured all four pennants by a collective fifty-nine games and won sixteen World Series games against only three losses. No American League club mounted a sustained attack on New York's preeminence. The Red Sox, so powerful during the early years of the twentieth century, collapsed after winning the World Series in 1918 and did not become a threat to win another pennant until after World War II. The Athletics, a great team during two distinct stretches, never finished first after 1931 and spent most of their remaining seasons in Philadelphia in the league's second division. Other American League clubs advanced to the fore sporadically, but none save the Tigers came close to challenging New York's supremacy. They won pennants in 1934, 1935, 1940, and 1945 but then not again until 1968. Nor did any of the National League's pennant winners have much success against the Yankees in the World Series. After the Giants beat them in 1921 and 1922, the Yankees won eighteen Series against only five losses through 1960. Only the Cardinals beat them more than once, in 1926 and 1942.

By the time Ruth hit his last two World Series home runs in 1932, his monumental career was winding down. He had hit 46 home runs in 1931, but his annual totals dwindled to 41 in 1932, 34 in 1933, and 22 in 1934. After that season the Yankees negotiated his unconditional release so he could sign with the Boston Braves. Disheartened that the Yankees would not let him replace McCarthy as manager, Ruth understood that he would be in line to succeed Bill McKechnie as the Braves' manager. But this was not to be. Ruth, forty years old, out of shape, and cantankerous, played only twenty-eight games for Boston. He hit the final six home runs of his career for the Braves, including his last three—numbers 712, 713, and 714—in Pittsburgh on May 25. Five days later he retired acrimoniously after striking out and then hurting his knee chasing a fly ball. Boston severed its ties with the Babe, and he never got an opportunity to manage anywhere. Ruth's successor as the Yankees' offensive leader was Lou Gehrig. The two had formed a mighty combination for several seasons, "the greatest one-two punch in the history of the game," in the words of Gehrig's biographer, even though they were lukewarm friends at best. At a time when no one could win the Most Valuable Player Award more than once, Ruth won in 1923 and Gehrig in 1927. In 1931 Gehrig batted .341, tied Ruth for the league lead in home runs, and drove in 185 runs, still an American League record. Three seasons later he captured the Triple Crown, leading the league in batting average (.363), home runs (49), and runs batted in (165), but Mickey Cochrane, Detroit's player-manager, won the MVP Award.[43]

The Yankees of 1936–39 were such a steady team, so precise in their preparation and execution, that McCarthy was later derided as a "push button" manager who had to make very few decisions. Barrow had assembled a roster rich with dependable veterans, but he and McCarthy were also adept at introducing talented youngsters into the lineup. During these four years infielders Joe Gordon and Babe Dahlgren and outfielders Tommy Henrich and Charlie Keller assumed starting roles, but none of them had near the impact as Joe DiMaggio, a shy, slim rookie in 1936. Born on November 25, 1914, DiMaggio grew up in the protective cocoon of North Beach, San Francisco's impoverished Italian American neighborhood. He was a skilled batter even at a young age, but he did not love the game. He often declined to join neighborhood pickup games and even gave up baseball altogether for a while. Only when two friends decided in 1932 to organize the Jolly Knights, a semipro team with uniforms, did DiMaggio agree to play regularly. The team had a sponsor, Rossi Olive Oil, but when DiMaggio began to make a name for himself as the team's best player, other clubs, including one called Sunset Produce, slipped him a couple of dollars to play for them too. Scouts from the local Pacific Coast League teams began watching him, but it was DiMaggio's older brother, Vince, who got him a professional tryout. The San Francisco Seals had signed Vince, and near the end of the season one of the team's outfielders and its shortstop left early to commence a barnstorming tour in Hawaii. Manager Ike Caveney needed a shortstop, and Vince volunteered Joe. He played in three games, got some hits, and earned an invitation to spring training in 1933.[44]

DiMaggio played three seasons for the Seals, at least one and perhaps two more than necessary. He was so good, in fact, that the club's owners would not part with him until they were satisfied they would receive full value in return. In 1933, despite competition from many other young players, he hit his way onto the roster. Standing tall and still at the plate, he held the bat behind his right ear, shifted his weight at the last possible moment, and drove the ball hard with beautiful regularity. He made the team by this display of talent, but his brother did not, victimized by the owners' desire to cut costs. Joe opened the season in right field, but for several weeks his bat went quiet, and his batting average dropped below .250. In late May he began to hit, game after game, without interruption. By the time the streak ended after a record sixty-one games, the crowds at Seals Stadium were huge, the mayor had already given him a gold watch, and DiMaggio was a star. He ended the year batting .340, and experts guessed that the Seals could sell his contract for $50,000 or more, but the club rebuffed all comers. The following season DiMaggio started off even better, but in late June he fell stepping into his car and injured his knee. He was out of the lineup for six weeks, and his value as a prospect plummeted. Many Major League scouts lost interest, but not the Yankees. They made an unusual offer: $25,000 and five players to the Seals in exchange for DiMaggio, with the deal not to be consummated—and the cash not to be paid—until after the 1935 season, time enough to see if the knee had healed, which it did. The Seals got a new manager, Lefty O'Doul, a skilled batter who coached DiMaggio to his best season yet: a .398 batting average in 172 games, 178 runs scored, 154 runs batted in, and 34 home runs. O'Doul taught him how to pull the ball, how to play the outfield, and how to act like a star. Moreover, when the Yankees sent DiMaggio a contract for $5,625 for 1936, O'Doul brought in his friend, Ty Cobb, to negotiate for the youngster. Cobb's letters got the Yankees to raise their offer first to $6,500 and then to $8,500. DiMaggio signed, and in the spring he drove with two older players to St. Petersburg, Florida, to begin his Major League career.[45]

DiMaggio sprained his ankle in spring training and then burned it using a heat lamp for treatment, but once he made his debut on May 2, the Yankees began to pull away from their competition. The disappointment associated with the club's three straight second-place finishes in 1933, 1934, and 1935 faded away, and home attendance jumped by two hundred thousand in the first half of the season and by more than three hundred thousand overall. New York clinched the pennant on September 10, ending the race earlier than in any previous American League season, and finished with a record of 102-51. Gehrig won the Most Valuable Player Award again while DiMaggio hit .323 with 29 home runs and 125 RBIs. The Yankees won the World Series too, in six games over the Giants. The following season proved to be more of the same. DiMaggio hit .346 and led the league with 46 homers. Gehrig hit .351 with 37, and New York again won 102 games. In the World Series the Giants provided the opposition again, but this time they won only one game. The Yankees were clearly McCarthy's team now, but he was quick to credit catcher Bill Dickey for handling the pitching staff with skill and tact. In 1938 New York added Gordon and Henrich to the starting lineup and romped to the pennant after winning forty-eight games in July and August against only thirteen losses. Gehrig started slowly, and on May 1 McCarthy dropped him from fourth to sixth in the batting order. DiMaggio tailed off to .324, but it hardly mattered. The Yankees finished nine and a half games ahead of the Red Sox and then swept the Cubs in the World Series to become the first team to win three Series in a row. "I believe we are the greatest ball club ever assembled," McCarthy said. "We have the pitching, the power, the defensive play."[46]

This trio of championships would become a quartet, but before that happened, the Yankees suffered two tragedies. In January 1939 Jacob Ruppert died of a heart attack, brought on by complications from phlebitis, an inflammation of the veins in his left leg. Unmarried, Ruppert had prepared for his death by creating a trust to benefit two nieces and a long-time female friend. But Barrow still held enough stock to remain in charge. Once the season began, it became painfully obvious that Gehrig's ability to play had declined precipitously and that something was wrong. He had adjusted his game the year before to compensate for a loss of power and energy that some attributed to his having played every game since June 1, 1925, and he had still batted .295 with 29 home runs. But after the first month of the 1939 season, his batting average stood at .143. On the morning of May 2 he asked McCarthy to take him out of the lineup. He never played another game. No one yet knew how sick Gehrig was. It wasn't until June that doctors at the Mayo Clinic diagnosed him with amyotrophic lateral sclerosis, a degenerative and fatal neurological disorder. Dahlgren replaced Gehrig at first base, and the Yankees machine marched on, led by DiMaggio, who batted .381 and drove in 126 runs. Gehrig returned to Yankee Stadium on the Fourth of July for Lou Gehrig Appreciation Day, the occasion upon which he spoke movingly and said, "Today I consider myself the luckiest man on the face of the earth." The Yankees needed no such luck. They made a mockery of the pennant race and finished seventeen games ahead of the Red Sox. Competing in their fourth straight World Series, they swept the Reds. Some experts have ranked the 1939 Yankees as the best team of all time. Their triumph that year, especially given the adversity they had to overcome, seemingly put them in position to extend their unparalleled run of success for years to come.[47]

Whatever Kenesaw Landis thought in 1931 when Ruppert purchased the Newark Bears, thereby embracing Branch Rickey's idea on how to build a ball club, the commissioner still refused to acknowledge any of the benefits of a farm system. His opposition did not matter. At the owners' winter meetings that year he lost control over the process by which players were optioned to lower classifications, and a year later the owners removed his authority to prevent transfers between farm clubs owned by the same Major League club. All he could do afterward was harass clubs for technical violations of the complicated regulations governing the movement of players throughout the Minor Leagues, and the particular target of his scorn was Rickey. Landis had come to believe that the Cardinals were running two farm systems, one legitimate and the other sub rosa and therefore illegal. He levied fines against two farm clubs and declared seventy-four players controlled by St. Louis to be free agents, but he did not fine either the Cardinals or Rickey personally. To this sort of discipline, the Minor Leagues paid scant attention. At the 1940 winter meetings they acted in concert with the Majors to pass legislation legalizing working agreements and making farm systems a permanent part of the baseball establishment.[48]

Five

"Keen Competition throughout the Closing Month"

If Captain Leland MacPhail and his flamboyant pal, Colonel Luke Lea, had gotten their way, the "War to End All Wars" would have concluded with a spectacular denouement. In January 1919, just eight weeks after the Armistice, this pair of ne'er-do-wells, together with six others, finagled five days of leave, commandeered two automobiles, drove to Kasteel Amerongen in the Netherlands, and attempted to kidnap the former kaiser, Wilhelm II of Germany. Fearful that he might be tried for war crimes, Wilhelm had not only abdicated the throne in early November, but he had also fled to a safe haven in neutral Holland. For the high-spirited Lea and his keen accomplices, this was unacceptable. They hatched a plan to abduct the kaiser and deliver him to the Paris Peace Conference, where they hoped he would face the drumbeat of international justice. Lea was a native of Tennessee, a graduate of Columbia Law School, the founding editor and publisher of the *Nashville Tennessean*, and a former U.S. senator. When the United States declared war on Germany, he organized a volunteer regiment, the 114th Field Artillery, and became its commanding officer. MacPhail was new to Tennessee at the time, but he joined Lea's regiment, leaving behind a pregnant wife and a daughter. The regiment fought in the Meuse-Argonne offensive, the last Allied operation of the war, but that wasn't enough for Lea and his buddies. Fortified with maps taken from the French War Office and armed with passports, visas, and a journalist's credential secured by Brand Whitlock, American ambassador to Belgium, the Lea gang entered the Dutch castle on the evening of January 5. Having cut telephone wires as they advanced and surprised the guards, they were shown into the library, where they demanded that Count von Bentinck, the kaiser's host, produce his guest. The arrival of the Americans had not gone unnoticed, and when the conversation began to stall after Wilhelm refused their invitation to leave, Lea decided it was time to abort the mission. He and his pals piled into their cars, only to be confronted by a gathering of Dutch soldiers who for some reason let them pass. They sped back to a ferry across the Rhine and rejoined their regiment, mission not accomplished. Afterward the Dutch government protested these shenanigans, and the American government investigated, but no courts martial ensued. Lea received a reprimand, and MacPhail escaped without having to surrender a souvenir he had grabbed off a desk in the castle. It was an ashtray adorned with a pipe-smoking wolf, a brazen symbol of outrageous but typical behavior that MacPhail treasured the rest of his life.[1]

Born in 1890 in Cass City, Michigan, Leland Stanford MacPhail was the son of William McPhail, a banker, and his wife, Catherine. His father's ancestry was Scots, a fact the son later trumpeted by expanding "McPhail" to "MacPhail," and his given names resulted from his mother's friendship with Mrs. Leland Stanford, wife of the famous railroad entrepreneur and California politician. After the Stanfords' son, Leland Jr., died as a youngster, the McPhails named their son in his honor. Young Leland studied at the Staunton Military Academy in Virginia and won a place at the U.S. Naval Academy, but he decided to enroll at Beloit College in Wisconsin instead. He played football and baseball there but lasted only one year, transferring to the University of Michigan and then to George Washington University, where he got a law degree in 1910. Taking a position with Davis and Rankin, a Chicago law firm, he defended the Union Pacific Railroad in two hundred lawsuits stemming from the losses of perishable products immediately after the San Francisco earthquake of 1906. MacPhail lost every case, but even though they were reversed on appeal when the earthquake was defined as an "act of God," Davis and Rankin did not offer him a partnership, and he resigned. He joined a second firm, got married to Inez Thompson, and shifted careers by moving to Nashville to run a department store for one of his firm's clients. Shortly thereafter he was off to war.[2]

Ashtray secured, MacPhail returned to the United States in March, turned down a promotion to major, and left the army in April. His wife and children had spent the war with relatives in Florida, but a business opportunity found the family reunited in Columbus, Ohio. Son Lee MacPhail, born in 1917 while his father was overseas, remembered Columbus as the city "where our roots are. The same house on Woodland Avenue on Columbus's east side was our home for fifteen years," he recalled. Together with a man named Walter Jones, MacPhail organized the Standard Corporation, manufacturers of glass. Four years later he sold his interest and took over the Ohio Motors Agency, selling the Willys–St. Claire automobile and then the Willys-Overland just as its popularity was peaking. Moving on again, MacPhail entered the construction business, developing a project to build a medical office building near the Ohio State University Hospital. But this was 1929, the onset of the Depression, and the Medical Sciences Building was a financial disaster. Along the way MacPhail became an official of the Ohio Golf Association and a popular college football referee, handling many games for Ohio State and a brace of other schools, including Notre Dame. MacPhail had a booming voice, but since large crowds tended to drown him out, he devised a series of hand signals to indicate penalties and other calls, signals that soon became standard throughout the sport. When the printed program for one Ohio State game listed his name erroneously as Lawrence MacPhail, his friends jokingly began calling him Larry. It stuck. He would be Larry MacPhail evermore.[3]

Despite Ohio State's prominence as a college football power, Columbus did not neglect its heritage as a baseball town. After Ernest Barnard left the Columbus Senators for Cleveland in the middle of the 1903 season, business manager Bob Quinn ran the American Association club and guided it to the top of the league's standings. The team played at Neil's Field on Cleveland Avenue across the street from the Columbus Arsenal (later renamed Fort Hayes), and after the 1904 season the club bought the property and built Neil Park, a concrete-and-steel ballpark with a seating capacity exceeding ten thousand. The Senators not only finished first in 1905; they also led the league in attendance, drawing over 280,000 fans, far more than any other club in the league. But mediocrity soon set in. The Senators finished in the middle of the pack or worse for most of the succeeding twenty-five years. Garry Herrmann, president of the Cincinnati Reds, bought the Senators in 1926, and in September 1929 the club passed to the Reds' new board of directors, headed by enterprising businessman Sidney Weil. He was general agent in Cincinnati for the Ford Motor Company and also got involved in banking, garages, and dry cleaning. Weil augmented his wealth considerably during the stock market boom of the 1920s, but the crash in October 1929 sent him reeling toward bankruptcy. He held the Senators for only one season, during which they finished sixth. Fortunately a group of Columbus businessmen decided they wanted to buy the team, and they recruited MacPhail, who needed a job, to head their venture. Weil gave the group an option to purchase the club for $100,000, and MacPhail became president.[4]

MacPhail's first imperative was to secure a steady source of better players. He journeyed to Cleveland to talk with Indians general manager Billy Evans, his partner on some football officiating crews, but Cleveland had a satisfactory working relationship with the New Orleans Pelicans in the Southern Association. MacPhail then went to Chicago, but White Sox owner Charles Comiskey was out of town. By chance MacPhail ran into his former associate, Walter Jones, also a college classmate of Branch Rickey, who was running the St. Louis

Cardinals. Jones called Rickey and introduced MacPhail over the phone. The Cardinals were still building their farm system, and when Rickey expressed interest in the Senators, MacPhail requested a meeting. "How about three o'clock?" said Rickey, anticipating that MacPhail would take the train from Chicago and arrive in St. Louis the following day. "Fine," replied MacPhail, but he had no intention of waiting. He raced to an airport, hopped on a plane, and bounded into Rickey's office that afternoon. Rickey was impressed with MacPhail's energy, and he was also glad to oblige Weil's business associate since Weil was a friend engaged in Jewish philanthropic causes just as Rickey was involved in comparable Methodist programs. Within short order Rickey introduced MacPhail to Cardinals owner Sam Breadon, and a deal was struck. The Cardinals bought the Columbus club for $100,000 in February 1931, and MacPhail signed a new two-year contract as team president. MacPhail returned to Columbus and brought with him a new name for his team: the Red Birds.[5]

Larry MacPhail took control of his club as the fortunes of the Minor Leagues were plummeting. To counteract the effects of the Depression, some leagues and club owners tried to market their businesses in novel ways. Twelve of the nineteen Minor Leagues that began play in 1931 attempted to boost fan interest by dividing their seasons into halves and matching the first-half winner against the second-half winner in a playoff to determine the overall league champion. This idea for a split season, as it was called, was not new, stretching back to the 1891 Eastern Association. Split seasons continued to appear sporadically on Minor League schedules over the next few years, but after the birth of the National Association to govern the Minors in 1901, their use was concentrated in Class D leagues. There were some exceptions. The Class C South Atlantic League played several split seasons in the decade before the Great War but gave them up after resuming play in 1919. After the war the Class B Texas League adopted the practice, but starting in 1920 the Ft. Worth Panthers won six straight league championships, five of them contested as split seasons in which "Atz's Cats"—named after manager Jake Atz—won both halves of each pennant race, obviating the need for a championship series. The New England League brought the split season to Class B baseball in 1927, and in 1928 three of the four Class A leagues gave it a try. After the Class Double-A Pacific Coast League endured a runaway pennant race in 1927, it too adopted a split season for the first time since 1905. In all, ten leagues used split seasons in 1927, sixteen in 1928, thirteen in 1929, and fifteen in 1930. Thus when a dozen leagues adopted split seasons in 1931, the idea was not so much a novelty as it was a desperate attempt to stay in business during very tough times.[6]

In 1931 two leagues that aimed to play split seasons, the Palmetto League and the Rio Grande Valley League, disbanded in midseason anyway. Three leagues, the Pacific Coast League, the Western League, and the Three-I League, tried to abandon the split season but reverted to it in the middle of the summer when fans' interest and attendance lagged in the face of runaway pennant races. Six of the eight owners in the Piedmont League voted in midyear to split their season too, but the National Association's Board of Arbitration overturned this decision, ruling that the league's bylaws required a unanimous vote. The Middle Atlantic League, located in the coal country of West Virginia and western Pennsylvania, expanded from eight teams to twelve in 1931, but the season that resulted bordered on folly. The league was dubbed "Daily's Dozen" after President Elmer M. Daily, and collectively its teams lost an estimated $40,000. Two teams played in three different cities, and the last-place team finished fifty-one games out of first place. Desperate to win and draw fans, teams systematically violated league rules for acquiring players but were not penalized. In Columbus the Red Birds were not immune from the uncertain climate that ran throughout the Minors. MacPhail and his manager, former Major League outfielder Nemo Leibold, ran through players with abandon, searching for anybody who could help the team break a streak of twenty-three seasons without a pennant. Official league statistics indicate that more than fifty players wore the Red Bird uniform, including twenty-two pitchers, and the team sneaked into fourth place on the season's last day. Perhaps more significant, MacPhail was able to increase attendance substantially and to make money, the only club in the American Association to do so.[7]

On June 21, 1931, the Red Birds and the Minneapolis Millers, scheduled to play a doubleheader in Columbus, came close to playing a tripleheader. Minneapolis won the first game, 14–3. Just after the second game commenced, Leibold got into such an argument with umpire Larry Goetz that Goetz forfeited the game to the Millers. Rather than ending the day's play, the clubs agreed to a third game, which Columbus won, 9–1. No matter that the league later nullified this contest. The willingness of the clubs to go overboard to satisfy their fans was typical of MacPhail, who, from the day he took charge, was nothing if not relentless to make his new business a success. Before the season he had replaced advertisements for a local brewer's malt syrup on the outfield fence at Neil Park with drawings of huge cardinals, painted the center-field flagpole bright red, and added signs near both foul poles showing their distance from home plate. He dressed the park's attendants in red hats and neckties and played music through the announcing system before and after games. MacPhail allowed ladies to buy a pass for $3 that would gain them admission to any game for 5 cents, and he fashioned his own version of Branch Rickey's Knothole Gang, admitting boys under sixteen for free on weekdays. He also established the Knothole Gang band, a hundred pieces strong, with its players festooned in blue sailors' trousers and red berets. But all of this was just prelude. MacPhail's goal was to buck the Depression and build a new ballpark. He soon convinced Sam Breadon to buy Sunshine Park, a plot of land on which MacPhail built Red Bird Stadium, with grandstand seats for seventeen thousand fans and a total capacity of twenty thousand. Construction cost nearly $400,000 and proceeded at lightning speed, with crews working two and sometimes three shifts a day. The park opened ahead of schedule on June 3, 1932, with a crowd of more than fifteen thousand. The Knothole Gang band entertained, and the Camp Chase Drum and Bugle Corps played "The Star-Spangled Banner." MacPhail allowed no pregame speeches, but the list of dignitaries present was long and impressive. Commissioner Kenesaw Landis, for one, was mightily impressed. "There is nothing like it in the minor leagues of the country," he said, "and you have a park here that would make many of the major league clubs envious."[8]

Veteran baseball observers, according to the *Sporting News*, questioned the wisdom of building such a palatial baseball park during hard economic times, but MacPhail's bravado quickly paid off. He set ticket prices at $1.50 for a box seat, $1.00 for a reserved grandstand seat, 75 cents for an unreserved grandstand seat, and 50 cents for a spot in the bleachers. Within days after the park's opening the Red Birds attracted a crowd of 18,000, and in their first eighteen games they drew a total of 112,745. For the season Columbus set a new club attendance record—310,000—outdrawing the parent Cardinals by 31,000. The Knothole Gang was a success too, even though the kids had to sit in the bleachers if they wanted to avoid a 10-cent federal tax. What MacPhail accomplished was even more remarkable because construction of Major League ballparks had virtually ground to a halt. A dozen new or rebuilt ballparks had made their Major League debuts between 1909 and 1915, but after the opening of Yankee Stadium in 1923, a lull set in.[9]

The final game of the 1932 season at Red Bird Stadium featured a campaign speech by Democratic presidential candidate Franklin Roosevelt. There is no evidence to suggest that Roosevelt's ability to play baseball as a boy was anything more than rudimentary, but he was a fan, and he understood that being seen liking baseball could pay political dividends. Writing to James P. Dawson, baseball reporter for the *New York Times*, in 1937, Roosevelt confessed:

> When it comes to baseball I am the kind of fan who wants to get plenty of action for his money. I have some appreciation of a game which is featured by a pitcher's duel and results in a score of one to nothing. But I must confess that I get the biggest kick out of the biggest score—a game in which the batters pole the ball into the far corners of the field, the outfielders scramble, and men run the bases. In short, my idea of the best game is one that guarantees the fans a combined score of not less than fifteen runs, divided about eight to seven.

Historian Richard Crepeau wrote that when President Roosevelt accepted an invitation to attend the Washington Senators' 1933 home opener, just weeks after his inauguration, he praised the game for keeping up people's spirits during the Depression. The *Sporting News* in turn lauded him for his "prompt and courageous efforts . . . to restore public confidence and to rehabilitate the nation." In May he incorporated baseball terminology into the text of an early "fireside chat," a radio message to the nation. "I have no expectation of making a hit every time I come to bat," he said. "What I seek is the highest possible batting average, not only for myself, but for my team." To this the *Sporting News* replied, "A nation, schooled in baseball, should find it easy to play ball with President Roosevelt and join him in united team-play to beat the common enemy."[10]

Several of the Roosevelt administration's New Deal agencies, starting with the Civil Works Administration (CWA) and culminating with the Works Progress (later Work Projects) Administration (WPA), paid particular attention to recreation and sports, including baseball. As the Depression worsened, recreation professionals noticed increased use of parks, baseball diamonds, swimming pools, and other such facilities and a lack of funds to maintain and repair them. Federal resources were brought to bear in this area despite complaints that tax money should not be used to help people play. Within a short period of time more than a million CWA workers improved roads and streets; sewer lines; airports and airstrips; schools; and over 3,500 parks, playgrounds, pools, stadiums, and athletic fields. The WPA was even more ambitious, employing more than 8.5 million people. Baseball historian Harold Seymour noted that by 1937 the WPA had spent half a billion dollars—about

10 percent of its budget—on parks and recreation, including 3,600 baseball fields and 8,800 softball fields, some new and many more renovated. By 1941 the list of WPA projects included 5,898 new athletic fields and playgrounds and 8,333 new recreational buildings, and a recreation survey in Chicago found 156 tax-supported diamonds among the city's 4,000 baseball fields. Some cities used federal monies to hold baseball clinics, often run by professional players. Pacific Coast League stars Jimmy Reese and Jigger Statz ran such a school in Santa Monica, California, and former pitcher Ed Walsh taught seventy thousand boys over a period of four months. Cardinals Terry Moore and Enos Slaughter ran a clinic at a St. Louis park that future Major League players Joe Garagiola and Yogi Berra attended.[11]

Many of the ballparks built or rehabbed by the New Deal were never intended for anything other than amateur baseball. Some began as amateur sites and later became homes to Minor League teams. Others were Minor League parks from their origins and set the precedent that privately owned clubs could play in publicly financed ballparks. The Levee Improvement Commission in Davenport, Iowa, sold $60,000 in bonds in 1930 to fund construction of a city-owned ballpark for the Blue Sox in the Mississippi Valley League. Two years later CWA funds paid for an upgrade, including paint for the grandstand seats and the bleachers, a new outfield fence, and an access road with additional parking. In 1936 a PCL club that had begun as the Salt Lake City Bees and then became the Hollywood Stars moved to San Diego. The WPA built a wooden ballpark seating 11,500 for the city, and the team, owned by Bill Lane and renamed the Padres, played in it rent free. Projects like these spurred similar proposals in cities and towns throughout the country. To cite just a few: WPA funds built new ballparks in Carthage, Missouri; Superior, Wisconsin; Charlotte, North Carolina; and Pine Bluff, Arkansas. They renovated existing facilities in Stockton, California, and Anniston, Alabama, and they paid in part for a new park in Jersey City, New Jersey, even though the city did not have a Minor League team at the time. In 1935 Joseph F. Carr, promotions director for the National Association, proposed that the Public Works Administration (PWA), still another New Deal agency, appropriate $4 million to build five hundred ballparks. This did not come to pass, but some local officials began to anticipate federal funds as a matter of course. In 1940 Dan Daniel, reporting that officials in St. Petersburg, Florida, were debating where to locate a new ballpark, quipped, "T'hell with where it is, boys, but build it while you can still get a WPA grant." A year later a *Sporting News* editorial praised George and Julius Schepps, owners of the Dallas Rebels in the Texas League, for spending

$137,000 of their own money to build their club a new ballpark, noting that "few privately-owned stadiums are being built these days, most of them being community affairs financed through federal agencies."[12]

In Cooperstown, New York, the WPA spent $23,401 to help renovate a parcel of land once known as Elihu Phinney's cow pasture and later exalted as Doubleday Field, where, according to baseball's creation myth, Abner Doubleday had invented the game on a summer day in 1839. That the Doubleday story was untrue mattered not. Since 1907, when the Special Base Ball Commission, often called the Mills Commission, issued its report declaring that baseball had no precedent in the English game called rounders or any other European game and was a purely American invention, Cooperstown stood poised to assume its place not only as baseball's Garden of Eden, but also its Valhalla. Sam Crane, a Major League infielder in the 1880s who later became a sportswriter, was the first to suggest that baseball officials create some sort of memorial in Cooperstown to recognize the game's greatest players. The Cooperstown Chamber of Commerce, having failed to secure public funds to purchase the Phinney lot, did so with private money, and slowly residents of the village began to treat the field and its alleged stature with greater respect. The village bought the land in 1923, but it was not until 1933 that work commenced to improve the field, along with several adjacent parcels. About this time the Board of Village Trustees appointed Alexander Cleland as its representative to promote Doubleday Field as a shrine for the game. Cleland, who worked for Stephen C. Clark, a local millionaire and philanthropist, became the principal advocate for building a ballpark on the Phinney property and for constructing what became the National Baseball Hall of Fame and Museum just down the street. When organized baseball officials balked at funding the ballpark, Cleland and the village approached Lester W. Herzog, the state administrator of the WPA. He approved funds for the project, which included building a steel-covered grandstand and wooden bleachers, reseeding the field, installing a drainage system, and erecting a new outfield fence and stone walls at the field's entrance. By the summer of 1939, when the Hall of Fame staged its official opening and teams of Major League All-Stars played the first Hall of Fame game, to become an annual tradition, Doubleday Field seated ten thousand people.[13]

Letters and other communications about various aspects of baseball crossed Roosevelt's desk throughout his presidency. Some of these concerned proposed WPA projects. In 1939 James J. Mahaney, mayor of Batavia, New York, called the president on the telephone and appealed successfully for funds to build a ballpark in his city. In 1940 Roosevelt authorized construction of the All-Sports Stadium in Duluth, Minnesota. Other requests were turned down. The Washington Elite Giants, a club in the Negro Southern League, asked the president to throw out the ceremonial first pitch before their opening game in 1936, and the *Sporting News* asked him to present a gold watch to Lou Gehrig before the 1937 All-Star Game. Both were denied. A boys team volunteered to call themselves the NRA Eagles (after the National Recovery Administration, an early New Deal agency) in exchange for White House sponsorship, and a distillery asked to decorate the presidential box for Opening Day with its marketing materials. These also were refused. In 1941 the Brooklyn First Committee sent Roosevelt a telegram: "UNLESS YOU ATTEND BROOKLYN DODGERS PARADE THIS MONDAY BROOKLYN WILL SECEDE FROM THE UNION." Roosevelt did not, and neither did Brooklyn. Throughout his years in office Roosevelt attended a fair number of games, mostly the Senators' home openers. He once told owner Clark Griffith that if his paralysis didn't force him "to hobble up those steps in front of all those people, I'd be out at the park every day," and most observers believed him. Wrote sportswriter Harold C. Burr, "Roosevelt enjoys himself at a ball game as much as a kid on Christmas morning."[14]

Perhaps no game was more important to the survival of the Minor Leagues in the 1930s than an exhibition played five decades before in Oceanside Park on Nantasket Beach in Hull, Massachusetts, a small village on a peninsula jutting north into Boston Harbor. From its emergence as a primitive bat-and-ball recreation to its life as a mature sport, baseball had always been defined as a daytime activity. Indeed part of the romance attached to the game stemmed from adults' memories that as children they played baseball during long summer days and didn't stop until the sun set. Prior to 1880 no baseball game had ever been played at night. David Pietrusza, in his history of night baseball, noted that gaslights had been illuminating city streets since the 1820s, and arc lights, using an electrical charge, were glowing in Europe by 1876. Brightening a baseball field, though, had to wait until after Thomas Edison demonstrated the incandescent light in Menlo Park, New Jersey, in October 1879. Less than a year later, on September 2, 1880, the Northern Electric Light Company staged a demonstration night baseball game in Hull between two amateur teams representing rival Boston department stores, Jordan Marsh and R. H. White. The company erected three hundred-foot wooden towers five hundred feet apart around the lawn adjacent to the Sea Foam House resort and hung thirty-six lights from each pole. Two engines and three generators lit the bulbs as the teams took the field at 8:00 p.m. and played to a 16–16 tie. Three hundred spectators watched the game, and the *Boston Post* reported that "when the lamps were lighted after dark, the effect was fine."[15]

Over the next fifty years Minor League entrepreneurs experimented with night baseball at a wide variety of venues, but few saw night games as anything more than novelties. Some games were staged as if they were part of a carnival, and the primitive lighting technology they employed often added to this atmosphere. Early attempts to light Major League games proved even less successful. The Chicago White Stockings (later the Cubs) considered installing lights as early as 1883, but nothing came of the idea. Four years later the New York Metropolitans in the American Association engaged William Hibbard Johnson, president of the Edison Electric Light Company and the man who had first hung electric lights on a Christmas tree, to illuminate a game by placing lights on the ground beaming upward, but his plan did not prove workable. The Indianapolis Hoosiers of the National League tried to use gas lamps on poles in center field in 1888, but they proved too bright for players trying to catch fly balls and not bright enough for ground balls. Sometime in the late 1890s lights blazed at Sportsman's Park in St. Louis. Browns owner Chris Von der Ahe's venue doubled as a nighttime racetrack with lights, and on one particularly dark afternoon fans protested the continuation of the ball game by lighting matches. Suddenly Von der Ahe turned on the lights, allowing the game to be played to a conclusion. A few years later the Cahill brothers, a trio of inventors and owners of a Holyoke, Massachusetts, firm that manufactured floodlights, turned their attention to baseball. Together with several wealthy businessmen, George Cahill and Reds president Garry Herrmann organized the Night Baseball Development Company in 1908, and workers slowly erected five hundred-foot towers, each holding fourteen arc lights, around the Reds' home park, the Palace of the Fans. Herrmann scheduled an exhibition game for June 18, 1909, but his resolve to use Reds players in it wavered. Instead two local Elks lodges squared off before 4,500 fans. Reviews of Cahill's lighting system were mixed. Herrmann testified that "night baseball has come to stay," but sportswriter Ren Mulford dissented, saying, "It will be a long time before National and American Leaguers are fighting for championships under the glare of the electric lights."[16]

The breakthrough game that propelled night baseball from possibility to reality was played on June 24, 1927, in West Lynn, Massachusetts. General Electric (GE) engineers had been working for several years to develop a lighting system good enough to permit baseball to be played without compromise. For this game they mounted seventy-two lights, each one rated at 1,500 watts, on poles fifty feet high. In addition they pointed twenty-five lights upward, thereby illuminating not only the entire playing surface, but also the space above it. The Lynn Papooses and the Salem Witches of the New England League played a seven-inning game, and the lighting system was a hit. In attendance were more than five thousand fans, including lighting engineers from other cities and players from the Red Sox and the team visiting Boston at the time, the Senators. Washington outfielder Goose Goslin said, "It's just as good ball as they could play by daylight." The Lynn experiment persuaded several Minor League executives that night baseball was now a viable idea. In 1929 Lee Keyser, president of the Des Moines Demons of the Western League, told the National Association that his club would play a number of night games during the upcoming season. After a short career in advertising and journalism, he had purchased a half-interest in the team in 1921 and became club president in 1923, only to be frustrated at the small crowds the team attracted for weekday games. Years later Keyser remembered that his first inspiration was attending a night football game. The second came from a brochure showing how GE had lit the Boston Common so youngsters could play baseball there. Keyser also recalled how a glance at the moon convinced him that balls hit above a lighting system could still be seen. "I noticed how bright was the moonlight down here on the earth," he said, "and what was it? Nothing but light reflected from the sun. I was sure then that electric lights, striking downward on the ground, would cast a reflection into the air and illuminate the ball far above the field. That is exactly how it works, as anyone can see if he takes the time to look. The white underside of the ball, against a background of the dark night sky, is easy to follow."[17]

Keyser obtained permission for his experiment from his league, reeling from two successive lean years, in February 1930. He tested equipment from two companies and paid $19,000 for a system built by the firm that had worked with GE in Lynn, the Giant Manufacturing Company of Council Bluffs, Iowa. Years later Keyser remembered that settling on the poles was less scientific. "We begged tower poles from the telephone company and the light and power company," he said. "Then, it was decided to raise the towers over 100 feet in the air instead of 65 to 70 feet, to cut the glare on both the players and the spectators. And that's about how it was started." At the time, though, Des Moines sportswriter Sec Taylor described a much more sophisticated process. He wrote that the lights would be hung from six galvanized steel towers, each ninety feet high and ten feet square at their base, buried in ten feet of concrete. Two towers, each holding fourteen 1,000-watt bulbs, were to be placed at the back of the grandstand, one between home plate and first base and the other between home and third base. A second pair, each with thirty-four lights, was to be located outside the park beyond first and third, and the third pair, with twenty-four lights each, was put beyond the outfield fence in left field and right field. Each light fixture was made of copper and waterproofed to protect it from both rain and bugs. The bulbs were backed by silver parabolic reflectors and covered by stippled lenses to break up the light and reduce the glare. Each bulb, though rated at 1,000 watts, was overloaded to perform at 1,300 watts.[18]

Keyser scheduled his first night game for May 2, his club's home opener, but Marvin L. Truby, owner of the Independence (MO) Producers of the Western Association, beat him to the punch. His club played a night exhibition game on April 17 and a league game on April 28 before a thousand fans. Still, all the publicity went to the Des Moines game. The *Sporting News* estimated the crowd at ten thousand, including "hundreds of baseball club owners, managers, directors, and league presidents." Students from Drake University counted 3,311 parked cars, 676 with license plates from outlying counties and 46 from out of state. NBC put the final innings of the game on the radio, and three of GE's shortwave stations delivered the signal around the world. Keyser, whose electric bill for the evening was $25, spoke on the air and called night baseball "glorious and wonderful." Several baseball officials agreed. Dale Gear, president of the Western League, said, "The demonstration at night was very practical. I am confident that night baseball will succeed." Claude Davenport, the Demons' manager, added, "The lights have no effect on the players' actions. This talk about the pitcher having such an advantage on the batter is bunk. The white ball against the black background of the sky affords a fine target for the batter." Michael Sexton, National Association president, predicted that "this Des Moines game may be the first step in vastly changing playing conditions in the minors." The *Sporting News* called the game a "success" in its headline, but took a less enthusiastic view editorially, saying, "If there is any real merit in baseball played under artificial light, it will be proved. . . . We hope that baseball will not be pushed by the radicals who are seeking to change our notions of sports until it becomes like a thing of the circus, two performances in one day under the big tent." The weekly also disputed the assumption that night games would prove a panacea to the Minors' economic woes. "The attendance at Des Moines dropped from 10,000 the first night (Friday) to 1,200 the second night (Saturday)," said the editorial. "Surely at least 1,200 fans would have attended a game on Saturday afternoon—especially with the team winning the day before." Yet, just two weeks later, night baseball had spread to eleven cities, and eight night games in Des Moines had drawn an average crowd of 2,309. The Giant Manufacturing Company took an ad in the *Sporting News*, and simultaneously the Pyle-National Company of Chicago advertised that its lighting experts "can give you night lighting that brings in the crowd, not once, but night after night."[19]

William Bramham, president of two Minor Leagues and future head of the National Association, was probably not in the stands at Des Moines, but he did approve of the experiment and pushed to have lights installed in his leagues' parks. The first night game in Bramham's South Atlantic Association matched the visiting Charlotte Hornets against the Augusta (GA) Wolves on July 21, 1930. The Charlotte pitcher, Jim Mooney, struck out a league-record twenty-three batters, indicating perhaps that the lights were not bright enough. Four of the six teams in Bramham's other league, the Piedmont League, hurried to install lights, and the High Point (NC) Pointers won the race, hosting the league's first night game on July 8 before five thousand fans. Bramham ruled that clubs with lights would thereafter have to play all games at night except for doubleheaders, which would be day-night affairs. Two Piedmont clubs eschewed lights, but they were threatened with expulsion if they didn't put up their own lighting systems for the next season. Early in 1931 an ad for the Giant Manufacturing Company indicated that thirty-two Minor League clubs would use its lighting systems during the coming season, and a story in the *Sporting News* said that teams in sixteen leagues would play some games at night. Most of these reaped benefits at the box office. Six of the eight clubs in the Texas League installed lights in 1931, and the league set an attendance record. Still, lights were no sure panacea for every Minor League club's economic trouble. The Jersey City Skeeters in the International League abandoned night ball after trying it in 1930, unable to compete with the other night life of the New York metropolitan area. The South Atlantic Association, despite using lights in 1930, did not play in 1931 and did not resume play until 1936. But the progress of night baseball would not be halted. In July 1934 the Toronto Maple Leafs in the International League installed lights and drew more fans to their first night game than they had on Opening Day. General Electric announced in 1937 that it had developed standardized recommendations to help owners light their ballparks, and the *Sporting News* noted in 1939 that 70 percent of all Minor League games were being played at night.[20]

Two weeks after Red Bird Stadium opened in 1932, lights that Larry MacPhail had ordered were installed, and the team played its first night game at home before a crowd of twenty-one thousand. By this time night baseball was a fixture for most clubs in the other two Class Double-A leagues, the Pacific Coast League and the International League, but it was still a novelty in the American Association. Owners accustomed to decades of day baseball simply did not fully grasp the favorable economic implications of night games. MacPhail was different, and to ensure the success of this innovation, he embellished his club's night games with radio broadcasts, fireworks, special ticket prices, and other promotions. Fans responded enthusiastically. Moreover, after the 1932 season ended, it was MacPhail who persuaded his league's owners to split their teams into two divisions, with the winners of each division meeting in a best-of-seven postseason playoff to determine the league champion. The Red Birds finished first in the East Division in 1933 by twenty games and defeated Minneapolis, winners of the West, four games to two, in the playoff, but MacPhail was not around to enjoy this triumph. Early in the season Branch Rickey wanted to promote second baseman Burgess Whitehead to St. Louis, but MacPhail, who thought he might have a pennant-winning team on his hands, balked, relenting only when Rickey agreed to ship five players to Columbus. The Cardinals owned the Red Birds, but MacPhail took his job, to field a competitive team and make a profit, seriously. So perhaps his tangle with Rickey was inherent in the farm system relationship. But it was exacerbated by MacPhail's lavish lifestyle and his extremely well-appointed office, neither of which Rickey could abide. He worked behind the scenes to remove MacPhail as a Red Birds stockholder, and without stock MacPhail could no longer legally serve as president. Fired or not, he was out. A while later, other owners charged the Columbus club with exceeding the league's salary limits. Even though MacPhail's name was not mentioned in the complaint, he demanded that Commissioner Landis look into the matter. He did so and cleared MacPhail of any wrongdoing, and MacPhail did not remain out of baseball for long.[21]

In 1933, as the number of clubs playing at night continued to grow and seven of fourteen Minor leagues played split seasons, three other leagues introduced postseason playoffs. The International League separated its clubs into Northern and Southern Divisions, with the top two teams in each division meeting in a two-round playoff to determine its champion. The eight-team Texas League did not create divisions but still sent its top four teams to a two-round playoff. The idea to extend the season in this way was not

MacPhail's. It came to baseball from ice hockey, with antecedents in other sports even further back in time. Frank Shaughnessy proposed what became known as the Shaughnessy Playoff Plan when he was running the Montreal Royals in the International League in 1932. "Here in Montreal," he argued before Minor League club officials, "we have $1,800,000 sunk into a stadium and club and have been losing money steadily because of waning interest by the first of August. With the playoffs, it is confidently believed that we can keep up interest just as they do in hockey." After the 1936 season the league's owners installed him as the league's seventeenth president. "With playoffs," he argued as the game struggled against the Depression, "we would have at least four clubs, and sometimes as many as six, with something to play for towards the end of the season. We could get away from that dreadful apathy which settled on all clubs which were out of the race, and which killed interest for a month or more when there was a runaway pennant race." Opponents of the plan complained that it wasn't traditional, that fans would never accept it, and that it would cheapen the regular season, but the International League tried dividing into two divisions for 1933, and the American Association did so for that season and the next. By 1936 both had accepted the Shaughnessy Plan. The plan worked, and other leagues jumped to adopt it. "The fans are given better baseball," Shaughnessy told the *Sporting News* in 1940, "for the players hustle to the end of the season and club owners, instead of weakening their teams by sales, try to strengthen them, thus assuring keen competition throughout the closing month, whereas in the past, both interest and competition waned." In 1940, when forty-four Minor Leagues began play, all forty-three that finished the season used the Shaughnessy Plan.[22]

By 1933 the economic fortunes of Minor League baseball had bottomed out and begun to improve, albeit erratically. National Association president William Bramham reported in April that his office in Durham was being flooded with requests for help with organizing new teams. Only fourteen leagues began play that season, but all made it through to their scheduled conclusions. Some leagues that had reduced ticket prices in 1932 to boost attendance kept the cuts in effect. Others restored them and still found attendance rebounding. Strict adherence to salary limits played a role too. The Western League's salary rule was perhaps the tightest of all: just $1,200 a month to be split among a fourteen-player roster, with $100 reserved for the manager. Some clubs moved from one city to another midseason, but only one went out of business prematurely. The three Double-A leagues suffered the least during the

Depression and rebounded most quickly. During the four tough seasons from 1930 through 1933, no club in these three leagues quit, and only one pulled up stakes and moved to a new city, the International League's Reading (PA) Keys, who became the Albany (NY) Senators in August 1932. Each Double-A league had a couple of perennially strong teams: Columbus and Minneapolis in the American Association, Rochester and Newark in the International League, and San Francisco and Los Angeles in the Pacific Coast League. Bill James called the 1934 Los Angeles Angels the best Minor League team of the decade, and historian Bill O'Neal called them "the greatest team in Coast League history." They ran away from their opponents, winning sixty-six of their first eighty-four games, and forced the league's owners to divide the season in half after not doing so in 1932 or 1933. It was a move made in vain since the Angels dominated the second half of the season just as easily, winning seventy-one games against only thirty-two losses for an overall record of 137-50. Without a playoff between the winners of each half of the schedule, the league arranged a best-of-seven postseason series between Los Angeles and an All-Star team from the other seven clubs. The Angels won it in six games.[23]

In several ways the Pacific Coast League had begun to separate itself from the other two Double-A leagues. In the decade after the end of the Great War, it had prospered. Despite a widespread gambling scandal, several franchise shifts and ownership changes, and contentious league meetings (often featuring verbal and physical altercations over a host of business issues), the PCL produced several outstanding teams and tight pennant races that drew big crowds. Despite the universal draft, from which no Minor League was exempt, and the growing number of working agreements and farm systems, the PCL was able to assert its own identity, transcending simple subordination to the Majors within the structure of organized baseball and appealing as a unique attraction to players and large numbers of fans alike. The long, pleasant summers on the West Coast let the league play extended seasons that boosted both players' statistics and their salaries. The schedule, which often matched two teams for seven games over a six-day span, fostered intense rivalries. The league's preference for signing the rich baseball talent in the region, especially the San Francisco Bay area, helped too, as did the sheer geographic isolation of the league from its competitors. For many PCL fans the Majors were a distant and secondary interest, and other Minor Leagues mattered even less. Recalled one San Franciscan many years later, "As far as we were concerned, the Pacific Coast League was it." That drinking in the stands continued unabated during Prohibition did not hurt, but the league also developed a host of fine players.

Some of them went on to the Majors, but others were more than content to remain on the West Coast, making a good living, traveling well, and playing in good weather most of the time. Tony Freitas, a pitcher who enjoyed several stints in the league from 1929 through 1950, was one of many who made their careers on the West Coast. Speaking for himself but by implication for others as well, he told writer R. Scott Mackey in 1992, "The Pacific Coast League was where I wanted to play and where I belonged."[24]

Chewing gum magnate William Wrigley Jr., who purchased the Angels in part to serve as a farm team for his Cubs, was at the center of the tumultuous relations among PCL owners. He argued over territorial rights with owners of the Vernon Tigers, situated just a few miles south of downtown Los Angeles. In 1923 he led a contingent of owners in a dispute that eventually cost league president William H. McCarthy his job and got the league office moved from San Francisco to Los Angeles. Soon thereafter Wrigley conspired with Salt Lake City owner Bill Lane to transfer his Bees to Hollywood, where they became the Stars. This move had a domino effect. It caused the Tigers to abandon Vernon and move to San Francisco, already home to the Seals, but two teams in San Francisco meant PCL baseball at Recreation Park every day. This put economic pressure on the Oakland Oaks, who depended upon fans crossing San Francisco Bay to watch them play while the Seals were on the road. Wrigley cared more about his club's success than others' problems. The Angels won the 1921 PCL pennant months after he bought them, but they had a tough time securing a follow-up triumph. Opening the Los Angeles version of Wrigley Field in 1925 brought in additional revenue since the Stars became tenants of the Angels, and Wrigley told his staff to "spare no expense" in purchasing good players. The result was another championship a year later. As good as the 1926 Angels were, they paled in comparison to the 1934 club. By this time Wrigley was dead, succeeded by his son, Phil. The Angels won twenty-three of their first twenty-eight games and later won twenty of twenty-two. Playing twenty-six weeklong series, Los Angeles won twenty-three of these series and lost only three. Few of these Angels enjoyed substantial Major League careers, but the team included several Minor League stars, players who performed very well over several seasons in the league of their choosing. Had the league not selected a postseason All-Star team to play against the Angels, argued researcher Jamie Selko, at least nine Los Angeles players would have been selected to a true league All-Star team.[25]

As the wealthiest owners in the Pacific Coast League, the Wrigleys' control of both the Angels and the National League Cubs gave them a competitive advantage that other owners sought to emulate, even before the benefits of farm systems had fully unfolded. In 1935 the Portland Beavers forged an affiliation with the Detroit Tigers. At the same time, the Oakland club hooked up with the New York Yankees. The deal probably called for New York to lend the Oaks $5,000 in the spring, interest free for six months. At the end of the season the Oaks would either repay the loan or send the Yankees two players. Lane, known as "Hard Rock" Bill, was a tight-fisted businessman who had purchased the (SF) Mission Wolves in 1915 and moved them in turn to Salt Lake City, Hollywood, and San Diego. In each city he struggled to compete with the richer clubs and lost money year after year. In 1936 Lane agreed to make the Padres a Red Sox farm team. Some of these relationships lasted while others did not. Particularly solid was the pact struck between the Sacramento Solons and the Cardinals in 1936, even though Branch Rickey's habit was to spread out his top prospects among Sacramento, Rochester, and Columbus. One St. Louis prospect testified to the high quality of play a farm system could foster: "I honestly believe you could have taken our top talent in the minors [in 1942] and finished third in the National League behind the Cardinals and Dodgers." Other PCL clubs survived the Depression in a variety of ways. The Seals had a trio of owners known as the "Vanderbilts of Valencia Street," the location of Recreation Park, the team's home through 1930. Baseball historians Bill Weiss and Marshall Wright wrote that San Francisco was the richest team in the Minors in the 1920s, with a big chunk of the club's revenues coming from player sales to the Majors, but all three co-owners had skills that augmented the team's financial position. Just prior to the 1938 season the Mission Reds moved from San Francisco to Hollywood, without a team since Lane's move to San Diego. After renting Wrigley Field for one season for these new Stars, owner Herbert Fleischaker sold the club to a group of Hollywood personalities headed by Bob Cobb, part owner of the Brown Derby restaurant, and including Cecil B. DeMille, Robert Taylor, William Frawley, George Burns, Gracie Allen, and Gary Cooper. Their money financed construction of Gilmore Field, which opened in 1939.[26]

Far to the east, clubs often sought civic support to stay afloat, or they fashioned unusual ownership arrangements to bolster their economic prospects. Citizens in Williamsport, Pennsylvania, underwrote the finances of the Grays in the New York–Pennsylvania League to keep the team alive in 1931. In Springfield, Missouri, the Western Association's Cardinals sponsored "Merchants' Loyalty Night" in 1932, drawing 9,083. A year later the Johnstown (PA) Boosters' Association held the first in a series of dances and bingo nights to raise funds for its club in the Middle Atlantic League. Other organizations and citizens' groups assisted their cities' clubs in a variety of ways. The American Legion post in Greenwood, Mississippi, borrowed money to finance a new ballpark, and fans in Davenport, Iowa, raised $3,500 in 1937 to guarantee players' salaries. In 1940 the Chamber of Commerce of Rome, New York, gave $500 to the Colonels in the Canadian-American League to cover its losses. A year later the American Legion post in El Dorado, Arkansas, paid debts incurred by the Oilers in the Cotton States League and sold season tickets to recover its investment. Speaking no doubt for many, Gordon E. Kent, president of the Rome Chamber of Commerce, justified such actions by saying, "The city that supports a professional baseball team is recognized as a thriving community and thus gains indirect prestige for business and industries."[27]

Ownership of clubs in trouble often devolved upon prominent businessmen or government officials. Coca-Cola lent money to the Atlanta Crackers in the Southern Association and took over ownership in 1932, when the team was on the verge of bankruptcy. In 1933 the Louisville club in the American Association offered to sell ten-year bonds to the public at 6 percent interest to cover a $175,000 mortgage, but three years later a group of twelve businessmen had to come forward with $5,000 each to save the club. The Hutchinson, Kansas, club in the Western Association listed a thousand fans as stockholders in 1935. The club's attendance was twice the population of the town, and the growth of its treasury allowed purchasing new equipment and a bus. In 1940 the Union Mine Workers local in Pennington Gap, West Virginia, took over the town's club in the Appalachian League and changed its name from Bears to Miners. Leagues, too, reached out to prominent people for leadership. The long-time president of the Southern Association was a federal judge, John D. Martin, and another judge, Emmett Harty, became president of the Cotton States League in 1939. Perhaps most unusual was the situation in the Canadian-American League, where the president was a Catholic priest, Reverend Harold J. Martin, a former Minor League pitcher. Predictably not all owners weathered the economic storm on the right side of the law. Roger E. Baker, president of the Northeastern League and owner of the Worcester (MA) Rosebuds, was arrested and convicted in 1934 for misappropriating $200,000 from the leather goods company where he was assistant treasurer and using these funds to promote his league and its clubs. He was convicted and sentenced to twelve to twenty-two years in state prison. Pug Griffin, president of the Lincoln Links in the Nebraska State League, was implicated in a gambling scandal in 1935 and removed from office. In 1938 business manager Pat Flanagan and manager

Eddie Krajnik were accused of betting on a game played by their team, the Welch (WV) Miners in the Mountain State League. Both were fined and suspended. Seymour Weiss, one of Louisiana governor Huey Long's associates, once owned the New Orleans Pelicans in the Southern Association, but he was arrested and convicted of mail and tax fraud.[28]

Pacific Coast League teams built loyal fan bases by retaining the same players year after year, but nothing excited fans more than young prospects determined to advance to the Major Leagues. In the 1930s two of the PCL's best prospects had destiny on their side. Both were born in California, both came to prominence in the PCL, and both eventually were elected to the Hall of Fame. One was Joe DiMaggio, who went from the Seals to the Yankees, and the other was Ted Williams. Born on April 30, 1918, in San Diego, Williams grew up pretty much alone. His father, Sam, was a photographer who drank, and his mother, May, worked long, devoted hours for the Salvation Army. Ted turned to baseball and soon gave it his full and undivided attention. Encouraged by several surrogate fathers, he played at Herbert Hoover High, where he impressed coach Wos Caldwell by hitting two mammoth fly balls at the team's first tryout session. Williams starred at Hoover for three seasons, both at bat and on the mound, but hitting was his obsession. "Always," recalled his friend and third baseman Joe Villarino, "the conversation was about hitting." When Williams graduated with his class in February 1937 with a special commendation for his typing skills, he had already played half a season as a professional. His mother talked with Bill Lane, whose Padres played their first season in San Diego in 1936. She signed a contract in Ted's name, getting Lane to promise not to farm out her son for the next two years. He joined the club in the middle of the 1936 season, meeting his teammates, including Vince DiMaggio, as they were boarding a train for San Francisco. Williams hardly played at all for weeks, but he got into the lineup in August, when starting outfielder Ivey Shiver left the club to coach football at the University of Georgia. Williams hit respectably, batting .271, as the Padres finished in second place.[29]

Red Sox general manager Eddie Collins traveled to San Diego to observe two other prospects, but Williams also impressed him. "It wasn't hard to find Ted Williams," he said. "He stood out like a brown cow in a field of white cows." Collins asked Lane about acquiring Williams's contract, but Lane said he had to honor his deal with May Williams. He offered the Red Sox the opportunity to bid for the seventeen-year-old after the following season. That was 1937, when Williams hit .291 with 23 home runs as the Padres fell to third place but won the PCL playoffs. After the season Lane held several other clubs at bay while Collins persuaded Boston owner Tom Yawkey to make the deal by parting with the rights to four Minor Leaguers. Williams was now the property of the Red Sox, who took him to spring training in Sarasota, Florida. He picked up the nickname "Kid" as the Sox shipped him to Daytona Beach, where the Minneapolis Millers of the American Association trained. Minneapolis was Boston's farm team, and Williams, probably good enough to play in the Majors but woefully immature, was theirs for the season. Moreover, Williams benefited from the tutelage of Rogers Hornsby, a spring training coach, who impressed upon his student this important principle: "Get a good pitch to hit." A Millers' preseason press release presciently called Williams "another DiMaggio," but DiMaggio was a complete ballplayer even in San Francisco, while Williams had rarely demonstrated interest in any other facet of the game besides hitting. But hit he did. After a slow start in Minneapolis, he piled up enough offense to win the association's Triple Crown, batting .366, hitting 46 home runs, and driving in 142 runs. Over the winter the Red Sox dumped outfielder Ben Chapman, a four-time American League All-Star. Williams would start in left field for Boston in 1939.[30]

Williams's Triple Crown season was truly outstanding, but the club finished sixth. Minneapolis fans remembered with more fondness the 1933 season, when five Millers hit .332 or better and first baseman Joe Hauser led the league with 182 runs batted in and 69 home runs, a Minor League record. A native of Milwaukee, Hauser was called "Unser Choe," German for "Uncle Joe," and he was a fan favorite. Starting in 1918, he played in Providence and his hometown before putting in three seasons with the Philadelphia Athletics, but a broken kneecap in 1925 relegated him to the Minors. He rediscovered his batting stroke in 1930 and walloped 63 homers for the Baltimore Orioles in the International League before moving to Minneapolis two years later. Taking full advantage of the cozy dimensions of their home, Nicollet Park, the Millers were an offensive machine. After they won the association's 1932 pennant, General Mills, headquartered in Minneapolis, put a billboard on the outfield wall calling its Wheaties brand of cereal the "Breakfast of Champions" for the first time. In 1933 the Millers batted .303 as a team and hit nearly twice as many home runs as their nearest competitor, but they lost to Columbus in the playoffs. In other Minor League cities, where irregularly shaped ballparks, unbalanced schedules, and the uneven distribution of playing talent had traditionally led to unusual Minor League statistics, the decade of the 1930s proved to be no exception. Frank Demaree of the Angels scored 190 runs in 1934,

Robert Holland of the PCL's Seattle Indians hit 72 doubles in 1930, and Lyle Judy of the Springfield (MO) Cardinals in the Western Association stole 107 bases in 1935. Several pitchers assembled exceptional won-lost records too, led by Joe Kohlman, who finished 25-1 in 1937 for the Salisbury (MD) Indians in the Eastern Shore League. Kohlman lost his first decision before winning twenty-five in a row, but what distinguished the Indians even more was that on June 19 the league forced the team to forfeit its first twenty-one wins for violating league rules. The Indians' record dropped from 21-5 to 0-26, but they still recovered to finish first and won the league's playoff.[31]

Virgil Trucks, who later threw two no-hitters in the Majors, set the Minor Leagues on fire in 1938, when he was just a nineteen-year-old rookie. Pitching on Opening Day for the Andalusia (AL) Bulldogs in the Alabama-Florida League, Trucks struck out 20 batters. A month later he pitched a 1–0 no-hitter against the Evergreen (AL) Greenies, striking out 19. On June 4 he threw a second no-hitter, defeating the Dothan (AL) Browns, 6–0, and striking out 15. He finished the year with a record of 25-6 and an earned run average of 1.25, with 418 strikeouts in 273 innings. Two years later, pitching for the Beaumont (TX) Exporters in the Texas League, he threw his third no-hitter. Johnny Vander Meer, twenty-one years old in 1936, pitched for the Durham Bulls in the Piedmont League and led the Minors in strikeouts. He fanned 19 Norfolk (VA) Tars on June 19, 17 Portsmouth (VA) Cubs on July 14, 20 Asheville (NC) Tourists on July 23, and 16 Cubs twice more on his way to a total of 295. Other pitchers put up outstanding single-game performances. In 1930 Tommy Bridges of Evansville (IN) in the Three-I League and Dave Danforth of Buffalo in the International League each struck out 20 batters in a game. In 1939 Dixie Howell of Wilkes-Barre (PA) in the Eastern League had a 20-strikeout game against the Binghamton (NY) Triplets. Hitters also shone. Buzz Arlett hit 4 homers in a game for Baltimore twice in 1932, Lou Frierson of Paris (TX) in the West Dixie League hit 5 homers in a game in 1934, and Harry Nolan of Rayne (LA) in the Evangeline League hit 6 homers in a doubleheader in the same year. On August 6, 1930, Gene Rye of the Waco (TX) Cubs hit 3 home runs in the eighth inning of a game against Beaumont, and in 1934 the Buffalo Bisons in the International League hit 5 homers in one inning. In the Eastern League the New Haven Profs beat the Hartford (CT) Senators, 23–22, in 1930, and on Opening Day in 1932 the Albuquerque Dons in the Arizona-Texas League defeated the El Paso Texans, 43–15, even though El Paso scored 11 runs in the first inning. Perhaps the strangest game of the decade occurred on September 6, the last day of the 1930 season, when seven members of the Macon (GA)

Peaches in the South Atlantic Association combined to no-hit the Columbia (SC) Comers in a seven-inning game, the second half of a doubleheader.[32]

Life in the Minor Leagues was a mixture of cool romance and hot, sweaty work, with most of the expressions of romance coming from fans lucky enough to watch games without having to play in them. Thomas Wolfe captured this mood in his posthumously published novel *The Web and the Rock*: "If we go anywhere at this hour of day [three o'clock in the afternoon], it is good to go to the baseball game and smell the grandstand, the old wooden bleachers, the green turf of the playing field, the horsehide of the ball, the gloves, the mits [*sic*], the clean resilience of the ash-wood bats, the smells of men in shirt-sleeves, and the sweating players." Less poetic but just as evocative was this remembrance from journalist Adela Rogers St. John in her biography of her father, famed defense attorney Earl Rogers: "Every Sunday and sometimes Saturdays we tried to go to Chutes Park to see the Los Angeles Angels play baseball. One day someone started the yell that became a tradition in the Pacific Coast League for many, many years. Kill the umpire, we'll get Earl Rogers to defend you. I have to admit Papa loved it. He'd wave his hat and shout back to the fans."[33]

Some ballplayers undoubtedly shared this sunny point of view, but most tied their love of the game to their economic prospects. Charlie Metro, whose long professional career as player, coach, manager, and scout began in 1937, admitted to being "crazy" about baseball "as far back as I can remember." He tried out with the St. Louis Browns organization and came home with a contract for $60 a month, but he did not sign it until Jack Fournier, who ran the camp, agreed to give him $100 in cash so that he could buy his mother a washing machine. In the tough economic times of the 1930s Minor League ballplayers could make do, even with salaries as low as Metro's, but the living was anything but easy. Playing in Easton, Maryland, Metro lived in a boarding house and paid a quarter a night for his room and a quarter for each meal. Ollie Carnegie, an outfielder who turned down several contract offers in the 1920s, changed his mind in 1931 after losing his job in a steel mill and realizing that he could not support his family playing semipro baseball. Claiming to be twenty-seven when he was really four years older, he still went on to set several International League records during a twelve-season career with Buffalo. Many ballplayers used the pages of the *Sporting News* to look for work, including a young man whose advertisement read: "Third baseman, right-handed thrower and batter, 22 years old, six foot tall, 178 pounds, with semi-pro experience in

Rhode Island and Connecticut, wants tryout with club in Organized Baseball." Those who found work still had reason to complain. Bill Atwood, a catcher who earned a promotion to the Orioles in 1935, told what it was like to escape from toiling in the Middle Atlantic League: "It's like getting out of prison to get out of that league. You ride herky-jerky buses all over the country and then play at night under the worst lights in the country. . . . And the fans don't think a lot of beaning you with a pop bottle every now and then."[34]

Al Cohen, an outfielder who played only twenty-nine games in the National League, nevertheless reveled in how much better travel arrangements were in the Majors than in the Minors. In the Eastern League and the South Atlantic Association, he noted in 1932, players traveled in buses or their own automobiles, but in the Majors they went first class, rode in Pullman cars, and ate and stayed in the best hotels. "I'm getting a big kick out of sleeping in lower berths," he admitted, "and signing my name on checks in the dining room now." Cy Block, who played for Macon, agreed that life in the South Atlantic League was hard. "There's no room for sissies in the minors," he said. "You can't afford to get sick or lonesome," he added, and "You can't stand the food and the bus rides unless you're young and strong and have always before you the picture of yourself in a big league uniform." Block recalled one road trip when the Peaches finished a Saturday night game in Spartanburg at midnight and drove all night to arrive in Jacksonville, Florida, at 10:00 a.m. for a Sunday doubleheader beginning at 1:00 p.m. "We sit up all night," he said, "sing songs I can't repeat, drink a million cokes, and when we get out, our fannies are as flat as a phonograph record." Not surprisingly, this rough life sometimes brought players into contact with local law enforcement officials. In 1931 Tony Freitas, pitching for Sacramento in the Pacific Coast League, was arrested a second time for speeding and sentenced to five days in jail. The judge allowed him out after one day to pitch a game and then return to serve the balance of his time. The following year, Cubs farmhand Adolph Wrobel was sentenced to two years in the federal penitentiary in Leavenworth, Kansas, for violating the Dyer Act, a 1919 law making it a crime to transport stolen motor vehicles across state lines in interstate or foreign commerce. In 1934 an eighteen-year-old named Tommy Perry was hitchhiking from Missouri to join the Sioux Falls (SD) club in the Nebraska State League when he was stopped in Des Moines and forced to do two days' labor in the local jail.[35]

Some of this inappropriate behavior made its way onto the playing field. Climax Blethen, a pitcher with the Knoxville Smokies in the Southern Association, reacted to jeering fans by yelling some profanities and tossing a chew of tobacco at them. Fred Shoemaker, of the Oil City (PA) Oilers in the Pennsylvania State Association, spit tobacco juice in the face of an official scorer, and Burleigh Grimes, managing the Grand Rapids Colts in the Michigan State League in 1940, drew a $50 fine and a suspension for squirting tobacco juice in an umpire's face. Players' behavior was sometimes adversely affected when they did not receive their paychecks on time. The Rock Island (IL) Islanders in the Western League disbanded on July 17, 1935, following a players' strike for payment of back salaries. With strict club salary limits in place and individual salaries tumbling, some clubs tried to provide extra compensation by holding "appreciation days" or granting bonuses for participation in postseason play. Judge William Bramham ruled these emoluments illegal early in 1940, but his decision was overturned by a mail ballot of club owners just weeks later. Still, confusion could reign. Later that year all but two players on the Salisbury (MD) Cardinals in the Eastern Shore League refused to show up for a playoff game after learning they would not receive a percentage of postseason revenues. Clubs also grappled with the possibility that they might have to contribute to unemployment compensation funds after Wisconsin classified baseball players as workers eligible for this benefit. In some states clubs argued successfully that players did not qualify for unemployment benefits because their contracts covered them for the entire year even though they played and were paid only during the season. Other states called players seasonal workers who could draw unemployment pay during the off-season. Paul V. McNutt, administrator of the Federal Security Agency, suggested that organized baseball alter its standard contract to avoid further confusion. Clubs could argue that playing baseball was a full-time occupation, but the *Sporting News* pointed out that most Minor League players earned less than $100 a month, not as much as factory workers and "barely a living wage."[36]

While the argument over farm systems and working agreements had raged, the Minors had adjusted the five-tiered league classification system (Classes Double-A, A, B, C, and D) without rancor. Designed to group leagues together based roughly on the aggregate population of the cities in them, the system had remained static since the creation of Class Double-A in 1912. Leagues came and went, and some moved from one classification to another, but the basic structure remained intact. At the top of this hierarchy sat the three Class Double-A leagues: the American Association, the International League, and the Pacific Coast League. Just under them was Class A, populated in 1912 by just two leagues, the Southern Association and the Western League. The Eastern League, a new circuit that began play in 1916 using an old name, moved up from

Class B to Class A in 1919 but went out of business after the 1932 season. The Texas League, eager to ascend to the same status as the Southern Association, rose to Class A in 1921, and the New York–Pennsylvania League did so in 1933. So things remained until after the 1935 season, when the National Association recognized that the Minors were on a growth spurt. In April 1935 promotions director Joseph F. Carr had called baseball "the best 'depression buster' we have." Noting that the number of leagues had increased three years running, from fourteen in 1933 to an anticipated twenty-two in 1935, Carr declared, "You just try to find any other business that has expanded that much during the Depression." The *Sporting News* reported that attendance was very good in most leagues in 1935 and that the next season would see further expansion.[37]

At the National Association's 1935 winter meetings in Dayton, the Minors took note of their vigor. The leagues approved unanimously a proposal to create a sixth level in the classification system, Class A1, lodged between Double-A and A, and to place the Southern Association and the Texas League in it. Class A1 was intended for leagues whose cities had an aggregate population between 1.45 million and 1.75 million, and both these leagues, with teams in growing cities, qualified. The amendment creating Class A1 set a salary limit for clubs of $4,600 and a roster size of seventeen. Two years later the Minors agreed to establish Class E, "reaching out," according to the *Sporting News*, "to take in leagues which otherwise could not operate because [of] the amount of money required and the population necessary." Class E teams would play no less than four games per week with rosters set at thirteen and a monthly salary limit of $750, and officials estimated that as many as ten such leagues would emerge from amateur and semipro groups already playing. Many sandlot players sent inquiries to National Association headquarters in Durham, but only one Class E league organized. Local entrepreneurs in small towns and cities not yet under the umbrella of organized baseball apparently preferred to maintain their autonomy, but the Minors, at the end of the decade, seemed poised for a new era of prosperity.[38]

Branch Rickey's dismissal of Larry MacPhail from his position in Columbus in 1933 in no way diminished the St. Louis executive's enthusiasm for a big and vibrant farm system. Rickey's relationship with MacPhail had been a source of irritation, but it did not cause him to doubt the wisdom of his strategy, and he was quick to find other young administrators with whom he worked more felicitously. The Red Birds replaced MacPhail with George Trautman, a native of Bucyrus, Ohio, a graduate of Ohio State, and a veteran of the Great War.

Trautman had organized the 1926 U.S. Open golf tournament and the 1931 Ryder Cup competition at Scioto Country Club in Columbus. He also was Ohio State's assistant athletic director and the convention publicity director for the Columbus Chamber of Commerce. Even before MacPhail's ouster, Rickey had also been working with Warren Giles, another war veteran who had gotten involved in baseball when he attended a meeting in his hometown of Moline, Illinois, to discuss the city's team in the Three-I League. Giles was so outspoken in that forum that the club elected him president, a position in which he did well enough to move in 1923 to St. Joseph, Missouri, home to a team in the Western League. That's how he met Rickey. The Cardinals optioned Taylor Douthit to St. Joseph, but Rickey neglected to file the appropriate paperwork. When the Pittsburgh Pirates offered Giles $10,000 for the player, he declined, calling Rickey's error an "honest oversight." That good deed earned him a promotion to the Cardinals' Syracuse farm club, which moved in 1928 to Rochester. In the St. Louis office Rickey relied on young Bill DeWitt. At the age of ten, DeWitt was a "soda hustler" both at Cardinal Field and the Browns' home, Sportsman's Park. In 1916 Rickey, working for Browns owner Phil Ball, needed a new office boy, and DeWitt got the job at $3.50 a week. When Rickey moved to the Cardinals, DeWitt went with him. Rickey soon promoted him to a pair of secretarial positions and then, when DeWitt was twenty-three, to treasurer, where his duties included complete financial control of the farm system.[39]

That Minor League club owners did not object to becoming farm teams seemed to escape Commissioner Kenesaw Landis's attention, and in 1938 he took his last shot at Rickey, "that hypocritical preacher" he held responsible for what he still regarded as bad baseball policy. In the years since 1932, when Major League owners had curbed the commissioner's authority to regulate transactions among a Major League club's farm teams, Rickey had constructed an organization so elaborate that it almost defied description. So vast was Rickey's nexus that scholars have disagreed as to its exact extent. Historian Charles Alexander credited St. Louis with a dominant interest in thirty Minor League franchises in 1938, either through outright ownership or working agreements, and control of 732 players. Robert Burk provided some additional details, asserting that the Cardinals' empire grew from seven farm clubs and 203 players in 1928 to twenty-eight clubs in 1937, thirteen owned outright. By 1940, Burk wrote, Rickey's organization encompassed thirty-three clubs and 743 farmhands. G. Edward White put the numbers at fifteen clubs owned outright and seventeen linked by working agreements. Perhaps more important, the Cardinals had at least one team in every Class D league, and they controlled every team in both the Arkansas-Missouri League and the Nebraska State League. All of this roiled Landis, who believed that Rickey had spun a web so fine specifically to circumvent the rules. In the spring of 1938, according to David Pietrusza, Landis was prepared to act on his conviction that the Cardinals were running two farm systems, one legitimately within the rules and the other sub rosa and illegal.[40]

The object of Landis's scrutiny was the Cardinals' relationship with the Cedar Rapids (IA) Raiders in the Western League. Landis and his assistant, Leslie O'Connor, worked on this case for weeks, and in March 1938, while the St. Louis club was training in St. Petersburg, Florida, Landis summoned Rickey, St. Louis owner Sam Breadon, and several players to the commissioner's winter quarters in nearby Belleair for a hearing, during which the conversation became quite heated. In his finding, announced on March 22, Landis determined that while St. Louis was operating its own farm system, more or less in accordance with baseball law, the Cardinals were also funding a second farm system spreading down from Cedar Rapids to a quartet of Class D teams. Money passed from St. Louis through its Rochester farm club and then to Cedar Rapids. "It was obvious," Landis wrote, "that the Cedar Rapids expansion program could have been, and was, undertaken only in reliance upon somebody's underwriting it and those assurances had been given that the necessary funds would be supplied as and when required." This scheme gave the Cardinals control or at least influence over two clubs in the same league, a blatant conflict of interest in Landis's view. It also allowed St. Louis to fudge its way around rules governing roster sizes, salary limits, and per club draft restrictions. Moreover, Landis also found that in 1932 the Cardinals owned the Danville (IL) Veterans in the Three-I League while simultaneously having a working agreement with the Springfield (IL) Senators in the same league. That sort of control, he reasoned, attacked the integrity of the league's pennant race. Since "this is just as important in the Three-I League as it would be in the National or American League," Landis levied fines against Cedar Rapids, Springfield, and the PCL's Sacramento Senators, another Cardinals farm engaged in similar conduct. He also declared seventy-four St. Louis farm hands free agents, but he did not bar the Cardinals from bidding on these players again, nor did he fine either the St. Louis club or Rickey personally. "It is desired to take only the 'remedial and preventative action' inescapably required to terminate this situation," wrote Landis. "It is the Commissioner's hope and belief," he continued, "that this will suffice, without punitive action, to forestall the possibility of these or any other baseball organizations hereafter entering into any arrangement for the control of more than one club in a league."[41]

Minor League club owners reacted to Landis's Cedar Rapids decision decisively. At the National Association's 1939 winter meetings in Cincinnati, held in conjunction with the Majors' winter meetings for the first time since 1923, Minor League officials passed a package of amendments designed to legalize working agreements and to facilitate the movement of players within a Major League club's farm system. In previewing this convention, Edgar G. Brands noted that working agreements, though quite prevalent, were extra-legal, "not covered by any baseball law," and he stressed the significance of the amendment to be introduced by the Northeast Arkansas League that would define working agreements and permit "the right to make selections of unnamed players' contracts from the roster of the selectee club." Some American League club owners, allied with Landis on this issue, threatened to oppose any attempt to extend farming. To that, Rickey thundered, "What would happen if working agreements were disallowed entirely? I know what would happen. We'd go back to about fifteen leagues. That's what would happen to the minors." Nearly unanimously, the National Association approved the amendments. So, too, did the National League, but the American League, led by Senators owner Clark Griffith, turned them down. That left the final decision in the commissioner's hands. He not only voted "No," but he also refused National League president Ford Frick's call to poll each of the sixteen clubs separately. In explaining his vote, Landis fulminated, "That legislation didn't originate in the minors. It originated in the majors."[42]

Although the joint meetings at which Landis reaffirmed his opposition to legalizing working agreements lasted only forty minutes, the repercussions were profound. Many executives agreed with Rickey that the Minor Leagues, absent support from the Majors, might well have to contract to survive. National Association president William Bramham issued a statement suggesting that a series of conferences between the parties could iron things out, but Landis had not yet fired his final salvo. In January 1940 he found the Tigers guilty of much the same offenses. He declared five players on Detroit's Major League roster to be free agents, set eighty-seven Tigers farmhands free, and ordered the club to pay a total of $47,250 to fifteen others. Frick, not even an American League official, was exasperated. "Good or bad," he said, "you can't throw baseball's farm system out the window unless you've got something to take its place." Landis did have a plan. He wrote to each Major League club owner suggesting that they create centralized schools for the development of baseball talent. How this proposal would have saved Minor League teams as independent enterprises was unclear, but it didn't matter. Owners dismissed it, one calling it a step toward "socializing baseball." Just a few weeks later Bramham revealed that there had been 102 working agreements in place in 1939, clubs at each level, from the Majors on down, allying themselves with clubs at every level below. When the National Association held its 1940 winter meetings, the delegates acted again in concert to pass an amendment that would legalize working agreements. The proposal was introduced, amended, adopted, and sent to the Major League meetings the following week. There the wording was changed a bit before being approved by both Major Leagues, a vote that deprived Landis of a say. The amendment became part of baseball's rules when the Minors assented to the changes by mail ballot, and a dispute that had begun nearly two decades before was pretty much settled.[43]

Before Larry MacPhail left Columbus, he was involved in an unsuccessful attempt to buy the Reds, and hardly a year later he got another chance to run the club. Sidney Weil, the principal owner, had borrowed against his stock from Cincinnati's Central Trust Company, whose president, Charles Dupuis, sat on the club's board and exerted a considerable amount of influence on how to run the team. Weil grew weary of this interference, especially as the Reds finished last in 1931, 1932, and 1933. He resigned as president and signed his stock over to the bank. Dupuis also resigned from the club's board, and in their place came two new directors from the bank, Thomas Conroy and David Jones. They joined the club's secretary and treasurer, Joseph Meagher, and attorney Maurice Galvin. Upon Branch Rickey's recommendation, these four turned to MacPhail to be the fifth board member, electing him vice president and general manager and ceding to him complete authority to run the club. MacPhail wasted no time. He asked waivers on the entire roster to gauge other teams' interest in his players, and before spring training commenced in 1934, he completed seven trades. Realizing that true improvement could come only with more capital than the bank might be willing to advance, MacPhail approached Powel Crosley Jr., suggesting that he buy a majority share of the club. Crosley was a millionaire, having interests in automobiles, refrigerators, radios, and broadcasting. MacPhail convinced him to buy preferred stock worth $175,000 and take an option to buy 80 percent of the common stock. Shortly thereafter Crosley exercised part of this option to purchase 51 percent of the common stock. As a symbol of his ascendancy, he renamed Redland Field, calling it Crosley Field.[44]

With Crosley's financial commitment firmly in place, MacPhail set about to overhaul the entire Reds operation. He hired a young man named Frank Lane, whom he had known from his days as a football official, to begin building a farm system. Before the season started, the pair bought outright or devised working agreements with six Minor League clubs, including Toronto in the International League, Topeka (KS) in the Western League, Wilmington (NC) in the Piedmont League, Beckley (WV) in the Middle Atlantic League, Bartlesville (OK) in the Western Association, and Jeannette (PA) in the Pennsylvania State Association. Former Major League infielder Milt Stock joined the club as chief scout and director of tryout camps. MacPhail also spruced up the ballpark, as he had done in Columbus. Construction crews repainted the gray seats green and orange. Ushers and ticket takers wore new bright red uniforms. Painters removed unsightly advertisements on the left- and right-field walls, and the rebuilt scoreboard featured only two ads: big images of Crosley radios, with their dials tuned to WLW, one of the owner's stations. The revamped Reds showed no noticeable improvement on the field, even as MacPhail continued to trade for new players. Firmly convinced that publicity led to tickets sold, he allowed three radio stations to broadcast games, each for a rights fee of $2,000. He also announced that the Reds would become the first Major League team to travel by airplane from one city to another. On June 8, 1934, most of the team—some players refused to fly—boarded two chartered American Airlines Ford Tri-Motors for a flight from Cincinnati to Chicago. Accompanying the team was radio announcer Red Barber, equipped with a shortwave transmitter. He broadcast a report while the plane was in the air, got off with his engineer when the plane stopped in Indianapolis, and drove home.[45]

The Reds had committed to radio early. In 1924 they broadcast their Opening Day game from a booth on the roof of Redland Field, and in 1929 a broadcaster named Bob Burnette sat in this perch and aired approximately forty home games on WLW. A year later Harry Hartman, a colorful local sportscaster, convinced Weil that radio broadcasts during the week would not hurt ticket sales because the audience would be mostly women at home trying to learn the rudiments of the game. Weil allowed him to broadcast all weekday home games and every road game, handled from telegraphic transmissions, on WFBE, excluding only weekend home games to preserve the live gate. Hartman, 5 feet 6 inches and 320 pounds, brought an inventive vocabulary to his work, using words like "Bam!" and "Socko!" to describe hard-hit balls and becoming the first announcer to employ the phrase "Going, going, gone" when a batter hit a home run. Barber, a southerner with little experience broadcasting baseball, joined the Reds in March 1934 at spring training in Tampa. For some time he had been working for the University of Florida's radio station and using his vacation days to travel throughout the South and Midwest looking for full-time employment. When he signed to broadcast Reds games for $25 a week, MacPhail put him on WSAI, the lesser of Crosley's two stations, for seven home games and seventy-two road games, where Barber said "what I did was intentionally arrange for the sounds of the wire service to be in close proximity to the mike." Simultaneously, a third broadcaster, Oatmeal Brown, did some Reds games on WKRC.[46]

The 1934 Reds were worse than the 1933 edition, finishing last for the fourth straight year, forty-two games behind the pennant-winning Cardinals. Forty players appeared in at least one game, but only one regular hit over .300, and only two pitchers won more than ten games. If there was a light at the end of this very dark tunnel, it was twenty-three-year-old Frank McCormick, an outfielder who had borrowed $50 from an uncle to attend a Reds tryout camp in Beckley, West Virginia, and was rushed to the Majors in September after playing only 120 games in the Minors. MacPhail not only lacked patience with his players, but he also quickly grew disenchanted with manager Bob O'Farrell, discharging him in July. For a replacement, MacPhail selected Charlie Dressen, then managing Nashville in the Southern Association, after being impressed with his attention to detail and his personal sense of bravado. At the end of his playing career Dressen had thought about becoming a police officer, but he applied to take over the troubled Nashville club at midseason in 1932 by offering to accept no salary unless the club won more games than it lost with him at the helm. Owner Fay Murray consented to this unusual arrangement, and the Volunteers won thirty-nine games against thirty-eight losses, including a 12–8 win on the season's last day. Hired by MacPhail on July 29, Dressen worked no miracles, but he willingly evaluated the parade of players MacPhail trudged through the clubhouse and found favor particularly with McCormick, second baseman Alex Kampouris, and left-handed pitcher Lee Grissom.[47]

The Reds improved in each of the next two seasons. They finished sixth in 1935 and fifth in 1936, but MacPhail and Dressen did not fare so well. Under pressure from the board of directors, MacPhail resigned in September 1936. Dressen lasted less than a full season more, resigning in early September 1937 after learning that he would not be retained for 1938. Their mediocre record aside, the 1935 Reds made history on May 24, when they became the first Major League team to host a night game, defeating the Philadelphia Phillies, 2–1. Despite the success of night baseball in the Minors, Major League owners had spurned this innovation resolutely. In 1934 the *Sporting News* editorialized that "the pendulum is swinging the other way. . . . Night baseball is now definitely on the way out." MacPhail thought otherwise, and he was perhaps heartened when the same newspaper reversed its editorial stance just six months later. "Times are changing," the weekly admitted, "and baseball must keep step with the transformations." MacPhail made the same argument, but the National League had a rule against night baseball that required unanimity to overturn, and Charles Stoneham, owner of the New York Giants, seemed adamantly opposed. In this stance he allied himself with the commissioner, who told MacPhail at one point, "Young man, you can write this down. Not in my lifetime or yours will you ever see a baseball game played at night in the majors." MacPhail did not capitulate. Fully aware that the Reds had drawn only 206,773 fans in 1934, he prepared a forty-page proposal advocating night baseball and urged his National League colleagues to hear him out. "If we are permitted to play night games next season [1935]," he promised, "and you are dissatisfied, I'll never use the lights again." This pledge he offered despite being prepared to invest $150,000 on lights, all of it borrowed. The league approved MacPhail's plan. The vote was 7–0, with Stoneham abstaining, to allow night ball with several restrictions, including limiting each home team to no more than seven night games per season and, perhaps surprisingly, imposing a ban on any other nighttime activities at a ballpark. This latter restriction caused MacPhail to have second thoughts, but Crosley refused to let him back down.[48]

The inaugural Major League night game came adorned with all the hoopla MacPhail could muster. He awarded the lighting contract to General Electric, and the company installed 632 light bulbs costing $4.75 apiece, each of them 1,500 watts, on eight 130-foot towers. The bulbs produced light three times as bright as the illumination at any Minor League ballpark. Tickets for all seventeen thousand reserved seats for the game, scheduled for Thursday, May 23, sold out a week in advance. On Wednesday the Reds practiced under the lights and were pleasantly surprised by their brightness. The Phillies declined to work out, manager Jimmie Wilson arguing that a night workout would result in stiff muscles the next day. Come Thursday, though, the weather was cold and rainy, and the game was postponed. On Friday most players ate a late lunch at 4:00 and then headed to the ballpark, along with a paid crowd of 20,422, despite a temperature of fifty-eight degrees. MacPhail opened the show with fireworks, including one display of the Reds' logo and another of Old Glory. A marching band then entered the field, and at 8:30, President Franklin Roosevelt, five hundred miles away in the White House, pressed a gold telegraph key to turn on the lights. The *Cincinnati Times-Star* wrote that the effect "was so glamorous, so sudden, so utterly thrilling that a mighty roar arose from the stands as night was converted into day by the tremendous inundation of illumination." More fireworks blasted away, followed by the arrival of color guards and two American Legion marching bands. Ford Frick threw out the ceremonial first pitch, and the game began at 9:00. In its aftermath few participants offered unreserved praise, but sportswriter Tom Swope of the *Cincinnati Post* offered a reasonable perspective. "There were no errors on either side," he wrote, "several sensational bits of fielding dotted the contest, and there was just enough hitting to make for tense situations in almost every inning."[49]

The Reds played seven night games that season, drawing a total of 130,337 fans, helping the club to more than double its 1934 attendance. When the World Series champion Cardinals played one of their two night games in Cincinnati in July, railroads ran special trains into the city, and more than thirty-five thousand people crammed into Crosley Field from Ohio, Kentucky, Indiana, and West Virginia. Those without tickets overwhelmed the box office, and those who bought standing-room tickets wound up twelve deep and shoulder-to-shoulder all around the field, creating just enough mayhem to put a smile on MacPhail's face and more than a few additional dollars in the club's treasury. MacPhail's short-term strategy, though, was to reinvest profits in more promotions and renovations, much to the chagrin of stockholders, who preferred receiving dividends. Several board meetings erupted into shouting matches, with MacPhail daring the directors to do without him, and once, in September 1936, even slugging Crosley. It didn't help, either, that MacPhail's drinking sometimes got him into trouble, including a fistfight with a police officer in an elevator of Cincinnati's Netherland Plaza Hotel. Thus it was hardly a surprise when MacPhail submitted his resignation on September 18, 1936, effective November 1. In his statement MacPhail professed his admiration for Crosley. "There has not been a single instance in this entire time," he said, "when Mr. Crosley has not cheerfully supported every single move that I have attempted to make in the interest of the Cincinnati Baseball Club." The owner responded in kind, saying, "My personal association with Mr. MacPhail has always been most pleasant." Kind words aside, MacPhail was gone, returning to Grand Rapids to help his father and brother run a small-town banking and investment business. He would be out of baseball little more than a year.[50]

Six

"They Could Never Say He Wasn't a 'Real Jew'"

Hank Greenberg towered over his teammates. He stood head and shoulders over most of the other elites of the game too. A photograph taken by Tommy Sande of the AP before the start of the 1937 All-Star Game in Washington's Griffith Stadium shows seven members of the American League team lined up, all of them leaning on their bats. Left to right, they are Lou Gehrig, Joe Cronin, Bill Dickey, Joe DiMaggio, and Charlie Gehringer—five starters in the game to come—plus Jimmie Foxx and Greenberg, reserves. The American flag is fastened to the façade of the upper deck behind them. The grass appears lush. Cronin glances to his left. Dickey holds his catcher's mitt under his right arm. DiMaggio seems ready to walk away. Gehringer rests his left arm on his waist. All seven would one day be inducted into the Baseball Hall of Fame, but the look on the players' faces betrays their indifference to this photo opportunity. Only a few are looking at Sande's camera, and none but Gehrig can manage even a restrained smile. Greenberg is the exception. He faces the camera, peers into its lens, and has a serious look on his face. He alone among the seven is standing up straight, and that is what makes this photograph so startling. Greenberg appears to be nearly a head taller than anyone else in the picture. Foxx stands 6 feet tall and weighs 195 pounds, but the "Beast," as he was called, seems diminished standing next to Greenberg's 6-foot-3, 210-pound frame. And the others in the photo match up no better against their All-Star teammate. Playing first base for the Detroit Tigers, Greenberg was on his way to driving in 184 runs for the season, but on this day he would not even get into the game. Gehrig and Foxx were first basemen too. They played. "All I did," Greenberg wrote in his autobiography, "was sign autographs for a day and a half." Still, before the game he is the one standing erect, strong, and determined.[1]

Greenberg was more than an imposing ballplayer. He was smart, curious, and proud, and in Detroit, where he played most of his Major League career, he was an icon. By the late 1930s, as the United States began to crawl out of the Depression and the country turned to consider the horrific events unfolding in Europe, he was an inspiration. Greenberg was, in fact, the first great Jewish baseball player and, in the judgment of historian Peter Levine, "the greatest American Jewish sports hero of all time." How he lived his life, not only on the ball field but off it, and how he faced down antisemitism in perilous times buttressed the spirits of Jews and non-Jews alike. Children of Jewish immigrants to the United States often antagonized their parents when they took to baseball, and Greenberg was no exception. Moreover, East European Jews were often thought to be too small or frail to participate in sports without fear of injury. But Greenberg's talent and intense dedication overcame his parents' objections, and his physique—he was 6 feet 3 inches tall at age thirteen—crushed any notion that he was too weak for sports. Actor Walter Matthau, who grew up Jewish in New York while Greenberg was playing for the Tigers, remembered, "Hank's arms as looking like steel cables on a bridge." He continued, "When you're running around in the jungle of the ghetto on the Lower East Side, you couldn't help but be exhilarated by the sight of one of our guys looking like a Colossus." Another Jewish fan, who listened on the radio to the Tigers playing the St. Louis Cardinals in the 1934 World Series, remembered Greenberg's heroics in Game One, when he hit a home run off Dizzy Dean. "Because he was a hero," this fan recalled, "I was a little bit of a hero, too." A woman wrote to the *New York Times* after Greenberg's death in 1986 that he "was a beacon to *goyim* [non-Jews], too. I . . . grew up in Catholic Detroit," she continued. "To my classmates' recital of Jewish faults, I had always the last word: 'Yeah? What about Hank Greenberg?' And they could never say he wasn't a 'real Jew.'"[2]

Henry Benjamin Greenberg was born on January 1, 1911, in the Greenwich Village section of New York City. About a year later his family moved to a sixth-floor apartment on Perry Street. Greenberg's parents, David and Sarah, were born in Romania and met in New York. Both were Orthodox Jews who spoke Yiddish and learned English. David Greenberg owned the Acme Textile Shrinking Works, a company that shrunk cloth to be made into suits. This was a successful business, but the Perry Street neighborhood became a tough place to live, especially for Jewish families. Many moved away, and the Greenbergs did too, when Henry was about six or seven, to a sixteen-room house that David built across the street from Crotona Park in the Bronx. Greenberg had learned about baseball at Public School (P.S.) 13 in Greenwich Village, and he began to play in earnest at his new school, P.S. 44. He joined other boys playing baseball and basketball at school and in the park, an athletic paradise full of fields and facilities. Except for the time these boys had to spend in the classroom, playing sports was a morning-until-sundown activity, twelve months a year. "I'd fill my pockets with fruit and candy and stay down at the ballpark all day," Greenberg remembered. "We would break for lunch and sit up in the stands and have a little water with our food and that was good enough." This fascination with sports bothered both Greenberg parents, who wanted their four children to go to college, and it particularly upset David Greenberg, who insisted that dinner be served promptly when he got home from work. "Imagine how I felt," he told the *Sporting News* in 1940, "when we had to wait evening after evening because Hank was across in the park playing ball—and the game was in the seventh inning!" Hank brushed his parents' objections aside. He showed disdain for his father's lawn by building a sliding pit in the backyard, and once he got so tired playing three-on-three basketball for hour after hour that he confessed to his friends, "I'm groggy. I'm groggy." Somebody in the gang misheard this rare admission, and "Bruggy" became his neighborhood nickname.[3]

New York's mass transit system in the 1920s had not grown enough to make travel in the Bronx easy. When Greenberg and his friends went to high school, the best way to get there was to walk, first to Morris High School Annex and then to the new James Monroe High, a forty-minute trip on foot. Greenberg played basketball and soccer and gave football and the shot put a try, but his love was baseball. One of his coaches, Tom Elliffe, was so bent on winning the city baseball championship that he didn't hesitate to augment his roster with non-students, some several years older than his legitimate players. Another coach may have been John F. Condon, also known as "Jafsie"—after his initials—who would become famous for serving as the intermediary between the Charles Lindbergh family and Bruno Richard Hauptmann, later convicted of kidnapping the Lindberghs' baby son. Greenberg graduated in February 1929, intending to enroll at New York University (NYU) and continue playing baseball there. He was distracted, though, by New York Yankees scout Paul Krichell, who had come one day to watch a Monroe pitcher and got a good impression of Greenberg as well. Over the summer Greenberg continued to work on his batting stroke at Crotona Park, swatting line drives to whoever would catch them, but when he thought about joining a group that shagged flies at the Polo Grounds for the New York Giants, someone told him not to bother. The Giants had already scouted him, he learned, and had found him wanting. Greenberg knew he was tall and ungainly. He lumbered around the bases. Even as a Major Leaguer, when he swung at a pitch and missed, he tended to stumble toward the front of the batter's box. Yet despite being rejected by the Giants, Greenberg persevered. He joined a semipro team called the Bay

Parkways, and his slugging for them got his name published as "Hyman Greenberg" in the *New York Times*. Other scouts besides Krichell showed up to watch the Parkways play, and soon Greenberg, still bent on becoming a college student in the fall, found himself virtually sequestered in East Douglas, Massachusetts, playing first base in the semipro Blackstone Valley League.[4]

The scout who hustled Greenberg out of New York City was former pitcher Jean Dubuc, a Vermont native of French-Canadian heritage who had been implicated tangentially in the Black Sox scandal. Dubuc—people pronounced his name as if it were "Gene Dubuque"—had pitched nine seasons in the Majors with the Cincinnati Reds, the Tigers, the Boston Red Sox, and the Giants. After the 1919 season, when Dubuc still showed promise, Giants manager John McGraw released him unexpectedly. Only months later did a possible explanation emerge. Pitcher Rube Benton testified before a grand jury that Dubuc had received a telegram during the World Series urging him to bet on the Reds, underdogs to the Chicago White Sox. Benton speculated that the telegram had come from Sleepy Bill Burns, one of the gamblers allegedly behind the plot to have the White Sox throw the Series and a fellow resident with Dubuc of the Ansonia Hotel in New York. Dubuc admitted receiving the telegram, but he avoided the wrathful justice of Commissioner Kenesaw Landis and finished his career in the Minors. By 1927 he was living in Providence, Rhode Island, where he coached the Brown University baseball and hockey teams while scouting for the Tigers throughout the Northeast. That's how he got to New York to see Greenberg, so impressive that Dubuc wanted to hide him from scouts for other teams. East Douglas was a company town controlled by Walter Schuster, owner of the Schuster Woolen Mills. He owned the baseball club too. Greenberg stayed in a hotel owned by Schuster, ate in a restaurant owned by Schuster, and once, when he decided to go home because he wasn't playing, accepted $175 from Schuster, who urged him to come back the following weekend, which he did.[5]

After the East Douglas season was over, Greenberg returned to New York, expecting to go to college in the fall of 1929, but before classes began, he had to mull over contract offers from four Major League teams. The Washington Senators (for whom Greenberg had worked out during the season) and the Pittsburgh Pirates wanted him, and so did the Tigers. Most surprising, though, was the interest shown by the Yankees. Krichell visited the Greenberg home more than once and took Hank to meet Ed Barrow, the Yankees' general manager. Barrow's gift of free passes to several games helped Greenberg plan his baseball future in an unexpected way. Sitting with Krichell, he got to watch Gehrig up close and realized that the Yankees would not need a first baseman for quite some time. Thus, even though the Yankees outbid the Tigers by $1,000, Greenberg was inclined to sign with Detroit. Dubuc offered him $3,000 cash and another $6,000 to be paid after his freshman year of college. Greenberg discussed the deal with his father, who now understood that baseball was not just a kids' game but a business. He gave his consent, provided that the Tigers amend the contract to pay $6,000 up front and the remaining $3,000 when Greenberg graduated four years later. Dubuc agreed. David Greenberg invested the money for his son in American Tobacco stock, but this was the fall of 1929, and a month later the investment was worthless. Hank started school at NYU, but by the end of his first semester he was ready to play baseball full time. "I've got to play," he told his father. "College can wait." He wrote to Detroit owner Frank Navin and received a railroad ticket to the Tigers' spring training camp in Tampa, Florida.[6]

Greenberg's contract called for him to be placed on a club no lower than Class Double-A, but the Tigers had expected the youngster to complete four years of college before beginning his career. Navin convinced the nineteen-year-old that he would be overmatched at the highest level of Minor League play and would do better at Hartford (CT) in the Class A Eastern League. But even that was too much. Greenberg batted only .214 in 17 games before being sent down to Raleigh, North Carolina, in the Class C Piedmont League. There he learned how to be a professional ballplayer, hitting .314 in 122 games with 19 home runs. He also earned a quick trip to Detroit at the end of the season and got into one game for the Tigers as a pinch hitter. His next season was much the same: a brief stop with Beaumont in the Class A Texas League, followed by demotion to Evansville (IN) in the Class B Three-I League, where he hit .315 with 15 homers and a league-leading 41 doubles. In 1932 he was a Beaumont Exporter for the entire season, the Texas League's All-Star first baseman, and the winner of its Most Valuable Player Award. Texas League teams took some road trips by train. They were not air-conditioned, of course, but still, in Greenberg's memory, train travel "was one step closer to the dream of playing major league ball where all the teams traveled by train." The Exporters finished first in the first half of the season and second in the second half and defeated the Dallas Steers, three games to none, to win the league championship. Greenberg hit .290 and drove in 131 runs. He led the league with 123 runs scored and 39 homers. Winning the league championship put Beaumont in the Dixie Series, a best-of-seven competition against the Chattanooga Lookouts, champions of the Southern Association. Greenberg hit a home run to win Game One, but the Lookouts took the next four. Over the winter Greenberg signed a contract for 1933 at $600 a month, with the expectation that he would play his next season in Detroit.[7]

The team that Hank Greenberg hoped to join had come to life in 1894, when Ban Johnson revived the Western League and put a team in Detroit that newspapers began to call the Tigers. In 1900 Johnson executed his plan to transform the Western League into the American League and considered dropping Detroit. He was not convinced that Detroit was large enough to support Major League baseball, but owner James D. Burns, a Democratic politician, would have none of it. The Tigers survived, but a year later the league president journeyed to Detroit to settle a dispute between Burns and manager George Stallings. Stallings agreed to sell his share of the club and resign, but Johnson wanted Burns out too. He negotiated the sale of the franchise to railroad and insurance executive Samuel Angus, who brought with him his chief bookkeeper, Frank Navin, the man who would make the Tigers champions. Navin was, in the opinion of many observers, tight-fisted ambition personified. Fred Lieb, who knew him well, expressed the minority view, calling Navin "a warm friendly man, exceedingly loyal, who loved life, had a whimsical sense of humor, and was one of the most charitable of club owners." Others were less sympathetic, holding to the opinion, clichéd as it was, that Navin was one of those guys who had "ice water in his veins." Angus was more than willing to let Navin run the club's day-to-day affairs. In fact, when Angus decided to sell the Tigers after only two seasons, Navin found a prospective buyer, Michigan lumber millionaire William C. Yawkey. Then, when Yawkey died suddenly before the deal was done, Navin persuaded the deceased's son, twenty-eight-year-old William H. Yawkey, who reportedly had been left $10 million, to complete the transaction. Yawkey paid Angus $50,000 for the club. Navin jumped from club secretary to secretary-treasurer and received $5,000 in club stock, a 10 percent share, for his deal-making.[8]

Before the 1907 season began, Yawkey lent Navin $20,000 to acquire a half-interest in the club. The Tigers won the first of three straight pennants that year, their attendance jumped more than 70 percent, and Navin cleared about $50,000. He assumed the club presidency, and a decade later, when Yawkey died in 1919 at age forty-three, a victim of the influenza pandemic, Navin bought another sliver of the team, just enough to keep control. The rest of Yawkey's share, now part of his estate, was purchased for $500,000 by John Kelsey and Walter Briggs, both rich from Detroit's burgeoning auto industry. The city's population more than doubled between 1910 and 1920, when, with 993,678 inhabitants, it was the fourth-largest city in the United States, a fact upon which Navin capitalized. He expanded the Tigers' ballpark, Bennett Field, from 8,500 seats to 10,000 in 1908 and added another 3,000 seats two years later. Two years after that he tore the whole place down and started over, spending $500,000 to build Navin Field, a steel-and-concrete ballpark seating 23,000. More than 24,000 fans showed up on Opening Day 1912, foreshadowing that the Tigers' season attendance would no longer loiter among the league's lowest. Yet Detroit's 1909 pennant was its last for a quarter century. The club regularly finished in the first division early in this period, but even a hundred-win season in 1915 did not result in another flag. After the Tigers finished sixth in 1926, Navin hired George Moriarty as manager. He brought the team home in fourth place, but only once in the next five seasons did Detroit finish above the .500 mark. That was in 1932, the year before Greenberg became a regular.[9]

Navin accumulated some of the capital he used to improve Bennett Field and then build Navin Field once the Tigers began playing home games on Sundays and drawing large crowds. Sunday baseball defied more than two centuries of cultural opposition to recreation on the Sabbath and risked the possibility of criminal prosecution since some city officials considered Sunday baseball illegal. Law enforcement officials sometimes arrested players during Sunday games, but some clubs fought back in court. They also began to schedule Sunday games at parks located outside city limits and therefore beyond the reach of municipal ordinances. Once the National League absorbed four clubs from the American Association after the 1891 season, the league amended its rules to allow Sunday games at local option. The first Sunday game in the National League was played on April 17, 1892. State law still prevented games in Massachusetts, Ohio, New York, and Pennsylvania, but the rules by which the National League created its schedule each season had begun to change.[10]

Even before the Western League became the American League, Sunday baseball was a staple of its schedule. Johnson's intention, though, was to move several clubs to larger cities, and when they did so, Sunday games became more difficult. Starting in 1899 and continuing through 1903, the Detroit club had played a small number of games on Sundays, but it had avoided serious legal troubles by using small ballparks outside the city limits, where Burns found sympathetic judicial authority. Bennett Field was more commodious, and in 1907 Yawkey decided to take a chance by playing a Sunday game there. He announced that a game postponed by rain a month earlier would be made up on August 18, a Sunday. "The adjoining property owners are all friends of the club," wrote one newspaper before the game; "the police commissioner has pledged himself not to interfere, the sheriff is Jimmie Burns, a former owner of the club and a good sport, while the prosecuting attorney and the mayor have made no objections." The game went off without incident before the second-largest crowd of the season, some ten thousand. Navin said, "We have conducted one game for the purpose of learning definitely whether or not the public wishes the Sunday game. A glance at the gathering in the stand of itself is sufficient to show that Sunday ball draws a representative crowd." The Tigers could squeeze in only one more Sunday game in 1907, but thereafter Sunday baseball became a regular feature of the Detroit home schedule and an easy way for Navin to boost his club's revenues and build what he hoped would be a championship team.[11]

The promotion of Hank Greenberg, a Jewish American, to Detroit in 1930, albeit briefly, showcased the broad ethnic diversity of baseball rosters in the middle of the twentieth century. Such was not always the case. As historian Frederick Ivor-Campbell pointed out, the men who had transformed baseball from an amateur pursuit to a professional game decades before were primarily Americans of English heritage. Thus it was no surprise that the rosters of National Association clubs in 1871, its inaugural season, were populated with such names as Bass, Birdsall, Brainard, Pratt, and Wright. Although one of the association's best pitchers was Dick McBride, an Irish American, and its best hitter was Levi Meyerle, a German American, most of that season's best players had surnames commonly identified as English. Boston's second baseman, Ross Barnes, for example, finished third in the league in batting average and on-base percentage and led the league in runs scored, while his teammate, pitcher Albert Spalding, led the league in wins and finished second in earned run average and strikeouts. If Spalding is grouped with the four other individuals sometimes (but erroneously in one case) called "fathers" of the game (Daniel Adams, Alexander Cartwright, Henry Chadwick, and Harry Wright), he would be linked with two Englishmen (Chadwick and Wright) and two Americans of English descent. Within a few years, though, baseball's ethnic mix grew more pronounced, mirroring the diversity in the waves of immigrants arriving on America's shores. McBride and Meyerle, two of the game's first stars, were quickly joined by substantial numbers of Irish Americans and German Americans. Many of these early players were the sons of immigrants, and their baseball skills afforded them the chance to rise above the economic status of their parents. Harold Seymour noted that Irish Americans played ball in such numbers that some observers thought they had a special talent for the game, while other fans argued the relative merits of Irish American ballplayers against German Americans. Indeed Lee Allen, who compiled data on the ethnicity of nineteenth-century players, wrote that early teams sometimes split into Irish and German squads to play each other on St. Patrick's Day.[12]

In the National League's first decade about 40 percent of its players were Irish American. As in other occupations, Irish American ballplayers were often stereotyped as prone toward rowdyism and excessive drinking, but some Irish American players were among the young game's very best. King Kelly was so popular that Irish fans gathered in sections of ballparks designated "Kerry Patches" to watch him play. Three early Giants stars were Irish. Pitchers Tim Keefe and Mickey Welch each won more than three hundred games, and first baseman Roger Connor was the leading slugger of his day even though he never hit more than seventeen home runs in a season. The Baltimore Orioles' roster in the 1890s was full of Irish Americans, including Dan Brouthers, Hugh Jennings, Joe Kelley, Willie Keeler, and John McGraw, and their manager was Ned Hanlon. Yet, by the end of the century, the percentage of Irish American players in the Majors had declined to about 20 percent, while German Americans, as a group, were ascendant. They accounted for nearly 30 percent of Major Leaguers during the first two decades of the twentieth century, and many of them became star players, including pitchers Addie Joss, Ed Reulbach, and Rube Waddell; catcher Wally Schang; and shortstop Honus Wagner, long regarded as the best player in National League history. Babe Ruth was the grandson of German immigrants and could converse in German, and Lou Gehrig spoke German with his parents, even in the presence of his wife, who spoke only English. In 1912 outfielder Charlie Stengel made his debut with the Brooklyn Dodgers. He became known as "Casey" because his hometown was Kansas City, but his original nickname, discarded after the outbreak of the Great War, was "Dutch."[13]

German American parents encouraged their sons to play baseball, and so did Italian American parents. "The children [of Italian immigrants]," commented one writer in 1906, "almost immediately become Americans. The boy takes no interest in 'Boccie.' . . . Like any other American boy, he plays marbles, . . . and when there is no policeman about, baseball." So many new Americans changed their names after immigrating that identifying the first Italian American to play Major League baseball is problematic, but cultural historian Lawrence Baldassaro believed that the first such player of note was Ed Abbaticchio, an infielder who broke in with the Philadelphia Phillies in 1897. "Abby" or "Batty," as he was sometimes called, especially in newspapers, was unusual in that he graduated from college as an accountant before deciding to play ball. He had a moderately successful nine-year career, but he hardly initiated a trend. Through the 1920s only twenty other Italian Americans played in the Majors. Most prominent, at least before Tony Lazzeri, who debuted in 1926, were Ping Bodie, born Francesco Stefano Pezzolo, and Babe Pinelli, born Rinaldo Angelo Paolinelli. Bodie got his Anglicized surname from Bodie, California, the town where his parents settled before moving to San Francisco. He hit 30 home runs in the Pacific Coast League in 1910 and was drafted by the White Sox. His outsized personality and wit exceeded his playing ability. Some scholars have suggested that Ring Lardner used Bodie as a model for Jack Keefe, the main character in *You Know Me, Al*, but Lardner himself dismissed this idea. Nor is it certain that Lardner penned the famous line about one of Bodie's failed stolen base attempts: "Ping had larceny in his heart, but his feet were honest." Pinelli shortened his name, as Bodie had changed his, both to fit into the narrow columns of newspaper box scores and to make what were perceived to be difficult foreign names seem less strange and more American. Pinelli was a good-fielding third baseman who hit .306 in 1924 with the Reds and got some consideration for the National League's Most Valuable Player Award. Burdened by a fiery temper, he nevertheless became a Major League umpire after his playing career was over. In the 1956 World Series he was behind the plate during Game Five, when Don Larsen of the Yankees pitched a perfect game.[14]

African Americans played baseball, too. Enslaved men, some of whom reminisced for the Federal Writers' Project in the 1930s, remembered playing ball before the Civil War. In the North, organized clubs of African Americans played baseball games in the 1850s, and just after the war, Black clubs traveled to play intercity games against both Black and white opponents. Yet, when one of the most prominent Black clubs, the Pythian Base Ball Club of Philadelphia, applied for membership in 1867 in the organization governing baseball throughout Pennsylvania, the application was denied. Jim Crow descended on baseball as the game itself shifted from an amateur pastime to a professional business, and individual Black players soon felt the wrath of race-based exclusion. Historian Leslie Heaphy counted over seventy African Americans on the rosters of white professional teams before 1890, including Bud Fowler, who played for more than thirty clubs in several states, and William White, who played one game for the National League's Providence Grays in 1879. Moses Fleetwood Walker signed a professional contract in 1883 with the Toledo Blue Stockings. Toledo joined the American Association in 1884, and Walker caught in 42 of the team's 110 games. His brother Welday played in five games in the outfield. But the tide was already turning. Cap Anson, manager of the National League's Chicago White Stockings (later the Cubs) objected to playing an exhibition game against Walker and the Blue Stockings in 1883, and he objected again in 1887 when Chicago was supposed to play against the Newark Little Giants of the International League with both Walker and George Stovey, also African American, on the roster. Directors of the Minor League ordered the league secretary to "approve of no more contracts with colored men." Walker and Stovey and a few others played a few more seasons, but the International League's decision put a so-called color line firmly in place.[15]

The first Jew to play professional baseball was Lipman Emanuel Pike, born in New York in 1845 to a family of Dutch heritage. He and his older brother Boaz played for amateur teams while they were still very young, and in 1866, as some amateur clubs were starting to compensate players secretly, the Athletic Club of Philadelphia paid Pike $20 a week to play second base. The Athletics' success was built on power, and Pike was part of their arsenal. Once he hit six home runs in a game the Athletics won, 67–25. In 1871 Pike left his third club, the Brooklyn Atlantics, one of the best clubs in the country, to join the National Association's Troy Haymakers as both player and captain, a role equivalent to today's manager. He lasted only four games at the helm, but he remained in the association as a player for all five of its seasons. Pike was a slugger with speed. Nicknamed the "Iron Batter," he was a league leader in home runs, runs batted in, and slugging average. In 1873, while playing for the Baltimore Canaries, he accepted a race against a horse named Clarence and beat the trotter at a hundred yards. The following year he played the outfield and managed the Hartford Dark Blues to a seventh-place finish. Pike moved to the St. Louis Brown Stockings in 1875 and stayed with this club when it moved into the National League in 1876, when he batted .323 with 19 doubles. In 1877 he managed Cincinnati for fourteen games and led the league in home runs with 4. Five other Jews played Major League baseball in the nineteenth century, including Leo Fishel, the first Jewish pitcher, but none had a career close to Pike's. After his death in 1893 the *Sporting News* published not just an obituary but a series of tributes attesting to his greatness as a player, and in

1911 Francis Richter, editor of *Sporting Life*, named Pike to his All-Star team for the decade of the 1870s.[16]

Between 1882 and 1914 more than two million Jewish immigrants arrived in the United States, coming mostly from Russia and other East European countries and settling largely in eastern cities. Many of these newcomers—close to 10 percent of all immigrants to America during this period—came from what Burton A. Boxerman and Benita W. Boxerman call "a premodern world." They wore distinctive clothes, observed the tenets of their religion, spoke Yiddish, and resisted the mainstream culture, adopting it slowly and with difficulty, if at all. These people came to the New World to escape harsh economic conditions, political repression, military conscription, and religious persecution. Afraid but hopeful, they lived in self-contained communities, like New York's Lower East Side, sometimes called ghettos. Their sons, much more willing to assimilate, often turned to sports, but with precious little green space in these neighborhoods, young boys interested in baseball had to improvise, turning streets into diamonds and odd pieces of wood into bats. Comedian George Burns, born Nathan Birnbaum in New York in 1896, remembered how he and his friends struggled to find a place to play: "When we played baseball, we used a broom handle and a rubber ball. A manhole cover was home plate, a fire hydrant was first base, second base was a lamp post, and Mr. Gitletz, who used to bring a kitchen chair down to sit and watch us play, was third base. One time I slid into Mr. Gitletz; he caught the ball and tagged me out." More of an impediment to these youngsters than the physical environment was the attitude expressed by so many of their parents that sports in general and baseball in particular were useless distractions that prevented children from studying and preparing to live successful adult lives. Baseball was good exercise for little boys, parents might concede, but those past a certain age should give it up. Ball playing was dangerous, and those who played it for a living were bums. Edward Israel Iskowitz, who grew up to become the song-and-dance man Eddie Cantor, recalled how parents and grandparents would censure a child by deriding him as "you baseball player, you."[17]

Only a few of these young second-generation New Yorkers ever had enough money to attend a Major League game, and even fewer played professional baseball. In the first decade of the twentieth century only five Jews made the Majors, and in the second decade only eleven did so. These players came mainly from the American South, where assimilation was somewhat easier and ball fields were plentiful. Barney Pelty, a right-handed pitcher nicknamed the "Yiddish curver," was born in Farmington, Missouri, about sixty miles south of St. Louis. His father, a cigar store owner, had left Prussia at the age of seventeen to avoid military service. Pelty won ninety-two games in the American League between 1903 and 1912. Erskine Mayer, also a right-hander, became the first Jewish pitcher to win twenty or more games in a season, a feat he accomplished twice for the Phillies in 1914 and 1915. Mayer was born in Atlanta. His maternal grandmother, a convert to Judaism, traced her ancestry back to the Mayflower. His father, born in Germany, was a concert pianist. With Jews making up about a third of New York's population in the 1920s, both the Giants and the Dodgers craved a Jewish ballplayer good enough to be a star. Giants manager McGraw told the *New York Tribune*, "A home run hitter with a Jewish name in New York would be worth a million." But the Giants' search proved unproductive. Mose Solomon, born on New York's Hester Street in the heart of the Lower East Side, hit well enough in the lower Minor Leagues to be nicknamed the "Rabbi of Swat," but he played only two games for the Giants in 1923. Andy Cohen, born in Baltimore and raised in El Paso, played three seasons at second base in New York, but he was a far cry from the Giants' answer to Babe Ruth, the "Sultan of Swat," as a gate attraction. Outfielder Harry Rosenberg also showed promise by hitting .368 in the Pacific Coast League in 1930, but after the Giants purchased his contract, he played in only nine Major League games, going hitless in five at bats.[18]

On June 27, 1923, Moe Berg, the son of Jewish immigrants from Russia, made his Major League debut for Brooklyn. Berg was a shortstop who had signed a $5,000 contract just the day before. Entering the game in the seventh inning, he got a hit, scored a run, handled five chances flawlessly, and caught a ninth-inning line drive, turning it into a game-ending double play. For the Dodgers Berg represented their best chance to do what McGraw had been attempting—finding a Jewish player good enough to entice fans to buy tickets—but for Berg playing in the Major Leagues was at first nothing more than a summer job. He had just graduated magna cum laude from Princeton, and his intention was to study languages at the Sorbonne. Berg already knew many languages, including Latin, Greek, French, Spanish, Italian, German, and Sanskrit, and he planned eventually to go to law school. So after batting only .186 in forty-nine games for Brooklyn, he left his parents' home in Newark, New Jersey, sailed to Europe, and settled in Paris for the winter. Berg got the education he wanted, but baseball intervened, leading him to complete law school at Columbia over several off-seasons. Demoted to the Minors in 1924, his mediocre offensive skills became the subject of baseball's pithiest scouting report, "Good field, no hit." Yet after he batted .311 in 1925 for the

Reading (PA) Keystones in the International League, the White Sox bought his contract. He remained in the Majors for fourteen more seasons, first as a utility infielder and then, after three Chicago catchers were hurt in the same game, as a catcher, a position he had never played before. "If the worst happens," Berg is alleged to have joked, "kindly deliver the body to Newark." Overcoming this lack of experience, he became a superb defensive catcher, but a knee injury limited any chance at significant offensive improvement. "Berg could speak eight [or ten or twelve] languages," goes a remark sometimes attributed to White Sox pitcher Ted Lyons, "but he could not hit in any of them." Berg was brilliant. His intellectual interests ranged from the classics, history, and literature to politics and science. Yet with Major League rosters full of poorly educated country boys, Berg got on exceedingly well with his teammates. Casey Stengel, a bit eccentric by his own admission, said, "Berg had all that knowledge and used them [*sic*] penetrating words, but he never put on too strong."[19]

After the 1932 season Berg, together with Lyons and outfielder Lefty O'Doul, accepted an invitation to teach baseball to university students in Japan. Organizing this venture was Herb Hunter, a former utility infielder who had taken Hunter's All-Stars, a squad of Major and Minor Leaguers, to Japan in 1920 and returned several times after that. In 1931 he led a team including Mickey Cochrane, Lou Gehrig, Lefty Grove, and O'Doul on a seventeen-game Japanese tour that saw the Americans go undefeated. The Japanese, Hunter reasoned, played baseball with dedication, but they lacked an understanding of the game's subtleties. Hence Berg, Lyons, and O'Doul gave clinics to players in Tokyo's Six-University League, spending five or six days at each school. Berg immersed himself in the Japanese language and culture on his voyage across the Pacific, and after the clinics were finished, he extended his stay, turning it into a round-the-world vacation. He toured sites in Japan and then went to China, Indochina, India, the Middle East, and Europe before returning home in February. Two years later he went to Japan again, this time as a member of an All-Star team featuring Ruth. Berg was no All-Star, but when Red Sox catcher Rick Ferrell turned down the trip, Berg took his place. Ruth, even though he was thirty-nine, was the star of the show, of course, and so at game time on November 29 no one noticed that Berg was not in the American dugout. He had another mission that day. Donning a kimono and slicking his hair back, he visited St. Luke's Hospital, one of the tallest buildings in Tokyo, ostensibly to pay a visit to Elsie Lyons, the American ambassador's daughter, who had just given birth. Berg entered the hospital and took the elevator to Lyons's floor, the fifth. But he didn't stop there. Discarding the flowers that were his supposed gift to the new mother, he jumped back into the elevator, rode it to the top floor, stepped out onto a piazza, and secretly climbed a staircase to the bell tower. Beneath lay a magnificent view of Japan's capital city. Berg reached beneath his kimono, pulled out a Bell and Howell movie camera, and shot twenty-three seconds of film, panning Tokyo's harbor and its military and industrial facilities. Japan, already at diplomatic odds with the United States, was extremely wary of American spies, but Berg, who undertook this risky business entirely on his own, blended into his surroundings so well that no one challenged him.[20]

When Hank Greenberg reported to the Tigers' spring training camp in San Antonio in 1933, he was surprised that manager Bucky Harris, who had replaced George Moriarty in 1929, told him to begin working out at third base. "There's nothing to it," Harris said. "You get out there and practice, and you'll do a great job." Greenberg had never played third, and he expected to make the Tigers' roster at first base. But Harris had persuaded Frank Navin before the 1932 season to spend $75,000 for Harry Davis, a slick-fielding Minor League first baseman, and the club could not give up on that investment. Greenberg struggled at third, and when the season opened, he mostly sat on the bench. Frustrated, he complained to Navin, at first without result, but after a few weeks Davis's bat went cold, and Harris, probably at Navin's insistence, wrote the rookie's name into the starting lineup on April 22. Greenberg hit his first Major League home run on May 6, by which time he had become a regular. The Tigers finished in the second division for the sixth year in a row, but Greenberg had a fine rookie season. He hit .301 in 117 games, with 12 home runs and 87 runs batted in. *Washington Post* sportswriter Shirley Povich lauded Greenberg's power, writing, "When this Greenberg hits a ball on the nose, it stays hit." Detroit's Jewish community embraced the newcomer heartily. Early in the season a group mobilized to give him a celebratory dinner and a Cadillac, but Greenberg declined the honors. As he wrote in his autobiography, "Nobody was rushing to give other rookies a dinner because of their religion. I just felt funny about it, and I always have." From players on other clubs Greenberg endured more than his share of the hazing typically directed at rookies. Some of this was traditionally based on ethnicity, but as Greenberg noted, "I was the only Jewish player who was making a name for himself, and so they reserved a little extra for me." Indeed. Even the player assigned to be his roommate did not take kindly to Greenberg's presence. Jo-Jo White, nicknamed for the way he pronounced the name of his native state, Georgia, continually tried to bait Greenberg into refighting the Civil War, even though Greenberg's family had been in Romania at the time. In one game White was thrown out trying to steal home with Greenberg at bat attempting to drive him in. "The next time you do that," the rookie said, "I'm going to hit you right on the head with the bat."[21]

Having completed one Major League season, Greenberg concluded during the winter that the Tigers should now offer him a Major League contract. Previously he had been paid as a Minor Leaguer, receiving a monthly salary that could have been reduced had he been sent down. Figuring that he was now worth $1,000 a month, he asked Navin for $5,500 for the five-and-a-half-month 1934 season. Navin demurred, offering $4,500, "more than a 25 per cent increase over your contract of last year." Greenberg had no leverage, except the improbable threat to withhold his services entirely, but he did not readily accept Navin's offer. The two argued until late February, when Navin told Greenberg on the telephone that he would "give you a $5,000 major league contract, and if the team finishes 1-2-3, I'll give you a $500 bonus." Detroit hadn't finished as high as third since 1924, but Greenberg accepted the compromise. When new manager Mickey Cochrane guided the Tigers to their first pennant since 1909, Greenberg made his money and in addition pocketed a loser's World Series share of $3,355. Moreover, Greenberg's performance on the field, batting .339 with 26 homers and 139 RBIs, plus his conduct off the field gave the opponents of antisemitism a new weapon in their fight against prejudice. Having grown up in a neighborhood where Jews were omnipresent, Greenberg himself was not terribly aware of antisemitism, but baseball was no different from any other sphere of American activity. Some early Jewish ballplayers had changed their names to avoid discrimination. Various Cohens, for example, according to historian Steven A. Riess, became Bohne, Cooney, Corey, Ewing, and Kane. In 1908 the *Sporting News* incorrectly called Giants rookie Buck Herzog a Jew, identifying him as a favorite of "long-nosed rooters." After sportswriter Hugh Fullerton began to question the integrity of the 1919 World Series, the same publication alleged that "a lot of dirty, long-nosed, thick-lipped, and strong smelling gamblers butted into the World Series." Automobile manufacturer Henry Ford, himself an anti-Semite, used the pages of his newspaper, the *Dearborn Independent*, to publish articles with such titles as "The Jewish Degradation of Baseball" and "Jewish Gamblers Corrupt American Baseball."[22]

In 1926 a Roman Catholic priest, Father Charles Coughlin, had begun to harness the power of radio to spread what became his own brand of antisemitism. Operating from a very small base, a parish in suburban Detroit with only twenty-five families, Coughlin became known as the "radio priest" for his messianic mastery of the still new medium. A skilled orator with a mellifluous voice, he simplified both religion and politics and transfixed his listeners. Coughlin infused his sermons, broadcast at first on Detroit station WJR and later nationwide on CBS, not only with orthodox religion, but also with a neo-populist critique of the Depression. At first he excoriated Herbert Hoover and supported Franklin Roosevelt, but after a while, his preaching against Wall Street and the power of American banks took on an overtly antisemitic cast, and the New Deal became, in his words, the "Jew Deal." Detroit was also the headquarters of the Black Legion, a murderous spinoff from the Ku Klux Klan, whose stated enemies included immigrants, labor activists, Communists, Catholics, African Americans, and Jews. Greenberg and his fans could not help but take notice of these developments in their city. He had already been cast in the *American Hebrew and Jewish Tribune* as "that elusive Jewish star," and on September 10, 1934, the *Detroit Free Press* took note of Rosh Hashanah, the Jewish New Year, with a page 1 headline that read "Happy New Year, Hank" in both English and Yiddish. Whether Greenberg should play baseball on this holy day became a concern for Jews everywhere and a test case for assimilation. Detroit newspapers approached an authority, Rabbi Joseph Thumim, who found references in the Talmud that would allow Greenberg to play. But Hank himself was far from sure. Even after spending the morning of the holy day in prayer at Congregation Shaarey Zedek, he searched his soul in the Tigers' clubhouse before donning his uniform. That he hit a pair of home runs in a 2–1 win over the Red Sox hardly dimmed the controversy. "When I got back to my hotel," he told teammate Marv Owen, "my phone rang half the night. I caught hell from my fellow parishioners, I caught hell from some rabbis, and I don't know what to do." Thus on Yom Kippur (September 18), the Day of Atonement and the most sacred holy day in the Jewish calendar, Greenberg opted not to play. He spent the day at Shaarey Zedek, where his arrival for morning prayers sparked spontaneous applause. That the Tigers had opened a substantial lead over the second-place Yankees in the pennant race hardly mattered. "I was a hero around town," Greenberg remembered, "particularly among Jewish people, and I was very proud of it."[23]

Led by Greenberg, second baseman Charlie Gehringer, and left fielder Goose Goslin—a trio nicknamed "the G Men" after the federal government's agents who spent the 1930s hunting down gangsters—the Tigers rebounded from their World Series defeat to the Cardinals in 1934 to win the pennant again in 1935. This time they were victorious in the Series, defeating the Chicago Cubs, four games to two. Greenberg led the team offensively. He hit .328 with 36 home runs and 170 runs batted in, a performance that brought him the American League's Most Valuable Player Award. Yet he got only six at bats in the World Series before breaking his left wrist in the seventh inning of Game Two, forcing the Tigers to rely on their superior pitching. After X-rays confirmed the preliminary diagnosis, Navin belittled the seriousness of the broken wrist: "Just don't worry about; it'll be all right." Greenberg took offense, but it hardly mattered because a month after the World Series, Navin died of a heart attack. Walter Briggs purchased all his late partner's shares to become the club's sole owner, and after the 1937 season he changed the name of Navin Field to Briggs Stadium. Greenberg thus had to negotiate his contract for 1936 with someone he had never met, and Briggs drove a hard bargain. He offered Greenberg $22,500, a nice raise, but Greenberg asked for $35,000, basing his demand on reports that White Sox outfielder Al Simmons had made $32,000 in 1933. "I was determined to make more money than Simmons," Greenberg recalled, but Briggs did not budge. Arriving at spring training without having signed a contract, Greenberg eventually gave in and signed at $25,000. "I didn't hold out to negotiate," he wrote. "But I had established a point with Mr. Briggs, with whom I felt I was going to have a long and, I hoped, friendly relationship. If I could play ball and have a good season, I knew that eventually I'd make up that extra $5,000 that I might have gotten in a compromise."[24]

Greenberg healed quickly enough to open the 1936 season, but in early May he broke the same wrist again after playing only twelve games and was done for the year. In 1937 he came back and put together what he called his best season. "I say this," he wrote in his autobiography, "because ballplayers appreciate that runs batted in are all that's important to a ball team. . . . And in 1937 I drove in 183 runs." He continued, "I was primarily concerned with and concentrated on driving in runs. I had always had my eyes set on beating Lou Gehrig's American League record. . . . It looked like it was going to stand a long time." By the All-Star break in early July Greenberg had 73 RBIs in sixty-seven games, more than respectable but not quite on Gehrig's pace. An assault on the league record might have been imminent, albeit distantly, but so too was Greenberg's first trip to the All-Star Game, as a reserve. New York Yankees manager Joe McCarthy, responsible for selecting the American League squad, had chosen three first basemen, but his starting lineup, save for pitcher Lefty Gomez, played all nine innings. That meant Gehrig at first base and not Jimmie Foxx or Greenberg. Gomez pitched three scoreless innings, and Gehrig homered, doubled, and drove in 4 runs as the American League won, 8–3. The victory did not placate Greenberg, though, who was angry because he did not get to play. "I took the hot train ride from Detroit to Washington and back," he wrote. "I was really annoyed," and he made American League pitchers pay the price. Greenberg drove in 31 runs the rest of July, 39 in August, 32 in September, and 8 in October, including 6 in one game, but he ended the season one shy of the league mark, and the Tigers wound up in second place.[25]

The idea that baseball's two Major Leagues should play a midseason All-Star Game originated with Arch Ward, sports editor of the *Chicago Tribune*. In 1933, when Chicago celebrated the centennial of its incorporation as a city by opening an international exposition or world's fair called "A Century of Progress," Ward believed that baseball should play a part. The city had hosted the World's Columbian Exposition in 1893, and "A Century of Progress," set to run for one summer but later extended for a second, was at least as grand. Incorporated in 1928 as a nonprofit enterprise and financed entirely by private funds, including a $10 million bond issue authorized on October 28, 1929, "Black Tuesday" during the stock market crash, the fair was a huge success, paying all its debts by the end of 1934 and making a profit. Almost forty-nine million people paid their way into the fairgrounds, 427 acres on Lake Michigan just south of downtown. They saw a wide array of attractions coordinated around a provocative color scheme that gave rise to the nickname "the Rainbow City." There were exhibits and pavilions that celebrated the wonders of foreign countries and the achievements of science and technology; a midway with rides and family entertainment; the Enchanted Island designed for children; the Sky Ride, enclosed cars 218 feet above ground strung between two steel towers; and the risqué allure of Sally Rand, she of the fan dance striptease. Visitors could also see replicas of the cabin of Jean Baptiste Point du Sable, a free black and Chicago's first permanent settler, and Fort Dearborn, built in 1803. After the fair closed, all its buildings were demolished, leaving only floods of memories and Ward's innovative contribution, the All-Star Game.[26]

Ward was a hustler from his first days in the newspaper business. After a short stint writing about sports for the *Dubuque Telegraph-Herald*, he enrolled at Notre Dame and became the school's first sports publicist, charged with promoting the football team and coach Knute Rockne. He moved to a newspaper in Rockford, Illinois, two years later and then to the *Tribune* in 1925. Ward's biographer called him a promoter, not a poet, and such was the case. He preferred editing to writing and publicizing to editing. In 1933 Chicago mayor Edward J. Kelly and officials of the fair wanted a sporting event to attract fans to the city, and Ward conceived of a contest matching the stars of the American League against the stars of the National League. He wanted baseball fans to help select the teams, and he cajoled fifty-five other sports editors around the country into helping with the balloting. In April 1933 Ward approached Will Harridge, Ernest Barnard's successor as American League president, with his idea. Ward suggested that profits for the game be donated to the Association of Professional Baseball Players of America (APBPA), a charity for indigent former players, and he pledged, rather recklessly, that the *Tribune* would cover all expenses in the event of rain. Harridge, normally a very cautious executive, said, "I am all for it." Ward next spoke to Cubs president Bill Veeck Sr., who was also enthusiastic. "That's the greatest idea to come into baseball in my time," Veeck said. American League owners approved the "Game of the Century" at a special meeting on May. They adjusted the league schedule to clear Thursday, July 6, for the game, but National League owners were more circumspect. The Braves and the Giants asked how their players could get to Chicago from Boston, the league's easternmost city, where they were to play a doubleheader on July 5. Cardinals owner Sam Breadon feared that the game and its charitable purpose would set a bad precedent. Ward convinced Breadon that other cities, including St. Louis, might host future games and reap their benefits, and league president John Heydler solved the scheduling dilemma by postponing the New York–Boston doubleheader. After that Ward and the two presidents signed a contract.[27]

On May 25 the *Sporting News* proclaimed, "For the first time in the history of the game an all-star team of each major league will meet on the diamond, with official sanction." But Ward's idea was not exactly new. In 1858, when baseball was still in its infancy, a three-game series at the Fashion Race Course in Queens, New York, matched the best players from several New York—that is, Manhattan—clubs against the best from several Brooklyn clubs. These were the first games for which an admission fee was charged, fifty cents, and the New Yorkers won the series, two games to one. In 1908 a fan wrote a letter to the editor of *Sporting Life*, a weekly newspaper published in Philadelphia, suggesting an All-Star Game of sorts as part of a baseball field day. Three years later, after Cleveland's star pitcher, Addie Joss, died of tubercular meningitis, a team of American League All-Stars played Joss's team, the Naps, in a benefit game that raised nearly $13,000 for his widow. In *Baseball Magazine* editor F. C. Lane campaigned for an All-Star Game as early as 1915, but club owners called this a ridiculous idea that would harm the prestige of the World Series. Ward's accomplishment was making the game happen. Sportswriter George Strickler, who worked for Ward on the *Tribune*, recalled years later that his boss had to badger Emil Fuchs, owner of the Braves, into approving the game. "Either we're going to announce there is a game," argued Ward, "or that we almost had one and didn't because of you." Fuchs capitulated. Richard Crepeau wrote that both Dan Daniel and the *Sporting News* were keen about the game. Daniel asserted that "what baseball needs is more showmanship, more innovations," and Taylor Spink hoped that the game would be "the dawning of a new era of enterprise."[28]

Fans responded enthusiastically, casting half a million ballots to help select two rosters of eighteen players each. Al Simmons of the White Sox, leading the American League in batting, got more votes, 346,291, than any other player in his league. The National League's leading hitter, Chuck Klein of the Phillies, led his league with 342,283 votes. Reaction was positive, too, when the National League announced John McGraw as its manager and the American League selected Connie Mack of the Philadelphia Athletics. McGraw had retired in the middle of the 1932 season, and these two venerable warriors had not faced each other since the 1913 World Series. Fans bought every seat in Comiskey Park plus an extra 2,250 bleacher seats put on sale two days before the game, played under bright blue skies and a hot sun. Each American League player wore his own team's home uniform, but the National League squad was outfitted in special gray uniforms trimmed in navy blue with the words "NATIONAL LEAGUE" across the chest. Both managers played coy by refusing to announce their starting lineups or pitchers ahead of time. McGraw was so secretive, in fact, that his batting order became clear to the fans only as the game progressed. The American League scored the first All-Star Game run in the second inning. Wild Bill Hallahan walked Jimmy Dykes and Joe Cronin, and Lefty Gomez singled Dykes home. Babe Ruth added to his team's lead in the third inning by hitting a two-run homer after Charlie Gehringer walked. The Nationals countered with two runs of their own in the sixth. Lon Warneke, who had replaced Hallahan, opened the inning with a triple that Ruth misplayed in right field, and he scored as Pepper Martin grounded out. Frank Frisch then hit a home run off Alvin Crowder to bring the score to 3–2, but the American League got one run back in the bottom of the sixth. Cronin singled, went to second on a sacrifice, and scored on a single by Earl Averill. The best left-handed pitchers in each league, the Giants' Carl Hubbell and the

Athletics' Lefty Grove, came in to pitch in the seventh, and each held the other team scoreless for the rest of the game. More than forty-nine thousand fans raised $51,000 for charity, and the thirty-eight-year-old Ruth, who snagged a Chick Hafey eighth-inning fly ball that could have been a game-tying home run, was generally adjudged to be the star of the game.[29]

The "Game of the Century" was a success in every way, but it was not until May of the following year that the leagues agreed to stage a second game. Owners at first declined to repeat what had happened in 1933, but Commissioner Kenesaw Landis described the first game as "a grand show" and called for its renewal. Baseball writers in New York waged such a campaign on behalf of their city that grudging approval followed. Moreover, if this second game proved successful, the owners agreed that an All-Star Game would become an annual ritual. Landis argued that the 1934 game should be played in a National League park, and after debate, the Polo Grounds, home of the Giants, won the honors. New York was celebrating what it called the tricentennial of organized sport in the city since lawn bowling had made its debut in lower Manhattan in 1634. If this were not reason enough to stage the game there, the fact that the Polo Grounds was the largest ballpark in the National League also was a factor. This game, too, was a sellout. Fifteen minutes before the first pitch, in fact, the gates closed as more than fifteen thousand fans sought entry in vain while more than forty-eight thousand fans were already safely inside. In the first and second innings these fans saw a display of pitching prowess that has never been equaled in any All-Star Game since. On the mound for the National League was Hubbell, on his way to winning twenty or more games for the second of five straight seasons. Hubbell was known as "King Carl" or "the Meal Ticket," and his best pitch was a screwball, a baffling breaking ball that moved down and away from right-handed batters. Leading off in the first inning, Gehringer singled, and Heinie Manush walked. Hubbell then struck out Ruth, Gehrig, and Foxx in succession. Simmons led off the second, and he, too, struck out, as did Cronin. Bill Dickey then broke the string by singling before Gomez also struck out. Hubbell had not only fanned six of the nine batters in the American League lineup. He had struck out five future members of the Hall of Fame in a row, a dazzling performance. That the American League won the game, 9–7, was almost beside the point.[30]

The 1934 game raised an additional $53,000 for the APBPA, and the publicity the first two contests generated was considered good for the economic health of the sport, especially during the Depression. When 69,812 fans showed up in Cleveland for the 1935 game, the "midsummer classic," as the All-Star

Game eventually came to be called, seemed to have become a fixture on the Major League schedule. Yet there were problems that threatened the game's future. Over the next few seasons, how the game was organized and how it was played underwent considerable tinkering that alienated fans. For the two first games fans had voted for their favorite players, but managers finalized the rosters. In 1935 and going forward from 1938 there was no fan vote at all, and managers picked their teams by themselves. In 1936 fans selected sixteen players per team, and each manager added five others, and in 1937 each manager selected his team upon the advice of his league's seven other managers. Starting in 1939, a new rule required that at least one player from each team be on its league's roster. In 1934 some observers had expected Mack and the Reds' Bill McKechnie, each league's senior manager, to handle the All-Star teams. But the leagues selected Cronin of the Senators and the Giants' Bill Terry because their teams had won pennants in 1933. Henceforth managers from the previous year's World Series handled the All-Star squads the following summer. The size of each team's roster increased steadily: eighteen in 1933, twenty in 1934 and 1935, twenty-one in 1936, twenty-three in 1937 and 1938, and twenty-five starting in 1939. Confusion reigned, too, about whether teams should treat the All-Star Game as an exhibition or play it to win. The press criticized the National League's managers for substituting liberally, but the American League took the game very seriously. In 1934 Mel Harder pitched five innings for the Americans, and in 1935 Gomez pitched six, leading to a rule limiting pitchers to three innings unless a game went into extra innings. The recently retired Ruth attended the 1935 game as a spectator, but in 1936 Boston's fans stayed away from the game at National League Park, perhaps because of the heat or perhaps because the club had massively mishandled the sale of tickets. In the days before the 1937 game speculation arose that this All-Star Game, the fifth in an annual series, might be the last, the novelty of the event having dissipated. But more than thirty-one thousand fans, including President Franklin Roosevelt and his entourage, endured a very hot day in the nation's capital to watch the game. Hank Greenberg's disappointment aside, this game is remembered most for a play in the third inning, when American Leaguer Averill rocketed a line drive off pitcher Dizzy Dean's left foot, breaking his toe. When Dean attempted to come back two weeks later before he was fully healed, he strained his pitching arm and effectively ended his career. The American League won the first three All-Star Games, but the Nationals snapped back to take three of the next five, including the 1940 game, played at last in Breadon's city at Sportsman's Park.[31]

Each of the first nine All-Star Games was broadcast live over at least two and sometimes three radio networks. NBC and CBS covered the first game in Chicago and the 1934 game in New York. The Mutual Broadcasting System began its coverage in 1935. Anticipating the first game, the *Sporting News* heralded CBS's plan, calling it "a most ambitious presentation . . . which will have Pat Flanagan, who has broadcast National League games for five years, and John O'Hara, who has been at the microphone at American League games for six years, giving the listeners all the details of the contest." Indeed an advertisement promoting the game featured photographs of Flanagan in a Cubs uniform and O'Hara in a White Sox uniform along with the encouragement "FANS, SUPPORT THIS BROADCAST BY TUNING IN!" CBS lined up a network of eighty-five stations for the game, "making it one of the biggest spreads ever given by radio for a sporting event." The *Sporting News* noted, too, that the broadcast "is sponsored by the brewers of Prima, described as America's finest beer, and the net proceeds [from the broadcast] will be donated to the fund for a home for old ball players, as will the profits of the game itself." NBC also employed two veteran announcers, Graham McNamee, who had broadcast his final World Series as a play-by-play announcer in 1931, and Hal Totten, who had started broadcasting Cubs games in 1924 and White Sox games a couple of years after that. Before the All-Stars gathered in Comiskey Park, the *Sporting News* acknowledged the ability of Flanagan and O'Hara "to analyze and describe the game," but after the fact, the baseball weekly criticized the announcers, focusing on McNamee and Totten. They "had difficulty naming the teams," said the review, "often confusing the Nationals with the Cubs and the Americans with the Yankees; few of them apparently knew the players well enough by sight to name them when they came to bat and twisted batting orders never were straightened out."[32]

Control of the rights to broadcast the All-Star Game resided with Commissioner Kenesaw Landis. He decided to contract with Prima to sponsor the 1933 game and to give broadcast rights to NBC and CBS in 1934 without charging any fee. The *Sporting News* objected to this largesse, saying, "The game should be sold, and big chains should not be handed this plum gratis," but Landis did the same thing in 1935. The rights to broadcast the World Series, though, he came to see as a commercial opportunity. Networks that carried the Series in the 1920s had done so without sponsorship. As late as 1934 NBC's policy was "not to broadcast commercially any World Series Games." An internal corporate memo argued that "we believe that major events of this nature should be broadcast as a service to our listening audience and should be secured by us as part of the program service that we render to different stations." Landis held this point of view initially, but the rigors of the Depression caused him to change his mind. In 1934 he sold sponsorship of the Series broadcasts to Ford for $100,000, with the players receiving $42,000 and the owners the rest. Ford contracted with both CBS and NBC to carry the games and paid at least some of the networks' costs. Landis and Ford renewed this arrangement in 1935, but the birth of the Mutual network raised Ford's costs prohibitively. The auto company backed away in 1936, and the Series went on the air for three years with no commercial sponsors. The networks were questioning whether they should bid for the rights to the Series directly, but NBC held fast to its earlier commitment. Thus when the commissioner signed a $100,000 agreement with the Gillette Safety Razor Company to broadcast the 1939 Series on Mutual exclusively, both NBC and CBS were taken aback. They pressured their affiliates to carry network programming and not the Mutual broadcasts, but some stations resisted and picked up the Series anyway. This dispute reached the Federal Communications Commission (FCC), already studying the extent of network control. In 1941 the FCC issued new Chain Broadcasting Rules that freed affiliates from network exclusivity when it did not serve the public interest. With nearly one-third of the nation's radios tuned to the World Series, depriving stations of the right to carry what many regarded as an event of national importance was no longer tenable.[33]

Simultaneously the commissioner also exerted control over which announcers would handle the Series. In 1932 he shunted McNamee away from play-by-play duties to a role that would later be called pregame host. At the same time CBS moved Ted Husing into a similar hosting role, but in 1935 Landis banned him entirely for criticizing the Series umpiring the year before as "some of the worst I've ever seen." In a meeting with the broadcasters before the 1935 Series, Landis alluded to Husing, saying, "There is one announcer, you gentlemen know him, who isn't here, and I don't have to go into that." Radio networks were not without some power of their own, though, and they sometimes balked at the commissioner's decrees. After the 1933 Series, for example, an internal NBC communication complained that Landis had expressed a preference for announcers "who were experienced in handling the play-by-play thru the season," but a year later the commissioner vetoed the same network's decision to add Detroit broadcaster Ty Tyson to its crew for the Series between the Tigers and the Cardinals. Landis was miffed that Tyson had predicted a Tigers victory and doubted whether the local announcer could avoid being "too excessively partisan" on a national broadcast. Mutual's debut in 1935 further complicated an already cloudy situation. Landis denied the new network, only three stations strong, permission to broadcast the Series unless Mutual officials could persuade WLW in Cincinnati to desert NBC and join them. John Clark, WLW's general manager, jumped at the chance to do so as long as Mutual agreed to add his announcer, Red Barber, to its team. Thus it was that Barber, after only two seasons announcing Reds games, got his first Series assignment. Memorably, he recalled the broadcasters' meeting with Landis hours before the start of Game One and the commissioner's admonition on how to report the game. "Report what the ballplayers do," Landis said. "Report what the managers do. . . . Report what the umpire does. . . . By report I mean you have the right to say what is going on, . . . but don't voice your own opinions. Don't editorialize. Report."[34]

By 1938 radio and baseball had reached a profitable, if uneasy, accommodation. Besides the All-Star Game and the World Series, thirteen of the sixteen Major League teams were broadcasting their home games on at least one station. Clubs were beginning to reap the benefits of charging rights fees, and stations, counting their advertising dollars, were beginning to weigh the advantages of preempting regular programming and broadcasting ball games instead. Early converts to radio—Cincinnati, Detroit (beginning regular broadcasts in 1927), the two Chicago clubs, and the Indians, who began regular broadcasts on WTAM in 1928—remained steadfast in their embrace of the new medium. Others wavered. Both St. Louis teams, the Cardinals and the Browns, tried radio and then backed away, banning broadcasts from Sportsman's Park in 1934, but they soon came back. The two Boston teams also started early—the Braves in 1925 and the Red Sox in 1927 with sportswriter Fred Hoey at the microphone. Both teams retreated, but by 1936 Hoey was broadcasting home games from both Boston ballparks over the Yankee network, twelve stations strong, throughout New England. In Philadelphia both the Athletics and the Phillies began broadcasting in 1936 with sponsorship from General Mills. Two years later the Pirates and the Senators gave in to pressure from fans and began broadcasting their home games.[35]

The exception to radio's growing acceptance in the baseball community was New York, home to three Major League teams. James R. Walker called Yankees owner Jacob Ruppert the "kingpin of the eastern anti-radio forces," but Charles Stoneham, owner of the Giants, wasn't far behind in loathing the new technology. Except for the odd game, all three clubs eschewed radio entirely. "The idea of spending money to provide a healthful form of outdoor recreation [ball games]," said Ruppert, "and then let everybody in free, of course [via radio], is ridiculous." In truth most Yankees, Giants, and Dodgers fans traveled to the ballpark via mass transit or even on foot, so the clubs had little incentive to promote their games beyond the city's limits. Stoneham even engaged in a legal battle to prevent the transmission of simple play-by-play accounts over wire services both from the Polo Grounds press box and from vantage points outside his ballpark. The Dodgers, inept on the field and in financial and administrative disarray since the death of owner Charles Ebbets in 1925, were more than willing to join their two richer and more successful neighbors in a complete ban of radio broadcasts, a five-year agreement not due to expire until 1939. Enter Larry MacPhail. On January 19, 1938, the Dodgers' directors attempted to resurrect their flailing business and hired him as executive vice president, giving him total authority. MacPhail secured a bank loan to refurbish Ebbets Field, wheedled additional funds from the directors to rebuild the roster, started planning to play games at night, and signed Babe Ruth as a coach and batting practice attraction. Before the start of the 1939 season MacPhail also broke the radio ban. He hired Barber, who had announced Reds games during MacPhail's tenure in Cincinnati; signed a deal with WOR (a 50,000-watt station); and sold broadcast rights to three sponsors, General Mills, Socony-Vacuum, and Procter & Gamble, for a fee of $1,000 per game. The Yankees and Giants were enraged, but they were forced to go along. Each began to broadcast home games only, and they made more money than the Dodgers did. But MacPhail put every Brooklyn game on the radio, beginning with spring training. Even before the Dodgers won the 1941 National League pennant, their first since 1920, MacPhail had cemented the synergy between baseball and radio. Brooklynites knew they could walk down any neighborhood street and hear Barber's gentle drawl describing the action whenever the Dodgers were playing.[36]

Six full seasons before Hank Greenberg became a full-time Major Leaguer, Ty Tyson began broadcasting all Tigers home games on WWJ, the radio station owned by the *Detroit News*. Sitting behind the microphone in the press box, Tyson was a native of Pennsylvania, a former student at Penn State, a veteran of the Great War, and the station's chief announcer. Tyson broadcast Detroit Symphony Orchestra concerts, bridge and tunnel openings, and University of Michigan football. WWJ enhanced its broadcasts with microphones positioned to pick up crowd noise, and Tyson became very popular. Over time he became known for the nicknames he bestowed on Detroit players. Charlie Gehringer was "Mr. Tiger." Pitcher Lynwood Rowe, already called "Schoolboy," became

"Schoolie" or "the guy who's playing hooky today," and Greenberg, never far from his heritage, was "Hankus Pancus." For seven years WWJ carried games without any commercial support as "a public service," Tyson explained, but in 1934 he began and ended each broadcast with the phrase, "Brought to you by Mobil Oil." When the Tigers reached the World Series that year and Commissioner Kenesaw Landis denied Tyson permission to broadcast the games nationally, Tiger fans objected, sending Landis six hundred thousand letters, some of them less than polite, and the commissioner relented, allowing Tyson to call the Series but only on WWJ. The following season, with the Tigers in the Series again, Landis changed his mind, and Tyson handled broadcasting duties for NBC. He did the 1936 Series too, working with Red Barber and Tom Manning, who had lost his job as the Cleveland Indians' regular-season broadcaster a few years before to Jack Graney, the first former player to become a broadcaster.[37]

After Frank Navin's death in 1935, Walter Briggs named his own son, Walter Jr. (called Spike), the club's treasurer, and he added to player-manager Mickey Cochrane's portfolio by making him vice president, a job equivalent to general manager. Cochrane was an "inspirational leader," in Greenberg's words, but he alienated other players when he purchased Al Simmons's contract from the White Sox in December and anointed his old teammate as a starting outfielder in place of Pete Fox, who had hit .385 in the World Series against the Cubs. Briggs expected much from Cochrane and his lineup, even though the Yankees, who had finished second in 1934 and 1935 and would win the pennant in 1936 and 1937, provided formidable competition. Cochrane suffered a nervous breakdown in June 1936, and coach Del Baker replaced him for several weeks. On May 25, 1937, the Tigers were in New York to face the Yankees. Cochrane hit a home run in the third inning, but in the fifth a breaking ball from pitcher Bump Hadley struck him in the head, and he collapsed. "I saw the ball roll in front of the plate and then Mickey fell on it, rolled over and cried, 'God Almighty!'" said Yankees catcher Bill Dickey. The pitch had fractured his skull in three places. Taken to St. Elizabeth's Hospital, Cochrane was in critical condition for several days. The *Sporting News* said he "lay between life and death," and doctors from the Mayo Clinic arrived to attend him. Nearly unconscious for ten days, Cochrane left St. Elizabeth's and moved to Henry Ford Hospital in Detroit, where he spent another six weeks as Baker guided the team again. In July Cochrane returned to the bench as manager, but he never played again. The Tigers finished second for the second year in a row, but they were thirteen games behind the Yankees.[38]

After the 1937 season Briggs increased the seating capacity of his ballpark to more than fifty-four thousand. Navin's last plan for expansion, unrealized at his death, would have provided for thirty-six thousand seats, but Briggs wanted even more. The Tigers had led the league in attendance in three of the previous four seasons, and Briggs sensed that his team's recent success would justify additional capacity. He extended the double-deck configuration, previously limited to the grandstand between the bases, all the way down both baselines and into the outfield. There was room for new seats in left field because Cherry Street, beyond the left field wall, had been rerouted earlier to build bleachers. Right field posed a tougher challenge. Trumbull Avenue, a major thoroughfare, could not be altered, but Briggs did not want to reduce the distance from home plate to the right-field fence too severely. The solution was a compromise. Right field was shortened from 367 to 325 feet, and the new upper deck was built overhanging the lower by 10 feet. Batters thus had a "home run porch" at which to aim. Detroit, a city once deemed too small to host Major League baseball, now boasted the second largest park in the Majors, behind only Yankee Stadium. Briggs's faith in his fans was rewarded. Attendance remained strong and would reach more than 1.1 million in 1940. On the field, though, the 1938 Tigers stumbled, and Briggs began to second-guess Cochrane, often telephoning him to berate his handling of the pitching staff. In early August, with the team stuck in fifth place, Briggs blamed Cochrane for two horrible losses to the Red Sox and fired him. Baker replaced Cochrane and pulled the club up to fourth place, but still sixteen games behind New York.[38]

By the time Cochrane was dismissed, Greenberg had already hit 37 home runs, a total that put him within reach of 60, Babe Ruth's single-season record. Greenberg felt the pressure early, starting perhaps when he hit four consecutive home runs in a doubleheader right after the All-Star break. He wrote, "In the latter half of the season, most of the publicity that Detroit got and, for that matter, most of the league publicity, centered on whether I could break Babe Ruth's record." In addition, "There was added pressure being Jewish. . . . I was representing a couple of million Jews among a hundred million gentiles, and I was always in the spotlight." Taking notice of the world situation, he added, "Of course, as time went by, I came to feel that if I, as a Jew, hit a home run, I was hitting one against Hitler." With five games to play, Greenberg's home run total stood at 58. Yet in two games against the Browns and three against the Indians, he failed to drive even one ball over the fence. "Some people still have it fixed in their minds," he wrote years later, "that the reason

I didn't break Ruth's record was because I was Jewish, that the ballplayers did everything they could to stop me. That's pure baloney. The fact is quite the opposite. So far as I could tell, the players were mostly rooting *for* me, aside from the pitchers." But he came up short. In 1939 Greenberg hit 33 home runs with 112 runs batted in, and in 1940 he won his second Most Valuable Player Award by leading the Tigers to the pennant. Against his will Greenberg moved that year to left field to allow Rudy York, another slugger, to play first base. Neither played defense more than adequately, but their offense more than compensated for any deficiencies in the field. Greenberg hit .340 with 41 homers and 150 RBIs, while York batted .316 with 33 home runs and 134 RBIs. The Yankees, uncharacteristically, started very slowly, dropping into last place in May, and despite a rush down the stretch, they could climb only to third place.[40]

The 1940 World Series matched the favored Tigers against the Reds, whom the Yankees had swept the season before. The two teams waged a seesaw battle, alternating wins until the Reds broke the pattern by pushing across two runs in the seventh inning of Game Seven on two doubles, a sacrifice bunt, and a sacrifice fly to win, 2–1. Greenberg did his part throughout, batting .357 and driving in 6 runs, but neither of his two singles in the final game helped produce a run. After the Series he faced a more serious problem. World War II had begun in Europe more than a year before. Germany had taken the Low Countries and France in the spring and appeared ready to invade England. In September Congress had passed and President Franklin Roosevelt had signed into law a bill authorizing the first peacetime draft in American history. Where each man registered for the draft did not matter, but the place he declared as his residence did. Anxious to avoid publicity, Greenberg registered in a small town in western New York, but he listed Detroit's Leland Hotel as his address. Come February 1941, he learned that the local draft board in downtown Detroit would have trouble meeting its quota and that he would, in a couple of months, be drafted. But the United States was not yet at war, and the draft commitment was for only one year. After being inducted, Greenberg joined the Fifth Division, Second Infantry Anti-Tank Company, at Fort Custer, Michigan, intent on doing his duty. In August Congress passed an amendment to the Selective Training and Service Act, exempting men over twenty-eight from the draft. Since Greenberg was thirty, he anticipated an early discharge, but his orders did not come through until December 5, and two days later the Japanese attacked Pearl Harbor. Greenberg had done his duty. He could have returned to his parents' home in New York with a clear conscience and let younger men do the fighting. But he did not. He left New York for Washington and enlisted in the Army Air Corps. "This doubtless means I am finished with baseball," he told the *Sporting News*, "and it would be silly for me to say I do not leave it without a pang. But all of us are confronted with a terrible task—the defense of our country and the fight for our lives."[41]

1. Ernest Barnard succeeded Ban Johnson as president of the American League and served until his death in March 1931. George Grantham Bain Collection, Library of Congress, Prints and Photographs Division, LC-DIG-ggbain-31078.

2. (*above*) Ban Johnson, founder and president of the American League, posed in his Chicago office as he resigned his position as league president in October 1927. AP/Shutterstock.

3. (*opposite top*) In its October 7, 1920, issue the *Sporting News* identified the eight Chicago White Sox players implicated in the conspiracy to fix the 1919 World Series: Hap Felsch, Chick Gandil, Joe Jackson, Eddie Cicotte, Claude Williams, Fred McMullin, Swede Risberg, and Buck Weaver. Wikimedia Commons.

4. Philadelphia Athletics catcher Mickey Cochrane tagged out Philadelphia Phillies third baseman Pinky Whitney in a close play during an exhibition game on April 1, 1933. The umpire was local John Quinn, two years before he began umpiring in the Major Leagues. National Baseball Hall of Fame and Museum.

FIX THESE FACES IN YOUR MEMORY

"CHICK" GANDIL

"HAP" FELSCH

JOE JACKSON

ALL PHOTOS © BY UNDERWOOD & UNDERWOOD

EDDIE CICOTTE

CLAUDE WILLIAMS

FRED McMULLIN

"SWEDE" RISBERG

"BUCK" WEAVER

EIGHT MEN CHARGED WITH SELLING OUT BASEBALL

5. Graham McNamee, shown here sitting in the stands and holding a microphone in his hands, broadcast his first World Series for Westinghouse in 1923. He broadcast twelve Series in all, his last in 1934 for NBC. National Baseball Hall of Fame and Museum.

6. Connie Mack, manager and co-owner of the Philadelphia Athletics, posed with two of his star players, catcher Mickey Cochrane (*left*) and pitcher Lefty Grove (*right*), just before the 1931 World Series. AP Photo.

7. *(above)* St. Louis Cardinals owner Sam Breadon, second baseman Rogers Hornsby, and business manager–field manager Branch Rickey worked together until the Cardinals traded Hornsby to the New York Giants after St. Louis won the 1926 World Series. National Baseball Hall of Fame and Museum.

8. *(opposite top)* Pepper Martin of the St. Louis Cardinals crossed the plate after hitting a two-run home run in the sixth inning of Game Five of the 1931 World Series. Martin drove in Frank Frisch, who had doubled, and gave the Cardinals a 3–0 lead over the Philadelphia Athletics. National Baseball Hall of Fame and Museum.

9. Born in 1910 in Arkansas, Jay Hanna Dean earned the nickname "Dizzy" while playing baseball in the army. He joined the Cardinals briefly in 1930 and won 134 games over seven seasons in St. Louis, leading the club to a World Series win in 1934. National Baseball Hall of Fame and Museum.

10. (*above*) Kenesaw Mountain Landis relinquished his position as a federal district court judge in Chicago to become the first commissioner of baseball in November 1920. An ardent fan, he gained a reputation for unflinching rectitude when he permanently banned eight members of the Chicago White Sox accused of involvement in the plot to throw the 1919 World Series. National Baseball Hall of Fame and Museum.

11. Babe Ruth joined the Yankees in 1920, having been sold to New York by the Boston Red Sox. Converted from a pitcher to an outfielder, Ruth played fifteen seasons for the Yankees, hitting 659 home runs and leading the club to seven American League pennants and four World Series championships. National Baseball Hall of Fame and Museum.

12. William G. Bramham, a North Carolina attorney and politician, was elected president of the National Association of Professional Baseball Leagues (the Minor Leagues) in 1932. He led the Minors through the Depression by imposing rules that forced club owners to demonstrate integrity and financial stability. He inscribed this photo to Minor League executive Elmer M. Daily. National Baseball Hall of Fame and Museum.

13. Slugger Babe Ruth (*left*), who often battled over his salary with the New York Yankees, here signing one of his contracts under the watchful gaze of general manager Ed Barrow (*standing*) and club owner Jacob Ruppert. National Baseball Hall of Fame and Museum.

14. After learning how to play baseball on the sandlots of San Francisco, Joe DiMaggio joined the San Francisco Seals in the Pacific Coast League late in the 1932 season as a shortstop. He moved to the outfield the next year and played three more seasons with the Seals before moving to the New York Yankees in 1936. National Baseball Hall of Fame and Museum.

15. On June 13, 1949, Stephen C. Clark, president of the National Baseball Hall of Fame and Museum, wielded the shovel during the groundbreaking ceremony to mark the start of construction of a museum addition. Bob Quinn, director of the Hall of Fame, stood on Clark's left. National League president Ford Frick and Ernie Lanigan, the Hall's curator, were on his left. National Baseball Hall of Fame and Museum.

16. Larry MacPhail began his baseball career in 1930 when he took an option to buy the Columbus club in the American Association and brokered its sale to the St. Louis Cardinals. He became the Red Birds' president and later moved to executive positions with the Cincinnati Reds in 1933, the Brooklyn Dodgers in 1938, and the New York Yankees in 1945. National Baseball Hall of Fame and Museum.

17. Frank Shaughnessy, a native of Montreal, played a few games in the Majors, but he made his mark as president of the International League from 1936 to 1960. He was an innovative thinker credited with proposing a postseason playoff system that helped to maintain fan interest late in the Minor League season and changed how leagues determined their champions. National Baseball Hall of Fame and Museum.

18. Five days before the first All-Star Game on July 6, 1933, National League manager John McGraw and American League manager Connie Mack announced that their starting pitchers would be each league's best left-hander, Carl Hubbell of the New York Giants (*left*) and Lefty Grove of the Philadelphia Athletics (*right*). Both managers, though, changed their minds. Hubbell pitched the last two innings for the Nationals, who wore special uniforms for the game, and Grove pitched the final three for the Americans. National Baseball Hall of Fame and Museum.

19. American League stars (*left to right*) Lou Gehrig, Joe Cronin, Bill Dickey, Joe DiMaggio, Charlie Gehringer, Jimmie Foxx, and Hank Greenberg posed before the start of the 1937 All-Star Game at Griffith Stadium in Washington DC. Photo by Tommy Sande. AP Photo.

20. Hank Greenberg broke into the Major Leagues with Detroit in 1933 and led the Tigers to the World Series in 1934. He led the league in runs batted in four times and home runs twice, and he was named the American League's Most Valuable Player in 1935 and 1940. In 1939, when this photograph was taken, Greenberg batted .312 with 33 homers and 112 RBIs. National Baseball Hall of Fame and Museum.

21. (*opposite top*) Following a call from his local draft board, Detroit Tigers star Hank Greenberg reported for induction into the army on May 7, 1941, and served until being discharged on December 5. Two days later the Japanese attacked Pearl Harbor, and Greenberg enlisted in the Army Air Corps. He missed three and a half seasons before returning to the Majors in July 1945. National Baseball Hall of Fame and Museum.

22. After Ted Williams received criticism for his 3-A Selective Service classification, a deferment based on his being his mother's sole support, the Boston outfielder decided to enlist in the navy. He went to a local induction center on May 22, 1942, where Lt. F. T. Donahue swore him in. National Baseball Hall of Fame and Museum.

23. (*above*) Yankees outfielder Joe DiMaggio enlisted in the army on February 17, 1943. Like many other Major League players, he did not see combat but instead played on service baseball teams intended to boost morale. In January 1945 he was assigned to Camp Kilmer, New Jersey, where he assisted in the development of the sports program by autographing baseballs for wounded soldiers and giving hitting and fielding lessons. National Baseball Hall of Fame and Museum.

24. St. Louis Browns owner Donald Barnes (*left*) kissed the ball that first baseman George McQuinn (*right*) snared to record the last out in the game that secured the American League pennant in 1944. The game was on October 1, 1944. From the Collections of the St. Louis Mercantile Library at the University of Missouri-St. Louis.

LEAGUE CHAMPIONS
BROWNS

25. (*above*) Before joining the navy, young Yogi Berra played the 1943 season for the Norfolk (VA) Tars in the Piedmont League. Berra batted .253 and hit 7 home runs in 111 games. AP Photo/Virginian-Pilot.

26. (*opposite top*) The St. Louis Browns' Don Gutteridge (*left*) began the 1945 exhibition season leading off in a game on March 21 at the team's wartime spring training camp in Cape Girardeau, Missouri. The catcher was Minor Leaguer Bob Comyn (*center*), and the umpire was Bill Grieve (*right*). From the Collections of the St. Louis Mercantile Library at the University of Missouri-St. Louis.

27. Two teams from the All-American Girls Professional Baseball League show their support for the war effort by forming a V for Victory before a game at Beyer Stadium in Rockford, Illinois. National Baseball Hall of Fame and Museum.

28. (*opposite top*) Following Happy Chandler's election, the new commissioner (*second from left*) posed with (*left to right*) Horace Stoneham, Larry MacPhail, and Branch Rickey. Special Collections and Archives, University of Kentucky.

29. Tom Yawkey (*seated, center*) bought control of the Boston Red Sox in February 1933. Seated next to Yawkey were former owner Bob Quinn (*left*) and American League president Will Harridge. Standing were Fred DeFoe (*left*), Yawkey's attorney and club secretary, and Eddie Collins, minority owner and the club's vice president and general manager. National Baseball Hall of Fame and Museum.

30. (*above*) Robert Murphy, head of the American Baseball Guild, and attorney Joseph Doherty examined a proposed contract that would have recognized the guild as a union representing Major League players, before a meeting with Pittsburgh Pirates executives on June 5, 1946. AP Photo.

31. Jorge Pasquel (*center*), president of the Mexican League, took over as manager of the Vera Cruz team on July 3, 1946. Here Pasquel is holding former manager Mickey Owen's son Charley. Former New York Giants player Danny Gardella (*left*) signed a lucrative contract with Pasquel but returned to the United States after one season. AP Photo.

32. Outfielder Danny Gardella played 168 games for the New York Giants in 1944 and 1945. Unhappy with the contract the Giants offered him for 1946, he contacted Jorge Pasquel, president of the Mexican League, who offered him a contract to play for Vera Cruz, giving him $5,000 to sign, an $8,000 salary, and an option for two more seasons. Disillusioned with living and playing conditions in Mexico, Gardella returned to the United States after the season but played in only one more Major League game. National Baseball Hall of Fame and Museum.

33. (*above*) Commissioner Happy Chandler (*left*), elected in 1945 but removed from office in 1951, had a special fondness for Philadelphia Athletics owner Connie Mack, known affectionately as the "Grand Old Man of Baseball." Special Collections and Archives, University of Kentucky.

34. (*opposite top*) From the time Bill Veeck started working for the Chicago Cubs in 1933 through his tenures as principal owner of the Minor League Milwaukee Brewers and three Major League teams (the Cleveland Indians, the St. Louis Browns, and the Chicago White Sox), he was a hands-on owner, speaking to fans' groups, selling tickets, engineering promotions, and, when needed, watering the grass, as shown here, at Milwaukee's Borchert Field in 1943. National Baseball Hall of Fame and Museum.

35. An outfielder from the University of Michigan, Dick Wakefield became known as the first bonus baby after he signed a contract with the Detroit Tigers in 1941 for a $51,000 bonus plus a new automobile for his mother. He played parts of nine seasons in the Majors and batted .293. National Baseball Hall of Fame and Museum.

36. Red Barber, a Mississippi native, began his baseball broadcasting career in Cincinnati in 1934. He moved to Brooklyn to handle Dodgers broadcasts in 1939 and, after feuding with Dodgers owner Walter O'Malley after the 1953 season, switched to the New York Yankees. National Baseball Hall of Fame and Museum.

37. Emanuel Celler served in the U.S. House of Representatives from 1923 to 1973 and was chairman of the House Judiciary Committee beginning in 1949. In 1951 Celler's subcommittee on study of monopoly power held hearings to examine the antitrust exclusion granted to organized baseball by the Supreme Court's 1922 decision in *Federal Baseball Club of Baltimore v. National League of Professional Baseball Clubs* (1922). New York World-Telegram and the Sun Newspaper Photograph Collection, Library of Congress, Prints and Photographs Division, LC-USZ62-127299.

38. (*opposite top*) Ford Frick left sports journalism in 1934, going to work as the head of the National League Service Bureau, the league's publicity office. He became league president later that same year and was elected baseball's third commissioner in 1951. National Baseball Hall of Fame and Museum.

39. Raised in Commerce, Oklahoma, Mickey Mantle played shortstop growing up but made his Major League debut as an outfielder for the New York Yankees on April 17, 1951. Anointed as the successor to Joe DiMaggio, Mantle was a powerful switch hitter who played eighteen seasons, hit 536 home runs, and won the American League Triple Crown in 1956. National Baseball Hall of Fame and Museum.

40. (*above*) Paul Jonas, director of sports at the Mutual Broadcasting System; Frank White, Mutual's president; Gordon McLendon, president of the Liberty Broadcasting System; and Lester May, Liberty's attorney (*left to right*) stood outside a December 4, 1950, meeting in which Minor League executives discussed the adverse effects of radio and television broadcasting on Minor League attendance. AP Photo.

41. (*opposite top*) St Louis Browns owner Bill Veeck met with Mayor Raymond R. Tucker on July 10, 1953, to discuss the club's future in St. Louis. Veeck was noncommittal, saying that he did not know if the Browns would leave or stay. From the Collections of the St. Louis Mercantile Library at the University of Missouri-St. Louis.

42. Dodgers owner Walter O'Malley (*left*) greeted Giants owner Horace Stoneham as National League president Warren Giles looked on. National Baseball Hall of Fame and Museum.

43. (*above*) When Henry Aaron left the Mobile, Alabama, neighborhood called Toulminville in 1952 to play with the Negro American League champion Indianapolis Clowns, he was an eighteen-year-old infielder who weighed 150 pounds. Two years later he made his Major League debut as an outfielder with the Braves, playing their second season in Milwaukee after having left Boston. National Baseball Hall of Fame and Museum.

44. (*opposite top*) After Horace Stoneham (*left*) moved the Giants from New York to San Francisco, he hired Jerry Donovan to be the club's business manager. Donovan was a former Pacific Coast League player who had worked for the San Francisco Seals, and he proved to be an important link between the Giants and the local community. National Baseball Hall of Fame and Museum.

45. National League club representatives met on March 18, 1953, in St. Petersburg, Florida, to vote on the proposed move of the Boston Braves to Milwaukee. *From left, standing*: James Gallagher of the Chicago Cubs, Horace Stoneham of the New York Giants, Bob Carpenter of the Philadelphia Phillies, Gabe Paul of the Cincinnati Reds, Louis Perini of the Braves, John Wilson of the St. Louis Cardinals, Walter O'Malley of the Brooklyn Dodgers, and Branch Rickey of the Pittsburgh Pirates. Seated (*left to right*) were National League president Warren Giles and Fred Fleig, the league's assistant secretary–treasurer. AP Photo/Preston Stroup.

46. (*above*) National League president Warren Giles, commissioner Ford Frick, and American League president Joe Cronin (*left to right*) smiled when they greeted each other at an off-season banquet. National Baseball Hall of Fame and Museum.

47. The men who secured a National League expansion club for Houston and named their team the Colt .45s were (*left to right*) R. E. Smith, Roy Hofheinz, George Kirksey, Craig Cullinan Jr., and Paul Richards, the team's first general manager. University of Houston Special Collections.

48. Attorney Bill Shea, chair of New York City mayor Robert Wagner's committee to bring National League baseball back to New York, talked to newsmen on July 27, 1959, about the formation of a third Major League to be called the Continental League, a venture that would include clubs in Denver, Houston, Minneapolis–St. Paul, New York, and Toronto. Seated next to Shea (*left to right*) were prospective club owners Craig Cullinan Jr. of Houston and Jack Kent Cooke of Toronto. AP Photo.

49. Calvin Griffith assumed control of the Washington Senators in 1955 and almost immediately began to consider offers to move the club elsewhere. The threat posed by the proposed Continental League forced the American League to consider expansion, and following the 1960 season the Senators moved to Minneapolis and became the Minnesota Twins. National Baseball Hall of Fame and Museum.

Seven

"It Would Be Best for the Country to Keep Baseball Going"

No one looked forward to the winter meetings of American League club owners in December 1941 more than Don Barnes. He and Bill DeWitt had led a group that purchased the St. Louis Browns in November 1936, but five seasons of woeful baseball coupled with prolonged economic hardship were enough to open the door to radical action. Barnes had a plan. He wanted to move his club to Los Angeles, transferring a Major League team for the first time since December 1902, when another American League franchise had moved from Baltimore to New York. Barnes crafted his proposal well. He persuaded the St. Louis Cardinals to pay him $350,000 to leave town. He also negotiated a deal with Chicago Cubs owner Phil Wrigley to displace Chicago's farm team in the Pacific Coast League, the Los Angeles Angels, and locate the Browns in the Angels' home, the West Coast version of Wrigley Field. DeWitt worked secretly with "the guy who wrote the American League schedules for fifty years, an old man who was in charge of the safe-deposit department of a bank in Boston," to draft a sample schedule that would have every other team make two trips to Los Angeles each season. In advance of the December meeting Barnes, a round-faced man who wore his hair slicked back without a part, talked confidentially to league president Will Harridge and spoke informally to his fellow owners. Perhaps the only trouble with Barnes's idea was its unfortunate timing. DeWitt recalled how he spent the Sunday before the league meeting opened at the Palmer House in Chicago: "We were in Comiskey Park watching the Bears and the Cardinals play football that day, and it was as cold as the devil. Somebody came in and said, 'Gee, they just had a flash on the radio that the Japs [*sic*] have bombed Pearl Harbor.' Me, I didn't know where the hell Pearl Harbor was; I never heard of Pearl Harbor." The meeting opened two days later, Tuesday, December 9, one day after President Franklin Roosevelt asked Congress for a declaration of war. Barnes made his presentation, but the Japanese attack and the fear it engendered made his argument moot. The owners defeated the Barnes plan unanimously. Even he voted against it.[1]

The financial challenge the Browns posed for Donald Lee Barnes dated back more than a decade. In April 1917, when Branch Rickey moved from the employ of Browns owner Phil Ball to begin working for the Cardinals, he left behind a second-division team with only one star on its roster. The 1922 Browns won ninety-three games and finished second, just one game behind the New York Yankees, but the club never won that many games again, and the black ink on its balance sheet soon turned to red. In 1933 St. Louis finished last, attracting only 88,113 fans. Ball lost $33,559, went through three managers, and then died in October. Ownership passed to his widow and their two children, with three trustees running the club for the estate. After the 1935 season, when the team drew only 80,922 fans, attorney Louis B. Von Weise, the trustee who served as club president, contacted Rickey and offered him a $25,000 fee to find a suitable buyer. Rickey took this task seriously, but the man most responsible for the resultant sale was his protégé, DeWitt, whom he had hired years before while running the Browns for Robert Hedges. Rickey had administered a stiff job interview, hired DeWitt at $3.50 a week, and had taken him with him to the Cardinals. DeWitt served serially as office boy, personal secretary, and administrative secretary and managed to earn a law degree attending Washington University in St. Louis at night. In 1935 the Cardinals named him club treasurer. An executive with Woolworth Stores made a bid to buy the Browns later that year but did not finalize a deal. DeWitt then talked to Barnes, whose daughter Anita had witnessed DeWitt's marriage to her friend. Barnes, president of the American Investment Company, was a millionaire casually interested in reviving the American League club in St. Louis. With DeWitt's assistance he assembled a large syndicate that bought the club in November 1936, but not Sportsman's Park, for $325,000.[2]

Barnes raised nearly a third of the purchase price by selling shares of stock to the public at $5 each. He commissioned a fan contest to create a new team emblem, a figure of King Louis IX of France, the saint after whom the city is named, and he hired DeWitt, who owned a small piece of the team, to be general manager. But the Browns' troubles on the field continued. The team lost 108 games in 1937 and landed in last place. Even as attendance increased to 123,121, Barnes insisted he was strapped for cash. He assessed the club's directors, all of them local business leaders, $5,000 each to support the club. In 1938 Bobo Newsom pitched 329.2 innings and won 20 games for the Browns, but they still finished seventh. Babe Ruth, retired since 1935, then offered himself as a candidate for manager, but DeWitt said no. He turned instead to young Fred Haney, a former infielder. His first season at the helm saw the Browns lose 111 games, finish an astounding 64½ games behind the first-place Yankees, and draw only 109,159 fans. Visiting teams complained that their share of the meager ticket revenues did not cover railroad fares and hotel bills. In response Harridge asked the other seven teams to help improve the Browns by selling them one quality player each for only $7,500. Barnes also completed a deal with the Cardinals to split the cost of installing lights at Sportsman's Park. The Browns played their first night game on May 24, 1940, before 24,827, their largest crowd in a dozen years and third-largest ever. But a league-imposed limit of only seven night games per season and two sixth-place finishes in 1940 and 1941 left the club in a precarious financial position, with the club's directors facing a loss of about $100,000 for the latter season alone. That's what caused Barnes to hatch his ill-fated plan to move the club to the West Coast.[3]

Harridge, the American League's third president, chaired the meeting at which club owners voted down the Barnes proposal, even though Harridge was recuperating from surgery. A man of solemn mien, he was a fit successor to Ernest Barnard, unflappable, reserved, and completely dedicated to his work. Born in Chicago, Harridge took a job after high school as an office boy with the Wabash Railroad and attended business college at night. Promoted to the ticketing department, he began booking trips for theatrical companies and sports organizations, including the American League, all of whose clubs used Robert McRoy, President Ban Johnson's personal secretary, to arrange their travel. When McRoy left in 1911, he recommended Harridge as his replacement even though the young man had never seen a baseball game. "I was scared to death when I reported for work," he recalled, but Johnson taught him the business of baseball. Harridge repaid this tutelage with fierce loyalty, but in February 1927, when league owners tried to nudge the erratic Johnson out of office, he took his anger out on his protégé and locked him out of the league office for several months because the owners had elected him league secretary. Johnson resigned in the fall, the owners elected Barnard president, and Harridge was able to return to work. After Barnard died in March 1931, Harridge got the job. "Outside of assigning umpires and ruling on occasional player disturbances on the field, there was little to do," he said, although meting out justice sometimes took a steely resolve. Just a year after taking office, Harridge proved his mettle when Carl Reynolds of the Washington Senators slid hard into the Yankees' catcher, Bill Dickey, who retaliated by punching Reynolds and breaking his jaw. Harridge fined Dickey $1,000 and suspended him for thirty days. In January 1940 Harridge's prompt "that the boys go a trifle socialistic for their own benefit" brought to the Browns pitcher Elden Auker, who won sixteen games, and outfielder Walt Judnich, who hit twenty-four home runs, but neither stanched the flow of red ink on the St. Louis club's balance sheet.[4]

Organized baseball quivered when World War II began. One Major League player, Philadelphia Athletics pitcher Chubby Dean, reacted to Germany's invasion of Poland on September 1, 1939, with resignation. He told James C. Isaminger, "I do not believe in war, but nevertheless, if we get into it, I will be the first to enlist and change from my baseball uniform to khaki." Baseball executives, on the other hand, were more equivocal. Some, including Clark Griffith, majority owner of the Senators, remembered how America's entrance into the Great War had unsettled their business. During the war he had led organized baseball's efforts to appear patriotic while simultaneously protecting its business interests. Two decades later, as Europe went to war again, organized baseball adopted roughly the same pose: reasserting its character as the patriotic National Pastime while also straining to protect itself as a business. The Minor Leagues felt the effect of the war first. Days after Hitler attacked Poland, Guy Moreau, business manager of the Montreal Royals in the International League and a captain in the reserves of Canada's Eighth Maisonneuve Regiment, was ordered to report for active duty. The following summer, as Congress debated a bill that would authorize peacetime conscription for the first time in U.S. history, the *Sporting News* reported that Major League clubs were refraining from purchasing young Minor Leaguers at prewar prices for fear they would soon be lost to the military. Nevertheless, in an editorial headlined "Uncle Sam Needs Only to Call," the weekly newspaper wrote, "Abner Doubleday did not originate baseball as a pastime or subterfuge for slackers and nothing is surer than the fact that it will not become such today." Misremembering what had transpired just a few years before, the editorial continued, "Baseball came out of the last war with its honor unsullied and with patriotism aflame, and if the nation again calls the game's participants to service, the response will be equally unselfish and enthusiastic. . . . There shouldn't be, and probably won't be, any plea for exemption based solely on the fact that those summoned desire to continue their diamond careers without interruption. Patriotic sacrifice can make no exceptions."[5]

The "determined group of private citizens" who advocated peacetime conscription crafted the bill that became the Selective Training and Service Act of 1940 to manage the transition from a peacetime economy to one poised for mobilization. Relying on voluntary enlistments, they knew, would be haphazard and chaotic as well as insufficient if war came. A draft could be fair and democratic if it were administered by autonomous local boards empowered to grant deferments to key personnel. Registration would be universal, but the draft itself would be selective, designed not only to build an army, but also to safeguard essential segments of the agricultural and industrial economy. Senator Edward Burke (D-NE) and Representative James Wadsworth (R-NY) introduced their bill in June in the face of substantial opposition. Yet a Gallup poll showed strong support for a draft, and the turn of events for the worse in Europe persuaded the Senate to pass the bill in August and the House a few weeks later. Males between the ages of twenty-one and thirty-six were called to register, subject to be drafted for one year of active duty, followed by ten years in the reserves. Men still could volunteer but for a term of three years, not one. About 6,400 local boards would run the draft, supervising registration, handling paperwork, and classifying men into categories. On October 29 a national lottery established a selection sequence based on dates of birth. Each local board then received a quota every month and had to decide whom to select. Although there were no official group deferments, the understanding was that single men without family responsibilities would be classified I-A and called first. Heads of families often were deferred, as were certain conscientious objectors, some students, and those deemed to hold key jobs in an expanding economy. Employers, of course, began to complain about these decisions, and the whole system suffered enormously as nearly 50 percent of those called failed physical, mental, or literacy examinations. After six months of operation four million men had been selected and classified, but only 402,000 had been inducted, far short of the goal.[6]

While Congress debated the bill authorizing peacetime conscription, the *Sporting News* endorsed a campaign to have Flag Day observed in every ballpark. After Frank Shaughnessy, president of the International League, suggested playing "The Star-Spangled Banner" before every Major League game, Ernest LaPointe, an army corporal stationed at Schofield Barracks in Hawaii, endorsed the idea, writing that the song was played before hockey games at New York's Madison Square Garden, and, he added, "I don't see any reason why they cannot do the same at a baseball game." Shaughnessy had "God Save the King" played in his league's Canadian cities beginning in 1940, and in 1941, before Pearl Harbor, playing the American National Anthem over public address systems and singing it became a fixture in many American ballparks. Overt patriotism was not, however, baseball's only reaction to the growing international crisis. Club executives were heartened to learn that players might wiggle around the coming draft. Playing baseball would not earn a deferment, but government officials asserted in September 1940 that players might be held exempt if they had "important" jobs during the off-season. Furthermore, if a player's number were to be called during the 1941 season, his induction might, at the discretion of his local board, be deferred until after the World Series. Or, stretching the intent of the forthcoming law just a bit more, a Major League player might have his induction deferred because the federal taxes he was paying on his salary might be considered a significant contribution to national defense. Owners considered increasing rosters to twenty-eight to take advantage of this possibility, but a *Sporting News* editorial was more calculating: "If baseball could function with 5,000,000 in uniform, 2,000,000 of them overseas, a little more than two decades ago, there is no reason why the game should be disturbed now by the prospect of less than a million in training this coming year."[7]

Eight days after the Cincinnati Reds defeated the Detroit Tigers in the 1940 World Series, professional ballplayers, along with millions of other men, registered for the draft. As Hank Greenberg registered in New York, Joe DiMaggio signed up in San Francisco and Bob Feller registered in Cleveland. Hugh Mulcahy, a pitcher for the Philadelphia Phillies and "26 years old, unmarried, and fancy free," signed up in Allston, Massachusetts. "To the nation," wrote Edgar G. Brands, these players "were only so many potential soldiers, marines, or sailors," but to club owners, they were "an investment to baseball of millions of dollars in human flesh." With a first call of draftees scheduled in a few weeks and others anticipated in the spring, "conscription-registered players," Brands wrote, "represent the big question mark of the 1941 season." Would ballplayers somehow be excused from military service? Would they be allowed to spread their required stint over two or more off-seasons? Would each team's losses to the draft be limited to, say, one or two players? Would the Majors be hit harder than the Minors? Club executives were not sure. They sought consolation in Brands's judgment that "no abandonment of baseball is contemplated, unless hostilities break out," but they attempted to remain patriotically correct. Reds president Warren Giles declared, "Baseball wants to do its part. We're not going to ask exemptions," and Bob Quinn, president of the Boston Braves, echoed him, saying, "Baseball will be right there as always and do whatever America wants it to do." Others hinted at a way to keep their business operating without alteration. Boston Red Sox owner Tom Yawkey explained that "people need relaxation and in time of stress are likely to turn to sports to let off steam," and Harry Grabiner, vice president of the Chicago White Sox, concurred, "We have to have some sports for the amusement of the public." Larry MacPhail, who joined the Brooklyn Dodgers in January 1938, was far blunter. "The one year of military service [required of draftees] could disrupt two years of their baseball careers," he complained, adding that "there should be a national ruling. Either the ballplayer goes when he's called or, like a college student, he goes when he finishes the season, or semester." He continued, "By doing nothing, the club owners are leaving the whole matter up to the ballplayers, getting them to stick their necks out. A ballplayer called up during the season shouldn't have to appeal to his draft board because that's going to hurt his popularity."[8]

Several club owners agreed with MacPhail and asked Commissioner Kenesaw Landis to send Griffith and a committee to ask the War Department how the draft would treat ballplayers. Landis refused. National League president Ford Frick, agreeing with the commissioner, asserted that "baseball is ready, yes eager, to do its duty in national defense. Baseball wants no favors in this respect. It expects no exemptions except such as the authorities may decide to favor it with." He continued, "We are not going to Washington with any appeal, or even with a request for information as to what the authorities intend to do with the players." Frick believed, too, that the draft would impose only a minor inconvenience. "I have gone over the draft," he said, "and doubt if in 1941 more than ten major leaguers will be taken into service." Speaking for the American League, Yankees president Ed Barrow, echoed Frick. "The American League is not going to send to Washington for information," he said, "nor is it going to appeal to the draft board to favor players." He continued, "Baseball never has been remiss in its duty and you will find it in the foreground in national defense." A few weeks later club owners decided to create a National Defense Service List, allowing them to place drafted players in a special category that would not count against a team's roster limit. Left without any protection, players had to deal with their draft boards as individuals, and confusion reigned. In November reports had Johnny Gorsica, born Gorczyca, moving to Canada so that he could enlist in the Polish Air Squadron, allied with Great Britain's Royal Air Force. But this was erroneous. Gorsica, who had pitched very well for Detroit in the World Series, was soon found in Beckley, West Virginia, living with his wife and son and working in a drug store.[9]

How local draft boards dealt with individual players varied from place to place. Greenberg had unknowingly registered with a board that had a small number of eligible men, so his low draft number, 621, suggested that he might be called early, but the first ballplayer drafted was Bill Embick, a Minor

League outfielder inducted in November 1940. The first Major Leaguer taken was Mulcahy, whose number, 246, got him inducted in March 1941. He asked for a deferment after buying his aged parents a house that he said they would be unable to maintain in his absence, but his local board said no. White Sox pitcher Johnny Rigney's case was convoluted. Engaged to Dorothy Comiskey, daughter of the team's founder, Rigney took a physical in spring training that revealed a perforated eardrum, a cause for disqualification. After a second physical in Chicago reversed that judgment, Rigney appealed for a deferment and then changed his mind and reported, only to have his induction physical affirm the original diagnosis. Rigney played the entire 1941 season with the White Sox and won thirteen games. New York Giants outfielder Morrie Arnovich seemed a candidate for induction too, but his second physical uncovered "dental deficiencies," upper and lower dental plates that made him ineligible for service. Greenberg's situation was more complicated. When he returned a questionnaire to his local board on February 14, he suggested that he should be deferred "because my years of earning power are limited and one year out of action will reduce my effectiveness considerably." Draft questionnaires were supposed to remain confidential, but Greenberg's answers reached the press and ignited a firestorm of controversy. He insisted that he did not have "any intention of trying to get out of military training," but even the three members of his local board divided on whether he had asked for a deferment. Further debate ensued after a doctor gave Greenberg a physical and classified him 4-F because of flat feet, unfit to serve except for limited duty. Greenberg again protested, "All I can add is that I am ready to report at any time that I am called." A second exam recommended that he be reclassified 1-A and left it to a medical advisory board to make a final decision. In the interim criticism continued unabated, one fan voicing the common-sense view that "if he's good enough to play baseball, he's good enough to march." On April 18 the medical board examined Greenberg and finalized his 1-A status. His local board then sent an induction notice, requiring him to report on May 7, after he had played only nineteen games. Greenberg said, "I never asked for a deferment. I made up my mind to go when I was called. My country comes first." And off he went to Fort Custer.[10]

MacPhail railed against the commissioner for his refusal to intercede on behalf of players exposed to the draft. "What's the judge getting $65,000 a year for?" he complained. "The least he could do is go to Washington and get a ruling, one way or the other, on how a ballplayer stands if he happens to be called in the middle of a season." Griffith thought MacPhail was overreacting.

He indicated that the War Department understood baseball's situation, the special nature of its business, and its value as entertainment during difficult times. "Yes," he told sportswriter Dan Daniel, "we deserve some consideration, but we are not going to the War Department to seek it." Yet behind the scenes, Griffith had already written to the White House, pleading baseball's case. He made two proposals: either limit each club to no more than one drafted player so long as the nation was not at war or assign to each club a drill sergeant who could train players so they could be deferred until after the 1941 season. General Edwin Watson, secretary to President Roosevelt, dismissed both ideas. He reminded Griffith that decisions on deferments were being left to local boards, and he noted that "the science of modern warfare is hardly that which can be attained on the baseball lot." The sport continued to put its patriotic foot forward. In February the National League announced that children of refugees would be admitted free to games. On May 18 the Yankees staged "I Am an American Day," with thirty thousand present for martial music and a speech on the advantages of the American way of life. In June the American League invited servicemen to attend games free of charge, and in July baseball donated net proceeds profits from the All-Star Game ($53,226) to the Army-Navy Recreation Fund of the United Service Organizations (USO). MacPhail also denied a request from the Brooklyn chapter of the America First Committee, a group opposed to intervention in the war, to hold a rally at Ebbets Field. On August 28 baseball supported "Defense Bond Day," yet another patriotic endeavor.[11]

Immediately before the season, "a year of utterly wonderful baseball," in the words of Robert Creamer, 162 of the 262 members of the Baseball Writers' Association of America polled by the *Sporting News* picked Cincinnati to finish first in the National League. Yet the Reds, after two straight pennants, faded to third place while St. Louis and Brooklyn staged one of the most exciting two-team races in league history. Sportswriter Leonard Koppett called this pennant race "hand-to-hand combat from start to finish," with the Dodgers pulling ahead on September 4 but never building a lead of more than three games. St. Louis won ninety-seven games, but Brooklyn won three more. Larry MacPhail had assembled a cast of veterans who brought Brooklyn a healthy dose of respectability after two decades of ineptitude. Brooklyn traded its way to success. Only shortstop Pee Wee Reese and outfielder Pete Reiser, one of the players Commissioner Kenesaw Landis freed from the St. Louis farm system in 1939, had played their first Major League games for the Dodgers. In the American League the Yankees rebounded from finishing second the year before by scorching their opponents and winning the pennant by seventeen games. New York proved that its farm system could bear Major League quality fruit, but the club's best player remained Joe DiMaggio, acquired by trade. The Yankee Clipper, as he was known, hit safely in a record fifty-six consecutive games, breaking the club record on June 17, the twentieth-century record June 29, and the all-time record, forty-four, on July 2. During his streak DiMaggio batted .408, hit 15 home runs, drove in 55 runs, and struck out only 5 times. Moreover, after going hitless on July 17, he hit safely in his next sixteen games. But DiMaggio did not win the batting title. Ted Williams of the Red Sox did by hitting .406, the highest American League batting average since George Sisler's .420 in 1922. Williams's feat abides in memory because he came into the last day of the season batting .39955, an average that would have rounded up to the magic mark of .400. Williams would have none of it. He played in both games of Boston's doubleheader in Philadelphia, getting 6 hits in 8 at bats.[12]

The 1941 World Series thus matched an American League champion that had won four of the previous five Series and eight of the last eighteen against a National League champion that had not won a pennant since 1920 and had never won a modern World Series. The teams split the first two games at Yankee Stadium. The Yankees won Game One, 3–2, with Bill Dickey and Joe Gordon getting two hits each and driving in all the runs. Red Ruffing, thirty-seven years old, beat Curt Davis, also thirty-seven. The Dodgers took Game Two by the same score with twenty-two-game-winner Whitlow Wyatt pitching a complete game while giving up nine hits. Moving to Ebbets Field, the Yankees won Game Three, 2–1, scoring both runs in the eighth inning on four straight singles, three of them by their outfielders. In Game Four Brooklyn took a 4–3 lead into the ninth inning. Kirby Higbe had started for the Dodgers, but he had been relieved in the fourth inning, and Hugh Casey had taken the mound with two outs in the fifth. Johnny Sturm opened the ninth inning by grounding out, and so did Red Rolfe. Casey's first pitch to Tommy Henrich was a ball, and the next two were called strikes. Henrich fouled off the fourth pitch and then took two more for balls. With the count full Casey threw a surprising breaking pitch. "I was fooled," Henrich said, and so was catcher Mickey Owen. Henrich swung and missed. "I committed myself too quickly," he admitted, but the ball got away from Owen far enough for Henrich to reach first safely. DiMaggio took advantage of this opportunity and singled. Charlie Keller doubled both runners home, and before the inning was over, the Yankees had scored two more runs. The Dodgers went quietly in the ninth, and the Yankees emerged with a 7–4 win and a three-games-to-one lead. The next day New York scored twice in the second and once in the fourth. The Dodgers answered with only one run, and the Yankees had their ninth World Series title.[13]

Organized baseball reacted to the surprise attack on Pearl Harbor with a mixture of shock and apprehension. Baseball officials were dismayed, even stunned, because the Japanese had long played the American game, often characterized as embodying the very essence of democracy and fair play. Baseball had arrived in Japan sometime after 1870, when several young American professors taught their university students the basics, and the game became popular quickly. Yet after Japan invaded Manchuria in 1931, relations with the United States began to deteriorate. Baseball began to think of itself not as a way to peace but as a respite from the difficulties the situation in the Far East and Europe presented. Journalists contrasted the pleasures of the game, especially the World Series, with growing troubles abroad and took consolation that America's separation from Europe was more than geographical. Richard Crepeau noted that an editorial cartoon published in the *Chicago Tribune* at the opening of the 1939 season depicted a seat in the upper deck as a "safe sanctuary from war hysteria." And yet the *Feather River Bulletin*, a small newspaper in northern California, warned that "the American boy learns how to use his eyes and his good right arm, and can use it in battle if he has to do so." Thus the hope that baseball might serve to lessen the threat of war shriveled as tensions between the United States and Japan escalated in the late 1930s, and the sneak attack on December 7 destroyed the idea entirely. How could it be, wrote Crepeau, "that a people who took so well to the game of democracy could now turn out to be the archenemy of the greatest democracy on earth?" After the United States declared war, the history of the previous few decades had to be rewritten. "After looking at the 70 years of Japanese baseball in retrospect," wrote the editors of the *Sporting News*, "this treacherous Asiatic land was really never converted to baseball. . . . [The Japanese] may have acquired a little skill at the game, but the soul of our National Game never touched them. No nation which has had as intimate contact with baseball as the Japanese could have committed the vicious, infamous deed of the early morning of December 7, 1941, if the spirit of the game ever had penetrated their yellow hides."[14]

Shortly after Pearl Harbor, William Bramham, president of the National Association, the governing body of the Minor Leagues, expressed his hope that "no tents should be folded until necessary." He continued, "We feel safe in saying that the outlook for the game is no more gloomy than that of any other line of endeavor—in fact, not as much so." Speaking at the winter meetings of the forty-one Minor Leagues that had played in 1941, Bramham concluded, "There is every reason to believe that if we keep our leagues intact, the federal, state, and municipal governments, as well as our patrons, will appreciate and support our efforts." Even in California, which some residents feared would be the target of a follow-up attack, Harry Williams, secretary of the Pacific Coast League, urged resilience. Faced with the possibility of blackouts and other disruptive inconveniences, he said, "We went to the trouble of teaching the Japs [*sic*] baseball, and we don't intend to let them obliterate it." The Major Leagues planned the 1942 season "with the idea the administration expected them to carry on as during the previous war." The leagues pledged $25,000 immediately to purchase equipment for army and navy sports programs and agreed to donate the proceeds from the All-Star Game that summer to the same fund. The New York clubs, a bit on edge that German forces might launch an attack on the East Coast, nevertheless proceeded without any "yammering about what the war might do to the game." Even though Ed Barrow offered Yankee Stadium to civil authorities as a bomb shelter, the clubs "take it for granted here that the war will do nothing for baseball, except possibly make attendance bigger, and perhaps curtail night competition." The *Sporting News* reinforced the view that baseball must go on. An editorial in January 1942 noted that soccer, rugby, and boxing continued in Great Britain and that "during the most critical days of the Moscow siege, a football match was played before a big crowd." The editors also quoted Branch Rickey, who said, "While our boys are fighting for democracy, we should not overlook the stay-at-homes. Industries are booming. Thousands and thousands are moving from rural districts to larger cities. Sports should play an important part while this war is going on."[15]

Early in 1942, Clark Griffith revived the Bat and Ball Fund, an effort he had directed during the Great War, and began ordering baseball equipment for shipment to military installations at home and overseas. Each destination would receive two packages: Kit A, containing three bats and a dozen balls, and Kit B, consisting of complete equipment for a catcher. "We are particular about sending complete catcher's paraphernalia," said Ford Frick, "because baseball wants every man behind the bat to get full protection when he is playing the game in this most hazardous of positions." Troops would also again be receiving copies of the *Sporting News*. But would there be a season about which to read? No one could yet be certain. House minority leader Joseph Martin (R-MA) said that baseball should keep going. "It would be foolish to do otherwise," he argued, and Congressman Wadsworth, co-sponsor of the draft bill, agreed. "I don't believe in draping the country in black," he said. Then in mid-January Landis, acting on his own initiative and without informing any club owners except Griffith, scribbled a note in pencil to President Roosevelt. He said, in part: "The time is approaching when, in ordinary conditions, our teams would be leaving for spring training camps. . . . I venture to ask what you have in mind as to whether professional baseball should continue to operate. Of course, my inquiry does not relate at all to individual members of this organization, whose status in this emergency is fixed by law operating upon all citizens." Roosevelt's response was quick and decisive, so positive and affirming that it immediately became known as the "Green Light" letter. While insisting that organized baseball must make its own decision, the president offered what he called "solely a personal and not an official point of view":

> I honestly feel that it would be best for the country to keep baseball going. There will be fewer people unemployed and everybody will work longer hours and harder than ever before. And that means that they ought to have a chance for recreation and or taking their minds off their work even more than before. . . . And, incidentally, I hope that night games can be extended because it gives an opportunity to the day shift to see a game occasionally. As to the players themselves, I know you agree with me that individual players who are of active military or naval age should go, without question, into the service. Even if the actual quality of the teams is lowered by the greater use of older players, this will not dampen the popularity of the sport. . . . Here is another way of looking at it—if 300 teams use 5,000 or 6,000 players, these players are a definite recreational asset to at least 20,000,000 of their fellow citizens—and that in my judgment is thoroughly worthwhile.[16]

In some small measure Roosevelt may have crafted his response to Landis to satisfy his own interest in baseball as a fan, but more broadly he was shrewd enough not to dismiss the public's view, as expressed in Gallup opinion polls and other ways, that sports should continue during the war. Roosevelt and Landis were far from friends. "Landis," Griffith once said, "wasn't much more welcome at the White House than the Japanese ambassador." Moreover, as Taylor Spink wrote of the commissioner, "His criticism of the Roosevelt Administration was that it didn't come to grips earlier with Hitler and the Japs [*sic*], and for not being better prepared when the big blow came." Nevertheless, when Landis asked the president to rule on baseball's fate, a request that could have been read as a challenge, the president refused to take the bait, noting in his letter that "you [Landis] will, of course, realize that the final decision about the baseball season must rest with you and the Baseball Club owners." Naturally the baseball establishment lauded the president's expression of support. Will Harridge read the letter with "deep appreciation." Barrow called it "glad tidings," and Don Barnes said, "It's the best news I've heard in two years." MacPhail noted that "President Roosevelt's letter has clarified the entire baseball picture." The *Sporting News* even suggested, far in advance of Opening Day, that Roosevelt be honored as baseball's Player of the Year for 1942. Further appreciation for the president's position came from outside the baseball business, not only in 1942, but throughout the war years. The *Chicago Sun* called his letter "the most notable contribution to baseball in our time." Congressman LaVern Dilweg (D-WI), a former three-sport collegiate athlete and professional football player, testified that baseball was important to those in combat who "hungrily await news of sports," and journalist Quentin Reynolds wrote, "Hitler has killed a great many things in the past few years. Do not let him kill baseball."[17]

Bolstered by the "Green Light" letter, organized baseball began the 1942 season as scheduled, augmented by a series of actions that demonstrated an enhanced commitment to the war effort. Larry MacPhail kicked off this campaign with a rousing speech at the annual dinner of the BBWAA's New York chapter. He called for everyone in the game "from Commissioner Landis to the peanut vendor" to take part of his salary in war bonds; suggested a second All-Star Game to raise additional money for the Bat and Ball Fund; and proposed that a few cents out of the price of every ticket sold be allocated toward the purchase of a B-17 bomber with a $300,000 price tag. The Major Leagues and the Minors announced that each player and umpire would wear a patriotic patch on his left shoulder to support "Hale America," a physical fitness program sponsored by the national Office of Civil Defense. The patch, in the shape of a shield, featured red and white vertical stripes topped by the word "Health" on a blue background. In Pittsburgh the design of a banner that flew from a downtown bank building to indicate that the Pirates would be playing at home that day was altered because it resembled the flag of Japan. The New Orleans Pelicans in the Southern Association painted their ballpark seats red, white, and blue. The Syracuse Chiefs in the International League renamed Municipal Stadium MacArthur Stadium in honor of General Douglas MacArthur, and the Indianapolis Indians in the American Association changed the name of

Perry Field to Victory Field. The Reds, accustomed to a fireworks show before the start of every night game, got their fans' approval to stop the pyrotechnics so that the explosives might be used by the military. Throughout the season, various clubs auctioned off autographed baseballs to buy war bonds and admitted fans who donated scrap metal in lieu of buying tickets.[18]

The sentence in President Roosevelt's letter that Landis could not have anticipated and certainly did not appreciate was the president's advocacy for more night games. The commissioner had resisted the spread of night baseball, but on this topic Clark Griffith was a convert to the other side, and he quite probably influenced the content of Roosevelt's response. Tending to view the expense of installing lights as a short-term cost rather than a long-term investment, other clubs had not flocked to follow MacPhail's initiative in Cincinnati. After the Reds played the first Major League night game in 1935, Tigers' owner Frank Navin said, "Why, this night game is baseball's ruination. It changes baseball players from athletes to actors. It's nothing more than a spectacle." Ed Barrow concurred. "I am more convinced than ever," he said, "that there is absolutely no future in electric lighted play." H. G. Salsinger summarized what others were thinking when he wrote simply, "Baseball was made to be played by daylight. It just isn't as good at night; it can't be. Infielders can't get a jump on the ball at night. Ground balls go through the infield that would be fielded in the daylight. You cannot see the spin of the ball at night—only a white object sailing at you. Night baseball is a much inferior game." This judgment, widely shared, dissuaded all other Major League clubs from duplicating the Reds' experiment until MacPhail took control of the Dodgers in 1938. As he had done before, he began by refurbishing a deteriorating ballpark, in this case Ebbets Field. After he secured a $200,000 bank loan, work crews repaired the dugouts and clubhouses, replaced broken seats, resodded the field, and gave everything a paint job. MacPhail had his ushers retrained too, but when someone asked him about night baseball, he said, "That's about number 10 on our list of priorities."[19]

Within a few days after the Dodgers started the 1938 season poorly, MacPhail reconsidered. He borrowed more money and contacted the General Electric Company to purchase a lighting system estimated to cost as much as $110,000, much more than he had paid in Cincinnati. "It's the best lighting plant science can produce and the best money can buy," he asserted. Once installed and tested, the lights were shown off to members of the press on June 14 to great reviews. The real show came the following night, with the Reds as the visiting team. MacPhail, true to form, turned the evening into an extravaganza. He invited local politicians, including Brooklyn borough president R. V. Ingersoll; baseball executives Gerry Nugent of the Phillies and Warren Giles of the Reds; and George V. McLaughlin, head of the Brooklyn Trust Company, the bank that held the club's notes covering its considerable debts. Reserved seats had sold briskly in the days leading up to the game. Twenty-five thousand general admission seats, including over three thousand in the bleachers, went on sale at 5:00, and well before game time, 9:20, the fire department ordered the gates closed, with 38,748 on hand and another 20,000 disappointed outside. The pregame festivities included fireworks, a marching band, a drum and bugle corps, and an appearance by Olympic champion Jesse Owens. Hired for $4,000, Owens raced against two players, broad jumped more than twenty-three feet, and ran over some low hurdles. Brooklyn's announcers, Red Barber and Al Helfer, raced too, with Barber easily defeating his three-hundred-pound partner. "Whether night ball is circus stuff or not," Dodgers executive secretary Jim Mulvey said, "tonight's crowd proves that it's what the public wants." The game itself was no circus as Cincinnati's Johnny Vander Meer pitched his second consecutive no-hitter, a feat never accomplished before or since. No one blamed the lights.[20]

Economist David George Surdam noted that the Dodgers drew an average of more than twenty-seven thousand for their night games in 1938, more than their average crowds for Sunday doubleheaders and more than their afternoon game on Memorial Day. Most owners still eschewed the innovation, but Will Harridge suggested that night baseball was on its way to almost universal adoption throughout the Majors. Connie Mack, owner of the Athletics, agreed. "Baseball must progress just as much as any other sport," he said. Other American League club owners may not have agreed, but they did approve night ball on an experimental basis in 1939, granting some clubs permission to play up to seven night games but none on Saturdays, Sundays, or holidays. Taking the initiative while other owners balked or stalled, Mack spent $105,000 on a lighting system mounted on eight towers around Shibe Park, home to both the Athletics and, since the middle of the 1938 season, the Phillies. Mack also had to persuade the Philadelphia zoning board since some citizens thought that lights or the sounds of radios tuned to the broadcasts of night games would disturb their neighborhoods. The results were spectacular. Mack told a pregame radio audience that "it's even brighter out there on the diamond than it is on a sunshiny day." Sportswriter Stoney McLinn agreed, writing in the *Sporting News* that "night actually was turned into day. The lighting was even. There were no shadows—no blank spaces or dead spots." Perhaps

Mack's mistake was scheduling the Athletics' first night game for May 16, a chilly evening that kept the crowd to fifteen thousand fans, but their second game, against the Yankees, attracted thirty-three thousand when a typical day crowd might have numbered about a tenth of that total. Not in favor of night baseball for quite some time, Griffith began to waver, but he still questioned the economics involved. Installing lights was expensive, as were electricity and maintenance. Risk-averse as were all owners, he also believed that while too few night games might not generate enough revenue to make an investment in lights profitable, too many might substantially cut into revenue by making the remaining day games on the schedule much less attractive.[21]

Slowly but seemingly inexorably night baseball debuted in one park and then another. The Phillies played their first night game on June 1, 1939. Bad weather kept the crowd to eight thousand as clubs began to understand that night games scheduled too early in the season might not be attractive. The Cleveland Indians, having installed lights at Municipal Stadium, but not League Park, set a record for attendance at a night game when 55,305 fans paid to see a 5–0 victory over the Tigers on June 27. Seven weeks later, on August 14, the White Sox debuted a $140,000 lighting system against the Browns. The situation in Sportsman's Park in St. Louis was complicated since the Cardinals were tenants of the Browns. Don Barnes wanted his team to play under the lights, but he could not afford to pay for them. Negotiations with the Cardinals dragged on, and lights were not installed until 1940. The Browns got to use them first on the same night that the Giants turned on the lights in the Polo Grounds, May 24. The Cardinals followed on June 4 as the Pirates were playing Forbes Field's first night game. Griffith continued to vacillate, but the success of the Indians and the White Sox finally convinced him to spend $130,000 to illuminate Griffith Stadium's enormous playing surface. After installing lights in 1941 and using them for the first time on May 28, Griffith began to lobby against the seven-games-per-season limit, arguing that the president's support for night games that defense plant workers on the day shift might attend should get the American League to alter its policy.[22]

Despite MacPhail's success in Brooklyn, night baseball made uneven progress in New York. Giants owner Charles Stoneham abstained when the National League voted to approve night baseball in 1935 and declined to play a night game against MacPhail's Reds in Cincinnati. At the same time, Yankees owner Jacob Ruppert kept his options open, saying, "If the National League test proves that night baseball is popular, and is needed, I will build an electric plant at the Stadium and urge the experiment on the American

League." Yet when MacPhail announced his plans for lighting Ebbets Field, both the Giants and the Yankees squawked that Brooklyn had an agreement with its two neighboring clubs to bar night ball from the entirety of New York. Besides, both clubs protested that New Yorkers were too sophisticated for night baseball. When the Dodgers played their first night game, MacPhail extended a special invitation to Giants manager Bill Terry, noting that the Giants had played a night exhibition game in the borough of Queens, not far from Ebbets Field, in 1932. Terry declined. While the Yankees consented to play at night in Shibe Park in 1939, the Giants remained firm in their determination not to. Horace Stoneham, who succeeded his father, did not reverse course until November 1939, when he announced at a luncheon at the New York Athletic Club that Westinghouse would install a lighting system at a cost estimated to be $125,000. The Giants played their first home night game on a cold, dreary evening before a disappointing crowd of 22,260. All box seats and reserved seats had been sold ahead of time, but day-of-game ticket sales were minimal. A number of Broadway celebrities, a rather steady part of Polo Grounds crowds over the years, came out for the occasion and left satisfied that New Yorkers maybe were too urbane for night ball. The Yankees continued to hold out. Barrow, talking dollars and cents, said, "The way I see it, a club which can draw without night baseball is a sucker to go for the lights. . . . I am afraid that the game under lights might turn out a passing fancy."[23]

Commissioner Landis and the club owners had to decide how to respond to the president's endorsement of night baseball in the "Green Light" letter. National League owners met in New York in late January 1942. Still unsure about the economics of night games, they suggested a fourteen-game maximum. American League owners argued about a fourteen-game minimum, with Griffith pushing for at least thirty-five night games. All Major League owners came together in February and agreed that no team would schedule more than fourteen night games except that Washington would be allowed twenty-one. Yet just after the season started, the government mandated that cities along the East Coast implement blackouts, turning off their lights one hour after sunset to avoid attracting enemy airplanes or submarines. This gave baseball the chance to move up starting times, transforming night games into twilight games and hoping to complete them while looking nervously at the clock. Twilight, specifically 6:30, became the starting time for the All-Star Game once the Majors moved it from the afternoon to attract working people and from Ebbets Field to the more spacious Polo Grounds because it was a benefit. With ticket prices set twice as high as in 1941, the game raised

$95,000 for the Bat and Ball Fund and the Army and Navy Relief Fund, even though bad weather held the crowd to 33,694. A thunderstorm delayed the start for an hour, turning this game, inadvertently, into the first night All-Star Game. Military authorities had originally dictated turning the lights out at 9:10, but just before the first pitch they agreed to allow play until 9:30, New York's blackout time. The American League squad scored three runs in the first inning and won, 3–1, with the final out recorded at 9:28. The Giants at first decided against playing any games at twilight, but on August 3 they hosted an exhibition against the Dodgers to benefit the Army Emergency Relief Fund. Begun at dusk, this game came to a premature end when umpire George Magerkurth called play precisely at 9:10, even though the Giants were losing, 7–4, with two men on base and nobody out in the bottom of the ninth. Fans howled at the Dodgers' faux victory, but a 150-person orchestra quickly took the field and played the National Anthem. This failed to placate the crowd, and the Giants decided against any further twilight games.[24]

When players reported for spring training in 1942, they sensed war encroaching on baseball. Anticipating that rosters for the coming season would look very different from those of 1941, the *Pittsburgh Press* published a list of young players, including Stan Musial, who might earn a starting job and become stars during "war ball." The *Sporting News* noted that "the wartime season of 1942 offers to rookies the finest opportunity in years for making good." Indeed some of the game's best players were already in the service, and others, classified 1-A by their draft boards, could anticipate being called soon. By one account sixty-one Major Leaguers were in the armed forces when the teams broke camp. By another reckoning rookies occupied seventy-nine of the Majors' four hundred roster spots on Opening Day. Baseball learned in February of its first war-related fatality. Gordon Houston, a Minor Leaguer before joining the Army Air Corps, died when his plane, a single-seater, crashed on a training flight at Ft. Lewis in Tacoma, Washington. On the field the war made its mark too. White Sox pitchers began their spring drills in Pasadena, California, by firing fastballs not into catchers' mitts but at a caricature of a Japanese soldier. Once the season began, playing the National Anthem before games became standard in every ballpark. Owners had to guess whether attendance would decline and decide if they should reduce players' salaries. When the Yankees opened training camp, only a dozen players showed up. The others, including Joe DiMaggio, were holding out, refusing to sign contracts calling for pay cuts. Players did sign eventually, of course, but owners' fears proved justified as Major League attendance fell to 8.55 million, a drop of nearly 12 percent. Only five clubs showed increases, most of them quite minimal. Trying to aid the war effort, the Majors contributed a portion of 1942 World Series revenues to the USO, and the Minors announced that clubs had raised $251,354 for various war agencies, not including about $380,000 in war bonds sold at games during the year.[25]

Less than a quarter of prewar Major Leaguers had been called to serve so far, but the draft status of some proved newsworthy throughout the war's first year. Ted Williams was one such player. He was single, but his draft board had originally classified him 3-A because he provided sole support for his mother. Yet in January 1942 Williams telephoned the Red Sox to tell them that he had been reclassified 1-A. He passed his physical and faced induction soon, but two weeks later the *Sporting News* reported that his local board's appeal agent had filed an appeal on the player's behalf. His mother was in poor health, he had sent her $5,000 in 1941, and he needed to play in 1942 to complete annuity payments that would provide for her future security. But the appeal failed, and Colonel J. E. Nelson, head of Selective Service in Minnesota, where Williams had registered, refused to intervene. The last resort was the President's Board of Appeal, essentially a request to have Roosevelt override the local board's decision. When the president did so, restoring Williams's 3-A classification, the public outrage was profound. Biographer Leigh Montville referred to the "Mr. Average Man" opinion poll in the *Boston Globe* and quoted one South Bostonian who said, "I am a bartender and a Ted Williams fan, but from now on you can count me off his list of supporters."[26]

Williams said he was confused. The *Sporting News* had reported that he had not initiated the appeal, and after the president's decision, Williams said, "I didn't want to get in wrong with anybody, so I let the local draft board handle the entire case. I didn't ask for it." In truth Williams had hired an attorney to guide the original appeal, and Colonel Nelson said that Williams himself requested the appeal to the president. Thinking about enlisting to end the controversy, Williams toured the Great Lakes Naval Station in Chicago, where Mickey Cochrane, now a navy lieutenant, ran the athletic program. Williams liked what he saw, especially when Cochrane suggested that playing Major League baseball before booing fans in every park might prove difficult. He took Cochrane's words as a challenge. Defiantly he announced that he would head south for spring training, earn big money, and enlist only after the end of the season. Despite editorial support from the *Boston Globe* and the *Sporting News*, the slugger began to reconsider when boos greeted him in several ballparks. Late in April a naval recruiter approached Williams. Secretly they toured the Squantum Aviation Training Station in Quincy, Massachusetts, and on May 22 Williams enlisted in the navy's new V-5 program, which offered men with no college education the chance to become pilots. Assured that he would not be called to active duty until after the season, Williams, along with teammate and fellow V-5 enlistee Johnny Pesky, had to attend night school for classes in mathematics, physics, and navigation. He finished the season by winning the Triple Crown, batting .356, with 36 home runs and 137 runs batted in. Deprived for the second year in a row of the Most Valuable Player Award, Williams reported for the Civilian Pilot Training Course at Amherst College on November 15.[27]

Williams was not alone. DiMaggio incurred the wrath of the fans and his boss when he held out for a better contract in the spring of 1942. "Doesn't he know there's a war on?" griped Ed Barrow. Following his outstanding 1941 season, DiMaggio thought he deserved a raise over his salary of $37,500. Barrow disagreed. He offered the Yankees' best player not a raise but a pay cut of $2,500, justifying this parsimony by contrasting his star with the young men who "had put on uniforms of olive drab for one one-hundredth the pay." The comparison was unfair, of course, and even insulting. DiMaggio had registered for the draft in October 1940, as required, and had been classified 3-A as a husband and a father. Nevertheless, Barrow's denigration stuck. While DiMaggio waited out the Yankees in a Florida beach house, soldiers stationed at nearby Camp Blanding mocked his refusal to sign a contract with an invitation "to a tryout with the 143rd Infantry, 36th Division, the fightingest [*sic*] regiment in this man's Army. The pay is only $21 a month, but that is far better than nothing." It was not until Barrow arrived in Florida that the two agreed on a contract calling for $42,000. Once the season started, fans expressed their discontent, particularly since DiMaggio got off to a horrible start. Named to the All-Star team mainly because of his work in previous seasons, he was booed at the game. It hardly mattered that his batting average recovered in the second half of the year or that he got seven hits in the World Series. When a San Francisco sportswriter reached DiMaggio during the off-season, the slugger refused to discuss what 1943 might bring. "Spring training won't concern me this year," he said, and on February 17 he enlisted in the Army Air Corps.[28]

One player feisty enough to fire back at fans who thought ballplayers were slackers was pitcher Paul Derringer. In remarks published in the *Sporting News* in March 1942, he said, "I doubt if there are very many players who are trying to duck their duty or not do their share." A Major Leaguer since 1931,

Derringer had punctuated his career with a series of altercations. In 1933, on his way to losing twenty-five games for the Reds, he threw an inkwell at Larry MacPhail, who had criticized him for not sliding on a close play at the plate. In 1936 a New York judge issued an arrest warrant after the pitcher allegedly assaulted a hotel guest who refused Derringer admission to a private reception. Three years later he and Dizzy Dean exchanged pregame punches and had to be separated by their teammates. Derringer's stridency was no surprise. He continued, "Here we find the public criticizing Ted Williams for accepting deferment from military service without knowing the facts. Do you think an appeal draft board would defer anybody if it didn't have solid facts to go on?" He also defended DiMaggio's holding out by saying, "I don't know of any lawyers, merchants, doctors or businessmen who aren't trying to make as much money as they can." Derringer then explained his own case. He had annuities and insurance policies that needed to be funded, and "if I can't play ball, I can't pay them." He had dependents, and the war had been brought "right to my doorstep, already" when "my wife's twin brother was killed the day after Christmas in the last flight he had to make before receiving his commission in the Air Corps." He concluded, "We [ballplayers] are no better or worse than anybody else in any walk of life. But we shouldn't be crucified unless we ask for special favors and I don't know of any ball player yet that's done that."[29]

Through the first five years of Don Barnes's ownership, the Browns lost almost five hundred games and roughly half a million dollars. A third of the way through the 1941 season Bill DeWitt fired Fred Haney and replaced him with Luke Sewell, who recalled years later that he thought the Browns' job "was probably the lowest job in the majors." He took it only after negotiating some control over team personnel and signing a contract for the remainder of 1941 and 1942. Sewell led the team to a tie for sixth place, but expenses still dwarfed revenues, and the organization tightened its belt by cutting ties with five farm clubs. Barnes appealed to his stockholders for additional capital, and Richard Muckerman, head of the City Ice and Fuel Company, invested substantially and became a vice president. In 1942 the team took a chance on a new second baseman, Don Gutteridge; a new shortstop, Vern Stephens; and a veteran pitcher, Boots Hollingsworth, who had spent 1941 in the Minors. All did well, as did outfielder Chet Laabs. The Browns finished 82-69, good enough for third place, their best finish since 1922. They made a profit, too, but were still nineteen and a half games behind the pennant-winning Yankees. New York's 1942 roster was nearly the same as it had been in 1941, and they were still the league's strongest team even though they lost the Series to the

Cardinals in five games. Teams had begun to lose a few key players to military service, but observers concurred that the overall quality of play in the Majors was not much diminished from the season before Pearl Harbor.[30]

Looking forward to 1943, Cleveland owner Alva Bradley expressed doubt that fans wanted wartime baseball to continue. "I would rather not open the ballpark next spring," he said, "than go out there and hear the wolves yelling, 'Why aren't you in the army, you big lug?' For my part," he continued, referring to Selective Service regulations, "I don't want any men on my club who aren't heads of families." J. Alvin Gardner, president of the Texas League, which suspended operations in 1943, struck a similar chord. Club owners, he said, "believed it was more important that the men build planes and tanks and work on the farms. . . . We would have taken up space in hotels, used transportation facilities needed in other lines and added to the food-rationing problem." Others disagreed. Ford Frick wrote, "Since the record is plain that to date in this war baseball has been useful, there's no reason for being shamefaced or apologetic about planning and scheduling the 1943 season." Two surveys undertaken by the Spokane (WA) Athletic Round Table showed broad support for baseball's continuance from fans and servicemen alike. Umpire Hap O'Connor, who had worked games in Japan, spoke for many when he said, "The Japs [*sic*] so envy us for our baseball prowess and our intense love of the game that to call it off during wartime would be like a tonic to them." Yet there would be problems with the quality of the game on the field from 1943 going forward. In February the War Manpower Commission listed more than sixty job classifications, including playing baseball, as nonessential, and told those working these jobs either to find essential work or prepare for induction. Early in the year organized baseball reported that 1,429 Minor Leaguers were on the National Defense Service List and that 115 American League players and 80 from the National League were already in the armed forces. Major League clubs, each allowed to carry forty players on the winter roster, listed an average of only thirty-two. The Phillies, with fourteen players in the service, had just twenty-three names on their roster.[31]

As the American economy mobilized, baseball travel had to change. Since Japan controlled 90 percent of the crude rubber supply that came to the United States before the war, the federal government found itself hard-pressed to outfit tanks, each of which required a ton of rubber, and battleships, each of which needed seventy-five tons. Three months before Pearl Harbor a first attempt to reduce wear on automobile tires—and hence conserve rubber—by rationing the distribution and sale of gasoline failed miserably. Forbidding sales at the pump between 7:00 p.m. and midnight simply sent drivers scurrying to filling stations before they closed for the evening. The next strategy, promulgated in January 1943, banned all pleasure driving. This prohibition was soon relaxed, but enough drivers switching to train travel coupled with a massive increase in military freight put a huge burden on the railroad system. Baseball responded after Joseph Eastman, director of the Office of Defense Transportation (ODT), urged the Majors to "give careful consideration to the problem of how your basic travel requirements can be met without a waste in space or mileage." During the second half of the 1942 season teams reduced the number of railroad cars they occupied by abandoning luxurious drawing rooms and confining themselves to cars with upper and lower berths. In 1943 both Major Leagues adjusted their schedules so that each club made only three long road trips instead of four. The Red Sox, for example, finished their last western swing to Chicago, Detroit, St. Louis, and Cleveland by playing eight straight games against the Indians, including three doubleheaders, before finishing their road trip in New York and then coming home.[32]

More significant, Commissioner Kenesaw Landis called an emergency owners' meeting in January 1943 to create what became the Eastman-Landis line, limiting how far teams could travel for spring training. "We don't need any orders," Landis said. "We want to do, and will do, what everyone will agree is the decent thing to do." In addition to delaying the start of spring training and moving Opening Day back one week, Landis's plan mandated that all teams, except for the Browns, would abandon both Florida and California and train east of the Mississippi River and north of the Ohio and Potomac Rivers. A well-established tradition thus fell to the exigencies of war. The Red Sox soon announced that they would train at Tufts College, where there was an indoor batting cage. Their players would live at Boston's Hotel Kenmore and take a six-mile trolley ride to the campus each day. The Cubs and the White Sox said they would hold camp at the French Lick Springs Hotel in Indiana, less than three hundred miles south of Chicago. The Cubs laid out a diamond on the resort's golf course while the White Sox planned to use a public park a few miles away. Other clubs soon made similar arrangements. The Cardinals and Browns stayed relatively close to St. Louis, the Cardinals in Cairo, Illinois, and the Browns in Cape Girardeau, Missouri. Several clubs clustered in Indiana. The Pirates considered Hot Springs but settled for Ball State Teachers College in Muncie. The Indians thought about Marietta College in Ohio before opting for Purdue University in West Lafayette, where there was a huge field house with a dirt floor. The Tigers occupied a Minor League park in Evansville, and the Reds settled on Indiana University in Bloomington, where there was an indoor dirt floor. Other clubs chose the Middle Atlantic region. The Athletics camped in Wilmington, Delaware. The Phillies selected Hershey, Pennsylvania, and the Senators picked the University of Maryland in College Park. The rest found spots in the Northeast: the Braves at the Choate School in Wallingford, Connecticut; the Yankees in Asbury Park, New Jersey; the Giants at the former John D. Rockefeller estate in Lakewood, New Jersey; and the Dodgers at Bear Mountain, New York, where they could use facilities at West Point.[33]

The end of winter came slowly, so many teams needed indoor facilities for limited drills, including calisthenics and weight lifting, and long underwear and ear muffs when they went outside. The A's rode sleighs to their indoor workouts, and several Dodgers tried skiing. Some teams hired physical trainers or track coaches to lead them in indoor conditioning. The Reds used a muscle relaxation specialist who had helped train the University of Tulsa football team, and the Phillies brought in Harold Bruce, once a trainer of Olympic athletes. Outfielder Danny Litwhiler appreciated what Bruce accomplished. "We were probably in as good a shape as any team as far as conditioning is concerned," he said. Yankees manager Joe McCarthy demurred, saying, "Indoor training is of little help," and Cubs manager Jimmie Wilson was even more succinct when he said, "Calisthenics stink as a baseball conditioner." A few southern players requested permission from their clubs to stay home and train there. When exhibition games began, teams were allowed to travel only short distances unless they were playing against military or naval teams. None of these arrangements proved to be more than marginally satisfactory or close to Major League standards, but players knew they had to persevere, and with just a few changes spring training in the north lasted for three seasons. The Giants stayed in New Jersey hotels in 1943 and 1944 and moved into the Rockefeller mansion in 1945. The White Sox, victimized by spring floods at French Lick, shifted to Terre Haute in 1944. The Yankees moved to Atlantic City, and the Braves, after two seasons at Choate, went south to Georgetown University. Tigers pitcher Virgil Trucks, reflecting on three springs in Evansville, spoke for many when he said, "It wasn't an ideal area for spring training, but since the circumstances called for that, nobody complained about it, [and] we all went about our jobs."[34]

The issue of the *Sporting News* dated February 25, 1943, provided a multifaceted portrait of baseball's travails entering the second wartime season, at the end of which both leagues would announce losses over $200,000. The lead story on page 1 covered Joe DiMaggio's enlistment, and the headline read "DiMaggio Takes Cut—from $40,000 to $50.00 a Month." A note on page 4 announced that General Mills had decided not to sponsor any radio broadcasts during the season. A reader poll on page 7 asked fans, "Should the Game Go On?" with cash prizes going to the best letters on either side. Most extraordinary, perhaps, were the ads. Someone recently discharged from the U.S. Army sought a position as a bat boy. Another from Meridian, Mississippi, offered for sale a complete ballpark lighting system since the Southeastern League would not operate in 1943. Two Minor League clubs sought players, while the Cardinals searched for more. "If you are now a FREE AGENT and have previous professional experience," read the club's ad, "we may be able to place you to your advantage on one of our clubs. We have positions open on our AA, B and D classified clubs." The *New York Times* called this ad "probably without precedent in the history of baseball," but St. Louis owner Sam Breadon admitted, "These are unusual times." Indeed historian David Finoli called 1943 "one of the most bizarre seasons on record." More than two hundred Major Leaguers were now in the service, including a fair number of the game's best players. Some of the lesser teams began to think optimistically, but as the season wore on, the two clubs with the deepest farm systems rose to the top and repeated as champions. The Cardinals finished first again in the National League, winning 105 games, and the Yankees prevailed in the American League, 13½ games ahead of Washington. The Browns regressed and finished seventh. Only Vern Stephens hit over .280, and Chet Laabs's home run total dropped to 17. The Yankees beat the Browns seventeen times against only five losses and turned the tables on the Cardinals in the World Series, winning it four games to one.[35]

The government's restrictions on the use of rubber for nonmilitary purposes had not affected the game on the field in 1942, but 1943 was a different story. A. G. Spalding & Bros. made the balls for both Major Leagues, and the company had enough inventory to last beyond the first wartime season. Baseball officials, though, were concerned that offensive production had declined steadily since 1939. With so many good hitters absent from the game, Commissioner Landis decided to introduce a livelier ball in 1943. Spalding developed sixteen different samples, the U.S. Bureau of Standards tested them, and a committee composed of Landis, Will Harridge, and Warren Giles selected the "balata ball" as the winner. The ball had a center composed of granulated cork covered by two layers of balata, the hard material used to cover golf balls. The yarn surrounding the balata was wound tighter too, in the hope that batting averages and home runs would rise dramatically. In addition the ball's horsehide cover came from a domestic source since the war had cut off shipments of European horsehide, and its substitute, Bolivian horsehide, was also no longer available. Prior to the season the *Sporting News* editorialized, "Pity the poor man on the mound," but the balata ball proved to be a dud. The overall batting average in the Majors stayed about the same, but home runs in 1943 dropped from 1,071 to 905 and total runs scored from 9,995 to 9,694. Historian William B. Mead noted that eleven of the season's first twenty-nine games were shutouts and that the first eleven games featured no home runs at all. The Cooper Union Institute of Technology then retested the balata ball and found it 25.9 percent less resilient than the 1942 ball. Spalding blamed a substandard rubber cement used to adhere one layer of the ball's interior to the next. The American League decided to use the balata ball until a better batch could be made, but the National League switched back to a supply of 1942 balls that Spalding still had in stock. Fortunately the War Production Board eased its restrictions after the season, and Spalding introduced yet another new ball, with a core made from synthetic rubber and a new cork, that had its intended effect.[36]

The Southeastern League's decision not to play in 1943 was symptomatic of the Minors' struggle. Minor League baseball had peaked in 1940, when forty-three leagues played the entire season, but in 1943 that number dropped to nine, reminding club owners and league officials of the nadir of the Depression. The National Association had extended President William G. Bramham's contract in December 1939 and raised his annual salary to $25,000, and the leagues' trust in their leader seemed well placed. After the 1940 season he reported that 4,520 players, a record total, had been reserved for 1941. Despite "the most unseasonable weather . . . the game had ever encountered," two national political conventions that kept fans home listening to the radio, "more or less war hysteria," and a decline in total attendance of one-third, only one league, the Arkansas-Missouri League, had disbanded prematurely. Bramham said he would "confidently look forward" to the following season and that the military draft was "not a cause for alarm." The Minors held steady in 1941. Forty-one leagues finished the season before Pearl Harbor, but only thirty-one began play in 1942, and five of those went out of business before July 4. Not only were more able-bodied athletes being called to military service than Bramham had anticipated, but the exigencies of wartime mobilization, including restrictions on night games and travel, put significant crimps in attendance and in the quality of play. Most rosters included some players either too old or too young for the service, some classified 4-F by Selective Service, and some with day jobs in defense-related industries. Late in the 1943 season Bill Sarni caught thirty-three games for Los Angeles in the Pacific Coast League. Emblematic of the growing manpower crisis, he turned sixteen on September 19. Bramham was not to blame for this decline, but when his health deteriorated, International League president Frank Shaughnessy mounted a challenge to his leadership. Six of the nine active leagues were prepared to vote for change, but Bramham ruled that inactive leagues could vote too, and they returned him to office for another five years.[37]

In November 1943 Senator Scott Lucas (D-IL), responding to yet another suggestion that organized baseball, after two years of war, should suspend operations for the duration, argued the contrary. In a speech on the Senate floor he said that the game, while using only an "infinitesimal" part of the nation's manpower, was making valuable contributions to the war effort, including raising more than $1 billion from the sale of war bonds, giving more than $2.1 million to various war funds, paying nearly $2.3 million in admission taxes, and donating over $250,000 to buy sports equipment shipped overseas. He noted that 151 National League players were already in the service, and of the 263 reserved for the coming season, eighty-five were pre–Pearl Harbor fathers, twenty were over thirty-five years of age, another thirty-one were over thirty, thirty-seven were classified 4-F, and ten had been ordered to report for induction. Baseball did not quit, but it limped into the 1944 season, with the government calling still more ballplayers either to military service or to work in war-related industries. Yankees manager Joe McCarthy threw up his hands when a reporter in spring training asked him to predict his club's starting lineup. "How could I possibly do that?" he complained. "Why I couldn't tell you who will be here next Tuesday." Indeed five of the Yankees' eight starters in 1943 (pitchers excluded) had been different from those in 1942, and six in 1944 were different from those in 1943. Manpower problems affected every Major League team, and more than three thousand Minor Leaguers were also in the military. Ten Minor Leagues started the season, and all finished, but finding enough skilled players at every level of professional play had become a problem. Selective Service had adjusted its criteria for drafting men several times so that there seemed at times to be just two classifications: 1-A (eligible to be called) and 4-F (physically unable to perform). Baseball cringed when government officials suggested putting all 4-Fs into a special labor pool because 4-Fs populated every Major League roster. The Giants, last in 1943, began the 1944 season with sixteen players in that classification, the most in the National League. The Browns started with eighteen 4-Fs, thirteen of whom remained on the roster for the bulk of the season.[38]

To fill out their 1944 rosters, clubs turned to superannuated players too old to be drafted and then, in a spectacular display of desperate naiveté, to the very young. The Browns' regulars included two infielders and two outfielders thirty-two or older, and a handful of American League starters on other teams were thirty-eight or older: Tigers outfielder Doc Cramer, Red Sox outfielder Bob Johnson, A's first baseman Bill McGhee, and Senators first baseman Joe Kuhel. Washington's catcher, Rick Ferrell, called upon to handle a pitching staff featuring four knuckleballers, turned thirty-nine just after the season ended. Starters in the National League were not quite so old, but a fair number of reserves and pitchers were at least thirty-five, topped by Dodgers pitcher Curt Davis, who started twenty-three games and turned forty-one in September. Brooklyn's roster, in fact, showed the lengths to which a club would go to find players capable of performing at the Major League level. The Dodgers ran through twenty-four pitchers, including eighteen-year-old Ralph Branca. Nineteen started at least one game, but twelve pitched in no more than ten games. Brooklyn used twenty-nine position players, including Paul Waner, forty-one, and his brother, Lloyd, thirty-eight. Ten players took a turn in the outfield for the Dodgers, and only two of them played more than sixty-five games. Another ten handled second base. Two of them, Eddie Basinski and Barney Koch, were only twenty-one, as was the Dodgers' first baseman, Howie Schultz, but the youngest man to play for Brooklyn was shortstop Tommy Brown, who would not turn seventeen until December. Brown made his debut on August 3, doubling, scoring a run, and making an error. He hit .164 for the season but remained in the Majors through 1953. It was the Reds, though, who brought the youngest player in baseball history to the Majors. He was fifteen-year-old Joe Nuxhall, a left-handed pitcher who relieved in the game on June 10, with the Reds losing, 13–0. Nuxhall lasted two-thirds of an inning, giving up 2 hits and 5 walks and being charged with 5 runs. He did not pitch in the Majors again until 1952.[39]

In January 1944 Will Harridge acknowledged that "the caliber of baseball is down—it could not be otherwise with so many great American League stars now in service." Yet when Alva Bradley suggested a month later that play should be suspended if it fell below a certain standard, Connie Mack responded, "That's just Bradley's idea," and Bradley himself quickly announced that he had been "misquoted." Still, the real possibility that the quality of play would be further diluted prompted Taylor Spink to write to President Roosevelt, arguing that baseball deserved special consideration. "As far as industry is concerned," Spink said, "I feel that it is a question of comparative valuation of the war effort involved. I believe these 2,000 players (in the majors and minors) when filling the recreational wants of the nation, are occupying a role that is just as valuable as they would be in performing in industry." White House press secretary Stephen Early dismissed this bold assertion. The president, he said, "would prefer to leave the matter from now on for determination under the regulations governing the manpower situation." Commissioner Landis took even more umbrage at Spink's brashness. Railing that the publisher spoke for no one other than himself, the commissioner reminded his listeners that baseball's position on its manpower woes was firm: "We ask no preferential treatment, and we would be disgraced if we got it." As if to demonstrate baseball's sincerity on this point, the Phillies announced in the middle of February that their twenty-eight-year-old president, Bob Carpenter Jr., a married man with two children, had become the first Major League club president to be drafted into the army.[40]

Prior to Opening Day 1944, when Spink's newspaper assigned Dan Daniel to write its preseason predictions, he had approached the task with a certain trepidation. "With a war on," he wrote, "the great players gone and many more bound to leave, the job confronting the 1944 baseball prognosticator is ten times as tough as it was in the days of peace." Daniel picked the Cardinals to repeat as National League pennant winners, calling them "overwhelming favorites." In the American League Daniel anticipated a "hot race" between the Yankees, the defending World Series champions, and the Senators. As for the Browns, Daniel said they "could finish in fifth place," but he consigned them to sixth, ahead of only Detroit and Philadelphia. Even if the *Sporting News*' Opening Day editorial, "Diamond Quality Remains Eminently High," was overly optimistic, all was not bleak. In January Landis and Judge Bramham appointed a postwar planning committee charged with figuring out how to funnel back into the game returning veterans, including Minor Leaguers, some of whose leagues had suspended operations. Allied military forces were winning significant victories in Europe and the Pacific, and baseball continued to do what it called its part to support the war effort. Contributions to the Bat and Ball Fund came from the All-Star Game: $81,275 from ticket revenues,

$25,000 from Gillette for radio rights, and a donation from the game's concessionaire. The Cardinals fulfilled Daniel's prediction by winning the National League pennant handily, but the American League race resulted in a huge upset. Led by Vern Stephens and pitchers Nelson Potter and Sig Jakucki, the surprising Browns played the rest of the league tough all season long. They won their first nine games, held first place at the All-Star break, and entered September in a four-team race with the Tigers, the Red Sox, and the Yankees. On the season's final day the Browns were tied with Detroit. The Tigers lost to Washington, but St. Louis beat the Yankees to capture the only pennant in the team's history. That the Cardinals went on to win what was called the "Streetcar Series," four games to two, was almost incidental.[41]

Landis missed attending the World Series, his first absence since he had become commissioner, and he had to listen to the games on the radio. Approaching his seventy-eighth birthday, he entered St. Luke's Hospital in Chicago on October 2, the day after the season ended and two days before Game One, to be treated for what was described as a severe cold. In fact Landis's health had been less than optimal for a very long time. He had been laid low by a serious bout with the flu in 1928, had undergone surgery for prostate cancer in 1936, and suffered repeatedly from bronchial difficulties that sent him to Florida each winter. His prostate trouble flared up again in 1942, and he often described his difficulties in graphic detail when he wrote to friends. This time his office kept his confinement secret for a few days, and Landis hoped to be discharged in time to cast one more vote against Franklin Roosevelt, running for an unprecedented fourth term as president. But whatever respiratory problems he had, they were complicated by a heart attack that left him weak and grumpy. Press releases from Landis's office downplayed the seriousness of his condition, and club owners were sure he would recover, even as he signed players' World Series checks. On November 17 an owners' committee voted to extend his contract, due to expire in January 1946, for an additional seven years, when he would be eighty-six. It was not to be. His birthday came on November 20, but his condition deteriorated until he died on November 25 of a coronary thrombosis. His body was cremated, and burial took place in Chicago's Oak Woods cemetery. Two weeks later the Baseball Hall of Fame's new Old-Timers Committee, convening for the first time at the winter meetings, elected him to the Hall. The two Major Leagues also agreed to rename their Most Valuable Player Awards, selected by the BBWAA, in his honor.[42]

The Browns' financial position did not improve much during the war years, even when they made the World Series. Home attendance rebounded to 255,617 in 1942, but the total in 1944 was only 508,644, fewer than 8,000 per date and fifth in the league. Just 960 people saw the team win the seventh game in its season-opening nine-game winning streak, and the season's only sellout, 35,518, came on the season's final day. Even the World Series games did not sell out. Receipts for the Series totaled $906,122, the lowest since 1939. Full shares for players on the winning team came to $4,626, but 10 percent of that came in war bonds, and half of the club's revenues had to go to war relief agencies. Bill DeWitt moaned, "Here we are losing money, and for once we get a chance to make some money in the World Series, and we have to give half of it away." Even though the club made a profit of $285,034, Don Barnes was ready to throw in the towel, and on August 10, 1945, Richard Muckerman, who owned 25 percent of the club, bought Barnes's 31 percent and was elected president. Barnes made approximately $200,000 on his original investment and said, after the sale, that he was considering a "trip to Europe to forget my experiences as a baseball magnate."[43]

Eight

"A Great Display of Tingling Patriotism"

The tiny craft were nicknamed "rocket boats," but the young sailor who liked almost nothing more than reading comic books thought he heard "rocket ships" and volunteered. Who wouldn't want to set off in a rocket ship, even on a dangerous mission? Besides, Seaman Second Class Larry Berra was bored. Months before, just after his eighteenth birthday on May 12, 1943, his hometown Selective Service board had notified him that he would soon be drafted. Berra had just recently begun playing baseball for the Norfolk (VA) Tars in the Piedmont League, and he was concerned that his first season was about to be truncated. Shrewdly he asked his draft board to transfer his paperwork from St. Louis to Norfolk, and the gambit worked. The papers took months to arrive in Virginia, so Berra finished the season with the Tars. During the summer they played an exhibition game at the Norfolk Naval Air Station, home of the navy's Atlantic fleet. Berra spoke with the manager of the air station team, who said that if Berra enlisted, he would get assigned to the air station, where he could play ball. After the season Berra passed his physical and joined the navy. He endured six weeks of basic training, but a summons from Norfolk never came. After a short trip home while his mother underwent surgery, Berra went to Little Creek, Virginia, for amphibious training during the day and movies and comic books at night. That's when he encountered the rocket boats. Technically each was an LCS(S), or Landing Craft Support, Small, thirty-six feet long, carrying a crew of one officer and six seamen, and armed with twin .50-caliber machine guns, two .30-caliber machine guns, forty-eight rockets, and a dozen smoke pots for deception. "I didn't think about it being dangerous," Berra told sportswriter Joe Trimble years later. "I was sick of hanging around all day. I wanted to be doing something," and he did, learning to fire the twin .50-caliber guns. After further training Berra's unit boarded an LST (Landing Ship Tank) bound for Boston; joined a convoy off the coast of Halifax, Nova Scotia; and sailed across the Atlantic to Glasgow, Scotland. Moving at last by train to Plymouth, England, Berra and his mates waited. Soon, they knew, it would be D-Day, and they would take part in the massive Allied invasion of northern France.[1]

For Berra, already sometimes called Yogi, the voyage across the Atlantic Ocean was a distant mirror of the trips his parents had taken several decades earlier. Berra was the son of Italian immigrants. His father, Pietro, had arrived in the United States in 1909, passed through the immigration station on Ellis Island, and declared that he was bound for St. Louis, there to visit an uncle. In fact his stop in St. Louis was brief. He went west to California and Colorado before returning to St. Louis and settling in a working-class neighborhood called "the Hill" or, more crudely, "Dago Hill." This clearly defined community was populated almost exclusively by Italian Americans, many of whom sought work with companies that produced bricks and other clay products. Pietro and his friend, Giovanni Garagiola, got jobs at the Laclede-Christy Clay Products Company. He saved enough money to send home and have a young woman named Paolina Longoni come to America. They were married at St. Ambrose, the Hill's parish church, and began a family that eventually included four boys and a girl. Lawrence, the youngest boy, was born Lorenzo, but both parents understandably struggled with English, and their attempts as new Americans to pronounce "Lawrence" came out as "Lawdies." So their youngest son was "Lawdies" at home and "Lawdie" on the street.[2]

Berra started playing baseball when he was about ten or eleven years old. "All the kids around my age who lived on Elizabeth Avenue made up a sports club that we called the Stags A.C.," he recalled, "and we played in the street, in the Shaw School yard, which was only two blocks away, and in Sublette Park, which was maybe half a mile away." Each block had its own club, and their baseball teams played one another regularly. "Every kid on the Hill belonged to a gang or a club," Giovanni Garagiola's son, Joe, said, and the *St. Louis Post-Dispatch* agreed, reporting in 1941 that about a thousand kids on the Hill belonged to nearly fifty neighborhood clubs. Most of their baseball teams had sponsors who provided complete uniforms or maybe just T-shirts, but no one outfitted the lowly Stags. Forced to be resourceful, they wore plain white T-shirts and old overalls, and they scrounged for equipment. Boys shared gloves and made do with splintered bats, and "everybody chipped in to buy a new ball once or twice a summer," Garagiola recalled. They even had a clubhouse, an empty garage that they rented for $12 a month, raising money by buying packs of cigarettes and small boxes of candy and reselling each item individually at a marked-up price. More ambitiously, they claimed an abandoned clay mine, then the neighborhood dump, as their own and converted it into a ball field. The Stags leveled the ground, dragged the infield, and even hauled in two rusty cars to serve as dugouts. Like many immigrant parents,

Pietro Berra frowned on his son's playing baseball, especially if Lawdie slid and ripped his pants. The game was hard for the father to understand, and it seemed frivolous. Moreover, the Stags seemed to do nothing except play, baseball in the spring and summer, soccer and football in the fall and winter. Young Berra, in fact, much preferred sports to school, and his lack of academic achievement further upset his father.[3]

A neighborhood woman introduced the Stags to Major League baseball. A St. Louis Cardinals fan, she sponsored Berra and his pals as members of Branch Rickey's Knothole Gang, which got them free seats in left field's upper deck for every Saturday home game at Sportsman's Park. Seeing Major Leaguers opened Berra's eyes to a world of possibility. "I used to worship the ballplayers," he said. "Watching them was the biggest thing in our lives." When the Cardinals were on the road, the Stags often went to the movies. One day, so the story goes, they watched a travelogue about India and fixed their eyes on a Hindu fakir who sat cross-legged as he charmed a snake and then stood up, walking away from the camera. "Hey," said Bobby Hofman, one of the Stags, "that yogi walks just like Lawdie Berra." Or maybe it was Jack McGuire Jr., another Stag, who saw Berra sitting cross-legged and said, "You look just like a yogi." In either case a new nickname was born, even as Yogi and his friends were beginning to play organized baseball. They participated in a summer-long YMCA tournament and finished second. The following year, still without a sponsor, the Stags broke up. Berra and Garagiola joined the Edmonds, sponsored by a restaurant, and finally got to wear complete uniforms. Berra left school after eighth grade for a series of menial jobs, but he set his sights on baseball as a career. He began to play American Legion ball, excelling at several positions and hitting the ball with power and authority. Post commander Leo Browne thought both Berra and Garagiola could play professionally, but Yogi, short, squat, and rather unorthodox, did not look like a ballplayer. The boys worked out several times at Sportsman's Park, and eventually Browne arranged formal tryouts for both with Rickey in attendance. Garagiola merited a Minor League contract with a $500 signing bonus, but Berra was not so fortunate. He balked when Rickey suggested a contract with no bonus. "I want the same as Joey's getting," Berra said, believing that he was a better ballplayer than his friend. Rickey grudgingly offered $250, but he also proffered this scouting report: "I don't think you can ever be a major league ballplayer. You're not built for this game."[4]

Berra was hurt. The St. Louis Browns had also given him a look and found him wanting. "Ever since I had been a little kid, I had been used to having the other guys laugh at me because of my looks and poke fun at me because I was so clumsy," he recalled, "but I had always been as good a ballplayer as any of them. . . . Now, for the first time, I didn't even have that." Garagiola went off to play professional baseball while Berra remained in St. Louis, working in a shoe factory and playing semipro ball for $5 or $10 a game. Unknown to him, Browne had also written to the New York Yankees, who came to St. Louis for the 1942 World Series. After the Series coach Johnny Schulte showed up at the Berra house. He offered Yogi a contract for $90 a month to play in Norfolk, plus a $500 signing bonus, exactly the sign of respect that Berra thought the Cardinals' proposal had lacked. Schulte saw no need to watch Berra play. He was acting upon instructions from George Weiss, the Yankees' farm director, who had known Browne from their time together in the Eastern League. Papa Berra signed the contract for his underage son, and Yogi waited for spring. Later that winter he received a telegram from Rickey, now running the Brooklyn Dodgers, asking him to come to spring training in Bear Mountain, New York, and sign a contract. It was too late. Yogi was Yankees property, but in Norfolk he learned that he would not receive his bonus unless he stuck with the club for the entire season. Berra made his professional debut on Opening Day, going 0-for-2. In August he put together two extraordinary games, 6 hits and 13 RBIs one day and 6 more hits and 10 RBIs the next. Facing the draft, he chose the navy, relishing the one week he would have off before reporting. When an officer told him the army would have given him a month off, Berra attempted to change his decision, but it was too late. "You're in the navy now," the officer said.[5]

Remembering his perilous trip across the Atlantic aboard LST492, Berra called it "awful. You would lie in your bunk and think what would happen if you hit a mine or were hit by a torpedo. . . . We were cannon fodder. I can now understand why old men send young men to war." In fact German U-boats did attack the eighty-ship convoy on its way from Halifax and sank two tankers. Once the seventy-two LCS(S) crews arrived in England, the navy decided that it needed only twenty-four for the D-Day invasion and reassigned the others. Berra remained with his rocket boat. Early on the morning of June 6 its crew and several others boarded the USS *Bayfield*, a Coast Guard transport that carried them toward the Normandy coast. At 4:30 a.m. the rocket boats were lowered over the side and, in Berra's words, "expendable as hell, we headed for Omaha Beach." The rocket boats' mission was to rendezvous with other boats near the coast and then head west toward Utah Beach. "We had maps showing where the German machine gun emplacements were," Berra said.

"Our job was to let them have it with rockets so that the GIs on LCVPs [Landing Craft, Vehicle, Personnel] following us would have a better chance making it onto the beach." As the rocket boats approached the beach, one launched a test firing to see if they were close enough to the shore. "Then we all joined in," Berra said, "and it was like nothing I had ever seen before in my life."[6]

D-Day was a Tuesday on which no games were scheduled in the American League and only two in the National League, the Philadelphia Phillies at Brooklyn and the Cincinnati Reds at the Pittsburgh Pirates. The newsflash announcing the Allied invasion came at 12:30 a.m., plenty of time for the Dodgers and Pirates to postpone their scheduled night games and for all fans to hear President Franklin Roosevelt's request that the day be dedicated to prayer. Four of the eleven Minor Leagues playing in 1944—the American Association, the International League, the Eastern League, and the Appalachian League—kept their gates closed on D-Day. In the Pacific Coast League, Hollywood and Portland postponed their games while San Francisco and Seattle played theirs. The Southern Association played a full schedule except for the game at Atlanta, postponed by rain. The Interstate League had only one game scheduled, and it, too, was postponed by rain. The Piedmont League played a full schedule, the Ohio State League played its only two scheduled games, and the PONY League played all its games but one.[7]

Prior to the Normandy invasion, news from the front intersected with baseball in various ways. The *Sporting News* took pleasure in noting how military commanders sometimes used baseball vocabulary to describe their operations. Army chief of staff George Marshall wrote that the army used "Play ball" as code during the invasion of North Africa in 1942 to signal "Fire away with all you've got." When the Allies decided in 1943 to invade Italy directly from Sicily instead of first attacking Sardinia or Corsica, General Dwight Eisenhower said, "We are playing in the big leagues. You can't hit a home run by bunting. You have to step up there and take your cut at the ball." On July 25, 1943, the public address announcer at Yankee Stadium interrupted the second game of a doubleheader between the Chicago White Sox and the Yankees to tell the crowd that Italian prime minister Benito Mussolini had resigned. Three days before D-Day, the crowd at the Polo Grounds in New York heard an announcement that the invasion had begun. The news was premature, of course, the result of an overzealous Associated Press teletype operator who had punched out the news for practice and transmitted it inadvertently. As a general rule the Office of War Information enjoined all broadcasters to safeguard the home front by never mentioning the weather during ball games. Brooklyn announcer Red Barber recalled that he would explain a rain delay by saying something like, "The game is stopped, and when it resumes, we'll let you know." Retired pitcher Dizzy Dean, broadcasting for both St. Louis teams, took a folksier approach, blurting out, "If you folks don't know what's holding up this game, just stick your heads out the window."[8]

Long before Allied troops secured the French beachhead, the daily responsibility for running organized baseball had fallen more and more to Commissioner Kenesaw Landis's reliable deputy, Leslie O'Connor. Soon after taking office in 1920, Landis had realized that he needed an assistant, someone without loyalty to any particular club. In February 1921 he went outside baseball to select O'Connor, a thirty-one-year-old attorney. A native of Chicago, O'Connor had enlisted in the army during the Great War. Assigned to the Judge Advocate Board for the Central District, he helped prosecute a man who claimed status as a conscientious objector. The case was assigned to Landis, who found the defendant guilty. "The judge rendered a decision in our favor," O'Connor recalled, "but pronounced it orally. . . . Our department was anxious to get it in the book as a precedent. Inasmuch as I had made shorthand notes of the judge's remarks in court, I wrote up the decision and persuaded him to sign it." After the armistice O'Connor was back in private practice when the telephone rang. "I need an assistant," the judge said when they met. "You know a lot of young lawyers. I thought you could give me the name of one." They talked for a half hour, and Landis asked him if he wanted the job. "I don't know anything about the administrative end of baseball," said O'Connor. "That's all right," replied Landis. "Neither do I—we'll learn together." Hired at a salary of $7,500 a year, O'Connor stayed with Landis throughout his tenure, writing decisions issued in the commissioner's name and running a very tight and efficient office. O'Connor did most of the investigative work for the commissioner's office and was, according to one observer, "thorough and merciless." One of his contributions was codifying the regulations governing the way the business operated. Another task was refining the index card system tracking the contract history of every player who signed a professional contract. By 1945 there were cards for over fifty thousand players, active and inactive, and on each, clerks used rubber stamps to record transfers, options, and other data vital to protecting the interests of players and clubs alike.[9]

When Landis died on November 25, 1944, organized baseball was befuddled. Never had the owners who employed the commissioner faced the reality of replacing one. Almost immediately O'Connor disavowed any interest in succeeding his deceased boss. "I have a short life to live," he said, "and I want none of that job. It's a killer." Yet at the owners' winter meetings in early December O'Connor agreed to serve as a member of a three-man advisory council that would take charge of the sport temporarily. Technically what the owners did was terminate the 1921 Major League agreement that created the office of commissioner and allowed the owners to hire Landis. The action taken on December 11 conferred "all the powers and duties of the commissioner" upon the new council, consisting of O'Connor and Will Harridge and Ford Frick, the presidents of the two Major Leagues. They would govern by majority vote except that "in any case involving a player's claim against the club or league," O'Connor would rule alone. The council was empowered to exercise its authority "until a new major league agreement shall be entered into between each of the major leagues and each constituent club of each major league, which agreement shall provide for a commissioner of baseball." That was the plan, but how it should come to pass caused some discussion. The Dodgers' Branch Rickey plus owners Clark Griffith of the Washington Senators and Horace Stoneham of the New York Giants suggested looking outside the sport for the next commissioner, someone, in Griffith's words, "who carries the confidence of the public." The Yankees' Ed Barrow, on the other hand, favored promoting from within. Still others argued that Landis had wielded too much power and that baseball should perhaps return to the pre-Landis National Commission, the unwieldy triumvirate consisting of the two league presidents and a third member elected by the other two.[10]

Baseball needed new leadership not only to administer its internal affairs, but also to continue the battle against those in the government who wanted to shut the sport down while the war was still on. Landis had done his best to position baseball as a patriotic endeavor, decreeing, as one of his final acts, that half the receipts from the 1944 World Series would be donated to war relief agencies and that players would receive 10 percent of their Series shares in war bonds. This was not enough to satisfy the critics, even though 260 of baseball's 400 current Major Leaguers had been classified 4-F (physically unable to perform) by their local draft boards. When President Roosevelt sent his State of the Union message to Congress in writing on January 6, 1945, he renewed his call for a national service act that Congress had rejected the year before as an unwarranted expansion of executive power. Roosevelt couched his request in benign terms. "I now again call upon the Congress to enact this measure for the total mobilization of all our human resources for the prosecution of the war," he wrote, but its intended targets were the nation's five million 4-Fs, who, the president said, could serve "in whatever capacity is best for the war effort." When James F. Byrnes, director of the Office of War Mobilization, closed all horse racing and dog racing tracks early in the year, he also asked Selective Service to revisit the draft status of all athletes, including the 4-Fs. Byrnes wondered how men declared unfit for military service could perform well as athletes, and he suggested that even legitimate 4-Fs might be fit enough for light military duty or factory work. Ford Frick and Clark Griffith met with Selective Service director Lewis Hershey to save the season, but Hershey exerted his own pressure. He declared that players classified 4-F by local draft boards would have their cases reviewed in Washington and that those with 2-A or 2-B occupational deferments needed to stay in their off-season jobs or risk being drafted. Congressman Andrew Jackson May (D-KY), chairman of the House Military Affairs Committee, also questioned baseball's continuation. "Any man who is able to play baseball is able to fight or work in a war plant," he said, as his committee considered what amounted to "work-or-fight" legislation. "If baseball has a morale value, it can be just as great played in the Army."[11]

Several Major Leaguers suddenly found themselves victims of this new hard line. In the words of baseball historian Richard Goldstein, "A number of ballplayers previously turned down by the armed forces [were drafted] simply because they were professional athletes." Phillies outfielder Ron Northey was the first. Deaf in one ear, Northey had failed two induction physicals, but in December 1944 Selective Service called him again. He failed a third time, yet in January was reclassified 1-A and summoned for induction. Cincinnati catcher Ray Mueller had a stomach ulcer that had kept him out of service. Called for reexamination early in 1945, he was found fit and inducted. So was Hugh Poland, who had played just a few Major League games in 1943 and 1944. He had injured his ankle, and the navy had rejected him when he tried to volunteer. Yet his draft board summoned him for a pre-induction physical in 1945. His file, he remembered, was marked with a big red "PA" for "professional athlete," but three doctors from the army, the navy, and the marines all rejected him. Just as he was about to leave the examination center, someone called him to another room. "Mr. Poland," said the fourth physician to look him over, "I'm going to tell you something. If you can play baseball on that leg of yours, you can go into the armed services." Poland protested that he had already been rejected. "That doesn't make a difference, you're a professional baseball player," said the doctor. "So I was in," Poland said. "And I was married, and I had two kids." Outfielder Danny Litwhiler's story paralleled Poland's. After suffering a knee injury in the Minors, he had been rejected six times but was summoned again in January. The same doctor who had seen him previously said, "You're rejected again. It's the same knee, it's never gonna be any different." But a captain followed up with Litwhiler and said, "Oh, I want to congratulate you. We've decided you should go in the service."[12]

Baseball's continuation during wartime had its defenders too. One was Senator Albert "Happy" Chandler (D-KY), who spoke against May's position. "It's foolish to discount the value of baseball as a morale factor," he said. "For that reason alone, those fellows would be more valuable playing ball than fiddling around at something else." Another was FBI director J. Edgar Hoover, who said that "there is no doubt about the wartime morale value of the game." A third supporter, not surprisingly, was Taylor Spink, who urged the owners to hire a new commissioner soon to lead this fight. In February the owners had appointed a four-man committee to evaluate potential candidates. Its members were Don Barnes of the Browns, Alva Bradley of the Cleveland Indians, Sam Breadon of the Cardinals, and Phil Wrigley of the Chicago Cubs. Meanwhile, Clark Griffith, Ford Frick, and Will Harridge were lobbying government officials to let their business continue. They proposed cutting rosters from twenty-five to twenty-two, reducing travel by 25 percent, and canceling the All-Star Game and, if necessary, the World Series. When Griffith visited the president in March, as he did every year to give him his annual pass, Roosevelt endorsed the game as he had done before. "I am all in favor of baseball," he told the press, "so long as you don't use perfectly healthy people that could be doing more useful work in the war." Later that month the "work-or-fight" bill failed to pass, and the War Manpower Commission decided that players working in war plants during the off-season would be free to leave those jobs to play ball through October. Byrnes endorsed this ruling, perhaps because the Allied war effort was progressing well, and early in April Vice President Harry Truman, soon to become president, also approved baseball's continuation.[13]

Even before Commissioner Landis died, baseball insiders speculated on who might succeed him if he retired at age seventy-nine when the basic agreement was set to expire in January 1946. One person mentioned was Judge Harry McDevitt, a friend of Philadelphia Athletics owner Connie Mack. Other potential candidates surfaced soon after Landis passed, including James Farley, former political adviser to President Roosevelt; Jimmy Walker, former mayor of New York; and Thomas Courtney, an Illinois Democrat who had just been defeated in a race for governor. John Drebinger noted in the *New York Times* that Courtney "has long been a close follower of baseball [who] owns one of the most extensive libraries on the game." The search committee cast a much wider net and considered such people as Frick, Herbert Hoover, Byrnes, Democratic National Committee chairman Robert Hannegan, Supreme Court justice William O. Douglas, Chandler, and former Ohio governor John Bricker. Branch Rickey pushed the committee to name a new commissioner quickly, but finding a consensus proved difficult, especially since owners were also unsure what powers the next commissioner should wield. After circulating a list of six candidates with their biographies attached, the committee called a joint meeting of both leagues for April 24, saying that it would have a recommendation. Yet when the owners convened, the committee's report included no recommendation and, in fact, no names. Pressured to produce a list of finalists, committee members cobbled together a list of eleven, not including Chandler. Many owners, including some who argued for hiring a temporary commissioner, had their say. They reduced the list to five—Chandler, Farley, Frick, Hannegan, and Ohio governor Frank Lausche—and began to vote. Farley and Frick were eliminated after the first ballot, and Lausche was dropped after the second. The tally on the third ballot was 11–4, Chandler over Hannegan, and Chandler was elected.[14]

Chandler's affection for baseball went back to his childhood, when he played catch with his father, followed the World Series by telegraph at the local railroad depot, and delivered copies of the weekly *Sporting News*, along with daily newspapers, to subscribers in his hometown, Corydon, Kentucky. He played football and baseball in high school, making a local name for himself as a pretty fair pitcher. He played, too, at Transylvania University in Lexington, where his coach, former Major Leaguer Jim Park, "put some polish on my game, showing me how to throw a better curve as well as a fastball." His outgoing disposition earned him the nickname "Happy," and his athletic prowess got him as far as semipro baseball. Chandler attended law school, got married, and entered electoral politics as a Democrat. He served first in the state senate, then as lieutenant governor and governor. In 1939 U.S. senator Marvel Logan died in office. Chandler resigned as governor, and his successor, Keen Johnson, appointed him to fill the vacancy. Chandler won a special election in 1940 to fill the balance of Logan's term and a full six-year term in his own right in 1942. Chandler was also a fan. He attended games at Cincinnati's Crosley Field and got to know Reds executive Larry MacPhail in the 1930s. During the war he was steadfastly in baseball's corner, even arranging a meeting with the president in 1943 so baseball officials could plead their case. He probably came to baseball's attention as a candidate to succeed Landis through the effort of John Gottlieb, a businessman who lived, as did the senator, at Washington's Mayflower Hotel. Gottlieb, who knew the owners of both the Cubs and the White Sox, appreciated Chandler's enthusiasm for baseball and suggested him to MacPhail, back in baseball as president of the Yankees after more than two years' service in the army. MacPhail advanced Chandler's name at the owners' April meeting, and the *Sporting News* called him the "perfect choice."[15]

Chandler was surprised when MacPhail called with news of his election, and he was attracted by the offer: a seven-year term at $50,000 a year plus expenses. Even though senators made only $10,000 a year, his initial reaction was to say no. "Larry," he said, "the war's not over yet. . . . I can't quit, I can't leave the Senate until we whip our enemies." MacPhail countered that baseball could wait. "So I accepted the offer," Chandler wrote, "with the understanding that I would not actively serve until I could in good conscience resign from the Senate." That did not happen until November. In the interim baseball owners and the commissioner-in-waiting met in July to understand the ramifications of the new Major League agreement under which Chandler would operate. Owners had set up a ten-man drafting committee in December 1944 and approved a new agreement in New York in February. One owner said their work was merely to "clarify the code," but the document that emerged went some distance toward curbing the power of the commissioner. Electing a new one, for example, would now require a three-fourths vote, not a simple majority, and the advisory council put in place after Landis's death would continue to review suggested amendments to existing rules. Individual owners recovered the right to sue the commissioner over an unfavorable ruling, and the commissioner's power to rule on any matter he considered "detrimental to baseball" was curtailed. MacPhail argued that "there has been no limitation of authority of the commissioner," but he added that Landis erred when he attempted to seize both "legislative and judicial authority. There was nothing in the rules or his contract to justify such interpretation." At the July meeting Chandler stated his opinion starkly. "I was elected unanimously," he said. "When I accepted, I assumed I would have full powers and I insist upon having full powers, and nothing short of it." To demonstrate the clout he expected to wield, he named Walter Mulbry from his Washington office as secretary and treasurer in the commissioner's office, and he shifted Leslie O'Connor to a new job, special assistant to the commissioner. In addition he moved baseball's headquarters from Chicago to Cincinnati, setting up shop on the twenty-sixth floor of the Carew Tower, at the time the tallest building in the city.[16]

The *Sporting News* published the 1945 American League schedule on March 15 and the National League schedule a week later. Each called for a total of 616 games, 154 per team, a regimen in place for good, it seemed, since 1920. Significantly nearly one-fifth of all games would be played at night, a stark contrast from just a decade before, when Cincinnati had introduced night baseball to the Major Leagues against substantial skepticism. Five clubs—the Boston Braves and the Red Sox, the Cubs, the Detroit Tigers, and the Yankees—still declined to install lights, but, as David Pietrusza wrote, "an orderly progression [toward night baseball] still seemed inevitable." At the winter meetings in December 1942, both leagues had reauthorized a maximum of fourteen night games per club for 1943 along with the Senators' twenty-one-game exception. Clark Griffith again argued for thirty-five or more night games to attract the hordes of wartime government workers then resident in Washington, but he did not get his way until July after showing that the average crowd for a night game at Griffith Stadium was fourteen thousand, far above the typical Senators' day game. In October 1943 government authorities had announced that German U-boats no longer posed a threat to shipping silhouetted against city lights, and they lifted the restriction on night games played along the eastern seaboard. This allowed both the Dodgers and Giants in New York and the Athletics and Phillies in Philadelphia to play night games in 1944. The Dodgers even donned satin uniforms, both home and away, believing the shiny fabric would provide improved visibility under the lights. At midseason in 1944 owners lifted all restrictions on night games, except on weekends, and the two St. Louis teams immediately pushed all their remaining midweek games to the evening. In 1945 the Cardinals scheduled forty-six night games, the Browns forty-three, and the Senators thirty-one plus four twilight/night doubleheaders. All other clubs, save the five holdouts, held to fourteen.[17]

The 1943 All-Star Game at Shibe Park was the first one scheduled at night. Game time was set for 8:45, but the Senators' Dutch Leonard did not throw the first pitch until 9:00 to accommodate the British Broadcasting Corporation, sending the game to servicemen around the world via shortwave radio. Managers Joe McCarthy of the Yankees and Billy Southworth of the Cardinals were responsible for selecting their entire squads. McCarthy picked five Yankees and then kept them all on the bench throughout the game, reacting to criticism that his league could not win without contributions from New York.

Fourteen players from the 1942 game were in the service, and eighteen made their debuts as the Americans won, 5–3. The game, called "a huge success" by the *Sporting News*, drew a near-capacity crowd and raised $115,174 for the Bat and Ball Fund. Players received a $50 war bond. The 1944 game at Forbes Field in Pittsburgh was also played at night. The National League won, 7–1, but the crowd was far short of capacity. Perhaps fans were disheartened that thirty players from the past two games were in the military. The 1945 game, set for Boston's Fenway Park, fell victim to further restrictions on wartime travel. On February 21 the Office of Defense Transportation (ODT) requested that all athletic teams cut their 1945 travel by 25 percent. The Major Leagues responded by consolidating the regular-season schedule somewhat, scrubbing the All-Star Game, and canceling the World Series unless the military situation improved. Ford Frick calculated that dropping the All-Star Game would save about five hundred thousand passenger miles. At the same April meeting at which owners elected Happy Chandler commissioner, they approved a plan first suggested by *Boston Post* sportswriter Jack Malaney to schedule a series of exhibition games over what would have been the All-Star break between geographically contiguous teams. ODT sanctioned seven of these games, all except the Tigers at the Pirates. Together, they raised $240,000, split between the National War Fund and the American Red Cross.[18]

Allocating proceeds from the All-Star Game and especially the World Series to war-related causes was often, in the words of historian Steven Bullock, "a disjointed and complicated affair." The Series, of course, could last from four to seven games, and officials also had to consider team travel and other expenses, ballparks with different seating capacities, and, not surprisingly, tax considerations that encouraged charitable donations. In 1942, for example, baseball executives determined that the World Series between the Yankees and the Cardinals would benefit both the USO and the American Red Cross. The scheme that evolved had the owners retaining all proceeds from Games One, Two, and Five and splitting the revenues from Games Three and Four, played in Yankee Stadium with almost twice as many seats as Sportsman's Park, with the two charities. The owners also agreed to donate all the receipts from Games Six and Seven, but the Cardinals spoiled that largesse by winning in five games. Players on the winning team received $6,193, a considerable sum, while the losers each received $3,352. According to Bullock, players had to promise to rebate their shares for the last three games, but none of these, it turned out, was played. In all, the 1942 Series donated $365,000 to the two charities, and other wartime Series followed much the same pattern.[19]

A complex slate of war relief games began in 1942 and continued, albeit in an abbreviated way, through 1945. These games almost always benefited the Army and Navy Relief Fund that provided support to families of those listed as missing in action. After the Dodgers hosted the Giants on May 8, 1942, every other team staged at least one relief game each season through 1944. The *Sporting News* lauded owners who marketed these games to maximize their charitable potential and criticized those who failed to live up to this obligation. Some clubs, for example, selected unattractive dates for their relief games to minimize their losses. In all, clubs donated more than $525,000 to the relief funds in 1942, far more than the goal of $250,000. Relief games in 1943, though, raised only $325,000, and in 1944, only a bit more than that, the novelty of these occasions having worn off as the number of Major Leaguers in the service increased. War bond sales were another way for clubs and players, using their celebrity, to contribute to the war effort. Clubs set up war bond booths inside ballparks, and, according to Bullock, Dodgers players went through the stands on Easter 1943, encouraging bond purchases that totaled over $75 million. Most unusually, the Brooklyn and New York chapters of the Baseball Writers' Association of America organized a unique auction that turned into, in Bullock's words, "a bond sale extravaganza." Cajoling business and civic leaders to attend a luncheon at the Waldorf-Astoria Hotel, they auctioned off the performances of thirty-six players, twelve each from the Dodgers, Giants, and Yankees, to form the War Bond League. Successful bidders pledged to purchase bonds in the amount of their bids and then to augment that amount based on the players' performances during the balance of the season. A single would cost winning bidders $2,500, a double $5,000, a triple $7,500, and a home run $10,000. Pitchers commanded $35,000 for a win and $50,000 for a shutout. In this way, former mayor Jimmy Walker, the master of ceremonies, persuaded attendees to part with an extraordinary amount of money.[20]

The Bat and Ball Fund, administered by Griffith and Frick, was more than window dressing on baseball's effort to appear patriotic. Recreational baseball in the armed services was an enormous enterprise, but the federal government was reluctant to support it by diverting resources critical to military and naval operations. Thus, it became the fund's goal to raise enough money to maintain fields, transport teams, and, in the words of *Washington Post* sports columnist Shirley Povich, provide equipment for "every post, on every front, home and foreign." In addition to purchasing baseball gear, tax-free, directly from manufacturers, the fund worked with Major and Minor League teams to pass on used equipment and foul balls returned by fans. The fund grew rapidly, especially in its first year, and by the end of 1942 had already supplied close to a hundred thousand balls, forty thousand bats, thirty thousand gloves, seven hundred bases, and four thousand sets of catcher's equipment. What military teams lacked were uniforms, "quite costly," according to the *Sporting News*, forcing officers in charge of athletic programs to scrounge as best they could. Despite the massive amounts of equipment the fund was able to provide, some service teams, including many overseas, didn't have enough. The army admitted that Special Services, the branch responsible for recreation, lacked the "flexibility needed to operate under varying conditions, especially in combat areas." Then, too, constructing and maintaining playing fields also could be a problem. Povich reported from the Marianas Islands in 1945 that soldiers and sailors were playing on fields abandoned by the Japanese. Despite these problems the Bat and Ball Fund worked. In Bullock's judgment, "Professional baseball organizations contributed financially to America's military effort while simultaneously satisfying the baseball appetites of soldiers and sailors."[21]

By winning the 1942 All-Star Game, the American League team got to play an army-navy All-Star team the following night in Cleveland. Managed by former Detroit manager Mickey Cochrane, the service team, composed "largely of famed big leaguers," in the words of Fred Lieb, lost, 5–0, before a paid crowd of 62,094 plus 2,000 soldiers and sailors who were admitted for free. These two games brought in total receipts of $255,000, with $62,000 being rebated to Cleveland fans in the form of war rationing coupons. Of the remaining money, $100,000 went to the Bat and Ball Fund and $93,000 to the Army and Navy Relief Fund. The Cleveland game served as a precursor to other similar fundraising exhibitions. In May 1943 Shirley Povich coordinated a game at Griffith Stadium between the Senators and the Norfolk Naval Training Station Bluejackets, perhaps the best service team, featuring several Major Leaguers. The Bluejackets won, 4–3, with the price of tickets going wholly to the purchase of war bonds. The game raised over $2 million—the second-largest gate for any sporting event to that date—and spurred others to think creatively along the same lines. In August a roster composed of the players selected in New York's War Bond League played a game featuring more auctions and war bond sales. Minor League teams did their bit too, albeit with a lower profile. One notable game in August 1943 matched a team of servicemen stationed on the West Coast against two Pacific Coast League teams, each for four and a half innings. Joe DiMaggio, recently inducted, helped draw twenty thousand fans, who donated $25,000 to buy athletic equipment. Negro Leaguers, too, sometimes played against white teams to support the war effort. In the spring of 1942 Wrigley Field hosted the Kansas City Monarchs, featuring pitcher Satchel Paige, against a team of Major Leaguers already in the service and captained by Dizzy Dean. The Monarchs won, 3–1, before a crowd of thirty thousand, the largest crowd at Wrigley that season.[22]

Many servicemen played baseball informally or in recreational leagues, but the very best, Major Leaguers included, were assigned, sometimes as "recreation specialists," to teams representing their units or the facilities where they were stationed. Commanders yearned, according to Richard Goldstein, "to carve out their own little athletic empires," and they were willing to manipulate regulations to make that happen. Tigers pitcher Virgil Trucks, for example, wanted to play for Cochrane and the Great Lakes Naval Training Station Bluejackets. Trucks had registered for the draft in Birmingham, Alabama, but Cochrane told him to get his papers transferred to a local board in Chicago. After doing so, he got his induction notice, ordering him to report to Great Lakes. The navy had several excellent teams, including the Great Lakes Bluejackets, two at Norfolk, and others at Bainbridge, Maryland, and Sampson, New York. The army tried to keep pace, but sometimes things went awry. Dodgers pitcher Kirby Higbe got processed into the army at Ft. Jackson, South Carolina, in just three hours because the fort's team had a game that afternoon. Pete Reiser, a star outfielder, nearly got discharged when he contracted pneumonia, but a colonel at Ft. Riley, Kansas, "looking forward to having a hell of a ball club here," ripped up the paperwork. Early in the war, military teams played each other in the United States and sometimes raised considerable amounts for war-related charities. In June 1942 army and navy All-Star teams, both full of Major Leaguers, played a five-inning game at the Polo Grounds before fifteen thousand fans. The navy won, 4–0. Another game later in the year occurred near the Panama Canal. The Atlantic Side All-Stars, led by Cardinals outfielder Terry Moore, defeated the Pacific Side All-Stars, as fans pledged $300,000 in war bond purchases.[23]

As more and more ballplayers joined the service and went overseas, the number of games played in both Europe and the Pacific grew commensurately. Most games matched American teams against each other, but an early fundraiser for the Red Cross pitted Americans versus Canadians at London's Wembley Stadium. In August 1943 Wembley hosted a doubleheader that drew 21,500 fans who contributed nearly $9,000 to the Duke of Gloucester's Red Cross and St. John Fund. The first game matched amateur American and Canadian teams. The second, touted as the first all-professional game in England since the Giants–White Sox tour of 1924, matched select squads from the U.S. Army team and the Eighth Air Force. After Germany surrendered in May 1945, military units organized a series of regional tournaments throughout Europe, leading to the GI World Series in Nuremberg. This best-of-five series matched the Seventy-First Infantry Division, whose roster included Major Leaguers, against the Overseas Invasion Services Expedition (OISE) All-Stars, with a roster that included Minor Leaguers and semipro players plus Negro League stars Leon Day and Willard Brown. The teams split the first four games before the OISE stars fashioned a major upset, scoring a run on a ninth-inning sacrifice fly to win, 2–1. The army got the jump on the navy when it came to baseball in the Pacific theater. In the spring of 1944 Chief of Staff George Marshall reacted to a report that 280 former professional baseball players were in the army but still serving stateside. Marshall ordered them overseas, and many went to Hawaii. The navy did not issue a similar directive until the spring of 1945, but long before that it had sent most of its best ballplayers to Hawaii, according to Goldstein, "to counter the army presence." Trucks remembered going home on leave late in 1944 and receiving a telegram as soon as he walked in the door ordering him to return to Great Lakes. The next day he boarded several planes and wound up in Hawaii to play in the Army-Navy World Series. The navy won eight games, the army two, and one ended in a tie. The navy then divided its players into two teams. They played one another on a string of islands just liberated from the Japanese. The army reinforced its roster with more players from the states and created three teams that toured in similar fashion. After Japan surrendered in September 1945, the navy brought its best players back to Hawaii, divided them into an American League squad and a National League squad, and played a seven-game series at Honolulu's Furlong Field.[24]

Before the war ended, more than four thousand players, both Major Leaguers and Minor Leaguers, had interrupted or ended their careers to serve in the armed forces. Many continued playing ball as part of their military duty, but others faced the brutal realities of combat. Two Major Leaguers, both of whom had played briefly, died in action. Elmer Gedeon, an outfielder with the Senators, died on April 20, 1944, when a Luftwaffe fighter shot down his B-26 Marauder over St. Pol, France. Harry O'Neill, who caught one game for the Athletics in 1939 and joined the marines in 1940, was killed on Iwo Jima on March 6, 1945. More than a hundred Minor Leaguers also lost their lives. Among them was Billy Southworth Jr., son of the Cardinals' manager. He flew twenty-five bombing missions over Europe before returning to the states for reassignment. On February 15, 1945, he took off from Long Island in a B-29 Superfortress, headed for Florida. One of the plane's engines quit. Southworth attempted an emergency landing, overshot the runway, and crashed. Minor League pitcher Bert Shepard was shot down in 1944 and woke up in a prisoner-of-war hospital, where German doctors had amputated his right leg below the knee. After the war he tried out for the Senators wearing an artificial leg, made the roster, and pitched in a regular-season game. Lou Brissie, another pitching prospect, survived artillery fire that broke his left ankle and right foot and came back to pitch seven seasons in the Majors. Less fortunate was Cecil Travis, who hit .359 playing shortstop for the Senators in 1941, his ninth year in the Majors, before being drafted and missing almost four full seasons. His feet froze during the Battle of the Bulge, and when he got back to the Majors, his form was off and his timing gone. "I just gave it up," he said, after retiring in the middle of the 1947 season.[25]

Among Major League owners, one who contributed most substantively to the war effort was Phil Wrigley of the Cubs. According to a 1943 profile in *Fortune*, the chewing gum magnate turned over five hundred thousand pounds of aluminum ingots, intended to be used for wrapping foil, to the Office of Production Management in March 1941. Shortly after Pearl Harbor he dismantled the huge electric "Wrigley" sign in New York's Times Square and shut off the floodlights illuminating the Wrigley Building in Chicago. He loaned Catalina Island, his personal fiefdom off the coast of Southern California and the Cubs' prewar spring training site, to the government for military training. He instructed workers in South America tapping trees for gum to tap also for rubber, and he converted a facility that packed chewing gum into one that packed K-rations, individual meals for soldiers in combat. In addition Wrigley, who had once called night baseball "just a fad, a passing fancy" but later changed his mind and ordered $185,000 of lights, steel, and wiring to be installed in Wrigley Field starting on December 8, 1941, had general manager Jim Gallagher call the War Department on that Monday morning to donate the material. None of these actions mattered very much in the long run, and some could have been keyed to a desire to see that the chewing gum business and the baseball business were not mothballed during the war, but Wrigley also sought a ready alternative to baseball if the sport were forced to shut down. He found what he wanted in women's softball, and in early 1943 he invested $100,000 to establish the All-American Girls' Softball League (AAGSL).[26]

The contract between the nonprofit league's board of trustees and the local officials in several cities who agreed to invest $22,500 to operate a team outlined three objectives: "to furnish additional means of healthful recreation to the public," "to create the incentive on the part of girls and women employed in war work to get out and play softball themselves," and "to keep all workers better satisfied with living in the community in which they are now located by furnishing additional entertainment which may now be available to them only in large cities." And yet when Wrigley commissioned Jimmy Hamilton, the Cubs' chief scout, to organize tryout camps in several cities, it became apparent immediately that the AAGSL would be no recreational league. On May 17 more than 150 players from twenty-six states and five Canadian provinces converged on Wrigley Field for spring training, and the number was cut to 60, four teams of 15 players each. Players signed personal service contracts with the league for amounts ranging from $40 to $85 a week. There was no reserve clause, but players agreed to abide by a code of conduct that governed appearance and behavior and required a chaperone to travel with each team. Despite publicity emphasizing that the league would exhibit "the highest ideals of womanhood," an image of acceptable female athleticism, Arthur Meyerhoff, who handled the league's promotional agenda at its inception, asserted that skill did not take a back seat to appearance. Starting on June 1, each team played a one-hundred-game schedule, with games six days a week, including doubleheaders on Saturdays. Tickets sold for sixty cents, less for children, and the teams also scheduled exhibition games at army and navy facilities, with service personnel admitted for free.[27]

To distance the league from recreational softball and to attract ticket buyers, Wrigley adjusted the playing rules to make the game look more like baseball. Nine players, instead of ten, took the field. The pitching distance was set at forty feet, not thirty-five. Base runners could take a lead and steal, and pitchers could start their delivery with only one foot on the rubber. Midway through the first season the league changed its name to the All-American Girls' Base Ball League (AAGBBL). The league lasted a dozen seasons (1943–54), and the playing rules continued to evolve, moving each season further from softball and closer to baseball. The diameter of the ball shrank from twelve inches in 1943 to nine inches in 1954. The length of the base paths grew from sixty-five feet to eighty-five. Pitchers threw underhand for four seasons, then sidearm for two, and then overhand as the pitching distance increased from forty feet to sixty feet. These changes excited and enticed some players but discouraged others. Tommie Thompson, a pitcher from South Carolina, complained, "I pitched underhand for three years and tried sidearm. I couldn't handle overhand pitching. It was the end of my career." Fortitude was never the issue. Players wore uniforms with short, full, flared skirts, and they slid with abandon. "We kind of looked at them [the uniforms] and realized if we were going to stay and play, we'd have to play in the skirts," recalled Dottie Kamenshek, the league's best hitter. Chet Grant, a former Notre Dame football player who managed in the league for three seasons, shed his initial skepticism at the quality of play these rules would foster. "You had to see it to believe it," he said, "and then you didn't."[28]

Wrigley sold his interest in the league to Meyerhoff after the 1943 season. For the next six years the league operated under his centralized administration, with clubs paying fees for promotion and advertising. After 1950 club owners bought Meyerhoff out, and the league began to decline. Wrigley's plan to place teams in Major League cities never came to fruition, except for a brief stint in Chicago, perhaps because organized baseball—that is, the men's game—never suspended operations during the war. Nor did the league achieve Wrigley's dream that its players would become as famous as other women athletic greats. The AAGBBL expanded to six teams in 1944 and to as many as ten in 1948, but in the main these teams played in smaller cities clustered in Illinois, Michigan, and Wisconsin. Attendance peaked in 1948 and tapered off after that. Only five teams played in 1954. More than six hundred women played in the league overall, and for many of them the chance to play stretched beyond being a wartime substitution to embrace opportunities for good incomes and better lives. As women's studies scholar Carol J. Pierman pointed out, the league persevered for a while even as the immediate postwar years brought pressure for women to retreat to traditional roles. During the war league games drew crowds by incorporating patriotic activities like blood drives, but in the 1950s American families moved to new suburban communities and started watching television for entertainment. Even exhibitions played at veterans' hospitals, drives to support the Red Cross, and tours, both national and international, could not keep the league afloat.[29]

By 1945 more than five hundred one-time Major Leaguers were in the service. Such was the state of baseball that sportswriter Warren Brown, as he anticipated the World Series between the Cubs and the Tigers, is said to have remarked, "I don't think either team is capable of winning." Yet these two clubs were fortunate. Most of their starters in 1945 had been their starters in 1944. Other teams had roster spots to fill in both these seasons, and sometimes they reached back into baseball's past to do so. Jimmie Foxx, who broke into the Major Leagues in 1925, had retired after batting just .226 for the Cubs in 1942. Yet he came back briefly with Chicago in 1944 and then signed with the Phillies in 1945. Foxx hit .268 in 89 games and even pitched in 9 of them. Outfielder Ben Chapman, a rookie in 1930, did much the same, playing and pitching for Brooklyn in 1944 and Brooklyn and the Phillies in 1945. Pepper Martin retired after the 1940 season but came back to play 40 games with the Cardinals in 1944. Babe Herman, out of the Majors since 1937, played 37 games in 1945 for the Dodgers and hit .265. Brothers Paul and Lloyd Waner doggedly hung on. Paul played 114 games in 1942, the year he turned thirty-nine, 82 games in 1943, 92 games in 1944, and 1 game in 1945. Lloyd, two years younger, sat out the 1943 season but played 34 games in 1944 and 23 in 1945. Al Simmons, whose first season was 1924, played 4 games in 1944 at age forty-two. Other players, not nearly stars, got one last chance in the Majors. Paul Schreiber had pitched sixteen innings for Brooklyn in 1922 and 1923. In 1937 he became the Yankees' batting practice pitcher, and in 1945 he was added to the roster and got into 2 games. Bill Steineke, a catcher, came up just short. Years after he got four at bats for the Pirates in 1931, the Yankees called him up from the Minors in 1944, when Rollie Hemsley was drafted. But Steineke never got into a game.[30]

Just before Opening Day in 1945 Taylor Spink predicted that the season would lead to "another all–St. Louis World's Series." Yet despite picking the Cardinals to win what would have been their fourth consecutive pennant, Spink argued that "the team with the greatest possibility for an upset is Chicago." And that's what happened. The Cubs, riding a ten-game winning streak, took over first place on July 8 and were never headed after that. The Cardinals kept the race close, in part by winning sixteen of the twenty-two games they played against Chicago. As the season neared its close, the Cubs led the Cardinals by one and a half games, but then the Cubs took doubleheaders from the Reds and the Pirates, their nineteenth and twentieth sweeps of the season, and won the pennant by three games. Looking at the American League, Spink figured that "the Browns will be tougher. They know they can win." But, he warned, "Detroit looks formidable." The Tigers took over first place on June 12 and never gave it up, despite late-season pressure from the Senators. The Browns finished in third place, six games behind. Their roster was substantially the same as the year before, but during the winter St. Louis paid the Memphis Chicks in the Southern Association $20,000 for the contract of Pete Gray, an outfielder who had lost his right arm in a childhood accident. Some observers regarded this move as a publicity stunt, but come Opening Day, Gray was in the starting lineup as the Browns' left fielder, and he got a single in four at bats. The hits proved hard to get, though, and Gray saw his playing time reduced. By the end of June he had appeared in only thirty-four games, and he finished the year batting .218. Moreover, the extra time he took to transfer the ball before throwing it gave Major League base runners a split-second advantage. First baseman George McQuinn recalled his displeasure, saying "There's no question that he cost us quite a few ball games." Still, come the last weekend of the season, the Browns had a chance to beat Detroit and force the Tigers into a one-game playoff against the Senators. Saturday's game was rained out, forcing a Sunday doubleheader. The Tigers did their job, clinching the pennant by beating the Browns in the first game, 6–3, before the second was canceled.[31]

The player most responsible for the Tigers' winning the pennant was Hank Greenberg. Following his reenlistment he spent more than three years serving his country and not playing Major League baseball. His decision, said the *Sporting News*, "gave the game and the nation a special thrill." As a sergeant, the rank he had when he left the army just a few days before, he went first to MacDill Field in Tampa and then to Officer Candidate School. After being commissioned as a second lieutenant, he went to the Flying Training Command in Fort Worth, Texas, there to be assistant athletic director responsible for inspecting training facilities at air bases around the country. He did not play baseball except for a war bond game in August 1942. Greenberg turned thirty-three in 1944, too old to be a pilot, but he got a transfer to accompany the first group of B-29s to go overseas. He spent a few months in China and India, contracted malaria in July, and was sent back to the States in October. Assigned to an office in New York, his job was to visit war plants where production was lagging and boost workers' morale. He was discharged in June, free to find out how badly his baseball skills had eroded. "It's hard for me to visualize I'm going to play baseball again," he confessed, but he rejoined the Tigers posthaste. The first Major Leaguer to return to the game from the war, he played in his first game on July 1 and hit a home run. In the season's final game the Browns led, 4–3, after eight innings. In the ninth Greenberg came to bat after an intentional walk. "The Browns had loaded the bases to pitch to me," he wrote in his autobiography, "because they were hoping I would hit into a double play." Instead he hit the second pitch just inside the left-field foul pole for a grand slam. The Tigers held St. Louis scoreless in the bottom of the inning, and the pennant was theirs. "It was fitting indeed," Fred Lieb wrote, "that a returned serviceman should decide a pennant race with his bat, on the final day of the season. Military men around the world will glory in his feat."[32]

Brown was wrong of course. Detroit was capable of winning the World Series, and they dispatched the Cubs in seven games. Greenberg batted .304 and hit two home runs. It was an exciting Series but one marked by "too much loose play, too many mental lapses, too many run-of-the-mine players," according to sportswriter Clifford Bloodgood. Had the twenty-four LCS(S) crews who had participated in the Normandy invasion still been in Europe in October 1945, they could have listened to the shortwave broadcast of the Series on the Armed Forces Radio Service, with Bill Slater and Al Helfer doing the play-by-play and Bill Corum supplying the color. But the crews had been dispersed and their boats retired in favor of larger craft. For two weeks after D-Day Yogi Berra and his mates remained on the *Bayfield*, relaying messages between Omaha and Utah Beaches, helping newcomers navigate through minefields, and dodging sporadic attacks from remnants of the Luftwaffe. After a brief rest back in Portsmouth, England, Berra's squadron headed for Bizerte, Tunisia, there to prepare for Operation Dragoon, the Allied invasion of southern France, in August. Their job, Berra recalled, was to fire upon a hotel in Marseilles occupied by the Germans. Once American troops landed and secured the area, Berra went ashore. "It was a wacky war," he said. "A half hour after we were getting shot at by the Germans, the French were welcoming us." The crew was soon sent to Naples and then to Oran, Algeria, but on New Year's Eve Berra boarded a troop transport bound for Norfolk and a month's leave at home. New orders then sent him to New London, Connecticut. He was assigned to take care of the base's movie theater, and eventually he joined the baseball team managed by former Major Leaguer Jim Gleeson. In the fall of 1945 he accompanied the base's football team to Yankee Stadium for a game against Tuskegee Institute and spent some time talking to Pete Previte, the Yankees' assistant clubhouse boy whom he would get to know quite well in the years ahead.[33]

Baseball followed the impending end of the war with great interest. Just before Nazi Germany launched the December 1944 offensive called the Battle of the Bulge, Major League owners held their winter meetings in New York. They anticipated the return of demobilized ballplayers by allowing clubs to increase the size of their rosters from forty to forty-eight during the off-season and from twenty-five to thirty during the season, with the proviso that reinstated players, those once on a team's National Defense list, could occupy one of these extra spots for up to one calendar year. However these owners would resolve their manpower problems, they faced the future knowing that their business had survived the war and rebounded, albeit slightly, from the worst of its economic dislocations. Total Major League attendance, after having been ravaged by the Depression, had inched back over 9 million in 1938 and peaked at 9.8 million two years later. But the war took its toll, and attendance continued to decline, falling to 7.5 million in 1943. The next year attendance went up to 8.8 million, and it rose again to 10.8 million, a new record, in 1945. Bolstered perhaps by the owners' aversion to cutting ticket prices, the sixteen Major League clubs made profits in every war year save 1943. They cleared a collective $978,000 in 1944 and made $1,212,000 in 1945. Robert Burk explained that profits were possible, even in lean years, because the federal government froze wages and salaries in 1942. The cumulative Major League payroll, as high as $3.65 million in 1939, contracted to $3.21 million in 1943 while the average individual salary dropped $900 during the same interval. Owners used the hardships of wartime to justify miniscule raises despite outstanding performances on the field. Stan Musial, to cite just one example, made $4,250 in 1942, his first full season, during which he hit .315 and drove in 72 runs. For that he won just a $1,000 raise.[34]

After Germany surrendered, Dan Daniel noted in the *Sporting News* that "the glorious termination of the struggle in Europe [will have] vast and important implications for all baseball" and "will do a lot to make rosters fairly static." Young players classified 1-A by Selective Service and not yet drafted "now may expect to be left to baseball," and those classified 4-F could anticipate remaining 4-F because "the War Department order requiring a Washington review of the cases of professional athletes rejected in the draft has been suspended." By June the baseball weekly was lauding the success of players who had already returned from the service, including Dave "Boo" Ferriss, a rookie pitcher with the Red Sox, and Tigers pitcher Al Benton. Ferriss, the first player to receive a baseball scholarship from Mississippi State, had signed with the Boston organization while still in college and played in the Minors in 1942 before he was drafted. He spent more than two years as a physical education instructor at Randolph Field in Texas, but, plagued by asthma that put him in the hospital for six weeks, he was discharged in February 1945. The Red Sox brought him to the Majors early in the season. He pitched shutouts in his first two starts, won his first start against every other club, and finished the season with a record of 21-10. Benton was no rookie, having pitched in the Majors in 1934 and 1935 for the A's and from 1938 through 1942 for Detroit.

He joined the navy after the 1942 season and spent most of his time playing ball in Norman, Oklahoma. Discharged early in 1945 because of migraine headaches, he won his first five starts for the Tigers before breaking a bone in his right ankle on May 24 and missing more than a month. He finished the season at 13-8 and pitched in three World Series games.[35]

Ballplayers came home from the war along with everyone else, and by the end of August a fair number of the game's stars had already traded one uniform for another and were again contributing on the field of play. "Home-from-War Aces Make A.L. Race Dogfight" said a late August headline in the *Sporting News*. Bob Feller, an early enlistee, had returned to the Indians, and Hugh Mulcahy, the first Major Leaguer drafted, was back with the Phillies. The Yankees welcomed back pitcher Red Ruffing, catcher Aaron Robinson, and outfielder Charlie Keller in their quest to pass the Tigers in the standings. Detroit was reinforced not only by Greenberg, but also by pitchers Tommy Bridges and Virgil Trucks. The law that governed how veterans would reenter the postwar workforce was not the GI Bill of Rights, as has sometimes been written, but the Selective Training and Service Act of 1940, the law that authorized the nation's first peacetime military draft. Section 8 of the law, as amended, read in part as follows:

> In the case of any such person [inducted into the land or naval forces under this Act] who, in order to perform such training and service, has left or leaves a position, . . . and who . . . is still qualified to perform the duties of such position, . . . such employer shall restore such person to such position or to a position of like seniority, status, and pay unless the employer's circumstances have so changed as to make it impossible or unreasonable to do so; . . . any person who is restored to a position . . . shall not be discharged from such position without cause within one year after such restoration.

That the draft law required inductees to serve only one year before returning to civilian life did not matter. Congress passed amendments several times after Pearl Harbor to meet the exigencies of wartime mobilization, but the protections for returning veterans did not expire until 1947. Facing this problem, baseball owners once again thought themselves a special case. Ballplayers were not factory workers. They did not occupy places on an assembly line. Their skills were not necessarily interchangeable. Understanding that playing the game competitively required talent and not just seniority, owners fashioned regulations they thought would meet the requirements of the law. Each veteran who sought reinstatement would need to apply within ninety days after being discharged. Any player who did so would not be guaranteed a roster spot, but he would get a trial of either thirty days during spring training or fifteen days during the regular season to demonstrate if he still possessed the skills needed for Major League baseball. If so, he could occupy a spot on the expanded roster for a year. If not, he could be waived and demoted to the Minors or given his unconditional release. Players sent to the Minors would receive Major League pay, with the parent club making up any difference, but those released would be paid for no more than their trial period.[36]

Of the more than five hundred veterans who played Major League ball before serving their country, about three hundred found spots on Major League rosters during the 1946 season. Among the rest, some retired, perhaps owing to age, and others willingly accepted spots in the Minors. A few, though, took issue with the owners' regulations, claiming lack of compliance with federal law. Tony Lupien was the most prominent player to do so. A 1939 Harvard graduate, Lupien was the regular first baseman for the Red Sox in 1942 and 1943 and the Phillies in 1944. He served in the navy in 1945 and was discharged in September, early enough to play in fifteen games before the end of the season and receive pay for nineteen days. Over the winter the Phillies acquired Frank McCormick, six years older than Lupien, from the Reds, and they sold Lupien's contract to the Hollywood Stars in the Pacific Coast League (PCL). Lupien protested that his demotion violated his reemployment rights. The Phillies contended that the few games Lupien played in 1945 satisfied their obligation to him, but Boston sportswriter Dave Egan was among those who disagreed. "The law of the land," Egan wrote in the *Boston Record*, "gives Tony Lupien the absolute right to reinstatement . . . not for fifteen days . . . but for one year," and he warned baseball that "this is the first recorded instance in sport of a war veteran being denied his rights, but I am sorry to say that it is not the last, for by the first of May the woods will be filled with veterans, wondering what happened to them and their supposed rights." Lupien considered legal action, but he was brought up short when the Stars sent him a contract for $8,000, the salary he expected from the Phillies, who, it appeared, were supplementing Hollywood's standard salary with money of their own. Realizing that while his cause might be just, his legal expenses would exhaust his reserves, Lupien declined to litigate and reported to the Stars. Assessing the benefits Lupien would enjoy in "glorious Hollywood," a *Sporting News* editorial wondered, "What, then, is Ulysses (Tony) Lupien squawking about?" But sportswriter Stan Baumgartner took a darker view, comparing Lupien to

Dred Scott, the plaintiff in the infamous pre–Civil War case, and calling the first baseman "another chattel."[37]

Early in the 1946 season the PCL schedule had the Seattle Rainiers and the Portland Beavers in Southern California to play consecutive week-long series against Hollywood and the Los Angeles Angels. Thereafter all four teams traveled north to play the second half of these home-and-home series, and on the long train ride Lupien had time to renew his acquaintance with Seattle's second baseman, Al Niemiec. Although Niemiec was six years older, the two had much in common. Both were from New England. Both had attended college, Niemiec at Holy Cross. Both had originally been signed by the Red Sox. Both had been in the navy. Niemiec played briefly for Boston in 1934 and for the A's in 1936, but he did better in the Pacific Coast League with San Diego (1938–39) and Seattle (1940–42) before joining the navy's preflight program. Discharged in January 1946, Niemiec rejoined his old club but sensed that with a new manager, Bill Skiff, his job was in jeopardy. Traveling north on the Pacific Coast Special, Niemiec confided in Lupien, and his fears were realized on April 22, when Seattle released him. Skiff and club vice president Torchy Torrance signed what amounted to a letter of recommendation, including the judgment that "Al still has a lot of fine baseball left," but they told Niemiec the club had decided to go with a roster of younger players. Niemiec was not placated. Almost immediately he filed a complaint with the local Selective Service office, claiming that his rights had been violated. The Selective Service System wrote to Seattle club president Emil Sick that Niemiec's dismissal was "without cause" and that he was still capable of playing at an acceptable level. The Rainiers disagreed, arguing that Niemiec had received a reasonable trial under baseball's regulations and had "demonstrated his inability to comply with the accepted standards of work performance and professional skill and proficiency required of our players and by clubs with which we were in competition." As a precaution Niemiec signed with the Providence Chiefs in the New England League on May 17, but his salary, $150 a month, was far below the $720 a month he would have earned in Seattle.[38]

Organized baseball regarded Niemiec's situation as no small matter. Torrance alerted league president Pants Rowland; William Bramham, head of the National Association, the Minors' governing body; and Commissioner Happy Chandler. Bramham, for one, was alarmed. Writing to all the leagues and clubs under his jurisdiction, he said that Niemiec "is one of the most dependable ball players that the club has had" and that "there is nothing in the record to reflect that he does not have the ability or background to continue in his former position." U.S. District Court judge Lloyd Black quickly agreed. He heard arguments in the case on June 15, including testimony from Skiff; announced his decision on June 21; and brought the parties back to court on June 24 to expand upon his ruling. He debunked the Rainiers' first argument, that "baseball is a quasi-public institution not operated primarily for profit," by referring to the league's articles of incorporation. He countered the club's second argument, that Niemiec no longer was "qualified to perform the duties of his position" by reasoning that Skiff "had no right to anticipate Mr. Niemiec's inability until it occurred. The employer may discharge at any time for cause," he continued, "but that cause must be something other than prediction or [the] hunch of the manager." Finally, Black dealt with the club's third argument, that Niemiec had waived his rights under the Selective Training and Service Act when he signed his contract, by noting that the employer, with complete control over the contract language, had failed in its obligation to write in clear and unambiguous language. "Any player reading this contract," wrote the judge, "would believe his rights were protected. Personally, after I have read it, I think his rights are protected." Black did not insist that Seattle rehire Niemiec but merely pay him a full season's salary. Chandler urged the club to pursue an appeal, with organized baseball bearing part of the expense, and the league's board of directors agreed to do so in July, but by the end of what proved to be a very profitable season, Seattle backed off. They satisfied the judgment against them, $2,905.36, in November.[39]

Yogi Berra rejoined the ranks of professional baseball players on May 12, 1946, when he reported to manager George Selkirk and the Yankees' top farm club, the Newark Bears in the International League. In a way Berra was lucky still to be in the New York organization. Months before, the Giants, on their way home from Boston, stopped in New London to play an exhibition game. Giants manager Mel Ott, watching batting practice with Jim Gleeson, his old friend, was impressed with Berra, despite his unorthodox approach at the plate. "Why, he made two hits on wild pitches," said Ott, who decided that the catcher had Major League potential. Back in New York, he offered Larry MacPhail $50,000 for Berra's contract. MacPhail almost said yes, but after consulting with veteran scout Paul Krichell, he put Ott on hold and summoned Berra to see him for himself. When the catcher walked into his office, MacPhail was aghast. "He looks like the bottom man of a bankrupt acrobatic team," he recalled, but when Berra asked about getting back the price of his train ticket, MacPhail surmised that he might indeed be a ballplayer. Figuring, too, that Ott had seen something worth nurturing, MacPhail decided to keep the young catcher. When Berra reported to the Newark club, Selkirk was not impressed, and neither was the clubhouse boy who handed him a uniform without a number and a cap too small. Berra balked at these snubs, but it was two weeks before he got into a game. Selkirk had an experienced catcher, Charlie Fallon, but he was thirty-one years old. The Yankees needed a replacement for the veteran Bill Dickey, who would retire after the season, and Berra, despite everyone's misgivings, appeared to be their best bet. Selkirk inserted him into the lineup as a pinch hitter on May 25. Berra played in seventy-six more games, some behind the plate and some in the outfield. He batted .314, hit 15 home runs, and drove in 59 runs while battling a broken thumb and a sprained ankle. The Bears finished tied for third in the eight-team league. They lost a one-game playoff to the Baltimore Orioles for third place and faced the first-place Montreal Royals in a best-of-seven semifinal series. The Royals won, four games to two, and went on to win the league championship over the Syracuse Chiefs and the Junior World Series against the Louisville Colonels of the American Association. Montreal, a farm team of the Dodgers, was led by a newcomer named Jackie Robinson.[40]

Nine

"The Smiling Young Man with the $1,000,000 Check Book"

Bob Quinn confessed to sportswriters invited to lunch at Boston's Copley Plaza Hotel in late February 1933 that he had run out of options. "I haven't got the money to continue," the Boston Red Sox owner said. "I have been carrying a load that very few men could have suffered without jumping out a window." Three other guests caught the writers' attention: American League president Will Harridge, Philadelphia Athletics coach Eddie Collins, and a young man identified as a "New York millionaire." Quinn then announced that he would be selling the Red Sox to that young man, just four days past his thirtieth birthday, for $1.2 million. The buyer's name was Tom Yawkey, the nephew and adopted son of William H. Yawkey, owner of the Detroit Tigers from 1904 until his death in 1919. Young Yawkey had inherited some money, reported to be $4 million, when his birth mother died in 1918 and an additional small sum when his adopted father died, but the remainder of his estate, $3,408,650, had been held in trust until he turned thirty on February 21, 1933. With all these millions now his—plus more when his adoptive mother died in July—Yawkey had more than enough to buy a Major League ball club. Where the desire to do so originated remained a bit of mystery. One story circulated in 1934 that Yawkey's wife, Elise, suggested that he do so. The key to the deal was Collins, who had met Yawkey in a dinner in 1928, the pair introduced to each other by Ty Cobb. Collins discovered that Yawkey was keenly interested in baseball, and Yawkey discovered that he and Collins had attended the same prep school, the Irving School in Tarrytown, New York, about twenty-five miles north of Manhattan. Yawkey told Collins that he wanted to buy a club, and when Quinn put up the Red Sox for sale, Collins brokered the deal. In return Yawkey named Collins vice president and general manager and gave him a small piece, perhaps 10 percent, of the club.[1]

According to researchers Mark L. Armour and Daniel R. Levitt, Yawkey told the Boston press corps that building up the Red Sox could not be done overnight. "It would be the height of folly to dump a lot of money into the thing all at once," he said. Yet the inexperienced owner did exactly that. He spent both time and money chasing championships but reaped precious little for his investments. Without players other teams wanted, Yawkey felt no compunction about sweetening transactions with substantial amounts of cash. His first deal in 1933 sent catcher Merv Shea and $50,000 to the St. Louis Browns for pitcher Lloyd Brown and catcher Rick Ferrell. Three days later he sent $100,000 to the New York Yankees for pitcher George Pipgras and third baseman Billy Werber. After the season Boston obtained three players from the Athletics, including star pitcher Lefty Grove, for two players and $125,000. Yawkey had Collins at his side, but the two locked horns dividing their responsibilities. They agreed to retain manager Marty McManus for 1933. Collins praised his work at season's end, but Yawkey dismissed him days later. The owner then further usurped Collins's authority by hiring Bucky Harris, just fired by the Tigers. Collins and Harris had not gotten along for years, and 1934 was no different. After the season Yawkey realized he had erred, and he approached Washington Senators owner Clark Griffith about Joe Cronin, the Senators' player-manager. Collins balked at this idea, but the general manager was beginning to understand the owner's belief in the power of his own fortune. Yawkey prevailed and got his man. Sportswriter Cy Peterman called him "the smiling young man with the $1,000,000 check book, . . . a fair-haired Santa himself," but Collins was more prosaic. Yawkey, he said, is "primarily in baseball for the kick he gets out of it. His other business interests are greater, materially, than his baseball venture, but he's the type who want to be successful in everything, even in his avocations."[2]

Adding the sums he paid for players to the purchase price for the club and combining them with the cost of refurbishing Fenway Park and then repairing it after a January 1934 fire brought Yawkey's investment in the Red Sox to more than $3 million after just ten months of ownership. Yawkey's first plan for the ballpark was cosmetic, but after consulting with the company that had designed Fenway, he decided on a more substantial reconstruction that eventually cost $1.5 million. Beginning after the 1933 season workers rebuilt the existing grandstand. They rebuilt the bleachers with concrete and connected them to the grandstand. They added steel to support a second deck, installed box seats at field level, moved home plate out toward the outfield, built a new press box, and erected a huge scoreboard in left field. Seating capacity increased from twenty-six thousand to thirty-eight thousand. Unafraid of the cost overruns, Yawkey said, "Renovate be damned. Let's build a new ballpark and have it right." The project employed more than seven hundred workers during the depths of the Depression and made Yawkey a local hero. Racing to finish before Opening Day, project managers were distraught when a fire broke out in the center-field stands. The five-alarm fire caused a quarter million dollars in damage, not all of which was covered by insurance. Yawkey forged ahead. He hired three hundred more workers, who collected overtime on round-the-clock shifts. A second, smaller fire in February led officials to suspect arson. Collins announced that "we are going to open this park on April 17 if we have to call out the state militia," but private guards provided the security to get the job done on time. Opening Day attracted 33,336 fans to see what Yawkey's money had wrought. They marveled at the green paint job that gave the entire park a fresh look, the wider seats, the reduction in foul territory that brought everyone closer to the field, and the electric scoreboard, standing, according to the blueprints, only 308 feet from home plate.[3]

Over the next few seasons Yawkey kept his checkbook open, but he was not rewarded with an American League pennant. After he spent another $300,000 before the 1935 season, the press dubbed his club the "Gold Sox" or the "Millionaires." They won just two games more than the year before. Yawkey persisted. In December he acquired Jimmie Foxx from the A's for two Minor Leaguers and $150,000 and then sent another $75,000 to Philadelphia for outfielder Doc Cramer and shortstop Eric McNair, even though Cronin played shortstop himself. Foxx had an outstanding season in 1936, but the Red Sox finished sixth, falling below .500 for the sixteenth time in eighteen years. Over the next winter Collins announced a change in strategy. He told *Baseball Magazine* that the club would make a commitment to developing its own stars through a farm system. "We have abandoned, definitely," he said, "the attempt to fight our way to a pennant by the purchase of ready-made players." The Red Sox had eight Minor League affiliations in 1936. They increased this number by three in 1937 but then fell back to eight in 1938, nine in 1939, and ten in 1940. Glenn Stout argued that Yawkey could have "created the most productive and extensive farm system in baseball" but that he "went only halfway," in contrast with other Major League clubs that had created farm systems sooner and built more affiliations. Moreover, by the time the Red Sox farm system began to produce Major League prospects, the veterans who had come to Boston via trade or purchase had long since passed their prime. Boston rose to fifth place in 1937, twenty-one games behind the first-place Yankees, and second place in 1938, again behind the Yankees. Foxx had another monster year in 1938 and won the American League Most Valuable Player Award. Arriving in New York to play a Memorial Day doubleheader, the Red Sox were in second place, two and a half games behind the Cleveland Indians and a game ahead of the Yankees. Before a crowd of 81,891, Boston lost both games. They dropped behind New York in the standings, fell to fourth place, and never got that close again.[4]

Attendance at Fenway Park had jumped up to 610,640 in 1934 and remained strong, but other teams simply did better at the box office. In 1938, for example, Boston finished fourth in league attendance behind New York, Detroit, and Cleveland. Yawkey's frustration built. At one point, learning that Jacob Ruppert might be interested in selling the Yankees, Yawkey contemplated buying them and selling the Red Sox, but the deal never materialized. The good news for Boston fans was that Bobby Doerr arrived to play second base in 1937, Ted Williams in 1939, and Dominic DiMaggio in 1940. The Red Sox purchased an option on Doerr's contract after he played with the Hollywood Stars in the Pacific Coast League (PCL) in 1934 and 1935. Collins picked up the option after seeing Doerr play on the same trip when he first took note of Williams. Doerr played the 1936 season in San Diego, also in the PCL. He made the Red Sox roster in 1937, but his season was abbreviated after he was hit in the head on April 26. Still, he had begun a career that would see him play in nine All-Star Games and be called, by Williams, the "silent captain of the Red Sox." DiMaggio, the youngest of three ball-playing brothers and the smallest, played for the PCL's San Francisco Seals starting in 1937. Two years later he finished second in the league in batting and won the Most Valuable Player Award. The Red Sox bought his contract for $75,000. The team's future looked bright, but two more second-place finishes in the next three years, 1939 and 1941, were the best they could do. After Pearl Harbor the club's performance was desultory: second in 1942, seventh in 1943, fourth in 1944, and back to seventh in 1945.[5]

Tom Yawkey was born in Detroit and raised in a Manhattan penthouse, attended by an array of servants that the fortune his uncle/adopted father had inherited could easily afford. Glenn Stout recalled an oft-repeated tale that had the youngster telling his aunt/adopted mother that he felt like the richest boy in the world. She filled several plates with beans and named each plate after the Vanderbilts, the Morgans, and other wealthy dynasties. Then she took one bean, put it in a bowl, and called it the Yawkeys. Still, that single bean was quite substantial, and young Tom lived a charmed life. While at Yale, where he was called Tim, he indulged his passion for fast cars and liquor, played class sports, kept to a close circle of friends, and graduated in 1925. Yawkey considered himself a New Yorker, and even after buying the Red Sox, he lived in New York's Hotel Pierre and maintained his offices at the Graybar Building. When in Boston, he lived in the Ritz Carlton Hotel, but whenever he could, he retreated to his family's estate on South Island in Georgetown County, South Carolina. His father had purchased twenty-five thousand acres on the coast and converted a former rice plantation into a lavish hunting and fishing retreat. William H. Yawkey entertained a brace of friends there, including Ty Cobb more than once. Tom preferred the South Island property for its seclusion and its rusticity. In fact, after the huge, thirteen-room house that his father built in 1915 was destroyed by fire in the summer of 1957, Yawkey mourned the loss of artwork, books, and sporting memorabilia, but he chose not to replace the house. On future visits he and his second wife lived in a pair of mobile homes. During the baseball season he would listen to Red Sox games by calling the Fenway Park receptionist from South Island and having her set down the telephone receiver next to a radio.[6]

In the decades before the Civil War, Georgetown County, centered on an area called the Waccamaw Neck, was rice country, where the production of this lucrative cash crop depended on the forced labor of Black slaves. The statistics are staggering. Toiling in a climate generously described as hostile and doing all the other tasks associated with this year-round enterprise, Georgetown County's slaves produced nearly half the rice crop of the entire United States. Before the American Revolution owners of these rice plantations enjoyed the highest per capita income in the colonies. Most of the plantations were self-sufficient, much of the planters' income was pure profit, and the profits were enormous. In the decades after the Civil War a small horde of northern millionaires, indulging their passion for relaxation and the sporting life, invaded Georgetown County and bought up a passel of former plantations. Newly rich though these men were, what they lacked was status, an American equivalent to aristocracy. Some bought English estates to compensate, some married their daughters to European gentry, and some purchased plantations whose heritage was being embellished by the emerging plantation myth, the romanticized retelling of southern history, embracing a devotion to the fictions of the Lost Cause. New York financier Bernard Baruch, a native of Camden, South Carolina, led the way, acquiring several plantations in the area and rechristening more than seventeen thousand acres Hobcaw Barony. Edward Porter Alexander, an ex-Confederate general, sold his property to William H. Yawkey, by then the owner of the Tigers. He built two homes and a stable on the property and turned former rice fields into a sportsman's retreat where young Tom learned to hunt, in his own words, "ducks, shore birds, woodcock, quail, turkey, and deer" and absorbed the culture of the segregated South.[7]

As Baruch, Yawkey, and others moved south, if only for a few months each year, they encountered the local population, some of whom had once been enslaved. The embers of the Civil War had not been fully doused, Jim Crow had begun to tighten its grip, and, according to historic preservationist Jennifer Betsworth, "Sectional tensions remained high." Residents of Georgetown County thus saw these new invaders as a mixed blessing. On the plus side, the Yankee interlopers were affluent enough to save endangered buildings from destruction and protect landscapes from subdivision. They employed craftsmen and laborers, some seasonally and some permanently, and pumped money into the local economy. On the other hand, locals felt a sense of loss as old residences were redefined as recreational playthings and agricultural lands became game preserves for the migratory rich. Winter residents restricted access to land they now owned and flouted conservation laws by overfishing and overhunting. According to Betsworth, one son of a former plantation owner resorted to trespassing and poaching on land that had once belonged to his family. It felt, he wrote, "like the rice fields and plantations had been stolen." Some Black residents undoubtedly shared these feelings, but there was a profound difference of course. Betsworth wrote that while "some northerners showed passing interest in the large numbers of African Americans who remained present, few noted the land's direct connection to slavery." Still, the new northern owners, hardly free of the racism that branded the South, often acted paternalistically. Archer Huntington, who with his wife, sculptor Anna Hyatt Huntington, built a house called Atalaya, employed Black workers to build "far more brick walls than any home needed." Dr. Henry Norris of Pennsylvania, the new owner of Litchfield Plantation, built an infirmary that offered Blacks free medical care, and Baruch wrote in his memoir that one reason he established a second home in his native state was to "do something for the Negro," hoping that he could help Blacks climb "both the educational and economic ladder."[8]

William H. Yawkey left no legacy as a philanthropist, but Tom Yawkey, both in Boston and South Carolina, did. Although he did not serve in the military during World War II, he donated five ambulances to the American Red Cross in 1942 for shipment to the Middle East. Three years later he gave $100,000, the largest single gift, to a campaign to improve medical care in Georgetown County by building a hospital, an institution he continued to fund throughout his life. Starting in 1953, he championed the Jimmy Fund of Boston's Children's Cancer Research Foundation, eventually making it the official charity of the Red Sox and donating millions to this cause. Yawkey's generosity was manifest. He paid his players well, bought some of them life insurance policies, and gave them bonuses. He set up college scholarships for Red Sox bat boys. He paid the medical bills for outfielder Jimmy Piersall when he was hospitalized in 1952 with mental illness. He contributed $25,000 to establish the Harry Agganis Foundation scholarship program after the outfielder died in 1955 at age twenty-seven. In Georgetown his money helped build a small African Methodist Episcopal church on South Island and houses for each family resident on the island. One newspaper reported in 1936 that "when a young couple gets married, he presents them with a house of their own." After Yawkey died in 1976, his will established a foundation to support the Tom Yawkey Wildlife Center, a donation to the South Carolina Department of Natural Resources of all twenty thousand acres of his land. According to the foundation's website, the center's "marshes, marine wetlands, forests, and sandy beaches play host to hundreds of species of coastal wildlife and serve as an undisturbed habitat for migratory birds, eagles, alligators, and many other endangered species."[9]

The milieu in which Tom Yawkey spent a good part of each year and the views of race relations endemic in Georgetown County, South Carolina, came into play in 1944, when Boston city council member Isadore Muchnick began to test whether Yawkey's benevolence crossed baseball's color line—that is, the unwritten agreement among club owners barring them from signing African American players. Both the Red Sox and the Braves required waivers to play home games on Sunday, and the city council needed to approve these waivers by unanimous vote each year. In a council speech Muchnick said, "I cannot understand how baseball, which claims to be the national sport . . . can continue a pre–Civil War attitude toward American citizens because of the color of their skins." Muchnick called upon the Massachusetts Commission against Discrimination (MCAD) to investigate the ball clubs' hiring practices. He also suggested in 1944 and again in 1945 that he would withhold his vote for Sunday baseball unless the Red Sox "notify the council before the issue date of said license that all players, regardless of race, color, or creed, will be treated in the American way and will be afforded an equal opportunity for positions on your team." Some scholars have suggested that Muchnick's motivation came from the changing demographics of Mattapan, the district he represented, from Jewish to Black, but in fact his district remained nearly all white until after 1950. A native of Boston's West End, Muchnick was a graduate of Boston Latin School, and he played hockey and lacrosse as an undergraduate at Harvard. After graduating from Harvard Law School in 1932, he opened his own law firm after larger firms said they would hire him if he agreed to change his name, deemed "too ethnic, too Jewish." He was, in the words of sportswriter Howard Bryant, "a classic East Coast liberal," a man who "possessed a skill and integrity that led him to be respected by both the Irish, who controlled city government, and the entrenched Yankees, who dominated Boston's cultural, legal, and financial world." Muchnick supported equal pay for women holding city jobs and a redistricting plan for the city's schools that would have led to some integration. "Both his children," Bryant wrote, "would marvel at the number of times their father would align himself with the underdog. . . . He consistently found himself on the minority side of issues."[10]

Scholars generally agree that the civil rights movement had its roots in the upheavals of World War II, but historian Rebecca Alpert found "the first sustained effort to call attention [to baseball's color line]" in 1933. She noted that two white newspaper columnists, Heywood Broun and Jimmy Powers, raised the issue at the annual dinner of the New York chapter of the Baseball Writers' Association of America and then in the pages of the *New York Daily News*. Two groups of newspapermen followed the New Yorkers' lead. The first included Wendell Smith of the *Pittsburgh Courier*, Sam Lacy of the *Washington Afro-American*, and other members of the National Negro Newspaper All-American Association of Sports Editors. The second consisted of Lester Rodney, Nat Low, and Bill Mardo, three sports editors for the *Daily Worker*, the official newspaper of the American Communist Party. Their persistence, sometimes working cooperatively and sometimes not, led in 1942 to an apparent promise from Bill Benswanger, president of the Pittsburgh Pirates, to give three African American players—catcher Roy Campanella, second baseman Sam Hughes, and pitcher Dave Barnhill—a tryout on August 4. Benswanger reneged, perhaps because of pressure from other owners, but those who sought to eradicate the color line felt they had won a small victory. In 1943 hints swirled that the Philadelphia Phillies might, with new ownership, sign Black players, but nothing came of these rumors. Early in 1945 Low's sources told him that the Brooklyn Dodgers' Branch Rickey "has actually been one of the most adamant magnates in the fight to break the Hitler-like ban on Negro players." Acting on this belief, he and Joe Bostic, sports editor for the Black newspaper the *People's Voice*, showed up unannounced at the Dodgers' spring training site at Bear Mountain, New York, demanding and getting an impromptu tryout for two players, first baseman Showboat Thomas and pitcher Terris McDuffie. Rickey, a staunch anti-Communist, watched the players and then excoriated Bostic. "I am more for your cause than anybody else you know, but you are making a mistake using force," he said. "You are defeating your own aims."[11]

Eddie Collins's first response to Muchnick was polite but firm. "I have been connected with the Red Sox for twelve years," he wrote on March 16, 1945, "and during that time we have never had a single request for a tryout by a colored applicant. . . . It is beyond my understanding how anyone can insinuate or believe that 'all ballplayers regardless of race, color, or creed, have not been treated in the American way' so far as having an equal opportunity to play for the Red Sox." Muchnick was not deterred, and neither was Smith. At Muchnick's request the journalist recruited three African American players—Sam Jethroe, Jackie Robinson, and Marvin Williams—to accompany him to Boston in April for a tryout with either or both Major League clubs. The Braves, through Bob Quinn, their president since 1935, flatly said no, but the Red Sox, through Collins, agreed, although they made the players wait four days beyond the scheduled date, perhaps because President Roosevelt died on April 12. "They are not fooling me," Muchnick told Smith. "These boys came here to get a tryout, and if they don't get one, it will simply be another mark against the undemocratic practices of major league owners and officials." Perhaps a newspaper column by Dave Egan critical of Collins forced the general manager's hand because on April 16, the day before Opening Day, the tryout took place. Coach Larry Woodall and scout Hugh Duffy, a star player in the 1890s, ran the show; manager Joe Cronin sat in the stands with Muchnick and Smith; and Collins either sat high in the stands out of view or absented himself entirely. After ninety minutes of shagging flies, fielding grounders, and batting practice, it was over. Duffy told the players, "You boys look like pretty good ballplayers. I hope you enjoyed the workout," and he said that the club would soon contact them, "probably in the near future."[12]

What happened as the tryout ended has been beclouded by an accusation that did not surface until thirty-four years later. Either the three players walked off the field without incident, or someone unknown, perhaps a voice from the back of the grandstand, yelled, "Get those n——s off the field." *Boston Globe* sportswriter Clif Keane, allegedly present at the time, recalled this obscenity for a *Globe* story written by Larry Whiteside in July 1979. No one else, including Muchnick, Smith, and the players, heard the same thing, and Keane's veracity has been sorely tested. In 2015 another Boston media figure, Tom Shaer, told Yawkey's biographer that at various times Keane had told three versions of the story: that he did not know who yelled, that he thought it was not Yawkey who did so, and that it was Yawkey. Adding an additional layer of uncertainty is that Keane himself was accused of bigotry. Whatever was said or not said, the three players came off the field without any expectation that a contract offer would follow, and they were proven right. A few days later Smith wrote to Collins, thanking him "for permitting the three Negro ballplayers whom I brought to work out at Fenway Park" and asking him "to let me know what decision, if any, has been made" about them. Collins responded two weeks later, apologizing that Cronin's broken leg, suffered in the third game of the season, "threw everything out of gear as far as our plans were concerned." Then, in an attempt to bring the whole matter to a close, Collins told Smith, "The one thing I fear . . . is tampering with any players who may be and have been under contract in several of the Negro Leagues. . . . We would want to be careful not to tamper with anyone else's property." Throughout this entire episode Yawkey remained silent. He was in Boston, but whether he was present in Fenway Park as the players worked out is not clear. He took no part in the tryout and perhaps no direct part in the decision not to offer any of the players a contract. The players expected nothing more. "It was kind of a dull day," recalled Jethroe. "There wasn't anything spectacular about it." Robinson added, "We shagged some flies in the outfield. Then we hit." When Duffy ended the workout, "That was that." The Red Sox declined the opportunity to do what no Major League club had done since 1884—namely, employ as a player any man clearly identified as African American. Whatever personal attitudes toward race Yawkey and Collins carried, the club they ran set no precedent in 1945 and would decline to cross baseball's color line for more than a decade thereafter.[13]

The immediate postwar years marked the beginning of a period of stunning economic growth in the United States and the rise of a coincident spirit of national optimism that historian James T. Patterson called "grand expectations." The Great Depression was over, the death struggle against the Axis had concluded triumphantly, and "millions of people," in Patterson's words, "thought that the American dream was alive and well." By the end of the 1940s the United States, with only 7 percent of the world's population, earned 42 percent of the world's income and produced half the world's manufacturing output. Per capita annual income in the United States was nearly double that of any of the next rank of nations. Americans also fully embraced the joys of unparalleled consumer consumption. "Between 1939 and 1948," according to Patterson, "clothing sales jumped three-fold, furniture four-fold, jewelry four-fold, liquor five-fold, household appliances, including TV, five-fold." Obliterating the distinction between "need" and "want," Americans did some catching up. They bought consumer goods out of reach for many before and during the war, including vacuum cleaners, refrigerators, electric ranges, and freezers. They dove into the purchase of new products such as electric clothes dryers, air conditioners, garbage disposals, long-playing record players, Polaroid cameras, and televisions. They latched onto conveniences like frozen foods and a wide array of products made from plastics. Most important, they bought automobiles and houses in record numbers. New car sales totaled 69,500 in 1945, 2.1 million in 1946, 5.1 million in 1949, and 6.7 million in 1950. New housing starts, averaging fewer than 100,000 per year during the year, jumped to 937,000 in 1946, 1.2 million in 1948, and 1.7 million in 1950. New units included public housing and private apartments, but they were mostly inexpensive, single-family homes designed for people no longer willing to double up with family or friends or otherwise endure substandard living quarters. Financed by government-backed mortgages, many of these homes were built in previously undeveloped areas known as suburbia. By 1960 Patterson wrote, one-third of all Americans lived in suburban areas. This tidal wave of prosperity did not engulf everyone of course, nor did it erase restrictions associated with class, ethnic, racial, and gender differences, but many Americans felt a sense of well-being, albeit soon tempered by the fears of the Cold War, that translated into, among other things, good times for the game still known as the National Pastime.[14]

To be sure, not all Americans shared in this prosperity, and its extent should not be romanticized. The postwar economy challenged farmers, and poverty, both rural and urban, proved resistant to amelioration if it was acknowledged at all. Racism, de jure in the South and other places and de facto throughout the country, stood undaunted, while the fight against sexism was not yet an idea whose time had come. Postwar prosperity also came with turmoil. American workers, both those who had remained on the home front during the war and those who had returned after serving in the armed forces, wanted a larger piece of the economic pie, and many recognized that joining a labor union was one way to achieve their goals. Union membership, thanks mostly to the spectacular growth of the Congress of Industrial Organizations (CIO) as it organized skilled, semi-skilled, and unskilled industrial workers, increased from 11.6 percent of total nonagricultural employment in 1930 to 26.9 percent in 1940 and 35.5 percent in 1945. Those organized into unions, although not "class-conscious in a Marxian sense," according to Patterson, "proudly identified themselves as 'working class.'" While many union members did not embrace the liberal social and political vision advanced by leaders like Walter Reuther, head of the United Automobile Workers, they nevertheless agitated throughout the war and after the peace came for higher wages and better working conditions. In 1944 alone, despite wartime's voluntary no-strike pledge, there were a record 4,956 work stoppages involving more than two million workers, nearly 5 percent of all those employed. Workers were motivated to strike, in part, because they "felt the sting of inequality." Corporations for which they worked reaped enormous after-tax profits during the war, and CEOs were more than handsomely compensated. Yet in late 1945, when the average annual salary for full-time workers was $2,190, according to Patterson, "around one-fifth of working families in American cities received less than $1,500 in total cash income for the year."[15]

The end of the war allowed organized labor to take the gloves off. The year 1946 saw a new record: 4,985 work stoppages involving 4.6 million workers. Union leaders across the industrial economy argued that wartime and postwar inflation justified wage increases of 30 percent. For workers at General Motors, for example, this would have meant an additional 33 cents per hour, but the company offered only 10 cents. A strike begun in December 1945 lasted 113 days and was settled when the two sides agreed to an increase of 18.5 cents. Average wages in manufacturing were stingy, labor leaders argued, but such workers were outearning farm workers, domestic workers, nurses and other hospital workers, and teachers, who earned an average of $1,995 yearly. In short, conditions were ripe for widespread labor unrest. In the spring of 1946 railroad workers went on strike, resulting in a national transportation shutdown. President Harry Truman threatened to seize the railroads and draft workers into the military, an ultimatum that soon brought the walkout to an end. Baseball players, especially those returning from the service to their prewar contracts, shared in this sense of dissatisfaction. They wanted and expected to experience a better life in the postwar era, and they saw, through a glass darkly, the economic gains achieved by organized labor, including increases in hourly wages, the right to bargain collectively, and the right to recover prewar jobs. In Pittsburgh a strike by 3,500 electric company workers forced an additional 100,000 people to stay home. The city's trolley system halted operations, street lights went out, and office buildings closed for fear of elevator failure. Mayor David Lawrence called the situation "a disaster."[16]

Watching this strife from Boston, Robert Murphy, a lawyer and labor relations professional, decided to approach members of the Pirates and offer them the chance to organize as the first chapter of the American Baseball Guild, a labor union he had just founded. Murphy was plowing ground long left fallow. Baseball players had tried to organize several times before but always without long-term success. The Brotherhood of Professional Base Ball Players, established in 1885 mainly to oppose the reserve clause, dwindled away after the Players League's one season, 1890. A decade later the Protective Association of Professional Baseball Players hoped to use the competition created by the new American League as leverage, but once the two Major Leagues came to an accommodation in 1903, it died out. A bit more successful, the Baseball Players Fraternity, organized by player-turned-attorney David Fultz starting in 1910, won some concessions on salaries and the reserve clause. In 1922 attorney Raymond Cannon, who had defended some of the Chicago White Sox for their role in fixing the outcome of the 1919 World Series, took charge of the National Baseball Players Association, with 225 members in the Majors and the Minors, but this group lasted barely a year. Further union organizing in the next two decades proved difficult, and CIO representatives who tried to unionize ballplayers during World War II made little headway. Murphy had an undergraduate degree from Harvard and a law degree from Northeastern, plus experience working for the National Labor Relations Board (NLRB) in Washington. Interested in baseball, he read with dismay that some Major League players were earning less than $3,500 a year, that they received no compensation during spring training, that they were bound in perpetuity to whatever club held their contracts by the reserve clause, and that they could be summarily cut with only ten days' notice.[17]

In Boston Murphy made friends with several members of the Braves whose complaints about salaries and other matters persuaded him and a colleague, Joseph Doherty, to register the guild at the city clerk's office. As clubs came to Boston to play either the Braves or the Red Sox, Murphy met with them in turn, gaining acceptance from some players and meeting with resistance from others, especially those who had grown up near southern mill towns, where opposition to union membership was deeply engrained. Murphy proceeded nevertheless. On April 16 his press release announcing the guild's formation listed four basic objectives: freedom of contract so a player would not be forced to join a club against his will; the right of a player to receive part of the purchase price if his contract was sold; the right to have disagreements about salary and other conditions of employment settled by collective bargaining and arbitration; and the right to join a union. Murphy did not attack the reserve clause directly, but his call for contracts not to be "one-sided" fooled no one.

Owners reacted immediately, Clark Griffith arguing that "baseball can't exist without the reserve clause." Murphy decided to try to organize the Pirates first, not only because they played in a strong union town, but also because they were in seventh place, struggling, and playing uninspired baseball. According to historian William Marshall, Pittsburgh had taken sixty-five players to spring training in 1946: twenty-two who had played in the Majors in 1945, seven Minor Leaguers, and thirty-six returning veterans hoping to reclaim their prewar jobs. In May the Pittsburgh roster included thirty-five players, including a few veterans. The Pirates fielded an old team, and manager Frank Frisch had trouble finding playing time for everyone. Moreover, players knew that the roster would have to be cut to thirty in June. Insecurity was rampant.[18]

The Pirates' majority stockholder was Barney Dreyfuss's widow, Florence, but day-to-day control of the club had fallen to son-in-law Bill Benswanger, an insurance executive and patron of the arts who joined the family business following the death of the Dreyfusses' son Sam in February 1931 and became president after Barney Dreyfuss died in February 1932. Murphy asked Benswanger in a telegram on May 15 for a meeting to discuss recognizing the guild and beginning collective bargaining. Benswanger agreed to meet on June 5 and expressed his belief that "the whole guild affair will be settled to everyone's satisfaction." Murphy declared that most of the Pirates were guild members, but the meeting with Benswanger did not go well, devolving into bickering. Murphy met with the players in their clubhouse before that night's game against the Dodgers "to tell them what kind of bosses they've got," and he demanded that Benswanger "be here in fifteen minutes or you won't have a game tonight." A heated discussion ensued, after which the players voted to play that night's game but not to take the field two nights later against the New York Giants if the club did not recognize the guild. Some newspaper stories joked about the prospect of a union for ballplayers, but Benswanger took the threat of a strike seriously. He consulted with Commissioner Happy Chandler and planned to put a surrogate team on the field if necessary, albeit one that would have included Frisch and coach Honus Wagner, then seventy-two years old. One current player, pitcher Rip Sewell, opposed the union, fed Benswanger inside information, and lobbied his teammates to reject a strike that would have extended beyond one game until the club recognized the guild. The Pirates met behind closed doors before the game against the Giants, took a strike vote, and announced that they would play. According to Marshall, twenty players voted to strike and sixteen voted against, but the team had agreed beforehand to walk out only if the strike got a two-thirds majority.[19]

Historian Lee Lowenfish, collaborating with former player Tony Lupien, wrote that Murphy had not wanted the Pirates to take a strike vote on June 5. More than twenty-six thousand fans were already in the ballpark, and Murphy was confident that if management continued to resist, the NLRB would rule in the guild's favor. Benswanger's intransigence, though, hardened attitudes among the players and forced the vote on June 7, giving the players only two choices, to strike or to play, and did not allow for a more nuanced response. Sewell led the opposition to a strike, but he also said that he was "in favor of any union for men who can't help themselves. But I'd hate to see baseball unionized, as a player has no limit on what he can earn in this game." Other players seemed to support the idea of a guild but were dismayed by Murphy's abrasive approach. Still others, like pitcher Ken Heintzelman, just back from the war, feared that a strike might adversely affect their careers. Veteran catcher Al Lopez resented Murphy's decision to have the Pirates bear the burden of being the first club to unionize. Third baseman Bob Elliott, the highest-paid Pirate, said, "There should be a way for the guild to get an agreement and avoid such an unpleasant thing. I say this as one who believes in the principles of the guild." Murphy's proposal for a $6,500 minimum salary certainly would have benefited several Pirates, including catcher Bill Salkeld. He had earned less than $6,000 in 1945, had to keep his family in a hotel during the season because of tight housing conditions, and was forced to borrow money to send them home to California after the season ended. Salkeld hit .315 and yet won only a $500 raise for 1946. After the strike vote Murphy filed charges against the Pirates with the NLRB, and the board set an election for August 21. In the interim Murphy filed similar complaints on behalf of the players on the three New York clubs and the two Boston clubs. He met with Braves players and told them that only 60 percent of the roster was making more than $5,000. In response the players decided to send a delegation to speak to owner Lou Perini about the guild's platform, including a proposal for some sort of player representation.[20]

In the months before Robert Murphy made his pitch to the Pirates, ballplayers, chagrined by crowded postwar rosters and what they perceived to be the unreasonable strictures of the reserve clause, were handed an unusual opportunity. Jorge Pasquel, a Mexican millionaire, offered a number of Major Leaguers substantial sums of money to jump their contracts—that is, to ignore the contracts they had already signed and the reserve clause contained therein and agree to play in Mexico. Pasquel, one of five brothers heirs to a large business empire anchored by a cigar factory and a customs brokerage firm, made no secret of his ambition. He wanted to elevate the Mexican League, an independent league outside the realm of organized baseball, into the equivalent of a third Major League and bring prestige to himself and his country. Mexico's baseball roots are deep but murky. Some sources point to July 4, 1889, as the date on which Treadwell Robertson, a railroad entrepreneur and former colonel in the U.S. Army, gave workers building the Monterrey-Tampico rail line a holiday they celebrated by playing a ball game in Cadereyta de Jiménez, a village in the state of Nuevo León. There is other evidence that American sailors played a ball game in Guaymas in 1877; that an American named Johnny Tyson, a foreman on a railroad project in Nuevo Laredo, demonstrated the game for interested workers and formed two teams, also in 1877; and that a club called "Mexico" was established in Mexico City in 1887. It is also probable that a Cuban family named Urzaiz landed at a Yucatán port in 1890, brought baseball equipment with them, and organized games among local youngsters. Fixing the birth of professional baseball in Mexico is far easier. In 1925 sportswriter Alejandro Aguilar Reyes and promoter Ernesto Carmona organized a five-team league that played a schedule beginning in June and concluded with a three-game playoff between the two teams tied for first. This league endured, but individual and team statistics, save for a list of pennant winners, are nearly nonexistent until 1937, when the Mexican League reached a certain stability. Teams during these early years—what scholar Peter C. Bjarkman called "Mexican baseball's lengthy prehistory"—sometimes supplemented their rosters with African American players and Cubans, including pitcher Martín Dihigo, whose no-hitter in 1937 may have been the country's first. Soon thereafter Pasquel got involved. After the Mexican League banned three executives for allowing their team, El Águila (the Veracruz Eagles), to forfeit the final three games of the 1939 season, Pasquel established Los Azules (the Veracruz Blues) as a possible replacement, but the league turned him down. Pasquel retaliated by forming his own league, the Mexican Major League, and after one season, during which Pasquel himself managed the Blues to the pennant, the new league replaced the old one and assumed its name. He and his brothers bought partial ownership of the league's other clubs and majority control of Mexico City's Delta Park, the best ballpark in the country. Not exactly behind the scenes, Pasquel ran the league well before he was officially elected president in 1946.[21]

Baseball fandom in Mexico was rampant and enthusiastic, but ballplayers native to Mexico were rarely highly regarded. No Mexican played in the Major Leagues until 1933. Baldomero "Mel" Almada Quirós, born in Huatabampo,

Sonora, and raised in Tucson and Los Angeles, was the first. He played with the Red Sox, Senators, Browns, and Dodgers from 1933 through 1939. He was followed by José Luis "Chile" Gómez Gonzales, born in Matzatlán, Sinaloa. He played for the Phillies in 1935 and 1936 and the Senators in 1942. Moreover, the quality of play in the Mexican League left much to be desired. When Agrario and Comintra, two teams sponsored by departments of the federal government, played for the league championship in 1935, only three hundred fans attended the final game. Thereafter the league changed its rules to allow each team to import four foreign players. Club owners looked to the United States, not to white players but rather to African Americans who had been barred from organized baseball since the late nineteenth century. Satchel Paige, generally acknowledged as one of the game's greatest pitchers, led a group of six African Americans to Mexico in 1938, confident that they could make more money south of the border than they could playing for Black teams in the United States. Paige and eight others, including future Hall of Fame members Josh Gibson and Cool Papa Bell, had played in the Dominican Republic the year before and had allegedly split $30,000, and Paige was pleased to sign a contract with Agrario for $2,000 a month. Five others came with him, but the season for Paige was a disappointment. Bothered by a sore arm, a condition he blamed on eating spicy food, Paige started only three games and completed none. Teammate Chet Brewer, also a pitcher, said Paige had hurt his arm the year before. "Those Mexicans found out he couldn't throw hard and just beat his brains out," he said. Yet when the pennant was on the line in the season's last game against El Águila, Paige started and pitched six scoreless innings before being lifted for a pinch hitter.[22]

Pasquel's motives for recruiting Black players, and later white players, were mixed. Perhaps he was driven simply by a desire to display the power of the family fortune, or perhaps he wanted to use baseball to boost the presidential candidacy of his friend, Miguel Alemán, whose election would have delivered a windfall for the Pasquels' business interests. Perhaps he just wanted the Mexican League to improve so much that it would be considered a de facto third Major League. Pasquel was a power broker, and he traveled often to the United States, carrying a diplomatic passport, thanks to Alemán. During the war he arranged draft deferments for two African Americans, Quincy Trouppe and Theolic Smith, so they could continue playing ball in Mexico, by promising Washington eighty thousand Mexican laborers to alleviate the manpower shortage. In 1944 he lured Rogers Hornsby, recently elected to the Hall of Fame, to Mexico to manage Los Azules, and in 1945 he spent $282,000 to get a firsthand look at white American players and at ballpark amenities he hoped to duplicate in Mexico. Pasquel's connection in the United States was *St. Louis Star-Times* sportswriter Ray Gillespie, who had first visited Mexico in 1937. Gillespie got Pasquel an apartment in St. Louis and started taking him to ball games. "Jorge Pasquel was a great baseball fan," he recalled, "very wealthy, one of the richest families in Mexico, estimated fortune $70 to $80 million." The pair went to Sportsman's Park, where Gillespie explained that St. Louis Cardinals shortstop Marty Marion, the National League's reigning Most Valuable Player, had been holding out for $15,000. "I'll give him twenty-five thousand to play for me," Pasquel retorted. When Gillespie explained why that would not be possible because he would be tampering with organized baseball, Pasquel dismissed his explanation, saying, "That's a monopoly." And so it began. Gillespie took Pasquel to Chicago and then to New York and other cities so that Pasquel saw more than fifty games. "There's only one way to do it [improve the Mexican League]," he told Gillespie, "and that's to offer more money. I believe that any man has the right to better himself, and ballplayers are no exception."[23]

Returning to New York in January 1946, Pasquel stayed at the Sherry-Netherland Hotel on Fifth Avenue and exercised three times a week at a nearby health club. There he met his trainer, Danny Gardella, a professional baseball player of slight stature and limited talent, especially defensively, who had been classified 4-F by his local draft board and played for the wartime Giants in 1944 and 1945. Pasquel was astounded that Gardella, who had batted .272 and hit 18 home runs in 1945, had to work during the off-season. He offered the outfielder a $5,000 bonus to sign a contract for $8,000 for 1946, plus options for the following two seasons. Gardella turned him down, preferring to take his chances with the Giants, even though they had offered him only a $500 raise to $5,000. Spring training did not go well. Gardella missed the train taking the team from New York to Miami. When he arrived at the Venetian Hotel, where the team was staying, he was broke, unshaven, and not properly dressed to enter the dining room, but he did so anyway. He refused to sign his contract and got into a row with team secretary Eddie Brannick, who refused his request for a cash advance. Dressed down by manager Mel Ott, Gardella stormed off, only to return a few hours later wanting to make amends and sign his contract. But it was too late. The Giants had released him. Gardella contacted Pasquel and became the first Major Leaguer, albeit one whose future as a player was quite uncertain, to jump to the Mexican League. He played left field and first base for Los Azules, made the midseason All-Star team, and finished the season batting .275 with 13 home runs. His club finished in seventh place in an eight-team league, and Gardella grew less content as the season dragged on. The ballparks and hotels were not what Pasquel had promised. Gardella spoke little Spanish, and the league played only three or four games a week, giving him too much free time. Even after his girlfriend flew to Mexico so the two could get married, Gardella remained morose. The club did not pay him a $500 bonus he had won in a contest, and near the end of the season Pasquel announced that salaries for 1947 would be cut. Gardella's Mexican adventure ended abruptly. A few hours after the final game, he and his wife flew to New York.[24]

Pasquel would have been thrilled if he had been able to sign one or more of baseball's stars. He approached pitchers Hal Newhouser (winner of the American League's Most Valuable Player Award in 1944 and 1945) and Bob Feller and outfielders Ted Williams, Joe DiMaggio, Hank Greenberg, and Stan Musial. By some accounts he offered Feller at least $300,000, Newhouser $350,000, and Greenberg $360,000, all for three years. They all turned him down, Feller doing so in a letter in which he wrote, "Sorry I cannot accept your generous offer due to present obligations." Pasquel also took a special interest in players on the Cardinals, whose owner, Sam Breadon, refused to pay any player more than $15,000, and whose general manager, Branch Rickey, believed that "a hungry ballplayer is a better ballplayer." As he did with Gardella, Pasquel promised the players he approached bonuses, long-term contracts, and first-class facilities, and by May 1946 he had signed three Cardinals—pitchers Max Lanier and Freddie Martin and infielder Lou Klein—and made offers to infielder Whitey Kurowski and the team's entire outfield: Enos Slaughter, Terry Moore, and Musial. Negotiations to snare Musial, who had missed only one season, 1945, to serve in the navy, were complicated. Pasquel used four surrogates: his brother Alphonso, former pitcher Roy Henshaw, catcher Mickey Owen (who had already signed to play in Mexico), and Gillespie. Musial apparently wavered more than once and eventually decided to stay with the Cardinals even though Pasquel's offer included a five-year contract at $25,000 per year, tax-free, plus a signing bonus that topped out at $50,000 in the form of five checks for $10,000 each tossed on the bed in Musial's apartment at St. Louis's Fairgrounds Hotel. In mid-June Musial told the press that he would remain with the Cardinals despite an offer "that was hard to turn down." Two years later sportswriter Frank Graham wrote that manager Eddie Dyer had swayed Musial by reminding him that he had a signed contract with St. Louis and that "an honorable man doesn't go back on his word."[25]

In all Pasquel lured twenty-three Major Leaguers to the Mexican League in 1946, including nine from the Giants, three each from the Dodgers and Cardinals, two from the Senators, and one each from six other clubs. Few of them enjoyed an experience as lucrative or as uncomplicated as they might have anticipated. Vern Stephens, who had led the Browns to the World Series championship in 1944 and had another good season in 1945, was Pasquel's prize catch, but he abandoned his Mexican sojourn almost before it began. The shortstop, who had led the American League in home runs in 1945, wanted a substantial raise to $17,500 for 1946, but the Browns countered with only $13,000. Stephens held out, content for a while to hit golf balls in Long Beach, California, his hometown. Pasquel called every day for two weeks, and Stephens reasoned that he could use an offer to play in Mexico to pry more money from St. Louis. He asked for an enormous amount—perhaps $75,000 per year for five years—and Pasquel agreed, sending $5,000 to Long Beach and putting the balance in an escrow account in a Mexican bank. Stephens flew south to join Los Azules. He played one game in Mexico City, driving in the winning run, and a second game a few days later after a 450-mile road trip. By one account these few days in a foreign country disillusioned Stephens. He complained about finding proper housing, he groused about the food, he hated the fact that the "C" on the shower faucet stood for *caliente*—that is, "hot" and not "cold"—and he had a tough time adjusting to breathing at altitude. Escape became the game plan. Stephens, who thought he was under surveillance, communicated with his father and with Browns scout Jack Fournier. He left the team in Monterrey for Nuevo Laredo, donned his father's overcoat, pulled a hat down over his eyes, and walked across the International Bridge into Texas before anyone in a position of authority recognized him. He rejoined the Browns, who were training in San Antonio, and signed a contract for what he had wanted. When Pasquel called offering him even more money, Stephens turned him down and returned what he had already been paid.[26]

Organized baseball recognized that both the American Baseball Guild and the Mexican League imperiled the sport's control of its work force through the reserve clause. Reaction to the insurgencies launched by Robert Murphy and Jorge Pasquel came swiftly and decisively. In April 1946 Clark Griffith told the *New York Times* that a players' union "would wreck baseball; knock it flat on its feet," that collective bargaining in baseball was "utterly impractical," and that "such things as paying a player a percentage of a purchase price and provisions for security, insurance, and bonuses already have been taken care of by baseball." He added that "the players are handsomely paid," and he concluded by agreeing that "the unions have done a fine job wherever they fit in, but this is one place where they do not fit." The *Sporting News*, prone to hyperbole whenever the National Pastime seemed threatened, editorialized that the postwar world was going through a social revolution and baseball was "passing through that social upheaval, along with bread baking and wheat growing, coal mining and steel puddling, railroading and meat production." Commissioner Happy Chandler announced that players who violated their contracts or the reserve clause would be banned from organized baseball for five years unless they returned to their teams before Opening Day. This threat did not dissuade Pasquel, who reasoned that a stiff penalty from Chandler would encourage players who jumped to Mexico to stay there, and he accelerated his recruitment efforts, snaring, perhaps most prominently, young Giants pitcher Sal Maglie and the veteran Mickey Owen. The problem with Pasquel's scheme was not the money he offered but rather the promised ballparks and living conditions that he could not deliver. Not even an appearance in Mexico by Babe Ruth, during which the aged slugger lauded Pasquel for his efforts, was enough. Alemán pulled back on his support after he was elected in July, and that strained Pasquel's resources. Some cities were too small to support the salaries they had to pay, and the one ballpark that approached Major League standards, Delta Park, had only twenty-three thousand seats. Clubhouses were inadequate; playing fields were poorly maintained; and the Americans had a tough time with travel, housing, and food. When Owen decided in July to quit and sneak back home, the end of Pasquel's adventure was in sight, even though Chandler declined to lift the catcher's suspension. Seven of the twenty-three Americans did not return to Mexico for the following season, and only seven played there beyond 1947.[27]

All three New York clubs sued Pasquel in state court, seeking injunctions against his efforts to sign their players, but baseball's hierarchy, wary of subjecting the reserve clause to legal scrutiny, sought to avoid litigation. "Judge Landis and I fought twenty-four years to keep baseball out of the courts," lamented Leslie O'Connor, the late commissioner's assistant and now general manager of the Chicago White Sox. Larry MacPhail, now running the Yankees for his co-owners, Dan Topping (heir to a fortune made in the tin industry) and Arizona real estate developer Del Webb, rushed forward with a plan to dodge additional legal entanglements. He suggested player representation on baseball's advisory council and a board of arbitration to resolve salary disputes. He also urged the players to revive a version of David Fultz's

Baseball Players Fraternity, even volunteering to help them do so. This idea, derided as a company union, was a violation of federal labor law, but the threat of Murphy's guild was very much alive. In response the owners met over the All-Star break and created the ad hoc Joint Major League Committee, whose members were MacPhail as chair, owners Sam Breadon, Phil Wrigley, and Tom Yawkey, and league presidents Ford Frick and Will Harridge. Given a broad mandate to address all the threats facing postwar baseball, the group convened seven times during July and August in Boston, New York, and Chicago and even issued what William Marshall termed "an almost revolutionary call" to open careful lines of communication with the players that went beyond Lou Perini's earlier meeting with some of his Braves. The committee asked each team to elect a player representative to serve as its spokesman on the labor issues before the game and for the player representatives in each league to select three to meet with the committee on August 5. Each league's group of eight met on July 29 and compiled a list of proposals that included, among other things, a minimum salary, money for spring training, a portion of the sale price going to a player sold, and the creation of a pension plan, something unheard of in baseball to that point. But player representatives in both leagues left the reserve clause alone.[28]

The player most associated with the development of the pension plan was Marty Marion, the Cardinals' tall, thin shortstop, nicknamed "Slats." He was a South Carolinian, born in Richburg, a dot of a town about forty miles south of Charlotte, North Carolina, but raised in Atlanta. When he was a boy, Marion fell down an embankment, suffered a compound fracture of his right leg, and was in traction for months. Still, he recovered to play high school and American Legion baseball and followed his older brother, Johnny, into the Minors. The Chattanooga Lookouts in the Southern Association gave him a quick trial in 1935 but cut him. Marion thought about studying architecture at Georgia Tech, but he attended a Cardinals tryout camp and won a measly contract offered by Frank Rickey, a scout for his brother, Branch. Marion climbed through the Minors for four seasons and took over as the Cardinals' starting shortstop in 1940, primarily because of his defensive skills. His childhood injury kept him out of the service, and he played a key role as St. Louis won three pennants and two World Series during the war. Teammate Danny Litwhiler said, "He just had fantastic hands," and it was those skills, not his .267 batting average with only 63 runs batted in, that earned him the National League's Most Valuable Player Award in 1944. After that season Breadon offered him a $1,000 raise to $13,000, but Marion wanted $15,000 and threatened not to play at all. Marion won, but he resented Breadon's stinginess, and since he was getting older and bothered by chronic back problems, he began to think about life after baseball. He spent a lot of time with the team's trainer, Doc Weaver, and, on the train to Boston for the 1946 All-Star Game, with Rip Sewell. As they talked and brought others into the conversation, they hatched the idea for a pension plan. Marion envisioned a plan funded annually from various sources: $100 from each player with five years' seniority, plus a lump sum payment of $500 from players reaching their tenth year; $2,500 from each Major League club; $50,000 from All-Star Game receipts; $100,000 from the World Series radio fees; and $160,000 from a series of in-season, interleague exhibition games. Marion figured to let this fund grow for a decade or so, after which five-year players would receive $50 a month for life and ten-year players, $100 a month.[29]

The six players who met with the owners committee on August 5 left with smiles on their faces. "They were very cordial," Cleveland pitcher Mel Harder noted, "and they wanted to help the situation." The players were pleased with the discussion of a minimum salary and a pension plan, but the reserve clause was not on the agenda. MacPhail called this omission "most gratifying," and Marion remembered years later that "we didn't think baseball could operate without the reserve clause." Whatever promises or suggestions MacPhail might have made to the players, he still had to prepare a draft report for the committee and a final version for the next owners meeting. He took the instructions given to the committee to heart and wrote an expansive, comprehensive planning document covering the labor question and other sensitive and even controversial matters. MacPhail admitted that baseball was a monopoly. He argued that the standard player contract needed revision and strengthening against potential legal challenges. He warned that the reserve clause would not hold up in court and could not serve as a basis for restraining orders against Pasquel's Mexican League challenge. He opined, too, that if Murphy had begun his unionization effort with Minor League players, he might well have succeeded. MacPhail went on, excoriating the owners for the haphazard way they organized and administered their business, calling it "an acute situation representing almost total confusion." This frank, even raw, draft drew the support of no one else on the committee, so what the owners saw a day later was a hastily expurgated version that earned their approval. Significantly, they created an executive council, composed of the commissioner, both league presidents, and two owners, charging it with the responsibility to rationalize the game, reconcile rules and regulations differences, create a unified publicity and promotional office, and work to maintain public confidence in organized baseball. As for the players, the owners also acknowledged them as a group speaking through their player representatives. They approved a minimum salary of $5,000 (well below Murphy's demand), adjusted separation pay from ten days' salary to thirty days', capped how much a player's salary could be cut from one season to the next at no more than 25 percent, extended disability protection, gave the players $25 a week for living expenses during spring training (an inadequate sum that quickly became known as "Murphy money"), and approved in principle a pension plan over the objection of owners burdened by poor attendance and unwilling to be forced to contribute.[30]

Sportswriter Red Smith offered his view in the *New York Herald Tribune* that the owners, by offering these few concessions, had "sought to forestall trouble by throwing the help a bone. They decided in advance how little they could offer and get by with." Murphy, who a few days before had learned that the Pirates had voted against joining the guild, 15–3, in an election run by the Pennsylvania State Labor Relations Board, predicted that players would not be content with committees dominated by owners. "The players," he said, "have been offered an apple, but they could have had an orchard." How the pension plan would work began to unfold during the World Series. The commissioner and the two league presidents agreed to donate their portion of the $175,000 radio rights fee paid by Gillette to initiate the plan, but when Chandler asked players on the Red Sox and the Cardinals to sign waivers surrendering part of their World Series shares, some Red Sox players hesitated. Only when Marion cautioned them to think about the years after they stopped playing and not be so concerned that their World Series bonuses, both the winners' and losers' shares, would be the lowest since 1918 did they agree. At the 1946 winter meetings owners formally agreed to allocate proceeds from both the World Series and the All-Star Game to the pension plan, as Marion had suggested, and to require a yearly contribution of $250 from every player to be matched by his club. At these same meetings, held concurrently with the Minor Leagues for the first time in three years and for the first time in a Minor League city, players made their presence felt. They demanded loosening the waiver rules so that players could move more easily from one organization to another and an end to scheduling doubleheaders after night games. The owners agreed to both. They also, perhaps responding to MacPhail's criticisms, signed a new Major–Minor League Agreement, replacing the old contract that was twenty-five years old and had been extended many times.[31]

By 1953 players had begun to wonder if the pension plan was adequately funded. Player representatives for each team, chosen in a variety of ways, met together several times a year, selected players to serve on the pension committee, and began to fashion an embryonic organization that became known as the Major League Baseball Players Association. Using minimal dues assessments from all Major Leaguers, they hired former Yankees traveling secretary Frank Scott, who was handling public appearances and endorsements for some players, to work part time as an administrator. Each league also had a player representative, the Yankees' Allie Reynolds and the Pirates' Ralph Kiner, designated to meet periodically with the owners. They arranged meetings with their respective leagues' owners the day before the 1953 All-Star Game in Cincinnati to discuss the pension and other grievances. Reynolds told the press that he "would be as much opposed to a labor boss in baseball as would the owners," but he did suggest that "the players have some kind of a liaison officer, to be a permanent member" of the commissioner's staff. That did not happen, so the players engaged a lawyer, J. Norman Lewis, to provide them with research and advice on salaries and pensions. Later that year Reynolds and Kiner brought Lewis with them to a pension committee meeting, but the owners forced Lewis to sit outside the meeting room. Kiner was incensed, and he carried his anger with him for years, complaining to historian Charles P. Korr in 1989 that "we were powerless, out there on a springboard with no help." Player representatives continued to meet, and Lewis continued to advise them. At the 1958 winter meetings in Washington, the players, with Lewis at their side, proposed the radical notion that each club set aside 20 percent of its gross revenues from all sources for its player salary budget. Frank Lane, general manager of the Indians, called this "the most preposterous demand the players have yet thought up," and an unnamed owner suggested giving the players "meal money during the season; no salary at all. Then, at the end of the year, just toss the twenty percent take into a room. I want to be there to see those players divide the money. That would be the greatest fight in history."[32]

The association's leaders dismissed Lewis in 1958, not because of the 20 percent proposal that the *Sporting News* called "exorbitant" but rather because he was, in their judgment, not doing enough to justify the retainer he was being paid. Besides, Phillies pitcher Robin Roberts, a graduate of Michigan State, a member of the pension committee, and the new National League player representative, believed that it was time for the association to open an office and hire full-time staff. He and Scott continued to address a number of issues with the owners, but they made little progress. In 1960 Scott submitted a report to the leadership on the benefits of a central office and recommended himself for a full-time position as "an active liaison man whose function" would be "to represent baseball matters and . . . [who would] be ready to travel between clubs to discuss whatever matter has arisen with a particular club." Roberts wanted more than this. He wanted the players to determine what the role of the central office would be, and he wanted whomever the association hired to retain a law firm. Roberts and outfielder Harvey Kuenn, the American League player representative, announced the opening of an office in New York, to be run by Scott, and the search for part-time legal counsel. The man who got that job was Robert Cannon, a Wisconsin judge and the son of Raymond Cannon, who had tried to organize the players in the 1920s. The *Sporting News* approved this selection, saying that Cannon would be realistic and would "make no demands, no public statements." He was not, by his own admission, an expert on pensions, and he voiced an attitude toward baseball's owners that was more conciliatory than some players wanted. Early on he declined to support an idea to hire a Washington lobbyist for the association, saying that he wanted to avoid doing anything that would "jeopardize the fine relationship existing between the players and the club owners." Cannon knew that running an office would cost money. He rejected the outlandish suggestion that the owners fund the association but recommended that support should come from World Series revenues, the same way the commissioner's office and the league presidents' offices were funded. In 1960, when he testified before a congressional committee for the first time, he said that he saw no need for legislative interference in baseball.[33]

Weeks before the start of the 1946 season Dan Daniel anticipated "a spirit of change, of brighter outlooks, and a fresh start." World War II was over, returning veterans were trying to reconstruct their civilian lives, and many ballplayers who had served their country were back competing for their old jobs. Baseball embraced a sense of renewal, and playing more night games seemed to some a way to point toward a future brimming with optimism. At the 1945 winter meetings in Chicago the two Major Leagues differed over whether to allow clubs to schedule an unlimited number of night games or cut back to prewar levels. The National League favored no restrictions, absent objections from the visiting team. American League owners acceded to requests from the Browns and Senators to host as many as thirty-three night games each, but they held all other clubs to no more than fourteen. Commissioner Happy Chandler decided that the two leagues should operate by the same rule, and he sided with the National League. Night baseball would no longer be a novelty. Spring training in warm weather also experienced a rebirth. Teams prepared to train once more in Florida and California, no longer confined, as they had been during the war, to sites east of the Mississippi River and north of the Mason-Dixon line. The *Sporting News* exulted in a headline, "Let It Snow! Clubs Set for Rush to Sunkist Zone." The Cubs opened a special camp in January in Lake Worth, Florida, for returning veterans and then held their full camp on Catalina Island. The White Sox, the Pirates, and the Browns also trained in California. All other clubs headed to Florida. As they gathered in baseball's traditional spring homes, Daniel admitted that "nobody pretends that those northern seasons were anything but synthetic representations of the real thing."[34]

When Major League clubs began spring training, traveling south and west for the first time since 1942, nearly a thousand players, each with a claim to a roster spot, assembled to bid for jobs. Clubs scrambled to find adequate housing and forced married players to leave their wives at home. By the time clubs headed north in early April, a surprising number of older military veterans had won back their positions. "A big factor," Daniel wrote, "is the remarkable form shown by many older regulars, back after two to four years in the service." Yankees manager Joe McCarthy voiced his surprise too. "When these men went into service, most of us said: 'Too bad, when they return to the big leagues, they will have lost their edge, their zest, and their ability to fight off younger opposition.' Well, it hasn't turned out that way at all." Still, those who had entered the military early found their return to baseball rather rough. Bill Embick, the first professional ballplayer drafted, never played again, his career limited to 103 games in 1940 in the Interstate League. Hugh Mulcahy was nearly thirty-two years old when he rejoined the Phillies on August 26, 1945. He pitched in 5 games that season, 16 in 1946, and 2 in 1947, with a combined won-lost record of 3-7. Battling both control and stamina issues, he struggled on in the Minors through 1951. Pitcher Johnny Rigney did not return to the White Sox until 1946. He pitched in 15 games that year and 11 the next before retiring. Outfielder Morrie Arnovich came back to the Giants in 1946, but he played in only 1 game, going hitless in three at bats. He played in the Minors for two more seasons, did some Minor League managing in the Cubs' farm system, and retired to run a sporting goods and jewelry store in his hometown, Superior, Wisconsin. Although Arnovich's parents had once wanted him to become a rabbi, he also coached the boys' basketball team at the local Catholic high school.[35]

Spring training in 1946 began with a rush. Before the Yankees opened camp in St. Petersburg and Bradenton, the club said that Pan American Airways would fly the team to Panama for exhibition games in late February and early March and that the Yankees would become the first team to use plane travel regularly throughout the season. The leagues announced that the 1946 All-Star Game, coming after 1945's cancellation, would be played at Fenway Park on July 9 and that the game's charitable beneficiary would not be the Bat and Ball Fund, a wartime endeavor, but the Baseball Welfare Fund. Schedule makers crafted a grid with eastern clubs making four trips west and vice versa, just as they had before wartime travel restrictions. When spring training opened with 383 exhibition games scheduled, a *Sporting News* headline crowed that "1,000 Crowd Major Camps in Greatest Job Scramble." Clubs took advantage of this waft of enthusiasm. Most decided to raise regular-season ticket prices anywhere from 50 to 100 percent. Reserved box seats would now cost between $2.00 and $2.50, general admission about $1.25, and bleacher seats between 60 and 75 cents. Near Opening Day an editorial in the *Sporting News* gushed, "That baseball's recovery from the war is completed was demonstrated during the spring training season, with its refurbished clubs, amazing turnouts, record enthusiasm, and fresh eagerness among the players." The newspaper predicted that "baseball is riding a boom wave that will carry it to heights hitherto unachieved." The start of the season bore out this optimism. Nearly a million fans poured through turnstiles during the first six days of play, heralding a season that "will be the greatest in the history of the game," sparked by "service returnees," who, "as a class, have been remarkably impressive." Indeed 40 percent, or fifty-seven players, of those who started on Opening Day in 1946 were reclaiming places they had occupied on Opening Day in 1941.[36]

Taylor Spink predicted that the Yankees would win the American League pennant, returning to the perch they had occupied for three of the previous five seasons and seven of the past ten. But he was wrong. Boston won the 1946 American League pennant handily, and the Yankees finished third, seventeen games behind. The Red Sox clinched the flag on Friday, September 13, when they defeated the Indians, 1–0. Coupled with a Detroit loss, Boston's ninety-seventh victory gave the Red Sox an unsurmountable lead over the Tigers and brought the club its first pennant since 1918 and its first with Tom Yawkey as owner. The team's victory party might have been a time for glee, but the champagne that night seemed to be spiked with frustration. Clinching the flag could have come days earlier, but the Sox had lost six in a row before the clincher. The team's slide was just steep enough to give the Boston press, rare with praise, another chance to fire a salvo at the club's perceived lack of fire. Back in spring training Red Sox manager Joe Cronin had rejoiced that his best four position players, including Ted Williams, had returned from the war unscathed and that his starting pitching looked to be above average. Cronin bristled, though, when he opened the *Saturday Evening Post* to see a story called "What's the Matter With the Red Sox?" in which veteran sportswriter Harold Kaese cited a "choir of critics" who believed that "there is nothing wrong with the Red Sox that a new manager wouldn't cure." The wound Kaese inflicted never healed. In the hotel elevator that September evening Cronin got into a verbal sparring match with Huck Finnegan of the *Boston American*, who had predicted that the Sox would swoon. The two were on their way to separate postgame celebrations since Yawkey, keenly aware of the relationship between the team and the writers, had booked the players' party in one banquet room and the press-only bash in another. To this affront Al Hirshberg of the *Boston Post* complained that the reporters were being treated like "scullery maids."[37]

No one can do more than guess what batting statistics Williams would have compiled if he had not spent three seasons in the marines. Nor could anyone at the time be sure if, by leaving the game at age twenty-four and returning at twenty-seven, he had left his best years in the cockpit. After his initial training at Amherst College late in 1942, he got his wings in May 1944 and was assigned to stay where he was as an instructor. In fact Williams did not go overseas until August 1945, two weeks after the United States had dropped two atomic bombs on Hiroshima and Nagasaki. With the war over, he got to play some baseball and was discharged in January 1946. In the season's early weeks it was clear that his time away had done him no harm. He was stronger and more confident and hitting well. In May and June he drove in 53 runs and hit 19 homers. In July he fashioned an all-time All-Star Game highlight by launching one of Rip Sewell's "eephus" pitches, thrown in a high arc like a slow-pitch softball, into the Fenway Park bullpen. Williams was such a dead-pull hitter that Cleveland manager Lou Boudreau resurrected a scheme tried five years before by Chicago's Jimmy Dykes. The "Williams shift" put all four infielders on the right side, moved the right fielder close to the foul line, and shifted the center fielder into right-center. It hardly mattered. Williams, at that point Boston's best player since Babe Ruth, finished the year batting .342 with 38 home runs and 123 runs batted in. Yet in September, as the team stalled, he drove in only 9 runs, prompting questions and comments that allowed his prewar feud with the press to fester again. Williams often resorted to off-color language, but in one tepid exchange he complained to Hy Hurwitz of the *Boston Globe*, "I get tired of looking at a little squirt like you," to which the sportswriter responded, "That makes us even, for I get tired looking at a big galoot like you."[38]

The Red Sox had to wait until after the season was over to know whom they would be playing in the World Series. James Carroll, St. Louis's unofficial betting commissioner—a euphemism for an illegal bookmaker or oddsmaker—had installed the hometown Cardinals as 7–10 favorites to win the National League pennant in March, but for the first time the race had ended in a tie, the Cardinals and the Dodgers both finishing at 96-58. Following their close battles with St. Louis in 1941 and 1942, the Dodgers fell off the pace considerably during the next three seasons. They finished twenty-three and a half games behind the Cardinals in 1943, forty-two games behind in 1944, and eleven games behind in 1945. Outfielder Dixie Walker was the only Brooklyn regular who played throughout the war. He hit .300 in 1945 and led the league with 124 runs batted in, but he was also thirty-four years old. In 1946 infielders Pee Wee Reese and Cookie Lavagetto returned from the navy and injury-plagued outfielder Pete Reiser from the army. Joined by two rookies, outfielder Carl Furillo and catcher Bruce Edwards, the reconstituted Dodgers engaged St. Louis in one of the tightest pennant races in league history. Brooklyn led by as many as seven and a half games in early July, but St. Louis pulled even on July 18. The teams entered September with the Cardinals ahead by two and a half games, and the Dodgers did not catch them until the Friday of the season's final weekend. On Saturday, September 28, both teams won, and on Sunday the Braves shut out the Dodgers, 4–0, and the Cardinals lost to the Cubs. A playoff would be necessary.[39]

Ever since Branch Rickey's farm system began to bear fruit, the Cardinals had been perpetual contenders for the pennant. St. Louis had finished first in 1926, 1928, 1930, 1931, 1934, 1942, 1943, and 1944 and had won the World Series five times. The Cubs edged them out in 1945, but the Cardinals reloaded in 1946. Stan Musial came out of the navy to play first base and bat .365. Red Schoendienst, discharged from the army for medical reasons, played second and hit .281. Marty Marion and Whitey Kurowski, both 4-F, held down short and third respectively. The outfield featured Terry Moore, Enos Slaughter (who batted .300 and drove in 130 runs), and Harry Walker, all discharged from the army, and the catcher was Yogi Berra's boyhood pal, rookie Joe Garagiola. The Cards' pitching staff was also outstanding. Howie Pollett, a twenty-game winner three times before joining the army, won twenty-one games and led the league in innings pitched and earned run average. Harry Brecheen, who won sixteen games in 1944 and fifteen in 1945, won another fifteen, as did Murry Dickson. The staff ERA, 3.01, was the best in the league. St. Louis also hired a new manager to replace Billy Southworth, who left after the 1945 season, emotionally crushed by the fatal crash of his son, an Army Air Corps pilot. The Cardinals turned to Eddie Dyer, a Rickey protégé who had retired in 1944 after running the St. Louis Minor League system. "Not every Cardinal liked Dyer," according to author Robert Weintraub, but he got the job done.[40]

The National League constitution required a series, not a single game, to break the tie. The toss of the coin to determine what would in a later day be called "home field advantage" in the best-two-out-of-three playoff took place in the league's New York office. Cardinals owner Sam Breadon, on the telephone from St. Louis, called "heads" and lost. Dodgers manager Leo Durocher then decided to play the first game at Sportsman's Park, with the second game and the third, if necessary, at Ebbets Field. But three games were not needed. In Game One Pollett held on gamely through all nine innings, giving up eight hits and three walks, but he won, 4–2, with Garagiola driving in a pair of runs. The game was marked by a surprisingly small crowd—26,012, about 8,000 shy of capacity—and by both dugouts barking incessantly at calls made by home plate umpire Beans Reardon. The Dodgers had arrived in St. Louis by train, and now they had to go back to Brooklyn the same way. The Cardinals' train made the trip in just twenty hours, but the *Dodger Special* was plagued by delays and took three hours longer. Dyer picked Dickson to start Game Two, and Durocher, whose pitching was somewhat overextended, went with lefthander Joe Hatten. He gave up five runs in less than five innings, and the Cardinals coasted to an 8–4 win, the Dodgers scoring three runs in a desperate ninth-inning rally that fell short. Brecheen replaced Dickson and let the tying run come to the plate before getting two strikeouts to end the game.[41]

The 1946 World Series was the only time that Ted Williams and Musial played against each other in games that mattered. Both were young, both had served their country, and both would receive their league's Most Valuable Player Award for their play in this first postwar season. Yet Williams batted .200 in the Series and Musial .222, and neither would play in a Series again. Walker and Boston's Wally Moses, a part-time outfielder, led their clubs in batting, but the real star was Brecheen, a thirty-two-year-old left-hander. Relying on a screwball, finesse, and pinpoint control, he shut out the Red Sox in Game Two, 3–0, to tie the Series at one game each. A week later, with his team down, three games to two, he gave up seven hits and pitched a complete game, winning, 4–1. The next day was an off-day, granted so that the Cardinals could have extra time to sell more tickets for Game Seven. The following morning Brecheen felt awful, his arm aching and his entire body depleted by the flu. Still, with the Cardinals ahead, 3–1, Boston got two men on with nobody out in the top of the eighth. Dyer called upon Brecheen to come in from the bullpen. Moses struck out, and Johnny Pesky lined out to right. Dom DiMaggio then doubled in two runs to tie the score before Williams popped out to second. In the bottom of the inning Slaughter singled to center, Kurowski botched a sacrifice bunt and popped out, and catcher Del Rice flied to left. With a count of 2-1 on Walker, Slaughter took off for second, and Walker hit safely into left-center field. What happened next became the stuff of legend. Slaughter scored the tie-breaking run, but students of the game have argued ever since whether to credit his base running or debit either center fielder Leon Culberson or relay man Pesky for a defensive lapse. Perhaps the most poignant reaction came from *St. Louis Post-Dispatch* sportswriter Bob Broeg, who, upon hearing the official scorers' decision, said, "Gentlemen, by scoring that a double, not a single, you've taken the romance out of a great play." Brecheen closed out the Sox in the ninth but just barely. Two men reached base before he retired the next three. The Cardinals were World Series champions again.[42]

After the Series ended, Dyer noted that both his club and the Dodgers, the club St. Louis had beaten in a playoff, owed their success to Rickey, a man whose approach to the business of baseball was vastly different from Tom Yawkey's. If the Red Sox owner saw any irony in this situation, it went unrecorded. After his club saw its hopes for its first World Series title since 1918 slip away, he reacted fatalistically. "If that's the way it had to be," he said, "there's nothing we could have done about it." Just after the Series he wrote checks totaling about $100,000, sending each player a percentage of his salary. "I did not give the boys bonuses," he said since these were prohibited. "It was just a salary increase." The future for the Red Sox looked bright, but they did not win another World Series in Yawkey's lifetime. In 1948 Boston tied the Indians for first place, but Cleveland won a one-game playoff. The following year the Red Sox came to the season's final weekend one game ahead of the Yankees, but New York beat Boston on both Saturday and Sunday to take the pennant, their first of five straight. The Red Sox would not return to the Series until 1967. Again they would face the Cardinals, and again they would lose in seven games. Boston did not exceed ninety-six wins, their total in both 1948 and 1949, until 1977, when the club won ninety-seven games in a season that finished more than a year after Yawkey's death.[43]

Ten

"Bright Colored Paper and Red Ribbons"

The idea, in the words of the man charged with executing it, "was to sell 'Beautiful Wrigley Field'; that is, to make the park itself so great an attraction that it would be thought of as a place to take the whole family for a delightful day." Phil Wrigley, principal owner of the Chicago Cubs since his father's death in January 1932, was convinced that a team's daily performance and daily attendance went hand in hand. Young Bill Veeck Jr. was cut from a vastly different cloth from his boss, but he thought this conclusion was "inescapable." Like Wrigley, he believed that "a team that isn't winning a pennant has to sell something in addition to its won-and-lost record to fill in those low points on the attendance chart." As a boy, Veeck, whose father had run the Cubs for Wrigley's father starting in 1919, was pretty much free to roam all over what was then called Cubs Park. "I am," he later claimed, with the extravagant flamboyance that characterized most of his life, "the only human being ever raised in a ballpark." After his father's death from leukemia in October 1933, Veeck returned to Kenyon College to finish football season, left school to move in with his mother and sister, and sought employment with the Cubs. Getting a job, first as an office boy and later as Wrigley's assistant, seemed quite natural. As an owner, Wrigley started slowly, in Veeck's memory. He made sure the ballpark was painted. He widened the box seats. He shooed away sidewalk vendors and newspaper boys. He put ushers outside to direct fans to the entrances, and he trained ticket sellers to be polite. All these changes helped, but "Beautiful Wrigley Field" did not come to pass until Wrigley put Veeck in charge of the project after the 1936 season.[1]

The Cubs had finished tied for second that year after winning the pennant the year before, and they anticipated a return to the World Series in 1937. Veeck's job was to make sure the ballpark was renovated—something beyond a paint job—and ready for the festivities. He hired Holabird & Root, Chicago's oldest architectural firm, to construct new outfield bleachers and new box and reserved seats down the left-field line. The bleachers were elevated twelve feet above the field but not so high as to obscure the view from the rooftops along West Waveland and North Sheffield Avenues, in left field and right field respectively, from where fans could watch games for free. Veeck also supervised building new offices behind center field and an equipment storage area under the bleachers for groundskeeping and concessions, his special passion. Early on he had worked in Wrigley's concessions stands and came, he wrote, "to understand the importance of space." Putting the beer and the coffee right next to the hot dogs, he argued, meant selling more of both. "I was even able to reduce it to a formula," he continued. "*One extra step costs you 10 percent of your gross.*" Thus when he installed new concession stands in 1938 and 1939, they were large, attractive, convenient, and furnished with state-of-the-art equipment. The highlight of this work, though, was a new center-field scoreboard that cost more than $100,000. Seventy-five feet wide and twenty-seven feet tall, it used magnetic numbers to display the line scores for the Cubs game and every other game being played in the Major Leagues. The system, a first, worked perfectly when debuted, even though the inventor, "a shy, hesitant, somewhat apologetic man," in Veeck's words, vanished just days before its installation. An additional novelty was using a yellow number, not a white one, to indicate the inning in progress.[2]

The renovations changed the dimensions of the playing field, but more than that, they added distinctive touches that transformed Wrigley Field into an iconic ballpark. The distance from home plate to the left-field foul pole, once 348 feet, increased slightly to 355 feet; the distance to straightaway center field shrank from 447 feet to 400 feet; and the distance down the right-field line jumped from 318 feet to 353 feet. Wrigley Field became known as a ballpark that favored pitchers, except when the wind was blowing out. And it was the wind that altered Veeck's most imaginative novelty. He recalled Wrigley's insistence that the renovated bleachers should bear "an outdoor, woodsy motif," so Veeck proposed that they plant some trees outside the park behind the bleachers. Wrigley, though, wanted trees in the bleachers, on the steps leading up to the scoreboard. Veeck acquiesced despite the impracticality and expense. "Just for openers," he wrote, "we had to build tree boxes into every step, which meant new concrete footings and new steel supports to carry the weight." That much accomplished, they planted eight Chinese elms, four ascending on each side of the scoreboard, only to have the wind blowing off Lake Michigan, less than a mile away, carry the leaves away. Wrigley was determined, so several other plantings ensued, all with the same result. At length the trees were abandoned, and what remained was the second part of this horticultural scheme: Veeck's suggestion to grow ivy on the new brick bleacher walls, reminiscent of the ivy-covered walls he had seen in a Minor

League ballpark in Indianapolis. Veeck scheduled the planting for after the 1937 season, but Wrigley insisted that the job be done immediately to impress some imminent invited guests. Veeck learned that ivy couldn't be planted overnight, so according to his account, he and groundskeeper Bob Dorr worked feverishly to string copper wire across the 1,003-foot wall and plant bittersweet that would crawl up the wire quickly as a stopgap. They later intermixed Baltic ivy and Virginia creeper, giving Wrigley Field a distinctive look that remained long after Veeck left the club.[3]

"By the time I was 12," Veeck remembered, "I decided that I was going to own a baseball team. . . . My life was going to be centered on baseball. It was inevitable." Early in 1941 Veeck left the Cubs when an opportunity arose. He put together a small group willing to come up with a small bundle of cash and assume the debts of the financially troubled Milwaukee Brewers in the American Association, a struggling franchise that had finished last in attendance and the standings in 1940. Acting on the beliefs he had honed in Chicago, Veeck began immediately to improve what would later be called the "fan experience." He repainted ancient Borchert Field, in use since 1887; refurbished the men's and women's restrooms; added music; and began an innovative program of promotional, in-game giveaways, most not announced beforehand. Fans had to come to the ballpark to learn what free gifts, including a steady supply of live animals, might be theirs. Working with new manager Charlie Grimm, who came with him from Chicago, Veeck turned over the roster several times, going through fifty-one players looking for winners. The Brewers could not escape last place in 1941, but they finished second in 1942 and first the next three seasons, and they led the league in attendance three years straight. The *Sporting News* named Veeck its Minor League Executive of the Year for 1942, but for most of his club's success, he was an absentee owner. Married and the father of three, Veeck could not be drafted. Yet after a dinner at Toot Shor's restaurant in New York with Barney Ross, a champion boxer who had retired from the ring and joined the marines, Veeck announced that he too wanted to enlist, not as an officer but as a private. The marines approved his application in November 1943. He went to boot camp, trained as an antiaircraft gunner, and went overseas in March 1944, first to Nouméa, New Caledonia, then to Guadalcanal, and in April to Bougainville in the Solomon Islands. There he was often sick and was severely injured, perhaps, in the words of biographer Paul Dickson, after "an artillery piece had fired prematurely and recoiled into Veeck's already compromised right foot (originally injured at Kenyon College), cutting a ragged gash to the bone." He spent the rest of the war in the hospital trying to heal and continued to direct Brewers' affairs from afar. In November 1946, back in the United States, he had his right leg amputated below the knee.[4]

Although the historical record is far less than clear, Veeck later claimed that after the 1942 season he had tried to buy the Philadelphia Phillies, a hapless club with unstable ownership receptive to a sale. The deal, if it ever existed, fell apart, Veeck wrote, after he revealed to Commissioner Kenesaw Landis his intention to replace the entire roster with African American players. The commissioner informed National League president Ford Frick, who had the league take over the franchise and sell it to someone else. After the war Veeck sold the Brewers and pursued the purchase of a Major League club, at first the Pittsburgh Pirates and then the Cleveland Indians. The Alva Bradley syndicate was ready to sell the Indians, and Cleveland fans, Veeck learned as he queried them walking around the city anonymously, wanted new ownership. The deal was finalized in June 1946 with Veeck and a large number of partners—including entertainer Bob Hope, born in London but raised in Cleveland—agreeing to a price of about $1.5 million. Veeck pioneered what he called a debenture stock arrangement that allowed him and his partners to put up very little cash. As in Milwaukee, his goals were to improve the club on the field and attract more fans to the ballpark. The changes he instituted were monumental. "When he took over," Dickson wrote, "the team had no radio broadcasts, no Ladies' Day, no posting of National League scores, and no telephone service for fans wishing to reserve tickets. All these things were changed within a matter of weeks." Veeck was a stickler for customer service. He refurbished the uniforms of the corps of ushers and stressed courtesy, paid particular attention to the hot dogs and mustard, and installed a new public address system. Plus he would appear, day or night, before any group within two hundred miles or so of Cleveland interested to hear him promote his ball club.[5]

Veeck entered the fray as an owner just as baseball began to boom. In 1946, the first postwar season, Major League attendance grew by more than 70 percent over the previous year to 18.5 million, a record for the second straight year. All sixteen teams saw their attendance rise, some of them remarkably so. The Phillies, jumping to fifth place in the National League after finishing seventh or eighth for thirteen consecutive seasons, nearly quadrupled their attendance from 285,057 to 1,045,247. Four other clubs—the Boston Braves, the Cincinnati Reds, the Boston Red Sox, and the New York Yankees—more than doubled theirs, with the New Yorkers becoming the first club to pass the 2 million mark at 2,265,512. Even the Philadelphia Athletics and the St. Louis Browns, long at or near the bottom in American League attendance, saw increases of 34 and a more modest 9 percent respectively. Total attendance rose again in 1947 to 19.9 million and in 1948 to 20.9 million and fell only slightly in 1949 to 20.2 million. Attendance at Red Sox and Indians home games rose for six years straight (1944–49), and Cubs attendance grew for four straight seasons (1944–47). These surges came when many Americans, without hesitation, regarded baseball highly. Public opinion polls in 1949 showed that 40 percent of Americans across the country said they "followed" Major League baseball, with higher numbers reported for those living in New England and the Mid-Atlantic region (47 percent), those living in the East-Central region (47 percent), those between the ages of twenty-one and twenty-nine (47 percent), those between the ages of thirty and forty-nine (42 percent), and men (49 percent).[6]

The Indians, who had drawn more than 900,000 fans just once before the war, went over 1 million in home attendance in 1946 and 1947 and drew 2,620,627 fans in 1948 to set a Major League record. Cleveland won the pennant and the World Series that year, but the Indians owed most of their box office success to Veeck. His marketing masterstroke, beyond the elaborate promotions that came to define his tenure as owner, was deciding to play every home game in spacious Municipal Stadium, with more than 77,000 seats. When the Indians had last won the World Series in 1920, they had played their home games in League Park, a small facility well east of downtown. Its capacity was 21,404 in 1946, and that's why Veeck abandoned it. The Indians had experimented with the bigger stadium in 1932 and 1933, but small weekday crowds were lost in its immensity. Veeck changed that, convinced that his Indians would draw crowds large enough to fill the place. Veeck worked to make the Indians better on the field, but stunts counted too. "Nobody in baseball is more aware of the fact that a ball club must sell baseball and win games," he said. "But you don't sell your baseball without dressing it up in bright colored paper and red ribbons." Veeck hired Max Patkin to coach first base as the former Minor League pitcher was turning occasional antics into a routine that would make him a baseball clown for years to come. He signed shortstop Jackie Price, who played in only seven games but entertained fans with a bag of between-inning tricks that included hitting a ball while suspended upside down. Veeck shot off fireworks; gave away nylon stockings and orchids to women; held a contest for batboy with a college scholarship as the prize; organized Don Black Night to support a journeyman pitcher and recovering alcoholic who had suffered a cerebral hemorrhage; and responded to Joe Earley, a fan who complained that there were too many celebrations honoring ballplayers past and present, by holding Good Old Joe Earley Night in his honor. Come the 1948 World Series, Veeck made sure that the club sold single-game tickets and not just blocks of three, too expensive for most fans. As a result, attendance for the three Series games in Cleveland totaled 238,491.[7]

After World War II ended, baseball moved into an era of unprecedented prosperity. The game's overall economic health could be measured by calculating net income for all sixteen Major League clubs combined (after taxes and before distribution of dividends). This figure had peaked at just under $2 million in 1930 but had never come close to $1 million throughout the rest of the decade. Consolidated net income in 1943 was a red number, $240,023, but it rose to nearly $1 million in 1944, $1.2 million in 1945, and nearly $4.9 million in 1946 and 1947. Margin of profit on gross operating income for all clubs, −2.7 percent in 1943, grew to 17.7 percent in 1946 and 16.2 percent in 1947. Only one American League club reported a profit of more than $50,000 in 1943, and two reported losses. By contrast, in 1946 all eight reported profits, only one (the Athletics) below $260,000. In the National League 1943 saw three clubs in the red and only two with profits greater than $36,000, but in 1946 only one team lost money, and three made more than $400,000. The Yankees set an American League record for profits in 1947 ($846,737) while the New York Giants did the same in the National League ($529,827), only to be bested by the Brooklyn Dodgers in 1948 ($543,201) and 1949 ($642,614).[8]

Postwar revenues gave clubs the chance to invest, more than ever before, in young and unproven players at a time when farm systems were expanding and to offer some players extra money just to sign a contract. Some sources indicate that baseball's first signing bonus may have been the $10,000 the Yankees reportedly paid pitcher Charlie Devens in 1932, but much more prominent was Dick Wakefield, an outfielder from the University of Michigan who signed with the Detroit Tigers in 1941 for a bonus of $51,000 plus a new Packard automobile for his recently widowed mother. Although his father had been a Major Leaguer, the son had played only one season of varsity baseball at Michigan before signing his contract. The twenty-year-old profited, perhaps, from the attitude expressed by Dan Daniel in the *Sporting News* that "it is better business to give $45,000 to one player, who has a real chance, than to dole out $5,000 apiece to half a dozen kids who will wind up in gas stations." After he got just 1 hit in seven pinch-hitting appearances, the Tigers sent him to the Minors. He returned to Detroit in 1943, made the All-Star team, and led the league with 200 hits. Service in the navy intervened. Injuries after the war, including a broken wrist and broken arm, took their toll, and his desire to train and play hard waned. Wakefield hung on until 1952 and batted .293 for his career, but he never became the star Detroit's investment envisioned. As the war wound down, other club owners embraced Daniel's point of view, at least somewhat. The Red Sox signed eighteen-year-old pitcher Dick Callahan for $15,000 in May 1944. The Washington Senators signed Dick Weik, a high school pitcher, for $20,000 in June 1945. The Red Sox also signed Ted Del Guercio, another pitcher, for $19,000 in July 1945, and the Phillies gave $7,500 to pitcher Lewis West, seventeen years old, in the same month. All four were assigned to Minor League clubs, and only Weik eventually made the Majors. A *Sporting News* editorial called these announcements part of an "epidemic of tremendous bonuses" but warned these youngsters that "money easily come by is money usually easily spent." The editorial continued with a cautionary note to club owners, saying that "if they feel that giving big bonuses to youngsters is an essential, well, it is their money." Yet as sportswriter Paul Hemphill noted years later, "Once bonus fever set in, there was no stopping it."[9]

Club owners couldn't help themselves. On the one hand, they were as committed as ever to holding down labor costs, both for untried youngsters and established veterans. On the other hand, they presumably wanted their teams to win games and attract fans who would buy tickets, still the major source of club revenue. While owners acknowledged that signing an untested player was a risk, they found self-restraint hard, especially in the heady seasons after the war, when some potential professional ballplayers, like thousands of other veterans, opted to use the GI Bill of Rights to attend college instead. Signing bonuses thus proliferated in number and grew in dollar amount as the talent pool shrank. Yet even as some players reaped the benefits of this largesse, owners' concerns for what would later be called "competitive balance" also grew. How could they, as analyst Steve Treder wrote, "forestall the ability of the wealthiest franchises (primarily, the Yankees, Dodgers, Red Sox, and [St. Louis] Cardinals) to buy up the best young talent and hoard it in their vast farm systems"? Attempts to reel in clubs that might offer bonuses with abandon surfaced at least as early as February 1945, when the Minor Leagues' committee to revise the Major–Minor League Agreement, chaired by Tommy Richardson, president of the Eastern League, began to consider a "radical overhauling," including such matters as "rights to pay bonuses," according to Fred E. Owens in the *Sporting News*. A month later Earl Mann, president of the Southern Association's Atlanta Crackers, warned that "we should try to do something about paying large bonuses to untried players." He added that "the majors are cutting each other's throats in this respect, and if a limit isn't put on this bonus situation, baseball is sounding its own death knell." But Minor League clubs in the higher classifications could play the bonus game too. Those part of a farm system could use money from the parent club to sweeten the contracts they offered prospects. Independent clubs, like the Crackers, could themselves proffer bonuses if they had the resources, once Commissioner Happy Chandler, brand new on the job and facing what the *Sporting News* called this "knotty" problem, made a controversial ruling allowing this practice in August 1945.[10]

The 1945 winter meetings muddled this complicated situation even further. In his annual report to the National Association, the Minors' governing body, President William Bramham decried the unbridled payment of bonuses as a step certain to lead to financial distress, and he urged that all bonuses be prohibited. Minor League officials listened and then took contradictory actions. One day they declined overwhelmingly to rescind the few rules allowing bonuses then in place, including Chandler's ad hoc amendment. The next day they voted, again overwhelmingly, to prohibit all bonuses and to send their resolution to the Major League meetings the following week in Chicago. Major League owners rejected the Minors' prohibition proposal, calling it illegal, and they did not take any concrete action of their own until meeting again in February 1946. They did not outlaw bonuses then but instead, according to Daniel, "[they] passed a regulation which makes it so tough to give a player anything extra that the bonus classification, except in the cases of players manifestly of big league caliber, will come pretty close to extinction." The proposed regulation would have defined a bonus player, for his entire career, as one whose initial contract "calls for $6,000 or more in the major leagues, in the minors $4,000 for Class AAA [established in 1946], and under that classification, on a pro rata scale." A club giving a player such a bonus would not be allowed to send him to the Minors without asking irrevocable waivers—that is, permission from every other club—and if the player passed through waivers, he would be subject to the draft for as long as he remained a Minor Leaguer. Chandler added extra teeth to this proposed rule, declaring that if a club violated these rules, club officials would be fined, and the player would become a free agent, with his club unable to sign him for three years. Yet although Bramham opposed bonuses, he called this proposed rule "unworkable," and the Minor Leagues declined to ratify it.[11]

Paying signing bonuses continued unabated through 1946. Bramham, in his final annual report, revealed that Minor League clubs had paid out more than $2 million in bonuses, "not counting cuts in postseason series, percentages of sale prices, and secret payments." Such financial recklessness, he said, threatened the life of the Minors. Given these developments, the quest to approve a rule controlling bonuses at the 1946 winter meetings succeeded. The amount that would trigger the bonus designation was set at $6,000 for a Major League contract, $4,000 for Class Triple-A, and so forth down to $800 for Class D; the other provisions suggested a year earlier were adopted as well. This rule did not last very long, nor did it dissuade clubs from offering signing bonuses large enough to require compliance with its tough terms. Owners streamlined the rule somewhat at the 1947 winter meetings and forced bonus players to sign affidavits attesting to the terms of their contracts, but criticism of the rule mounted. Some opponents focused on the idea that young players who received bonuses were being unjustly deprived of the chance to develop their skills at an appropriate level of play. Veteran players complained, too, that bonus signees often occupied roster spots without contributing much to their teams' success and that money paid to the untried was unavailable to boost the salaries of established players. Several owners called for the rule's repeal, but Browns general manager Bill DeWitt, one of the rule's co-authors, defended it for doing what it was intended to do, cutting total bonus expenditures by hundreds of thousands of dollars a year. Still, the signings continued. Reds president Warren Giles called paying huge bonuses "a very dangerous and extravagant practice [that] violates, in my judgment, all principles of sound business operation." At the 1948 winter meetings the Minor Leagues reacted. They considered many amendments to the rule but passed only one. Major League owners rejected that, but they agreed to establish a committee to study the problem.[12]

The committee met in January 1949 to discuss a wide range of proposals. Some were directed at the fear that Major League owners might be spending themselves into bankruptcy. Others tried to address the plight of fiscally prudent, independent Minor League clubs. The committee presented three amendments, all approved by both the Majors and the Minors. The first change, according to the *Sporting News Baseball Guide*, "revised the maximum non-bonus payments permitted to $6,000 for a major, Triple-A, or Double-A club; $4,500 for a Class A club and $3,000 for Class B, C, and D clubs." The second amendment, attacking the subterfuge inherent in hiding the size of a bonus by paying it out over time, "provided that if total salary and bonus in a contract extending beyond one year exceeded the specified maximums for one year, the bonus status prevails." The third "permitted a club obtaining a bonus player via the draft or on waivers to option the player one time within twelve months of his acquisition." Still, the critics were not satisfied. The Executive Council looked at the rule again in August 1949 but left it intact, perhaps because the call for repeal offered no clear alternative. Signings continued, as did complaints about ways to circumvent the rule, including signing a player's father to a scouting contract, paying off the family mortgage, or lavishing entertainment on the prospect and his family. At the Minors' 1949 winter meetings thirty-two leagues voted for repeal and twenty-six against, short of the three-fourths majority needed. The following week the American League voted for repeal, and the National League voted against. Chandler broke the tie by siding with the American League. That sent the matter back to the Minor Leagues, which again turned repeal down. In January 1950 the Pirates set a dubious record, signing pitcher Paul Pettit for $100,000, the highest bonus yet paid. Then at the 1950 winter meetings, the bonus rule met a sudden and overwhelming demise. Yet just four days after the rule was repealed, the spending continued. Catcher J. W. Porter, a star in American Legion baseball, agreed to a contract with the Chicago White Sox for $67,500.[13]

The opportunity the Servicemen's Readjustment Act of 1944, known as the GI Bill, afforded veterans to attend college inspired other young people, including high school baseball players, to do the same. The number of eighteen- and nineteen-year-olds enrolled in school—mostly in college—rose from 668,000 in 1945 to 1,134,000 in 1948 and to 1,817,000 in 1960. Colleges and universities conferred 216,521 degrees in 1940, 317,607 in 1948, 496,874 in 1950, and 476,704 in 1960. The GI Bill's benefits were modest: $65 a month for single veterans, $90 for those with dependents, and up to $500 a year for tuition and books, but the lure of a college education began to attract young men in unprecedented numbers. Organized baseball had to address the implications of this trend for its business. A rule approved in 1946 prohibited clubs from signing youngsters still in high school, but once prospects graduated and became eligible to sign a professional contract, the chance to go to college and play baseball there offered them another career path. Baseball had never shied away from college players, although in the early years of the professional game, players with a college education were quite rare. Connie Mack signed many collegians. From 1908 through 1914 his Athletics featured five players—Jack Barry, Charlie (called "Chief") Bender, Eddie Collins, Jack Coombs, and

Eddie Plank—who went directly from college to the Major Leagues. Complicating this situation were players like Christy Mathewson, who studied at Bucknell for three years but played professionally during the summers, and Lou Gehrig, who played in 1921 for the Hartford (CT) Senators in the Eastern League under the name "Lew Lewis" to preserve his eligibility at Columbia. Some arrangements were even more deceptive. As late as 1938 the University of Illinois declared star athlete Lou Boudreau ineligible after learning that the Indians were paying his parents $100 a week for promising that their son would sign a Cleveland contract upon graduation.[14]

Branch Rickey of the Cardinals announced that he intended to introduce a resolution at the 1934 winter meetings banning clubs from signing college players until they had finished their education. Nothing came of this proposal even as the *Sporting News*, noting that clubs in both leagues continued to sign college players, urged colleges attracted to football's "revenue-producing possibilities" to "pay more attention to baseball, a line of activity that does offer remunerative places for graduates who can demonstrate playing ability." College baseball coaches, including many former players, used their connections with the professional game to build their programs, yet they also grumbled when their players left to sign professional contracts. In February 1946 a four-man committee—Commissioner Chandler, Tigers general manager George Trautman, Art Ehlers, promotional director of the Minor Leagues, and Colgate baseball coach Eppie Barnes, president of the new American Association of College Baseball Coaches—considered a plan to restrict the signing of college players. Barnes spoke out, pursuant to a complaint from Coombs, the Duke baseball coach, that one of his players had left school after signing a contract. During the summer the *Sporting News* reported, prematurely as it turned out, that the dispute was "headed for an amicable agreement," even though International League president Frank Shaughnessy said that a college player should have the right to be the judge of his own career. At the 1947 winter meetings owners considered a far-reaching proposal that would have allowed no contractual relationships with college players either until they had completed their college eligibility or their class had graduated. Despite exhortation from Taylor Spink that "every boy, if possible, should have a college education, and this is as important to a ball player as to anyone else," owners tabled the proposal, and it died.[15]

Baseball needed more players. The postwar growth of the Minor Leagues created the demand. More young men going to college restricted the supply. Some who had played high school baseball gave it up upon entering the college classroom. Others played college ball for a while only to discover that they were not good enough to turn pro. Thus even as the number of Minor Leagues began to decline beginning in 1950, Major League owners refused to restrain themselves or their organizations from signing college players at will. Nor were they particularly keen to extend the agreement with the national high school federation to refrain from signing high school players. In 1950 owners appointed a committee to amend their 1946 agreement, claiming that colleges were swooping down upon high schoolers with scholarship offers, primarily to play football, before they graduated and before baseball clubs could contact them. The existing rule would not expire until December 1951, so owners empowered a new committee of eight, four from the Majors and four from the Minors, to ready a replacement. Approved at the 1951 winter meetings, the new rule allowed clubs to contact high school players while they were still in school and sign them as soon as their eligibility expired. Starting in 1953 high schoolers could be signed even while they were in school, but they were not eligible to play in organized baseball until their class graduated or they dropped out. The number of high school players signed under this new rule skyrocketed, as did the amount of bonus money clubs heaped upon them. One estimate was that clubs paid out $4.5 million in bonuses to high school and college players in 1952, with the Red Sox signing seventeen youngsters during one three-week period in midseason and spending close to $500,000 in bonuses during the year.[16]

Adding to the owners' concerns about their labor supply came uncertainties surrounding the outbreak of war in Korea in June 1950. Americans were not sure how to react. World War II was so fresh in everyone's memory that many people felt, as the American Civil Liberties Union noted, "a special deepening of their anxiety." Chicago sportswriter John Carmichael reported in the *Sporting News* that many owners did not think that baseball would get the same "green light" they had in 1942. Said one National League club official, "Anything like complete mobilization of industry is bound to curb baseball along with other professional sports." An American League executive agreed, saying that "unless American ends this thing in Korea or elsewhere by next spring, baseball won't open the 1951 season." Carmichael suggested that a prolonged war would threaten the financial viability of several Major League organizations. Clubs had prospered in the postwar years, he noted, but he wondered how much money owners had saved after expanding their farm systems, paying more scouts to sign more players at hefty bonuses, and upgrading their ballparks. Shortly after hostilities began, both Major

Leagues and the National Association scrapped plans for jubilee anniversary celebrations, thereby saving $150,000. After the 1950 season John Drebinger reported in the *New York Times* that clubs were unwilling to make trades. "No one," he wrote, "wants to risk trading for a youngster because by tomorrow he may be on his way to a military training base." Yankees manager Casey Stengel concurred, contemplating the uneasy future by saying, "How silly it is to sit here in Florida in December and try to dope out what will happen next summer in the American League." At the 1950 winter meetings Chandler said that baseball needed to be ready for any emergency "in the event of a third world war." The next day the commissioner restated his position on the war, saying, "I do not know that we are going to have total mobilization, and if we do have total mobilization, I do not know what the consequences would be. I don't think anyone could answer that now."[17]

The Selective Training and Service Act of 1940 was replaced by the Military Selective Service Act of 1948, the nation's second peacetime draft. It was extended to provide troops for Korea before passage of the Universal Military Training and Service Act in June 1951. This law provided an array of deferments, but baseball players merited no special treatment. Thus the first Major Leaguer called to serve after the North Korean attack was Phillies pitcher Curt Simmons, whose unit in the Pennsylvania National Guard was activated in August 1950. Yet organized baseball continued without interruption and without an equivalent to the "Green Light" letter. The government reasoned that the national economy could provide both "guns and butter," but baseball was not so sure, particularly when players were called upon to serve their country. Early on, a soldier in Korea wrote to the *Sporting News*, expressing his concern. "Some of these fellows [club owners]," he wrote, "are going to have a tough enough time finding ball players with all the able guys needed over here to help us fellows." In November 1951 the Cardinals reported that 95 of their Minor Leaguers were in the service. Three months later, that number had risen to 131, and new owner Fred Saigh said that 3 of these, all of them pitchers, would have been strong candidates to make the Major League roster for the upcoming 1952 season. Tom Poholsky had pitched in the Majors in 1950 and 1951 but would not rejoin the Cardinals until 1954. Harvey Haddix was drafted in September 1950 and did not make his Major League debut until August 1952. Jackie Cohan sustained wounds to his left leg in October 1951 and subsequently endured an amputation at the knee, settling for a job as a Cardinals scout.[18]

Baseball researchers have not determined exactly how many players in the Majors and Minors were called to military service during the hostilities, how many served in Korea, or how many were wounded. The *Sporting News* attempted to keep track in two regular columns, "Call to Colors" and "From Service Front." The National Defense Service List, created during World War II to protect players' roster rights, grew from four Major Leaguers during the winter of 1949–50 to seventeen a year later and forty-nine in December 1951. The first casualty in Korea was apparently Bob Ezell, a nineteen-year-old outfielder who had played for the Ventura (CA) Braves in the California League in 1950. A marine, he suffered shrapnel wounds and frostbite in January 1951 and was sent to southern California to recuperate. First to die was George Sulliman, a graduate of Yale, a second baseman in the Cardinals organization, and a marine lieutenant. On April 24, 1951, having been in Korea only three weeks, his platoon came under enemy attack, and he was fatally wounded while trying to clear a jammed machine gun. In all, twenty Minor Leaguers died in the service during Korea. The only former Major League player to die in Korea was Bob Neighbors, an outfielder who played seven games with the 1939 Browns. A pilot during World War II, he made the air force a career and flew a B-26 Invader in Korea. On August 8, 1952, his plane was hit by ground fire and went down. His body was never recovered, and he was declared dead at the end of 1953. Five active Major Leaguers saw service in Korea. Bobby Brown was a cardiologist selected in a special "doctor's draft" because he had not served during World War II. The other four—Jerry Coleman, Bob Kennedy, Lloyd Merriman, and Ted Williams—were jet pilots who faced danger regularly. Coleman had flown fifty-seven missions in World War II, and he flew another sixty-three in Korea. He was awarded two Distinguished Flying Crosses, thirteen Air Medals, and three Navy citations. "Merit badges," he called them. "I was just doing my duty."[19]

The 1946 season was the start of a remarkable, if short-lived, resurgence for the Minor Leagues. After bottoming out during the war, when only nine leagues limped through the 1943 season, ten in 1944, and twelve in 1945, the number of leagues skyrocketed to forty-three in 1946, fifty-two in 1947, fifty-eight in 1948, and fifty-nine in 1949, when teams played Minor League baseball in 438 cities and towns across the country. As the American population migrated south and west, Minor League baseball followed. The thirty-one leagues that were born in 1946 or reborn after a wartime hiatus placed teams in 222 cities or towns, 63 percent of them in southern or western states. Arizona added teams in six cities, including Phoenix for the first time since 1932 and Tucson for the first time since 1941. In California, between

1946 and 1949, thirteen small cities saw Minor League clubs resurrected, and nine others hosted Minor League clubs for the first time. The structure of the upper Minor Leagues changed. Most significant was the creation of a new classification, Class Triple-A, in which were placed the American Association, the International League, and the Pacific Coast League. Other leagues grew more robust and moved up in the Minors' classification system. In 1946 the Southern Association and the revived Texas League were elevated from Class A1 to Class Double-A. The South Atlantic League, dormant after 1942, came back to life in 1946 and rose from Class B to Class A. The Carolina League and the Florida International League, both Class C, became Class B in 1949. The Class D Evangeline League became a Class C league in 1949. Moreover, more than half of all Minor League clubs were now components of Major League farm systems. The Dodgers led the pack with twenty-five farm clubs, but no Major League team had fewer than nine affiliates. Total attendance in the Minors surged as well, from thirty-two million in 1946 to more than forty million in each of the next three years.[20]

Organized baseball confronted the population's move west when the Pacific Coast League (PCL) renewed its campaign to become a third Major League. The PCL had begun as an independent league, and its executives had never quite shed the lofty idea that their enterprise was unique. It was, of course. Most of its teams were located in large cities by Minor League standards, and the league played seasons that sometimes stretched to two hundred games. Even during the Depression the PCL had argued that it was robust enough to be elevated to Major League status, and in December 1944 the board of directors authorized President Pants Rowland to seek Major League status. At the 1945 winter meetings, just as the National Association was creating Class Triple-A, Rowland persuaded other Minor League presidents to approve a resolution "that the Pacific Coast League now become a major league and to be such beginning with the 1946 season, but provided that it must obtain approval of the commissioner of baseball, of the presidents of the two major leagues and the National Association and that it be accepted as a major league in Organized Baseball and remain therein." A four-person committee, including Rowland and three club owners, took this resolution to the Major League meetings the following week, but they were turned down. "Major league status is not a matter of legislative definition," read the statement accompanying the denial. "It depends upon the size of the parks, the baseball income available, and many other factors." Professing an interest in players' economic well-being, the Majors said that if the Pacific Coast League became a Major League, clubs in it would be exempt from having their players drafted by American and National League clubs. PCL clubs would still be able to draft players from lower classifications but might not be able to pay such players adequate Major League salaries. Thus "if the men whom they [PCL clubs] are thus able to draft from the minor leagues were not given major league opportunities and were also deprived of the chance to advance to long-established major leagues, an injustice would be done." As a consolation to the PCL, the Majors offered "the services, if desired, of a cooperating committee to further study the situation," but Rowland predicted that "the men who control major league baseball are merely postponing the inevitable."[21]

The Major Leagues also contended that several PCL ballparks did not meet Major League standards. Gilmore Field in Hollywood, Wrigley Field in Los Angeles, Seals Stadium in San Francisco, and Sick's Stadium in Seattle seemed close to adequate, but the other four were too small. The Oakland and Sacramento ballparks each held about 11,000 spectators, San Diego no more than 12,000, and Portland just about 12,500. In addition the Hollywood Stars and the Oakland Oaks were located so close to more robust franchises that many questioned their ability to succeed on the Major League level. In response PCL owners announced plans to expand the four small ballparks, but these projects were insufficient to sway the Majors. Los Angeles, the crown jewel in the PCL diadem, posed its own special problems. League officials feared that Los Angeles could become a Major League city all by itself. It was certainly large enough. The Browns, who had abandoned their plan to move to Los Angeles for the 1942 season, considered this idea again after the war. Angels owner Phil Wrigley would have received substantial compensation if the Browns or any other Major League club had moved to Los Angeles. Thus when the PCL's directors enabled Rowland to seek Major League status with the proviso that all clubs would agree not to transfer the right to operate in their cities to an American or National League club, Los Angeles had voted no. The PCL played the 1946 season as a Class Triple-A Minor League, drawing more than 3.7 million fans, a record. At that year's winter meetings Rowland advanced the same proposal, concerned not only about Los Angeles, but also San Francisco, where attendance that year, 670,563, set a Minor League record that would stand for nearly forty years. The Majors rejected the PCL again, but this time they offered a small concession, saying that if an existing Major League club wanted to relocate to a PCL city, "no such territory can be invaded unless the minor league and its club are paid such compensation as shall be mutually agreed upon as just and reasonable." PCL owners had agreed that unanimous consent would be required before a Major League team could move in, but such a promise would be hard to keep and harder to enforce.[22]

The war years had not been kind to National Association president William Bramham. The hardships the Majors faced had burdened the Minors too, including the loss of players to military service and war industries and the travel restrictions caused by gasoline rationing. At the Minors' winter meetings in December 1943 Bramham's contract was up for renewal. He was reelected unanimously but only after a number of leagues discontented with his leadership walked out in protest. Bramham lambasted his opponents, accusing them of creating discord, and criticism of his work continued. He suffered a mild stroke in September 1944 yet remained determined to see his responsibilities through the war. At the 1946 winter meetings Bramham, in deteriorating health, announced his retirement. The association kept him on as a consultant, but in July 1947 he died after suffering a heart attack. Anticipating Bramham's retirement, more than a dozen candidates tested the waters. Some of them were soon dissuaded after learning that Bramham's attractive salary might not be offered to his successor, but not George Trautman. He came to the job with sterling qualifications. When Larry MacPhail left Columbus in 1933, Branch Rickey recruited Trautman to run the Redbirds. After the 1935 season American Association owners elected him league president. He made his mark by taking a seat on the National Association's executive committee and chairing a postwar planning committee and the committee to revise the Major–Minor League Agreement. After the war he left the Minors to become executive vice president and general manager of the World Series champion Tigers. Bramham's retirement altered Trautman's career path again. When the balloting began, all the other aspirants withdrew, and he was elected unanimously and given a salary equal to his predecessor's.[23]

As if to celebrate baseball's postwar recovery, the Major Leagues and the Minors held their 1946 winter meetings jointly in Los Angeles. "Every visitor will be cared for in a first-class hotel," promised Oscar Reichow, the Hollywood Stars' business manager. Major League delegates, convening west of Chicago for the first time, stayed at the fashionable Ambassador Hotel. Minor League personnel lodged at the Biltmore, an even grander facility. Although there were controversies brewing just below the surface, "harmony," in the words of one researcher, "seemed to be the prevailing mood." Happy Chandler had replaced Kenesaw Landis without too much ado, and even though Bramham had thundered his way into retirement, Trautman took charge peacefully. Perhaps most significant, the Majors and the Minors approved a new Major–

Minor League Agreement, the basic document that coupled them together. The agreement it replaced was barnacled with scads of amendments. Over the years various committees had attempted a complete rewrite but always unsuccessfully. During the war the agreement, technically expired, had been extended several times on a year-to-year basis. Finally, in 1946 both sides examined the draft crafted by the latest committee and accepted it. No one had been quite sure how long the 1921 agreement was supposed to have lasted, but this new deal had a definite life span: five years with options to renew it built in. The Minors won substantial concessions, including the right to terminate the agreement upon a three-fourths vote of the association's membership. They also got the same limitations on the authority of the commissioner that the Majors had imposed when they hired Chandler.[24]

From a financial viewpoint the Minors had much to celebrate in the years immediately following the war. All three Class Triple-A leagues set attendance records in 1946. The American Association bettered its mark in 1947 and again in 1948. The International League and the PCL experienced slight dips in those two years but set another record in 1949. The twenty-four clubs playing Class Triple-A baseball reported a combined net profit of $884,911 in 1946 and $923,560 in 1947. Class Double-A did well too, jumping from a profit of $207,363 in 1946 to $741,899 in 1947. Unfortunately for most owners, these good times did not last. Class Triple-A clubs' earnings dropped to $598,549 in 1948 and $574,997 in 1949, and they lost $1,413,002 in 1950. Profits in Class Double-A declined as well, to $398,581 in 1948, $237,749 in 1949, and $120,410 in 1950. The lower classifications did less well throughout these years. Class A leagues made money in 1946 and 1949, Class B and Class C in 1946 and 1947, and Class D in 1946. But in 1950 leagues in these four classifications lost nearly $2 million combined.[25]

The *Official Baseball Rules* for 1949 contained seventy-one rules while those for 1950 contained but ten, nine playing rules and one covering official scoring. This massive consolidation developed pursuant to a special meeting of the Playing Rules Committee held on March 3, 1949, in Sarasota, Florida. "I don't know what will come out of this meeting," said Commissioner Chandler, who convened the group, "but there are some rules which can stand changing, especially some minor rules which the two leagues—American and National—interpret differently." The *Sporting News*, remarking that the "last general revision" dated from 1940, took note of "charges that the rules are written in arcane language, that a number conflict with each other, that clarification is imperative, and that various league interpretations should be incorporated in the code." The Sarasota meeting lasted nine hours and resulted in several changes for the upcoming season. One required the catcher to stand within the catcher's box during an intentional walk. A second required umpires to call a balk if a pitcher straddled the rubber without the ball in his possession or if he stood in position to pitch and dropped the ball. Another change outlawed the use of what the *Sporting News* called "the famous webbed 'claw' glove used by first basemen the past few years," but not until the 1950 season. More important, as the *Sporting News* noted, "the committee recognized the need of recodifying the rules as a whole," delegating this work to a three-man subcommittee. That group, which met throughout the summer, reported back to the full committee in November and published the new rule book early in 1950. The *Sporting News* called this new edition "the most drastic overhauling since 1904" and greeted it with acclaim. "The recodified playing rules are simple enough for a grade school student to understand," said the editors. "Their application has been made direct, the language is modern, and the grouping is practical. The work on the rules has been tedious and long. The committee charged with the task have done an excellent job."[26]

Consolidation and clarification meant changes, of course, perhaps the most visible of which was the attempt to regulate the height of pitching mounds at "15 inches higher than home plate." Only five Major League ballparks met that standard and required no alterations. Eight others had mounds that were too flat, and one, Wrigley Field, was too high. Washington's Griffith Stadium posed special problems. Because of the peculiar slope of the ground, its mound was only seven inches higher than home plate but fifteen inches higher than first and third bases. The club was given a year's dispensation to raise the level of the bases and adjust the mound accordingly. Umpires spoke to every club early in spring training to explain the new rule book and to emphasize that the new wording defining the strike zone, "between the batter's armpits and the top of his knees when he assumes his natural stance," was not substantively different from the old wording, "not lower than the batsman's knees, nor higher than his shoulders." As umpire Bill Stewart said, "There is no new strike zone. It is merely that for the first time the rule defining the strike zone has been worded correctly." The summary of the new rule book published in the *Baseball Guide* noted that "no change was made in the game itself," but how to interpret the committee's new verbiage continued to vex officials. Extensive amendments were made in November 1953, including restoring the sacrifice fly rule—that is, crediting a batter with a sacrifice and not a time at bat if his flyout drove in a run; requiring fielders to bring their gloves to the dugout at the end of each half-inning instead of leaving them lying on the field of play; and allowing laminated bats, a change expected to "give the batter more power." Rejected was a proposal to legalize the spitball, a pitch outlawed since 1920. Further smaller revisions were made for 1955, 1957, 1958, and 1959. One 1957 revision tried to speed up the game by mandating that the pitcher "deliver the ball to the batter within 20 seconds after he receives the ball" instead of "within 20 seconds after taking his pitching position." Another, surprisingly, codified the umpire's authority "to disqualify any player, coach, manager or substitute." Committee chair Jim Gallagher, former Cubs general manager, said, "Nobody ever noticed that the umpire wasn't given specific authority under the rules to eject a player, coach, or manager. . . . Now we have spelled it out."[27]

The adoption of the new rule book in 1950 and the ensuing amendments did not quell ongoing debate about equipment, playing rules, and umpiring. In 1947 Major League clubs interested in evaluating Minor League talent more accurately asked all the Minor Leagues to adopt a uniform ball, complaining that some Minor Leagues used a ball that was too lively. Nearly simultaneously others argued that it was the Major League ball that had become too lively. All leagues adopted a common standard for 1949, but the proliferation of home runs kept the discussion alive. "The rabbit ball? That's a lot of bunk," snapped Cincinnati Reds general manager Gabe Paul in 1954, adding, "There's no difference in the ball. It's just in the pitching, that's all." The bat, too, got a makeover, with the new rule allowing for laminated construction, deemed cheaper and more durable. The specifications for a bat went from made "entirely of hard, solid wood in one piece" in 1950 to "one piece of solid wood or formed from a block of wood consisting of two or more pieces of wood bonded together with an adhesive" in 1954. Outspoken in his opposition to this innovation, American League president Will Harridge said, "Once you open the door, there is no telling where the movement will end. If laminated bats, why not aluminum bats?" In 1948 National League president Ford Frick bucked up the authority of his league's umpires. In a booklet that Dan Daniel called the "Ten Commandments," Frick restated the umpire's power to eject players, coaches, managers, and even spectators. At the same time he reminded umpires that "your sole duty is to umpire a ball game as the representative of the entire National League, and so in all your actions and conduct keep in mind that your position calls for the settling of controversies on the ball field only, and not for starting them elsewhere."[28]

Official scoring changed too. In 1949 Frick, a former sportswriter, questioned the competence of some of the sportswriters who served intermittently as official scorers, and he suggested a smaller cadre of qualified scorers and a complete revision of the scoring rules. The 1950 rule book expanded the section on scoring from seven to fifteen pages, going from two rules, one defining terms and the second explaining how to complete the summary sheet for each game, to one rule with eighteen sections. The goal was accuracy and consistency, but standardization proved elusive. After the new rules took effect, the two Major Leagues still required their scorers to report games on different forms asking for different data. How to score a game properly remained complicated, and the Scoring Rules Committee approved amendments nearly every year, rewriting extensively in 1955 and again in 1957. The 1950 rule book, for example, greatly expanded the explanation of when to credit a batter with a base hit, but further lengthy revisions came in 1955, and a shorter change was added two years later. Another change concerned how to determine the winner of the "individual batting championship"—that is, the league leader in batting average—a subject not included in earlier rule books. In 1950 a player had to appear in two-thirds of his team's games and get at least four hundred official "times at bat" to be eligible for the batting championship. Two years later the minimum standard became "as many or more times at bat as the number of games scheduled for one club in his league during the season, multiplied by 2.6," and in 1957, it changed again to "as many or more total appearances at the plate in league championship games as the number of games scheduled for each club in the league that season, multiplied by 3.1." Similarly, the 1950 rules defined, for the first time, how to determine the winning and losing pitchers in a game, but these standards were rewritten in 1951 and altered a bit more in 1955 and 1957.[29]

Perhaps no rule engendered more controversy and required more emendation and explanation than the balk rule. The 1950 rule book defined a balk as "an illegal act by pitcher or catcher with a runner or runners on base, entitling all runners to advance one base," but what constituted an "illegal act" had been debated for more than a century. A balk rule was part of the National League's first rule book in 1876, and it was clarified or amended at least ten times before 1940. Starting in that season it became a balk "if the pitcher, in the act of delivering the ball, . . . drops the ball, either intentionally or accidentally." No one liked that change, including Frick, but it survived. In 1949, to minimize the chicanery inherent in the so-called hidden ball trick, a pitcher would be charged with a balk if he straddled the rubber without the ball in his possession. Even more controversially, the 1950 revision said, "If there is a runner or runners, it is a balk if the pitcher delivers the pitch from 'set position' without coming to a stop of one full second." Pitchers objected when umpires began enforcing this one-second pause strictly, the *Sporting News* noting that PCL umpires called fifty-nine balks during the first week of the 1950 season. After the 1952 World Series Branch Rickey accused Yankees pitchers of flouting this rule, saying he counted twenty-six balks, all uncalled, in just one game. Moreover, batters complained when they hit safely only to be called back to the plate because the umpire had called a balk but the pitcher had completed his delivery anyway. This last grievance was addressed in 1954, when the manager of the team at bat could "elect to accept either the balk penalty or the result of the batter's action." Left for dispute was Rule 8.05(c), requiring the pitcher "to step directly toward a base before throwing to that base," no one being able to state definitively what "step directly" meant.[30]

Simultaneously owners were continuing their struggle to find a way to control their labor costs. The bonus rule, passed in 1946 to restrain spending on untried players, had been repealed in 1950, after which clubs continued to spend with abandon. Baseball historian Brent Kelley wrote that between 1946 and 1950, "there had been a total of six reported bonuses of $60,000 or more; in 1951 alone, there were four." Minor League executive A. C. Gonzalez decried these expenditures, saying, "The practice of paying big bonuses is hurting the player as well as baseball." White Sox general manager Frank Lane agreed, saying that the bonus "has a demoralizing effect, not only on the players receiving the big money, but on others not so fortunate." As the extravagance continued, Texas League owner Dick Burnett offered a comprehensive but unrealistic plan that included eliminating farm systems, and newly elected commissioner Ford Frick said that something had to be done. In August he appointed Branch Rickey chair of a committee to devise a plan. "Their eventual recommendation," wrote Kelley, "was a return to a bonus rule, but a *new* bonus rule, one with teeth that could be enforced." At the 1952 winter meetings Bill Veeck proposed a rule to stop Major League clubs from signing any players lacking previous professional experience and to make every Minor League player subject to the draft after just one year of service. This would have served, he later wrote, "to make the American League decently competitive, . . . to distribute the talent more evenly, . . . and put an end to the absurd and ruinous business of handing out $50,000 and $100,000 bonuses to untried and untested kids just out of high school." Veeck's proposal was dismissed, but a new bonus rule was passed. It said that a bonus player would be a first-year player signing for more than a $4,000 bonus with a Major League club or a top Minor League club or for $3,000 with a lower-classification Minor League club. Major League bonus players would be required to spend two years on the parent club's roster. Minor Leaguers could not be moved up or down for a year. The rule empowered the commissioner to levy fines against clubs and executives, but no ceiling was imposed on the size of bonuses teams might offer.[31]

The new rule did not dissuade all clubs from continuing to offer bonuses. Prior to the 1953 season seven clubs signed a total of thirteen players. The Tigers signed three players, but only outfielder Al Kaline, signed out of a Baltimore high school for $35,000, proved to be a gem. The Pirates signed 1950 Heisman Trophy winner Vic Janowicz even though he had not played baseball in college. He played in eighty-three games over two seasons, batted .214, and returned to football with the Washington team in the National Football League. Pittsburgh also grabbed twin brothers, Eddie and Johnny O'Brien, college basketball stars. They failed to make the grade as infielders or as pitchers. Lane continued to complain, saying, "I know of no profession other than baseball where it is the practice to pay a novice a substantial sum merely because of what the employer hopes he might do." He pushed for an unrestricted first-year draft to solve the bonus problem, but at the 1953 winter meetings the bonus rule stayed, and the draft failed to pass. The group of bonus babies in 1954 included only six players, but third baseman Harmon Killebrew was among them. He did not become a regular until 1959. The bonus rule remained untouched after the season, but owners did approve an amendment prohibiting a club from signing any player who had completed his freshman year of college until his class had graduated or he turned twenty-one. In 1955 fifteen clubs signed twenty-two players for more than $4,000 and a number of others right at the limit for avoiding the bonus baby designation. The bonus players signed by National League clubs included one fine pitcher and one who became a superstar. In August the Cardinals signed Lindy McDaniel, who, after some years as a starter, became an excellent relief pitcher. In December 1954 the Dodgers signed Sandy Koufax, a first baseman–pitcher from the University of Cincinnati. Since Koufax had little control on the mound, the Dodgers used him sparingly in 1955 and 1956, and it took him several more seasons to harness his prodigious ability.[32]

By 1956 the first two groups of bonus babies signed under the 1952 rule had spent their mandatory two years on Major League rosters. Clubs could evaluate their progress and gauge how the system was working. Perhaps because the results were far less than spectacular, Kaline aside, clubs signed only four bonus players that year, but each of them would build a respectable Major League career. The following year clubs signed twenty-two players, the second-highest total yet, and paid out three of the six highest bonuses. The Milwaukee Braves gave $112,000 to eighteen-year-old catcher Hawk Taylor and $100,000 to infielder John DeMerit. The Reds signed pitcher Jay Hook for $65,000. By the middle of the season, though, owners were beginning to discuss the idea that the rule had run its course. Cardinals president August Busch led the opposition to it in the National League, and Tigers general manager John McHale did so in the American. Busch claimed that this "most stupid regulation" was unrealistic and that it worked a hardship upon novice players. McHale argued that the rule had failed to help the less wealthy clubs, that it was unenforceable, and that it had created bad blood between clubs who accused each other of cheating—that is, signing players for less than $4,000 and then paying them additional money under the table. Sportswriter Joe King called the bonus system a failure because, in the case of too many players, "what had appeared to be a dollar sign was only a question mark." Thus at the 1957 winter meetings, Major League owners voted to abolish the bonus rule "to protect club owners against themselves." No other rule took its place. The two leagues squabbled about the status of current bonus babies as the rule expired. The American League wanted them liberated immediately so that clubs could send them to the Minors. The National League insisted that the two-year restriction be honored. In January 1958 the leagues agreed that players signed under the rule could be farmed out immediately.[33]

The death of the second bonus rule meant that clubs could spend huge sums on new players with abandon, and they were quick to do so. In July 1958 the *Sporting News* reported that data from fourteen of the sixteen clubs indicated that they had spent at least $3.25 million on players getting bonuses of $10,000 or more and probably as much as $5 million when the bonuses of those getting less than $10,000 were added in. These figures alarmed club officials, some of whom asked where the money to sustain this system would come from. Frick admitted that paying bonuses so indiscriminately was "a crazy thing" and that the practice had gone "haywire." One solution, just a suggestion during the summer, was for an unrestricted draft exposing all players who had finished their first year of professional play. That would curb the bonus frenzy, some said, but others called the idea "somewhat socialistic." Nevertheless, at the 1958 winter meetings, the first-year draft proposal passed. Any free agent signed after December 5, 1958, could be drafted after his first professional season if he was not placed on a Major League club's expanded roster. A drafted player would have to spend the following season on the roster of the club drafting him. Still, over the following months clubs offered bonuses of $40,000 or more to twenty-two players, including three who each received $100,000. By the end of the 1959 season thirty-nine first-year players were on Major League rosters. Spending continued, and at the 1959 winter meetings the first-year draft was softened, allowing clubs that drafted bonus players to send them to the Minors. Some club executives began to discuss the idea that the best way to solve this long-standing problem, paying too much for untried talent, would be a universal free-agent draft—that is, drafting players before they signed a professional contract—but others regarded such a plan as illegal.[34]

Given all these uncertainties, it is not surprising that Major League club ownership was a bit unstable in the immediate postwar years. William Marshall, in his study of the seasons from 1945 through 1951, divided the owners into several groups, somewhat overlapping. He characterized four of them as gentleman sportsmen who used their inherited wealth to anchor the business of baseball during the Depression, the war years, and beyond. Walter Briggs, who had bought complete control of the Tigers following Frank Navin's death in 1935, developed a reputation for benevolence as one of these four. Yet if the profile of the sportsman-owner suggests that he remained behind the scenes and let others run his team, Briggs did not do so. He fired manager Mickey Cochrane during the 1938 season after haranguing him for quite some time. When Commissioner Landis released nearly a hundred Detroit farm hands in 1940 because the organization had connived to bury them in the Minors using fake contracts and other subterfuges, some pointed at Briggs's general manager, Jack Zeller, as the plot's mastermind, but Briggs did not fire Zeller, thereby suggesting that Briggs was part of the plot. That same season he insisted that the club acquire several veterans in a bold attempt to mortgage the future and finish first. Briggs, already a polio victim, had suffered a stroke, and he said, "My life is not certain. I want to be the head of a winning ball club before I'm called out at the plate." The Tigers did win the pennant in 1940, and they won it again in 1945, thanks, in part, to Hank Greenberg's return to the lineup from military service in July. After the 1946 season, though, when Greenberg led the league in home runs, Dan Daniel erroneously reported that the slugger wanted to finish his career with the Yankees, bolstering his story with a photograph showing Greenberg holding up a Yankees jersey. Greenberg protested that the photo was not new and dated from a war benefit game played in New York in 1943, but Briggs chose to believe that his star player was ungrateful. "Get rid of him," he told new general manager Billy Evans, and Evans did so, selling Greenberg's contract to the Pirates for $75,000, an amount well above the waiver price.[35]

Phil Wrigley was another of the gentleman sportsmen, and so were Boston's Tom Yawkey and the Reds' Powel Crosley. The Cubs owner never saw his team win the World Series nor capture another pennant after 1945. A shy man who rarely went to the ballpark, he had such a diversified fortune that, in the opinion of Glenn Stout, "he came to believe that somehow his wealth was not the sole product of genealogy, but instead tangible evidence that he himself possessed special gifts and could achieve success in fields for which he had no experience whatsoever." After the war, Wrigley steadfastly rejected installing lights at his ballpark, and he dabbled in odd ideas like hiring a University of Illinois psychologist, whose theories were interesting but embryonic at best, to work with Cubs players. Yet over his long tenure he became one of the sport's insiders, acknowledged as a sage businessman to whom others often turned for advice. Yawkey, whose stewardship of the Red Sox bordered on paternalism, was similarly unsuccessful as an owner. He ran the team as his personal fiefdom, hiring and retaining front office personnel whose cronyism sometimes outpaced their competence. Yet Yawkey's millions put him in baseball's inner circle too. Crosley had supported two significant baseball innovations, air travel and night baseball, but after the Reds won the pennant in 1939 and 1940, they would not reach the World Series again until 1961. Crosley lived a private life and spent much time away from Cincinnati. Less clear is the role he played in his club's 1953 decision to alter its nickname from "Reds" to "Redlegs." General manager Gabe Paul's announcement included no explanation, but the *Sporting News* speculated that "the political significance of 'Reds' in international affairs was responsible for the change." Ohio, mimicking the federal government during the Cold War, had its own Un-American Activities Committee.[36]

Marshall characterized four other owners as the "old guard," men and their families in some cases who stood for continuity and tradition: the Mack family in Philadelphia, the Griffiths in Washington, the Comiskeys with the White Sox, and the Stoneham family in New York with the Giants. Connie Mack was baseball's most senior citizen. He had played in the Major Leagues starting in 1886, managed since 1894, owned part of the A's since 1901, and served as team president since 1937. By the end of the war he was planning to divide operational control of the club between two of his sons. As he wrote, "I have trained my sons to keep the tradition going, and I hope they will train their sons to follow in the path of their grandfather." After much family strife Mack's sons forced their father to retire as manager in October 1950, his reputation soiled by rampant stories that his memory was failing and that he fell asleep on the bench during games. Said one observer, "He should have known the parade had passed him by." Even before Charles Comiskey died in October 1931, nominal control of the White Sox had passed to his son, Lou, and team secretary Harry Grabiner, who had worked for the club since 1905. Lou Comiskey spent money to improve the team. He put in place a plan to build a farm system but, suffering from heart disease, died in July 1939. Grace, his widow, took over as president. She gave each of her children, Dorothy, Gracie Lou, and Charley, various but uncertain roles running the club but ruled, in the words of historian Richard C. Lindberg, "with a velvet fist," running off Grabiner in 1945. In some ways Charley, also called Chuck, was the heir apparent, but his mother never quite surrendered the reins, and before she died in 1956, she muddied the waters by transferring 54 percent of her stock to Dorothy and only 46 percent to Chuck. The siblings battled in court for a messy two years, and their dispute led eventually to majority control of the club passing out of the family's hands.[37]

Clark Griffith bought 10 percent of the Senators in 1911 and an additional 40 percent in 1920, backed by William Richardson, a Philadelphia grain merchant. Clark and Addie Griffith had no children of their own, but Addie's brother, James Robertson, and his wife, Jane, had seven, and James struggled with alcoholism. In 1922 the Griffiths took in two of the Robertson children, Calvin and Thelma, who, although they were never adopted, changed their last name to Griffith. The Senators thus became a family-run club. Calvin became vice president, and several siblings assumed other executive positions. John Jachym, who purchased Richardson's shares in 1950, wanted to be an active owner and introduce modern business practices, but Griffith froze him out. Jachym gave up and sold his shares to Gabriel Murphy, who agreed to be a silent partner. He, in turn, sold enough shares to Griffith to make his friend the majority owner. When Griffith died in October 1955, Calvin became president, controlling 52 percent of the club, essentially debt-free. Horace Stoneham inherited the Giants from his father Charles, who had bought the club in 1919 for $1 million. "The most costly franchise in baseball has changed hands," read the press release, but the purchaser was a surprise. Charles Stoneham had no previous interest in baseball. He was a man about town who, in the words of researcher Bill Lamb, "embodied a Jazz Age stereotype—cutthroat businessman by day, boozy bon vivant by night." Stoneham's chief business was operating a bucket shop, a sleazy establishment where customers could claim to be investing in the stock market but were really placing bets against the broker on whether a stock's price would rise or fall. When Bright's disease took his life in 1936, the club passed to Horace, who had apprenticed in the baseball business from the bottom up, including stints in selling tickets, groundskeeping, and secretarial work. Horace Stoneham generally remained out of sight, but he participated in league meetings fully and built a powerful offensive club that nevertheless failed to contend throughout the war years. In 1948 Stoneham hired Leo Durocher as manager, prying him away from the Dodgers in midseason in a move that shocked fans everywhere.[38]

The other eight clubs, five in the National League and three in the American, were controlled by a new generation of capitalists, men who, according to Marshall, "were looking at the game as a financial opportunity and operated their clubs as businesses." Six of the eight were burdened by competing in two-team cities, and the other two, the Dodgers and Yankees, played in a three-team city. First to change hands during the war years were the Phillies, a club victimized by undercapitalization and unimaginative leadership since Gerry Nugent became club president in 1932. Expenses perennially outstripped revenues, and in late 1942, with Nugent $160,000 in debt to the National League and two years behind in rent at Shibe Park, where the Phillies had been playing since 1938, Ford Frick ousted Nugent and quickly found a buyer, William Cox, a millionaire sportsman in the lumber business who took over the club when some of its debts were forgiven. He hired Bucky Harris as manager in 1943 but fired him in July. Harris told a group of sportswriters that Cox had been betting on the Phillies. Commissioner Landis investigated, and Cox was banned and forced to sell. The new owner was multimillionaire Bob Carpenter Sr., president of the DuPont Chemical Company. He installed his son, Bob Jr., as president. In Boston a trio of construction company owners, Lou Perini, Guido Rugo, and Joe Maney, bought 73 percent of the Braves in 1944 from Bob Quinn. After selling the Red Sox to Yawkey in 1933, Quinn had joined the Braves in 1935 as president and part owner, his $200,000 stake financed by majority owner Charles Adams, who also owned the Boston Bruins hockey team and Suffolk Downs, a racetrack. Perini and his partners, known sometimes as the "Three Steam Shovels," had each held a minority position since 1941. Quinn remained president for less than a year. He was replaced by his son, John, who ran the Braves as the new owners invested heavily in a farm system, a scouting staff, and substantial upgrades to Braves Field, grown old since opening in 1915.[39]

Like the Phillies, the Browns underwent two ownership changes in the immediate postwar years. After the Japanese attack on Pearl Harbor forced Don Barnes to abort his plan to move to Los Angeles, he had to look elsewhere for an influx of cash. He found it in the person of Richard Muckerman, a minority owner since 1939. Muckerman not only acquired additional stock in 1942; he also bought out Barnes and became majority owner in August 1945, retaining Bill DeWitt and his brother, Charlie, to run the club. Muckerman invested heavily, buying his ballpark, Sportsman's Park, from the Phil Ball estate, and then renovating it, building a park for the club's farm team in San Antonio, and constructing a new spring training facility in Florida. Attendance did not support these expenditures, and Muckerman wound up heavily in debt. He sold controlling interest in the club to the DeWitts in February 1949, but the terms of the deal revealed how undercapitalized the new owners were. The brothers put up only $75,000 of their own money while borrowing $300,000 from the American League and $650,000 from Muckerman himself. Just a few months before the Cardinals had gotten new owners too. Sam Breadon, majority owner since 1920, was suffering from prostate cancer. In November 1947 he sold his interest to Fred Saigh, a St. Louis attorney, and Robert Hannegan, a Democratic political operative. The terms of the deal were astounding. Saigh and Hannegan secured nearly the total purchase price, just over $4 million, through loans from two St. Louis banks, the wife of a former minority owner, and Breadon himself. Their own stake included just $10,000 in cash and $50,800, described as the club's surplus cash. In other words, as Marshall wrote, "The purchasers essentially used the team's existing assets to acquire the club." Just a year later Hannegan's hypertension got the best of him, and he asked Saigh to exercise his right of first refusal to buy him out, producing an alleged offer of $1.2 million from Bostonian Joseph P. Kennedy for his share. Saigh was forced to match it, much to his displeasure. "He was only in it a season," Saigh complained about Hannegan, adding, "I haven't thought too much of the Kennedys since that time."[40]

Three other clubs left family control during these same years. The Dreyfuss family sold the Pirates in 1946 to a syndicate including banker Frank McKinney, real estate developer John Galbreath, attorney Tom Johnson, and popular singer Bing Crosby. McKinney sold out during the 1950 season, and Galbreath became president. The Dodgers' situation was much more complicated. Brooklyn was a club shackled by a tangled ownership profile even before the deaths of co-owners Charles Ebbets and Ed McKeever in 1925. After the 1942 season George McLaughlin, a banker who had been de facto running the Dodgers for the Ebbets and McKeever estates, announced that the club had hired Branch Rickey, who had recently left the Cardinals, as president and general manager, and Walter O'Malley as the club's chief counsel. Within a short period of time they found investors sufficient enough to buy out both estates. The Yankees, too, were owned by an estate, that of Jacob Ruppert, who had died in 1939. He had no children and left the bulk of his considerable assets to a collection of relatives, with the ball club passing intact to a pair of nieces and Helen Weyant, Ruppert's longtime companion. Four trustees ran the club for these three heirs, and Ed Barrow became team president. The estate proved to be much more complicated than originally anticipated, and by 1944 tax obligations and outstanding debts forced a sale. Larry MacPhail, just as he was being discharged from the army, was interested. He did not have enough money to make a bid by himself, but eventually he found two partners, Dan Topping and Del Webb. They bought the Yankees in January 1945 for $2.85 million. Each owned a third of the club, but Topping and Webb funded much of MacPhail's investment and installed him as president. Three tumultuous years later, however, MacPhail was out. He had arranged, but not yet implemented, an initial public stock offering that would have made 50 percent of the club available and raised approximately $3 million. Topping and Webb nixed the proposal, desirous of avoiding attendant public scrutiny, and bought out their partner for $2 million.[41]

As these new owners and ownership groups took shape, 1948 set a high watermark for Major League attendance, but this prosperity did not last. Attendance in most cities declined in 1949, dropped steadily during the early 1950s, and remained relatively stagnant after that. The Yankees, to give just one example, saw their attendance drop every year from 1949 through 1954 and hover around 1.5 million or less after that, even though the club won ten American League pennants and seven World Series between 1949 and 1960. The year 1949 was rough in Cleveland too. Just a year after winning the Series, the Indians saw attendance drop by four hundred thousand as they fell to third place. When they were eliminated from the pennant race, Bill Veeck devised a bizarre promotion. On September 23 he staged a mock burial of the 1948 pennant, a pregame ritual that began with the owner, dressed in black and wearing a top hat, driving a hearse in a funeral procession. Beyond the center-field fence the cortege lowered a real casket into the ground near a cardboard tombstone that read "1948 Champs." Manager Lou Boudreau and his coaches shoveled dirt into the grave while the team's traveling secretary, Rudie Schaffer, read the last rites from the *Sporting News*, widely known as the "Bible of Baseball." Veeck knew that he was an oddity and an outcast, neither a gentleman-sportsman nor part of the old guard nor a new capitalist. He just loved baseball and wanted to be a part of it, but his personal financial situation cut into his passion. His wife, from whom he had long been estranged, filed for divorce, and once the petition was granted, Veeck was in dire straits. Needing cash to put in trust for his children, Veeck, despite his enthusiasm, decided to sell the Indians to a group of Cleveland businessmen headed by insurance executive Ellis Ryan. Veeck's partners received close to a two-to-one return on their investment, beyond the profits they had already extracted, and Veeck himself cleared nearly $500,000, subject only to a 25 percent capital gains tax. Veeck's experiment in Major League marketing, his iconoclastic approach in a hidebound business, was over, but he would be back.[42]

Eleven

"Il A Gagné Ses Épaulettes"

When Red Barber reported for work on September 30, 1947, he walked into Yankee Stadium knowing he would soon witness something that had never happened before. The World Series between the New York Yankees and the Brooklyn Dodgers would be televised. Gillette and Ford had joined forces to pay $65,000 for sponsorship rights, even though each game would be shown to an estimated audience of only half a million fans watching on nine stations in four markets: New York, Philadelphia, Washington, and Schenectady, New York. Larry MacPhail, one of the Yankees' three co-owners, did not approve. He had anticipated, according to Dan Daniel, that an all–New York World Series without television "would produce the most emphatic sellouts in the history of baseball." Commissioner Happy Chandler took the opposite tack. At first, he wired NBC, CBS, and Mutual that rights to the Series could be had for $100,000. Convoluted negotiations followed. Chandler turned down a bid that met his price from Brooklyn's Liebmann Breweries, as well as an offer from Ford for a ten-year, $1 million contract. Before settling with Gillette and Ford, he also said that an $85,000 offer from a New York auto accessories business had arrived too late. Barber would not be the television broadcaster. That job belonged to radio veteran Bob Stanton, assisted by Bill Slater and Bob Edge, also experienced radio announcers. Barber and Mel Allen would handle the radio broadcasts, but Barber, who had announced Major League baseball's first televised game, recognized the import of the moment. "The radio broadcast of the 1947 World Series was the big assignment in all sports," he wrote later, but "it would never be as dominant again. Television was small, but it was like a little touch of pregnancy. It grew rapidly."[1]

Television was still very much a novelty in American homes, but the new medium and baseball were already acquainted. Philadelphia Athletics manager Connie Mack gave Philco's experimental station the first documented baseball interview on television in February 1937. In March 1939 the manager of the Los Angeles Angels in the Pacific Coast League (PCL) and several players were interviewed in a Mutual television studio. The game recognized as the first to be televised was a college matchup between Princeton and Columbia at Baker Field in New York on May 17, 1939. Produced by NBC and its parent company, RCA, and broadcast on W2XBS, the telecast could be seen on about four hundred receivers in the New York area and at the RCA facility in Rockefeller Center. Producer Tom Hutchinson and director Burke Crotty utilized just one camera, positioned on a platform erected on a hill above the third-base line, that yielded an indistinct and confusing image of the action. Barber's turn, a one-game experiment on August 26, 1939, came shortly after he moved from broadcasting Cincinnati Reds games to Ebbets Field. W2XBS again handled the production, this time using two cameras, one at field level just to the left of home plate and a second in the upper deck above third base, near where Barber sat. NBC's fee, so to speak, was paying to install a television receiver in the press room so that reporters and club officials could watch as Barber called the action between the Dodgers and the Reds and did three non-scripted commercials, one for each of the Dodgers' radio sponsors (Ivory Soap, Mobil Oil, and Wheaties). After the game, the first of a doubleheader, Barber rushed down to the field to conduct on-camera interviews with both managers and several players. To commemorate his effort Barber asked for an inscribed silver cigarette box that NBC sent him, along with a bill for $35. "I still have it," he wrote in 1970, "and it is worth more to me than the thirty-five dollars it cost me in 1939."[2]

The second professional game televised, on Opening Day 1940, confirmed that the new medium was here to stay. The PCL's Hollywood Stars lost to the Seattle Rainiers, but several entertainers showed up to pose for the camera, and traffic slowed around a shop where fans could watch the game on a receiver positioned in the display window. Three weeks later the opener between the Dodgers and the New York Giants became the first game to be shown on an embryonic television network. A General Electric relay station in Schenectady transmitted the broadcast from New York City to Metropolitan Hospital in Mount McGregor, New York. Telecasts of other games from Ebbets Field continued occasionally throughout the season, and in 1941 the Dodgers telecast about one game a week. Commercial television began on July 1 that year, and the first commercial program broadcast was the game between Brooklyn and the Philadelphia Phillies, shown on NBC's commercial station, WNBT. The Bulova Watch Company paid $4 to include a video version of its radio time signal on the broadcast, and other sponsors soon agreed to pay NBC's going rate, $90, to support one hour of weekend programming or roughly $210 to sponsor an entire Major League game. Commercial television retreated during the war, but WBKB in Chicago began televising Cubs home games in 1946 and aired about four games a week in the second half of the season. WNBT televised the second game of the National League playoff that year between the Dodgers and the St. Louis Cardinals, but Chandler and Gillette were unable to come to an agreement on a deal to televise the World Series. Stations affiliated with three networks—NBC, CBS, and the DuMont Television Network—angled to sponsor games in 1947 even as Major League owners attempted to make sure that players would not share in any revenues accruing from television. That year ten of the sixteen Major League teams telecast at least some home games. All three New York teams signed to show all seventy-seven home games—the Dodgers on CBS, the Yankees on DuMont, and the Giants on NBC.[3]

Walter Lanier "Red" Barber cut his teeth on radio at the University of Florida. After a housemate asked him to read a research paper, "Certain Aspects of Bovine Obstetrics," on the campus radio station, WRUF, the station offered him a job that included handling the Gators' opening football game in 1930. So bad that he got pulled from the broadcast, he earned a second chance after watching team practices and learning about the game from an assistant coach. Barber was smitten. "For the three summers of '31, '32, and '33," he later wrote, "I rode buses at night to save hotel bills, went into barbershops for a bath, shave and fresh linen, and auditioned for the announcing staffs of WBT in Charlotte, WSB in Atlanta, WHAS in Louisville, all the stations and networks in Chicago, and always, always WLW in Cincinnati." When MacPhail expanded the Reds' radio presence in 1934 to include this station, whose 500,000-watt signal could be heard throughout the South, Barber got a job, starting with broadcasting the first Major League game he saw. Over time he developed a reputation as a colorful but precise broadcaster whose charming southern vernacular found a huge audience, especially among the Dodgers faithful after he followed MacPhail to Brooklyn. Barber asserted that "the most important fact the sports announcer can broadcast is the score," and to that end he kept a three-minute egg timer on hand in the radio booth as a prompt. Barber broadcast the World Series every year from 1935 through 1943, but in 1944 he refused Gillette's offer to break his contract and move from the Dodgers to the Yankees and Giants. That ended his Series work until 1947, when Chandler decided that the principal announcers for the teams playing in the Series had to be on the Series broadcasts.[4]

Barber's partner in 1947, Mel Allen, graduated from the University of Alabama with a degree in political science and entered law school, all the while serving as the public address announcer for Crimson Tide football games.

When an emergency arose in 1935, Allen got his first broadcasting experience calling that autumn's game between Alabama and Auburn. After finishing law school and passing the bar exam, he went to New York, ostensibly for a vacation but truly to audition since veteran CBS announcer Ted Husing had heard his work and liked it. Allen got a job at $45 per week that included some sports plus narrating soap operas; reading commercials; and, on May 6, 1937, interrupting *The Kate Smith Hour* to announce that the *Hindenburg* had crashed. Two years later, when the three New York teams ended their self-imposed radio boycott, General Mills summoned Arch McDonald from Washington to announce Giants and Yankees games and sent Allen south to replace him. That arrangement did not last. Washington Senators owner Clark Griffith preferred former pitcher Walter Johnson to Allen, and Allen returned to New York just in time to take over for McDonald's unfortunate assistant, who was fired after calling Ivory Soap "Ovary Soap" on the air. After the season McDonald soured on New York and went back to Washington, and Allen replaced him as the lead broadcaster for both Yankees and Giants games. He worked with Barber on the World Series in 1940 and 1942 before Uncle Sam called. After serving in the army, Allen resumed his career in 1946. Both the Giants and the Yankees wanted him exclusively, but MacPhail, now with the Yankees, won out by telling him that the Yankees' broadcaster would travel with the team to cover road games live.[5]

Barber remembered the 1947 Series as "the most exciting," and the *Sporting News* called it the "biggest, richest, and perhaps wildest." It was also the first to use six umpires on the field, and once it ended, it was the first time since 1924 through 1926 that three straight Series had gone seven games. The Yankees won their eleventh championship by taking the first two games at home, winning the crucial fifth game at Ebbets Field, and triumphing in the decisive seventh game. Brooklyn fans recalled for a long time the defensive gem of the Series: left fielder Al Gionfriddo's one-handed spear of Joe DiMaggio's fly ball nearly 415 feet from home plate with two runners on base and the Dodgers ahead, 8–5, in the sixth inning of Game Six. Even more famous, though, was Game Four, when Yankees right-hander Bill Bevens took a no-hitter into the ninth inning, only to lose his pitching gem when pinch hitter Cookie Lavagetto, coming to bat with two out and two men on base as the result of walks, doubled off the right-field wall to score two runs and win the game, 3–2. No World Series pitcher had ever thrown a no-hitter nor come as close as Bevens did, despite the ten walks he surrendered, and Allen and Barber treated the unfolding drama differently. Allen, as voluble as Barber was restrained, called the first four and a half innings. He respected the tradition that no one mention a no-hitter in progress for fear of jinxing the outcome, while Barber, taking over in the middle of the fifth, said to himself, "What right did I have to withhold any statistic of the game because of a superstition?" He also recalled Commissioner Kenesaw Landis's instructions, before Barber's first World Series in 1935, simply to report what was happening on the field. So at the end of the inning he gave the totals: "The Yankees, two runs, six hits, and one error; the Dodgers, one run, no hits, and two errors." Bevens lost the game, and the next day he told Barber, "Red, you didn't have a thing to do with it. It was those bases on balls that did it."[6]

Before the Series MacPhail explained why he opposed televising the Fall Classic. He said, "I am not interested in furnishing a free show for every tavern with a television set. I believe it would be harmful to the gate." He was wrong. Televising the Series did not depress attendance. Every game was a sellout. Game One, in fact, attracted 73,365 fans, a record, but one that lasted only a few days until Game Six drew 74,065. The Series set a record for total attendance too, 389,763, and for net receipts, $2,021,348.92. This figure included $175,000 for radio rights and the $65,000 Chandler negotiated for television rights. A full share of the players' pool for members of the winning team was $5,830, and for the losers, $4,081. Mutual Broadcasting assembled a network of more than four hundred stations to hear the radio broadcasts. Nearly three-quarters of all homes with a radio—and more than 90 percent in New York—listened to one or more games. James L. Conners reviewed the work of Allen and Barber in the *Sporting News*, lauding them for providing "crisp, accurate, lively, and colorful descriptions" and for being "noticeably fair and objective." He called Barber "not only an accurate reporter, but a sound commentator, an original phrasemaker, and a chuckling humorist—an unusual and almost unbeatable combination." Stanton's work on television did not draw similar critical attention, but the telecasts were popular. RCA distributed a thousand free tickets to each game at its Exhibition Hall at Radio City, and the sale of television sets in the New York area rose 25 percent as a result of the Series. Babe Ruth may have watched too, since RCA and the Yankees had given him a television just a few months before. Presciently the *Sporting News* noted that "now there has developed still another medium, in time, to become one of the most powerful of all, except the newspaper, in spreading the gospel of the game—television."[7]

Early in 1947 Pittsburgh owner John Galbreath enticed Hank Greenberg to join the Pirates by offering him $100,000, a sum, Galbreath said, that would make the former Detroit Tigers slugger the highest-paid player of all time. Greenberg agreed, but he wanted $40,000 in salary plus the right to buy $75,000 in Pirates stock that the club would repurchase after the season for $135,000, thus allowing Greenberg to declare $60,000, for tax purposes, as a capital gain and not regular income. Galbreath agreed and gave Greenberg and his wife a ride to spring training in his private plane. There Greenberg took under his wing young Ralph Kiner, who had led the National League in home runs in 1946, his rookie season. The two became fast friends. Greenberg made Kiner a better hitter, and they both profited when the Pirates erected an inner fence at Forbes Field, reducing the distance to the left-field stands by at least twenty feet. The area behind the fence, known first as Greenberg Gardens and later Kiner's Korner, helped the veteran hit 25 home runs and the youngster, 51, tied for the league lead. Galbreath's largesse was symptomatic of the postwar era. The *Sporting News* reported in February 1946 that the total Major League payroll was "creeping up toward a $5,000,000 total," when, "not so very long ago," the entire National League payroll was less than $700,000. "Optimists," the weekly continued, "insist that the game is moving into an era of unprecedented prosperity." Just a year later, though, the same publication suggested that "salary spirals, unless halted, threaten to shake the financial foundations of the major leagues." Said one anonymous owner, "Something is going to crack." Greenberg's contract may have paid him more than any other player. Joe DiMaggio and Ted Williams apparently did not sign their first $100,000 contracts until 1949, and Stan Musial, not until 1958. Bob Feller signed a contract with the Indians in 1947 for $70,000 plus attendance bonuses that might have pushed his paycheck to $100,000 either that season or the next, when Cleveland won the World Series.[8]

The converted B-24 that Greenberg and his wife boarded with Galbreath left LaGuardia Airport in New York and landed in Miami because the Pirates would be training in Miami Beach. Ten other clubs trained in Florida in 1947, but the Indians and the Giants broke new ground by setting up their spring training operations in Arizona. Major League owners were beginning to realize that a growing part of the American population was moving south and west and that the geography of the National Pastime was no longer so national in scope. Before buying the Indians, Bill Veeck owned a ranch near Tucson, where he watched the Chicago White Sox and the Cubs play an exhibition game on their way east from California to start the 1946 regular season. Once he purchased the Cleveland club, Veeck announced that the Indians would train in Tucson if he could persuade another club to come to Arizona with him. The Giants agreed to do so in August, but they picked Phoenix as a site, about 110 miles to the north. The Cubs moved their spring camp to Mesa, a Phoenix suburb, in 1952, and when a fourth club, the Baltimore Orioles, began training in Arizona in 1954—first in Yuma, 150 miles to the west, and then in Scottsdale, another Phoenix suburb—spring baseball had what was called the Cactus League to rival Florida's Grapefruit League.[9]

Galbreath also offered Greenberg the chance to travel by air on road trips. Air travel had been part of baseball's future since 1929, when Cleveland general manager Billy Evans, while turning down an offer to buy an airplane for his club, predicted that all teams would one day travel by air and that the Major Leagues might eventually be adjusted to include one or two cities on the Pacific coast. Following the Reds' pioneering flight in 1934, ball clubs traveled by plane sporadically. The Boston Red Sox flew from St. Louis to Chicago on July 30, 1936; the Cardinals hopped a mail plane from Boston to Chicago in September 1938; and the Dodgers flew from St. Louis to Chicago on May 7, 1940. In 1946, when the Yankees and the Red Sox announced that they would fly regularly, they gave players the option to travel by train. A stormy flight from Chicago to St. Louis persuaded several Red Sox players to do just that. "Boys," said first baseman Rudy York, "I've made my first and last air trip." Outfielder George Metkovich concurred, saying "I've flown plenty, but this is my finale. I'll tell you I was scared more than I've ever been in my life before. From now on, I'm a railroad man." The Yankees used a plane called the "Yankee Mainliner," supplied by United Air Lines. Capital Airlines transported thirteen of the sixteen Major League clubs on some trips in 1953. The next season Branch Rickey announced that the Pirates would travel exclusively by air. Rickey bought $3 million in insurance for his club and an additional $2 million for players' families. By 1958, 90 percent of all team travel was by air, even though air travel was still dangerous. At the 1957 winter meetings, the American League announced the creation of a "Rehabilitation Plan," allowing any club losing seven or more players in a major disaster to buy the contracts of players from other clubs. Each of the other seven clubs would have to prepare a list of twelve available players, but no club could lose more than three. League president Will Harridge also announced the purchase of a $1.875 million group accident insurance policy to cover player purchases under the plan.[10]

Baseball in these early postwar years has retained the image of a golden age despite declining attendance, ballparks that were beginning to show advanced wear and tear, and the departure of five Major League clubs from their longtime homes for what they hoped would be greener pastures. The resilience of this romantic description rests on nostalgic memories focused, at least in part, on the success of the three New York teams over the eleven-year period beginning in 1947, during which they won a combined seventeen pennants and nine World Series. Many writers of popular baseball history sustained this narrative, including Roger Kahn, a sportswriter who covered the Dodgers for the *New York Herald Tribune*. He immortalized members of this team in his elegiac *The Boys of Summer*, and his later book, *The Era, 1947–1957: When the Yankees, the Giants, and the Dodgers Ruled the World*, "centers on the three great baseball teams that played in New York City from 1947 through 1957, when New York was the capital of the world." Two of these teams did have national followings, but attendance figures for these years belie their hallowed reputation. Kahn admitted as much, writing that "from the start of the Era to the end, attendance declined sharply at all three New York ballparks. In 1947, about 5.5 million tickets were sold for New York baseball. In 1957, the total was 3.2 million." Indeed falling attendance was a stunning problem throughout Major League baseball, not just in New York. The Boston Braves' attendance peaked in 1948 and dropped to 281,278 in 1952. The Cubs drew 1,364,039 fans in 1947 and 670,629 in 1957. The Pirates topped out at 1,517,021 in 1948 and bottomed out at 469,397 in 1955. In the American League Cleveland's attendance dropped to 722,256 in 1957. The St. Louis Browns never reached 1 million and fell to 247,131 in 1950, while the Senators hit 1 million once in 1946 and plummeted to 425,239 in 1955. Only when the Braves moved to Milwaukee, the Browns to Baltimore (where they became the Orioles), the Philadelphia Athletics to Kansas City, and two of the New York clubs to the West Coast was this downward slide halted.[11]

If organized baseball needed a leader to provide a steady hand during postwar uncertainty, Happy Chandler was perhaps not the best man for the job. Nearly every year of his tenure was tainted by controversies large and small that alienated him bit by bit from one executive after another and from the press. Just after Major League club owners elected him to succeed the late Kenesaw Landis as commissioner of baseball in April 1945, the senator from Kentucky upset his constituents by suggesting that ballplayers should not bet on horse racing, a sport that had gone dormant during the war and was looking to recover. In July he met with several American League umpires, including Ernie Stewart, and suggested that their salaries and working conditions could stand to be improved. He asked Stewart to circulate a few ideas among a small group of umpires by letter, but when Stewart did so, league president Will Harridge found out and demanded that Stewart retire, effective immediately. Chandler learned quickly that some matters would be beyond his authority. He could not force Harridge to rescind what amounted to Stewart's dismissal, even though the umpire had acted, not as a labor organizer, but as a representative of the commissioner. Several years later Stewart recounted his firing, and he quoted Harridge as saying, "When Mr. Chandler learns to run his office and let me run the American League office, he is going to be a lot better off." But Chandler persisted. Before he resigned his Senate seat on November 1 and took office officially, he rocked the boat again by suggesting that the umpires working the World Series deserved compensation beyond what was stipulated. Upon hearing this, some owners floated the idea that they wanted to buy out his contract immediately, just as he was beginning on the job, and Red Sox owner Tom Yawkey volunteered to fund the ouster himself since the league treasuries could not afford to do so. Reporters, too, took umbrage when Chandler moved his office from Chicago, the seat of Landis's domain, to Cincinnati.[12]

Chandler spent good portions of 1946 dealing with the threats posed by Robert Murphy's American Baseball Guild and Jorge Pasquel's Mexican League. By early 1947 he was also ensnared in the growing rivalry between Branch Rickey's Dodgers and Larry MacPhail's Yankees. The two had once been teacher and student, but according to Lee Lowenfish, "MacPhail was jealous that his one-time mentor had usurped his place as the mastermind in Brooklyn." After the Yankees finished the 1946 season with an interim manager, rumors swirled that MacPhail had approached Leo Durocher, the Dodgers' manager since 1939, as a replacement, or perhaps that Durocher had advanced his own name. MacPhail hired veteran manager Bucky Harris instead, but at the same time he named Charlie Dressen a Yankees coach. Dressen, who had played in the Majors from 1925 through 1933 and managed for MacPhail in Cincinnati from 1934 through 1937, had been a Dodgers coach and Durocher confidant since 1939 with one brief hiatus. When Rickey replaced MacPhail in Brooklyn after the 1942 season, he fired Dressen, apparently to show his disapproval of the coach's penchant for betting on horse races. That exile lasted just a few months, but when Dressen got his job back in July 1943, it came with a greatly reduced salary. Despite raises in the ensuing years, Dressen never made up the difference, telling Dan Daniel in November 1946 that he wanted "to get away from Brooklyn because for no good reason, I lost $14,000 in salary over there." Rickey offered him a contract for 1947 and 1948 at a reported $14,000 per year, but Dressen gave only verbal, and not written, assent. He thought himself free to sign with the Yankees, but Rickey cried foul, firing off a memo to MacPhail. The Yankees' executive responded rather sharply but only after he had signed Dressen. Making a tense situation even worse, another Dodgers coach, Red Corriden, active in baseball since 1908, announced his resignation at the 1946 winter meetings, and he too signed a contract with the Yankees.[13]

It fell to Chandler to unsort this mess, but before he could do so, more complex questions surrounding Durocher's lifestyle surfaced. The Dodgers manager was nothing if not flamboyant, both on and off the field. Baseball historian Jeffrey Marlett crystalized the aspects of Durocher's personal life that made him a lightning rod for publicity. "Along the way," Marlett wrote, "Durocher kept company with movie stars, entertainers, and an entire retinue of shady underworld characters. He had legal difficulties, four divorces, and fights with fans, jilted women, and angered husbands, fathers, and boyfriends." Rickey, who employed Durocher despite the attendant exasperation, put it more succinctly, saying that his manager "possessed an infinite capacity for immediately making a bad thing worse." Rickey's 1942 edict that the Dodgers refrain from gambling, the same decree that led to Dressen's firing, had little effect on Durocher. His close friend was professional gambler George Raft, whose movie career often had him portraying a gangster. Raft lived in Durocher's apartment when he was in New York, and Durocher wintered in Raft's Hollywood home. Raft had been on baseball's radar at least since 1941, when he bragged about winning $100,000 betting on baseball and Durocher had given his friend four box seats to the World Series. In 1944, while Durocher was at spring training, Raft used the manager's apartment to host a gambling party during which a wealthy participant was bilked out of $12,000 in a dishonest crap game. The big loser complained to the district attorney, and although no charges were filed, the police leaked the story to the newspapers. Two years later syndicated columnist Westbrook Pegler, acting on information that linked Durocher with racketeer Joe Adonis and a check-cashing scam, published stories exposing the Raft-Durocher connection and its implications. Rickey was worried, but he decided not to confront Durocher directly. Instead he ordered his assistant, Arthur Mann, to inform Chandler.[14]

Sources agree, somewhat inexplicably, that Chandler knew nothing of Durocher's antics until Mann paid a visit to the commissioner's Cincinnati office in November. From there Chandler summoned Durocher to a meeting at which he ordered him to cut off contact with Raft, Adonis, and other undesirables. The manager said he would, but then he stunned Chandler by announcing that he had fallen in love with actress Laraine Day, whom he planned to marry as soon as she got a divorce from her husband, with whom Durocher had tangled in the intimacy of Day's bedroom. The couple's liaison, even after they were married, incurred the wrath of the Diocese of Brooklyn's Catholic Youth Organization (CYO), an enormous athletic program that supported the Knothole Gang, Rickey's scheme for turning boys into dedicated Dodger fans. Spring training in 1947 proved even more momentous. According to William Marshall, the Dodgers fed Durocher a steady diet of inflammatory newspaper clippings, conniving to have him, rather than Rickey, continue the feud with MacPhail. Harold Parrott, the Dodgers' public relations director and traveling secretary, as well as Durocher's ghostwriter for the *Brooklyn Eagle*, wrote a column on March 3 saying that the upcoming three-game exhibition series between the Dodgers and the Yankees in Caracas, Venezuela, would be played for blood. "I want to beat the Yankees," Durocher wrote, even though he never saw his column before it was published, "because MacPhail knows in his heart that I love Brooklyn, always wanted to manage there and regard Branch Rickey as my father." Things got even muddier when the two teams returned to Havana, where the Dodgers were training, for additional games. Durocher spied two prominent New York gamblers, Memphis Engelberg and Connie Immerman, sitting in box seats MacPhail had given them, with the Yankees' co-owner positioned just rows behind. "If I even said 'Hello' to one of those guys," Durocher complained, "I'd be called up before Commissioner Chandler and probably barred."[15]

MacPhail exploded, denied the implication of Durocher's outburst, claimed that Engelberg never bet on baseball, and filed a complaint with the commissioner's office accusing Durocher and Rickey of slander and libel, conduct detrimental to baseball. Chandler had to intervene again. He scheduled a hearing on this dispute for March 24 in Sarasota. Just before that date he indicated that he might have prejudged the case, saying that "somebody may wind up getting kicked out of baseball," while bragging that he could handle this matter without flinching. He had signed death warrants as governor of Kentucky, he said, "so I'm not going to be timid when I get ready to take action." Rickey was not present in Sarasota, and the Dodgers seemed unprepared to rebut MacPhail's charges. Durocher felt uneasy having attorney Walter O'Malley represent both the Dodgers and him, but he was relieved when MacPhail accepted the manager's apology for the fiery column, saying, "Forget it, buddy, it's over." But it wasn't. Chandler pressed Durocher about playing high-stakes card games with his own players, and MacPhail insisted that Chandler had not handled his earlier complaint against Rickey. Chandler called a second hearing for March 29 in St. Petersburg. There Rickey took responsibility for the statements about the gamblers near MacPhail's box, but Arthur Patterson, the Yankees' traveling secretary, admitted that he might have supplied those tickets. The commissioner then counseled separately with the representatives of each club, both Rickey and MacPhail taking issue with how they thought Chandler might be leaning. His decision came on April 9, less than a week before Opening Day. Chandler fined Parrott $500 for the newspaper column. He fined the clubs $2,000 each for conducting their controversy in public, and he suspended Durocher for one year for not living up to "the standards expected" of managers and for a series of "publicity-producing affairs." Finally, getting back to the matter that started the whole fracas, the commissioner found that Dressen had violated his verbal agreement to coach with the Dodgers and suspended him for thirty days.[16]

Nothing about Happy Chandler's term as commissioner abides in popular memory more prominently than the role he played in the integration of organized baseball engineered by Branch Rickey and Jackie Robinson. The basic story is so compelling. As Steven A. Riess noted, "The Jackie Robinson story is to Americans what the Passover story is to Jews: it must be told to every generation so that we never forget it." Rickey, acting from complicated motives—including his desire to build a winning team, his interest in making money, and his ethical and religious convictions that led him to want to right a historic wrong—operated behind a veil of subterfuge. He met Robinson in Brooklyn on August 28, 1945; told him that coach Clyde Sukeforth had brought him to Brooklyn to offer him a chance to play for the Dodgers organization; and got him to sign an agreement accepting a $3,500 bonus and a salary of $600 a month that would soon be offered by the Montreal Royals, Brooklyn's International League farm club. That signing took place on October 23 in the Montreal office of Royals president Hector Racine, and Robinson planned to join the Brooklyn organization for spring training in Daytona Beach, Florida, in February. Historian Jules Tygiel wrote that the reaction of the nation's sportswriters to Rickey's decision was intense but that his supporters "easily outnumbered his detractors." Most Major League owners were less vocal. Indians owner Alva Bradley proclaimed that "colored players have never been discriminated against in the major leagues," but Connie Mack, Chandler, Ford Frick, and Will Harridge all declined to comment. Minor League officials were decidedly less positive, with Eastern League president Tommy Richardson complaining to Chandler about Rickey that "some of these fellows lay the eggs and after they're broke they expect someone else to take them and put them back together."[17]

Robinson and his wife, Rachel, made their way cross-country from California at the end of February. It was a perilous journey during which Jim Crow buffeted them as they neared their destination. Daytona Beach was regarded as a southern town more liberal than most, but the Royals trained in nearby Sanford, where residents made clear their displeasure at Robinson's arrival. Several other towns, some citing local ordinances, refused to allow the Royals to play. During spring training Robinson moved from shortstop to second base and hit poorly, but on April 15 he became the first African American to play a regular season game in organized baseball in the twentieth century. The Royals opened on the road against the Jersey City Giants, winning, 14–1, before a capacity crowd of more than twenty-five thousand. Robinson grounded out to short in his first at bat, but he followed that with four straight hits, including a three-run homer and a bunt single, and he scored twice on balks. As the Royals' road trip continued, Robinson's batting average tumbled. Once the team came home and especially after the Robinsons moved into an apartment in Montreal's East End, he became more comfortable at the plate and began to reveal his potential. Montreal had finished first in 1945, but only three Royals from that team had returned in 1946, and manager Clay Hopper, a native of Mississippi, was new too. Robinson's presence proved crucial as the Royals won the pennant again. The rookie hit .349, led the league in runs scored with 113, stole 65 bases, and led all second basemen in fielding percentage. The Royals defeated both Newark and Syracuse in playoff series to advance to the Junior World Series against the Louisville Colonels in the American Association. Montreal won that too, four games to two. As fans stormed the field in celebration, they chanted about their new hero, "Il a gagné ses épaulettes" (He has earned his wings). Sam Maltin, a Canadian, a socialist, a sportswriter for the *Montreal Herald*, a stringer for the *Pittsburgh Courier*, and the Robinsons' neighbor, put it more prosaically. "It was probably the only day in history," he wrote, "that a black man ran from a white mob with love, instead of lynching on its mind."[18]

To call Robinson "the first," as many have, obscures the rich tradition and long history of African Americans playing baseball on their own terms. After Jim Crow shackled America, Blackball, as some have called it, persisted. The first professional Black team, paid salaries in lieu of carving up gate receipts, came to be known as the Cuban Giants. Organized in 1884, they developed a routine that had them using the Argyle Hotel, a lavish resort in Babylon, New York, as their summer home and the San Marcos Hotel in St. Augustine, Florida, as their winter base. Absent a league, they improvised a schedule against Major League, Minor League, semipro, and amateur teams and other all-Black clubs. After a decade or so the balance of power in Blackball shifted somewhat to Chicago and the Midwest. The best Black clubs began to barnstorm extensively, sometimes playing white professional clubs and sometimes engaging in multigame series billed as "Colored Championships," but the standard for determining the best Blackball club remained uncertain. One club making a bid to be declared supreme was organized by Frank Leland. They were called the Chicago Union Giants, Leland's Union Giants, and then the Leland Giants, and they became successful because of Rube Foster, their pitcher, manager, and booking agent. His specialty, besides pitching, was putting together barnstorming schedules that allowed players to display their talents before large crowds against both Black and white clubs. Foster split from Leland after the 1909 season to organize his own team, the Chicago American Giants. They won several championships, but Foster's goal was to determine a true national Black baseball champion through a league. Thus he and other midwestern club owners created the Negro National League in February 1920. Foster suffered a mental breakdown in 1926, and the league he founded folded after the 1931 season. A second Negro National League began play in 1933 and lasted through 1948. The Negro American League, founded in 1937, proved more durable than the others, lasting until 1960. Foster hoped for a Negro World Series too, but it never became a financial success as teams played limited league schedules and still depended on robust barnstorming for economic survival.[19]

The jewel mounted in the center of every Blackball season was the East-West All-Star Game played in Chicago. In 1933 Cum Posey, co-owner of the Homestead (PA) Grays, perennially one of the strongest clubs, met with two Pittsburgh sportswriters to discuss the idea of a North-South All-Star Game to be played at Yankee Stadium. This game never happened, but Gus Greenlee, owner of the Pittsburgh Crawfords and Posey's rival, grabbed the idea and persuaded certain writers to lease Comiskey Park for an East-West Game. The first one, played on September 10, attracted a crowd of twenty thousand. Fans selected each team, casting votes by clipping ballots printed in African American newspapers and mailing them in. Despite the Depression, vote totals topped a million in the first few years and rose to over seventeen million in

1939, and attendance eventually rose to capacity too. In several years a second game was played in Cleveland, New York, or Washington. Except perhaps for boxing matches involving heavyweight champion Joe Louis, the East-West Game became Black America's favorite sporting event. Fans came to Chicago from around the country, arriving on special trains from New York, Kansas City, and New Orleans. The Grand Hotel and others on Chicago's South Side were booked solid. Restaurants filled, department stores sold game tickets to drive customers inside, and nightclubs hopped with crowds thrilled to see the nation's greatest entertainers perform. "You didn't go to Chicago to sleep," recalled Monte Irvin, who played in his first East-West Game in 1941. Negro Leaguers conceptualized their game as a serious opportunity to exhibit their skills. They played hard to win. The game attracted both the Black and white press and front office personnel as well. It became a showcase for Blackball's talent, and it embodied, in the words of historian Larry Lester, "the spirit and life of Negro League baseball, serving to entertain, educate, and ultimately provide a forum to integrate our national pastime many years later."[20]

Rickey was planning to promote Robinson to the Major Leagues in 1947. He decided that both the Dodgers and the Royals would train in Havana, away from segregated Florida. Robinson, still on the Montreal roster, was joined by three other African American players: pitchers Don Newcombe and Roy Partlow and catcher Roy Campanella. Rickey also wanted spring training to make a profit. Brooklyn played the Braves in Havana and the Yankees in Havana and Venezuela. He also arranged for the Dodgers and Royals to play games in Panama's Canal Zone against local clubs and against each other. Rickey and manager Leo Durocher learned that several southern-born Dodgers, bent on not playing with an African American, signed a petition urging Rickey not to promote Robinson. Durocher confronted the rebels in a midnight meeting in the kitchen of the army barracks where the team was staying, making it clear that Robinson would make the team. "He's going to win pennants for us," he said. "He's going to put money in your pockets and money in mine." The Major League club and the farm club also played one another eight times in Havana. Rickey's strategy was obvious: to demonstrate Robinson's abilities to his future teammates. "I want you to be the most conspicuous player on the field," Rickey told him. Journeying north to Brooklyn, the two teams played on April 10, the day after Chandler had suspended Durocher. During the game Rickey issued a press release announcing that "the Brooklyn Dodgers today purchased the contract of Jackie Roosevelt Robinson from the Montreal Royals." All this was done with Chandler's approval. While initially cool to the idea that Robinson—or any player—should be "the first," the commissioner had been impressed with Robinson's 1946 season in Montreal and more than a bit willing to take Rickey's side after Major League owners voted, fifteen to one, not to support the Brooklyn club. "It isn't my job," Chandler wrote in his memoirs, "to decide which colors can play big league baseball. . . . So bring him in. Transfer Robinson."[21]

Collectively the Major Leagues dragged their feet on desegregation. After Jackie Robinson made his Major League debut on April 15, 1947, other clubs added African Americans to their rosters, but it took more than a dozen years for the last team, the Boston Red Sox, to integrate. Playing first base for the Dodgers on a cold day in Brooklyn, Robinson went 0-for-3, but after reaching base on an error in the seventh inning, he scored his first Major League run. The home team defeated the Braves, 5–3, their first of ninety-four wins, which brought the club its first pennant since 1941. Over the course of the season the first African American to play professional baseball in the twentieth century made his presence felt, putting together a hitting streak of fourteen games in May and another of twenty-one games starting in mid-June. For the year he hit .297 with 12 home runs, and he led the league with 29 stolen bases. Both the Baseball Writers' Association of America (BBWAA) and the *Sporting News* named him National League Rookie of the Year. In August 1947 Dan Bankhead, an African American pitcher, played his first game for the Dodgers. The next year catcher Roy Campanella played for Brooklyn, followed in 1949 by pitcher Don Newcombe. Both put together outstanding careers. Campanella, a professional at fifteen, played ten seasons for Brooklyn before being paralyzed in an auto accident. He won the Most Valuable Player (MVP) Award three times and was elected to the Hall of Fame in 1969. Newcombe won 149 games over ten seasons, including 20 or more three times. He also hit 7 home runs in 1955 and 15 home runs in his career. When Ford Frick complained that pitchers were habitually underrepresented in MVP voting, the BBWAA created the Cy Young Memorial Award to honor the season's best pitcher. Newcombe was the first winner, in 1956, and he won the MVP Award too. The Dodgers had a fine team in the postwar years, including pitcher Carl Erskine, first baseman Gil Hodges, shortstop Pee Wee Reese, and centerfielder Duke Snider, all white. Two other Black players also contributed to their success. Pitcher Joe Black won the Rookie of the Year Award in 1952, and second baseman Jim Gilliam did the same the following year. This club, more or less intact for a decade or so, brought the Dodgers more baseball glory than ever before, including additional pennants in 1949, 1952, 1953, 1955, and 1956, near misses in 1950 and 1951, and Brooklyn's only World Series championship in 1955.[22]

Two American League clubs integrated in 1947 as well. Bill Veeck, after buying the Indians in 1946, signed one African American player the next year and a second in 1948. Unlike Branch Rickey, who refused to compensate Robinson's club, the Kansas City Monarchs, Veeck dealt directly with Effa Manley, owner of the Newark Eagles, and agreed to purchase the contract of twenty-three-year-old second baseman Larry Doby for $15,000. Doby signed an Indians contract on July 5 and pinch-hit two days later, striking out. The following day, he started at first base in the second game of a doubleheader and singled in four at bats. Doby faced prejudice from teammates, opponents, and Cleveland fans, who besieged Veeck's office with angry letters. He hit only .156 for the season but made the starting lineup in 1948 in the outfield. In July Satchel Paige, the legendary Negro Leagues pitcher, joined Doby on the Cleveland roster, despite his advanced age. Together they played significant roles as the Indians won the pennant and the World Series. Doby became the first African American to hit a home run in the Series, and Paige made one relief appearance. Two weeks after Doby's 1947 debut the Browns introduced two Black players, Hank Thompson and Willard Brown, both obtained from the Monarchs. St. Louis was described as a "southern city," and the stands at Sportsman's Park had been desegregated only three years before, but the Browns were mired in last place, and general manager Bill DeWitt admitted that "we believe our colored boys will help us at the gate." The experiment did not work. Thompson had a rough past and a problem with alcohol. Brown admitted to being twenty-six but was several years older. Both were shunned by teammates, and neither performed well on the field. Thompson played his first game on July 17, going 0-for-4. Brown made his debut two days later, hitting into two double plays with the bases loaded. St. Louis fans did not flock to the ballpark, and those who did show up subjected the pair to racist taunts. Occasional spurts of offense mattered not enough, and the Browns sent them both back to Kansas City in August. Thompson was batting .256 at the time and starting at second base, but when he asked DeWitt to explain why he was being cut, the response was, "There are things I can't discuss."[23]

In general the remaining National League clubs integrated sooner than their American League competitors. Thompson stayed with the Monarchs through the 1948 season and then signed a contract with the Giants. He began 1949 with Jersey City in the International League and was batting .296 when he was called up to the Majors, playing his first game and starting at second base on July 8. Monte Irvin played in the same game, pinch-hitting in the eighth inning and drawing a walk. He batted only .224 in thirty-six games, but two years later he hit .312 and led the league in runs batted in with 121. The Braves were next. Sam Jethroe was one of the three players who had worked out for the Red Sox in 1945, but none of them got a contract offer. The Dodgers signed Jethroe, nicknamed the "Jet," in 1948 and sold his contract to the Braves in 1949. Jethroe made his Major League debut on April 18, 1950, and won the Rookie of the Year Award, even though he was thirty-three years old. The Pirates, who had considered offering several Black players a tryout in 1942, integrated on April 22, 1953, when Carlos Bernier, a Black Puerto Rican, entered the game as a pinch hitter in the eighth inning and was hit by a pitch. For the Cubs shortstop Ernie Banks played his first game on September 17, 1953, followed three days later by Gene Baker. Banks became a regular in 1954 and played his entire nineteen-year career with Chicago. First baseman Tom Alston became the first Black player for the Cardinals on April 13, 1954. He went hitless in four at bats. The Reds broke their color line four days later when Puerto Rican Nino Escalera pinch-hit in the seventh inning, followed immediately by another pinch hitter, Chuck Harmon, an African American. The Phillies were the last National League team to integrate when Chico Fernandez opened at shortstop on April 16, 1957. He was followed by John Kennedy, an African American who appeared as a pinch runner on April 22, 1957. He played in only five games, two others as a pinch runner, and went hitless in two at bats. The Phillies did not have Black players in their regular lineup until 1960.[24]

The White Sox became the third American League club to integrate. Orestes Miñoso Arrieta, called "Minnie," had broken in with Cleveland in 1949 and was traded to Chicago in April 1951. A Cuban considered Black, he made his debut for the White Sox on May 1. Sam Hairston was the first African American to play for Chicago, pinch-hitting and then catching on July 21. The first African American to play for the Athletics was Bob Trice, the A's starting pitcher on September 13, 1953. He lost that game but won his next two starts. Carlos Paula, another Cuban, became the first Black to play for the Senators when he started in left field on September 6, 1954. Washington did not have another Black player on its roster until 1957. The Yankees did not integrate until April 14, 1955, when Elston Howard entered the game against the Red Sox in the sixth inning. No Black player appeared in the Tigers' lineup until Ozzie Virgil on June 6, 1958. Virgil, a Dominican who had played the previous two seasons for the Giants, started at third base. Doby became the second

Black Tiger in 1959. Finally, the Red Sox, who could have been the first club to integrate, became the last to do so on July 21, 1959, when Elijah "Pumpsie" Green entered the game as a pinch runner and then played shortstop against the White Sox. Boston's second Black player was Earl Wilson, who made his debut on July 28. The club's first African American regular was outfielder Willie Tasby in 1960, by which time such players as Henry Aaron, Banks, Willie Mays, and Frank Robinson were established stars in the National League.[25]

Integration came to the Minor Leagues fitfully, more grudgingly in the South than the North. After Robinson broke the color line in the International League, three other leagues integrated in 1946: the Class B New England League, the Class C Border League, and the Class C Canadian-American League. John Ritchey, a catcher known as "Johnny Baseball," broke the color line in the Pacific Coast League on March 30, 1948. A twenty-five-year-old catcher described in the *Sporting News* as "of Negro-Spanish descent," he entered the San Diego Padres game against Los Angeles as a pinch hitter and grounded out, thus becoming the first Black man to play in the league since 1916. Campanella became the first Black player in the American Association when he was sent down from Brooklyn to join the St. Paul Saints in May 1948 after playing three games with the Dodgers. He played thirty-five games for the Saints, batting .325 with 13 home runs and 39 runs batted in, forcing Brooklyn to recall him on July 2. A *Sporting News* headline in 1950 asked "How Soon Will South Use Negro Players?" but despite large crowds turning out to watch the Dodgers play preseason exhibition games in several southern cities, the two Class Double-A leagues, the Texas League and the Southern Association, did not integrate until 1952 and 1954 respectively. Dick Burnett, owner of the Texas League's Dallas Eagles, decided to integrate his team to keep pace with the National Football League, whose New York Yankees, with three Black players, had just become the Dallas Texans. Burnett feared that Dallas sports fans would accept integration and leave his team behind if it remained all white. The Eagles were a Cleveland affiliate, so Burnett consulted with Indians general manager Hank Greenberg, but neither of the two prospects they identified panned out, the first not even showing up for spring training. Burnett spoke with Greenberg again and signed right-handed pitcher Dave Hoskins, who had integrated the Class A Central League in 1948. Hoskins started for the Eagles on April 13, 1952. Nat Peeples was the only African American to play in the Southern Association before it went out of business after the 1961 season. He played two games for the Atlanta Crackers on April 9–10, 1954, but he was soon optioned to the Jacksonville Braves in the Class A South Atlantic League.[26]

Hoskins had played his first Central League game for the Grand Rapids (MI) Jets on August 1, 1948. He batted .393 in forty-six games while enduring harsher treatment than he later experienced in the Texas League. The next Class A league to integrate was the Eastern League. The Wilkes-Barre (PA) Barons signed outfielder Fred Thomas, a Black Canadian who made his debut on July 4, going hitless in the first game of a doubleheader and getting two singles in the nightcap. Thomas played only twelve games, batting .268, before being released. The Class A Western League dropped its color line in 1950, when the Denver Bears signed Panamanian Pablo Bernard. He played second base on Opening Day and was optioned to Ventura (CA) in the Class C California League in May. The South Atlantic League integrated in 1953. Two players, Elbert Israel and Fleming Ready, played for the Savannah Indians, and three others, Aaron, Horace Garner, and Felix Mantilla, played for Jacksonville. Years later Aaron remembered that summer: "I don't recall ever feeling that our lives were in imminent danger," he wrote, "but we took nothing for granted." Garner, looking back, said, "I wouldn't live that summer over again for a million dollars." Emblematic of leagues resistant to change was the Class C Cotton States League, with teams in Arkansas, Louisiana, and Mississippi. When the Hot Springs (AR) Bathers announced their intention in 1953 to sign two African American pitchers, brothers named Jim and Leander Tugerson, league owners voted to seize the franchise and put the club out of business. Hot Springs retreated, but short of pitching in May, the Bathers brought up Jim Tugerson from the Class D Mountain States League. League president Al Haraway forfeited a Bathers' game to the Jackson (MS) Senators, and Hot Springs backed down again. Tugerson sued Haraway, the league, and its clubs, alleging a conspiracy to deprive him of the right to fulfill his contract and challenging the legality of segregation more than a decade before passage of the 1964 Civil Rights Act. He lost, but the next year the league, having lost two Mississippi teams, relented. This dose of liberality was short-lived. Reduced to five clubs and beset by severe financial problems, the league went out of business after the 1955 season.[27]

Erasing organized baseball's color line afforded players from the Spanish-speaking Americas enhanced opportunities to play. Some Latinos, going back to Esteban Bellán in 1871, had been deemed light skinned enough not to be excluded from the National Pastime. Among this number were Cuban pitcher Adolfo Luque, Spanish American catcher Al Lopez, and Mexican outfielder Mel Almada. Historian Adrian Burgos Jr. counted fifty-five players, the majority from Cuba, who played in the Majors before 1947, but, Burgos wrote, "the more talented were playing outside organized baseball during this early period," including José Méndez, Cristóbal Torriente, and Martín Dihigo, all future members of the Hall of Fame. The post-Robinson years were different. Starting with Miñoso, who debuted with the Indians on April 19, 1949, thirty-seven Afro-Latino players reached the Major Leagues through the end of the 1959 season. Ten had played previously in the Negro Leagues, and the rest came up through the Minors. All these players had to negotiate a complicated cultural and racial landscape. Some were criticized for self-identifying as Latino and denying their blackness. Some were alienated from their teammates, both Black and white. Others, perhaps all, were befuddled by the intricacies of Jim Crow. Communication was a problem for those who spoke only Spanish, and the lack of familiar cuisine imposed an enduring burden for all. Most particularly, Latino players were susceptible to being branded as insular, hot-headed, lazy, and lacking mental acuity. Vic Power remained on the roster of the Yankees' top farm club for three years because general manager George Weiss decree that "the first Negro to appear in a Yankee uniform must be worth having been waited for." Roberto Clemente Walker, a Puerto Rican whose baseball cards identified him as "Bob," objected when his English was rendered in print as "I no play so gut yet. Me like hot weather, veree hot."[28]

Integration also meant, perhaps inevitably, the demise of the Negro Leagues. In 1945 there were four such leagues, the Negro American League, the Negro Southern League, the second Negro National League, and the brand new United States League, a recent creation of Branch Rickey and Gus Greenlee. One by one, they went out of business. Once Robinson signed his Montreal contract, Negro Leagues clubs saw their primary reason for being slip away—namely, providing a setting for the best players barred from organized baseball to exhibit their skills before appreciative audiences. As the door to the Major Leagues cracked open, the best young Black prospects could now aspire to something new, and fans who had supported this enterprise took notice. By the end of 1948 Manley acknowledged that "the Negro fan would rather watch Doby, Robinson, Campanella, and Paige than a Negro League game any time." Black teams hoped they could still provide opportunity for young players not yet signed by organized baseball and a way for players too old for the Majors to finish their careers, but the fan base to watch these players disappeared. "The fans deserted us to go see the boys on the white teams," Manley said, "deserting us like they say rats desert a sinking ship." The United States League lasted two seasons, the Negro National League expired in 1948, and the Negro Southern League limped to an uncertain finish in 1950. Clubs changed hands and cities, desperate to retain an audience. Starting in 1953 Syd Pollock, running the Indianapolis Clowns, a team somewhat similar to basketball's Harlem Globetrotters, signed Toni Stone, Connie Morgan, and Mamie Johnson, three talented women, as gate attractions, but this could not stem the tide. The Negro American League split into two divisions, East and West, in 1949 and went back to a single division in 1952. In 1958 the league was down to four teams, and in 1960 it went out of business. A final East-West Game played in Yankee Stadium in August 1961 served as a sad swan song.[29]

Happy Chandler weathered the storm surrounding Leo Durocher's suspension and Jackie Robinson's rookie season, and 1948 proved rather calm for him as well. The following year, though, the hard line he dictated against the players who had jumped to the Mexican League—five-year suspensions—backfired. Some owners blamed him for the lawsuits filed by Danny Gardella and others, arguing that once the threat posed by the Mexican League had dissipated, the commissioner should have mitigated the suspensions and worked toward reinstatement. Chandler did forgive Mickey Owen, getting the catcher to agree not to sue organized baseball in return for receiving extra service time for his pension, but no one else got a deal. Owners habitually had wanted to avoid courts of law, but Chandler was adamant, telling a dinner crowd at the University of Florida in April 1949 that he would fight against the jumpers "until the Supreme Court tells me I'm wrong." Yet in June, after a federal appellate court refused to reinstate players whose lawsuits were pending, Chandler, stating that it was "clear that I could act under no compulsion," reduced the bans from five years to three. Some players dropped their suits, but Gardella did not, and the owners held Chandler responsible for prolonging their legal difficulties. Thus when the commissioner asked the owners to extend his contract at the 1949 winter meetings, more than two years before his seven-year term was due to expire in April 1952, he was not dealing from a position of strength. Pirates president Frank McKinney spoke highly of Chandler's tenure, but Will Harridge, a stickler for doing things the way they had always been done, countered that Commissioner Kenesaw Landis had never received a new contract more than a year in advance. The motion to renew Chandler's contract failed, 11–5, but the owners gave him a $15,000 per year raise as a vote of confidence. Over the next few months, though, grumbles solidified into grievances, and support for Chandler's continuance wilted. At the 1950 winter meetings a new contract came to a vote three times and never came close to garnering the three-fourths super-majority needed to pass. The first vote was 9–7 in Chandler's favor, and the second was 8–8 when Cleveland owner Ellis Ryan changed his vote because he thought Ohio governor Frank Lausche might be open to accepting the job. On the third ballot the vote reverted to 9–7, still three votes short. Chandler took the rebuke personally. He refused at first to leave office before his term expired but, after some discussion, agreed to resign on July 31, 1951, by which time organized baseball was facing its greatest political threat since the antitrust actions brought by the outlaw Federal League.[30]

The politician who best embodied the challenge confronting baseball was Emanuel Celler, a Dodgers fan, a Democrat, and a member of the House of Representatives from New York's Fifteenth Congressional District. Celler was born in Brooklyn in 1888, graduated from Columbia University in 1910 and Columbia Law School in 1912, and began practicing law by defending a Polish American immigrant accused of voting without being a citizen. In 1922 New York City's tax commissioner persuaded Celler to run for Congress in a district a Democrat had never represented. Given virtually no chance to win, Celler organized an aggressive grassroots campaign. He distributed rulers and ink blotters to public schools; used a sound truck to make half a dozen street-corner speeches each day; and sent a tin of cocoa, compliments of a friend, to every house in the district. The result was an Election Day upset. Celler won by 3,111 votes out of 44,289 cast over the incumbent and three other candidates. Devoting his time in Congress to immigration, civil rights, and civil liberties, he rose through the House's hierarchy to become chair of the Committee on the Judiciary following the dramatic Democratic win in 1948 that returned Harry Truman, against the odds, to the White House. On July 11, 1949, this committee authorized the creation of the Special Subcommittee on Study of Monopoly Power with Celler himself as chair. Monopoly was a subject in which the congressman had been interested for many years, having introduced several bills dealing with investigating AT&T, the motion picture industry, and foreign loans made by American banks. By 1951 this subcommittee included, as one of several members of note, Peter Rodino Jr., later chair of the Judiciary Committee during the Watergate era, and, as associate counsel, John Paul Stevens, later associate justice of the Supreme Court.[31]

Despite encouraging written words from Truman to all government agencies that "I strongly favor the objectives of the Celler committee," the subcommittee got off to a rough start. Critics wondered if it was just investigating monopoly or taking on the entirety of American big business. "I was interviewed and photographed," Celler recalled, "and, above all, denounced. . . . How did I even dare question bigness in business? How could I ever suggest that the bigness of business should be looked at with a critical eye?" Nevertheless, the subcommittee began its work in earnest with hearings on the general problem of monopoly power, calling more than fifty witnesses, including executives from Metropolitan Life Insurance, DuPont, and General Electric, and then homing in on the steel industry. The subcommittee next studied the newsprint industry, noting that an acute shortage of newsprint was having an adverse effect on the business fortunes of small newspapers, followed by a look at the aluminum industry and its three corporate giants, Kaiser, Reynolds, and Alcoa. Then, Celler wrote, "came the baseball inquiry. . . . If I thought storms had broken furiously over my head before, I knew better when these hearings started. Never had such controversy raged. Never had so many columns been filled with torrents of words." Baseball seemed vulnerable on so many fronts, including the refusal of Major League owners to consider expanding their business beyond two leagues and sixteen teams all located no further west than St. Louis, but the "center of the storm," Celler noted, "was the 'reserve clause.'" Three congressmen had filed bills to protect baseball and other professional sports from antitrust regulation, thereby codifying the 1922 Supreme Court decision that held organized baseball exempt. These bills were sympathetic to the sport, but once an investigation began, baseball officials worried, it could veer off in any direction and look critically at labor relations, farm systems, territorial rights for Minor League clubs, and radio and television broadcasting policies. "That organized baseball today is 'big business,'" Celler wrote, "cannot be denied."[32]

In May 1951 Celler explained to *Sport Magazine* why his subcommittee would be targeting baseball. He told interviewer Charles Dexter that "there have been charges that Organized Baseball is a monopoly" and that the 1922 court decision had been challenged by several lawsuits, including Danny Gardella's. He noted that "I personally have no desire to harm Organized Baseball. I want to strengthen the game," but he added that "we plan to look into every aspect of the business operations of the game, for proof or disproof of the charges that it is controlled by a monopoly." To the *New York Times* Celler sounded threatening. "In my opinion," he said, "baseball is now operating in violation of the anti-trust laws. . . . We should not permit matters to drift any longer. Baseball is one of the finest things in American life, but it is in danger." Speaking to announcer Bob Wolff on a Washington DC radio station,

Celler clarified his position, saying, "If the reserve clause is essential, so be it. If it is illegal, something must be done about it. . . . I don't know the answer. Our study will be so oriented as to inquire into the facts." His tone was more ominous when he said, "We may recommend remedial legislation," but "we may have to recommend prosecution by the Department of Justice, particularly if we find the reserve clause is evil. . . . Nobody wants to muddy waters, but sometimes a boil must be lanced to cure the patient and that's the situation now." Baseball executives were uncertain how to react to the impending hearings. The *Sporting News* called the committee's agenda a challenge and urged the sport's hierarchy to "marshal its forces to meet the test." Yet the editors of *Sport Magazine* sensed that baseball executives were simply aghast. Their editorial read in part: "As in every previous instance where a threat was leveled against the controversial reserve clause in the standard player contract, spokesmen for the game fell over their own feet trying to stave off any action. Some of the boys implied colorfully that anybody who said that the reserve clause was unconstitutional was no better than a dirty hound dog. Worse than a Communist, yes, sir."[33]

Originally scheduled to open on June 28 and then July 9, but delayed by more pressing congressional business, the subcommittee's inquiry into baseball was massive. There were sixteen days of hearings spread over two weeks in late July and early August and two more weeks in October. Transcripts of the hearings plus exhibits and appendixes ran to 1,643 published pages, and they were followed months later by a 232-page report summarizing the subcommittee's findings. Weeks before the first witnesses testified on July 30, Dan Daniel interviewed Celler and speculated that the investigation would probe "far deeper than the question of the reserve clause." Reporting that Celler had conferred with attorneys representing organized baseball and the two Major Leagues, Daniel wrote that "the public is going to learn a lot about the operation of leagues and clubs in both the majors and minors." He suggested: "The hearing, it is indicated, will develop a detailed financial analysis of the major and minor league clubs, seeking to reveal their profitability and the extent of interlocking controls, such as might be exercised through farm clubs and extensive scouting systems that give parent clubs apparent player monopolies and majority votes in league affairs." Finally, Daniel laid out just how far the subcommittee might reach, including "a study of the commissioner's powers, those of the league heads and club owners, the rights and status of players, real estate holdings, handling of concessions, privileges given some radio and television stations and denied others, financial arrangements for the airing of games, and the game's responsiveness to the wants of the public as reflected in gate receipts and other channels."[34]

Following an opening statement in which Celler asserted his desire "to preserve the integrity of baseball, which has traditionally been considered our national pastime," the subcommittee heard from four witnesses during the first week of testimony: Ty Cobb, Ford Frick, Harry Simmons (described in the record as a "baseball historian and publicity director of the International Baseball League"), and George Trautman, head of the Minor Leagues. Cobb's testimony was supposed to be brief, but he enchanted the members with stories about his career, including his wrangles over salary, while denying that baseball was a business. "It is rather doubtful," he said. Cobb supported the reserve clause, but he admitted that he had once talked to a reporter on the telephone when he had "never had a chance to collect my thoughts" and suggested that the clause could stand an amendment. "I told him," Cobb said, "that possibly at the end of a . . . certain period if he [a player] had contractual troubles with his ownership, . . . they should . . . have a committee or a board of the most constructive thinking owners in the league . . . and he would have a chance to sweeten his contract." Yet Cobb declined to agree that the reserve system "looks like peonage." Frick spoke for the balance of the first morning and all day on July 31. Before taking questions, he read an eight-thousand-word statement in which he defended the reserve system as "basically . . . a long-term contract which is nothing unusual where distinctive personal services are contracted for. I read in the papers that [entertainer] Milton Berle has just signed such a contract for 30 years. . . . Neither is there anything exceptional in the player's inability . . . to negotiate with any other club. . . . I understand, for instance, that where there is a binding exclusive contract for unique personal services, there is a long-established principle of law which affords the employer the right to enjoin the performer from rendering those services to anyone else." The next morning Simmons presented a history of the game, followed by Trautman, whose statement congressmen interrupted frequently as he explained the structure of Minor League baseball and such arcane practices as waivers, options, territorial rights, and the intricacies of the farm system.[35]

At the end of the first week of testimony Congressman Celler released a statement announcing that "the baseball inquiry has not yet progressed to the state where definite conclusions can be drawn." He added, "In order to see the picture and see it whole, such factors in organized baseball as the operations of the reserve clause, the geographical locations of major league clubs, the drafting of players by the major leagues from the minors, the farm system, the waiver rules, the powers of the Commissioner, and the types of covenants operating all the clubs must be closely examined. . . . Therefore, the vital question remains to be clarified: Are the unique properties of organized baseball so paramount as to warrant exemption for baseball from the operation of the anti-trust laws?" To continue probing these questions during the second week of hearings, the subcommittee called Happy Chandler, rather suddenly the former commissioner of baseball. He was scheduled to testify for two days on August 6 but spoke for less than four hours. Absent a prepared statement, he spent most of his time explaining and defending his tenure as commissioner, including the suspensions he imposed upon players who had jumped to the Mexican League and his role in stifling the development of Robert Murphy's American Baseball Guild. He said he had also hired two former FBI agents to guard against corruption in the game because the commissioner "represents first the people of the country in the protection of the integrity of baseball as a sport." Almost as an aside, Chandler defended the reserve clause. "I think it is not too objectionable to anybody," he said. He also noted that he had tried to be innovative, suggesting that the two Major Leagues combine their umpiring staffs and that baseball give serious consideration to expansion. "I would have loved to organize a third major league or even a fourth," he said. "I think baseball should make a survey and realign the whole thing," indicating that such cities as Baltimore, Milwaukee, Houston, Dallas, San Francisco, Los Angeles, Seattle, and maybe even Portland could support Major League clubs. Representative Kenneth Keating (R-NY) asked Chandler about his ouster. "I attribute it only to the fact that I was required to get twelve votes, and I got only nine," Chandler replied, adding that "it was the only election that I was ever in where I got a majority and did not win."[36]

The final witness during the second week of hearings was Representative Bud Herlong Jr. (D-FL), former president of the Florida State League and one of the three congressmen who, along with one senator, had introduced bills to grant baseball legislative exemption from antitrust scrutiny. He called Minor League baseball "not even a business at all" but "a community enterprise," and he explained the precarious finances of Class D baseball. "It costs a Class D team to put a team on the field and operate for a year approximately $40,000," he said. "The average income to a Class D team from its concessions and from the gate receipts amounts to about $30,000 a year. So in the overall picture your teams in Class D will average losing $10,000 a year." He also explained how broadcasting Major League games on radio stations in Minor League cities adversely affected attendance. "The total attendance at the ballpark that year [1949] in Leesburg was 49,958," he said. "In 1950 they started putting these games of the day on the radio and people all afternoon would listen to baseball games. . . . They got a tummyful [*sic*] by night and did not go out to the ball game. . . . In 1950, with a much better ball club, we had an attendance of 30,000." Yet Herlong defended the reserve clause, and he supported congressional action to codify the 1922 Supreme Court decision. He had introduced his bill, he said, because "I do not know what someone else is going to believe because members of the Supreme Court quite often disagree." When Celler asked if "baseball and those interested in baseball are qualified to adopt self-regulatory rules and for that reason you want some degree of exemption from the antitrust laws," Herlong agreed, saying, "That is right. They are qualified to do that, because while they are in a strict sense competitors, at the same time they must cooperate for their mutual good and for the advancement of the game because the public has an interest in it." After Herlong finished, chairman Celler announced, "It is our plan to resume these hearings in the fall after the World Series."[37]

That 1951 World Series, according to Stan Baumgartner, "proved to be an anticlimax." The Yankees defeated the Giants, four games to two, to snare their third consecutive win. As Baumgartner noted, no other team had won more than two Series in a row except for the Yankees themselves, winners of four straight from 1936 through 1939. Overall it was the Yankees' fourteenth Series win in eighteen appearances and their fourth victory over the Giants against only two losses. What tempered Baumgartner's enthusiasm for the Series was that, for the second consecutive year, it followed a National League pennant race that he called "sensational." On August 11 the second-place Giants had lost to the Phillies, while first-place Brooklyn, playing a doubleheader in front of two experimental television cameras that captured these games in color for the first time and broadcast them to some ten thousand viewers, won the first game against the Braves, and took a thirteen-and-a-half-game lead over their crosstown rivals. Even though Boston came back to win the second game, the lead, down to thirteen games, seemed insurmountable, a near-fatal blow being rendered against a hated foe. Yet it proved all too fragile and, in retrospect, illusory. The Dodgers limped home the rest of the way, winning twenty-four games and losing twenty-three, while the Giants won a stunning thirty-seven games, including six of seven against Brooklyn, and lost only seven times. Still, the Giants never occupied first place alone. On the last Friday of the season, September 28, New York was off, and Brooklyn lost to the Phillies, falling into a tie. Both teams won on Saturday, the Giants beating Boston, and the Dodgers shutting out Philadelphia. On Sunday the Giants won again while the Dodgers required an excruciating fourteen innings and a Jackie Robinson home run to set up the improbable: the second playoff in National League history.[38]

The National League had rejected a proposal in 1949 to reduce its playoff format from best-of-three to a single game, and it retained a coin toss to determine which team would open with a game on the road and then play the climactic one or two at home. Dodgers manager Charlie Dressen won the toss and elected to play the first game at home. That gamble failed as the Giants, carried on the momentum they had built during the season's final weeks, won at Ebbets Field, 3–1. The next day at the Polo Grounds the Dodgers turned the tables, 10–0, behind four home runs and a six-hitter from Clem Labine. On October 3 Brooklyn took a 4–2 lead into the bottom of the ninth inning. Starter Don Newcombe gave up singles to Alvin Dark and Don Mueller. Monte Irvin fouled out, and Whitey Lockman doubled Dark home. Dressen replaced Newcombe with Ralph Branca, and Giants third baseman Bobby Thomson hit Branca's second pitch, a high fastball, over the head of Andy Pafko into the lower deck of the left-field stands for a three-run, game-winning, pennant-clinching home run. Baseball had never seen this before, such a stunning end to a stunning pennant race. "The Giants win the pennant!" screamed Russ Hodges, their radio announcer, repeatedly. "There is no way to tell it," wrote Red Smith in the next day's *New York Herald Tribune*. "The art of fiction is dead." And yet, there was still more to the story, hidden, except for rumors, for decades. In 2001 *Wall Street Journal* reporter Joshua Prager finally got those involved in the conspiracy to talk, confirming that, starting on July 20, the Giants employed an elaborate system to steal the catcher's signs and relay to any batter who wanted such assistance information about the next pitch. The club positioned a reserve infielder with a telescope in a window of the center-field clubhouse. A buzzer relayed what the spy saw to the Giants bullpen. From there someone sitting in the bullpen signaled the batter. When Prager published his findings in a book, the headline on the book review in the *New York Times* was "The Giants Steal the Pennant." But on to the World Series they went.[39]

When the Celler subcommittee resumed its hearings on October 15, the testimony was less than compelling. Twenty-four witnesses appeared over eight days, and three others submitted written statements. No one spoke out against the reserve clause, but no one supported legislation to protect baseball's exemption from antitrust scrutiny. Fred Hutchinson, the American League's player representative, called the reserve clause "a necessary and reasonable provision for the preservation of organized baseball." Pee Wee Reese concurred, saying that "without the reserve clause, I do not think that baseball could operate." Phil Wrigley declared that he "would not be in favor of baseball being exempt from the antitrust laws." Some subcommittee members suggested that the bills being considered were too broad to fix whatever legal problems baseball might have. Several witnesses discussed whether baseball was in restraint of trade by restricting Major League status to sixteen clubs in two leagues or by refusing to allow existing clubs to move to the West Coast. Clark Griffith argued that allowing the Pacific Coast League to become a Major League was premature. "In the first place," he said, "they have to have adequate baseball parks. They have to have the populations that would warrant that." Others disagreed, none more creatively than Larry MacPhail. He argued that "if you reduced the farm system to sensible proportions and limited the number of farm clubs any major league organization could have—so that the weak clubs could compete on an equal basis with the rich and the strong clubs—there is no reason at all why you could not have six major leagues." Testifying by letter, Leonard Roach, supervisor of Los Angeles County in California, put things more succinctly. "The issue as I see it," he wrote, "is whether Los Angeles, the third city in the nation, is to become a member of the major-league families, or to be made the victim of this conspiracy between major and minor leagues to keep major-league baseball from Los Angeles."[40]

As the hearings concluded on October 24, Celler offered closing remarks. "The problems before us are complex," he said. "For that reason the subcommittee will not attempt any hurried solution." He announced that the "subcommittee and its staff will make a thorough analysis of our record, and it is expected that early in the next session of Congress we will be able to make public the result of our deliberations." In an editorial the *Sporting News* commended the subcommittee for "conducting the hearing with decorum"—that is, avoiding television—and for allaying the "considerable apprehension" with which baseball approached the hearings. On the contrary, the editors wrote that "one of the most beneficial aspects of the Washington hearings was the light . . . shed upon baseball operations and policies," and they concluded that "baseball cannot help but be the gainer from the better understanding of its problems that the hearings brought to the fans." The subcommittee's report, filed in May 1952, recommended "no legislative action at this time."

More specifically the report came to four conclusions: first, that Congress should not pass legislation condemning the reserve clause; second, that the three bills before the House be reported unfavorably, thus keeping baseball's relationship with antitrust law unchanged; third, that the federal government should not establish an agency to regulate baseball; and fourth, that the legal future of the reserve clause should be left to the courts. The *Sporting News* said that "the committee's basic conclusions . . . should fill every executive . . . with a deep sense of responsibility." On May 28 Frick wrote to Celler to thank him for the subcommittee's efforts. "I would be remiss," he wrote, "if I did not express to you my appreciation of a job well done." He added, "I think you will agree with me that all the men in baseball showed a keen willingness to do anything they could to make a great game an even greater one."[41]

The Celler subcommittee's hearings were not televised, but more and more baseball games were. Red Barber was devoted to the craft of play-by-play on radio, but he was being pulled in other directions. In July 1946 CBS had hired him as its director of sports, a position that combined extensive broadcasting with administrative responsibilities. In addition to handling New York Giants football games, he produced and hosted a children's sports quiz show; college football bowl games; the 1948 Winter Olympics from St. Moritz, Switzerland; and the CBS *College Football Roundup*, which incorporated play-by-play from any number of games across the country. One result of these obligations was that 1947 marked Barber's last season as the full-time radio broadcaster for the Dodgers. In 1948 he hired Ernie Harwell to join him as a Dodgers broadcaster. The club began live broadcasts of all its away games that same year, but Barber did not take his first road trip until July. When Gillette purchased the rights to televise the 1948 World Series, the safety razor company employed Barber as its lead broadcaster. The following year Barber partnered again with Mel Allen to broadcast the Series on radio, and the two would pair once more for the 1951 Series, but this time on television. In 1950 Barber hired Vin Scully to replace Harwell, who left Brooklyn to broadcast Giants games. By that summer turmoil with the Dodgers' ownership structure overshadowed changes in the radio booth. Two Brooklyn businessmen, Andrew Schmitz, an insurance executive, and John Smith, chairman of Pfizer Chemical, had helped Walter O'Malley and Branch Rickey buy the estates of Charles Ebbets and Ed McKeever, but O'Malley and Rickey ceased seeing eye-to-eye. Through a complex negotiation, Rickey left the club. He sold his share of the team to O'Malley, whose control of the Dodgers, plus the election of a new commissioner to replace Chandler, transformed organized baseball in the 1950s.[42]

Twelve

"A Sound If Not Spectacular Choice"

He gave his middle name as Christopher, a saint's name, but Ford Frick's pals in the press box sometimes called him Cuthbert after another saint, a seventh-century Anglo-Saxon monk known for his piety and diligence. Dan Parker of the *New York Daily Mirror* fashioned the nickname, even once reserving a spot in the New York Yankees spring training press box for "F. Cuthbert Frick." Parker was a presence, standing 6 feet 4 inches and weighing 240 pounds, while Frick was more of a drone. The small-town Indiana native was not a great writer, but he did his job quickly. One colleague, Marshall Hunt, remembered that "Frick, with his lightning touch, could bat out an overnight story in eight minutes flat, right there at the ballpark, put it on the wire, and he was through for the day." Another friend, Tommy Holmes of the *Brooklyn Eagle*, credited Frick with "a mind that works with lighting precision. On sports assignments he invariably would be packing up his portable typewriter while the rest of us were struggling to get into the second paragraph." Robert Boyle, who profiled Frick in *Sports Illustrated*, wrote that "by the time most of the writers on the road were climbing out of bed, Frick had already finished breakfast and was busy at the typewriter." Yet Frick was no hermit. Fred Lieb, another sportswriter, remembered that friends called Frick "'the barber.' He always has liked people," Lieb recalled, "felt the good ones far outnumbered the bad ones, and that if you give a person a fair shake, you are likely to get a fair shake in return." Frick came to New York in 1923, when sports writing was in its mythical golden age. Bill Farnsworth, Frick's boss as sports editor of the *New York American*, introduced him to the rest of the fraternity—glittering names like Heywood Broun, Ring Lardner, W. O. McGeehan, Grantland Rice, and Damon Runyon; slightly lesser lights like Frank Graham, John Kieran, Lieb, and Sid Mercer; and the real workhorses, Dan Daniel and Bill Slocum. "I was goggle-eyed and scared to death," Frick said. Graham testified that his friend "never wrote a poor story and, very often, his was the best story in town," but Frick himself demurred. "I was a helluva typist," he said. "Maybe I wasn't a good writer, but I could type."[1]

If Frick the reporter—and later the baseball executive—had any fault, it was that he loved baseball too much. "Indiana youngsters of my generation were born to baseball," he wrote in his memoir, adding, "For us it was baseball by default." This was a boyish attitude, but he carried it with him into maturity. In a 1932 radio commentary he admitted that "all of us, mature and gray and harassed, are only boys grown older." Baseball was his passion, and he its fervent evangelist. As his biographer noted, he even wrote "an article for a music teachers' magazine that emphasized the rhythm and grace of the pickoff and the double play." Growing up in Brimfield, a village in northeast Indiana, Frick and his playmates had two local baseball heroes. One was Ed Morley, "a long-armed, loose-jointed chap, who had a fastball to make opposing batters' eyes pop, and a good curve to go with it." Morley was no more than a semipro pitcher, but he brought home $25 a game plus railroad fare, and "to us youngsters that was the clincher." Besides, he owned the town's print shop and produced its four-page weekly newspaper. "It was in his shop," Frick wrote, "that I first got the smell of printer's ink in my nostrils, and the lure of reporting news in my heart." Brimfield's other baseball god was Burt Inks, who pitched in the National League in the 1890s. He was "big stuff," Frick admitted, even though Inks retired with a losing record. Another early baseball thrill may be apocryphal. Frick recalled a time when the Chicago Cubs came to neighboring Kendallville to play an exhibition game in 1907. Catcher Johnny Kling was one of the last players to saunter toward the ball field. Motioning toward young Ford, he asked, "Hey, kid, want to go to the ball game? Just carry these shoes for me, and when we get to the gate you just walk in with us." The historical record fails to show that such a game took place, but Frick carried the memory with him and was not disappointed, upon meeting his hero in 1937, that Kling did not recall the incident. In 1950, when Frick gave a college commencement address, he called baseball "an integral part of our American life. . . . It has, through the years, been a simple living example of democracy at work. It is as American as the cornfields of Indiana." Six years later, in his introduction to *The Fireside Book of Baseball*, he noted that this anthology collected stories "that held a particular fascination, in many cases, for me. There are some that are about my boyhood heroes."[2]

The Frick family came to the United States from Switzerland and settled in Noble County, Indiana. Jacob Frick, born in 1853, married Emma Jane Prickett in 1875. They had five children: Sophronia, called Frona; Gertrude; Barbara, who died in infancy; Ford; and Clara. Ford's middle name was probably

Christian, in honor of his grandfather, even though he used "Christopher" or just the initial "C" throughout his life. The only boy in the family was a whiz in school. He finished eighth grade early and graduated from high school at fifteen. Following a week-long commencement celebration, he went to Fort Wayne to take typing and stenography classes at the International School of Business and got his first newspaper job at the *Fort Wayne Journal-Gazette*. After a year he enrolled at DePauw University in Greencastle, Indiana, trying out unsuccessfully for the baseball team but occupying several key editorial positions on the school newspaper. He worked his way through school, waiting on tables at his fraternity house. "The only money I had was a five dollar bill my uncle gave me at Christmastime in my sophomore year," he told Boyle. He also wrote freelance stories for newspapers in Indianapolis and Terre Haute and occasionally for the *Chicago Tribune*. After graduation, though, he found a teaching position, not a newspaper job, in Walsenburg, Colorado, about 160 miles south of Denver.[3]

Frick's connection in faraway Walsenburg was school superintendent S. M. Andrews, who had lived with the Frick family when he was principal of the Brimfield school. Arriving in the summer when school was out, Frick played ball for a semipro team. "I was a first baseman but couldn't throw," he later told sportswriter Jerome Holtzman. In the fall he began teaching high school English and journalism, wearing glasses, his sister recalled, to look a bit older. He also roomed with Andrews and met the girl next door, Eleanor Cowling, who in 1916 became his wife. The Fricks moved to Colorado Springs, where Ford taught high school and then business English at Colorado College before leaving the classroom to become sports editor of the *Colorado Springs Gazette*. During the Great War he left the newspaper for a job with the War Department rehabilitating wounded soldiers. After the armistice he went back to journalism with the *Colorado Springs Telegraph* and to teaching, and he opened an advertising agency. His big break came in June 1921, when nearby Pueblo suffered an enormous natural disaster. Heavy rains flooded several creeks that flowed into the Arkansas River. Rushing water surged into the city, collapsing several levees, and many people died. Frick hired an airplane to survey the damage, some of which was caused by a lumber yard fire. His reporting, published over several days, was precise, detailed, and vivid. He avoided the sensational and got his words to press well before reporters for the Denver newspapers and the Associated Press, whose planes erred by landing in Pueblo and getting stuck in the mud. Somehow Frick's enterprise crossed the desk of Arthur Brisbane, managing editor of William Randolph

Hearst's *New York American*. Brisbane invited Frick to New York, offered him a job, and the small-town boy found himself, for the rest of his life, as it turned out, in the big time.[4]

The world of New York journalism in the 1920s was a whirl of excitement, awash with newspapers, magazines, publishers, editors, writers, photographers, and cartoonists, many of whom had come from far away to seek fame and fortune, armed with sketch pads, Graflex View cameras, Corona typewriters, and ready quips. These folks, both in and out of sports, comprised a pretty fast crowd, and Frick made no effort to keep up. His writing lacked staying power, and he consciously adopted a style that placed ballplayers above criticism. Years later, when he had a chance to address a gathering of reporters who covered the Minor Leagues, he advised them to remember that "you are the eyes and ears of the kids who think the game is great and the men playing it are honest. Remember that ridicule, for the sake of a funny line, or comedy at the expense of someone's pride, never paid dividends." Extra money in Frick's pocket came from his arrangement with Christy Walsh, a sports cartoonist turned agent, to become a ghostwriter for Babe Ruth. Walsh, who got into ghostwriting by penning stories about the 1919 Indianapolis 500 under the byline of war hero Eddie Rickenbacker, figured out that he would be better off paying others to do the writing and syndicating the results. He added more players as clients and recruited Slocum and Frick to write for Ruth. The Yankee great reportedly preferred Slocum's work to Frick's, but when Walsh and Ruth decided to produce *Babe Ruth's Own Book of Baseball* in 1928, Frick did most, if not all, of the work, albeit without getting credit on the title page. He had moved, too, from one Hearst paper to another, the *New York Journal*, and from there got his baptism in broadcasting when Hearst purchased a radio station. Frick first went on the air as a last-minute substitute, but his voice, clear and distinctive, brought several offers. The National Broadcasting Company (NBC) paired him with Graham McNamee to announce the 1930 World Series, and this led to a fifteen-minute evening show on WOR and other radio obligations that jammed his daily calendar. In 1931 he was part of an experiment to broadcast New York baseball. Four stations aired a Brooklyn Dodgers game, McNamee on WEAF, Ted Husing on WABC, Sid Loberfeld on WMCA, and Frick on WOR.[5]

Frick kept up a murderous pace for four years, covering the Yankees for the *Journal*, doing a news broadcast at noon, a sports news broadcast at 6 p.m., his own show at 7 p.m., and hosting *Andre Kostelanetz Presents*, a weekly concert of light classical music. He even called his newspaper column "Ford Frick's

Broadcast" and adorned it with a photograph of him talking into a microphone. All this work raised his profile in media-savvy New York, including a friendship with New York Giants manager John McGraw and another job offer. In 1922 the National League had established a "Service Bureau" to handle what Edward Bernays, who invented the phrase, called "public relations," especially requests for information from the press. Cullen Cain, formerly of the *Philadelphia Public Ledger*, founded the bureau, but he left in 1934, after suddenly losing his eyesight. McGraw summoned Frick to an owners' meeting in February, and the league offered him the job. His tenure was brief, less than a year, but in that time he authorized production of the first *National League Green Book*, matching the *American League Red Book*, media handbooks that compiled team directories, rosters, schedules, and a host of statistics and other useful data. John Heydler, National League president on an interim basis in 1909 and continuously since 1918, retired abruptly in December. Several names surfaced as potential replacements, but Heydler, much respected, endorsed Frick, and he was elected unanimously. He became the league's ninth president and, at age thirty-nine, its second youngest, while absorbing the pay cut that came with the job.[6]

Ford Frick had no administrative experience, so he played to his strengths. He vowed to stay close to his newspaper colleagues and cultivated his friendship with Dan Daniel, who could be counted upon to get Frick's point of view into print. He continued to write preseason columns, hosted an annual spring training dinner for club officials and reporters, and often watched games from the press box. He also realized that baseball needed promotion, especially during the Depression. He expanded the Service Bureau and urged clubs that did not already have one to create "information departments" to feed a steady diet of baseball news to journalists and broadcasters. Aware that the league had ignored its fiftieth anniversary in 1926, he was determined to celebrate its sixtieth, asking each club to stage a birthday party paying homage to the league's history. Most prominently, Frick played a key role in the creation of the National Baseball Hall of Fame and Museum. The finding of the Mills Commission that baseball had been invented in Cooperstown, New York, gained traction in 1932, when an old baseball was discovered in a trunk in neighboring Fly Creek. The trunk had belonged to Abner Graves, the man who claimed he had been present when Abner Doubleday laid out the first baseball field in 1839, and the ball found among his possessions was identified, erroneously, as the "Doubleday baseball." John Heydler and others had supported Cooperstown philanthropist Stephen C. Clark's effort to build a museum to celebrate the game's origins, but it was Frick who added the idea of a hall of fame, to honor the game's best players, to the project. One day before meeting Alexander Cleland, Clark's assistant, to discuss how the National League might support the opening of the museum, Frick happened to visit the National Hall of Fame of Great Americans, an outdoor sculpture garden on the Bronx campus of New York University. "I was much impressed," he wrote, even though he doubted the Doubleday story, "and had a notion that a Baseball Hall of Fame would be great for the game." In August 1935 the Baseball Writers' Association of America (BBWAA) agreed that its members could vote to elect members, and, after much complication, the inaugural class of immortals—Ty Cobb, Walter Johnson, Christy Mathewson, Babe Ruth, and Honus Wagner—was announced in February 1936.[7]

Frick's first major test as league president came when he was forced to confront the instability of the Boston franchise, a club that, over more than three decades, had searched in vain for excellence on the field and stability in the front office. By the time Frick got involved in the Braves' plight, the club's financial situation was close to desperate. To raise money club president Emil Fuchs announced a plan late in 1934 to construct a portable track to stage greyhound races at Braves Field after ball games. "It would not interfere with baseball at all," Fuchs said. Frick declared his opposition. He said, "There will be no dog racing in any of our parks so long as baseball is played there." Fuchs then proposed that the Braves lease Fenway Park for their home games, thus no longer playing baseball at Braves Field, which they did not own, but Red Sox owner Tom Yawkey said no. Commissioner Landis did not approve either. In February 1935 the league stepped in, signing an eleven-year lease for Braves Field and turning it over to the Braves, with dog racing specifically prohibited. That bought Fuchs additional time to concoct another scheme. Ruth had turned forty in February, and the New York Yankees had released him. Fuchs saw an opening that he thought would boost attendance. He signed Ruth to a $25,000 contract, hinting that he might manage the team in 1936, but the slugger lasted on the roster only until the beginning of June, hitting his final six home runs as a Brave. By the end of the month Fuchs knew he had to sell. He resigned as president, but finding a buyer proved difficult. In November the league took control of the team and its debts. In December, after some additional squabbles, the league accepted a bid from Bob Quinn in partnership with millionaire Charles Adams, but Adams's ownership of a racetrack rankled Frick, who believed that baseball and gambling should not mix. Thus in 1941 Quinn, representing a large group, acquired Adams's share of the club.[8]

Besides handling Boston's ownership situation, Frick burnished his spurs as league president by handling a number of varied matters well, always keeping in mind his desire to promote the game and make it more attractive to fans. He was a cautious supporter of night baseball, attending the first Major League night game in Cincinnati in 1935 and calling it "swell." He passed his first test as a player disciplinarian early in the same year after Cubs shortstop Billy Jurges tangled with Pittsburgh Pirates base runner Cookie Lavagetto, who thought Jurges had spiked him. Frick fined and suspended Jurges as the instigator, as well as Cubs pitcher Guy Bush, who came out of the dugout to join the fray, but he did not fine Lavagetto. "Frick," wrote the *Sporting News*, "appreciates the fact that a little scrapping now and then helps, rather than hurts, the game, and apparently he acted with that in mind." Frick continued Heydler's prohibition against players' fraternizing on the field, and while he supported his league's umpires, he refused to yield when Dolly Stark, a popular umpire, sat out the 1936 season in a salary dispute. Frick enjoined managers from rushing the field to protest ball-and-strike calls, saying that "fans come to the park to see ball games, not to sit in on stupid, time-consuming arguments at the plate." He also instructed umpires to enforce the balk rule strictly, and when George Barr did so against Dizzy Dean, the St. Louis Cardinals pitcher called Frick and Barr "the two greatest crooks in baseball." That earned Dean a messy suspension that Frick later regretted.[9]

By 1939 feisty play in the league had gotten out of hand, some thought, and Frick reacted. In July Giants first baseman Zeke Bonura chased base runner Leo Durocher into right field after Durocher, Brooklyn's player-manager, stepped on Bonura's foot. A brawl ensued, augmented by fans throwing beer bottles from the stands. A few days later Jurges tangled with umpire George Magerkurth. Both threw punches, and Frick, after imposing heavy fines and suspensions, instructed umpires to clamp down. He also advocated use of early versions of batting helmets and took action against teams whose pitchers threw "beanballs," pitches umpires deemed thrown deliberately at batters' heads. Frick ruled that offending pitchers should be ejected, as they had been in the American League for years, and managers fined. A year later he included "body balls" in the ban after Dodgers pitcher Les Webber, instructed to walk Cardinals star Stan Musial, decided to hit him instead of throwing four balls. Frick guided his league through the uncertainties of each season's schedule during World War II; restrictions on spring training and travel; and dissatisfaction with the balata ball, introduced after the federal government began to ration rubber. As the 1944 season began, he continued to tout the game he loved for its positive effect on wartime morale, referring to "the thousands of men far from home, in camps and on the seas—eager to find out the score, to know who pitched . . . details that bring them a touch of America as they knew it before war entered their lives." Thus after Commissioner Landis died in November, sportswriters advanced Frick's name as his successor because they believed baseball needed an insider to provide continuity as the sport faced the possibility that there would be no 1945 season. John Drebinger pointed to Frick as the favorite in the *New York Times*, and Dan Daniel did much the same in the *Sporting News*. Frick may have harmed his chances when he visited Selective Service officials early in 1945, violating Landis's unwritten policy that executives should not go to Washington except when summoned. In addition, once it became clear that baseball would be allowed to play a fourth wartime season, the urgency to elect an insider diminished, and Senator Happy Chandler's candidacy drew additional support. The search committee also seemed to favor an outsider for the job, and when owners began to vote on the committee's report in April, Frick's name failed to survive the first ballot. Still, the owners tasked Frick with drafting the press release announcing Chandler's election, and they also asked him to help the commissioner-elect understand the job he had just accepted.[10]

Six years later the situation was different. Frick's biographer asserted that the league president played no role in the owners' decision not to renew Chandler's contract and force his resignation before his term was up. Nor did Frick advance his own name as a possible replacement. "I have the best job in the history of the National League," he told a crowd at Toots Shor's New York restaurant, "and I am quite content to stay with it." At least one executive disagreed. Walter O'Malley, fully in control of the Dodgers after buying out Branch Rickey, was beginning to assert himself as one of the game's leaders, and he identified Frick in early July as someone with the qualities needed, "a judicial temperament, administrative ability, an awareness of public relations and a firm belief baseball is the national sport and must be sustained as such." Taken in this context, Frick's appearance on July 31 before Congressman Emanuel Celler's (D-NY) Special Subcommittee on Study of Monopoly Power stood as an audition. Before the first of what would be fourteen congressional appearances he would make over the next fourteen years, Frick exuded confidence, asserting that "a better game will come out of the hearings" and that "the committee will . . . open a new highway for baseball through the years ahead." After reading his opening statement on July 30, 1951, he submitted to hours of questions the following day. Congressman Patrick Hillings (R-CA) pressed him on the absence of Major League teams on the West Coast, and Celler grilled him on the five-year penalties Chandler had imposed on players who had jumped to Jorge Pasquel's Mexican League. Frick parried these questions as well as he could, and when he returned for additional testimony in October, he admitted that "a great deal of good has come from these hearings," adding that "I believe baseball has profited very much from this discussion . . . on things that we can correct probably within our own organization." Arguing the impracticality of expanding the two Major Leagues beyond eight clubs each, he suggested that the Pacific Coast League (PCL) might one day become the foundation of a third Major League, an idea that Vincent X. Flaherty, columnist for the *Los Angeles Examiner*, dismissed as "babble."[11]

By October 1951 Frick had the job he had not sought, commissioner of baseball, bestowed upon him by a process far more protracted than club owners had anticipated. After voting in December 1950 not to extend Chandler's contract, owners appointed a four-man search committee—Lou Perini of the Braves, Ellis Ryan of the Cleveland Indians, Del Webb of the Yankees, and Phil Wrigley of the Cubs, asking them to conclude their work by early February. In the *Sporting News* Edgar G. Brands reported in January that the committee was "finding the task a difficult one" because "few, if any [of the nominees] combine the qualifications necessary." Owners met in March to consider the committee's four finalists: political operative James Farley; Ohio governor Frank Lausche; George Trautman, head of the Minor Leagues; and Chandler, whose supporters pushed his reelection one more time. They voted only on Chandler and again failed to elect him to a second term. The list of candidates ballooned, especially once Chandler agreed to resign. O'Malley grew impatient. He said, "I simply make the point that any organization is going to do its best only when it has the top executive to correlate all its activities. For that reason I call for a commissioner as soon as it is possible to elect one." The Dodgers owner said he did not have a preferred candidate, but, he added, "If Ford Frick were nominated, there is a man whom I certainly would not be opposed to." In August owners cut a list of forty down to eleven and agreed to select a commissioner before the end of the month. Their surprise choice was Major General Rosie O'Donnell, recently returned from Japan, where he commanded the Fifteenth Air Force, but his election was vetoed by President Harry Truman, who insisted that O'Donnell remain on active duty. Finally, on September 20, Frick got the job. Meeting in Chicago, owners went into executive session at 11:35 a.m. They cast sixteen ballots, most of them ending as a standoff between Frick and Warren Giles of the Cincinnati Reds, who eventually withdrew. Frick was elected at 10:18 p.m. "They made a sound if not spectacular choice," wrote Joe Williams in the *New York World–Telegram and Sun*.[12]

Frick signed a seven-year contract at $65,000 per year, and he reacted calmly to his election. "I didn't seek this job," he said, "didn't particularly want it, but now that I have it, I am going to give it the best I have, and I'm going to be the commissioner 24 hours a day." The *Sporting News* outlined the problems facing him: the reserve clause, "which is under pressure from the federal government"; "realignment and expansion of the major leagues because of vast population increases in California and Texas, especially"; "the question of television and radio and its effect on attendance"; and, given the outbreak of hostilities on the Korean peninsula, "the manpower problem caused by Selective Service." In his own press conference Frick said that "the problems will not be too different from those that daily confront a major league president," adding, "I feel I've had a measure of success in the National League job I am giving up. Well, I just used horse sense and managed to get along pretty well with the people in our league." He announced his intention to move the commissioner's office from Cincinnati to New York. He agreed that "the effects of big league [radio and television] broadcasts on minor league attendance are one of the big problems in baseball" but declined to discuss the matter in detail. "Remember," he said, "I'm a new man on this job." Frick expressed "no cause for alarm" about baseball's decrease in attendance since the heady postwar seasons, but he indicated, in answer to a question about the future of the Pacific Coast League, that "nothing stands still, and it is the same with baseball. . . . In the past half-century there have been vast changes in the size and importance of American cities. Changes in the baseball structure are inevitable." Those looking for strong leadership might have been disappointed, though, when Frick announced in December that he would not cast a tie-breaking vote in favor of new regulations if the two leagues disagreed. The issue at hand was a proposal at the winter meetings to cut the size of a Major League roster from twenty-five to twenty-three. The National League voted to approve the reduction, but the American League voted no. Frick cast his vote for the status quo.[13]

President Harry Truman was a baseball fan, and so was Dwight Eisenhower, the Republican who succeeded him in 1953. Six days after the Japanese surrender in 1945 Truman, who had become president upon Franklin Roosevelt's death on April 12, went to Washington's Griffith Stadium to watch the Senators beat the St. Louis Browns, 4–1. Roosevelt had not seen a game since Opening Day in 1941, so Truman's appearance was a sign that peace had returned. The president wore a tan gabardine suit, a brown and green tie, and a new Panama hat. When his black limousine drove through the right-field gate, the navy band played "Hail to the Chief," and the crowd of 20,311 gave him a tumultuous ovation. Truman threw out two first pitches to please the photographers, and he tossed both left-handed, even though he was ambidextrous. Two Senators, Buddy Lewis and George Myatt, snagged them. Truman also signed thirty-one balls throughout the game, acceding to every player's request for his autograph. While in office, Truman saw sixteen games at Griffith Stadium, more than any previous president, and he remained a fan after leaving the White House and returning to his home in Independence, Missouri. Eisenhower had played both high school baseball and football in Abilene, Kansas, and he intended to do the same as a cadet at West Point, but a knee injury suffered in a 1912 football game cut his athletic career short. Ike, as he was called, may have played professional baseball before and during his years at West Point—the evidence is hazy—but he carried his fandom with him throughout his life. Eisenhower attended Opening Day all eight years of his presidency, plus Game One of the 1956 World Series. His decision in 1953 to forego the presidential opener in favor of beginning a golfing vacation in Augusta, Georgia, caused some consternation, but rain postponed the game, and Eisenhower was back in Washington to do the honors when the Senators opened play three days later.[14]

The style of play these presidents and millions of other fans watched in the 1950s was, in the words of Bill James, "perhaps the most one-dimensional, uniform, predictable version of the game which has ever been offered to the public." James wrote that "every team approached the game with the same essential offensive philosophy: get people on base and hit home runs." The National League, which had set a record for home runs in 1950, did so again in 1951, 1953, and 1955. The American League bested its 1950 record in 1956 and 1959. From 1951 through 1960 Eddie Mathews of the Braves hit more home runs (338) than any other National Leaguer, and Mickey Mantle of the Yankees led the American League with 320. Simultaneously, from 1951 through 1960 only four National Leaguers and four American Leaguers batted .350 or better. The number of strikeouts, on the rise since the end of the war, continued to escalate. The National League, having set a record in 1950, topped that mark every year from 1952 through 1960. American Leaguers struck out a record number of times in 1955, 1956, 1957, 1958, and 1959. League leaders sometimes stole fewer than 30 bases. No player stole more bases than the Giants' Willie Mays did when he stole 40 in 1956 until Luis Aparicio of the Chicago White Sox swiped 56 in 1959 and 51 in 1960 and the Dodgers' Maury Wills stole 50, also in 1960. Led by Aparicio, the White Sox were the only team to steal more than 100 bases in a season. They did so four years in a row, 1957 through 1960, and were known as the "Go-Go Sox." The Cardinals stole only 18 bases in 1953, the 1953 Browns only 17, and the 1957 Senators just 13. Every team, according to James, sought big players, put a premium on home runs, and sacrificed speed, defense, and grace.[15]

The players who broke this mold, more than any others, were Mays and Mantle, both rookies in 1951 and both exceptional enough to be short-listed on any reasonable selection of the best players of all time. Many readily echoed Mays's teammate and manager Bill Rigney, who called him "the greatest player I ever saw, bar none." Casey Stengel, Mantle's manager, said simply, "He should lead the league in everything." Mays, born in Westfield, Alabama, in 1931, was the son and grandson of ballplayers locally prominent in the Jim Crow South. He played football and basketball in high school and baseball for local semipro teams, and he joined the Birmingham Black Barons in the Negro American League for three seasons before signing with the Giants in 1950. He integrated the Interstate League with the Trenton (NJ) Giants and spent the early weeks of the 1951 season with the Minneapolis Millers in the American Association before being promoted to the parent club in May, just past his twentieth birthday. After going hitless in his first twelve at bats, he homered off the Braves' Warren Spahn on May 28 and, thanks to the encouragement of manager Leo Durocher, was in center field to stay. Mays led the Giants to the pennant and won the National League Rookie of the Year Award, but he missed most of the 1952 season and all of 1953 in the army. Returning to the Giants, he was quickly recognized as a star among stars. In the 1950s alone he led the league in batting and home runs once, in slugging average three times, and in stolen bases four times. He was named to the All-Star team perennially, won four Gold Glove Awards, and was named Most Valuable Player in 1954. His speed and his defense added to his luster, capped off, perhaps, by his brilliant, over-the-shoulder, back-to-the-plate catch against Vic Wertz of the Indians in Game One of the 1954 World Series.[16]

Mantle, also born in 1931, learned the game from his father, Mutt, who loved baseball so much that he named his first son after Hall of Fame catcher Mickey

Cochrane without realizing that Cochrane's given first name was Gordon. Mantle attracted the attention of Yankees scout Tom Greenwade, who had to wait until the youngster graduated from high school in 1949 before signing him for a $1,100 bonus plus $400 for the rest of the season. Mantle played two seasons in the Minors and enjoyed a September call-up to New York in 1950 before joining the parent club at the start of the 1951 season. Mantle's talent was so prodigious that Stengel anointed him as Joe DiMaggio's successor, but Mantle had trouble adjusting to big league pitching. The Yankees sent him down to the Kansas City Blues in the American Association, where he batted .361 and hit 11 home runs in forty games before coming back to the Yankees in August. Playing next to DiMaggio in Game Two of the 1951 World Series, he injured his knee and missed the rest of the Series. His rise to stardom slowed, but his talent was undeniable, highlighted by several monster home runs, including one in Griffith Stadium in 1953 that traveled an estimated 565 feet. Two years later he hit three homers in the same game, each of them clearing the 461-foot sign and landing in the Yankee Stadium bleachers. Injuries nagged him throughout his career, but during the decade of the 1950s he led the league in home runs four times and slugging average twice. An annual selection to the American League's All-Star team, he won the Most Valuable Player Award in 1956 and 1957 and finished second in the voting in 1960. His best season, 1956, saw him capture the Triple Crown, leading the American League in batting average, home runs, and runs batted in, the first player to do so since Ted Williams in 1942 and 1947.[17]

Both Mays and Mantle were called five-tool players. They could hit for average, hit for power, field, throw, and run, but they were the exception, not the rule. Baseball in the 1950s was sluggish and unimaginative. According to James, "A baseball game was not a clash of opposing philosophies or unlike skills, but rather a simple test of quality, a day-to-day worry about which pitcher had his control and which one would slip a pitch into the wheel-house of the other's behemoth and how many men would be on base." Games also began to take longer to play, with the time of an average nine-inning game increasing from 2:05 in 1946 to 2:34 in 1960. Concern over slow games was not novel, going back at least to 1909, but Dan Daniel raised the issue anew in 1949, asserting that "the customers may start complaining." Ford Frick admitted that "the two-hour contest is pretty much a thing of the past," but he asserted that "the fans have not complained." Pitchers were at fault, some said, as they pointed to "so much three-and-two pitching" and "so many bases on balls." In fact the number of walks in both leagues dropped during the 1950s, but the grumbling continued. In 1950 Indians general manager Hank Greenberg groused that "there's no reason in good sense for an average game lasting more than two hours," but American League president Will Harridge countered that he had "never received a protest from a patron against the length of time it was taking our players to contest championship games." A few years later pace of play replaced time of game as the issue. Harridge changed his mind, and at the 1955 winter meetings American League owners adopted a rule limiting a manager to one visit to the mound per pitcher without removing him. A year later one rules change required that "the pitcher shall deliver the ball to the batter within twenty seconds after he receives the ball," and a second mandated that "the batter shall not leave his position in the batter's box after the pitcher comes to the Set Position, or starts his windup." One National League owner condemned these changes as "ridiculous and silly" while Reds general manager Gabe Paul asked, "If people want a short game, why do they come out to doubleheaders?" A majority of fans responding to a 1957 *Sporting News* poll expressed "no objection to the so-called long game [if] the contest is action-packed and exciting."[18]

One explanation advanced for teams' overreliance on home runs to generate scoring was the condition of the baseball itself, specifically the widespread belief that the ball used in the Major Leagues was a "rabbit ball." In 1947 Edward Hubbert, whose company sewed the covers onto the balls manufactured by Spalding for both Major Leagues, acknowledged that "the 1947 ball is the liveliest in the history of the game," meaning that "any strong young man with a bat in his hand can hit a home run these days." Yet less than a year later a Spalding official contradicted Hubbert by calling his assertion "just a lot of hot air" and adding that there is "nothing to that jackrabbit stuff." Players, managers, and coaches agreed. "The hitters are going for distance now," Pirates coach Bill Burwell said. "They want a home run." Paul concurred, saying, "That rabbit ball? That's a lot of bunk. It's just in the pitching." The experts also debated how to pitch in these offensive times. One theory was speed, more fastballs, especially after Cleveland's Bob Feller was clocked in August 1946 (by new army technology called a lumiline chronograph) throwing 98.6 miles per hour. Many pitchers took the opposite tack, according to National League umpire Beans Reardon, who said in 1947, "I never saw so many knucklers, sliders, spinners, changes of pace, curves, and fast ones in my life." There were other suggestions, too, for easing the pitcher's burden. Years before the 1950 rules revisions Feller had urged standardizing the height and slope of pitching mounds. Burt Shotton, managing the Dodgers in 1947, recommended widening home plate from seventeen to twenty inches. Former Minor League club owner Jack Corbett advocated use of his invention: a convex pitching rubber that would allow pitchers to push off without scratching a hole in the dirt. Former pitcher Bucky Walters, coaching for the Giants, offered a simple remedy. He said, "If they want to do something for the pitchers—and this I think they should do—then let them raise the seams on the ball," making it easier to grip and easier to spin.[19]

Pitchers fought back, of course, using a variety of tactics. In 1946 Daniel reported that an increasing number of pitchers were experimenting with a knuckleball. Throwing at batters to back them away from the plate flared up too. "World War II is over," Oscar Ruhl wrote in the *Sporting News*, "but the baseball war is just starting. . . . Baseball is getting back to the scrappy, fiery days when it caught the imagination of the fans, back to the spirit that built it into a great national pastime." Bean balls, as they were called, became a persistent problem. Wes Ferrell, with a reputation for throwing what pitchers called dust-off pitches, said he would not hit his grandmother, "but I might brush her back a bit with one high and inside." The number of batters hit by pitched balls each season did not come close to the levels endured in the first years of the twentieth century, but totals began to tick upward in the 1950s. League presidents gave their umpires authority to warn offending pitchers and fine them $50, and most players began wearing some form of head protection while batting. Branch Rickey, general manager of the Pirates after leaving the Dodgers, required his players to wear plastic helmets in 1952. The National League mandated either helmets or plastic cap liners in 1957, and the American League followed suit a year later. More radical was the idea that the spitball, banned since 1920, be legalized. Burleigh Grimes, the last of the legal spitball pitchers, urged the rules change to "give the poor pitchers a lift" and "take them out of their misery." The rules committee rejected this plea, even though Ford Frick argued for the spitter as National League president in 1949. He did so again as commissioner in 1955. A *Sporting News* poll of eighty-four players, coaches, and managers endorsed the change too, but members of the rules committee stood firm in opposition. The strike zone also came in for criticism. Some argued that all umpires should be required to define the zone uniformly, while Cubs manager Stan Hack, not alone, pleaded for a larger strike zone because "there are too many singles hitters swinging for home runs." He added, "A pitcher can't afford to throw down the middle. So he's trying to keep the pitch inside the strike zone and at the same time keep it inside or out or high or low, and not many can do that."[20]

When Danny Gardella and his wife returned to the United States after the 1946 Mexican League season that had left him so dissatisfied, he hoped to play ball again, but Commissioner Happy Chandler's five-year ban was still in effect. Gardella hooked on with the Gulf Oilers, a New York semipro team, only to watch helplessly as the Cleveland Buckeyes of the Negro National League canceled a game against them, not wanting to take any risk by playing against a banned player. News of the canceled game reached attorney Frederic Johnson, author of a 1939 law review article questioning whether the reserve clause could withstand serious legal challenge. Gardella and Johnson met, and in September they filed suit in federal court against organized baseball, seeking $100,000 in damages, an amount that would be trebled under antitrust law provisions if they won. As legal preliminaries commenced, Gardella took a job as a hospital orderly, earning $36 a week. Johnson argued before district court judge John Bright that Chandler's suspension had truncated Gardella's career and that the reserve clause he violated when he signed with Jorge Pasquel was an antitrust violation, a conspiracy in restraint of trade and commerce. Baseball officials knew that the Supreme Court had ruled in 1922 that "the exhibition [of baseball], although made for money, would not be called trade or commerce in the commonly accepted use of those words," but they worried that more recent agreements to broadcast games on commercial radio and television might bring that decision under question. Bright died before he could rule on whether Gardella's suit should advance to trial, and his successor, Henry Goddard, dismissed the case in July 1948. He said he did not have authority to overturn Supreme Court precedent, but he noted that the 1922 decision might be reversed on the grounds Johnson had advanced. Baseball's attorneys sought to settle with Johnson, but he demanded $200,000 as he appealed Goddard's ruling to the U.S. Court of Appeals for the Second Circuit. In February 1949 that court reversed Goddard's decision and allowed the suit to proceed to trial. Writing for the 2–1 majority, Judge Jerome Frank said, "We have here a monopoly which, in its effect on ballplayers like the plaintiff, possesses characteristics shockingly repugnant to moral principles that, at least since the War Between the States, have been basic in America, as shown by the Thirteenth Amendment to the Constitution, condemning 'involuntary servitude.'"[21]

Baseball officials acted stunned by Frank's ruling and, using Cold War rhetoric, wrapped their rebuttal in the American flag. Branch Rickey called opponents of the reserve clause persons with "avowed Communist tendencies who deeply resent the continuance of our national pastime." Senator John

Bricker (R-OH), Rickey's close friend, linked baseball to traditional American values "while the marching hordes in China are spreading the doctrine of communism" and called the Gardella case a sword of Damocles hanging over organized baseball. Chandler ridiculed the notion that players were burdened by servitude. "No major league player receives less than $5,000 a year," he said, "and some of them get close to $100,000." Several prominent sportswriters, including Shirley Povich and Dan Daniel, agreed. Yet behind the scenes baseball was worried. In 1946 Chandler had told the owners that the reserve clause could not be used in court as the basis for a restraining order preventing a player from breaking his contract. In January 1949 he offered hope to Mickey Owen that reinstatement from his ban for playing in Mexico was just "around the corner," and in June, amid complicated legal developments in suits brought by other players, he reduced the suspensions of everyone who had jumped to Mexico from five years to three, making them eligible to return to their former teams. Before the trial on the Gardella lawsuit began, Johnson angled for a settlement, realizing that his client could not collect damages since he had made more money in Mexico than he had with the Giants. He had the court order Chandler to give a deposition, and he grilled him. The commissioner argued that his job was to enforce discipline because the players had "joined a group who said they were going to kill baseball in the United States," but Johnson got him to admit that baseball was not in economic distress and that the recent World Series had earned the business $150,000 from radio and an additional $65,000 from the emerging television market. After Chandler's second day of testimony, baseball's lawyers approached Johnson about a deal. Gardella was reluctant, but he agreed to drop his lawsuit in exchange for a cash payment later revealed to be $60,000, half of which went to Johnson, and to have his contract transferred to the Cardinals, whose new owner had helped arrange the settlement. In 1950 Gardella went hitless in one Major League at bat for St. Louis before being sent to the Minors.[22]

Gardella had not won at trial, but the settlement he reached led others to consider filing their own lawsuits. At least three players did so along with a Minor League club owner, all of them claiming that the reserve clause violated federal antitrust law and impinged upon their right to make a living. Jack Corbett had been a Minor League player in Indiana as early as 1904; a manager of the Asheville Tourists, who won the pennant in the North Carolina State League in 1915 with future novelist Thomas Wolfe as their batboy; and an owner of several clubs starting with the Atlanta Crackers in the Southern Association in the 1920s. Corbett moved to California in the late 1930s to become president of the San Diego Padres in the Pacific Coast League, and in 1948 he purchased the El Paso Texans in the Arizona-Texas League. A year later he signed seven players from the Mexican League to contracts with the Texans, only to have National Association head George Trautman nullify them on the grounds that Chandler and Dr. Eduardo Quijano Pitman, Pasquel's successor as league president, had agreed that organized baseball and the Mexican League would henceforth respect each other's contracts. "I had the contracts approved by the minor league office," Corbett told the *Sporting News* when he announced that he would be suing both Chandler and Trautman, "but the rights to the services of the players were denied me. I have sent them a bill for $100,000, which I consider a fair value for the players." Corbett contended that he had signed the players before Chandler and Quijano had made peace. He retained the same attorney who had represented Gardella. "When the suit is filed," he said, "it will be for triple damages, under the antitrust law, so it will be for $300,000." Filed in Cincinnati because that's where the commissioner had his office, Corbett's suit alleged that Chandler had no authority to enter into an agreement with Quijano because such an action, along with the reserve clause, would "monopolize or attempt to monopolize trade or commerce among the several states and with foreign nations" in violation of the Sherman Antitrust Act of 1890, as amended. For good measure Corbett also asserted that the reserve clause was contrary to Article IX, Chapter 55, of the UN charter, "which provides that each United Nation must improve labor conditions and adhere to fundamental freedoms."[23]

Former Major League pitcher Jim Prendergast was the next to sue. He had meandered through the Minors for years after signing a contract in 1934 just after graduating from high school. Drafted by Cincinnati after the 1941 season, he saw his career interrupted by the war. He enlisted in the army, attended Officer Candidate School, was commissioned as a second lieutenant, played some army baseball, and saw combat in France, Austria, and Germany. In 1946 he reported to spring training with the Reds, but they sent him to their top farm club, the Syracuse Chiefs in the International League, where he pitched very well. His record was 17-10 in 1946 and 20-15 in 1947, with twenty-four complete games and 257 innings pitched. After these two promising seasons the Braves purchased his contract, and he made the Major League roster in 1948, appearing in ten games before being sent down to Milwaukee in the American Association on June 30. He stayed with the Brewers for the balance of the season and the first half of the next before trying to restart his career, without much success, back in Syracuse. His record with the Chiefs, over a season and a half, was 13-23 with a 5.50 earned run average. Syracuse sent him a contract for 1951 cutting his monthly pay from $1,100 to $750. Prendergast refused to sign, and the Chiefs traded him down a level to the Beaumont (TX) Roughnecks in the Texas League. Rather than uproot his family for very little money, the pitcher retired and promptly contacted attorney Johnson and his two young associates, William and Michael Kunstler, brothers who later earned celebrity for defending civil-rights and left-wing political activists. The lawsuit they filed on April 30, 1951, in the Northern District Court of New York claimed that the reserve clause had prevented Prendergast from selling his talents elsewhere after the 1946 season and gave him no recourse after Syracuse tried to demote him to Beaumont. Johnson claimed that Prendergast had lost $50,000 in potential earnings, so the suit sought $150,000 in damages.[24]

One day later another former pitcher, George Toolson, filed his own lawsuit in federal district court in Los Angeles, seeking $350,000 in damages. Toolson had played three sports in high school and college and received a $2,500 bonus in 1942, when he signed a contract with the Red Sox, who sent him to Greensboro, North Carolina, in the Piedmont League, where he pitched only sixty-three innings. Promoted to Louisville in the American Association in 1943, Toolson injured his knee and suffered control problems. He joined the Army Air Corps after the season, serving mostly as an athletic trainer playing baseball and basketball at Williams Field in Higley, Arizona. He returned to Louisville after the war and pitched for the Colonels for three seasons before being traded to the Kansas City Blues, the Yankees' farm team in the American Association. Before the season the Yankees transferred him to the Newark Bears in the International League, and in June, to the Oakland Oaks in the Pacific Coast League, but injuries plagued him there, as they had throughout his career. In 1950 the Yankees demoted him to the Binghamton (NY) Triplets in the Eastern League, but Toolson refused to report, and he was put on the ineligible list. While his situation was being determined, he pitched, thanks to a conditional assignment, for the Pacific Coast League's San Francisco Seals, who returned his contract to Binghamton after the season. Toolson consulted attorney Howard Parke, a boyhood friend, and decided to sue the Yankees, challenging the reserve clause and questioning the 1922 Supreme Court decision.[25]

The third player to file a lawsuit aimed at the reserve clause was Minor Leaguer Walter Kowalski, an outfielder with the New Castle (PA) Indians in the Middle Atlantic League. He had signed a contract in the fall of 1942 with the Lockport (NY) White Sox in the PONY League, but faced with the near certainty that he would be drafted, he enlisted in the Army Air Corps in 1943 and missed three baseball seasons. He played for Lockport in 1946 and then had his reserve rights assigned to the Dodgers. They sent him to the Kingston (NY) Dodgers in the North Atlantic League, where he played third base, hit .318, and led the league with 24 triples. Brooklyn promoted him to Class A during the winter but sent him down to Class B, the Asheville Tourists in the Tri-State League. This meant a pay cut that was made worse when Kowalski injured his ankle and was sent to the Trois-Rivières (QC) Royals in the Class C Canadian-American League. Here he led the league in hits and was named an All-Star, good enough to be promoted to Class A for 1949, this time with the Greenville Spinners in the South Atlantic League, but again he failed to make the roster. Sent down to Class B, he hit .280 for the Newport News (VA) Dodgers in the tough Piedmont League, which included twenty-five future Major Leaguers. He began the 1950 season in Class A, was sent down again to Class B, and then had his contract assigned to the Johnstown (PA) Johnnies, a club without a Major League affiliation in the Middle Atlantic League. Kowalski seemed mired in the lowest levels of Brooklyn's large farm system. Moreover, he came to believe that the Dodgers had promoted him to Class A simply to shield him from being selected in the Minor League draft. In the midst of the 1951 season he had Maurice Koodish, one of Corbett's lawyers, file suit for $150,000, asserting that Brooklyn had wronged him and that organized baseball had provided no relief.[26]

In the ensuing months Prendergast's suit made little progress amid a backlog of cases in upstate New York. Toolson's suit came before Judge Ben Harrison, and on November 6, 1951, he ruled, as Judge Goddard had in the Gardella case, that, as a district court judge, he did not have authority to overturn a Supreme Court decision. "I am bound by the decision of the Supreme Court," he wrote. "It is not my function to disregard such a decision because it is old. If the Supreme Court was in error in its former opinion or changed conditions warrant a different approach, it should be the court to correct the error." Corbett's suit and Kowalski's had been consolidated, and in December Judge John Druffel ruled, as Harrison had, that he lacked jurisdiction to reverse the Supreme Court. All three plaintiffs, their suits dismissed without having come to trial, appealed to the appropriate circuit courts of appeals. The Ninth Circuit affirmed Harrison's decision in December 1952, and the Sixth Circuit did the same with Druffel's ruling in February 1953. All three plaintiffs were undeterred and appealed to the Supreme Court, which agreed to hear the cases, bundled together as *Toolson v. New York Yankees*, in October. In three hours of oral argument spread over two days, attorneys for the plaintiffs argued that the 1922 decision should be overturned, while Raymond Jackson, representing organized baseball in the Kowalski and Corbett cases, answered a question from Justice Hugo Black by asserting that "baseball wasn't ruled commerce in 1922 and it isn't now." The court announced its decision on November 9. By a vote of 7–2, the justices agreed with the decisions of the lower courts that dismissed the lawsuits. These judgments were affirmed, said the court, "on the authority of *Federal Baseball Club of Baltimore v. National League of Professional Baseball Clubs* . . . so far as that decision determines that Congress had no intention of including the business of baseball within the scope of the federal antitrust laws." In the months that followed Prendergast's suit and five others, filed after Kowalski began his legal quest, were dismissed on the basis of the court's decision in *Toolson*.[27]

In 1949 all Major League teams except the Pirates televised some, if not all, of their home games. The Browns televised five games that season, the Detroit Tigers thirty, and the Cardinals thirty-five. Every other club save Pittsburgh aired the full slate of seventy-seven home games. No club televised even one road game, and none would do so until 1953. Television, even in its infancy, had begun to influence baseball, both on and off the field, in ways that neither television moguls nor baseball executives could yet imagine. The two businesses were engaged in a courtship propelled by television's need for low-cost programming and baseball's hope for additional revenue impelled by the sport's fear that televising games would affect attendance adversely. As with radio, sponsorships provided the financial cushion to make this relationship work. The simplest arrangement had sponsors paying rights fees to teams and then contracting with television stations to broadcast games, including advertising time—that is, commercials. In 1949 baseball's television sponsors included five breweries, two tobacco companies, two car companies, one gasoline company, and one manufacturer of radios and televisions, Philco. For their money, to give one example, Chesterfield cigarettes, sponsoring the Giants, received the following: six commercials, either thirty or fifty-five seconds long, which aired before the game, after the second, fourth, sixth, and eighth innings, and after the game; short mentions after every half-inning; signage at the ballpark; and an in-game shot of the broadcaster lighting up a Chesterfield. Some sponsors paid to have home runs rebranded as, say, a "Ballantine Blast" after the beer or a "White Owl wallop" after the cigar. By 1950, according to James R. Walker and Robert V. Bellamy Jr., "advertisers were spending more than

$20 million to sponsor baseball on radio and television, much of the money going to television to cover its much higher production costs."[28]

Baseball and television felt compelled to embrace each other right away. As Walker and Bellamy noted, nine of the country's eleven television stations in 1947 broadcast either Major League or Minor League baseball, with two stations showing both American League and National League games. During the summer, baseball telecasts filled nearly half of all television time. Two years later, when only 2.3 percent of American households owned a television set, thirty-one of the seventy-seven stations showed baseball, and over half of those aired Minor League games. Stations craved baseball, and so too did companies that manufactured televisions. They used the sport to push consumers to buy their first set. David Sarnoff, whose company, RCA, produced both radios and televisions and ran NBC, said much later that "we had to have baseball games and if they demanded millions for the rights, we would have had to give it to them." These early stations were independently owned and operated, and they looked to baseball, especially night baseball, to provide programming far less expensive than anything they could have produced themselves. Starting in 1947, though, four companies ABC (American Broadcasting Company), CBS, DuMont, and NBC—strove to transform television into a medium of significance and consequence. They began linking stations across the country into networks and offering them programs designed to be broadcast simultaneously from coast to coast, primarily in the evening. Conflict with baseball was inevitable, and it came quickly. As Walker and Bellamy wrote, "NBC and CBS could not sell a national audience to advertisers when their own stations in New York, the nation's largest market, were carrying the Dodgers (on WNBT) or the Giants (on WCBS) instead of the network's programs." To address this dilemma networks tried to amend their contracts with sponsors by continuing to carry afternoon baseball games and shifting night games to independent stations in the same market. Sponsors objected to this bifurcated arrangement, and within a few years local stations that had joined networks had pretty much abandoned telecasting baseball games. In New York, for example, independent station WPIX, not a network affiliate, claimed in 1953 to be broadcasting "more sports than any other station in the country."[29]

The uneasy relationship between baseball and network television echoed similar discomfort between baseball and network radio. Starting in 1948 Gordon McLendon, a young Yale graduate and navy war veteran, began broadcasting Major League games on a collection of radio stations in the Southwest.

Two years later his buccaneering enterprise, the Liberty Broadcasting System, was showcasing games every day over 250 stations in thirty-three states. Wary of copyright law and organized baseball's displeasure, McLendon did not broadcast games live. Instead he used the practice called "re-creation," incorporating inventive audio techniques originating in a radio studio to simulate the sounds of the game and the ballpark. McLendon argued that when he re-created play-by-play accounts obtained from teletype transmissions or from observers using binoculars on rooftops, he was passing on to listeners information that had already been made public. Baseball took no action against him at first, even though McLendon's business seemed to violate at least the spirit of Rule 1(d), part of the Major–Minor League Agreement adopted in December 1946. It stated that "no major league club shall consent to or authorize a broadcast or telecast (including rebroadcast or network broadcast) of any of its games to be made from a station outside its 'home territory' and within the 'home territory' of any other baseball club." The rule also meant, according to Walker, "that any complaining major or minor league team could tell any other major league team to remove any broadcasts of its games from stations within a fifty-mile radius of the complaining team's home park." Rule 1(d) was intended to give Minor League clubs some protection, but it also attracted attention from the Department of Justice as a restraint of trade. The National Association of Broadcasters also objected, arguing that the rule prohibited stations from giving their listeners the baseball broadcasts they wanted to hear. Liberty Broadcasting continued to grow, and organized baseball came to an uneasy accommodation with McLendon. In 1950, though, Mutual began radio transmission of a "Game of the Day," over 520 stations, which had organized baseball's support, in part because it avoided Sunday games and night games. McLendon lost his chief sponsor, Falstaff Beer, which moved to Mutual, and by 1953 Liberty was out of business.[30]

The first telecast of the World Series in 1947 drew mixed reviews, but R. W. Stewart in the *New York Times* highlighted what would make baseball on television so appealing. "Despite the limitations of the scene reproduced by the electronic cameras," Stewart wrote, "those in the tele-bleachers were getting a more intimate view of the game than those actually in the ballpark." In 1948 Gillette purchased exclusive television rights to the Series for $140,000, according to the *Sporting News*, and worked with Mutual, which had no television network, to cobble together two groups of stations, nineteen in the East to show the games played in Boston and twelve in the Midwest to show the games in Cleveland. Gillette estimated that 93 percent of the televisions within reach of these stations' signals watched some part of the Series. Gillette bought the rights again in 1949, for $200,000, and made the telecasts available to any station connected to AT&T's new coaxial video cables, which spanned the East and the Midwest. Almost every station signed up, even though Gillette refused to pay them for airing the telecasts, which included Gillette commercials. Station managers reasoned that they could not risk offending their viewers by declining to broadcast the Series. In 1950 DuMont and Chevrolet lost a bidding war against Mutual and Gillette that pushed the rights fee for televising the Series to $800,000, with all three networks carrying the telecasts. This unprecedented sum attracted the attention of the leagues' player representatives, Marty Marion of the Cardinals and Detroit's Fred Hutchinson. They wanted a substantial cut of this money, perhaps for the new players' pension plan. After some hesitation Commissioner Chandler met with them on November 8 and offered to allocate the bulk of the rights fees, from both radio and television, to the pension plan. Club owners ratified this deal a week later, but in December, when these same men voted not to renew Chandler's contract, he blamed their decision on the pension deal. As a lame duck, Chandler followed through by signing a six-year contract with Gillette and Mutual for $6 million, most of which went to fund the pension plan.[31]

This deal included not only the World Series, but also the All-Star Game, which, to that point, had not attracted nearly the same interest from television. Chandler's office had contacted NBC about televising the 1948 game in St. Louis, but that network declined because "we have no cable connection with St. Louis as yet." Instead a local station, KSD-TV, produced the first All-Star Game telecast but only for its local audience. NBC again said no in 1949, but CBS paid $25,000 to televise the game, played at Brooklyn's Ebbets Field. Before signing its six-year deal, Gillette bought the rights to the 1950 game in Chicago and contracted with NBC to televise it. Some owners voiced their approval for the big contract Chandler had engineered. Others expressed concern that he had sold the rights to the sport's two premier events at 1950 prices while the number of homes owning televisions was skyrocketing. This criticism was muted, however, since, as sportswriter Dan Parker noted, "it's the ballplayer's money." When the Dodgers and Giants finished tied at the end of the 1951 regular season, a truly national coaxial cable network was in place, making the best-of-three playoff the first games shown on television coast to coast. CBS showed the first game, picking up the feed from WOR-TV, the New York station that showed Dodgers games. NBC showed

Games Two and Three, buying the rights from WPIX, which showed Giants games. NBC partnered with Gillette in 1951 and began televising the World Series exclusively. The following year the only affiliates not connected to the transcontinental transmission were in Brownsville, Texas, and Albuquerque, New Mexico. This measure of stability gave the technology behind the scenes a chance to improve the quality of the broadcasts. Producers and directors experimented with new camera positions and advanced lenses plus on-screen graphics to convey additional information. In 1953 *Variety* called NBC's effort a "workmanlike job."[32]

Televising regular-season games nationally had yet to happen, but in 1953 DuMont executive Thomas McMahon hatched a plan to do just that. Unwilling to attract antitrust scrutiny—sure to come if he dealt with the Majors as one entity—McMahon negotiated with teams individually. His goal was to protect the revenues of those clubs already invested in television and to calm the fears of those who had but dipped their toes into this mighty ocean. He planned to black out games in the home teams' markets, so as not to cut into ticket sales, and to assuage the fears of the Minor Leagues by giving them a share of the financial pie and televising games only on Saturday afternoons, when few Minor League games were played. This "game of the week" concept came to fruition, but DuMont lost out in its execution to ABC, struggling to acquire enough affiliates to remain financially viable. ABC's plan, initiated in 1953, kept games off the air in every Major League city, but only three teams signed up, and only eighteen affiliates, mostly in the South and West, showed the seventeen games available. ABC persevered, bolstered by its decision to sign Dizzy Dean, who had developed a well-earned reputation as baseball's most colorful radio announcer, as one of its broadcasters. In 1955, as a few Americans were beginning to buy new television sets that could receive programs broadcast in color, CBS nudged ABC aside, still negotiating with clubs one by one and still blacking out games in Major League cities and Minor League markets when games were in progress. A year later Dean and his partner, Buddy Blattner, broadcast the home games of seven teams, including all three New York clubs, on 175 stations. In Hawaii, where a live telecast was not possible, films of Saturday's games aired on Sunday afternoons. NBC joined the fray in 1957, signing the Braves, Cubs, Pirates, and Senators and continuing CBS's blackout policy. NBC hired Lindsey Nelson, a veteran broadcaster of college football games, to handle play-by-play and former player and manager Leo Durocher, with enough charisma to counter Dean, as his partner. By 1957, according to Walker and Bellamy, broadcasting was paying baseball $9.3

million per year in rights fees for the World Series, the All-Star Game, two Saturday games of the week, and a plethora of local telecasts. Baseball on television had become a fixture.[33]

Television's revenue potential seduced Major League club owners, but the emergent ubiquity of the television signal gave them what the *Sporting News* called the "video jitters." Philadelphia Phillies president Bob Carpenter believed that television would be "the greatest boost the game ever had." Phil Wrigley thought television would serve baseball as a promotional device once owners grew to accept it. Cardinals co-owner Robert Hannegan agreed, saying, "Television is going to produce tremendous things for baseball." Others were not so sure, according to the *Sporting News*. Sportswriter Tom Meany warned in 1947 that "television does not constitute a problem for baseball yet, but it inevitably will." Dodgers executive Branch Rickey added his own dash of uncertainty. "What to do about television," he mused in 1948, "I do not pretend to know." The fear ensnaring many was that television would torpedo attendance. On this point Meany was in the minority. He argued that "television will not keep the fan out of the ballpark any more than radio broadcasts did." He continued, "It should, as radio did, act as a stimulant to entice the non-fan to lay his dough at the wicket and see a game from the stands." Ed McAuley of the *Cleveland Press* disagreed, saying, "Listening to a game, a man may desire to see it. But seeing it from his easy chair, at no cost and free from parking problems, he might decide that only a darned fool would make the trip to the ballpark." Rickey put the case against television more succinctly. "Radio created a desire to see something," he said in 1953. "Television is giving it to them." Fred Saigh, Hannegan's partner, accepted television as a fait accompli but saw it as a destabilizing economic force that baseball had to contain. "If we must have baseball on television," he said, "then the tie-up must be controlled so that baseball doesn't suffer at the gate by offsetting the loss in attendance by exacting a heavy fee from firms sponsoring TV." Saigh argued that since rights fees helped home teams recoup revenue lost from tickets not sold, some television money should go to visiting clubs, who also took a cut when fans stayed home. "That is a socialistic theory, pure and simple," groused Brooklyn president Walter O'Malley. "All he [Saigh] asks," O'Malley huffed, "is to share in the other fellow's enterprise."[34]

Minor League officials expressed little ambivalence about the perilous effects of television. In 1948, just after the Braves and Red Sox announced their first television packages, Frank Shaughnessy complained on behalf of two International League clubs, the Jersey City Giants and the Newark Bears, both of them overwhelmed by telecasts of New York's three Major League teams. Jersey City, with a population of 360,000, had about six hundred taverns, 90 percent of them newly equipped with televisions and, night after night, showing ball games. Other Minor League cities were similarly burdened, including Baltimore, within fifty miles of Washington, and Milwaukee, barely ninety miles north of Chicago. During the 1948 All-Star break in St. Louis two television committees, composed of Major and Minor League owners, met, but the Minors' plight received "only token consideration." At the 1948 winter meetings the Minors voted unanimously "to ban radio and TV telecasts beyond fifty miles from the station," but the Majors voted this down. A year later the New England League admitted that it had gone out of business because of television, and officials from other leagues considered whether the Minors should simply eliminate all franchises located within fifty miles of any station broadcasting Major League games. The Pacific Coast League raised an additional concern: once coaxial cable reached the West Coast, fans there could watch complete games from the East in the afternoon and "be so surfeited with baseball that they would be unlikely to attend games in their own ballparks" in the evening. PCL president Pants Rowland urged his league's clubs to minimize the number of their own televised games too. Bill Corum of the *New York Journal-American*, a sportswriter and a radio personality, put the matter bluntly, writing that "it is plain as plain can be that the big leagues can't go on eating their own young, the minor leaguers, indefinitely, without serious results to their own digestion." But there seemed to be no workable solution as the Majors netted $2.3 million from local broadcasts in 1950. At that year's winter meetings the Minors again approved a plan to restrict Major League broadcasts, including banning them entirely on any day when a local Minor League team was scheduled to play a home game, but the Majors hardly took this idea seriously. Perhaps out of desperation, the Kansas City Blues announced they would play all their Wednesday, Saturday, and Sunday games in 1951 during the afternoon.[35]

Rule 1(d) of the Major–Minor League Agreement had addressed the concerns of Minor League club owners that broadcasting Major League games on radio or television into Minor League cities and towns would ruin Minor League baseball. As early as 1931 a *Sporting News* editorial noted that the Junior World Series between the International League's Rochester Red Wings and the St. Paul Saints of the American Association was "not as well attended as predictions had been made for it." The culprit, the editorial said, was the

Major League World Series "as the fans of the cities in which the Class AA games were played seemed to get more of a thrill from the radio stories sent out of St. Louis and Philadelphia than they did from their home games." The Department of Justice's investigation of Rule 1(d) did the Minors no favors. Under federal pressure baseball amended the rule in 1949 by reducing the restriction on broadcasts to times when a Minor League game was under way and then dropped the rule entirely in 1951. The Minors, believing that the threat from television was at least as great as that from radio, looked to Congress for relief. Senator Edwin Johnson (D-CO) was not only president of the Western League, but also chair of a subcommittee that considered a bill he introduced in 1953 to allow Minor League clubs to ban broadcasts in their home territories without violating antitrust law—that is, to reinstate the provisions of Rule 1(d) without liability. Ignoring the conflict-of-interest position he occupied, Johnson spoke in favor of this bill as a baseball executive would, saying that "unless Congress comes to our rescue, we are through." Several witnesses, including Ford Frick, George Trautman, and Shaughnessy agreed. Al Haraway, president of the Cotton States League, was even more emphatic. "We've survived for fifty-one years in flood, famine, wars, and even yellow fever epidemics," he said, but television competition in the future might be something else again. Johnson's bill made it out of committee, but with the complications inherent in Congressional business, it died on the Senate floor. Rule 1(d) was never revived.[36]

Commissioner Frick was as befuddled by baseball on television as anyone else in a position of authority or influence. After Saigh renewed his complaint for relief for visiting clubs prior to the 1952 winter meetings, adding to it a suggestion for a one-year moratorium on televised baseball, Frick sympathized and created a joint Major League–Minor League committee, with Shaughnessy as chair, to develop a broadcasting policy. "The committee is to have its findings ready by the time the major leagues hold their joint meeting in Boston on the eve of the All-Star game in July," Frick said. His own position was murky and uncertain. As networks began to negotiate with clubs about televising their home games, Frick stood on the sidelines. "I cannot see how I could become involved," he said before admitting that "I do not know what our policy should be with regard to television." Testifying before the Johnson subcommittee, the commissioner agreed that "the major leagues cannot exist without the minor leagues," but he also said that "we have no objection to television going into towns that want to see baseball where baseball is not being played or where baseball is being played." The Shaughnessy committee commissioned a survey about television's effect on the Minors, but it did not report in July or even at the 1953 winter meetings. Meanwhile, Frick floated a plan to create a "game of the week" broadcast in which all teams would be involved. Estimates forecast $2 million in potential revenues, with half to be shared with the Minors, but the Justice Department objected. In the fall of 1954 Frank Lawrence, owner of the Portsmouth (VA) Merrimacs in the Piedmont League, organized a coalition of Minor League teams to file suit against Frick and the Major League clubs, alleging breach of contract for allowing broadcasts that invaded Minor League territory and arguing for a strict fifty-mile radius on Major League telecasts. Frick explained that such a restriction would violate antitrust laws, but in December he persuaded the Majors to amend agreements with their Minor League clubs, including underwriting most of the costs of Minor League spring training and paying part of Minor League managers' salaries. "This is by far the most important piece of legislation passed at these meetings," Frick said. "It can well be the means of survival for many clubs in lower minor league classifications."[37]

In December 1957 CBS announced that it would augment its Saturday afternoon game of the week with a game each Sunday afternoon. The network signed four American League teams (the Baltimore Orioles, Chicago, Cleveland, and New York) and two National League teams (Cincinnati and Philadelphia) for $100,000 each. Bill MacPhail, CBS's director of sports and the son of baseball executive Larry MacPhail, said that "CBS Television is not granted the right to broadcast the two Games of the Week over any television station in any city where a minor league team is playing an afternoon game, nor over any television station located within fifty miles of any other minor league game." The Sunday package, shown on 103 stations—fewer than Saturday's 159—began on June 1 with the Reds at the Phillies. Buddy Blattner and Dizzy Dean flew from St. Louis to Philadelphia after their Saturday game to do the Sunday broadcast. Early in 1959 NBC responded to the CBS challenge by announcing plans for its own Sunday game. NBC asked viewers to "join us for all fifty games this year," while CBS boasted that fans could "see two games every weekend on the CBS-TV Game of the Week." ABC, out of network baseball since 1954, resurrected its Saturday game of the week in 1960, thus giving viewers in markets not blacked out access to 123 games across three networks. Still the smallest of the three, ABC chose not to compete directly with its rivals. It broadcast its games at 4 p.m. (ET), even showing several games from Kansas City, Philadelphia, and Washington on a tape-delayed basis. After one season ABC gave up on this experiment and sought to attract viewers on late Saturday afternoons with a new program, a ninety-minute magazine-style show called *Wide World of Sports*.[38]

In 1953 one Minor League club owner wailed, "If you think it's rough in Korea, you ought to be in the minor leagues," but Major League club owners refused to acknowledge any responsibility for the harm televised games appeared to be doing to the Minors. Rickey argued that some communities simply weren't big enough or prosperous enough to support Minor League baseball, while Gabe Paul went much further, calling Minor League club owners "just plain lazy." As the decade plodded on, the plight of the Minors seemed only to get worse. Attendance began falling in 1950 to 27.6 million, a drop of more than 7 million from the previous year. Paul Fagan, owner of the PCL's San Francisco Seals, said, "We do feel that major league broadcasts are a very strong factor and especially so when they infringe upon our time limits and place such severe emphasis on the word 'major' in their announcements." The number of leagues declined too, from fifty-eight in 1950 to thirty-eight in 1953 and twenty-two in 1960. Many leagues that went defunct were of recent origin, suggesting that the Minors' postwar expansion had been overly ambitious, but a few had sturdy histories. A 1954 poll of Minor League owners about financial reform revealed wide support for controlling both radio and television broadcasting of Major League games into Minor League territory. Virgil Wacks, president of the Mountain States League, added that "A four-year survey reveals that ninety-nine per cent of fans who listen to games or see them on TV do not go to games the same night, because nobody, nowadays, has room in his system for more than two hours of baseball in a single day." In August 1956 Frick appointed a "save the minors" committee to oversee a $500,000 stabilization fund, aimed primarily at clubs in the lower Minor League classifications. Horace Stoneham conceded that the fund's intention was "to give the minors real professional help," and Bill DeWitt, who administered the fund, said, "Let's get rid of all this negative thinking in baseball. Let's talk about what's right with this game and quit harping on what's wrong." Nearly simultaneously, though, when CBS announced its plan to begin telecasting a Sunday game of the week, Shaughnessy called this a potential "death blow." When his league's owners authorized his use of $350,000 to pursue legal and Congressional action, Frick was sympathetic, saying, "Believe me, if it were up to me, I'd issue an order at once, barring the Sunday telecasts. But my hands are tied." The stabilization fund was replaced in 1959 with the Player Development and Promotion program, nearly $1 million a year to help struggling franchises on a sliding scale: $22,500 for clubs in Class Triple-A down to $3,000 for clubs in Class D. Some leagues scrambled to maintain enough members to continue play, and total Minor League attendance fell to 12,171,848. In July 1959 the PCL's Portland Beavers sued organized baseball for $1.8 million, alleging loss of revenue from the televising of Major League games in Portland. A federal district court judge ruled for baseball, and in September 1960 the U.S. Court of Appeals for the Ninth Circuit upheld the district court's judgment, saying that "if professional baseball is to be brought within the pale of federal antitrust laws, the Congress must do it."[39]

Thirteen

"I Have Long Desired to See California"

Henry Aaron was just a few months past his eighteenth birthday and, in his own words, "was learning more about America." The team for which he was batting cleanup and playing shortstop, the Indianapolis Clowns of the Negro American League, had been on the road for several weeks. They had no home field, in fact, and were no more from Indianapolis than the Harlem Globetrotters basketball team was from Harlem. Aaron had joined the Clowns in Winston-Salem, North Carolina, for what was euphemistically called spring training. "There wasn't much training involved," he recalled, "and the weather in Winston-Salem didn't feel like any spring I'd ever known. The wind ripped across the field without mercy, cutting right through the threadbare shirt I practiced in." To Aaron, "just a nuisance" to his teammates, "a raggedy kid who was in the way," everything was new. He had never been outside the city limits of Mobile, Alabama, without his parents until Ed Scott, the part-time Clowns scout who had been tracking the youngster on the city's sandlots since 1950, put him on a train in March 1952, with Aaron carrying a duffel bag containing two sandwiches, a baseball, and a glove. After a few exhibition games the team opened its meandering season with a long bus trip to Texas and Oklahoma and then came back east through Missouri, Tennessee, North Carolina, South Carolina, and Maryland. The day after a Saturday game at Baltimore's Memorial Stadium, a doubleheader at Griffith Stadium in Washington was rained out. Aaron and his teammates had breakfast in a nearby restaurant, and after they finished eating, they heard the kitchen staff breaking all the plates the Black ballplayers had used. "Here we were in the capital in the land of freedom and equality," Aaron said in his autobiography, "and they had to destroy the plates that had touched the forks that had been in the mouths of black men. If dogs had eaten off those plates, they'd have washed them."[1]

Henry Louis Aaron's life to that point had been constricted by racism. He was born in an area of Mobile called Down the Bay and raised in nearby Toulminville, both segregated by law and custom. His biographer, Howard Bryant, suggested that Aaron probably did not have a substantive conversation with a white person until joining the Boston Braves' farm club in Eau Claire,

Wisconsin, in June 1952. In addition, before he signed with the Clowns, Aaron had barely played organized baseball of any kind. The sport of choice in Toulminville was fast-pitch softball because that was what the recreation department offered. Central High School, which expelled Aaron for chronic truancy, had a softball team, not a baseball team, and so did his new school, the Josephine Allen Institute. It mattered not much. Inspired by seeing Jackie Robinson play an exhibition game in Mobile in 1948 and hearing him give a talk, Aaron dismissed education and set his sights on a baseball career. "It had to work," he said later. "There wasn't anything to fall back on." Scott watched Aaron play for local industrial teams, starting when he was sixteen, but that was enough. The scout contacted Clowns owner Syd Pollock in the fall of 1951 and got Aaron a contract calling for $200 per month. Scott told Aaron, "Treat the Clowns like a minor league club, a stop on your way to the big money—$5,000 a year in the majors." Aaron took the advice to heart. Although he was not much of a fielder, his hitting more than compensated, leading his Clowns teammate Ray Neil to exclaim, "Already in 1952, Hank Aaron was the best hitter I'd ever seen. He had more wrist strength and a quicker bat at age eighteen than most great hitters in their primes." Aaron played just fourteen games for the Clowns, his hitting so spectacular that Pollock appended a note to a letter he wrote to Braves farm director John Mullen, alerting him that "we got an 18-year-old shortstop batting cleanup for us." The word got out. Scouts flocked to Clowns games, but Pollock acted quickly, selling Aaron's contract to the Braves on June 11 for $10,000. At the time the youngster was leading the league in batting, hits, runs, doubles, home runs, runs batted in, and total bases.[2]

Aaron flew to Eau Claire from Chicago, remembering the short trip as "the first flight of my life, and the worst flight." His new team, the Bears, played in a town that was nearly all white, with just seven Blacks among its thirty-five thousand residents. Aaron would be living among whites and playing with and against them, all for the first time. He fought homesickness and loneliness. "I had the feeling that people were watching me," he wrote, "looking at me as though I were some kind of strange creature. . . . There was nothing in my experience that prepared me for white people." On the field, though, he fit in right away, getting two hits in his first game and hitting his first home run about a week later. Good enough to be selected to the league's All-Star team, Aaron batted .336 for the season and won the Northern League's Most Valuable Player award. For 1953 the Braves, having moved to Milwaukee from Boston, promoted him and two other Black players to Jacksonville, just as the South Atlantic League was integrating. "I don't recall ever feeling that our lives were in danger," Aaron wrote, "but we took nothing for granted." It was a rough year, so much of it ruled by Jim Crow, but Aaron responded with perseverance, and he put together a great season, while moving from shortstop to second base. In July the *Sporting News* pegged both Aaron and his double-play partner, Felix Mantilla, as having "a strong chance to make the majors." Aaron's defense was woeful, but at the plate he sparkled. He hit .362 and led the league in batting, runs, hits, and runs batted in, missing out only on the home run title. He was named to the All-Star team and, for the second straight year, earned the Most Valuable Player award. Manager Ben Geraghty did not worry that Aaron led the league's second basemen in errors. "He told some writers," Aaron said, "that I'd make people forget Jackie Robinson." In the off-season Aaron played winter ball in Caguas, Puerto Rico, and moved from shortstop to the outfield.[3]

Looking ahead to the next season, Milwaukee sportswriter Red Thisted wrote that "Aaron is near the top of the list of [manager] Charlie Grimm's prospects for the 1954 Braves, but whether he will make the big team, and at what position, has nearly everyone on a limb." A return to second base got ruled out on the day after Christmas, when the Braves sent six players and $100,000 to the Pittsburgh Pirates for second baseman Danny O'Connell. The Milwaukee outfield seemed crowded too. Billy Bruton was set in center field and Andy Pafko in right, and a trade with the New York Giants brought Bobby Thomson to play left. That left Jim Pendleton and Aaron as reserves, at best. But Pendleton held out for a better contract and showed up at spring training overweight, and Thomson broke his ankle in three places on March 13. Aaron spent his spring crushing the ball, and suddenly he was a starter, even though he had not yet signed a Major League contract. That happened as the Braves traveled north to open the season in Cincinnati. Life for Black ballplayers in the Majors was still far from easy. Hotels and restaurants in several National League cities still discriminated, and some of Aaron's teammates resented his presence on the roster. Postwar Milwaukee, Bryant wrote, was a contradictory city, known, on the one hand, for tolerance and high quality of life but, on the other, as "one of the most severely segregated cities in the country." Looking back, Aaron explained why he believed Black players in the 1950s were so much better than their white counterparts. "It was because we had to be," he wrote. "And we knew we had to be. There was too much at stake for us to screw it up." The 1954 Braves did not live up to predictions that they would win the pennant. They had an up-and-down year and finished in third place, eight games behind the New York Giants. Aaron, too, performed inconsistently. After Grimm moved him to the cleanup spot in the lineup, he responded at one point by getting only 5 hits in 41 at bats. Still, he hit .280 for the year with 13 home runs and 69 runs batted in, numbers that would have been a bit higher had he not broken his ankle on September 5 while sliding into third base after hitting a triple.[4]

The decade during which Henry Aaron became a Major Leaguer has been tagged too often by too many as a time when not much happened. Nothing could be further from the truth. Wedged in between the unspeakable horrors of World War II and the political and cultural upheavals of the 1960s, the 1950s were a time of profound change affecting nearly every aspect of American life, including professional baseball. In 1950 the population of the United States stood at just over 151 million, and the birth rate, long depressed, was rising to levels not seen since the 1920s. The baby boom began, not surprisingly, shortly after the war ended as young married people, many of them veterans, started families. According to historian James T. Patterson, "In May 1946, nine months after V-J Day, births increased from a low in February of 206,387 to 233,452. In June they rose again, to 242,302. By October they numbered 339,499 and were occurring at a record rate." Births in 1946 totaled 3.4 million, a record, but not one that wouldn't be broken. There were 3.8 million births in 1947, 3.9 million in 1952, and more than 4 million in every year from 1954 through 1960 and beyond. As the American population grew, it got younger. Median age dropped from 30.2 years in 1950 to 29.5 years in 1960. Similarly the population under eighteen rose from 31.0 percent in 1950 to 35.7 percent in 1960. Simultaneously Americans were migrating from the East and the Midwest to the South and the Southwest. California's population grew by 48 percent between 1950 and 1960 to 15.8 million. Texas grew by 24 percent to 9.6 million. Growth in Florida and Arizona was even more astounding. Florida's population increased by 78 percent from 1950 to 1960 and Arizona's by 73 percent during the same decade. At the same time the population of eastern states, and especially eastern cities, stagnated or declined. In 1940 the ten most populous cities in the United States included eight of the ten Major League cities. Pittsburgh dropped out of the top ten in 1950, and Boston dropped out in 1960. Moreover, no city hosting Major League baseball in 1950 showed a gain in population ten years later. By contrast the population of metropolitan Atlanta from 1950 to 1960 grew by 51 percent, Los Angeles by 61 percent, Houston by 62 percent, Dallas–Ft. Worth by 67 percent, and Phoenix by 152 percent.[5]

Postwar families, many of whom moved out of cities to the suburbs, created a new, middle-class, American lifestyle fueled by a sturdy belief in the American way of life and a robust faith in the American dream. Compared to previous generations, they earned more, ate and dressed better, got more schooling, and lived more comfortably. Parents faced life optimistically, believing in both science and religion; rejoicing that prayers to combat polio were answered by the Salk vaccine, deemed "safe, effective, and potent" in 1955; and trusting that government would help keep them safe from communism and foster an environment so their children would live even better lives. This lifestyle depended, perhaps too idealistically, on the conformity of the nuclear family, steady fathers, stay-at-home mothers, and college-bound children. It was a lifestyle characterized by a commitment to both public spending for national defense and education and private spending for a wide variety of new consumer goods. The archetypal suburbs in which this lifestyle unfolded were three Levittowns, the first on New York's Long Island, built by the eponymous Levitt and Sons. Their houses were simple: a living room, a kitchen, two bedrooms, and a bathroom, erected on a concrete slab and sold for less than $10,000 with no down payment and no closing costs. Levitt refined the construction process, dividing it into twenty-seven steps, with a different crew assigned to each, so that, at peak, thirty houses a day were completed. Levittown, twenty-five miles east of Manhattan, included 17,400 homes and 82,000 residents, albeit none of them Black. It was at the time the largest housing development constructed by a single builder. Each home sat on a small plot of land where homeowners could grow a lawn, flowers, and trees. The streets were curved and given names ending in "road" or "lane." Levitt also built swimming pools, playgrounds, baseball diamonds, and seven "village greens," common areas for recreation and small retail stores. In addition he sold land at cost for public schools. So popular was this concept that on one day in March 1949, according to urban historian Kenneth T. Jackson, 1,400 contracts were signed, some by families that had been waiting in line four days for the opportunity.[6]

Living in suburbia almost certainly required buying an automobile: drive to work, drive to shop, drive for recreation. A family could shelter their car in a carport or park it in their own garage, often attached to the house, purchase gasoline and maintenance at nearby service stations, buy groceries at convenient supermarkets, and shop for almost everything else at nearby shopping centers (sometimes called "plazas" or "malls"), dozens of stores ringed by ample free parking. Even going to the movies, a staple of Depression-era and wartime recreation, could be done from an automobile parked at an open-air drive-in theater. Many suburban families, living in inexpensive homes financed with affordable mortgages, were able to save money for discretionary purchases, including, in some cases, family travel during the breadwinners' paid vacations. When President Dwight Eisenhower signed the Federal-Aid Highway Act of 1956 into law, construction began on the forty-one-thousand-mile National System of Interstate and Defense Highways, and travel became easier. Families could stay in "cabins," "tourist courts," or increasingly in "motels"; eat lunch at a White Tower, a McDonald's, or some other fast-food outlet; and have dinner at a Howard Johnson's—all reasonably priced. Simultaneously, though, suburban families found it increasingly satisfying to spend leisure time at home, gardening, cooking on a barbecue, visiting with neighbors, playing backyard games, and providing playtime for children. Homes in Levittown were equipped with central heating and a fireplace, and some homeowners were able to install air conditioning, making indoor recreation more comfortable. Families could invite guests for dinner. They could listen to music, play cards and board games, and discuss current events. More and more, though, families found their leisure time focused on watching television.[7]

As baseball attendance, both in the Major Leagues and the Minors, began to recede from the highs of the immediate postwar years, the number of television sets in the United States began to skyrocket. Television manufacturers sold about 7,000 sets before the war, 3.6 million between 1942 and 1949, and 6.1 million in 1950 alone. That number jumped to 10.3 million in 1951, 20.4 million in 1953, 30.7 million in 1955, and 41.9 million in 1958. Baseball officials believed that a fair number of these sets were tuned regularly to Major League games. Thus, as television stations and networks began to broadcast more games, Major League executives blamed their declining attendance on the new medium. Minor League officials echoed this complaint. Yet, according to James R. Walker and Robert V. Bellamy Jr., "There is one serious problem with all the anti-television hysteria of the late 1940s and early 1950s: minimal baseball was on television outside major league markets during the period of most rapid decline." From 1948 to 1952, in fact, the Federal Communications Commission issued no new licenses, and there were only 108 stations on the air. Early research by Jerry Jordan, a college student whose father was executive vice president of a prominent advertising agency, contended that a team's record, more so than television, determined attendance, but Jordan's data were limited and open to interpretation. Moreover, as Walker and Bellamy wrote, "The emergence of television was an easy causal explanation for any positive or negative change in the culture: a convenient 'post hoc ergo propter hoc' rationalization." It took a while for critics to suggest that television itself—and not televised baseball—might be the culprit. John Drebinger explained that "the novelty of the thing, the fact that it offers many other attractions—the Milton Berles, Jimmy Durantes and the like—could also have contributed much to keeping folks at home evenings, when otherwise they could be going out to the ballpark." National League president Warren Giles agreed, saying, "Owners of television sets are not going to turn off their television programs merely because baseball games are not being shown."[8]

As the American population moved south and west, the Pacific Coast League (PCL) pursued its dream of becoming a third Major League. Midway through the 1947 season PCL president Pants Rowland suggested that his league could prepare better for Major League status if it were awarded special consideration and made exempt from the draft for a period of five years. Frank Shaughnessy, president of the rival International League, excoriated this idea, but Bob Cobb, vice president of the PCL's Hollywood Stars, said, "There is no way we can build up to major league caliber if the majors are permitted to come out here each year and take the cream of the players we develop." Rowland took his proposal to the Minor Leagues' 1947 winter meetings. He said that the PCL would change its name to the Pacific Major League (PML) and occupy a position below the Majors but above Class Triple-A. Its clubs would not draft any players from the two other Class Triple-A leagues and would pay enhanced prices for players drafted from lower classifications. In exchange PML players would be protected from the Major League draft until they had accumulated six years of service time instead of the standard four. Even before the winter meetings convened, Frank Lane, president of the American Association, the third Class Triple-A league, expressed his opposition, and Rowland's idea failed to garner approval from the required three-fourths of the Minor Leagues. The Majors turned it down as well, despite Rowland's warning. "I do know that the Pacific Coast League should be a major league right now," he said, "but if it isn't so recognized, a lot of kibitzers who think there's going to be an invasion of Los Angeles and San Francisco [by the Majors] may as well mute their trumpets."[9]

The Majors released a statement in response, saying that "at present there appears to be no minor league which is entitled to major league classification" but added that "the major leagues further believe that minor leagues or clubs applying for major league classification must assume responsibility for any necessary adjustments of territorial rights of others, must have adequate population, income and park facilities and must establish that operation once the major league status requested is practical and justified." This convoluted language was not directed just at the PCL. It was also designed to dissuade existing Major League clubs from moving west, and it worked, at least for a while. In July 1948 Edwin Pauley, a wealthy oilman, gave up his quest to buy the St. Louis Browns and move them to Los Angeles. He calculated that he would have to spend $2.75 million for the Browns, $2.5 million to displace the Minor League Angels, and $500,000 to each of the other seven PCL owners. "I wouldn't want to buy the Browns or any other club for $8,750,000," he said. The Majors' impediment, though, did not prevent Rowland from asking again for special draft privileges in December 1948. When the Majors again said no, Edgar G. Brands wrote that "the death knell for aspirations of the Pacific Coast League to major league recognition was sounded." Still, there was a chance that someone would try to do what Pauley had not or that one of the existing Major Leagues might expand and pick off one or more PCL cities. Commissioner Happy Chandler had hinted at this possibility in 1947, eyeing Hollywood, Los Angeles, Oakland, and San Francisco, but while the National League voiced its approval, the American League did not. Chandler fleshed out his idea later, suggesting two ten-team leagues to "see if it works," and then two twelve-team leagues that would eventually be split into three eight-team leagues. Hearing this, Paul Fagan of the San Francisco Seals advanced the radical idea that the PCL should kiss organized baseball good-bye, withdraw from the National Association, and become an "outlaw" league, but other owners, afraid of the consequences, declined to go along.[10]

There things stood until the summer of 1951, when the House Judiciary Committee's Subcommittee on Study of Monopoly Power began its hearings on organized baseball, including its reluctance to move the Major League game west, and heard testimony from National League president Ford Frick. He acknowledged in his opening statement that "the time is coming, in the foreseeable future, when cities like those on the Pacific coast or in other sections of the country will be able to have major league baseball if they so desire," and he testified that elevating an entire league would be less disruptive than selecting one or two existing clubs for promotion or moving existing clubs to the West Coast. But when questioned by Congressman Patrick Hillings (R-CA), representing part of Los Angeles County, Frick was less clear on how establishing a third Major League might be accomplished. "I do not believe," he said, "that a major league can spring up overnight. I do not believe that the mere labeling of a league with the name 'major league' per se makes it a major league in its performance, in its actions, and everything else." When Frick mentioned population and distance as two impediments to change, Hillings countered, asking Frick if "you are not just using this particular theory of yours, that a third major league would be much more desirable than to transfer some franchises from a few cities out there, as an excuse to prevent the expansion of major league baseball to the west coast?" A week later the subcommittee heard from Damon Miller, secretary and business manager of the Seals. He admitted that "our own league was never too definite on just exactly what they wanted. They [the owners] have all wanted something but some of us wanted a little more than some of the other clubs." But he insisted that "the San Francisco club would not be satisfied with anything less than a complete elimination of the draft and a complete elimination of the minor-league designation."[11]

Before the subcommittee's second round of hearings in October, the PCL voted unanimously to withdraw from the National Association unless it received draft exemption. Al Wolf of the *Los Angeles Times* understood that this ultimatum posed a serious risk to both the Majors and the PCL, where attendance had begun to fall, but Frick, by then baseball's new commissioner, defused the situation by announcing the creation of the "Open classification," above Class Triple-A, and a pathway for an Open league to become a Major League. Qualifications to reach the Open classification were substantial, including agreement from at least six of eight club owners, financial stability, removal of salary limits, average annual total attendance of 2.25 million for five consecutive seasons, aggregate population of 10 million, and combined park capacity of 120,000. In return clubs in an Open league would receive several benefits. Their players would be exempt from the draft until they accrued five years of service, they would draft from lower classifications right after the Majors, and they would have first call on drafted players returned from the Majors. In November Frick disclosed how an Open league could advance to the Majors. All eight clubs would have to apply together. Aggregate population for the league's cities would have to exceed 15 million, and every ballpark would need a seating capacity of at least 25,000. In addition average attendance would have to be more than 3.5 million for the three years preceding application. The league would have to play a 154-game schedule, accept all the agreements binding the Majors to the Minors, adopt the uniform Major League players' contract—that is, the reserve clause—and join the players' pension plan. The PCL met these benchmarks in most ways but fell short on attendance. Fagan had a solution: retain good players, pay higher salaries, expand and improve ballparks, and draw larger crowds. It didn't work. Fagan could not push the PCL to spend enough to attract sufficient fans to meet the attendance standard. Other owners were far less willing to invest as heavily as Fagan proposed, and in 1953, his cash depleted, Fagan put the Seals up for sale. The PCL became an Open league without him, but its dream to become a Major League faded away.[12]

Braves president Lou Perini owned one of baseball's oldest franchises, but even he had begun talking about expansion. In 1948 Perini spoke to the Milwaukee Athletic Club as president of the American Association's Milwaukee Brewers, a team the Braves had bought in 1946 "because we were in desperate need of a farm club." In his speech he predicted that "Milwaukee will be in a major league within five years." He surmised that the Major Leagues would react to the entreaties of the Pacific Coast League by expanding to two twelve-team leagues. "San Francisco and Los Angeles are ready for big league baseball, and Oakland and Hollywood will be taken in, too, because of the natural rivalry," but he added, "we can't run [a league] with ten teams." Perini told his audience that "Milwaukee will be the first after the Coast cities," and he identified Montreal, Baltimore, and Houston as the three cities that would likely complete the new alignment. Later in the year he formalized this proposal, saying it "would make the majors truly national in scope." Perini suggested, too, that part of the deal would require the three Class Triple-A leagues to consolidate into two. "It's not a fair deal," he admitted, "but should we penalize the fans of San Francisco and Los Angeles by preventing them from seeing major league baseball?" Three years later, responding to a comment by Chicago Cubs owner Phil Wrigley that "the entire map of Organized Ball should be reorganized so that baseball can keep pace with the growth of the nation," Perini reiterated his grand scheme. "Now—not when world conditions are settled, but NOW—is the time," he said, calling again for two twelve-team leagues, a revamping of the Class Triple-A alignments, and an examination of "whether it is timely to include clubs in such neighboring countries as Canada, Cuba, and Mexico." Facing the transportation problem inherent in expansion, Perini said simply, "Airplanes annihilate space."[13]

Perini first voiced these thoughts as his team was on the upswing. Since he and his two partners, Guido Rugo and Joe Maney, had bought out the club's other stockholders in 1944, the Braves had become a better team after decades of ineptitude. Commencing a spending spree that paid dividends, the Braves lured Billy Southworth away from a short retirement, signing him to manage with a three-year contract worth about $100,000. They bulked up their scouting staff and added eleven farm clubs in 1946 and two more in 1947. They refurbished Braves Field, installed lights, and designed special "sateen" uniforms for players to wear during night games. Over a short period of time in 1946 Perini engineered twelve deals, remaking the roster. That season began inauspiciously. New green paint on grandstand seats had not dried by Opening Day, and about five thousand fans left Braves Field with damaged clothing. The club promised them reimbursement, but it took all season to wade through some thirteen thousand claims, many bogus, and cover nearly $6,000 in cleaning bills. Red Sox owner Tom Yawkey lent the Braves Fenway Park until the paint dried, and the team, beset by injuries, finished fourth, over .500 for the first time since 1938 and in the first division for the first time since 1934. In 1947 a much healthier roster finished third, led offensively by third baseman Bob Elliott and right fielder Tommy Holmes and on the mound by right-hander Johnny Sain and left-hander Warren Spahn. During the off-season Boston bolstered its roster by acquiring two veterans, outfielder Jeff Heath from the Browns and second baseman Eddie Stanky from the Brooklyn Dodgers, the latter tasked with mentoring young shortstop Alvin Dark. Southworth signed a five-year contract extension worth $250,000 and did his best juggling an assemblage of journeymen and youngsters. The starting rotation was a bit thin, prompting *Boston Post* sports editor Gerry Hern to pen a short piece of doggerel that has been remembered as "Spahn and Sain, and pray for rain." Spahn won only fifteen games, but Sain led the league with twenty-four wins. The Braves won the pennant, their first since 1914. And yet a double anticlimax followed. The Braves anticipated an unprecedented matchup against the crosstown Red Sox, but they finished in a tie with the Cleveland Indians and lost the one-game playoff, 8–3. The World Series was a disappointment too, the Indians beating Boston, four games to two.[14]

The Braves fell as quickly as they had risen. The decline may have begun with Southworth, who battled alcohol and whose brusque managerial style alienated his players. One coach quit over the winter, and spring training in 1949 was rife with disruptions. Sain stopped talking to his manager, and Spahn asked to be traded. Southworth came close to blows with a radio announcer and a player he might have asked to spy on his teammates. Many older Braves, especially the war veterans, were upset that the club signed bonus pitcher Johnny Antonelli for far more money than they were making. Southworth tangled with Perini during a telephone call, and on August 16 the club announced that it had granted the manager a leave of absence for the rest of the season. Coach Johnny Cooney took over. The Braves limped home in fourth place, and the players voted Southworth only a one-quarter share of the World Series money that went to each league's top four finishers. The next two seasons were no better. Southworth returned to the helm but lasted only a season and a half. Perini broke up his club by trading Stanky and Dark to the Giants in December 1949, sending Sain to the New York Yankees in August 1951 for a young pitcher named Lew Burdette and $50,000, and shipping Elliott to the Giants before the start of the next season. Holmes, who replaced Southworth in June 1951, proved bereft of managerial talent, and Charlie Grimm, Milwaukee's manager, replaced him midway in 1952. That year the Braves finished seventh, thirty-two games out of first place. Moreover, attendance had plummeted. Even in 1948 the Braves did not outdraw the Red Sox, and the decline after that was precipitous, down to 1,081,795 in 1949, 944,391 in 1950, 487,475 in 1951, and an alarming 281,278 in 1952. Perini and his two brothers now owned all the club's stock, and they lost more than $1 million over three seasons. These years of decline gave them plenty of time to ponder whether Boston was still a city large enough to support two Major League teams.[15]

Even before Perini whetted Milwaukee's appetite for a Major League club, rumors floated throughout the baseball world that other franchises might be on the move and that the future of the sport's multi-team cities might be in doubt. In 1947 the *Sporting News* reported that real estate developer Robert Rodenberg, owner of the Baltimore Colts in the All-America Football Conference, was interested in buying the Browns and moving them to Baltimore. Other groups from other cities, including Los Angeles, were similarly interested, but when Richard Muckerman sold the Browns to the DeWitt brothers, the club stayed put. Phil Wrigley thought that Los Angeles was not yet ready for a Major League club because "the city lacks a first class public transportation system," but he admitted that "if I had to choose between selling the Chicago and Los Angeles franchises, I would sell the Chicago Cubs. Los Angeles, I believe, has a greater future." The Milwaukee County Board of Supervisors authorized building a new ballpark good enough to attract a Major League club in 1947, and voters approved bond issues to fund construction in 1950. Perini intended to have the Minor League Brewers move into this new County Stadium, but after the 1952 season he gave Boston a subtle ultimatum. "I have no plans to move the Braves," he said, "but I wouldn't be so stubborn as to go along this way for ten years." Milwaukee was aflame with Major League fever and chose not to wait. A statewide campaign began to buy the Brewers from Perini and move them out of the way to Toledo, Ohio. Politicians demanded that the county rescind Perini's lease and search for another Major League club, and the city cheered when the Browns' newest owner offered Perini $750,000 to allow the St. Louis club to move to Milwaukee. Perini turned the offer down, but he was spooked again when Milwaukee offered the Cardinals $4 million to come north. National League owners certainly did not want to abandon St. Louis, so they urged Perini to act quickly. He did. On March 18, 1953, with spring training already underway, the Boston Braves became the Milwaukee Braves, consummating baseball's first franchise shift since 1903.[16]

The terms under which Bill and Charlie DeWitt bought the Browns in 1949 presaged the club's continued financial instability. Heavily in debt from the purchase, the brothers disposed of players to acquire cash. Richard Muckerman had sold his top farm club to the Detroit Tigers, and the DeWitts followed this path, reducing the St. Louis farm system from twenty clubs to eleven. The brothers also pursued legal action, unsuccessfully, to try to evict the Cardinals, their tenants, from Sportsman's Park, claiming that the intricacies of the Cardinals' sale from Sam Breadon to Fred Saigh and Robert Hannegan in 1947 had violated the terms of their lease. On the field the postwar Browns returned to their traditional place at or near the bottom of the standings. After winning their only pennant in 1944 and finishing third in 1945, they dropped to seventh in 1946 and eighth in 1947. In the DeWitts' two seasons as owners the Browns won fifty-three games in 1949 and fifty-eight in 1950, good for seventh place each time. The owners even employed a hypnotist, Dr. David Tracy, to improve performance, without much success. Just after his hiring the Browns lost two games, 20–4 and 29–4. The roster was not completely bereft of good players. Pitcher Ned Garver won twelve games in 1949 and thirteen in 1950. Third baseman Bob Dillinger batted .324 in 1949 and led the league with 20 stolen bases for the third year in a row. Roy Sievers batted .306 in 1949 and won the Rookie of the Year Award. Home attendance lagged far behind every other American League club, falling to 270,936 in 1949 and even less in 1950. As one season rolled into the next, the DeWitts' investment looked increasingly less rosy.[17]

Waiting in the wings was Bill Veeck. Out of baseball reluctantly since selling the Indians in November 1949 as part of a divorce settlement, he wanted back in. In May 1951 one of his friends was in St. Louis, and he learned from Saigh that the DeWitts were financially strapped and might be getting ready to sell. Hearing this news, Veeck got to work, putting together a group to take an option on buying the Browns. The DeWitts owned 58 percent of the club, but Veeck insisted that he be able to buy at least 75 percent to take advantage of special tax breaks. He approached 1,400 individual Browns stockholders but struggled to get what he needed until one board member sold him 8,572 shares. The deal was announced in early July, and the next day Veeck watched his new team lose both ends of a doubleheader to the Indians. Veeck was a true fan, a skilled baseball executive, and an innovative marketer without peer, but the challenge the Browns presented proved beyond his flair. The promotions, designed to attract a crowd, win or lose, began right away. Veeck gave every fan a free beer or soft drink one night and set off fireworks after the game. He gave women free orchids, as he once had in Cleveland. He started a pregame radio show allowing fans to call in with questions and comments. On August 19 he staged his most famous stunt, having 3-foot-7-inch Eddie Gaedel lead off in the bottom of the first inning in the second game of a doubleheader celebrating the fiftieth anniversary of the American League. Gaedel's appearance was legal—Veeck had signed him to a contract and added him to the roster—but league president Will Harridge was livid, and his anger was shared by other club owners, who accused Veeck of making a travesty of the game and their business. Still, five days later it was "Grandstand Managers Day" at Sportsman's Park. Fans coming through the gates were given a placard with a green "yes" on one side and a red "no" on the other so that they could vote and help manager Zack Taylor make decisions during the game. Attendance picked up during the second half of the season, but the Browns fell back into eighth place, forty-six games behind the pennant-winning Yankees.[18]

The next two seasons were no better. Veeck's biographer wrote that his goal was to drive the Cardinals out of town, but he hardly had the resources to do that. His ownership group was undercapitalized, and the contract he signed with Falstaff Beer to broadcast games paid the Browns on a sliding scale: $250,000 for winning the pennant down to $1 for finishing seventh or eighth. Veeck tried to get under Saigh's skin. He challenged the third-place Cardinals to a postseason game for charity that Saigh nixed, and he signed a bunch of ex-Cardinals: Rogers Hornsby as manager, Marty Marion as a player-coach, Harry Brecheen as a pitcher-coach, and Dizzy Dean as a broadcaster. Hornsby antagonized his players and proved to be a disaster, but Marion's record after he replaced Hornsby was even worse. After the 1952 season Veeck went to the winter meetings determined to upset the apple cart even more. He proposed that Major League clubs be prohibited from signing any player lacking previous professional experience and that every Minor League player be eligible for the draft after only one year of service. Both ideas seemed to target the very successful Yankees, and both died an angry death. And when American League owners approved a two-year deal guaranteeing visiting teams a modest share of television revenue, Veeck balked unless the visitor's share was raised to 50 percent. The Yankees took umbrage again, and Veeck lost again. Defeated, he rebelled—and sacrificed revenue—by refusing to allow any Browns road game to be televised by the home team. The Yankees retaliated by refusing Veeck permission to televise any of their games with the Browns, and they got the Indians and Red Sox to do so too. In January 1953 Saigh pleaded no contest to income tax evasion and was sentenced to fifteen months in prison. Looking for financial relief, he received bids for the Cardinals from two groups interested in moving the club to Houston, and he found a coterie of Milwaukee businessmen willing to move them there. Saigh wanted St. Louis to remain a National League city, and he yielded to league pressure to sell the club to the Anheuser-Busch brewery. Veeck now knew he could no longer compete, but he had alienated so many other American League owners with his demeanor and his behavior that his newest idea—to move the Browns—was met with stony opposition.[19]

Perini shut Veeck out of his first choice, Milwaukee, but Veeck had already been talking to parties in Baltimore, including Mayor Thomas D'Alesandro Jr., who wanted people to call Baltimore a Major League city; Jack Dunn III, owner of the International League's Orioles; and attorney Clarence Miles, who had little interest in baseball but believed that a Major League club would benefit the city. Miles organized a group that agreed to buy a 20 percent share of the Browns, and Veeck pledged to raise additional capital by selling stock to the public. National Brewing Company offered $300,000 to broadcast the team's games and an additional $350,000 to compensate Washington Senators owner Clark Griffith for loss of television revenue with a new team just forty miles away. But opposition to the proposed move built too. St. Louis mayor Joseph Darst threatened a lawsuit, and George Trautman, head of the Minor Leagues, argued that a move so close to Opening Day would disrupt the International League's schedule. Philadelphia Phillies president Bob Carpenter called Veeck's plan "asinine," and the Yankees said they would support it only if "certain conditions were met" but declined to say what those might be. When Veeck and D'Alesandro presented their plan to league owners on March 16, 1953, they were turned down with only one other club, the Chicago White Sox, supporting them. Veeck was stunned. "It would have been a good move financially," he said. Owners questioned the financial details, feared lawsuits, and worried about the schedule. Harridge blamed the rejection on the lack of time before Opening Day, but *New York Times* sportswriter Arthur Daley called the opposition "a disgraceful demonstration of spite and malice," designed "to impoverish him and drive the nettlesome Veeck from the game."[20]

Veeck's situation in St. Louis became more precarious. In April 1953 he sold Sportsman's Park to the Cardinals for $800,000 plus an extra $300,000 for moving expenses since the Veeck family had been living in the ballpark. The Browns began the season with a rebuilt roster and a hint of optimism, but by July they had settled in seventh place. At one point they lost twenty home games in a row, a Major League record. Fans fully grasped the despair of the team's lame-duck position and quit buying tickets. When rookie Bobo Holloman pitched a no-hitter in his first Major League start on May 6, just 2,473 fans were there to see it. The sparse crowds became legendary, as did Veeck's quips about his predicament. "It's a good thing I brought my car," he said one night. "I can drive all these folks home after the game." More seriously, the feud between Veeck and the Yankees spilled out onto the field on April 28. The teams brawled after a hard slide into second base. Six players were subsequently fined, and Yankees co-owner Del Webb hardened his resolve to get Veeck out of the league, at one time suggesting that new ownership should move the franchise to Kansas City or Los Angeles. Miles firmed up his group's financial commitment, but at a September owners meeting when Veeck and Mayor D'Alesandro again asked permission to move the Browns, again they lost. Webb exited the meeting grinning. D'Alesandro was crushed, but within a day he had worked out a deal with the league. The Browns would move to Baltimore, but they would do so without their iconoclastic owner. The league gave the Miles group forty-eight hours to find enough money to buy out Veeck, and they did so. When they agreed to acquire the Minor League Orioles for $350,000 and to compensate the International League with a $48,749 indemnity, the American League approved the deal unanimously, brushing aside a last-minute offer from a Los Angeles group that included Webb and aircraft manufacturer Howard Hughes. The Browns played their last home game on September 27, losing, 2–1, in twelve innings to the White Sox. First baseman Ed Mickelson drove in the Browns' only run, and the game came to an end with the teams using discolored baseballs, the supply of new balls having been exhausted. Veeck left baseball again, but despite all his operating losses, he received $12 for every share for which he had paid $7 and thus cleared a 38 percent profit.[21]

Away from his office in Shibe Park, Connie Mack, president, treasurer, and manager of the Philadelphia Athletics, had to deal with two families. They did not get along. He and his first wife, Margaret, had two sons, Roy and Earle, and a daughter, Marguerite. Mack and his second wife, Katherine, had four daughters and one son, Connie Jr. It was the elder Mack's desire to have all three sons succeed him in running the A's, but the path to do so was complicated. Following the deaths of original co-owner Ben Shibe's two sons, Tom in 1936 and Jack a few months later, Mack, who had been treasurer since 1901 and held 50 percent of the club's 1,500 shares, bought 141 shares from Jack's estate and became president too. After the war he decided to bring his sons into the business. Roy, the eldest, became secretary; Connie Jr. was named assistant treasurer; and Earle, already a coach, was appointed assistant manager. Mack also began dispersing his shares among his wife and his sons but not his daughters. Roy, Earle, and Connie Jr. each got 163 shares, and Katherine got 100, with Mack retaining 302 shares for himself. Katherine objected so strenuously on behalf of their four daughters that she and her husband separated for a time. There were Shibe heirs, too, who owned 609 shares, just over 40 percent of the club. In various disputes they sided with Connie Jr. and his mother and voted their 872 shares together. After the 1949 season this alliance exerted its muscle and ousted two longtime coaches over the senior Mack's objection. In May 1950 the Shibe-Mack group relieved Earle as assistant manager and gave his job to former player Jimmy Dykes. The battle continued. In August Earle and Roy bought out Katherine, Connie Jr., and the several Shibe heirs. This stock, according to Mack's biographer, "went into the treasury" so that Connie Sr., Roy, and Earle owned all the active shares and had complete control of the club. Privately the sons urged their father to retire as manager, and when he did, they named Dykes manager for 1951. Connie Sr. remained president in name, Roy became executive vice president-treasurer, and Earle vice president–secretary.[22]

Like the DeWitt brothers and Veeck, the Mack brothers did not have enough money to run a Major League club. To finance their purchase of the stock held by the Shibe-Mack coalition, they took a $1.75 million loan from Connecticut General Life Insurance and secured the loan with a mortgage on Shibe Park. Both baseball and insurance executives wondered about this deal, but the Philadelphia banker who put it together thought that club revenues were sufficient to make it work. Besides selling tickets to their own games, the A's had two tenants. The Phillies paid them somewhere between $75,000 and $120,000 a season in the postwar years, and the Philadelphia Eagles professional football team paid them roughly $50,000–$80,000 per year. Shibe Park concessions, run by Jacobs Brothers Penn Sportservice during the games of all three teams, brought the A's about $200,000 a year. In addition the A's and the Phillies sold their radio and television rights as a package, splitting about $450,000, and the A's in 1954 made another $100,000 from national telecasts. Club profits for the years 1947–49 totaled $450,000. In 1950 the Macks spent $300,000 to improve the ballpark, including putting in new box seats, and $100,000 on a new electrical plant. The brothers pared the farm system, kept a keen eye on salaries, paid themselves modest salaries, and plowed everything else back into the club, paying shareholders no dividends. Thus mortgage payments of $200,000 per year to retire the Connecticut General loan seemed not out of reach.[23]

The A's on the field did not do much to enhance the value of this investment. In the first five postwar seasons the team had finished eighth, fifth, fourth, fifth, and eighth. Attendance peaked in 1948 at 945,076, when the team made a run at first place, and dropped to 309,805 two years later. In his dotage the elder Mack had tried to reassert his control by making two trades, both disastrous. In October 1949 he traded promising second baseman Nellie Fox to the White Sox for catcher Joe Tipton, and in December he sent four players and $100,000 to the Browns to acquire two players, including Bob Dillinger. Mack hoped that Dillinger's skill stealing bases would push the A's higher in the standings, but the outfielder refused to hustle. "You are not worth the money we spent on you," Mack said to him when he sold him to Pittsburgh in July 1950. The A's were not without a few good players. In 1951 and 1952 first baseman Ferris Fain won consecutive batting titles, and pitcher Bobby Shantz won eighteen and twenty-four games. Outfielder Gus Zernial led the league in home runs and runs batted in 1952 and hit 42 homers the next year. But the team finished sixth in 1951, fourth in 1952, seventh in 1953, and eighth in 1954, sixty games behind the Yankees. The financial calculations undergirding the mortgage began to unravel. The Macks lost $315,000 in 1950, just about broke even in 1951 and 1952, and lost almost $100,000 in 1953, after which Roy said, "We can't stand another year as bad as the last one." Making the mortgage payments now required turning over the Phillies' rent to the insurance company. Having enough cash on hand for day-to-day operations meant taking an additional loan from Jacobs Brothers. Earle and Roy began bickering, sometimes threatening to buy out one another with money neither had. The club announced that attendance in 1954 would have to reach 550,000 for the club to survive, but a "Save the A's" campaign did not pan out, and tickets sold totaled only 304,666.[24]

Early in 1954 at least one homegrown offer to buy the club took shape, promising to keep the A's in Philadelphia if the Macks agreed to sell all their stock. Roy, though, wanted to be part of any new ownership group and become club president at last. From outside the city in July came several other proposals, including one from Arnold Johnson, a Chicago millionaire acting on behalf of several Missouri business groups who wanted Major League baseball in Kansas City. He offered $3.375 million, but he insisted that he would move the club. Connie Sr. and Earle, who wanted to retire, expressed interest in Johnson's offer, but Roy tried to hang on. League owners met several times during the fall to consider the Macks' situation, unsure of Roy's intentions. More than once the league extended deadlines to give Roy time to raise funds to buy the entire club, but when he was unable to do so, the league authorized Johnson on October 12 to finalize his deal. Roy had no choice. He consented but asked for a few days to contemplate giving up what had been the family's business for more than half a century. During that interval a new Philadelphia syndicate emerged, proposing to buy the club, keep it in its home city, and retain Roy in a senior capacity. He signed an agreement with this group on October 17, only to get a telegram from Johnson that night, gilding the Kansas City offer with what seemed to be better terms, including front office jobs for both Roy and his son, Connie Mack III. Johnson met Roy on October 18 and came to an agreement, a situation that led to confusion when league owners assembled again on October 28. There the deal with the Philadelphia syndicate failed to get approval, and Will Harridge's assistant said, "The meeting adjourned to permit the Macks to return to Philadelphia to work out their own problems." Roy's failure to inform Earle and their father about his deal with Johnson caused further confusion and resentment. Johnson met with both and got their approval. When league owners met again on November 8, Roy urged approval of the Johnson deal. Five clubs voted yes, but moving a franchise required six votes. After much discussion the Tigers switched their vote, and the Philadelphia Athletics became the Kansas City Athletics.[25]

Three Major League clubs had picked up and moved, but none had come close to landing in California, the Golden State, part of the American dream at least since the time of Abraham Lincoln. A few weeks before he was assassinated, the sixteenth president wrote to a friend, "I have long desired to see California; the production of her gold mines has been a marvel to me, . . . and nothing would give me more pleasure than a visit to the Pacific shore." Baseball fell in love with California early. Residents of the state capital organized the Sacramento

Base Ball Club in 1859, and two amateur clubs played the first organized game in the state on February 22, 1860. The first enclosed ballpark on the Pacific coast opened in 1868, and the next year the Cincinnati Red Stockings, on tour demonstrating the wonders of professional baseball, played six games in San Francisco, plus one cricket match, and one in Sacramento, winning them all handily. Between 1887, when organized Minor League baseball came to the state, and the end of World War II, there were clubs in fifty-two California cities and towns, including Los Angeles. By 1950 it had become the fourth largest city in the United States with a population of nearly two million. The several ideas to move the Browns west certainly whetted Los Angeles's appetite for Major League baseball, but once those plans failed to materialize, how best to become a Major League city remained unclear. As the Pacific Coast League's hope to become a third Major League faded, Los Angeles reconsidered attracting an existing club, especially after Milwaukee, Baltimore, and Kansas City had done so, or encouraging the Majors to expand beyond two eight-team leagues. In this confusion one fact stood out. Transportation to and from California was not an issue. "You see," Branch Rickey said in 1948, "what with fast trains and planes, transportation no longer can be a determining factor in considering extension of the major league sphere."[26]

Walter O'Malley probably encountered California for the first time when the Dodgers signed a working agreement with the Hollywood Stars in 1948, but he later told Vincent X. Flaherty that he did not begin to think about Los Angeles as a potential home for the Dodgers until about five years before it happened. O'Malley admitted that it was manager Charlie Dressen who "might have planted a seed." Before Rickey left Brooklyn, he, too, talked to Stars executive Bob Cobb about Los Angeles as a Major League city, even though he said in 1948 that "nothing has been presented that requires change." Lou Perini came to see things differently, of course, but O'Malley favored stability. He voted against the Braves' move twice before Perini overcame his objections. O'Malley's concern about his club, from his earliest days on the Dodgers' board of directors, was the condition and uncertain future of Ebbets Field. In 1946, its thirty-sixth year of operation, the bill for maintenance and improvements ate up more than half the team's profits. Ebbets was small. Its aisles were too narrow and the number of its exits insufficient, said Brooklyn's building commissioner, to allow the Dodgers to rent it out for championship boxing. By 1946 O'Malley was consulting with a civil engineer and an architect about either renovating Ebbets Field substantially or finding another Brooklyn location where the Dodgers could play. Over the next few years the club's situation became more dire. After peaking in 1947, the Dodgers' attendance declined and then stagnated around 1.1 million per year, despite the team's persistent excellence on the field. Brooklyn was declining economically. Manufacturing was leaving, key department stores were closing, and the borough's sole daily newspaper, the *Brooklyn Eagle*, ceased publication in January 1955. Families who had worn Dodgers fandom as a birthmark for decades were moving to the suburbs. When once they could take public transportation to reach the ballpark, now they had to negotiate a lack of arterial highways, crumbling city streets, and woefully inadequate parking. Even important games failed to draw huge crowds. The first game of the 1951 playoff against the Giants was not a sellout. Neither were the sixth and seventh games of the 1952 World Series against the Yankees. And so O'Malley's goal, according to biographer Andy McCue, "remained his new stadium with the amenities he thought would be needed to attract more fans, whether in Brooklyn or elsewhere."[27]

In the upper reaches of Manhattan Giants owner Horace Stoneham was battling much the same problems as O'Malley. Decades before, the Giants had been the toast of New York, and the Polo Grounds, aside from the bright lights of Broadway, the place to be for those who wanted to be seen. While the Yankees and Dodgers were mired in mediocrity at best, the Giants under manager John McGraw reached for excellence yearly. Giants shortstop Bill Dahlen, traded from Brooklyn after the 1903 season, captured the spirit of these years when he said, "It has always been my ambition to play in New York City. Brooklyn is all right, but if you're not with the Giants, you might as well be in Albany." McGraw retired midway through the 1932 season, when he was, according to Charles Alexander, "a fat and sickly old man nearing sixty." First baseman Bill Terry succeeded him and led the Giants through one more burst of glory, winning the pennant in 1933, 1936, and 1937 but losing the World Series all three times. Long before, the Yankees and their sustained run of success had become the darlings of New York's fans, and the Dodgers found new life with Larry MacPhail and then Rickey in charge. Meanwhile, the Giants wandered through the 1940s mostly in the second division. The postwar Giants were a team of sluggers with poor pitching until Leo Durocher, immediately after his arrival in the middle of the 1948 season, persuaded Stoneham and his son-in-law, club vice president Chub Feeney, to rebuild the roster with the succinct evaluation, "Back up the truck." The Giants finished third in 1950, just five games out of first place, and in 1951 the club's stunning upset of the Dodgers became known as the "Miracle of Coogan's Bluff," referencing the terrain upon which the Polo Grounds sat.[28]

Three seasons later the Giants won the pennant again. Led by Willie Mays and Johnny Antonelli, obtained from the Braves in the trade for Bobby Thomson, the Giants won 97 games and finished 5 games ahead of the Dodgers. Mays batted .345 and hit 41 home runs. Antonelli, never effective as a Boston bonus baby, won 21 games and led the league with a 2.30 earned run average. Waiting in the wings for a World Series showdown were the Indians, heavy favorites after winning an astounding 111 games. Yet the Giants swept the Series, with substitute outfielder Dusty Rhodes hitting a pinch-hit, extra-inning, three-run home run to win Game One and hitting a second homer to seal the win in Game Two. His heroics aside, this World Series will forever be remembered for the catch Mays made in the eighth inning of the first game when Vic Wertz smashed a towering line drive to center field. According to writer Arnold Hano, who was sitting in the bleachers, "Mays turned full around, head down, running as hard as he could" to the deepest recesses of the ball field. "He caught the ball, and then whirled and threw, like some olden statue of a Greek javelin hurler, his head twisted away to the left as his right arm swept out and away." The odd configuration of the Polo Grounds helped immortalize Mays's catch. Rebuilt after a fire in 1911, the ballpark was shaped like a horseshoe, measuring 280 feet down the left-field line, 258 feet to right, and an extraordinary 483 to center. It was also, as anyone could see, even more decrepit than Ebbets Field, showing its age in antiquated seating and amenities and desperately in need of repairs and remodeling. Stoneham knew he had a parking problem too, and he also realized that nearby public housing projects had persuaded middle-class white fans that going to see a Giants game had become risky business. The club drew 1,155,067 fans while they were winning the 1954 pennant but only 824,112 the next season.[29]

Both O'Malley and Stoneham indicated that they wanted to keep their clubs where they were. Stoneham, reticent most of the time, seemed to have given some thought to two schemes. One would have asked the Yankees to allow the National Leaguers to share Yankee Stadium, much as the two clubs had shared the Polo Grounds before 1923. The second would have sought public funding, an unlikely prospect, to build a new ballpark in which both New York clubs would play. Neither scheme came close to materializing before Stoneham, after the 1955 season, began to consider something more drastic: moving the Giants to Minneapolis. He had seen the Braves prosper in Milwaukee, attracting rabid fans eager to make the transition from Minor League baseball, and he thought he could do the same in the city where the Giants' Class Triple-A team, the Millers, played and where he held territorial rights that would make a move easier. Stoneham disclosed his intentions in a confidential conversation with O'Malley in March 1957, but publicly he said nothing. The Dodgers' owner, on the other hand, offered to use private funds to build a new ballpark in a Brooklyn location where two subway lines and the Long Island Railroad converged if the city would use its power under Title 1 of the 1949 Federal Housing Act to condemn the site and sell the land to the Dodgers. This plan needed approval from Mayor Robert Wagner and a bureaucrat named Robert Moses, a man who held no elective office but was so embedded in numerous city and state planning positions that no public works project in New York could be commissioned without his authorization. Moses had little use for O'Malley and less for his proposal, arguing that a private enterprise like a ball club could not benefit from public funds set aside for slum clearance. Moses offered the Dodgers instead the chance to build a ballpark not in Brooklyn but in a section of Queens called Flushing Meadows. He and O'Malley butted heads for many months, locked in a tangled dance of death played out in the newspapers, New York's city hall and other municipal offices, and the New York State legislature.[30]

In November 1954 San Francisco voters approved a bond issue authorizing $5 million for a big new ballpark intended to accommodate a Major League team. The Pacific Coast League's dream to become a third Major League was gone, so the city's leaders had to decide whether to woo an existing team or wait for the possibility of expansion. Francis McCarty, president of the board of supervisors, made some informal inquiries to clubs that might be candidates to move west. New mayor George Christopher, taking office in January 1956, was more aggressive. The campaign to attract a team gathered steam when O'Malley revealed during spring training that he had bought Wrigley Field in Los Angeles and the PCL's Angels, giving him territorial rights in that city. McCarty approached Stoneham in New York, and Christopher encouraged Los Angeles mayor Norris Poulson to bring the Dodgers to southern California. Both mayors apparently agreed that getting two clubs to move would be easier than grabbing just one. In May Christopher, O'Malley, and Poulson huddled secretly in Los Angeles with Matthew Fox, head of a pay-per-view television company that O'Malley thought would solve baseball's television problem. A week later the San Franciscans met with Stoneham in New York and convinced him that their city would be a better home for his team than Minneapolis. Commissioner Ford Frick tried to intervene, suggesting that baseball's internal politics required that the parties proceed cautiously, so Christopher was guarded when he told the press that the city would soon present Stoneham with a letter of intent outlining the terms of an offer. For two months the mayor pressed his case. Stoneham, called to testify before a congressional subcommittee and asked if he would move the Giants "if a suitable proposition is made," said, "I would recommend it to our board, yes." The formal offer arrived, and on August 9 the Giants' board approved the move, 8–1, with only M. Donald Grant, a Wall Street broker, opposed.[31]

The Dodgers' odyssey to Los Angeles was even more convoluted, exacerbated by the complete lack of empathy between O'Malley and Moses. As if to hint at what the future might hold, O'Malley announced in August 1955 that the Dodgers would play seven home games in 1956 in Jersey City, New Jersey. In December 1956 he sold Ebbets Field to a developer who leased it back to the Dodgers. Prior to buying Wrigley Field, he and his daughter visited Los Angeles, ostensibly to buy a small airliner for the Dodgers but also to visit an area called Chavez Ravine, which, he had been told, might be a suitable site for a ballpark. O'Malley held his cards close to his vest. His negotiations with Los Angeles authorities were less than definitive. The owner appeared willing to deed Wrigley Field to the city in exchange for access to land at Chavez Ravine. He would build a ballpark with private funds, provided that the city would supply the land, grade the site, build access roads, and exempt the operation from certain taxes. New York tried to get back into the game, but O'Malley remained noncommittal, declining to announce his intentions before the same congressional subcommittee that had interrogated Stoneham or anywhere else. Wagner and Moses did not quite grasp that the Dodgers would abandon their home, while Los Angeles authorities could not imagine why O'Malley would not come to their city. Extraneous matters intruded too, all the way up to October 7, 1957, when the Los Angeles city council approved a contract to which O'Malley did not assent until he heard about the affirmative vote. He announced his decision to move his club on October 8, but even this did not settle the situation as legal battles and political infighting over the site for a new ballpark continued for some time, including a June 1958 referendum on the deal that the city and the Dodgers won with 51.8 percent of the vote.[32]

The Braves' experiment in Milwaukee proved to be a rousing success. Third baseman Eddie Mathews said, "I don't think any city has ever gone as crazy over a baseball team as the city of Milwaukee." The Braves held an open house on March 15, 1953, that drew ten thousand people, and Opening Day, cold and rainy, attracted bands, dignitaries, and tailgaters, starting a new tradition. Newly minted Braves fans flocked to County Stadium in such numbers that attendance passed 1952's total on May 20. For the season the Braves drew 1,826,397, a league record that opened the eyes of other owners, and in 1954 they surpassed two million in attendance, a standard they met for the next three seasons. Lou Perini banned televising home games and allowed fans to carry in their own beer and liquor. On the field the relocated Braves never finished a season with a winning percentage below .500, and they immediately became a rival to the Dodgers. General manager John Quinn built a young, powerful roster that Charlie Grimm managed until Fred Haney replaced him in May 1956. The solid infield included Joe Adcock at first base, Danny O'Connell, followed by Red Schoendienst at second, Johnny Logan at shortstop, and Mathews at third. The outfield featured Billy Bruton, a rookie in 1953; Henry Aaron, a rookie in 1954; and Wes Covington, a rookie in 1956. Del Crandall was the catcher, and Warren Spahn remained the anchor of the pitching staff throughout the decade, complemented by Lew Burdette, who bedeviled batters with rumors that he frequently threw a spitball. The star, of course, was Aaron, who quickly began to live up to an early scouting report that called him "one of the finest hitters God ever put on this earth." Over five seasons (1955–59), Aaron led the league in hits twice and won two batting titles; led the league in runs, home runs, runs batted in, and slugging average once; won the 1957 Most Valuable Player Award; and played in every All-Star Game. Milwaukee finished second in 1953, third in 1954, and second in 1955 and 1956. They won the pennant in 1957 and beat the Yankees in the World Series, four games to three. Burdette won three of those games, and Aaron batted .393 with 3 home runs. The following year they repeated as National League champions but lost the Series to the Yankees in seven games. In 1959 the favored Braves finished in a first-place tie with the Dodgers, who recovered from a seventh-place finish the year before. In the National League's third best-of-three playoff the Dodgers won the first two games and deprived the Braves of becoming the first team to win three straight National League pennants since the Cardinals in 1942–44. Only 18,297 fans showed up for the second game, played in County Stadium in the rain.[33]

Following the departure of the American League's Baltimore Orioles to New York after the 1902 season and the two years of the Federal League's Terrapins, the Dunn family kept professional baseball in Baltimore alive. Jack Dunn found and developed Babe Ruth before selling his contract to the Red Sox, and Jack's grandson, Jack III, assumed control of the Orioles after his grandfather died in 1925. They were a perennially successful Minor League club, but not a Major League one. Starting in 1916 Dunn's Orioles played in what had been the Terrapins' wooden ballpark until it burned down in 1944, victimized by fireworks gone awry. Dunn then secured the use of Municipal Stadium, built for football, and converted it to baseball, albeit with short distances down both foul lines. He enlarged it to seat more than 52,000, and in 1946 the Orioles set an International League attendance record, attracting 620,726 fans, even as the park was being completely rebuilt with reinforced concrete and renamed Memorial Stadium. When Bill Veeck set his sights on Baltimore as a new home for his Browns, he negotiated with Dunn for his territorial rights, agreeing that Dunn would get stock in the Major League club and a five-year personal services contract, while Veeck would acquire the Minor League club and dispose of it. Once the Clarence Miles group acquired the Browns, Dunn became the Orioles' first traveling secretary. Unfortunately for Baltimore fans, the relocated team proved to be no better than the team they had been in St. Louis. They lost their first game, 3–0, in Detroit before winning their home opener, 3–1, over the White Sox. Success, though, was not to be. The 1953 Browns had finished 54–100. So did the 1954 Orioles. After the season, general manager Art Ehlers pulled off the largest trade in baseball history, sending six players to the Yankees in exchange for ten New Yorkers, but the 1955 Orioles improved by only three games. In 1958 Larry MacPhail's son, Lee, became general manager. He enhanced the farm system and the scouting department and began to develop Major League talent. The Orioles improved slowly, achieving their first winning record in 1960, when they finished in second place.[34]

American League owners worried that new A's owner Arnold Johnson would be beholden to Del Webb and Dan Topping, who owned the Yankees and their top farm club, the Kansas City Blues. Johnson had done several business deals with the pair, including acquiring a substantial interest in the Automatic Canteen Corporation, a large vending machine company. In 1953 Johnson bought Yankee Stadium and Blues Stadium for $6.5 million. He leased them back to the Yankees, sold the land underneath Yankee Stadium to the nonprofit Knights of Columbus, took a lease back on that land, and sublet it to the team. Once he decided to buy the A's, he persuaded the city government to buy Blues Stadium, enlarge it, and provide certain financial incentives. Webb and Topping helped by refusing to sell their territorial rights in Kansas City until voters approved a bond issue to fund this municipal endeavor, and Webb's construction company did the work on the ballpark. This cozy relationship continued once Johnson took charge of the Athletics. Over the next five seasons the two clubs made sixteen trades involving fifty-nine players, many of whom contributed to the Yankees' success in several pennant races. The A's on the field struggled to overcome their Philadelphia birthright. In Johnson's five years at the helm, they finished sixth once, seventh three times, and eighth once. In 1955, 32,147 fans turned out to watch former president Harry Truman throw out the ceremonial first pitch, and attendance that year was strong, 1,393,054, but it declined steadily and never surpassed that number again. Johnson did well financially, but his tenure as club president came to a sudden end. During spring training in 1960 he suffered a cerebral hemorrhage while driving away from the ballpark and died the next morning. His executors put the club up for sale. Chicago insurance executive Charlie Finley bought out the Johnson estate in December 1960 and secured the remaining stock in February 1961. Capitalized at $1 million in 1955, the club sold for $4 million.[35]

The San Francisco Giants opened the 1958 season on April 15, defeating the Los Angeles Dodgers, 8–0. They played at Seals Stadium, the former home of the PCL club. Horace Stoneham had paid the PCL to terminate the Seals, a Red Sox farm team, and grant him territorial rights to his club's new home. He compensated the Red Sox by transferring ownership of his Minneapolis franchise in the American Association to them, and he established the Phoenix Giants in the PCL as his top farm club. The Giants finished third in 1958 and 1959 and third in attendance both years, behind the Dodgers and the Braves. Their new ballpark, Candlestick Park, opened in 1960. After opening on the road, the Dodgers made their home debut on April 18, defeating the Giants, 6–5. They did so before a crowd of 78,672 in the Los Angeles Coliseum, a venue with a configuration unsuited to baseball. The Dodgers slumped to seventh place in 1958, but they rebounded in 1959 and defeated the White Sox in the World Series, four games to two. Dodger Stadium, the ballpark of Walter O'Malley's dreams, opened in 1962. The larger picture, though, was even more significant. The West Coast had acquired what it had sought for so long, Major League baseball, while the city of New York had lost two of its three teams and stood bereft.[36]

Fourteen

"Henry, Don't Go Out There"

Bill Shea was not the sort of lawyer who represented clients in a court of law. "Around his office," read his obituary in the *New York Times*, "people jokingly speculated whether he even knew where the courthouse was." Nor was he the sort of lawyer who toiled in the library and the classroom, making his mark as a legal scholar. Instead, wrote historian Michael Shapiro, "He was the sort of lawyer whom powerful men trusted with their secrets and whom they could rely upon as a go-between." In December 1957 Robert Wagner, mayor of New York, appointed Shea and three other political insiders to a committee charged with a responsibility that, a year previously, few had imagined would become necessary: bringing National League baseball back to their city, following the departure of the New York Giants and the Brooklyn Dodgers for California. Wagner's committee was formidable. James Farley, chairman of the board of the Coca-Cola Export Corporation, former postmaster general, and former Democratic National Committee chairman, had once been advanced as a possible successor to Happy Chandler as commissioner of baseball. Bernard Gimbel was chairman of the board of Gimbel Brothers, a chain of department stores; president of the New York Convention and Visitors Bureau; and Hank Greenberg's father-in-law. Clinton Blume, who had pitched for the Giants in 1922 and 1923, was a real estate developer, one of the men responsible for putting together the package that became Rockefeller Center. But Shea was the committee's face and the one who did its work, and he was ideally suited to the task. Years later, journalist Nicholas Pileggi anointed him "the city's most experienced power broker, its premier matchmaker." He was, Pileggi added, "a man who has spent forty years turning the orgies of politicians, bankers, realtors, union chiefs, underwriters, corporate heads, utility combines, cement barons, merchant princes, and sports impresarios into profitable marriages." But the task before him was daunting.[1]

Born in New York in 1907, William Alfred Shea earned an athletic scholarship to New York University, but he remained a Violet for only one year before transferring to Georgetown, where he played football for one season and basketball for three. After graduation he earned a law degree from Georgetown Law School and got his first job with the New York firm of Cullen and Dyckman. There he met George McLaughlin, Brooklyn's Democratic Party leader and president of the bank that controlled the Dodgers' finances. The two developed a firm friendship. Shea then went to work for the New York State Insurance Department, got involved in Democratic politics, and in 1941 became a founding partner of Manning, Hollinger, and Shea, specializing in real estate and corporate law. *Sports Illustrated*'s Roy Terrell called him "a brawny, fast-talking Irishman," and Shea's *Times* obituary described him as "a burly affable man with a firm handshake for messengers and moguls alike." Shapiro wrote that Shea "smiled easily and comported himself without pretense." He never held elective office, but Pileggi called him "the unofficial chairman of the state's unofficial permanent government [who] labored quietly in a political twilight somewhere between the private interest and the public good." Less charitably journalists Jack Newfield and Paul DuBrul later called Shea's merged law firm, Shea and Gould, "a factory of legal graft" helping clients in "getting around the law without breaking the law." Shea's office was located in Manhattan, and he maintained a legal residence in Brooklyn, but he spent most of his time at a ten-room house in Sands Point, an affluent suburb on Long Island's north shore. Shea played golf; had a small stake in a prewar semipro football team; and counted among his friends some of the big names in sports, including Branch Rickey and Walter O'Malley. His wife, Nora, had a sports connection too. Her father, Long Tom Shaw, was a former bicycle racer turned "turf man"—that is, a bookmaker, at the time a legal profession.[2]

The effort to keep National League baseball in the nation's largest city had begun in the spring of 1957 before the Giants and Dodgers had made known their intentions to move. Rumors about their departure were rampant when McLaughlin suggested he might broker a deal to buy the Giants for $2.75 million and keep them in their ancestral home. Horace Stoneham said no, and when McLaughlin then proposed raising $5 million to fund a new team in New York as a not-for-profit organization, league president Warren Giles told him that New York already had two teams. Once those two teams decided to leave, McLaughlin approached Rickey, chairman of the board of the Pittsburgh Pirates, about that club's availability, but the former Dodgers executive was forced to tell McLaughlin that "money can't buy a franchise." Pirates owner John Galbreath worried, Rickey said, that his reputation in Pittsburgh would be trampled, as O'Malley's later was in Brooklyn, if he let his team move. As chair of the mayor's committee, Shea started to look at other franchises. He listened to reports that the Cincinnati Reds were threatening to move to New York, but one executive dismissed this idea, suggesting that Reds owner Powel Crosley was merely exerting some pressure "to get a little more action out of the city officials in Cincinnati." (In fact Crosley was looking for additional parking around Crosley Field, and in January 1958 the Cincinnati city council appropriated $2 million for 2,600 parking spaces.) The Philadelphia Phillies also said no to Shea, as did the St. Louis Cardinals. Shea dangled before these owners the prospect of improvements to Ebbets Field, the ballpark the Dodgers had abandoned, but still got no takers. He was heartened when New York's Board of Estimate, overseeing the city's budget and contracts, gave its preliminary endorsement to a plan to build a new ballpark, perhaps in Flushing Meadows, a site in Queens that O'Malley had rejected before deciding to leave. Shea called a change in baseball's rules to allow a franchise in one league to move without getting permission from the other league "a step in the right direction," but he admitted in April 1958 that "so far there is no active interest."[3]

Shea switched gears, embracing an idea that had been percolating for at least a decade. Why, he asked, should the National League confine itself to only eight clubs? But when he could garner no significant support for expansion, he moved quickly to yet a third scheme: establishing a third Major League with a New York club as its centerpiece. "Since it has now become apparent that the National League means to do nothing," he told a press conference on November 12, 1958, "we have decided to go on a new tack." Establishing a third Major League had been Rickey's idea as early as 1953, but it was Shea who brought it to life. He told the gathering that prominent citizens in Dallas, Denver, Houston, Miami, Minneapolis–St. Paul, and Toronto—all cities ignored by the Major Leagues—had already expressed interest in owning franchises. Commissioner Ford Frick, just back from a trip to Venezuela, attended the press conference and reacted to Shea's news variously. "Baseball," he said, on the one hand, "is not going to be sledge-hammered into putting a club in New York because of a threat of a third league." Yet he also seemed to express support for a club in the city. "I would like to see two majors of twelve clubs each, with East and West sections," he said, "but if it could be done with a third major league, I certainly wouldn't oppose it." More plaintively he added, "Why haven't they [the potential owners] or the committee come to see me?" Shea worked for months to assemble financing for his new venture. He was encouraged in May 1959, when the two Major Leagues said they would "favorably consider" applications for a third league, and in June he identified the New York franchise's three wealthy owners, including Joan Payson, a minority owner of the Giants and the co-owner of Greentree Stable, a thoroughbred racing enterprise, with her brother, John Hay Whitney, owner of the *New York Herald Tribune*. A few weeks later Shea told Wagner that the new league would be a reality within two years, and in late July he announced its formal creation with five franchises so far—in Denver, Houston, Minneapolis–St. Paul, New York, and Toronto—set to begin play in 1961. "I believe in the good faith of the major leagues," he said, "and that they will not go back on commitments they already have made."[4]

Having a club in New York, Shea knew, was essential if the new league were to come to life, and having robust ownership there and elsewhere was equally important. The original New York group had included financier George Herbert Walker Jr., whose uncle had donated the Walker Cup to amateur golf; Dwight Davis Jr., whose father had given the Davis Cup to international tennis; and Dorothy Killam, whose personal fortune amounted to at least $135 million. When Killam withdrew, Payson replaced her, bringing along even more resources, plus her business partner, M. Donald Grant. Entrepreneur Jack Kent Cooke held the Toronto franchise. He had been a musician, an athlete, and the owner of a radio station, a magazine, and baseball's Toronto Maple Leafs, champions of the International League in 1954, 1956, and 1957. In Houston George Kirksey, once a sportswriter/publicist, organized thirty-five of the city's wealthiest men into the Houston Sports Authority (HSA), a group headed by oilman Craig Cullinan Jr., grandson of the founder of Texaco Oil. The HSA worked to pass a referendum in November 1957 authorizing the expenditure of public funds to build a multipurpose stadium with a dome to protect the games within from the oppressive Houston climate. The Denver franchise went to Bob Howsam, whose farming background included growing alfalfa and raising bees. While he was a student at the University of Colorado, he married the daughter of politician Edwin Johnson, who took Howsam to Washington as his administrative assistant when he was elected to the U.S. Senate. Johnson was also president of the Western League, and he brought Howsam into the baseball business. After running the Class A league for his father-in-law, he bought one of the league's clubs, the Denver Bears, and through a complicated transaction turned them into a Class Triple-A club in the American Association. In the twin cities of Minneapolis–St. Paul interest in Major League baseball was kindled first by the possibility of the Giants' moving there and then by reports that the Senators might consider abandoning Washington. Unwilling to wait, Wheelock Whitney Jr., a young investment banker, put together an ownership group, with support from the

Dayton department store chain, Hamm Brewery, Pillsbury, and the *Minneapolis Star-Tribune*, to join the new league.[5]

Meeting at Galbreath's farm outside Columbus, Ohio, in May 1959, Major League owners laid out ten "principles of operation" that a third league would have to meet to earn organized baseball's endorsement, including ballparks seating at least twenty-five thousand, a schedule of at least 154 games, and a commitment to accept the uniform Major League players' contract, with the reserve clause embedded therein. Shea's resources to meet this challenge included the venerable Rickey, named president of the new venture, now called the Continental League, in August, and two congressional subcommittees renewing their concern with baseball's antitrust status, regarded by some as a historic wrong that needed correction. Even at seventy-seven, Rickey was a force to be reckoned with. He had survived one heart attack and battled Ménière's disease, and he walked with a cane, but the crusader in him was as feisty as ever. Meeting with baseball officials immediately after his appointment as Continental League president, Rickey declaimed, "We want your cooperation, we need your cooperation, we demand your cooperation." Congressman Emanuel Celler (D-NY), chair of the House Judiciary Committee and its Antitrust Subcommittee, had revived his interest in baseball's legal standing when the Dodgers left his beloved Brooklyn. He was joined by Estes Kefauver (D-TN), a member of the Senate Judiciary Committee and chair of its Antitrust and Monopoly Subcommittee. Kefauver had introduced a bill in February 1959 to give organized baseball and the other major sports partial protection from antitrust regulation but limit the number of players any baseball organization could keep under contract. Rickey testified before the Kefauver subcommittee in August. In his extemporaneous answers he seemed to belittle critics of organized baseball's protected position outside antitrust regulation, but he knew that he must be a critic too because a third league would collide with the sport's sanctioned monopoly status in several ways. Both Celler and Kefauver supported the idea of a third league, and so too did Vice President Richard Nixon, who wanted baseball to expand internationally. Shea, though, preferred not to seek legislative relief to make the Continental League a reality. He was optimistic, saying that "baseball must realize that, with the general growth of the country and the demand of so many municipalities for major league baseball, the expansion to a third league is inevitable." Yet by October Shea was more circumspect. "You can see under the table," he said, "certain things that are happening that I don't think are exactly happenstance, or just happening from nowhere."[6]

In January 1960 the *Sporting News* published a front-page story with the headline "Players' Pay Soars to All-Time High." Dan Daniel reported that the sixteen Major League clubs would pay salaries during the coming season totaling nearly $10 million. The New York Yankees' payroll in 1959, he wrote, had been about $700,000, with Mickey Mantle earning about $78,000, "but now a club with a $600,000 payroll is not unusual." New York general manager George Weiss questioned the wisdom involved. "There isn't another enterprise in these United States," he said, "which, recognized as a business, is so oblivious of the principles of safe financial operation as is baseball." He went on to say, "We are not opposed to paying a man $100,000 a season, as we did to Joe DiMaggio, just so long as he is a $100,000 player in skills and in popular appeal." Because the Yankees finished third in 1959, "few Bombers are in line for merit increases," Weiss said, but other clubs anticipated paying more in 1960 to reward performance in 1959. "The Detroit club is very generous in its player payroll," said Tigers president Bill DeWitt, who believed that American League batting champion Harvey Kuenn would seek an $18,000 raise to $50,000. The San Francisco Giants expected their payroll to increase by about $100,000 to a total of $500,000, and the Baltimore Orioles planned to give substantial raises to two young pitchers, Milt Pappas, from $11,000 to $15,000, and Jerry Walker, from $8,500 to $13,500. Daniel gave several reasons to explain these increases and others like them. "Club owners and operating officials are responsible for some of the upward trend," he wrote. "They have been talking too much for their own good. . . . This process of talking too much has to do with assertions in both leagues that as much as $500,000 has been refused for a player's contract." Another factor was the scarcity of quality players. "We are told," Daniel wrote, "that major league prospects are more and more difficult to locate." Also to blame was "the bonus incubus," an idea that "if it is good economy to give a seventeen-year-old kid fifty grand, why isn't it better economy to reward the veterans properly?" But, Daniel concluded, "behind all of the other factors stands one which has been dominant, and strongly fought by the owners, through the decades. The players have been underpaid ever since the American League came into the field in 1901. The players have not received their just dues at any time, and they are not getting them now."[7]

If baseball was suffering from a shortage of quality players, as Daniel alleged, the emergence of the Continental League might exacerbate this problem. Branch Rickey did not think so. The league had opened its own offices in New York in November 1959, and from there he and Bill Shea continued to attack the four practical challenges organized baseball had thrown down in front of them: nailing down three additional cities and ballparks, creating a pension plan to match that of the two existing leagues, clarifying how teams would obtain players, and settling territorial rights questions raised by infringing upon established Minor League clubs. Various cities submitted applications for the three remaining franchises, and three were approved: Atlanta and Dallas–Ft. Worth in December and Buffalo in January 1960. "As for ballparks," Rickey added, "we'll have them." His optimism was bolstered in April, when New York City's Board of Estimate gave final approval to the issuance of bonds to build the stadium in Flushing Meadows. The pension question was also resolved in January. Each club would commit around $80,000, Shea said, and would assume responsibility to pay benefits for service time accrued in the American and National Leagues, splitting costs as appropriate. Rickey believed that obtaining players would be easy too, that there would be "plenty of talent available for a different league." Traveling extensively in early 1960 from one baseball city to the next, he predicted that a third league's demand for talent would not exhaust the supply. "A fourth major league is just around the corner," he said. "As soon as we get underway, it will be ready to fall into place." Rickey reflected on how Ban Johnson's creation of the American League had affected the market for players. "In Ban's time," he said, "we had seventy million people. Now we have 180 million people. Out of quantity comes quality. . . . With more major league opportunity, I have no fear there will be sufficient young men to meet the challenge." Later on he made much the same point by saying that "there are players all over the world."[8]

Rickey's plan to get the Continental League off the ground involved dividing radio and television revenues equally and creating a player pool—that is, sharing scouting expenses and putting all prospects into a "grab bag" from which they could be drafted. This thought, said a *Sporting News* editorial, "is laudable, but the consequences must be feared. Such a revolutionary plan is bordering on socialized baseball. It could destroy individual initiative. . . . We respect Rickey's genius, but in a nation of free enterprise, this common pooling of talent does not seem to be the answer." Expecting to work within the existing reserve system, the Continental League hoped to obtain some players from American and National League organizations, but it also carved out a special relationship with a dormant Minor League recently reborn. A group of prominent North Carolina businessmen had approached experienced Minor League executive John Moss in the fall of 1959 to explore reviving the Western Carolina League, which had played from 1948 through 1952. Moss accepted the job, but when he went to the 1959 winter meetings to seek working agreements with Major League organizations for his eight clubs, he got no offers. He then approached Rickey, and the two concluded a deal by which the new Minor League would develop talent for the new Major League. Rickey offered Moss and his owners generous terms, which they accepted. Each Western Carolina club would receive $7,500 to subsidize player salaries and an additional $7,500 for spring training expenses, plus money to pay the manager's salary and some to maintain facilities. Without any players of their own, Moss's clubs intended to stock their rosters by reaching out to free agents, both veterans and young players whose careers might have been cut short prematurely, and by staging tryout camps. Rickey assisted this process by hiring two former players he knew well, Burt Shotton and Al Todd, and Harvey Stratton, baseball coach at Catawba College, to help Moss evaluate talent.[9]

On January 24, 1960, Rickey spoke at the Diamond Dinner, the annual banquet hosted by the Milwaukee chapter of the Baseball Writers' Association of America (BBWAA). Determined, if not defiant, he declared that "the Continental League is as inevitable as tomorrow morning although not as imminent." Anticipating troubles that he would later call "an accumulation of blocks and stoppages," he was resolute, saying, "I prefer turbulent progress rather than quiet stagnation." Progress, though, was hard to find. Two weeks prior to Rickey's speech Commissioner Frick had reasserted his support for the expansion of Major League baseball. "I've always been for it," he said, and "if most baseball people want it done through a third league, I'm for it." But, he warned, "certain things must be done before the Continental League qualifies under the rules," and those certain things included satisfying the Minor Leagues upon whose territory the new league would infringe. In February Houston's potential owners learned how onerous these terms could be. After much discussion, the Houston Buffaloes in the American Association rejected an offer for their territorial rights from the Houston Sports Authority. The Buffs had set a price of $262,500 plus $25,000 a year for five years to compensate club president Marty Marion. The HSA's counteroffer—based in part on Walter O'Malley's suggestion that he might sell the new league his rights to Montreal for $150,000—was $184,000, a sum that Buffaloes chairman Russell Rowles called "unsatisfactory." Alternatively, when the Sports Authority proposed that the two groups merge their equity into one organization, Rowles said only that he did not have authority to discuss such an idea. A week later Weiss dismissed a suggestion that the Continental League's New York club might play temporarily in Yankee Stadium, saying that "there will be no sanctuary for the New York club of the Continental League in Yankee Stadium even for a day."[10]

In March Frick intervened but not for the better. According to Russell Buhite, who played in the Western Carolina League before becoming a historian, the commissioner ruled that the league-to-league relationship Rickey had crafted with Moss was contrary to baseball's rules, and he told the reborn Minor League that it could not become part of organized baseball connected to the Continental League because the Continental League was not yet part of organized baseball. "If the Western Carolina League wanted to operate with working agreements between its clubs and the clubs already in Organized Ball, . . . that could be worked out. . . . But they cannot pool players or make arrangements with teams not yet in Organized Ball." Furthermore, he said, the Continental League could not become part of organized baseball until it satisfied all its territorial rights questions. Rickey stormed about indignantly, but these obstacles could not be blustered away. Houston's situation was not unique. Frank Shaughnessy, president of the International League, wanted $1 million each to compensate his clubs in Toronto and Buffalo, and the American Association wanted $850,000 for Minneapolis–St. Paul and smaller claims for other league cities. Continental League owners blanched at the threat of this financial hit. Jack Kent Cooke argued that a proper fee for Toronto should approximate the $48,749 the Orioles had paid the International League when the Browns had moved from St. Louis. Shea was so upset at these roadblocks that he issued an ultimatum. Either "help us or suffer the consequences," he said, hinting that the league would seek relief from Congress or "take affirmative steps of our own." To this threat Frick asked, "Just what has the Continental League done toward meeting the requirements?"[11]

As the calendar dawned on a new decade, baseball fans could not know how their sport would be transformed over the next twelve months. In retrospect the *Sporting News Baseball Guide* called 1960 "a year of startling change and historic developments" during which "probably never before were so many momentous decisions and events involving Organized Baseball compressed into a similar span." News during the 1959–60 off-season including demolition of Ebbets Field; awarding the contract to build the Los Angeles Dodgers' new ballpark to Vinnell Constructors; and a rare trade involving two superstar outfielders, Harvey Kuenn moving from the Tigers to the Cleveland Indians in exchange for Rocky Colavito. Fans also read stories that the game's two greatest stars in the previous decade would be absorbing pay cuts. The Cardinals' Stan Musial had volunteered to take a $20,000 cut, down to $80,000, and Ted Williams of the Boston Red Sox insisted that his pay be reduced from $125,000 to $90,000. A poll of sportswriters, one representing each club, picked Willie Mays of the San Francisco Giants as the game's most exciting player, edging out Chicago White Sox shortstop Luis Aparicio, five votes to four. Major League scouts considered organizing a union designed to improve their salaries, provide job security, and create a pension plan. Following the resignation of Will Harridge, Joe Cronin, former player, manager, and general manager, was elected president of the American League. National League president Warren Giles defended his decision not to renew the contract of umpire Vic Delmore because of "my personal opinion that he did not have sufficient ability to continue as a major league umpire." Reds pitcher Jim Brosnan incurred the wrath of Indians general manager Frank Lane by publishing a piece in *Sports Illustrated* in which, according to Dan Daniel, "he held [manager Solly] Hemus and general manager Bing Devine of the Cards up to ridicule." Lane announced that "no player on the Cleveland club would be permitted to compete with the working press." The White Sox decided to put players' names above the numbers on the backs of their uniforms, an innovation that the *Sporting News* called "a step toward making baseball more enjoyable for the man who pays his way at the gate." Rumors floated that new Milwaukee Braves manager Charlie Dressen might ask outfielder Henry Aaron to switch to second base. Yankees manager Casey Stengel announced that Roger Maris, obtained by trade from the Kansas City Athletics in December, would start in right field.[12]

Baseball tradition shattered when the National League season opened on Tuesday, April 12, and the American League began six days later. Since 1904 the two Major Leagues had almost always begun play on the same day except for some years when the Senators were given the honor of hosting Opening Day one day before anyone else and inviting the president of the United States. Fred Lieb said the National League's early start was "knocking down another precedent," and he noted that "the big distances between the eight National League cities was given as the main reason" for doing so. Bob Burnes explained that the extra week would put "some air in the schedule to allow teams to travel to and from the West Coast more comfortably." He pointed to several occasions in 1958 and 1959 when "the Giants or Dodgers would stop off in Chicago or St. Louis, en route to or from the Coast, for a Monday or Tuesday contest. Fans protested that 'the Giants and Dodgers were in and out of town before we knew it.'" The 1960 schedule had other quirks. The six National League clubs not located in California made four trips to the West

Coast, correcting an inequity from the previous two seasons when some teams traveled west only three times but played prolonged series in Los Angeles and San Francisco. The Giants went to Los Angeles for games on Thursday, Friday, and Saturday, April 28–30, but both teams had off on Sunday, May 1, because Mary's Hour, a Catholic celebration, had booked the Los Angeles Coliseum for that date. Several clubs in both leagues departed from the tradition of playing doubleheaders on Memorial Day, the Fourth of July, and Labor Day by scheduling night games on those holidays. The Senators and Orioles played an unusual four-game series in early June with games in Washington on June 3 and 5 and games in Baltimore on June 4 and 6. The Orioles, in their seventh season in Baltimore, played only two games at home after Sunday, September 4, virtually ceding use of Memorial Stadium during the season's final month to the National Football League's Colts.[13]

The annual preseason poll of BBWAA members conducted by the *Sporting News* had the Giants winning the pennant, but the Pirates got off to a fast start, winning twelve of their first fifteen games. San Francisco played well too, and, later on, so did Milwaukee, but after May 30 Pittsburgh was out of first place for only one day. The Pirates developed a reputation for coming from behind to win. On June 18, for example, Dodgers pitcher Danny McDevitt came within one out of finishing a three-hit shutout, but Pittsburgh scored three runs in the ninth inning and one in the tenth to win, 4–3. Pittsburgh reached the All-Star break with a record of 49-30, with one additional rain-slogged game against the Giants called a tie, stopped by the league's 12:50 a.m. curfew with the score at 7–7. At the end of June outfielder Roberto Clemente was batting .341 with 52 runs batted in, and shortstop Dick Groat was hitting .334. Pitcher Vernon Law's record was 11-3, and Bob Friend was 9-5. The Yankees, seeking to return to the top of the American League after being displaced in 1959 by the White Sox, who were favored to repeat, were a less certain two and a half games ahead of the Orioles. Chicago and Baltimore held first place for much of the first half of the season, with New York falling as far as fourth. Through June 4 the Yankees were 20-20. Ten days later they were 29-21, having won two from Boston, three of four from Chicago, two from Cleveland, and two from Kansas City. This streak came to an end on June 15, when New York, too, played a 7–7 tie, a game against the Athletics called in the bottom of the thirteenth inning after a thirty-minute rain delay. The Yankees' power hitting sparked their surge. They hit 46 home runs in June and scored 165 runs. Maris hit 14 homers that month, and Mickey Mantle added 12. New York had a solid defensive infield, and Stengel managed a pitching staff short of stars except for Whitey Ford.[14]

As the season unfolded, it was clear that the dissolution, albeit slow, of baseball's color line had transformed the style of play prevalent in the 1950s, especially in the National League, moving away from a lumbering emphasis on home runs, strikeouts, and consequent low batting averages and toward speed with its attendant advantages. According to historian Lawrence Hogan, "Blacks not only excelled in the big leagues, they changed the way in which baseball was played. Black athletes reintroduced speed and base running into a game that for three decades had been dominated by power hitters." Moreover, as the percentage of Black Major Leaguers rose throughout the decade, they earned more than a proportionate share of spots on All-Star Game rosters, and they produced an even higher percentage of what Mark L. Armour called star-quality seasons. Because the National League integrated faster than the American, the differences between the two were substantial. By 1960 half of the star players in the National League, by Armour's definition, were Black, while the American League would take another decade to reach this mark. Between 1947, when Jackie Robinson made his debut, and 1960, Black players led the National League in stolen bases twelve times, the American League only three. Black players led the National League in batting average four times and slugging average six times. They led the league in home runs four times and runs batted in six times. By contrast, Larry Doby was the only Black player to lead the American League in any of these categories. He won the slugging title once, led the league in home runs twice, and led in runs batted in once. Black players won the National League Rookie of the Year Award nine times in these fourteen seasons and the Most Valuable Player Award nine times. No Black player won either award in the American League. Beginning with Robinson, National League rosters added a Black future member of the Hall of Fame nearly every year. The American League had only Doby and Minnie Miñoso.[15]

The All-Star Game, receipts from which funded the players' pension plan, gave the National League an annual showcase to display the talents unshackled by integration. In fact, from 1959 through 1962, the leagues played two games each year, and the Nationals won five of these eight with one game ending in a tie. The American League had won eight of the first twelve games through 1944 and then four more consecutively from 1946 through 1949. After that, as the color line collapsed, the worm turned. The National League took four in a row and six of seven. The 1950s featured two extra-inning games and one shortened by rain. In 1950 Red Schoendienst hit a home run in the fourteenth inning to break a 3–3 tie and propel the Nationals to victory in the first nationally televised All-Star Game. Five years later Musial hit a home run in the twelfth inning to give the Nationals a 6–5 win. The start of the 1952 game at Shibe Park was delayed twenty minutes by rain and stopped for close to an hour after the fifth inning before being called, with the Nationals ahead, 3–2. In 1959 pitcher Robin Roberts, the National League's player representative, concerned about the pension fund, suggested two games per year. Walter O'Malley endorsed this idea, but many others did not, arguing that a second game would dull the luster of the first and that fans would accuse the players of greed. Encouraged by the commissioner, players approved the proposal, and owners gave their consent too. Thus there were thirteen games played between 1950 and 1960, and the Nationals won nine. National League All-Stars hit 21 home runs and scored 64 runs during the decade. African Americans hit 6 of these homers and drove in 18 runs. The American League squads hit 13 homers and scored 50 runs. Doby was the only Black player to hit a home run for the Americans and the only one to drive in a run, although Cubans Miñoso and Vic Power each drove in 2 runs, and Mexican Roberto Ávila González drove in 3.[16]

Lurking close to the surface as the 1960 season began was the lament from the Senators that Washington, a city with a long baseball history, was no longer a fit place for Major League play. Clark Griffith had died in 1955, and Calvin, his "adopted" son, succeeded him as club president. The younger Griffith had long expressed anxiety about the Senators' future. Clark had supported the move of the St. Louis Browns to Baltimore, but Calvin had not, fearing an adverse effect on attendance from a team situated only forty miles away. He was additionally concerned about his ballpark, with the smallest capacity in the league, and the deteriorating residential area in which it was located. More pointedly he openly blamed declining attendance not on his team's poor performance but on the evolving racial makeup of the neighborhood in which Griffith Stadium was situated. During the 1956 World Series representatives from Los Angeles asked Griffith to consider moving there. That overture came to nothing. The next year, after Horace Stoneham decided not to move to Minneapolis, representatives from the Metropolitan Sports Area Commission, which had built Metropolitan Stadium, a ballpark suitable for Major League play, approached Griffith about moving to the Twin Cities. Griffith expressed his enthusiasm but remained noncommittal. The Senators played an exhibition game at the Met in July 1958, but Griffith told the Kefauver subcommittee that he planned to stay in Washington "[as long] as is humanly possible." Other owners opposed the Senators' suggested move. They argued that the National Pastime needed a presence in the nation's capital and, more practically, that abandoning Washington might move Congress to legislate against baseball's antitrust exemption. Nevertheless, Griffith announced after the 1959 World Series that he wanted to move. On behalf of the Continental League, Bill Shea was outraged. "They knew we had the stage set to move into Minneapolis," he said. At this point league president Joe Cronin, Griffith's brother-in-law, entered the fray, announcing the creation of a committee to study not relocation but a new notion: expansion.[17]

Growing the Majors beyond two leagues with eight teams each was not a new idea. As early as 1948 Lou Perini had predicted expansion to a pair of twelve-team leagues. In 1951 Ford Frick voiced his support in the *Sporting News* for "a change in the organic law of the game that would enable cities to move up the ladder to higher classifications, as do players, when they qualify." He continued: "Suppose we grant full major league status, or partial major recognition, to the Pacific Coast League at present. What assurance would we have that in another ten years, some other big minor, whose cities may have had a big populations increase would not want similar promotion? . . . A change in the baseball map is inevitable." In 1952 Phil Wrigley argued for four Major Leagues. "We keep crying about lack of material," he said. "But it's our own fault. We don't make it financially attractive enough for youngsters to make baseball a career. There just aren't enough jobs at the top." Wrigley hired Bill Veeck, no longer a Major League owner, as a $1,000-a-month special assistant "to expedite the movement of major league ball to the Coast." The American League responded in December 1953 by appointing a committee headed by Frank Lane "for an exploratory survey of possible new major league territory." A few months later Lane expressed his belief that "the answer to greater baseball prosperity is to expand each of the two big leagues into ten-club circuits." He added, "I believe when expansion comes it will be a two-city single area invasion," like Los Angeles and San Francisco or Houston with Dallas–Fort Worth or Kansas City along with Minneapolis–St. Paul.[18]

There were naysayers of course. Clark Griffith had been one. When Hank Greenberg, general manager of the Indians, extolled the possibility of Major League baseball on the West Coast, Griffith cautioned him, "Henry, don't go out there. . . . It's cold and it's damp. . . . In 1905, I pitched in Portland, and boy, was it cold." Early in 1955, though, Lane credited Greenberg with conceptualizing three draft 162-game schedules for a ten-team league. "I don't believe we'll be using any of them until 1957, but that doesn't mean it can't happen in 1956." Yet the *Sporting News* soon editorialized that "evidence accumulates that there is no early prospect of further changes in the major league map." The National League, the weekly said, "has turned down any idea of an increase to ten clubs," and the American League's Realignment Committee has "set up minimum standards [that are] formidable obstacles." Nothing happened quickly, and in May 1957 Frick urged the owners to adopt a "thoughtful long-range program" to expand their membership. "The issue is expansion," the commissioner said, "and not a realignment of the clubs we now have." Meeting the day before the 1958 All-Star Game, owners discussed "the possible shift of Washington to one of four cities hungry for big league ball—Minneapolis, Houston, Dallas and Toronto" and "the return of National League ball to New York." Perini, perhaps impatient, said, "I can't see any reason why we can't increase the league to ten or even twelve clubs and take care of some of the cities hungry for big league ball." Yet again nothing happened, and after the owners' meeting at the Galbreath farm in May 1959, the *Sporting News* declared that "for the present, at least, the possibility of increasing the membership of either or both present circuits from eight clubs to ten is as dormant as the emery ball." To this news Larry MacPhail, retired, reacted with a warning. The Major Leagues, he said, should "expand or regret it." He continued, "There are cities . . . that are crying for big league status and deserve it. There are others. As many as a dozen." But he cautioned against the Continental League. "A third league simply couldn't make a go of it. . . . It would crumble of its own weight; in fact, [it] would never have a chance of succeeding."[19]

When Branch Rickey heard about Cronin's committee, he met with him right away and came away disgruntled. "I never heard so much solicitude in my life," he said, "about my knee, my heart, my wife, my children, my present, my past, my future." But the American League president shared scant details about what he intended. What Cronin had in mind, wrote his biographer, was adding two teams to create two nine-team leagues. In this scenario the American League would add two clubs, one in New York and one in Minneapolis, with the New York club then shifting to the National League, an arrangement that would require interleague play for scheduling purposes. The National League was not interested. At the 1959 winter meetings Warren Giles declared that "there is not sufficient sentiment at the present time to consider expansion of the National League." Shea also complained about Cronin's proposal, saying that "vague promises of American League franchises had proved a surprisingly effective means of forestalling the early completion of Continental League membership." He and Rickey threatened to begin play outside organized baseball if necessary, despite all the difficulties that would entail, but he also looked to Congress for antitrust relief that would make a third league's life easier. That did not come. Kefauver introduced a new bill in May 1960, but after hearings at which Rickey testified, the whole Senate sent the bill back to committee, effectively killing it. Organized baseball knew that its dispensation from antitrust regulation remained intact, including control of its labor supply through the reserve clause and control over territorial rights against which Rickey had railed. The crushing blow toppling the Continental League came suddenly in July, when the National League leapfrogged ahead of the American and announced that it would expand in 1962. Although Shea called this "a hopeful sign," it was anything but. Rickey met with leaders of both leagues, but he could not stem the tide against his upstart enterprise. Shea announced that "we have no thought of disbanding," but he had no answer to the indemnification quandary and no arrows left in his quiver to fight against expansion. When the National League's formal and stunning announcement came on August 2, the eight owners of the Continental League franchises gave their grudging assent and disbanded. If New York were to return to the Major Leagues, a third league would not be the vehicle with which to do so.[20]

The Pirates started the second half of the 1960 National League season slowly, losing three of five games at home and then four of six on a trip to the West Coast. Briefly the Braves snuck into first place by two percentage points, and both the Dodgers and Cardinals put together good streaks to pull close to the lead. Pittsburgh reasserted itself, but St. Louis proved to be the Pirates' most dogged challenger. The Cardinals crept within three games of first place in mid-August, and they swept a three-game series in St. Louis at the end of the month. The Pirates, though, had built a solid margin, winning seventeen of twenty-three games in one stretch, including several games by coming from behind. They clinched the pennant on September 25. Dick Groat, who won the league's Most Valuable Player Award, hit .325, and Roberto Clemente, who hit .314, led the team with 94 runs batted in. Vernon Law finished with twenty wins, good enough to capture the Cy Young Award, and Bob Friend won eighteen. The American League race remained a three-team battle throughout July and August among the Yankees, Orioles, and White Sox. New York finished August with eight wins in ten games, but Baltimore hung on and even jumped into first place on September 4, just ahead of the Yankees. Thereafter the New Yorkers won twenty-two of their final twenty-six games, clinching their eleventh pennant in fourteen seasons. They led the league with 193 home runs. Mickey Mantle hit 40 and Roger Maris hit 39. Maris also led the league with 112 runs batted in and won the Most Valuable Player Award. Fourteen Yankees pitchers were credited with wins, but no one won more than fifteen games. The regular season closed on Sunday, October 2. The Yankees beat the Red Sox, 8–7; the Pirates beat the Braves, 9–5; and before a crowd of 4,768 at Griffith Stadium the second-place Orioles defeated the Senators, 2–1, in what would soon be known as the last home game played by this franchise in the nation's capital. Seen through a distant rear-view mirror, four numbers from the final day of play stand out: 7 complete games, including 2 by losing pitchers; 71 strikeouts, an average of 4.4 per team; total attendance of 124,693, or 15,587 per game; and an average game time of 2:16. But the season provided so much more. There were three no-hitters. The Cubs' Don Cardwell no-hit the Cardinals, and Lew Burdette and Warren Spahn both threw no-hitters against the Phillies. Spahn also recorded his 2,000th strikeout on July 15 and his 50th shutout on August 30. Henry Aaron hit his 200th career home run on July 3, the Cubs' Ernie Banks his 250th on June 30, Mantle his 300th on July 4, and Ted Williams his 500th on June 17. Williams, named Player of the Decade by the *Sporting News* in August, hit 21 more homers, including 1 in his final Major League at bat on September 28.[21]

Baseball historians regard the 1960 World Series as one of the most astounding. The Pirates had not reached the Series since 1927, when the Yankees beat them in four games straight, but this time Pittsburgh defeated New York, four games to three, even though the Yankees scored a record 55 runs to 19 for the Pirates. Moreover, the New Yorkers also set records for most hits in a seven-game Series, most extra-base hits, most total bases, highest batting average, and highest slugging average. Yet the Yankees lost, and stunningly so. The Series opened in Pittsburgh, and the home team won Game One, 6–4, behind Law, who pitched seven innings and gave up 10 hits but only 2 runs. Art Ditmar started for New York and lasted one-third of an inning. Pittsburgh tallied 3 runs in the first and 2 in the fourth on a home run by second baseman Bill Mazeroski, and its defense squelched the Yankees by turning 3 double plays. The next day New York's powerful bats came to life. They battered starter Friend and five relievers to win, 16–3. Center fielder Mantle led the Yankees' offense with 2 home runs, good for 5 runs batted in.

The Yankees continued to pound the Pirates' pitching when the Series moved to New York. They won Game Three, 10–0, scoring 6 runs in the first inning and 4 in the fourth. Mantle hit another home run, and second baseman Bobby

Richardson, who would finish the Series with a record 12 RBIs, added a grand slam. Whitey Ford pitched a complete game, surrendering 4 hits, while the Pirates' starter, left-hander Vinegar Bend Mizell, gave up 4 runs in one-third of an inning. Law helped Pittsburgh even the Series by winning Game Four, 3–2. He drove in the Pirates' first run in the fourth, tying the score, and gave up 2 runs in 6.1 innings. Stengel tried Ditmar again in Game Five, but again he was found wanting, yielding 3 runs in 1.1 innings. Pittsburgh won, 5–2, with third baseman Don Hoak and Mazeroski each driving in a pair of runs.

Back in Pittsburgh the Yankees' bats exploded again as they won Game Six, 12–0. New York got 17 hits and scored 5 runs in the third inning and 2 each in the sixth, seventh, and eighth. Richardson drove in 3 runs, and four others drove in 2 each, including Ford, who pitched another complete game, giving up 7 hits. That sent the Series to a seventh game for the fifth time in six seasons. Pirates manager Danny Murtaugh sent Law to the mound for a third start, and Casey Stengel countered with Bob Turley, who had won Game Two while giving up 13 hits. This time he was not so fortunate. First baseman Rocky Nelson hit a two-run homer in the first, and when catcher Smoky Burgess opened the second with a single, Turley was gone, relieved by Bill Stafford. The Pirates added 2 more runs and led, 4–0. New York scored its first run in the fifth, when first baseman Bill Skowron hit his second home run of the Series, and the Yankees chased Law in the sixth and took the lead, 5–4, on left fielder Yogi Berra's three-run homer off reliever Roy Face. In the top of the eighth inning New York stretched its lead to 7–4. Catcher John Blanchard drove in a run, and third baseman Clete Boyer doubled in the second. In the bottom of the eighth the Pirates finally got to Bobby Shantz, who had relieved Stafford in the third and pitched five scoreless innings. Three straight singles drove Shantz from the mound and led to 5 runs. Shortstop Groat drove in the first, right fielder Clemente the second, and backup catcher Hal Smith (who had entered the game in the top of the inning) hit a three-run homer over the left-field wall. The Pirates now led, 9–7, but the Yankees were not through. They tied the score in the top of the ninth. Mantle drove in a run with a single and Berra a second with a groundout. In the bottom of the ninth Mazeroski led off against Ralph Terry, the fifth Yankees pitcher. He hit the second pitch over the left-field wall, winning the game, 10–9, and the Series with it. Mazeroski's jubilant gallop home, his batting helmet in his hands, his arrival at home plate greeted by fans who had invaded the playing field, celebrated what has remained one of baseball's iconic moments.

The announcement following the owners' meeting on August 2, 1960, at the Conrad Hilton Hotel in Chicago had revealed the weakness of the Continental League's position, but the entire drama took several more months to play out. "The Continental League comes to Chicago with their hats in their hand," Bill Shea had said. "We know we have no control over what is to happen." In the morning Major League owners met with their prospective new partners and treated Branch Rickey with respect. After lunch, though, owners from the two established leagues convened again while Rickey, Shea, and their Continental League owners were left to wait in an anteroom as supplicants. "We weren't used to losing," said Wheelock Whitney, "but we knew we didn't have any cards to play." The end to Shea's dream came quickly. Walter O'Malley explained what he believed would happen. Expansion, not a third league, would be the path to the future. "All expansion business will be done under Continental League franchise holders," O'Malley said, declaring that the Major Leagues had agreed to expand by four teams, with four more to be added later. Ford Frick rejoiced at this news. "Peace, it's wonderful," he said. "I have always favored expansion, and this is the best way." The Continental League owners cheered too, anticipating that they would soon have franchises within the existing Major League framework. Shea thought so, too, and called the day "the greatest baseball event in fifty years." Initial press reports said that Houston and Toronto would join the American League, and Minneapolis–St. Paul and New York, the National League. In fact, though, owners in the established leagues were far from unanimous on how they would proceed. O'Malley, wielding influence as his league's most powerful owner, had his eyes on Houston and New York. Joe Cronin and Del Webb, the head of the American League expansion committee, craved Houston and especially southern California, aiming to pry away some of the riches going exclusively to the Dodgers. Then, too, the American League had to deal with Calvin Griffith's request to move the Senators, a plea complicated by uncertainty in Kansas City following Arnold Johnson's death and hints that the Indians might want to move too.[22]

After the Chicago meeting Rickey told Jack Kent Cooke, "You know, of course, that the internal expansion idea does not have my support as the best solution," and he later wrote to O'Malley that "it is my set opinion that internal expansion, so-called, is completely illogical." Nevertheless, the two leagues persisted. On October 9 Webb met with George Kirksey during the World Series and tried to extract a commitment to have Houston join the American League, but Craig Cullinan, whose money was funding the Houston initiative, preferred the National League. The next day O'Malley and Warren Giles announced that both Houston and New York had applied for National League membership. Owners approved both cities a week later and authorized these new clubs to begin play in 1962. The American League, stung by this preemption, did not sort out its affairs for a while. On October 26 Cronin and his owners met in New York and voted to expand in 1961. Griffith would move the Senators to Minneapolis–St. Paul, where they would become the Minnesota Twins. One expansion team would replace them in Washington, and the other, owners hoped, would go to Los Angeles. O'Malley objected, citing Major League Rule 1(c), and Frick agreed that, according to this rule, the American League could not place a team in Los Angeles without the unanimous consent of owners in both leagues. Negotiations ensued with Frick, Giles, and O'Malley engaging with Cronin, Webb, Griffith, Tigers owner John Fetzer, and Webb's partner Dan Topping. O'Malley was adamant, not conceding until the two sides agreed to seek amendments to Rule 1(c) that would permit either league to install a club in a city with more than 2.4 million people without the other league's consent. This solution would allow the American League to invade Los Angeles and the National League to return to New York, but the details of this compromise were not worked out entirely until several more days of harried negotiations took place at the 1960 winter meetings in St. Louis. The American League exacted some revenge by using a rules technicality to deny Houston and New York the chance to establish farm systems in 1961, but O'Malley struck back too. He forced the new Los Angeles team, the Angels, to play in Wrigley Field, the old ballpark that he owned, and to sign a four-year lease that included paying an annual rent of $200,000 or 7.5 percent of revenues, assuming all maintenance costs, and surrendering all receipts from parking and concession sales.[23]

The American League scurried to find owners for its two expansion franchises. In Washington competition to control the new Senators centered on two groups, one headed by retired general Pete Quesada, a World War II veteran and head of the Federal Aviation Agency, and the other by retired admiral John Bergin, head of Graham-Paige, a corporation that once manufactured automobiles but now had its business in real estate, including control of New York's Madison Square Garden. Webb and Topping supported Bergin, but Cronin was Quesada's friend, and his group got the nod in November. The situation in Los Angeles was more complicated. Immediately after the league's decision to expand, Hank Greenberg announced that he would leave his position as vice president–treasurer of the White Sox and assemble an ownership group that would include former player Ralph Kiner, San Diego banker C. Arnholt Smith, and Bill Veeck. O'Malley was none too pleased to have the showman Veeck as a potential competitor, but Greenberg said, "I'm not interested in O'Malley's opinion, but only those of the people of Los Angeles." Still, O'Malley's negotiating strategy included so many roadblocks that Greenberg withdrew. Speculation then turned to a group led by movie cowboy, recording star, and businessman Gene Autry and his partner in various radio stations, former Stanford football player Bob Reynolds. They beat out a late bid from Charlie Finley, who soon turned his attention to the Athletics. Both new clubs spent more than $2 million to acquire their basic rosters in a special player distribution held, after delays, on December 15. Each American League club prepared a list of fifteen eligible players culled from its forty-man roster. Each new club then selected, in order, ten pitchers, two catchers, six infielders, four outfielders, and six players irrespective of position. Neither Washington nor Los Angeles could take more than four players from any one club, and no existing club could lose more than seven players. In addition both new clubs selected one player from the farm system of each existing club at the standard draft price, $25,000.[24]

In the National League expansion proceeded more leisurely since the new clubs would not begin play for another year. In Houston Cullinan's group relied on his wealth, but unwilling to assume full control, he added the financial heft of oilman Bob Smith, perhaps the richest man in Texas, and the political power of Roy Hofheinz, a local official with wide influence. Kirksey, not rich enough to invest heavily, remained in charge of promotions. Before he was shunted aside, he crafted an advertising deal with the Colt Firearms Company and suggested naming the team the Colt .45s. Smith and Hofheinz objected, saying that Houston fans should pick the team's nickname. Kirksey acquiesced and conducted a poll, and after sorting through thousands of ballots, he determined that the name garnering the most votes was Colt .45s. In New York, where the vicissitudes of the Continental League had been felt most acutely, Shea rejoiced. Despite the collapse of Rickey's dream, he had kept his eye on the prize and engineered the return of National League baseball to his city. Even before the embryonic league folded, Joan Payson and the wives of the other potential owners for this new club banded together as a committee to ask the public to suggest a name for the new team. Officially they would be the New York Metropolitan Baseball Club, but about 1,500 letters poured in, offering 468 suggestions for a nickname. The women brought in an advisory committee composed of twelve sportswriters. They narrowed the list of names to ten and asked the public to vote again, but they did not limit the choice to the preferred ten. A thousand letters arrived, most suggesting names far beyond the list of finalists. Some wanted the team called the Continentals or the Skyliners or the Jets or the Burros (for the city's five boroughs). Payson preferred the Meadowlarks, a reference to Flushing Meadows, where the team would play, but the name that got the most votes, thirty-two, and the one the owners adopted was the Mets.[25]

By the time Bill Mazeroski's fly ball sailed over the left-field fence at Pittsburgh's Forbes Field to win the 1960 World Series, **Ernest Barnard**, second president of the American League, had been in his grave for thirty years. Long gone, he was nearly forgotten. His crisp, efficient guidance, calming the league's roiling waters after the reluctant and forced resignation of Ban Johnson, its founder, was but a distant memory. Johnson's name lives on. He was elected to the National Baseball Hall of Fame in 1937 and the Hall of Fame at Marietta College, his alma mater, in 1984. He had donated funds to begin construction of the college's fieldhouse, and it was named Ban Johnson Arena. The Jayhawk Collegiate League, a summer league within the National Baseball Congress, named its team in Liberal, Kansas, the BeeJays in his honor, and the Ban Johnson Amateur Baseball League began playing in the greater Kansas City area in 1927. No such acclaim for Barnard. No award bears his name, nor does his statue stand outside any ballpark. In 1946 the Hall of Fame established the Honor Rolls of Baseball, designed to commemorate executives, managers, umpires, and sportswriters. Barnard was one of thirty-nine people so honored. Nine of them were later inducted into the Hall of Fame itself, but not Barnard. Will Harridge, who succeeded Barnard in 1931, resigned as president in December 1958 and was named chairman of the board, a largely ceremonial post. He died in 1971 and was elected to the Hall of Fame posthumously a year later. Joe Cronin, elected to the Hall of Fame in 1956, followed Harridge. He was the only person to start his baseball career as a player and advance to manager, general manager, and league president. He moved the American League office from Chicago to Boston, hired Emmett Ashford, the Majors' first Black umpire, and retired in 1973, unwilling to accede to Commissioner Bowie Kuhn's desire to move the league office to New York.[26]

The presence of the Mack family among baseball's hierarchy lasted until 1961. The health of **Connie Mack** was already deteriorating when he and his sons, Roy and Earle, negotiated, over a protracted period of time, to sell the Athletics in November 1954. Mack spent the rest of the winter in Florida. He journeyed to Kansas City, the A's new home, for Opening Day. He went there again in July for a reunion, where he was greeted by nine of his former stars: Home Run Baker, Jack Barry, Mickey Cochrane, Eddie Collins, Jimmie Foxx, Lefty Grove, Mule Haas, Bing Miller, and Al Simmons. "The poor man had failed considerably since I had seen him before," Barry said. In October Mack fell out of bed, broke his hip, and required surgery, but he recovered. In February 1956 he fell out of bed again, and a priest administered the last rites of the Catholic Church. He died peacefully on the afternoon of February 5. His one-page will, filed for probate on February 16, valued his estate at $60,377.40, before taxes, the bulk of which was a $38,000 life insurance policy. For his willingness to sell the family business to the group headed by Arnold Johnson, Roy Mack had received a one-ninth interest in the Kansas City Athletics. He remained in Philadelphia and signed a three-year contract with the Phillies to guide the maintenance of their ballpark, once Shibe Park but now Connie Mack Stadium. He also supervised the Athletics' spring training camp in West Palm Beach, Florida. He died in February 1960. Roy's brother, Earle, left baseball after the sale and went into the construction business. He died in February 1967. When Charlie Finley bought control of the A's in December 1960, he bought only 52 percent of the club, the stock held by Johnson's estate. Two months later he exercised an option to buy the remaining 48 percent, making him the only American League owner besides Boston's Tom Yawkey to control the entirety of a club's stock. Selling these shares were Nathaniel Leverone, a business associate of Johnson's, Patrick Leverone, and Johnson's brother Earl, who together owned 28 percent, and, holding 20 percent, Margaret McGillicuddy, Earle's widow.[27]

After the demise of the Continental League **Branch Rickey** flew from Chicago back to Pittsburgh and told Wheelock Whitney that he had plans. "I will keep busy," he wrote. "I intend to bring another club to World Series status." He offered advice, perhaps unsolicited, to the new National League club in New York, but in June 1961 he suffered a heart attack, his second, serious enough to put him in the hospital for more than six weeks. If he had hoped for a larger role with the Mets, this health crisis forbade it. A few months later he took a telephone call from Jackie Robinson in which the former Dodger told the man who had helped facilitate the desegregation of organized baseball that the BBWAA had elected Robinson to the Hall of Fame in his first year of eligibility. Rickey joined Robinson in Cooperstown in July 1962 to celebrate and then went home to take another phone call, this time from Cardinals owner August Busch. Complaining that his club had not played in the World Series since 1946, Busch asked, "Would you be interested in coming to the

Cardinals to work as a senior consultant?" Thus began the last chapter of Rickey's baseball life, made difficult by the uncertainty about what a senior consultant was supposed to do. Rickey moved back to St. Louis, close to old friends and family, but his relationship with Cardinals general manager Bing Devine was uneasy at best. Rickey saw promise on the St. Louis roster, and he was right. The Cardinals won the World Series in 1964, but their journey to the pennant was tumultuous. Busch fired Devine in August of that year and told Rickey in October that his services were no longer needed. Except for the accolades, his most remarkable baseball career was over. A year later Rickey went to Columbia, Missouri, to be inducted into the Missouri Sports Hall of Fame. His acceptance speech was, as always, memorable, but before he could finish, he paused, staggered, and struggled to say, "I don't believe I'm going to be able to speak any longer." He collapsed and lost consciousness. A doctor administered mouth-to-mouth resuscitation that kept Rickey alive. Rushed to a hospital, he lingered in a coma for almost a month before dying on December 9, 1965. He was inducted into the Hall of Fame in 1967.[28]

The tenure of **Kenesaw Landis** as commissioner remained the yardstick against which the performance of each of his successors has been measured. The force of the wording on his Hall of Fame plaque, "His integrity and leadership established baseball in the esteem, respect, and affection of the American people," remained strong, but as time went on, arguments over certain aspects of his tenure came to the fore. Jerome Holtzman called Landis "a crusty federal judge [who] gave birth to the fiction that the commissioner is a fire-belching Solomon. During his twenty-four-year reign, he was the first and last court of recourse." Over time, though, how much authority Landis had and how he had brandished his power became the subject of intense scrutiny. Questions surrounded his treatment of the Black Sox and his opposition to the development of farm systems. Most acutely debate raged over charges that he had refused to speak out or act against segregation in organized baseball. This argument came to a head in 2020 when the political attention of the nation embraced questions of police misconduct and racial injustice. Barry Larkin, Terry Pendleton, and Mike Schmidt, recipients of the Most Valuable Player Award, questioned the plaque's formal name, the Kenesaw Mountain Landis Memorial Baseball Award. "Why it is on there?" Larkin asked. Said Schmidt, "If you're looking to expose individuals in baseball's history who promoted racism by continuing to close baseball's doors to men of color, Kenesaw Landis would be a candidate." Pendleton added, "This is 2020 now and things have changed all around the world. It can change for the better." The membership of the BBWAA responded by voting overwhelmingly to remove Landis's name from the award. "We will no longer be associated with the Landis name, and the MVP plaques will be nameless in 2020," BBWAA president Paul Sullivan said.[29]

When Larry MacPhail, Dan Topping, and Del Webb bought the Yankees in January 1945, MacPhail became club president–general manager, and **Ed Barrow** was elevated to chairman of the board, a new position. "Mr. Barrow and I are in full accord on the policy of the club," MacPhail said, "and he will continue to direct affairs until such time as I can permanently take over my new duties." That time came quickly, and Barrow was shunted aside. He retired at the end of 1946, accepting a year's salary as severance. MacPhail took over with his customary swagger. He moved the club's offices to prominent space on Fifth Avenue, just across the street from the Plaza Hotel and close to a number of fine restaurants where he and Topping could enjoy extended lunches and happy hours. He also decided that the best way to handle Barrow's office files and, in fact, all the club's records dating back to the time when they were known as the Highlanders was to throw them away. Fortunately the maintenance man responsible for emptying the waste baskets thought otherwise. He salvaged everything, took it home, and began looking for a buyer. He sold some items to a New York book dealer and some to a dealer in New Haven, Connecticut; he gave some endorsed and canceled checks to friends as souvenirs. The book dealer later peddled what he had to a retired news editor at the *New York World–Telegram and Sun*. He kept the collection for about two years and eventually, according to Yankees historian Marty Appel, "the material trickled into a larger marketplace." Barrow chafed at retirement even though his health was failing. He attended Babe Ruth Day at Yankee Stadium in April 1947. Topping gave him a watch at an old-timers' game in 1948, and in 1950 he was the guest of honor at that season's Old-Timers' Game, receiving a television set as a gift to mark his long tenure with the club. Barrow also served on a Hall of Fame selection committee that later became the Veterans Committee. He himself was elected to the Hall in September 1953, three months before his death.[30]

When **Larry MacPhail** testified before Congressman Emanuel Celler and the Subcommittee on Study of Monopoly Power on October 24, 1951, he was listed in the table of contents as "former club owner, Bel Air, Md." Indeed the end of his baseball career had come suddenly. As the Yankees exulted in their clubhouse following their triumph in the 1947 World Series, MacPhail, never shy, stormed to the center of the room and proclaimed his resignation. "I'm through. I've got what I wanted, and I'm through," reported the *New*

York Times. "I can't take any more of this. My health won't stand it." In truth, MacPhail and his co-owners, Topping and Webb, had disagreed about how much authority MacPhail should cede to George Weiss, who was running the Yankees' farm system. So MacPhail's retreat to his own farm in Maryland was not unexpected. He had purchased a dairy farm in 1941, converted it to breed Black Angus cattle, and then switched again to breeding and racing thoroughbreds, adopting maize and blue from the University of Michigan as his racing colors. With his heart set on producing a colt that would win the Kentucky Derby, MacPhail invested heavily. That dream went unfulfilled, and in 1952, just fifteen months after becoming a father once again at the age of sixty, he bought Bowie Race Track, spending considerable sums on its renovation and development, as he had with ballparks in Columbus, Cincinnati, and Brooklyn. Running Bowie was fun, but the breeding end of the business brought him more satisfaction and more income. He never returned to baseball except to analyze the sport's ills and suggest cures for them in *Life* magazine in 1958. MacPhail battled cancer twice, enduring a severe course of radiation on his throat and then surgery on his colon. As he advanced in age, his behavior became erratic, and he needed constant medical care. He found it in a veterans' hospital in Miami, where he enjoyed eating daily servings of ice cream and watching a huge American flag waving just outside his window. Ravaged by a lifetime of smoking and drinking, he died on October 1, 1975, and became yet another of baseball's primal forces to be inducted into the Hall of Fame posthumously in 1978.[31]

Hank Greenberg retired as a player following the 1947 season. He was proud of how he had played. "I guess I was tough to handle," he wrote. "I played hard, I tried my best. I was always looking to overachieve, and I guess a lot of people didn't like that." He was proud, too, of how he had managed his finances. "By the time I closed out my career, I had saved $300,000. I only made $447,000, so in all those years I spent $147,000," he recalled, but he soon learned that there were better ways to invest than Treasury bonds. After striking up a friendship with Bill Veeck at the 1947 World Series, he declined an offer to play for the Indians, but he agreed to learn the baseball business and become club vice president. He later ran the farm system and became general manager after Veeck sold the Indians to Ellis Ryan. In this position he advocated for expansion to the West Coast, desegregated the Indians' spring training accommodations in Tucson, and made sure that the club stayed in integrated hotels on the road. In 1956 the BBWAA elected him to the Hall of Fame. "It's just too wonderful for words," he said. "I'm deeply grateful and humble for this honor." After the Indians finished in sixth place in 1957, criticism from fans and the press persuaded the club to fire Greenberg. After a short while he became part of a seven-man syndicate led by Veeck and Chicago businessman Arthur Allyn that bought the White Sox in March 1959. That arrangement lasted until June 1961, when Allyn bought out his partners. Greenberg remained as general manager, but he resigned in August, ending his baseball career, and he eventually moved to Beverly Hills. He went back to Detroit in 1983 for a ceremony at which his number 5 was retired, and he died in September 1986 after a lengthy struggle with cancer.[32]

When **Don Barnes** sold the Browns in August 1945, he said, "I think I have accomplished my three big ambitions in coming into baseball. I finally saw a St. Louis American League team win the pennant; I saw Sportsman's Park jammed on the last day of the 1944 season for a Browns game; and I am leaving the Browns in sound financial condition." He left baseball but remained at the head of the American Investment Company, a business he had founded to finance the installment sales of automobiles. Deeply involved in various civic and charitable organizations after selling the club, he was widely regarded as "the elder statesman of the consumer finance field" and served as president of the National Consumer Finance Association. Barnes died in St. Louis on July 20, 1962, of complications following abdominal surgery.[33]

Yogi Berra enjoyed a storied Major League career as a player, manager, and coach and was elected to the Hall of Fame in 1972. After his retirement he became one of America's most beloved personalities, with a reputation burnished by a seemingly endless bundle of off-beat comments and observations, often grammatically incorrect but perceptive, dubbed "Yogi-isms." Honored in St. Louis, his hometown, during the 1947 season with a Yogi Berra Night, he began his speech by saying, "I want to thank everyone for making this night necessary." Berra had made his Major League debut late in 1946, but he did not become the Yankees' starting catcher until 1949. Ungainly and unorthodox, he nevertheless developed into one of the game's finest catchers, both offensively and defensively, taking an approach to baseball that was perhaps best encapsulated by one of the quotations attributed to him: "Half this game is ninety percent mental." Berra played with the Yankees from 1946 through 1963. He batted .285 for his career and hit 358 home runs. He won the American League Most Valuable Player Award three times and played for ten teams that won the World Series (1947, 1949, 1950, 1951, 1952, 1953, 1956, 1958, 1961, and 1962). He retired after the 1963 season, and the Yankees named him manager to replace Ralph Houk, who had replaced Casey Stengel after the

Yankees lost the 1960 World Series. Berra's Yankees, an aging team, won the pennant in 1964 but lost the World Series, and he was fired. The crosstown Mets called, and Berra answered, signing on as a player-coach. He played in only four games in 1965 but remained a Mets coach through several managerial changes, finally getting his chance at the helm after Gil Hodges died of a heart attack in 1972. Berra managed the Mets for three and a half seasons, winning the 1973 pennant, but he was fired in August 1975. He returned to the Yankees as a coach and then as manager in 1984 and for one month in 1985, and he finished his baseball career as a coach for the Houston Astros (formerly the Colt .45s). In retirement his humble celebrity spread through a number of television commercials that played off his personality, and his Yogi-isms became so ubiquitous that he was said to have said, "I never said most of the things I said." As a legend and an icon, he was pleased when the Yogi Berra Museum and Learning Center opened on the campus of Montclair State University in Little Falls, New Jersey. Berra died in September 2005.[34]

Tom Yawkey never won the World Series as owner of the Red Sox. At his death in 1976 the club and Fenway Park were part of a trust he had created to control his charitable donations. The two living trustees were his widow, Jean, and James Curran, an accountant in Yawkey's New York office. Joseph LaCour, who had also worked for Yawkey, became a third trustee, and the trio soon appointed a six-member advisory board to run the ball club. In October the trust announced its intention to sell the Red Sox to a thirteen-person group—including Haywood Sullivan (a member of the advisory board) and team trainer Buddy LeRoux as general partners and Jean Yawkey as one of eleven limited partners—for an estimated $15 million. There were other bids, including at least one offering more money, and in December the American League refused to approve the sale, declaring that the purchasing group lacked financial stability. In March 1978 the Sullivan-LeRoux group fashioned a new bid with Jean Yawkey as a third general partner. The league approved this deal in May, but within three years the general partners were fighting among themselves. Yawkey eventually bought out LeRoux, and when she died in February 1992, John Harrington, chief executive officer of the trust, took control of the club and became team president. Tom Yawkey was elected to the Hall of Fame, posthumously, in 1980, but his role in his club's resistance to desegregation drew renewed scrutiny in 2006. The Boys and Girls Clubs of Boston named its new center in his honor, but in 2018 the Boston Public Improvement Commission accepted the club's proposal to rename Yawkey Way, a street adjacent to Fenway Park, returning it to its previous name, Jersey Street.[35]

Bill Veeck owned three Major League clubs in his colorful career—the Indians, the Browns, and the White Sox—but he owned the White Sox twice. The group he put together in 1959 bought the 54 percent of the White Sox owned by Dorothy Rigney, Charles Comiskey's granddaughter, and left Chuck Comiskey, Rigney's brother, holding the other 46 percent of the club's stock. With Veeck in charge the White Sox won the pennant in 1959, but they lost the World Series to the Los Angeles Dodgers. In 1960 Veeck introduced two innovations that eventually became standard in baseball: names on the backs of players' uniforms and fireworks launched from the scoreboard after a White Sox home run. Various ailments forced Veeck to sell his share of the club to Arthur Allyn in June 1960, and in December Allyn bought out Chuck Comiskey, ending his family's long involvement in baseball. Veeck retired to a farm in Maryland, but he could not remain inactive. For a while he ran Suffolk Downs, a racetrack near Boston, and wrote a book about his experience, *Thirty Tons a Day*. The White Sox struggled financially. John Allyn, who had bought the club from his brother, was near bankruptcy, and Veeck put together a group of more than forty investors to reacquire the club in 1975, saving it from being moved to Seattle. Several American League owners opposed the deal, claiming that it relied too much on borrowed money. But they disliked Veeck too. He raised additional cash, but the owners voted no again, changing their minds only after Detroit owner John Fetzer said, "Look, I don't like it any more than you do that we're allowing a guy in here who has called me a son-of-bitch over and over. But, gentlemen, we've got to take another vote." And they did, approving the sale, 10–2. Veeck took charge just days before arbitrator Peter Seitz abolished the reserve clause, and the emergence of what came to be called free agency exposed the lack of Veeck's resources. Additional health issues compounded his problems, and in 1980 he sold the club to Jerry Reinsdorf, a Chicago real estate developer, and Eddie Einhorn, a television executive. In his final years Veeck returned to Wrigley Field, sitting in the bleachers as a fan. He died in January 1986 and was elected to the Hall of Fame, posthumously, in 1991.[36]

After Walter O'Malley assumed control of the Dodgers, he went to war to rid the club of all things Rickey, even imposing a $1 fine on anyone he caught uttering the man's name. **Red Barber**, beloved by Brooklyn fans, fell victim to this purge. O'Malley's biographer wrote that the two had a complicated relationship. "O'Malley and I never had an argument," Barber wrote. "We never had anything open. It was just a combination of small things that kept growing and growing." What created the final chasm between the two was O'Malley's cavalier reaction to news that Barber and Mel Allen would be broadcasting the

1953 World Series on the radio. Gillette had made this announcement without negotiating with the announcers, and Barber was incensed. He told O'Malley how he was being treated, and the owner dismissed him, saying, "That's your problem." On the spot Barber decided not to return to the broadcast booth at Ebbets Field. A few days later he signed on with the Yankees, even though he knew he would play second fiddle to Allen and deal more with television than he would prefer. Barber and Allen remained partners until the Yankees fired Allen after the 1964 World Series. Barber lasted two more seasons, his dismissal coming perhaps because on a chilly day during the 1966 season, with the Yankees on their way to their first last-place finish since 1912, he called his viewers' attention to the "smallest crowd in the history of Yankee Stadium." Barber commenced a very active retirement in Key Biscayne, Florida, writing books and a newspaper column and broadcasting occasionally on local radio and television. In 1978, when the Hall of Fame created the Ford C. Frick Award to be presented annually to a broadcaster for "major contributions to baseball," Barber and Allen were jointly its first recipients. Starting in 1981 Barber enthralled a whole new audience when he agreed to join the National Public Radio show *Morning Edition* and converse live with host Bob Edwards for four minutes every Friday morning. Edwards preferred a scripted show, but Barber was delightfully serendipitous, talking as much about opera, philosophy, and his beloved camellias as sports. He asked to be off the broadcast set for October 9, 1992, and died thirteen days later.[37]

In 1963 **Ford Frick** announced that he would retire as commissioner when his contract expired in two years. Frick had stood as the public face of baseball for more than a decade, not only in front of Congressional committees, but also before increasingly critical media, but his authority was limited and his pronouncements often uncertain. Baseball had continued to struggle in its relationship with television, not solved until passage of the Sports Broadcasting Act of 1961. As the plight of the Minors continued, Frick urged action, but nothing happened until May 1962, when the Player Development plan replaced the Player Development and Promotion program. Under this new structure the Major Leagues took control of the Minors, guaranteeing the survival of at least a hundred Minor League clubs by agreeing to pay the bulk of players' salaries throughout a consolidated league structure. Most famously Frick got caught up in the controversy over how to acknowledge records achieved in the additional games added to the regular-season schedule because of expansion. Frick had suggested separate categories for records set during the new 162-game seasons and perhaps the use of "some distinctive mark" when appropriate. Yet after Roger Maris hit his 61st home run in the Yankees' final game of the 1961 season, surpassing Babe Ruth's single-season total of 60, Frick's sensible concern gave way to the erroneous idea that he had mandated an asterisk be placed next to Maris's name. Frick was elected to the Hall of Fame in 1970. Four years before, he had spoken against Ted Williams's suggestion that the Hall induct the best players from the Negro Leagues, arguing that they were not qualified because they had not played ten years in the Major Leagues. Victimized by several strokes in the 1970s, Frick died in April 1978.[38]

Henry Aaron played for the Milwaukee Braves until they moved to Atlanta after the 1965 season, for the Atlanta Braves from 1966 through 1974, and for the American League's Milwaukee Brewers in 1975 and 1976. Along the way he picked up the nickname "Hammerin' Hank" for his prodigious ability at the plate, but he was more often called the "Home Run King" after he surpassed Babe Ruth's record of 714 career home runs. Aaron finished the 1973 season with 713 homers, and his quest to exceed Ruth drew intense media attention and virulent, bigoted antagonism expressed in bags full of racially charged hate mail and death threats. He tied Ruth on Opening Day in 1974, and he broke the record on April 8 against the Dodgers' Al Downing. At Aaron's request the Braves traded him to the Brewers after that season. He hit 22 homers in his final two years, finishing with 755, a total not exceeded until Barry Bonds did so in 2007. After he retired, Aaron worked as the Braves' vice president for player development and later served as a senior vice president. He had wide business interests and promoted the Hank Aaron Chasing the Dream Foundation, helping gifted children achieve their potential. The Braves honored Aaron by retiring his number in 1977 and unveiled two statues of him, one that stood at Atlanta–Fulton County Stadium and was later moved, as did the Braves, to Turner Field, and a second installed at SunTrust Park, later Truist Park, the Braves' home starting in 2017. He was elected to the Hall of Fame in 1982. In 1999 Major League Baseball created the Hank Aaron Award, given each year to one player in each league deemed to have achieved the season's best overall offensive performance. At his death Aaron held the Major League records for total bases and runs batted in, was second in at bats, and third in hits. He won the National League home run title four times, although he never hit more than 47 in a season, was selected as an All-Star in every season except his first and last, and won three Gold Glove Awards for defensive excellence in the outfield. He died in 2021.[39]

Bill Shea did not seek an executive position with the team that became the New York Mets, nor did the Mets offer him one. Once the club received a certificate of membership from the National League in March 1961 and the New York General Assembly approved public funding for a private purpose, the construction of a new ballpark, in the same month, Shea's baseball work was essentially over. The Mets hired George Weiss as president and Casey Stengel as manager soon after both had been cut loose by the Yankees after the 1960 World Series. The Mets played their first two seasons, 1962 and 1963, in the Polo Grounds, the Giants' old home. Ground was broken for Flushing Meadows Park on October 28, 1961. In February 1963 Mayor Robert Wagner signed a bill changing the ballpark's name to William A. Shea Municipal Stadium. It opened in April 1964 and was the Mets' home until the final game of the 2008 season. Shea was inducted into the Mets Hall of Fame in 1983. He died in October 1991, and his law firm, Shea and Gould, lasted until 1994, when it dissolved in acrimony. Late in 2008 demolition of Shea Stadium began, preceded by an auction of its artifacts, and the Mets began playing the 2009 season in their new home, CITI Field.[40]

Acknowledgments

Any publishing project taking as long as this one to come to fruition compels its author to recognize with profound thanks the dozens of friends and compatriots whose generous assistance has provided essential aid and support along the way. My first thanks go to the late Dorothy Seymour Mills, who encouraged my work when it was just an idea; to Dan Ross, former director of the University of Nebraska Press, who helped turn the idea into a contract; and to academic historians and dear friends Dick Crepeau, Larry Gerlach, and Sam Regalado, who continually assured me that my reach had not exceeded my grasp. My thanks go, too, to Elaine Engst and Lorna Knight at the Carl A. Kroch Library at Cornell University, who allowed me unprecedented access to the Harold Seymour Papers, and to John Rawlings, former editor of the *Sporting News*, who encouraged me to believe that I could complete this project while also working for him.

For help with photographs I am grateful to the following: Katie Boudreau, Deerfield Academy; Charles Brown and Alyssa Persson, University of Missouri –St. Louis, Mercantile Library; Nadia Clifton, University of North Carolina at Chapel Hill, Wilson Special Collections Library; Emily Deal, Vince Lee, Bethany Scott, and Greg Yerke, University of Houston Special Collections; Chris Eckes, Cincinnati Reds; Jason Flahardy, University of Kentucky Archives; Stephen Grinch, Otterbein University; John Horne and Cassidy Lent, National Baseball Hall of Fame and Museum; Kraig Kitchin, Radio Hall of Fame; Matthew Lutts, Associated Press; Gary Mitchem, McFarland Publishing; Gio Papanicolaou, Shutterstock; Arielle Petrovich, Beloit College; Sara Pezzoni, University of Texas at Arlington Special Collections; David Pietrusza; Beth Piwkowski, Cleveland State University Special Collections; Jacob Pomrenke, SABR; Amy Purcell, University of Louisville Archives and Special Collections; David Rodriguez, Redux Pictures; Mark Rucker, Transcendental Graphics; and Steve Steinberg.

Other heartfelt and deserved thanks go to Marshall Adesman, Rich Applegate, Jean Ardell, Mark Armour, Gary Arnold, Bill Ballew, Cryder Bankes, Carlos Bauer, Roland Baumann, Gary Bedingfield, Dick Beverage, Charlie Bevis, Clifford Blau, David Bohmer, Bob Buege, Gene Carney, John Carvalho,

Stuart Chambers, Jennifer Chan, Merritt Clifton, Casey Coleman, Everett Cope, Tim Copeland, Bill Deane, Jonathan Dunkle, Jeff Ecker, Chris Eckes, Morris Eckhouse, Mike Emeigh, Brian Englehardt, Bruce Esser, Gary Fink, Rob Fitts, David Fleitz, Cynthia Franco, Chris Gallutia, Rob Garratt, Jim Gates, Rai Goerler, John Grabowski, Karl Green, Craig Greenham, Rex Hamann, Michael Haupert, Leslie Heaphy, John Heer, Don Heidenreich, Bill Hickman, Judith Hiltner, Stuart Hodesh, Bob Hoie, Brett Honeycutt, Paul Huffman, Rick Huhn, Rob Hurtt, John Husman, Bob Jansen, Harry Jebsen, Michael Jesse, Lloyd Johnson, Dave Kelly, Bob Kerler, Dave Kindred, Francis Kinlaw, Leonard Koppett, Chuck Korr, Herm Krabbenhoft, Graig Kreindler, Sean Lahman, Bill Lamb, Allison Levin, Dan Levitt, Lee Lowenfish, Christopher Luettger, Victoria Luther, Bill Marshall, Bob Mayhall, Neal McCabe, Jimmy McColery, Andy McCue, Chuck McGill, Jim Meier, Stacey Merx, Dawn Mitchell, Peter Morris, Dan Nathan, Mitchell Nathanson, Rod Nelson, Skip Nipper, Bill Nowlin, Jeff Obermeyer, Darrol Pierson, Bobby Plapinger, Jacob Pomrenke, Ben Rader, John Rall, Tom Reinsfelder, Greg Rhodes, John Rosengren, Robert Rubin, Bobby Ruffin, Mark Sandheinrich, Joe Santry, Gabriel Schechter, John Schleppi, Fred Schuld, Stuart Shea, Terry Shea, Tom Shieber, Dave Smith, Gary Smith, Ron Smith, Dennis Snelling, Lyle Spatz, Glenn Stout, John Thorn, Stew Thornley, Steve Treder, Michel Vigneault, Daniel Vivian, Linda Wachtel, Jim Walker, Bob Warrington, Irwin Weil, Paul Wendt, Jim Wheeler, Frank White, Tim Wiles, Laura Wilkerson, Kat Williams, Saul Wisnia, Ryan Woodward, Lewis Wyman, Al Yellon, John Zajc, and Tom Zocco.

It is also a pleasure to thank the staff of the University of Nebraska Press, including senior acquisitions editor Rob Taylor, whose patience knows no bounds; senior project editor Sara Springsteen, who kept us on schedule; and copyeditor Bojana Ristich.

Finally, to my family: my late parents; my wife Donna; our daughters Katie and Sarah; our sons-in-law Jason Meyers and Justin Hartman; and our grandsons Andy, Patrick, Joey, and Max. As Brian Wilson and Tony Asher wrote, "God only knows what I'd be without you."

Notes

PROLOGUE

1. *Sporting News*, April 2, 1931.
2. *Cleveland Press*, March 31, 1931; *Sporting News*, April 2, 1931.
3. Lane, "New President," 339–40; *Sporting News*, November 10, 1927.
4. Lane, "New President," 341.
5. O'Neal, *The American Association*, 206; Madden and Stewart, *The Western League*, 52–53; L. Johnson and Wolff, *Encyclopedia of Minor League Baseball*, 2nd ed., 123–24.
6. L. Johnson and Wolff, *Encyclopedia of Minor League Baseball*, 2nd ed., 123–24. See also Lane, "Brooklyn's New Business Manager," 301; *Sporting News*, March 26, 1936. See also Costello, "Bob Quinn."
7. Lane, "Brooklyn's New Business Manager," 301; Longert, *Addie Joss*, 28–29.
8. Lane, "New President," 341.
9. Seymour, *The Early Years*, 94, 144–47; N. J. Sullivan, *The Minors*, 6–24; Hoie, "The Minor Leagues," 510; L. Johnson and Wolff, *Encyclopedia of Minor League Baseball*, 3rd ed., 136, 141.
10. Finch, Addington, and Morgan, *The Story of Minor League Baseball*, 18; L. Johnson and Wolff, *Encyclopedia of Minor League Baseball*, 3rd ed., 136, 141; Seymour, *The Early Years*, 108–9; D. A. Sullivan, *Early Innings*, 128–30; *Spalding's Official Baseball Guide for 1883*, 58–60 (cited hereafter as *Spalding Guide*); *Spalding Guide for 1884*, 47–51.
11. *Spalding Guide for 1887*, 101–6; Burk, *Never Just a Game*, 100–101, 121–22; Alexander, *Our Game*, 62–63; Rader, *Baseball*, 77–78; House Judiciary Committee, *Organized Baseball*, 36. See also Blau, "The Major League Draft."
12. Murdock, *Ban Johnson*, 9–29.
13. Finch, Addington, and Morgan, *The Story of Minor League Baseball*, 17; L. Allen, *The American League Story*, 4–6; Seymour, *The Early Years*, 307–8; Murdock, *Ban Johnson*, 30–42.
14. Allen, *The American League Story*, 7–11; Murdock, *Ban Johnson*, 43–48; Seymour, *The Early Years*, 308–14. See also Buege, "The Birth of the American League," 6–9.
15. Murdock, *Ban Johnson*, 58, 67, and chapters 7–8.
16. Lane, "New President," 341, 374; L. Johnson and Wolff, *Encyclopedia of Minor League Baseball*, 3rd ed., 178; O'Neal, *The American Association*, 3–4; Wright, *The American Association*, 3; House Judiciary Committee, *Organized Baseball*, 42;

Finch, Addington, and Morgan, *The Story of Minor League Baseball*, 17–21; N. J. Sullivan, *The Minors*, 44–46. See also Green, "1901," 6–8.

17. Lane, "New President," 374; O'Neal, *The American Association*, 4–5; Schneider, *The Cleveland Indians Encyclopedia*, 339.
18. F. A. Lewis, *The Cleveland Indians*, 4–31; Eckhouse, *Legends of the Tribe*, 1–6; Koppett, *Koppett's Concise History of Major League Baseball*, 83; Dewey and Acocella, *The Ball Clubs*, 206–9; Lieb, *The St. Louis Cardinals*, 21–23; Thomas, "Frank DeHass Robison and Matthew Stanley Robison," 142; Cash, *Before They Were Cardinals*, 255; Eisenbath, *The Cardinals Encyclopedia*, 397; Schneider, *The Cleveland Indians Encyclopedia*, 11. See also Egan, *Base Ball on the Western Reserve*; and Hetrick, *Misfits!*
19. F. A. Lewis, *The Cleveland Indians*, 32; Eckhouse, *Legends of the Tribe*, 6; Associated Press, June 29, 1934 (Charles Somers clipping file, *Sporting News* Research Center); *Sporting News*, November 10, 1927, and January 14, 1932; Murdock, *Ban Johnson*, 48–50. See also Schuld, "Charles W. Somers."
20. Bernstein, "Barney Dreyfuss"; Boxerman and Boxerman, *Ebbets to Veeck to Busch*, 29–32; D. M. Daniel, "Dreyfuss," 439–40; Bailey, "Barney Dreyfuss Buys Pittsburgh"; Lieb, *The Pittsburgh Pirates*, 44–45, 48–49; *Sporting News*, December 16, 1899.
21. Murdock, *Ban Johnson*, 46–66; L. Allen, *The American League Story*, 25–26; Seymour, *The Early Years*, 307–24; Enders, *100 Years of the World Series*, 12; Abrams, *The First World Series*, 52. See also Miskowiec, "1902," 12–15.
22. N. J. Sullivan, *The Minors*, 42, 45–46; D. A. Sullivan, *Early Innings*, 256–57, 267–68; Alexander, *Our Game*, 86; L. Johnson and Wolff, *Encyclopedia of Minor League Baseball*, 3rd ed., 189, 196; Burk, *Never Just a Game*, 157.
23. L. Johnson and Wolff, *Encyclopedia of Minor League Baseball*, 2nd ed., 133–35.
24. Wright, *The International League*, 1ff; Madden and Stewart, *The Western League*, 1–76; Bryson and Housh, *Through the Years with the Western League since 1885*, 19; Wright, *The American Association*, xi, 1–3, 10; O'Neal, *The American Association*, 3–4; Nelson, *The Golden Game*, 12–18; Zingg and Medeiros, *Runs, Hits, and an Era*, 2–17; L. Johnson and Wolff, *Encyclopedia of Minor League Baseball*, 2nd ed., 91, 92, 123–27, 134–41; N. J. Sullivan, *The Minors*, 58.
25. Seymour, *The Early Years*, 84, 106, 145, 165, 297, 298, 341, 343; Seymour, *The Golden Age*, 10, 27–31, 33–37, 263; Dewey and Acocella, *Biographical History of Baseball*, 366–67, 523–24. See also Lamberty, "Harry Clay Pulliam," 22–23; and Ginsburg, "John Kinley Tener," 26–28.
26. Cook, *August "Garry" Herrmann*, 5–6; L. Allen, *The Cincinnati Reds*, 74–75; *Reach Guide for 1904*, 116–17; *Sporting News*, April 30, 1931.
27. Wright, *The Southern Association*, 5–78, 105; L. Johnson and Wolff, *Encyclopedia of Minor League Baseball*, 3rd ed., 145, 196; *Sporting News*, January 25, February 8, and February 22, 1934; O'Neal, *The Southern League*, 1–24; *Reach Guide for 1908*, 139–48; *Reach Guide for 1909*, 163–81; *Spalding Guide for 1909*, 29–31; *Spalding Guide for 1912*, 7–11. See also Nowlin, "1907," 40–42; and Pajot, "1908," 45–48.

28. Light, *Cultural Encyclopedia of Baseball*, 176, 253, 771–72; Seymour, *The Golden Age*, 199–206; N. J. Sullivan, *The Minors*, 59–60, 65–77.
29. N. J. Sullivan, *The Minors*, 60–63, 76; L. Johnson and Wolff, *Encyclopedia of Minor League Baseball*, 2nd ed., 193–211.
30. Leavengood, *Clark Griffith*, 114–16; Seymour, *The Golden Age*, 245–55; Murdock, *Ban Johnson*, 119–26; L. Johnson and Wolff, *Encyclopedia of Minor League Baseball*, 2nd ed., 213–14; *Reach Guide* for 1919, 8.
31. *Spalding Guide* for 1919, 39–40; *Reach Guide* for 1919, 272–81; L. Johnson and Wolff, *Encyclopedia of Minor League Baseball*, 3rd ed., 206. See also Pomrenke, "1918," 118–21.
32. *Reach Guide* for 1920, 19–21, 261–63; *Reach Guide* for 1921, 12–13, 194–95; N. J. Sullivan, *The Minors*, 65–66; L. Johnson and Wolff, *Encyclopedia of Minor League Baseball*, 3rd ed., 206.
33. Pietrusza, Silverman, and Gershman, *Baseball*, 632–33; Dewey and Acocella, *The Ball Clubs*, 209–13; Eckhouse, *Legends of the Tribe*, 12–14; F. A. Lewis, *The Cleveland Indians*, 51–63, 76–79; Schneider, *The Cleveland Indians Encyclopedia*, 324, 339–40; Longert, *Addie Joss*, 124–25; Beverage, "Farm Systems and the PCL," 1; *Sporting News*, November 10, 1927.
34. *Sporting News*, December 3, 1942; Murdock, *Ban Johnson*, 83; F. A. Lewis, *The Cleveland Indians*, 77–79, 83–87, 107–34; Schneider, *The Cleveland Indians Encyclopedia*, 324, 340.
35. Seymour, *The Golden Age*, 264–68; Pietrusza, Silverman, and Gershman, *Baseball*, 730; *Sporting News*, June 11, 1952; Murdock, *Ban Johnson*, 167–72.
36. Huhn, *The Sizzler*, 5–26, 40–41; Seymour, *The Golden Age*, 259–61; Pietrusza, Silverman, and Gershman, *Baseball*, 1042–43; Murdock, *Ban Johnson*, 159–63.
37. Seymour, *The Golden Age*, 262–63; Murdock, *Ban Johnson*, 163–64.
38. Seymour, *The Golden Age*, 24, 263–64; Murdock, *Ban Johnson*, 145, 156–57; Dewey and Acocella, *Biographical History of Baseball*, 369.
39. Seymour, *The Golden Age*, 265–68, 311–12; *Sporting News*, June 11, 1952; Murdock, *Ban Johnson*, 167–72.
40. Seymour, *The Golden Age*, 269–73; Murdock, *Ban Johnson*, 172–78. See also Pomrenke, "1919," 123–27.
41. Seymour, *The Golden Age*, 294–304; White, *Creating the National Pastime*, 91–101. See also Carney, *Burying the Black Sox*; and Pomrenke, *Scandal on the South Side*.
42. Seymour, *The Golden Age*, 311–18; Murdock, *Ban Johnson*, 180–82; Pietrusza, *Judge and Jury*, 161–66; *Sporting News*, November 11 and 18, 1920.
43. Voigt, *American Baseball*, 201–2; Pietrusza, *Judge and Jury*, 166–72; Leuchtenburg, *The Perils of Prosperity*, 89; Alexander, *Our Game*, 119; Crepeau, *Baseball*, 20; *Sporting News*, November 18 and November 25, 1920.
44. Murdock, *Ban Johnson*, 145–52, 159–63, 221–25; Schneider, *The Cleveland Indians Encyclopedia*, 325.
45. *Sporting News*, December 3, 1942; *Reach Guide* for 1928, 21; *Reach Guide* for 1929, 115; *Reach Guide* for 1930, 15; *Reach Guide* for 1931, 15, 17; *Cleveland Press*, March 28, 1931; Murdock, *Ban Johnson*, 231–36.

46. Reach Guide for 1932, 11–13, 224–33; Spalding Guide for 1932, 11–14, 220–27; Sporting News, April 2, 1931; L. Allen, The American League Story, 127–28.
47. Murdock, Ban Johnson, 236–37; Cleveland Plain Dealer, March 31, 1931; Sporting News, April 9, 1931; Spencer (IN) Evening World, March 28 and April 1, 1931; Owen (IN) Leader, April 8, 1931.
48. Spalding Guide for 1932, 11; Reach Guide for 1932, 13; Pietrusza, Silverman, and Gershman, Baseball, 438–39, 691–93.

1. "THE BALL PLAYER IS A FORTUNATE MAN"

1. New York Times, April 15, 1931.
2. Sporting News, April 23, 1931; New York Herald Tribune, April 15, 1931; A. H. Levy, Joe McCarthy, 145–48.
3. Sporting News, April 23, 1931; New York Herald Tribune, April 15, 1931.
4. Nash, The Life of Herbert Hoover, 1:1–29; Burner, Herbert Hoover, 16, 18; Hoover, The Memoirs of Herbert Hoover, 1:21; R. N. Smith, An Uncommon Man, 16; Mead and Dickson, Baseball, 64, 66, 68; Creamer, Babe, 318–19.
5. Lieb, Connie Mack, 228–29; Voigt, American Baseball, 207; Kuklick, To Every Thing a Season, 61; Kashatus, Connie Mack's '29 Triumph, 129–30.
6. Jordan, The Athletics of Philadelphia, 104; Macht, Connie Mack: The Turbulent and Triumphant Years, 553, 620–21; Mead and Dickson, Baseball, 60 (with Williams quotes and Hoover quote); Kennedy, Freedom from Fear, 76–77.
7. Appel and Goldblatt, Baseball's Best, 272; Stuart H. Chambers, email messages to author, October 9, 2003; "51st Regiment, Massachusetts Infantry (Militia)," Family Search, https://familysearch.org/wiki/en/51st_Regiment,_Massachusetts_Infantry_(Militia), accessed June 2021; Lieb, Connie Mack, 3–5, 6–11, 17; Roy, History of East Brookfield, Massachusetts, 243; Sporting News, February 15, 1956. See also Macht, Connie Mack and the Early Years of Baseball, 8–20, 22–28.
8. Lieb, Connie Mack, 12–27; Mack, My 66 Years in the Big Leagues, 18–19; Macht, Connie Mack and the Early Years of Baseball, 29–51, 60–61.
9. Philadelphia Evening Bulletin, February 1956 (date uncertain; Connie Mack clipping file, Sporting News Research Center); "Sports: The Monumental Mack," Newsweek, December 28, 1942, 78; Lieb, Connie Mack, 28–31; Nemec, The Great Encyclopedia of 19th-Century Major League Baseball, 165; unidentified newspaper clipping (Mack clipping file); Macht, Connie Mack and the Early Years of Baseball, 53–56, 61.
10. Lieb, Connie Mack, 32–42; Macht, Connie Mack and the Early Years of Baseball, 67–107; Dewey and Acocella, The Ball Clubs, 453–55, 574–75. See also Seymour, The Early Years, chapter 19; and Koszarek, The Players League.
11. Lieb, Connie Mack, 42–50, 62; Mack, My 66 Years in the Big Leagues, 21; Macht, Connie Mack and the Early Years of Baseball, 108–83.
12. Jordan, The Athletics of Philadelphia, 12–17; Dewey and Acocella, The Ball Clubs, 419–20, 595–96; Paxton, "The Philadelphia A's Last Stand," 133; Kuklick, To Every Thing a Season, 15–16; Macht, Connie Mack and the Early Years of Baseball, 181–85, 190–93, 197–203, 212–13; Lieb, Connie Mack, 66.

13. Ritter, *The Glory of Their Times*, 121, 199; Lieb, *Connie Mack*, 52; Koppett, *The Man in the Dugout*, 68–71; *Sporting News*, February 15, 1956.
14. Kuklick, *To Every Thing a Season*, 34–36, 51; Paxton, "The Philadelphia A's Last Stand," 133; Jordan, *The Athletics of Philadelphia*, 69–71; Lieb, *Connie Mack*, 180–97; Macht, *Connie Mack and the Early Years of Baseball*, 659–72; Macht, *The Grand Old Man of Baseball*, 2; Dewey and Acocella, *The Ball Clubs*, 444–45.
15. Kuklick, *To Every Thing a Season*, 112, 53; Lieb, *Connie Mack*, 199–206; Jordan, *The Athletics of Philadelphia*, 85–91.
16. Jordan, *The Athletics of Philadelphia*, 87–100; Lieb, *Connie Mack*, 206–38; Kuklick, *To Every Thing a Season*, 59–62.
17. Galbraith, *The Great Crash*, 12–13, 17, 189; Kennedy, *Freedom from Fear*, 35–37.
18. Kennedy, *Freedom from Fear*, 11, 43–44, 56, 65–69; McElvaine, *The Great Depression*, 76.
19. James, *New Bill James Historical Baseball Abstract*, 120–22; Seymour, *The Golden Age*, chapter 21.
20. James, *New Bill James Historical Baseball Abstract*, 159; Alexander, *Breaking the Slump*, 27–33; Koppett, *Koppett's Concise History of Major League Baseball*, 179–81; Burk, *Much More Than a Game*, 40–41; *Sporting News*, February 5, 1931.
21. Appel and Goldblatt, *Baseball's Best*, 343–44; Dewey and Acocella, *Biographical History of Baseball*, 426; Pietrusza, Silverman, and Gershman, *Baseball*, 1037–39 (with Mack quote). See also Stein, "Al Simmons."
22. Appel and Goldblatt, *Baseball's Best*, 90–92; Pietrusza, Silverman, and Gershman, *Baseball*, 218–20 (with Mack quote). See also Bevis, *Mickey Cochrane*; and Bevis, "Mickey Cochrane."
23. W. H. Daniel, *Jimmie Foxx*, chapters 1 and 2; Appel and Goldblatt, *Baseball's Best*, 158–60; Pietrusza, Silverman, and Gershman, *Baseball*, 376–78. See also Bennett, "Jimmie Foxx."
24. Dewey and Acocella, *Biographical History of Baseball*, 259–60; Pietrusza, Silverman, and Gershman, *Baseball*, 635–37; Kaplan, *Lefty Grove*, chapters 1–5. See also Mead, *Two Spectacular Seasons*; and Kaplan, "Lefty Grove."
25. J. R. Walker, *Crack of the Bat*, 21–23; C. Smith, *Voices of the Game*, 6–9 (emphasis in original). See also Douglas, *The Early Days of Radio Broadcasting*, 1, 117–18.
26. J. R. Walker, *Crack of the Bat*, 25–30; Barber, *The Broadcasters*, 24; C. Smith, *Voices of the Game*, 10–11; C. Smith, *Voices of Summer*, 8–9; Douglas, *The Early Days of Radio Broadcasting*, 121–24.
27. J. R. Walker, *Crack of the Bat*, 31–41; Ham, *Broadcasting Baseball*, 43; Barber, *The Broadcasters*, 30–32; *Sporting News*, October 8, 1931.
28. Ham, *Broadcasting Baseball*, 64; Lardner, *The Lost Journalism of Ring Lardner*, 138; J. R. Walker, *Crack of the Bat*, 22; J. R. Walker, "The Baseball-Radio War," 54; Light, *Cultural Encyclopedia of Baseball*, 72; *New York Times*, May 26, 1923; *Sporting News*, May 18, 1939. See also Nathan, *The McFarland Baseball Quotations Dictionary*, 47–48.
29. J. R. Walker, *Crack of the Bat*, 48, 82, 86–87; Light, *Cultural Encyclopedia of Baseball*, 602; Bush, "1929," 206; *New York Times*, December 9, 1931.

30. J. R. Walker, *Crack of the Bat*, 10, 87–93; *Sporting News*, June 30, 1932, and February 8, 1934; *New York Times*, December 17, 1932, and February 4, 1934. See also Sussman, "1932," 223; LeMoine, "1934," 237; Sussman, "1935," 242; Keeney, "1936," 245; Long, "1938," 255; Light, *Cultural Encyclopedia of Baseball*, 602.
31. J. R. Walker, *Crack of the Bat*, chapters 4, 6, and 8; "Wheaties Baseball," *Broadcasting*, April 15, 1935, 39; "Baseball Trophies Will Be Awarded by General Mills," *Broadcasting*, May 1, 1936, 20; "Sports Sponsors in Scramble for Baseball, Grid Campaigns," *Broadcasting*, February 15, 1937, 16. See also *New York Times*, January 11, 1934, and *Sporting News*, February 15, 1934, April 18, 1935, May 21, 1936 (with Wheaties ad; emphasis in original), May 4, 1939, and September 5, 1940.
32. *Sporting News*, January 8, 1931.
33. Seymour, *The Golden Age*, 122–23, 125.
34. Cresap, "1911 Ball Liveliest of 'Em All," 9–10; Bartlett, *Baseball and Mr. Spalding*, 146–47, 229–31.
35. "The Lively Controversy over the Lively Ball," *Literary Digest*, October 5, 1929, 78–81; *Sporting News*, February 12, 1931; *New York Times*, February 6, 1931.
36. *Sporting News*, February 12, 1931.
37. Burk, *Much More Than a Game*, 40–41; Rabinowitz, "Baseball and the Great Depression," 49; House Judiciary Committee, *Study of Monopoly Power*, 1599, 1600, 1615, 1636.
38. *Official Baseball Rules*, printed in *Spalding Guide* for 1930; *Official Baseball Rules*, printed in *Spalding Guide* for 1931.
39. *Official Baseball Rules*, printed in *Spalding Guide* for 1908; *Official Baseball Rules*, printed in *Spalding Guide* for 1926; *Spalding Guide* for 1931, 16; *Reach Guide* for 1931, 17–18. See also Nemec, *The Rules of Baseball*, 112, 203.
40. Seymour, *The Early Years*, 104–15; Burk, *Much More Than a Game*, 24; Seymour, *The Golden Age*, 348–50; *Sporting News*, November 27, 1930, and February 26, 1931.
41. F. L. Allen, *Since Yesterday*, 31; *Sporting News*, January 22, January 29, February 5, February 26, and April 16, 1931; Kaplan, *Lefty Grove*, 157.
42. *Sporting News*, January 22, January 29, February 5, February 12, February 19, February 26, March 12, March 19, March 26, and April 2, 1931.
43. Jordan, *The Athletics of Philadelphia*, 111; Kaplan, *Lefty Grove*, 139; *Sporting News*, April 9 and April 16, 1931; *Reach Guide* for 1932, 19, 21, 23.
44. *New York Times*, June 25, 1931; *Sporting News*, April 23, May 14, and May 21, 1931.
45. Kennedy, *Freedom from Fear*, 82–89.
46. Leuchtenburg, *The Perils of Prosperity*, 255; Jordan, *The Athletics of Philadelphia*, 113; House Judiciary Committee, *Study of Monopoly Power*, 1599, 1600, 1615, 1636.
47. Lieb, *Connie Mack*, 248–52; Macht, *The Grand Old Man of Baseball*, 17–20, 57–59.
48. Lieb, *Connie Mack*, 252–55; Macht, *The Grand Old Man of Baseball*, 102–4; *Sporting News Baseball Guide: 2006 Edition*, 344–45.

2. "SO YOU'RE THE GODDAMNED PROHIBITIONIST"

1. Polner, *Branch Rickey*, 4–8; Mann, *Branch Rickey*, 7–8; Lowenfish, *Branch Rickey*, 15–17, 121.
2. Polner, *Branch Rickey*, 7–22; Mann, *Branch Rickey*, 8–25; Lowenfish, *Branch Rickey*, 14–19.
3. Polner, *Branch Rickey*, 23–34; Lowenfish, *Branch Rickey*, 19–25.
4. Polner, *Branch Rickey*, 35–46; Lowenfish, *Branch Rickey*, 25–40.
5. Polner, *Branch Rickey*, 46–62; Lowenfish, *Branch Rickey*, 40–60.
6. Polner, *Branch Rickey*, 63–75; Lowenfish, *Branch Rickey*, 53–59, 61–66, 70–74, 77–87; Dewey and Acocella, *The Ball Clubs*, 495, 516–17.
7. Golenbock, *The Spirit of St. Louis*, 75–77; Mann, *Branch Rickey*, 83–93; Lowenfish, *Branch Rickey*, 82–90; Dewey and Acocella, *The Ball Clubs*, 496.
8. Alexander, *Rogers Hornsby*, 9–33.
9. Lieb, *The St. Louis Cardinals*, 68–70; Alexander, *Rogers Hornsby*, 37–48; Polner, *Branch Rickey*, 66.
10. Polner, *Branch Rickey*, 76–78; Mann, *Branch Rickey*, 95–98; Lowenfish, *Branch Rickey*, 102–6.
11. Lieb, *The St. Louis Cardinals*, 71–73; Dewey and Acocella, *The Ball Clubs*, 496; Polner, *Branch Rickey*, 79; Golenbock, *The Spirit of St. Louis*, 84, 88–90; *Sporting News*, May 18, 1949; *St. Louis Globe-Democrat*, February 21, 1943 (with Breadon quote); Lowenfish, *Branch Rickey*, 109–12, 115–16, 119–20.
12. Lieb, *The St. Louis Cardinals*, 74–76; Golenbock, *The Spirit of St. Louis*, 89–90; *St. Louis Globe-Democrat*, February 21, 1943; Polner, *Branch Rickey*, 79; Fetter, *Taking on the Yankees*, 136–37; Lowenfish, *Branch Rickey*, 120–21. See also Stockton, "Singing Sam," 77, 132ff.
13. Golenbock, *The Spirit of St. Louis*, 90; *Sporting News*, January 21, 1948, and May 18, 1949; Polner, *Branch Rickey*, 80–81 (with Burnes quote); Lieb, *The St. Louis Cardinals*, 76–78; Fetter, *Taking on the Yankees*, 138; Lowenfish, *Branch Rickey*, 121–24.
14. L. Johnson and Wolff, *Encyclopedia of Minor League Baseball*, 3rd ed., 164; Dewey and Acocella, *Biographical History of Baseball*, 52; Cobbledick, "The Cleveland Indians," 223–25; Polner, *Branch Rickey*, 62; Fetter, *Taking on the Yankees*, 121–22; Noguchi, "'The Residue of Design,'" 36–41. See also House Judiciary Committee, *Organized Baseball*, 44–46; and Blau, "Optional Assignments."
15. Burk, *Much More Than a Game*, 37; Polner, *Branch Rickey*, 82–84; Fetter, *Taking on the Yankees*, 134–35, 138–40; Lowenfish, *Branch Rickey*, 122–23; L. Johnson and Wolff, *Encyclopedia of Minor League Baseball*, 3rd ed., 304; *New York Post*, November 13, 1934 (with Breadon recollection); *Sporting News*, December 1, 1932. See also Stockton, *The Gashouse Gang*, 19–23.
16. Appel and Goldblatt, *Baseball's Best*, 195; *Sporting News*, January 18, 1934, and February 19, 1977; Lowenfish, *Branch Rickey*, 110; James and Neyer, *Neyer/James Guide to Pitchers*, 229; unidentified newspaper clipping (Jesse Haines clipping file, *Sporting News* Research Center).

17. Appel and Goldblatt, *Baseball's Best*, 38; *St. Louis Star*, May 29, 1929 (with Bottomley/Brundidge quote); Lane, "The Man Who Put the Punch in the World's Champions," 487–88; Lowenfish, *Branch Rickey*, 118–19, 141.
18. Alexander, *Rogers Hornsby*, 56–105; Lowenfish, *Branch Rickey*, 113, 125, 131, 133–34, 147, 149; Dickson, *Baseball's Greatest Quotations*, 189.
19. Alexander, *Rogers Hornsby*, 64, 69–70, 80–81, 92, 99–105; Polner, *Branch Rickey*, 89–90; Lowenfish, *Branch Rickey*, 145–46, 149–51, 154.
20. Dewey and Acocella, *The Ball Clubs*, 498; Runyon cited in Reisler, *Guys, Dolls, and Curveballs*, 221; Alexander, *Rogers Hornsby*, 111–20, 123–26; Lowenfish, *Branch Rickey*, chapter 7.
21. Lieb, *The St. Louis Cardinals*, 128–48; Lowenfish, *Branch Rickey*, 155, 157–59; Pietrusza, Silverman, and Gershman, *Baseball*, 458.
22. Barthel, *Pepper Martin*, 5–20 (with *Philadelphia Inquirer* quote); *New York Daily News*, October 12, 1931; *Sporting News*, October 15, 1931 (with Martin/Brundidge quote); Bloodgood, "'Pepper' Martin," 494.
23. *Sporting News*, August 6, 1925, October 1, 1942, and February 8, 1950; *St. Louis Post-Dispatch*, October 1, 1944; Barthel, *Pepper Martin*, 20–39.
24. Lieb, *The St. Louis Cardinals*, 148–50; Barthel, *Pepper Martin*, 40–44; Lowenfish, *Branch Rickey*, 208–14.
25. Bevis, *Mickey Cochrane*, 82, 84–85; L. Allen, *The World Series*, 128; Lowenfish, *Branch Rickey*, 214–16.
26. Barthel, *Pepper Martin*, 65–97 (with quotes from Carmichael and Isaminger and newspaper headline); Bevis, *Mickey Cochrane*, 86–91 (with Kieran quote); Lowenfish, *Branch Rickey*, 216–19.
27. Light, *Cultural Encyclopedia of Baseball*, 798–99; Lieb, *The St. Louis Cardinals*, 154–56; Lowenfish, *Branch Rickey*, 219–22.
28. Gregory, *Diz*, 22–33.
29. Gregory, *Diz*, 33–34, 36–38, 42–52; *Sporting News*, August 28 and October 9, 1930.
30. Gregory, *Diz*, 51–67; Lowenfish, *Branch Rickey*, 209–11.
31. Gregory, *Diz*, 68–75; Barthel, *Ducky Medwick*, 1–9.
32. Barthel, *Ducky Medwick*, 6–30.
33. Barthel, *Ducky Medwick*, 31–48; *Sporting News*, July 7, 1932.
34. Kennedy, *Freedom from Fear*, 86–91, 98–103; Leuchtenburg, *Franklin D. Roosevelt and the New Deal*, 17; Lowenfish, *Branch Rickey*, 222–25, 229; Lieb, *The St. Louis Cardinals*, 160–62.
35. Lowenfish, *Branch Rickey*, 225–31; Pietrusza, Silverman, and Gershman, *Baseball*, 316.
36. Creamer, *Babe*, 369–71; Gregory, *Diz*, 95–97, 100–105; Barthel, *Ducky Medwick*, 49–51; Lowenfish, *Branch Rickey*, 231–35. Attendance figures come from Tiemann and Palmer, "Major League Attendance," 107.
37. Lowenfish, *Branch Rickey*, 235–49; Gregory, *Diz*, 125–26, 140, 151–53, 167–77, 192–95.

38. Gregory, *Diz*, 237–38 (with Tom Meany column); Lowenfish, *Branch Rickey*, 241–53; Fleming, *The Dizziest Season*, 7, 279; Barthel, *Ducky Medwick*, 91. See also Lieb, *The St. Louis Cardinals*, 164.
39. Auker with Keegan, *Sleeper Cars and Flannel Uniforms*, 52–54; Lowenfish, *Branch Rickey*, 252, 255–56; Gregory, *Diz*, 208–17.
40. Barthel, *Ducky Medwick*, 78–79; Lowenfish, *Branch Rickey*, 256–57; Auker with Keegan, *Sleeper Cars and Flannel Uniforms*, 52–54; Gregory, *Diz*, 218–31.
41. Barthel, *Ducky Medwick*, 79–84; Gregory, *Diz*, 213–38.
42. Pietrusza, *Judge and Jury*, 339–41; Fleming, *The Dizziest Season*, 309 (with Gallico quote); *Sporting News*, October 11, 1934; Lowenfish, *Branch Rickey*, 258–59.
43. Gregory, *Diz*, 239; Lowenfish, *Branch Rickey*, 251, 260–63; Lieb, *The St. Louis Cardinals*, 175–83.

3. "THE INTRICACIES OF ORGANIZED BASEBALL"

1. See, for example, the dust jacket of Pietrusza, *Judge and Jury*; the photo sections in Holtzman, *The Commissioners*, and Honig, *Baseball America*; and Landis's obituary in the *New York Times*, November 26, 1944.
2. Pietrusza, *Judge and Jury*, 1–12; J. G. T. Spink, *Judge Landis*, 1–9.
3. Pietrusza, *Judge and Jury*, 14–28; J. G. T. Spink, *Judge Landis*, 10–14.
4. Pietrusza, *Judge and Jury*, 29–41 (with Lippmann quote and *Saturday Evening Post* description). See also "Chicago Federal Building," Emporis, http://www.emporis.com/en/wm/bu?id=132232, accessed June 2021.
5. Voigt, *American Baseball*, 142; Lieb, *Baseball As I Have Known It*, 116; Helyar, *Lords of the Realm*, 7; White, *Creating the National Pastime*, 106; Seymour, *The Golden Age*, 368; Pietrusza, *Judge and Jury*, xv, 20, 94, passim (with Pringle quote).
6. Pietrusza, *Judge and Jury*, 47–93 (with Pringle quote); Chernow, *Titan*, 537–41.
7. Pietrusza, *Judge and Jury*, 109–37.
8. Pietrusza, *Judge and Jury*, 109, 136–37, 153–54; B. Lamb, "John T. Powers"; Voigt, *American Baseball*, 142; Light, *Cultural Encyclopedia of Baseball*, 252–53; House Judiciary Committee, *Organized Baseball*, 50–54; *Sporting News*, March 26, 1947, and January 7, 1948; Seymour, *The Golden Age*, 199–205.
9. Seymour, *The Golden Age*, 203–12; Pietrusza, *Judge and Jury*, 154–55; House Judiciary Committee, *Organized Baseball*, 54–56; Levitt, *The Battle That Forged Modern Baseball*, 182–85.
10. Levitt, *The Battle That Forged Modern Baseball*, 185–87; Pietrusza, *Judge and Jury*, 156–57 (with Landis quote); Seymour, *The Golden Age*, 212; Light, *Cultural Encyclopedia of Baseball*, 253; J. G. T. Spink, *Judge Landis*, 34–35; House Judiciary Committee, *Organized Baseball*, 56.
11. Levitt, *The Battle That Forged Modern Baseball*, 223–46; Pietrusza, *Judge and Jury*, 157; Lowenfish and Lupien, *The Imperfect Diamond*, 88; Seymour, *The Golden Age*, 212–13, 230–32; Light, *Cultural Encyclopedia of Baseball*, 254; House Judiciary Committee, *Organized Baseball*, 56–57; *Sporting News*, February 10, 1916. See also Abrams, *Legal Bases*, 53–58; and Hailey, "Anatomy of a Murder."

12. A. H. Spink, *The National Game*, 345; Stout, *The Cubs*, 4–5; Findling, "Chicago Cubs," 56–59; Cash, *Before They Were Cardinals*, 10; Pietrusza, Silverman, and Gershman, *Baseball*, 533–34; Solomon, *The Baseball Timeline*, 35.
13. Lansche, *The Forgotten Championships*, 9–13; Adams poem in Dawidoff, *Baseball*, 20; Pietrusza, Silverman, and Gershman, *Baseball*, 29–31; Appel and Goldblatt, *Baseball's Best*, 11–12; Stout, *The Cubs*, 26–27, 30–31, 37–38; Benson, *Ballparks of North America*, 86–87; Holtzman and Vass, *Chicago Cubs Encyclopedia*, 12–14, 300–303, 325–27; Wrigley as told to Crissey, "Owning a Big-League Ball Team," 24–25, 129–30.
14. Weisberger, *When Chicago Ruled Baseball*, 18–20, 152–53; Lindberg, *White Sox Encyclopedia*, 10–29, 312, 428–32, 434–44; Holtzman and Vass, *Chicago Cubs Encyclopedia*, 26–27, 353–54; Lindberg, "Chicago White Sox," 540–41. See also Wilbert and Hageman, *The 1917 White Sox*.
15. Lindberg, *White Sox Encyclopedia*, 25–27; Dewey and Acocella, *The Ball Clubs*, 151–54; W. F. Lamb, "The Black Sox Scandal," 506–24. See also Carney, *Burying the Black Sox*; and Pomrenke, *Scandal on the South Side*.
16. Seymour, *The Golden Age*, 329–30; Pietrusza, *Judge and Jury*, 173–75; B. Lamb, "Gene Paulette"; James, *New Bill James Historical Baseball Abstract*, 136–38.
17. Pietrusza, *Judge and Jury*, 169–72; *Reach Guide* for 1921, 44, 194, 203; Seymour, *The Golden Age*, 406–7; House Judiciary Committee, *Organized Baseball*, 59–61.
18. White, *Creating the National Pastime*, 280–81; Seymour, *The Golden Age*, 406–7; Blau, "Optional Assignments"; L. Johnson and Wolff, *Encyclopedia of Minor League Baseball*, 3rd ed., 206; Fetter, *Taking on the Yankees*, 122–23; House Judiciary Committee, *Organized Baseball*, 59–61; *New York Times*, December 18, 1921; *Reach Guide* for 1922, 243–45; *Reach Guide* for 1921, 44, 194, 203.
19. Seymour, *The Golden Age*, 407 (with first Landis quote); Hoie, "The Minor Leagues," 512; *Reach Guide* for 1922, 252 (with second Landis quote). See also Marren, "1921," 140–41.
20. Hoie, "The Minor Leagues," 512; Seymour, *The Golden Age*, 408–9; *Reach Guide* for 1922, 243, 245; *Reach Guide* for 1923, 272, 293; *Reach Guide* for 1924, 20–21, 297–98.
21. *Reach Guide* for 1923, 272, 293, 493–94; Seymour, *The Golden Age*, 408–9; Pietrusza, *Judge and Jury*, 373–74 (with McCarthy quote); *Reach Guide* for 1925, 16, 260; Hoie, "The Minor Leagues," 512; Burk, *Much More Than a Game*, 45; *Reach Guide* for 1922, 243, 245; *Reach Guide* for 1924, 20–21, 297–98.
22. Seymour, *The Golden Age*, 409; Pietrusza, *Judge and Jury*, 374; Hoie, "The Minor Leagues," 513; Burk, *Much More Than a Game*, 45; *Reach Guide* for 1931, 13–15, 169; L. Johnson and Wolff, *Encyclopedia of Minor League Baseball*, 3rd ed., 308; *New York Times*, January 10, January 15, January 18, and January 21, 1931; *Sporting News*, January 15, January 22, January 29 (with Foster quote), February 5, September 22, and October 8, 1931, October 12, 1933, October 8 and October 15, 1936, February 2 and October 12, 1939.
23. Creamer, *Babe*, 240–43; C. Smith, *Voices of the Game*, 8–9; Pietrusza, *Judge and Jury*, 229–30.

24. Light, *Cultural Encyclopedia of Baseball*, 62; Seymour, *The Early Years*, 32; Rucker and Bjarkman, *Smoke*, 13; Figueredo, *Cuban Baseball*, 7, 25–26; Echevarría, *The Pride of Havana*, 4, 100, 135–36; Tygiel, *Baseball's Great Experiment*, 13–16; Heaphy, *The Negro Leagues*, 135–37, 139–40; Seymour, *The Golden Age*, 191 (with Johnson quote); Cole, "Ersatz Octobers," 80.
25. Creamer, *Babe*, 131–32; Smelser, *The Life That Ruth Built*, 86, 106, 132; Seymour, *The Golden Age*, 191–92.
26. Smelser, *The Life That Ruth Built*, 156–57, 204–5; Echevarría, *The Pride of Havana*, 138; Creamer, *Babe*, 219–20, 236, 245.
27. Creamer, *Babe*, 246–57; Smelser, *The Life That Ruth Built*, 227–31, 242–43; Pietrusza, *Judge and Jury*, 229–40.
28. Seymour, *The Golden Age*, 393; Pietrusza, *Judge and Jury*, 232, 235, 238–39 (with Landis quote); Creamer, *Babe*, 255 (with Ruth quote); Burk, *Much More Than a Game*, 18–19; J. G. T. Spink, *Judge Landis*, 106; *Reach Guide for 1923*, 493.
29. *St. Louis Post-Dispatch*, March 24, 1964; J. G. T. Spink, *Judge Landis*, 89–90; Pietrusza, *Judge and Jury*, 176; Lowenfish, *Branch Rickey*, 130.
30. Seymour, *The Golden Age*, 186–87. See also House Judiciary Committee, *Study of Monopoly Power*, 657–58; and House Judiciary Committee, *Organized Baseball*, 44–46.
31. Burk, *Much More Than a Game*, 37; House Judiciary Committee, *Organized Baseball*, 60; Seymour, *The Golden Age*, 418–19.
32. Burk, *Much More Than a Game*, 37–39, 44–48; House Judiciary Committee, *Organized Baseball*, 65–72; Seymour, *The Golden Age*, 419–20; *Sporting News*, December 10, 1931; J. G. T. Spink, *Judge Landis*, 191–92, 198–201, 211.
33. Polner, *Branch Rickey*, 83; Kennedy, *Freedom from Fear*, 85–87, 91–92; Leuchtenburg, *Franklin D. Roosevelt and the New Deal*, 1–3, 13–15; Leuchtenburg, *The Perils of Prosperity*, 247–49, 252–54, 262–63.
34. House Judiciary Committee, *Organized Baseball*, 143; *Sporting News*, October 31, 1929; L. Johnson and Wolff, *Encyclopedia of Minor League Baseball*, 2nd ed., 219; Hoie, "The Minor Leagues," 512; O'Neal, *The Pacific Coast League*, 224; Dobbins, *The Grand Minor League*, 25–27; Mackey, *Barbary Baseball*, 108–10.
35. Hoie, "The Minor Leagues," 512; *Reach Guide for 1925*, 420; L. Johnson and Wolff, *Encyclopedia of Minor League Baseball*, 2nd ed., 96–97, 257–328.
36. L. Johnson and Wolff, *Encyclopedia of Minor League Baseball*, 2nd ed., 268–71; *Sporting News*, February 12, February 19, March 5, March 19, April 16, May 4, July 30, August 6, August 31, and October 1, 1931.
37. *Sporting News*, October 22, December 3, and December 10, 1931, January 7, January 14 (with Landis quote), July 21, July 28, November 3, and December 8, 1932; *New York Times*, January 4, July 18, July 20, July 23, October 24, December 6, and December 10, 1932. See also House Judiciary Committee, *Study of Monopoly Power*, 1351–91.
38. *Sporting News*, December 29, 1932; Sumner, "William G. Bramham," 116–17; Holaday, *Professional Baseball in North Carolina*, 3.

39. Sumner, "William G. Bramham," 117; *Sporting News*, December 29, 1932, and December 11, 1946.
40. Sumner, "William G. Bramham," 118; Finch, Addington, and Morgan, *The Story of Minor League Baseball*, 28; L. Johnson and Wolff, *Encyclopedia of Minor League Baseball*, 3rd ed., 328, 332; *Reach Guide* for 1932, 109; *New York Times*, December 4, 1931; *Sporting News*, December 10, 1931, December 11, 1946, and July 16, 1947. See also *Baseball Blue Book* for 1932, 66–67.
41. L. Johnson and Wolff, *Encyclopedia of Minor League Baseball*, 3rd ed., 328, 332; *Reach Guide* for 1934, 145; Finch, Addington, and Morgan, *The Story of Minor League Baseball*, 29; *Sporting News*, October 20, December 8, and December 15, 1932.
42. Addington, "'We Shall Not See His Like Again,'" 381; Finch, Addington, and Morgan, *The Story of Minor League Baseball*, 29–33; *New York Times*, May 17, 1932, and November 17, 1933; *Sporting News*, April 28, 1932, May 31, June 7, and June 14, 1934, and December 11, 1946.
43. *Sporting News*, May 5 and July 14, 1932, May 10 and July 12, 1934, February 7, July 18, and November 28, 1935, December 10, 1936, May 20, December 2, and December 9, 1937, December 15, 1938, November 9, November 30, and December 7, 1939, February 22 and June 13, 1940; L. Johnson and Wolff, *Encyclopedia of Minor League Baseball*, 2nd ed., 278, 282, 286, 291, 297, 305, 312, 321.
44. Spink J. G. T. Spink, *Judge Landis*, 152, 209, 212, 242; Sumner, "William G. Bramham," 119; *Reach Guide* for 1938, 159; *Spalding-Reach Official Baseball Guide* for 1940, 163; *Sporting News*, November 30, 1939.
45. Burk, *Much More Than a Game*, 63; *Sporting News*, February 13, 1936, and February 3, 1938; *Reach Guide* for 1936, 161–62.
46. Sickels, *Bob Feller*, 1, 15–27; *Sporting News*, April 2, 1936; House Judiciary Committee, *Organized Baseball*, 72.
47. Sickels, *Bob Feller*, 30–36ff, 49–59.
48. Pietrusza, *Judge and Jury*, 359–61 (with Landis quote); Burk, *Much More Than a Game*, 64; House Judiciary Committee, *Study of Monopoly Power*, 673, 680; *New York Times*, April 1, 1938; *Sporting News*, December 1, 1938.
49. Burk, *Much More Than a Game*, 51; *Sporting News*, December 14, 1939 (with Daniel quote).

4. "THE YANKEES NEED BUILDING UP"

1. Levitt, *Ed Barrow*, 9–10; Barrow, *My Fifty Years in Baseball*, 10–12; *Sporting News*, November 19, 1936, and December 23, 1953.
2. Levitt, *Ed Barrow*, 10–17; Barrow, *My Fifty Years in Baseball*, 12–24; *New York Sun*, December 19, 1935; *Pittsburgh Sun-Telegraph*, November 11, 1953.
3. Levitt, *Ed Barrow*, 19–24; Barrow, *My Fifty Years in Baseball*, 24–33; *Sporting News*, May 17, 1950, and December 23, 1953; Hittner, *Honus Wagner*, 36–39.
4. Levitt, *Ed Barrow*, 25–36; Barrow, *My Fifty Years in Baseball*, 35–48; Pietrusza, *Lights On!*, 9–10; DeValeria and DeValeria, *Honus Wagner*, 34; Light, *Cultural*

Encyclopedia of Baseball, 792; *Sporting News*, July 16, 1898; Gershman, *Diamonds*, 55; Heaphy and May, *Encyclopedia of Women and Baseball*, 22; *Reach Guide* for 1902, 112.

5. Levitt, *Ed Barrow*, 35–51; Barrow, *My Fifty Years in Baseball*, 44–51; Dorward, "Ed Barrow's Toronto Years," 101–5.
6. Levitt, *Ed Barrow*, 54–71; Barrow, *My Fifty Years in Baseball*, 49–62; *Sporting News*, April 2, 1904, and May 17, 1950; Dewey and Acocella, *The Ball Clubs*, 236–37; Appel and Goldblatt, *Baseball's Best*, 26; Dorward, "Ed Barrow's Toronto Years," 105–7.
7. Levitt, *Ed Barrow*, 71–84; Dorward, "Ed Barrow's Toronto Years," 107–8; *Sporting News*, December 8, December 15, and December 21, 1910, December 21, 1911, November 19, 1936, and May 17, 1950; Barrow, *My Fifty Years in Baseball*, 61–63; O'Neal, *The International League*, 52.
8. Levitt, *Ed Barrow*, 84–110; Barrow, *My Fifty Years in Baseball*, 63, 65, 71, 75–76, 81–86; *Reach Guide* for 1912, 249.
9. Levitt, *Ed Barrow*, 118–26; Barrow, *My Fifty Years in Baseball*, 86–88; Creamer, *Babe*, 143–48; *Reach Guide* for 1918, 167.
10. Levitt, *Ed Barrow*, 125–26; Stout and Johnson, *Red Sox Century*, 122–23; Creamer, *Babe*, 24–37; Smelser, *The Life That Ruth Built*, 3–14.
11. Smelser, *The Life That Ruth Built*, 12–36; Creamer, *Babe*, 37–52.
12. Creamer, *Babe*, 53–81; Smelser, *The Life That Ruth Built*, 38–49.
13. Creamer, *Babe*, 126–30, 152–54, 165–66; Ritter, *The Glory of Their Times*, 145; Zingg, *Harry Hooper*, 157–61.
14. Creamer, *Babe*, 192–204; Levitt, *Ed Barrow*, 146–48, 150–59; Stout and Johnson, *Red Sox Century*, 118–19; Barrow, *My Fifty Years in Baseball*, 101–7; Lieb, *The Boston Red Sox*, 178–82; Zingg, *Harry Hooper*, 180–84; M. T. Lynch, *Harry Frazee*, 65–66, 74–85.
15. Barrow, *My Fifty Years in Baseball*, 108; Levitt, *Ed Barrow*, 162–63; Stout and Johnson, *Red Sox Century*, 145–49; Lieb, *The Boston Red Sox*, 182–83; M. T. Lynch, *Harry Frazee*, 106–7; Stout, *Yankees Century*, 87–92; Creamer, *Babe*, 217–27.
16. Fetter, *Taking on the Yankees*, 27–31, 54–56; Stout, *Yankees Century*, 67–68; Graham, *The New York Yankees*, 24–26; Levitt, *Ed Barrow*, 182.
17. Stout, *Yankees Century*, 67–71; Graham, *The New York Yankees*, 26–31; Levitt, *Ed Barrow*, 181–82.
18. Graham, *The New York Yankees*, 35–42; Stout, *Yankees Century*, 76–81; M. T. Lynch, *Harry Frazee*, 74–83, 93–94.
19. Stout, *Yankees Century*, 87–94; Creamer, *Babe*, 217–27; Levitt, *Ed Barrow*, 170–74, 177–78; Stout and Johnson, *Red Sox Century*, 150–52; Lieb, *The Boston Red Sox*, 183–84; Barrow, *Fifty Years*, 108–10; M. T. Lynch, *Harry Frazee*, 120–24, 128, 151.
20. Levitt, *Ed Barrow*, 187–88, 189–91, 193–94; Gallagher and LeConte, *Yankee Encyclopedia*, 315; Dewey and Acocella, *Biographical History of Baseball*, 253; Stout, *Yankees Century*, 94–95; Pietrusza, Silverman, and Gershman, *Baseball*, 525; Barrow, *My Fifty Years in Baseball*, 126–32.

21. Creamer, *Babe*, 237–43; Stout, *Yankees Century*, 96–101; Fetter, *Taking on the Yankees*, 15–18; Tiemann and Palmer, "Major League Attendance," 106–8; House Judiciary Committee, *Study of Monopoly Power*, 1599–600.
22. Stout, *Yankees Century*, 104–7; Graham, *The New York Yankees*, 73–94; Levitt, *Ed Barrow*, 195, 200–209; Barrow, *My Fifty Years in Baseball*, 134–40; Murdock, *Baseball between the Wars*, 41; Dewey and Acocella, *The Ball Clubs*, 371; Light, *Cultural Encyclopedia of Baseball*, 775; P. Morris, *A Game of Inches: The Game behind the Scenes*, 29–35.
23. Goldblatt, "San Francisco Giants," 369; Robinson and Jennison, *Yankee Stadium*, 12–13 (with Lieb quote); Fetter, *Taking on the Yankees*, 75, 79–80, 82–84; Stout, *Yankees Century*, 96–97; Hynd, *The Giants of the Polo Grounds*, 242.
24. Fetter, *Taking on the Yankees*, 47–48, 69–75; Bevis, *Sunday Baseball*, 195–96.
25. Graham, *The New York Yankees*, 99–100, 198–99; Levitt, *Ed Barrow*, 212–14; A. H. Levy, *Joe McCarthy*, 79–81, 83–84, 86. See also Berger, "Earle Combs."
26. Thornley, *Baseball in Minnesota*, 60–61; Barrow, *My Fifty Years in Baseball*, 143; Levitt, *Ed Barrow*, 187–89, 206; Eig, *Luckiest Man*, 38–39.
27. Eig, *Luckiest Man*, 3–38.
28. Eig, *Luckiest Man*, 39–68.
29. Murdock, *Ban Johnson*, 116, 175–76, 210–11, 221–22; Seymour, *The Golden Age*, 264–69, 307, 312, 317–18; Pietrusza, *Judge and Jury*, 165–67, 230–38, 292. See also Miskowiec, "1926," 178.
30. Fetter, *Taking on the Yankees*, 88; Levitt, *Ed Barrow*, 224–25; Gallagher and LeConte, *Yankee Encyclopedia*, 121; A. H. Levy, *Joe McCarthy*, 175–76; Stout, *Yankees Century*, 116–18; *Sporting News*, January 22, 1947. See also Gluekstein, "Tony Lazzeri."
31. Stout, *Yankees Century*, 118–20; R. M. Cohen and Neft, *The World Series*, 114–19; Creamer, *Babe*, 305–8; Smelser, *The Life That Ruth Built*, 336–41.
32. R. M. Cohen and Neft, *The World Series*, 120–27; Stout, *Yankees Century*, 120–35. See also Krabbenhoft, "Lou Gehrig's RBI Record: Striving to Get It Right"; and Krabbenhoft, "Lou Gehrig's RBI Record: 1923–39."
33. House Judiciary Committee, *Study of Monopoly Power*, 1599–602; Fetter, *Taking on the Yankees*, 165–70.
34. Stout, *Yankees Century*, 138, 140–43; Levitt, *Ed Barrow*, 231–32, 248, 249; Graham, *The New York Yankees*, 107; Pietrusza, Silverman, and Gershman, *Baseball*, 316, 532, 645; *Sporting News*, October 21, 1937, January 22, 1947, and December 23, 1953.
35. D. M. Daniel, "DiMaggio, Lazzeri, Moore Deals Stand Out in Barrow's Recollection," 411; Stout, *Yankees Century*, 120, 138, 172; Smelser, *The Life That Ruth Built*, 360, 467; Seymour, *The Golden Age*, 409; Levitt, *Ed Barrow*, 264–65 (with Barrow quote).
36. *New York Times*, November 13, 1931; *Sporting News*, November 12 and 19, 1931; Graham, *The New York Yankees*, 187–88; Barrow, *My Fifty Years in Baseball*, 179; Stout, *Yankees Century*, 148. See also Levitt, *Ed Barrow*, chapter 19.
37. L. Johnson and Wolff, *Encyclopedia of Minor League Baseball*, 2nd ed., 272–75;

Levitt, *Ed Barrow*, 277–79; Pietrusza, Silverman, and Gershman, *Baseball*, 314; Boxerman and Boxerman, *George Weiss*, 4–7; G. M. Weiss, "The Man of Silence Speaks," 28; *Sporting News*, December 27, 1945.

38. Levitt, *Ed Barrow*, 277–78; G. M. Weiss, "The Man of Silence Speaks," 28–30; Boxerman and Boxerman, *George Weiss*, 7–24; *Sporting News*, February 16, 1933, and December 27, 1945; L. Johnson and Wolff, *Encyclopedia of Minor League Baseball*, 2nd ed., 215–55.
39. Pietrusza, Silverman, and Gershman, *Baseball*, 314; L. Johnson and Wolff, *Encyclopedia of Minor League Baseball*, 2nd ed., 256; Boxerman and Boxerman, *George Weiss*, 18–19, 25, 31–32; G. M. Weiss, "The Man of Silence Speaks," 30; "Champion Dollar Guy," 69; *Sporting News*, December 27, 1945, and February 1, 1956; Levitt, *Ed Barrow*, 278–79.
40. A. H. Levy, *Joe McCarthy*, esp. pp. 77, 99–101, 144–49, 156–57; Koppett, *Koppett's Concise History of Major League Baseball*, 183; Levitt, *Ed Barrow*, 253–57.
41. Creamer, *Babe*, 359–64 (with Williams quote); Sherman, *Babe Ruth's Called Shot*, 82–87; T. Wolf, *The Called Shot*, 255–57.
42. Creamer, *Babe*, 364–68; Sherman, *Babe Ruth's Called Shot*, 99–113, 140–57; T. Wolf, *The Called Shot*, 276–83; Montville, *The Big Bam*, 311; Isaacs, "Babe Ruth's Called Shot," 221–29 (with Drebinger comments). See also Walsh, "Babe Ruth and the Legend of the Called Shot."
43. Creamer, *Babe*, 383–402; Eig, *Luckiest Man*, 188–89.
44. H. Levy, *Joe McCarthy*, 295; Cramer, *Joe DiMaggio*, chapters 1–3.
45. Cramer, *Joe DiMaggio*, chapters 4–6.
46. Stout, *Yankees Century*, 164–72; Lieb, *The Detroit Tigers*, 230–31.
47. Stout, *Yankees Century*, 172–77; Levitt, *Ed Barrow*, 317–18, 327–29; Eig, *Luckiest Man*, 233–36, 241–319.
48. Pietrusza, *Judge and Jury*, 361–66; *Sporting News*, January 23, 1936, December 30, 1937, June 9, 1938, November 30, December 7, and December 14, 1939; *Spalding-Reach Official Baseball Guide* for 1941, 147, 149.

5. "KEEN COMPETITION"

1. Warfield, *The Roaring Redhead*, 9–23; MacPhail, *My Nine Innings*, 16–18; Mann, "The Larry MacPhail Story," 70; Sher, "Larry MacPhail," 64–65. See also Berger, "Larry MacPhail."
2. Warfield, *The Roaring Redhead*, 3–8; MacPhail, *My Nine Innings*, 15–16.
3. Warfield, *The Roaring Redhead*, 24–26; MacPhail, *My Nine Innings*, 3–5; Mann, "The Larry MacPhail Story," 70.
4. Rhodes and Snyder, *Redleg Journal*, 239; Warfield, *The Roaring Redhead*, 26; McKelvey, *The MacPhails*, 8; *Sporting News*, September 26, October 3, and October 17, 1929.
5. Warfield, *The Roaring Redhead*, 26–27; McKelvey, *The MacPhails*, 8–9; Lowenfish, *Branch Rickey*, 205–7; Mann, "The Larry MacPhail Story," 71; *New York Times*, February 19, 1931.

6. L. Johnson and Wolff, *Encyclopedia of Minor League Baseball*, 2nd ed., 220–78; O'Neal, *The Pacific Coast League*, 7, 10, 51; House Judiciary Committee, *Study of Monopoly Power*, 1641.
7. L. Johnson and Wolff, *Encyclopedia of Minor League Baseball*, 2nd ed., 268–70, 273–74; *Sporting News*, July 2, July 9, July 16, July 23, July 30, October 29, and December 24, 1931; *New York Times*, July 21, 1931; Warfield, *The Roaring Redhead*, 27–28; *Reach Guide for 1932*, 121–29.
8. L. Johnson and Wolff, *Encyclopedia of Minor League Baseball*, 2nd ed., 271; *Sporting News*, June 25, 1931, and June 9, 1932; Warfield, *The Roaring Redhead*, 28–31 (with Landis quote); McKelvey, *The MacPhails*, 9–10.
9. *Sporting News*, June 30 and July 7, 1932; Warfield, *The Roaring Redhead*, 29–31.
10. Pietrusza, *Lights On!*, 104; Roosevelt, "Letter on Baseball, Sports, and Sportsmanship" (with Roosevelt letter to *New York Times*); Crepeau, *Baseball*, 71 (with *Sporting News* quote); *Spalding Guide for 1934*, 11 (with short Roosevelt quote).
11. Kennedy, *Freedom from Fear*, 175–76, 212–13; Leuchtenburg, *Franklin D. Roosevelt and the New Deal*, 120–23, 125–26; *Sporting News*, April 14, 1932; K. S. Davis, *FDR*, 305–14, 466–71; Seymour, *The People's Game*, 69–70; Howard, *The WPA and Federal Relief Policy*, 14–129. See also Federal Works Agency, *Final Report on the WPA Program*, esp. 51–53, 62; and Wong, "FDR and the New Deal on Sport and Recreation," 173–91.
12. Benson, *Ballparks of North America*, 1, 128–29, 160–62; Montville, *Ted Williams*, 29; *Sporting News*, June 4, 1931, December 21, 1933, January 24, 1935, December 23, 1937, February 17, November 17, and December 29, 1938, February 16, 1939, March 21, 1940 (with Daniel quote), February 6 and August 7, 1941; *New York Times*, February 20, 1935.
13. Kossuth, "Boondoggling, Baseball, and the WPA," 56–68. See also Block, *Baseball Before We Knew It*, esp. chapters 1–4; and Vlasich, *A Legend for the Legendary*.
14. Benson, *Ballparks of North America*, 27; *Sporting News*, March 14, 1940; Mead and Dickson, *Baseball*, 71, 75, 191, 199–200 (with Roosevelt and Burr quotes).
15. Pietrusza, *Lights On!*, 1–4 (with *Boston Post* quote); Light, *Cultural Encyclopedia of Baseball*, 509; Eddleton, "Under the Lights," 37–42; Metcalf, "Organized Baseball's Night Birth," 47–49. See also White, *Creating the National Pastime*, chapter 5.
16. Pietrusza, *Lights On!*, 10–16, 28–33 (with Herrmann and Mulford quotes); Dewey and Acocella, *The Ball Clubs*, 123; Eddleton, "Under the Lights," 38.
17. Pietrusza, *Lights On!*, 46–50, 53–54; Eddleton, "Under the Lights," 39; Metcalf, "Organized Baseball's Night Birth," 47; *Sporting News*, March 2, 1933, and December 15, 1948.
18. *Sporting News*, February 13, March 13, and April 17, 1930, December 15, 1948.
19. Pietrusza, *Lights On!*, 55–56; Eddleton, "Under the Lights," 39–40; Metcalf, "Organized Baseball's Night Birth," 47–48; unidentified newspaper clipping (Marvin Truby clipping file, *Sporting News* Research Center); *Sporting News*, April 17, May 8, May 22, and May 29, 1930.

20. *Sporting News*, April 17, 1930, February 26, March 5, April 2, and November 5, 1931, July 12, 1934, December 30, 1937, December 7, 1939; Sumner, "William G. Bramham," 119, 121; Pietrusza, *Lights On!*, 72–73; *New York Times*, May 24, 1932.
21. Warfield, *The Roaring Redhead*, 31–39; Holland, "The Great MacPhail," 60; Mann, "The Larry MacPhail Story," 71–72; Lowenfish, *Branch Rickey*, 234–35; *Sporting News*, May 25, June 22, July 6, and August 7, 1933; *New York Times*, June 15, 1933.
22. *Sporting News*, February 16, 1933, September 20, 1934, December 19, 1935, November 5, 1936, February 2 and October 24, 1940, December 14 and 21, 1960. See also Bevis, "How the Shaughnessy Plan Redefined Success in Sports," 27–39.
23. *New York Times*, January 24, April 11, and April 14, 1933; *Sporting News*, April 17, May 12, and May 19, 1932, February 16 and April 20, 1933; L. Johnson and Wolff, *Encyclopedia of Minor League Baseball*, 2nd ed., 264–82; O'Neal, *The Pacific Coast League*, 65–67; James, *The New Bill James Historical Baseball Abstract*, 161.
24. *Sporting News*, March 3, 1932; Mackey, *Barbary Baseball*, 46.
25. Mackey, *Barbary Baseball*, 41, 54, 65–68, 71, 80, 108–11; O'Neal, *The Pacific Coast League*, 65–68; James, *The New Bill James Historical Baseball Abstract*, 161; Selko, *Minor League All-Star Teams*, 63–64.
26. Mackey, *Barbary Baseball*, 11–12, 14, 40, 44, 49; O'Neal, *The Pacific Coast League*, 73, 262–63; *Sporting News*, January 28, 1937, and January 19, 1939; Levitt, *Ed Barrow*, 298; Dobbins, *The Grand Minor League*, 110, 112; Broeg and Miller, *Baseball from a Different Angle*, 232 (with quote from prospect); Weiss and Wright, *100 Greatest Minor League Baseball Teams*, 196; Benson, *Ballparks of North America*, 170–71.
27. *Sporting News*, March 19, 1931, September 8, 1932, November 2, 1933, May 2 and December 5, 1935, July 22, 1937, October 10, 1940, January 2, 1941.
28. E. J. Kahn, *The Big Drink*, 167; *Sporting News*, February 9, 1933, October 18, 1934, February 14, May 2, and December 5, 1935, February 27, March 19, and April 16, 1936, June 17, June 24, and November 4, 1937, August 4, 1938, January 19, 1939, June 27, July 4, and July 11, 1940; Irey, *The Tax Dodgers*, 94–95, 109–10; T. H. Williams, *Huey Long*, 374–75, 798.
29. Seidel, *Ted Williams*, chapters 1–2; Montville, *Ted Williams*, chapters 1–3.
30. Seidel, *Ted Williams*, chapter 2; Montville, *Ted Williams*, chapters 2–3.
31. *Spalding Guide* for 1934, 132–39; Benson, *Ballparks of North America*, 234; Pietrusza, Silverman, and Gershman, *Baseball*, 479; L. Johnson and Wolff, *Encyclopedia of Minor League Baseball*, 2nd ed., 295, 298.
32. L. Johnson and Wolff, *Encyclopedia of Minor League Baseball*, 2nd ed., 267, 271, 275, 282, 291, 305, 321; Pietrusza, Silverman, and Gershman, *Baseball*, 1146.
33. Wolfe, *The Web and the Rock*, 26; St. John, *Final Verdict*, 107.
34. Metro with Altherr, *Safe by a Mile*, 1, 24–25; *Sporting News*, March 24, 1932, October 31, 1935, October 30, 1976.

35. *Sporting News*, August 27, 1931, April 17 and July 14, 1932, May 17, 1934, November 14, 1940.

36. *Sporting News*, February 2 and 16, 1933, September 19, 1935, December 7, 1939, January 11, February 8, March 14, March 28, August 1, and September 12, 1940, September 11, 1941; *New York Times*, July 18, 1935, December 1 and 5, 1939.

37. L. Johnson and Wolff, *Encyclopedia of Minor League Baseball*, 2nd ed., 11; *New York Times*, April 7, 1935; *Sporting News*, September 12, 1935.

38. L. Johnson and Wolff, *Encyclopedia of Minor League Baseball*, 2nd ed., 11; Sussman, "1935," 241; *Sporting News*, November 28, 1935, January 9, 1936, December 9, 1937, January 6 and October 27, 1938, July 22, 1943; Wright, *The Texas League*, 198.

39. *New York Times*, June 25, 1963; Pietrusza, Silverman, and Gershman, *Baseball*, 412; Lowenfish, *Branch Rickey*, 156; Lieb, *The St. Louis Cardinals*, 91; *St. Louis Globe-Democrat*, December 7, 1931.

40. Pietrusza, *Judge and Jury*, 362; Alexander, *Breaking the Slump*, 149; Burk, *Much More Than a Game*, 36, 50; White, *Creating the National Pastime*, 286–88; *Sporting News*, January 14, 1937. See also Lieb, *The St. Louis Cardinals*, 84–86; and House Judiciary Committee, *Study of Monopoly Power*, 977–1049.

41. J. G. T. Spink, *Judge Landis*, 232–36; Burk, *Much More Than a Game*, 64–65; Pietrusza, *Judge and Jury*, 362–66; House Judiciary Committee, *Study of Monopoly Power*, 673–80.

42. Long, "1939," 264, 266, 268; *Sporting News*, November 30 and December 7 and 14, 1939.

43. Waddell and Nowlin, "1940," 271–74; *Spalding-Reach Official Baseball Guide* for 1941, 147, 149; *Sporting News*, February 1, 1940; House Judiciary Committee, *Study of Monopoly Power*, 681–87.

44. Warfield, *The Roaring Redhead*, 40–51; Dewey and Acocella, *The Ball Clubs*, 186–87; Pietrusza, *Lights On!*, 104.

45. Warfield, *The Roaring Redhead*, 51–53; L. Johnson and Wolff, *Encyclopedia of Minor League Baseball*, 2nd ed., 279–82; Rhodes and Snyder, *Redleg Journal*, 260–61.

46. Light, *Cultural Encyclopedia of Baseball*, 602; Warfield, *The Roaring Redhead*, 51; C. Smith, *Voices of the Game*, 19–20, 27–28; J. R. Walker, *Crack of the Bat*, 55–56, 73–74; Rhodes and Snyder, *Redleg Journal*, 240–41, 260; Barber and Creamer, *Rhubarb in the Catbird Seat*, 182–200.

47. Dewey and Acocella, *The Ball Clubs*, 187–88; Pietrusza, Silverman, and Gershman, *Baseball*, 739–40; Warfield, *The Roaring Redhead*, 53–55.

48. Dewey and Acocella, *The Ball Clubs*, 188–89; *New York Times*, July 31, 1930; Pietrusza, *Lights On!*, 84, 104–6; Warfield, *The Roaring Redhead*, 57–58; *Sporting News*, February 8 and August 23, 1934; Rhodes and Snyder, *Redleg Journal*, 265. See also LeMoine, "1934," 235.

49. Pietrusza, *Lights On!*, 109–17 (with *Cincinnati Post* quote); Warfield, *The Roaring Redhead*, 58–59; Rhodes and Snyder, *Redleg Journal*, 265–66 (with *Cincinnati Times-Star* quote).

50. Rhodes and Snyder, *Redleg Journal*, 264–71; Dewey and Acocella, *The Ball Clubs*, 188–89; Warfield, *The Roaring Redhead*, 61–68; McKelvey, *The MacPhails*, 17–19. See also Barber and Creamer, *Rhubarb in the Catbird Seat*, 194–95.

6. "NEVER SAY HE WASN'T A 'REAL JEW'"

1. *Sporting News*, January 30, 1957; Greenberg, *Hank Greenberg*, 97 and photo section following p. 138. See also Krabbenhoft, "Hank Greenberg's American League RBI Record."
2. Levine, *Ellis Island to Ebbets Field*, 132; Riess, "From Pike to Green"; Edelman and Kupferberg, *Matthau*, 14–15; Kempner, *The Life and Times of Hank Greenberg* (with quote from "another Jewish fan"); Greenberg, *Hank Greenberg*, xv, 5, 282 (with *New York Times* quote).
3. Greenberg, *Hank Greenberg*, 1–7; Rosengren, *Hank Greenberg*, 13–16, 19–20, 75; *Sporting News*, November 7, 1940.
4. Greenberg, *Hank Greenberg*, 8–10, 13–15; Rosengren, *Hank Greenberg*, 18–28; unidentified newspaper clipping, May 2, 1935 (Hank Greenberg clipping file, *Sporting News* Research Center); Berg, *Lindbergh*, 254–63, 265–69. See also Alexander, *John McGraw*, 337.
5. Simon, *Green Mountain Boys of Summer*, 50–54; Seymour, *The Golden Age*, 300, 307, 338; Greenberg, *Hank Greenberg*, 15–16; Rosengren, *Hank Greenberg*, 28–29.
6. Greenberg, *Hank Greenberg*, 16–19; Rosengren, *Hank Greenberg*, 30–34; Fitzgerald, "Hank Greenberg," 29.
7. Greenberg, *Hank Greenberg*, 20–36; Rosengren, *Hank Greenberg*, 37–38, 42–54; Fitzgerald, "Hank Greenberg," 29, 85.
8. Lieb, *The Detroit Tigers*, 28–35, 38–41, 55; *Sporting News*, April 28, 1900; Riess, "Detroit Tigers," 606–7; Dewey and Acocella, *The Ball Clubs*, 235–36; Murdock, *Ban Johnson*, 47; Okkonen and Jones, "Francis J. Navin," 535; Levitt, *Ed Barrow*, 62.
9. Dewey and Acocella, *The Ball Clubs*, 239–42; Riess, "Detroit Tigers," 608, 610–11, 613, 615–16; Lieb, *The Detroit Tigers*, 105, 173; Klier and Rubenstein, *Who Really Made Your Car?*, 89, 262; Benson, *Ballparks of North America*, 134–36.
10. Bevis, *Sunday Baseball*, 11–17, 24–28, 34–56, 75–115, 271; Riess, "Professional Sunday Baseball," 95; *Constitution and Playing Rules of the National League of Professional Base Ball Clubs* (1876), 18; Thorn, *Baseball in the Garden of Eden*, 174; Melville, *Early Baseball*, 113; *Constitution of the National League of Professional Base Ball Clubs* (1878); Seymour, *The Early Years*, 135–47; Nemec, *The Great Encyclopedia of 19th-Century Major League Baseball*, 165–67; *Sporting Life*, March 18, 1885; Nemec, *The Beer and Whiskey League*, 19–25.
11. Bevis, *Sunday Baseball*, 136–38, 167–69, 271–72; *Sporting Life*, August 24, 1907; *Detroit Free Press*, August 19, 1907.
12. Nemec, *The Great Encyclopedia of 19th-Century Major League Baseball*, 7–23; Ivor-Campbell, "The Many Fathers of Baseball"; Seymour, *The Early Years*, 334; L. Allen, *The Hot Stove League*, 22.

13. R. F. Peterson, "'Slide, Kelly, Slide'"; Gerlach, "German Americans in Major League Baseball."
14. Gerlach, "German Americans in Major League Baseball," 29; Baldassaro, "Before Joe D"; Pietrusza, Silverman, and Gershman, *Baseball*, 100–101; Yardley, *Ring*, 168.
15. Hogan, *Shades of Glory*, 5–11, 43–65; *Narrative of the Life of Frederick Douglass*, 44; Blight, *Frederick Douglass*, 507–8; Swanson, *When Baseball Went White*, 4, 9–18; Brunson, *Black Baseball*, 1:225, 2:587, 837–38; Heaphy, *The Negro Leagues*, 10, 12; McKenna, "Bud Fowler."
16. Boxerman and Boxerman, *Jews and Baseball*, 8–12; Riess, "From Pike to Green," 117; Schaefer, "Lip Pike" (with *Sporting News* obituary and Richter All-Star team).
17. Boxerman and Boxerman, *Jews and Baseball*, 37–39, 83 (with McGraw's *New York Tribune* quote); Riess, "From Pike to Green," 119–21 (with Cantor quote); Burns, *The Third Time Around*, 9–10.
18. Boxerman and Boxerman, *Jews and Baseball*, 83–93; Riess, "From Pike to Green," 122–26.
19. Boxerman and Boxerman, *Jews and Baseball*, 104–7; Pietrusza, Silverman, and Gershman, *Baseball*, 82–83; Dawidoff, *The Catcher Was a Spy*, 39–44, 48–57; Nathan, *The McFarland Baseball Quotations Dictionary*, 39.
20. Dawidoff, *The Catcher Was a Spy*, 76–81, 87–96; Reaves, *Taking in a Game*, 53–59, 63–72; *Sporting News*, January 1, 1931; Fitts, *Banzai Babe Ruth*, 203–7.
21. Greenberg, *Hank Greenberg*, 36–42 (with Povich quote), 46; Rosengren, *Hank Greenberg*, 3–4, 57–64, 69–72.
22. Greenberg, *Hank Greenberg*, 47–50, 53; Rosengren, *Hank Greenberg*, 73–74; Riess, "From Pike to Green," 122–24 (with *Sporting News* and *Dearborn Independent* quotes).
23. Kennedy, *Freedom from Fear*, 227–32, 240; Leuchtenberg, *Franklin D. Roosevelt and the New Deal*, 100, 277; Greenberg, *Hank Greenberg*, 57–62; Rosengren, *Hank Greenberg*, 1–12, 87–90; Bak, "The Dark Days of the Black Legion."
24. Dewey and Acocella, *The Ball Clubs*, 243–44; Greenberg, *Hank Greenberg*, 85–86, 89–91; Rosengren, *Hank Greenberg*, 104–33; Lieb, *The Detroit Tigers*, 227–28.
25. Greenberg, *Hank Greenberg*, 91, 94–97; Rosengren, *Hank Greenberg*, 135, 143–47.
26. "Century of Progress Exposition," Encyclopedia of Chicago, http://www.encyclopedia.chicagohistory.org/pages/225.html, accessed July 2021.
27. Littlewood, *Arch*, 3–5, 18–39, 66–71; Pietrusza, Silverman, and Gershman, *Baseball*, 471–72, 1198; Vincent, Spatz, and Smith, *The Midsummer Classic*, xi.
28. Littlewood, *Arch*, 67; *Sporting News*, May 25, 1933; P. Morris, *A Game of Inches: The Game on the Field*, 135–36, 177; Seymour, *The Early Years*, 25; Seymour, *The Golden Age*, 193–94; Pietrusza, Silverman, and Gershman, *Baseball*, 578; Solomon, *The Baseball Timeline*, 167; Holtzman, *No Cheering in the Press Box*, 157–58; Crepeau, *Baseball*, 111.

29. Littlewood, *Arch*, 71–75; Vincent, Spatz, and Smith, *The Midsummer Classic*, 3–9; Alexander, *Breaking the Slump*, 71–72, 287.
30. Littlewood, *Arch*, 75–76; Vincent, Spatz, and Smith, *The Midsummer Classic*, 10–16; Alexander, *Breaking the Slump*, 84; Pietrusza, Silverman, and Gershman, *Baseball*, 529; *New York World-Telegram*, July 10, 1961.
31. Vincent, Spatz, and Smith, *The Midsummer Classic*, 17–49; "Boos for the All-Star Game," *Literary Digest*, July 20, 1935, 34; Gregory, *Diz*, 332–36. See also *New York Times*, July 10 and 11, 1935.
32. *Sporting News*, June 29 and July 13, 1933; *New York Times*, October 1, 1931. See also C. Smith, *Voices of Summer*, 7–20.
33. J. R. Walker, *Crack of the Bat*, chapter 5. See also *Sporting News*, July 5 and September 27, 1934, July 4 and October 10, 1935, August 31 and November 9, 1939; *New York Times*, September 24, 1933, September 27, 1934, September 20, 1935, September 27, 1936, November 4, 1937, November 6, 1939.
34. J. R. Walker, *Crack of the Bat*, 97–99; *New York Times*, October 1, 1931, and September 28, 1932; Pietrusza, *Judge and Jury*, 338–39; C. Smith, *Voices of the Game*, 36–37; Barber, *The Broadcasters*, 79–83.
35. J. R. Walker, *Crack of the Bat*, 48, 63–64, 67, 86, 90–91, 161–62, 166.
36. J. R. Walker, "The Baseball-Radio War, 1931–1935," 55–56; Appel, *Pinstripe Empire*, 184–86, 204–5; Levitt, *Ed Barrow*, 284, 323–25; *New York Times*, October 10, 1935, February 15 and 25, 1936; *Sporting News*, March 12 and April 23, 1936; J. R. Walker, *Crack of the Bat*, 52–54, 166–68; Dewey and Acocella, *The Ball Clubs*, 89–90; Warfield, *The Roaring Redhead*, 69–82; Hynd, *The Giants of the Polo Grounds*, 313–14.
37. J. R. Walker, *Crack of the Bat*, 67–68; C. Smith, *Voices of Summer*, 25–27; Ham, *Broadcasting Baseball*, 90–91. See also Ulrey, "Jack Graney."
38. Dewey and Acocella, *The Ball Clubs*, 244; Greenberg, *Hank Greenberg*, 51; *Sporting News*, June 3, 1937 (with "life and death" quote); Bevis, *Mickey Cochrane*, 142–43; Lieb, *The Detroit Tigers*, 231.
39. Gershman, *Diamonds*, 230–31; Riess, "Detroit Tigers," 618; Lieb, *The Detroit Tigers*, 233–34.
40. Greenberg, *Hank Greenberg*, 96, 110, 116, 117, 121, 128–39.
41. Greenberg, *Hank Greenberg*, 143–49; Rosengren, *Hank Greenberg*, 210–21, 233–37; Kennedy, *Freedom from Fear*, 459; *Sporting News*, December 18, 1941.

7. "KEEP BASEBALL GOING"

1. *Sporting News*, November 19, 1936, and December 18, 1941; Leavengood, *Clark Griffith*, 258; Mead, *Even the Browns*, 33–34; Green, "1941," 281. See also Dewey and Acocella, *The Ball Clubs*, 519–20; and Borst, "Baltimore Orioles," 473.
2. Lowenfish, *Branch Rickey*, 83–84, 259; Dewey and Acocella, *The Ball Clubs*, 517–19; Borst, "Baltimore Orioles," 471, 475; *Sporting News*, October 26, 1933, December 5, 1935, November 19, 1936, March 4, 1982.

3. Dewey and Acocella, *The Ball Clubs*, 519; Borst, "Baltimore Orioles," 472; *Sporting News*, January 11, February 1, February 8, February 15, and May 30, 1940, August 14, 1941.
4. Pietrusza, Silverman, and Gershman, *Baseball*, 471–72; *Sporting News*, January 11, 1940, and April 24, 1971; *New York Times*, April 10, 1971; Green, "1941," 278.
5. *Sporting News*, September 7, 1939 (with Dean quote), August 29 and September 5, 1940; Dewey and Acocella, *The Ball Clubs*, 576–79; Grahek, "Clark Griffith," 760; Leavengood, *Clark Griffith*, 114–16.
6. Gietschier, "'Uncle Sam Needs Only to Call'"; Clifford and Spencer, *The First Peacetime Draft*, 5, 220; Flynn, *The Draft, 1940–1973*, 13–48, 117; Langer and Gleason, *The Challenge to Isolation*, 682; Klein, *A Call to Arms*, 81; Rosengren, *Hank Greenberg*, 200.
7. Crepeau, *Baseball*, 205; *Sporting News*, May 23, August 1, October 3, and October 31, 1940; Light, *Cultural Encyclopedia of Baseball*, 474.
8. *Sporting News*, October 24, 1940; Creamer, *Baseball and Other Matters*, 121–22, 124–25.
9. *Sporting News*, November 7, November 14, December 12, and December 19, 1940.
10. Rosengren, *Hank Greenberg*, 211–21; *Sporting News*, November 28, 1940, February 13 and May 15, 1941; Classification History (SSS Form 102) for William Harry Embick, Hugh Noyes Mulcahy, John Dungan Rigney, Morris Arnovich, and Henry Greenberg, World War II Selective Service Records, Records of the Selective Service System, 1926–1975, National Archives, St. Louis MO; Creamer, *Baseball and Other Matters*, 122–23, 126–35; Greenberg, *Hank Greenberg*, 143–45.
11. Creamer, *Baseball and Other Matters*, 125 (with MacPhail quote); Crepeau, *Baseball*, 210–11 (with Daniel quote); *New York Times*, February 2 and June 10, 1941; Vincent, Spatz, and Smith, *The Midsummer Classic*, 50; *Sporting News*, August 28, 1941.
12. Creamer, *Baseball and Other Matters*, 4, 51; Koppett, *Koppett's Concise History of Major League Baseball*, 205–6; Appel, *Pinstripe Empire*, 219–22.
13. Creamer, *Baseball and Other Matters*, 310.
14. Crepeau, *Baseball*, 196–203 (with *Chicago Tribune* cartoon and *Feather River Bulletin* quote); Reaves, *Taking in a Game*, xv–xix; *Sporting News*, December 18, 1941.
15. *Sporting News*, December 18 and 25, 1941, January 1, 1942. See also Terkel, *"The Good War,"* 25–27, 35–36.
16. Leavengood, *Clark Griffith*, 258–59; *Sporting News*, January 8 and 22, 1942, May 31, 1950; *New York Times*, January 9 and 17, 1942; Pietrusza, *Judge and Jury*, 432; Hubler and Drazen, *The Nats and the Grays*, 34–37.
17. Leavengood, *Clark Griffith*, 259; Bazer and Culbertson, "Baseball during World War II," 114–19 (with *Chicago Sun*, Dilweg, and Reynolds quotes); Pietrusza, *Judge and Jury*, 432 (with Spink quote); *Sporting News*, January 22, 1942; Goldstein, *Spartan Seasons*, 34.
18. Bullock, *Playing for Their Nation*, 28; Goldstein, *Spartan Seasons*, 37–38, 63–64;

Sporting News, February 12, 1942; *New York Times*, February 3, May 21, August 27, September 2, September 20, September 25, and September 28, 1942. See also D. Parker, "The World of Sports."

19. Pietrusza, *Judge and Jury*, 388, 389, 434; Pietrusza, *Lights On!*, 32, 77–78, 107–8, 119, 139, 141, 157, 159, 162–64; Lieb, *The Detroit Tigers*, 44; Light, *Cultural Encyclopedia of Baseball*, 512; Warfield, *The Roaring Redhead*, 72–74.
20. Pietrusza, *Lights On!*, 120–31 (with MacPhail quote); *New York Times*, May 23 and 26, 1938; Surdam, *Wins, Losses, and Empty Seats*, 233–34.
21. Surdam, *Wins, Losses, and Empty Seats*, 234–37 (with first Mack quote); Pietrusza, *Lights On!*, 135–39 (with second Mack quote); *Sporting News*, July 7 and December 22, 1938, February 16 and May 25, 1939, March 14, 1940; *New York Times*, May 16 and 17, 1939.
22. Light, *Cultural Encyclopedia of Baseball*, 511–13; Pietrusza, *Lights On!*, 139–61; Surdam, *Wins, Losses, and Empty Seats*, 238–43; *New York Times*, October 21, 1931; *Sporting News*, November 14, 1940.
23. Surdam, *Wins, Losses, and Empty Seats*, 221, 226–27, 234, 238–39; Pietrusza, *Lights On!*, 121, 142, 148; Warfield, *The Roaring Redhead*, 76–78; *New York Times*, September 24, 1932, November 15, 1939, May 25 and 30, 1940.
24. Pietrusza, *Lights On!*, 164–69; *New York Times*, April 30, May 16, May 19, and August 4, 1942; *Sporting News*, August 13, 1942; Vincent, Spatz, and Smith, *The Midsummer Classic*, 56–59; Goldstein, *Spartan Seasons*, 124–28. See also Wells, *Baseball's Western Front*, 13, 67.
25. Finoli, *For the Good of the Country*, 13–14, 17; *Sporting News*, February 19, February 26, April 16, and August 20, 1942; Gilbert, *They Also Served*, 43; Goldstein, *Spartan Seasons*, 31; *New York Times*, November 1 and 13, 1942.
26. *New York Times*, November 26, 1942; *Sporting News*, January 8, January 15, January 22, January 29, February 26, and March 5, 1942; Cavanaugh, *Season of '42*, 7; Montville, *Ted Williams*, 99–101.
27. Montville, *Ted Williams*, 102–8; *Sporting News*, March 5, March 12, March 19, and May 28, 1942.
28. Montville, *Ted Williams*, 95; Cramer, *Joe DiMaggio*, 188, 198, 200; Cavanaugh, *Season of '42*, 6–7; Goldstein, *Spartan Seasons*, 150.
29. *Sporting News*, March 19, 1942; Berger, "Paul Derringer."
30. Mead, *Even the Browns*, 45–49, 67–72; Dewey and Acocella, *The Ball Clubs*, 520; Borst, "Baltimore Orioles," 472–73.
31. *New York Times*, November 26, 1942, January 16, January 24, February 4, February 9, February 15, February 16, February 28, March 25, and March 26, 1943; *Sporting News*, January 7, 1943.
32. Kennedy, *Freedom from Fear*, 624; *Sporting News*, October 7, 1943; Perrett, *Days of Sadness, Years of Triumph*, 133–34; Polenberg, *War and Society*, 14–19; Goldstein, *Spartan Seasons*, 99; *New York Times*, October 8, 1942.
33. Goldstein, *Spartan Seasons*, 99–120; *Sporting News*, January 7, 1943; *New York Times*, December 9 and 31, 1942, January 6, 1943.

34. Goldstein, *Spartan Seasons*, 97–123; Mead, *Even the Browns*, 73–76.
35. *Sporting News*, February 25, 1943; Bullock, *Playing for Their Nation*, 29; *New York Times*, February 24, 1943; Finoli, *For the Good of the Country*, 53; Mead, *Even the Browns*, 99–109.
36. Goldstein, *Spartan Seasons*, 131–34; Mead, *Even the Browns*, 78–79; Finoli, *For the Good of the Country*, 58–59, 145; *Sporting News*, March 18, March 25, and April 22, 1943, January 6, 1944.
37. L. Johnson and Wolff, *Encyclopedia of Minor League Baseball*, 3rd ed., 313–39; *Sporting News*, November 28 and December 5, 1940.
38. *New York Times*, November 16, 1943; Goldstein, *Spartan Seasons*, 156–57; Mead, *Even the Browns*, 118, 140–41; Finoli, *For the Good of the Country*, 143.
39. Mead, *Even the Browns*, 141–42; Finoli, *For the Good of the Country*, 143–44.
40. *New York Times*, January 5, February 2, February 3, February 4, February 8, February 12, and February 15, 1944; *Sporting News*, February 17, 1944.
41. *Sporting News*, April 20 and 27, 1944; *New York Times*, January 4, January 5, and January 11, 1944; Vincent, Spatz, and Smith, *The Midsummer Classic*, 68; Mead, *Even the Browns*, 129–87.
42. Pietrusza, *Judge and Jury*, 444–52; *Sporting News*, October 5, October 12, October 19, October 26, November 23, November 30, December 7, December 14, and December 21, 1944.
43. Mead, *Even the Browns*, 186; Dewey and Acocella, *The Ball Clubs*, 520; Borst, "Baltimore Orioles," 475; *Sporting News*, August 16, 1945. See also Pajot and Erion, "St. Louis Browns Team Ownership History."

8. "A GREAT DISPLAY OF TINGLING PATRIOTISM"

1. Pessah, *Yogi*, 45, 48–49, 53; Barra, *Yogi Berra*, 27–34; Trimble, *Yogi Berra*, 42; DeVito, *Yogi*, 34–42; Berra with Horton, *Yogi*, 141–44; Berra and Fitzgerald, *Yogi*, 19, 66–71; Nowlin, "Yogi Berra and the D-Day Invasion," 58–60.
2. DeVito, *Yogi*, 1–6; Barra, *Yogi Berra*, 3–7; Berra with Horton, *Yogi*, 150; Berra and Fitzgerald, *Yogi*, 33–34; Pessah, *Yogi*, 20.
3. Berra and Fitzgerald, *Yogi*, 35–38; DeVito, *Yogi*, 11–14; Mormino, *Immigrants on the Hill*, 199; Barra, *Yogi Berra*, 9–10, 14; Pessah, *Yogi*, 18–19.
4. Berra and Fitzgerald, *Yogi*, 38–40; Barra, *Yogi Berra*, 15–23; DeVito, *Yogi*, 15, 20–22, 26–27, 29–32; Pessah, *Yogi*, 18–19, 24–28, 31–32.
5. Barra, *Yogi Berra*, 22–41; Berra and Fitzgerald, *Yogi*, 62–63; Trimble, *Yogi Berra*, 33–40; DeVito, *Yogi*, 32–37; Pessah, *Yogi*, 39–51; *Sporting News*, May 13, 1943.
6. W. H. Parker, *We Called Ourselves Rocketboatmen*, 46–47, 70–71; Berra with Horton, *Yogi*, 144; Barra, *Yogi Berra*, 34–37; DeVito, *Yogi*, 42–43; Pessah, *Yogi*, 54–57.
7. Goldstein, *Spartan Seasons*, 39; *New York Times*, June 7, 1944; *Sporting News*, June 15, 1944.
8. *Sporting News*, September 16, 1943; Goldstein, *Spartan Seasons*, 38–40.
9. Pietrusza, *Judge and Jury*, 175–76; *Chicago Daily Tribune*, February 5, 1921; *Sporting News*, April 5, 1934, and February 5, 1966; *Chicago Tribune*, January 22, 1966; *New*

York Journal-American, December 21, 1944, and September 30, 1959; *Washington Post*, February 5, 1921; Simons, "Twenty-Four Years with the Judge," 331–32, passim; *Cleveland News*, December 13, 1944; *Philadelphia Evening Bulletin*, January 29, 1960.

10. *New York Times*, November 28, 1944; *Chicago Daily Tribune*, December 12, 1944; Marren, "1944," 299–300; Marshall, *Baseball's Pivotal Era*, 14.
11. Marshall, *Baseball's Pivotal Era*, 16; Dallek, *Franklin D. Roosevelt*, 547, 599; *New York Times*, January 5, January 19, and January 24, 1945; Roosevelt, "State of the Union Address"; Goldstein, *Spartan Seasons*, 200–201.
12. Goldstein, *Spartan Seasons*, 203–7; Marshall, *Baseball's Pivotal Era*, 16.
13. *Sporting News*, February 1, February 8, and February 22, 1945; Marshall, *Baseball's Pivotal Era*, 17; Goldstein, *Spartan Seasons*, 202; Finoli, *For the Good of the Country*, 221; *New York Times*, January 26 and April 8, 1945.
14. *New York Times*, September 2 and November 26, 1944, January 4, April 24, and April 25, 1945; Marshall, *Baseball's Pivotal Era*, 17–21.
15. Chandler with Trimble, *Heroes, Plain Folks, and Skunks*, 13–14, 23, 27, 161; Marshall, *Baseball's Pivotal Era*, 24–27; *Sporting News*, May 3, 1945.
16. Chandler with Trimble, *Heroes, Plain Folks, and Skunks*, 173–74, 176–81; *New York Times*, December 13, 1944, February 4, May 2, and July 13, 1945; Marshall, *Baseball's Pivotal Era*, 37–41; *Chicago Daily Tribune*, May 4, 1945.
17. *Sporting News*, March 15 and 22, 1945; Bush, "1942," 289; Pietrusza, *Lights On!*, 163–65, 168, 176–78; *New York Times*, July 14 and December 25, 1943, February 25, July 12, and July 13, 1945; Okkonen, *Baseball Uniforms of the 20th Century*, 49.
18. Pietrusza, *Lights On!*, 171; Vincent, Spatz, and Smith, *The Midsummer Classic*, 62–75; *Sporting News*, July 8 and 22, 1943, March 1 and July 26, 1945; *New York Times*, June 4, 1943, May 22, 1944, February 22 and May 13, 1945; Burk, *Much More Than a Game*, 71.
19. Bullock, *Playing for Their Nation*, 31–32; R. M. Cohen and Neft, *The World Series*, 191. See also *Sporting News*, September 3, 1942; and D. M. Daniel, "Major Leagues Have Proud Record in War and Relief Enterprises," 327–28.
20. Bullock, *Playing for Their Nation*, 32–37, 151; *Sporting News*, May 21, 1942; Mead, *Even the Browns*, 5–6; *New York Times*, March 31, April 14, and June 5, 1943; Goldstein, *Spartan Seasons*, 75–77.
21. Bullock, *Playing for Their Nation*, 37–39, 71–73, 144 (with Povich quote); *Sporting News*, March 15, 1945.
22. Pietrusza, *Lights On!*, 170–71; Finoli, *For the Good of the Country*, 12, 16; Bullock, *Playing for Their Nation*, 39–45; *Sporting News*, July 16, 1942 (with Lieb quote); Rosengren, *Hank Greenberg*, 242–43. See also Radford, "Navy World Series"; and "The Game's the Thing: Organizing Military Baseball," Puget Sound Navy Museum, http://www.pugetsoundnavymuseum.org/navy-baseball-in-wwii/, accessed July 2021.
23. Goldstein, *Spartan Seasons*, 225–36; Bullock, *Playing for Their Nation*, 45–47; Jacobson, *Pete Reiser*, 131–33.

24. Bullock, *Playing for Their Nation*, 47–48; Bedingfield, "The 1943 All-Pro Game in England"; Bedingfield, "The 1945 GI World Series"; Goldstein, *Spartan Seasons*, 236–43; Nowlin, "The 1945 All-Star Game," 212–14.
25. Bedingfield, "When Baseball Went to War"; Goldstein, *Spartan Seasons*, 248–49, 254; Shepard, "Lt. Bert Shepard"; Nowlin, "Lou Brissie's Amazing Comeback"; Pietrusza, Silverman, and Gershman, *Baseball*, 1141.
26. "'Chewing Gum Is a War Material,' says Phil Wrigley," *Fortune*, January 1943, referenced in Fidler, *The Origins and History*, 29–33; Pietrusza, *Lights On!*, 98–99. See also Steele, "Philip Wrigley."
27. Fidler, *The Origins and History*, 31, 33, 34, 36, 44, 181, 199, 349; *Sporting News*, April 22, 1943; Candaele, "The History of Women's Baseball," 161–64.
28. Fidler, *The Origins and History*, 9, 17, 35–36, 71–72.
29. Fidler, *The Origins and History*, 36, 69, 168–69; Pierman, "The All-American Girls Professional Baseball League."
30. Burk, *Much More Than a Game*, 72; Nathan, *The McFarland Baseball Quotations Dictionary*, 132 (with Brown quote); Mead, *Even the Browns*, 214–16, 236; Pietrusza, Silverman, and Gershman, *Baseball*, 194–95, 377–78, 489–90, 716–17, 1037–39, 1195–98.
31. *Sporting News*, April 12, 1945; Mead, *Even the Browns*, 208–10, 223, 230–33; Marshall, *Baseball's Pivotal Era*, 29–32; *New York Times*, September 30, 1944; Kashatus, *One-Armed Wonder*, 89–91, 98–102, 109–13, 117–19; Lieb, *The Detroit Tigers*, 260–62; Goldstein, *Spartan Seasons*, 209–10.
32. Rosengren, *Hank Greenberg*, 235–39, 241–46, 249–70 (with *Sporting News* quote); Greenberg, *Hank Greenberg*, 148–55; *Sporting News*, October 4, 1945 (with Lieb quote).
33. Bloodgood, "The Tigers," 235–36; *Sporting News*, October 4, 1945; Barra, *Yogi Berra*, 36–44; W. H. Parker, *We Called Ourselves Rocketboatmen*, 126–59; Pessah, *Yogi*, 57–63.
34. *Sporting News*, December 7 and 21, 1944; *New York Times*, December 14, 1944; Burk, *Much More Than a Game*, 73–74; *New York Daily News*, March 4, 1946. See also House Judiciary Committee, *Study of Monopoly Power*, 1599, 1600, 1615, 1636.
35. *Sporting News*, May 10, June 7, 1945; Nowlin, "Dave Ferriss"; Nowlin, "Al Benton."
36. *New York Times*, August 6, 1945; *Sporting News*, August 30, 1945, and February 7, 1946; Selective Training and Service Act of 1940, Pub. L. 76–783, 54 Stat. 885 (1940); Goldstein, *Spartan Seasons*, 269–70; Burk, *Much More Than a Game*, 83; Marshall, *Baseball's Pivotal Era*, 86; Turner, *When the Boys Came Back*, 55.
37. Anton and Nowlin, *When Baseball Went to War*, 7; Burk, *Much More Than a Game*, 83; Day, *Clubhouse Lawyer*, 193–95; Lowenfish and Lupien, *The Imperfect Diamond*, 129–32; *Sporting News*, March 7, 1946 (with Baumgartner quote); Bevis, "Tony Lupien" (with Egan quote).
38. Lowenfish and Lupien, *Imperfect Diamond*, 133–34; Day, *Clubhouse Lawyer*, 206–8; Nowlin, "Al Niemiec"; Obermeyer, "Disposable Heroes."

39. Obermeyer, "Disposable Heroes"; Niemiec v. Seattle Rainier Baseball Club, 67 F. Suppl. 705 (W.D. Wash. 1946); *New York Times*, June 22, 1946.

40. *Sporting News*, May 16 and June 5, 1946; *Newark Star-Ledger*, May 26, 1946; *Rochester Democrat & Chronicle*, May 26, 1946; Barra, *Yogi Berra*, 41–43, 45–48; Trimble, *Yogi Berra*, 55–57, 59–60; Pessah, *Yogi*, 64–68, 71–75; Rampersad, *Jackie Robinson*, 156–57.

9. "THE SMILING YOUNG MAN"

1. *Sporting News*, March 2 and 9, 1933, March 6, 1957; Nowlin, *Tom Yawkey*, 1, 4–8, 14; Stout and Johnson, *Red Sox Century*, 175–78, 181–82. See also Armour, "Tom Yawkey"; and Huhn, *Eddie Collins*, 270–74.
2. Armour and Levitt, *Paths to Glory*, 112; Nowlin, *Tom Yawkey*, 13, 19–21, 46–48 (with Peterman and Collins quotes); Stout and Johnson, *Red Sox Century*, 184, 187–89; *Sporting News*, October 5, 1933.
3. Stout and Johnson, *Red Sox Century*, 186–87, 189–91; Nowlin, *Tom Yawkey*, 16–17, 39–41.
4. Stout and Johnson, *Red Sox Century*, 197–210 (with Collins quote).
5. Tiemann and Palmer, "Major League Attendance," 107; Nowlin, "Bobby Doerr"; Pietrusza, Silverman, and Gershman, *Baseball*, 289, 294; Contois, "Dom DiMaggio"; Barney and Barney, "Boston Red Sox," 514–17; Dewey and Acocella, *The Ball Clubs*, 59–60; Stout and Johnson, *Red Sox Century*, 197–210ff; Nowlin, *Tom Yawkey*, 49–72ff.
6. Stout and Johnson, *Red Sox Century*, 179–83; Nowlin, *Tom Yawkey*, 26–38, 59, 114, 191–93; *Sporting News*, December 2, 1943.
7. G. C. Rogers, *The History of Georgetown County*, 325, 339, 343, 409, 434–35, 454, 485–87, 489–90; Joyner, *Down by the Riverside*, 1–2, 22–23, 33–35, 41; *Greensboro (NC) Daily News*, April 2, 1937; Betsworth, "Reviving and Restoring Southern Ruins," 57.
8. Betsworth, "Reviving and Restoring Southern Ruins," 60, 63, 73; G. C. Rogers, *The History of Georgetown Country*, 490, 496 (with Baruch quote). See also South Carolina Plantations website, https://south-carolina-plantations.com, accessed July 2021.
9. Nowlin, *Tom Yawkey*, 17, 91, 115–17, 120, 126, 130, 132, 158, 164, 175, 286, 333–34. See also "Yawkey Foundation Conservation and Wildlife Support," Yawkey Foundation, https://yawkeyfoundation.org/giving/conservation-wildlife, accessed July 2021.
10. H. Bryant, *Shut Out*, 23–24, 27–29, 33–38; *New York Times*, March 10, 1945; Nowlin, *Tom Yawkey*, 106; Tygiel, *Baseball's Great Experiment*, 43; Rampersad, *Jackie Robinson*, 119; Eig, *Opening Day*, 135; Alpert, *Out of Left Field*, 163–64; Norwood and Brackman, "Going to Bat for Jackie Robinson," 124–25; Stout, "Tryout and Fallout," 12.
11. Kennedy, *Freedom from Fear*, 857; Alpert, *Out of Left Field*, 134–62; Lowenfish, *Branch Rickey*, 361–63; Stout, "Tryout and Fallout," 14.

12. Huhn, *Eddie Collins*, 302–5; Stout and Johnson, *Red Sox Century*, 240–42; Stout, "Tryout and Fallout," 14, 18; H. Bryant, *Shut Out*, 28–30.
13. Huhn, *Eddie Collins*, 306–7, 345; Nowlin, *Tom Yawkey*, 107–13, 126, 420–38 (with Keane recollection); Stout and Johnson, *Red Sox Century*, 242–44; Tygiel, *Baseball's Great Experiment*, 44 (with Jethroe and Robinson quotes); Armour, *Joe Cronin*, 153–56; H. Bryant, *Shut Out*, 2–12, 31–33, 52–62; Wendell Smith to Eddie Collins, April 27, 1945, and Eddie Collins to Wendell Smith, May 11, 1945, Wendell Smith Papers, National Baseball Hall of Fame Library.
14. Patterson, *Grand Expectations*, 61–81; Jackson, *Crabgrass Frontier*, 232–33.
15. Patterson, *Grand Expectations*, 40–43; Polenberg, *War and Society*, 159–61.
16. Patterson, *Grand Expectations*, 43–44; Marshall, *Baseball's Pivotal Era*, 64.
17. Giglio, *Musial*, 126; Patterson, *Grand Expectations*, 43; Lowenfish and Lupien, *The Imperfect Diamond*, 139–40; Koszarek, *The Players League*, 41–47; Light, *Cultural Encyclopedia of Baseball*, 769–70. See also McKelvey, *Mexican Raiders*, 26–36; and *Sporting News*, December 17, 1931, August 4, 1932, February 11 and 18, 1937.
18. Marshall, *Baseball's Pivotal Era*, 64–67; Lowenfish and Lupien, *The Imperfect Diamond*, 139–42; Weintraub, *The Victory Season*, 179–81; Turner, *When the Boys Came Back*, 136–38; *New York Times*, April 18 and 22, 1946; *New York Daily News*, April 18, 1946.
19. Benswanger, "Professional Baseball in Pittsburgh," 27, 32; *New York Times*, May 3, May 16, and June 5, 1946; Marshall, *Baseball's Pivotal Era*, 67–71; Lowenfish and Lupien, *The Imperfect Diamond*, 141–47; Turner, *When the Boys Came Back*, 139–44.
20. Lowenfish and Lupien, *The Imperfect Diamond*, 145–47; Marshall, *Baseball's Pivotal Era*, 71–72.
21. Vaughn, "Jorge Pasquel"; Bjarkman, *Diamonds around the Globe*, 267–77; Iber, "Mexico," 76–78; Virtue, *South of the Color Barrier*, 73–85. See also McKelvey, *Mexican Raiders*, 41.
22. Virtue, *South of the Color Barrier*, 58, 60–62, 67.
23. Bjarkman, *Diamonds around the Globe*, 277–79; Virtue, *South of the Color Barrier*, 112, 115–16; Holtzman, *No Cheering in the Press Box*, 337–49 (with Gillespie quotes).
24. Marshall, *Baseball's Pivotal Era*, 45; Virtue, *South of the Color Barrier*, 125–27; McKelvey, *Mexican Raiders*, 61, 85–93; Weatherby, "Danny Gardella."
25. Marshall, *Baseball's Pivotal Era*, 49; Virtue, *South of the Color Barrier*, 74; McKelvey, *Mexican Raiders*, 45–46; Bjarkman, *Diamonds around the Globe*, 277–79; Giglio, *Musial*, 127–31. Scholars disagree on the money Pasquel offered to various players. I have relied primarily on Marshall and secondarily on Virtue and McKelvey.
26. Marshall, *Baseball's Pivotal Era*, 50–52; Virtue, *South of the Color Barrier*, 125–36; McKelvey, *Mexican Raiders*, 95–102; Armour, "Vern Stephens."
27. *New York Times*, April 22, 1946; *Sporting News*, June 19, 1946; McKelvey, *Mexican Raiders*, 66, 170–71; Marshall, *Baseball's Pivotal Era*, 49, 52–56, 59–63.

28. *Sporting News*, May 23, June 19, and July 24, 1946; Warfield, *The Roaring Redhead*, 155–63; Turner, *When the Boys Came Back*, 140; Marshall, *Baseball's Pivotal Era*, 74–75; Lowenfish and Lupien, *The Imperfect Diamond*, 147–48.
29. Marshall, *Baseball's Pivotal Era*, 75–76; Weintraub, *The Victory Season*, 43–44, 206–7; Corbett, "Marty Marion."
30. Marshall, *Baseball's Pivotal Era*, 78–81 (with MacPhail and Marion quotes); Korr, *The End of Baseball as We Knew It*, 15–16; Weintraub, *The Victory Season*, 268–73; House Judiciary Committee, *Study of Monopoly Power*, 1625–28. See also Pappas, "The MacPhail Report of 1946," 2–4.
31. Weintraub, *The Victory Season*, 274 (with Red Smith quote); Marshall, *Baseball's Pivotal Era*, 81–82, 97–98; *Sporting News*, October 16, December 4, and December 11, 1946; Nechal, "1946," 309–10.
32. *Sporting News*, July 22 and December 10, 1953; Korr, *The End of Baseball as We Knew It*, 17–20; Mike Lynch, "1958," 3.
33. *Sporting News*, December 10, 1958; Korr, *The End of Baseball as We Knew It*, 20–24.
34. *Sporting News*, January 3 (with first Daniel quote) and February 7, 1946 (with second Daniel quote); Bokser, "1945," 305–6.
35. *Sporting News*, February 7 and April 4, 1946 (with Daniel quote); C. P. Rogers, "Hugh Mulcahy"; Berger, "Morrie Arnovich."
36. *Sporting News*, January 10, January 17, February 14, February 28, April 18, and April 25, 1946; Vincent, Spatz, and Smith, *The Midsummer Classic*, 76; Weintraub, *The Victory Season*, 98.
37. *Sporting News*, April 18, 1946; Weintraub, *The Victory Season*, 17–18, 293–94 (with Hirshberg quote); Stout and Johnson, *Red Sox Century*, 247–50; Turner, *When the Boys Came Back*, 201–2; Armour, *Joe Cronin*, 163–65; Montville, *Ted Williams*, 128.
38. Montville, *Ted Williams*, 108–25; Stout and Johnson, *Red Sox Century*, 247–50; Weintraub, *The Victory Season*, 292.
39. *Sporting News*, March 7, 1946.
40. Pietrusza, Silverman, and Gershman, *Baseball*, 185, 819; Koppett, *Koppett's Concise History of Major League Baseball*, 217; Stout, *The Cubs*, 186–88; Weintraub, *The Victory Season*, 40–50; Lieb, *The St. Louis Cardinals*, 196.
41. Markusen, "Tiebreakers," 252; *Sporting News*, October 2, 1946; Weintraub, *The Victory Season*, 308–16; Turner, *When the Boys Came Back*, 213–21.
42. Montville, *Ted Williams*, 125–32; Giglio, *Musial*, 139–43; Turner, *When the Boys Came Back*, 225–55; Weintraub, *The Victory Season*, 322–83 (with Broeg quote).
43. Nowlin, *Tom Yawkey*, 109–13, 126, 420–38; H. Bryant, *Shut Out*, 2–12, 52–62; Turner, *When the Boys Came Back*, 221.

10. "BRIGHT COLORED PAPER AND RED RIBBONS"

1. Veeck with Linn, *Veeck*, 40; Dickson, *Bill Veeck*, 14, 41, 47; Angle, *Philip K. Wrigley*, 61; Corbett, "Bill Veeck."
2. Dickson, *Bill Veeck*, 47–49; Veeck with Linn, *Veeck*, 37–38, 42–49 (emphasis in original in Veeck quote); Shea with Castle, *Wrigley Field*, 159–64, 167.

3. Shea with Castle, *Wrigley Field*, 165–66; Benson, *Ballparks of North America*, 93; Veeck with Linn, *Veeck*, 42–43; Dickson, *Bill Veeck*, 48. See also *Chicago Tribune*, September 12, 1937.
4. *Chicago Tribune*, May 3, 1959, quoted in Dickson, *Bill Veeck*, 26; Corbett, "Bill Veeck"; L. Johnson and Wolff, *Encyclopedia of Minor League Baseball*, 3rd ed., 314, 322, 332, 337, 340; Dickson, *Bill Veeck*, 55–58, 67–68, 87–89, 93–104.
5. Veeck with Linn, *Veeck*, 171–72; Pietrusza, *Judge and Jury*, 420–24; Jordan, Gerlach, and Rossi, "A Baseball Myth Exploded"; Tygiel, "Revisiting Bill Veeck"; Neyer, *Rob Neyer's Big Book of Baseball Legends*, 28–30; Dickson, *Bill Veeck*, 105–12, 357–66; Macht and Warrington, "The Veracity of Veeck," 17–20; Dewey and Acocella, *The Ball Clubs*, 219–20; Light, *Cultural Encyclopedia of Baseball*, 164; Corbett, "Bill Veeck"; Odenkirk, *Of Tribes and Tribulations*, 163–64, 170–73.
6. Tiemann and Palmer, "Major League Attendance," 107; Strunk, "The Quarter's Polls," 538–39.
7. Benson, *Ballparks of North America*, 105–7, 110–11; Gershman, *Diamonds*, 96, 98–99, 143–44; Dickson, *Bill Veeck*, 113–14, 117, 120, 151–54; Corbett, "Bill Veeck"; Odenkirk, *Of Tribes and Tribulations*, 174–77.
8. House Judiciary Committee, *Study of Monopoly Power*, 1599, 1600, 1615.
9. *Sporting News*, July 7, 1932, July 3, 1941, July 25, 1945; Corbett, "Dick Wakefield"; Hemphill, "Whatever Happened to What's-His-Name?," 152.
10. Marshall, *Baseball's Pivotal Era*, 254; Treder, "Cash in the Cradle," 1; *Sporting News*, February 15, March 15, August 16, and September 27, 1945.
11. *Sporting News*, December 6, 13, and 20, 1945, February 7 and March 7, 1946 (with Daniel quote); *Sporting News Baseball Guide* for 1946, 184; Bokser, "1945," 307.
12. *Sporting News*, October 30, December 4, and December 25, 1946, April 14, May 5, June 2, June 16, July 7, August 11, November 24, December 8, December 15, and December 22, 1948; *Sporting News Baseball Guide* for 1947, 146; Nechal, "1946," 311; Montgomery, "Georgia's 1948 Phenoms," 72–73; *Sporting News Baseball Guide* for 1948, 90; *Sporting News Baseball Guide* for 1949, 92.
13. *Sporting News*, January 12, January 19, February 2, February 16, April 6, August 24, September 14, September 21, December 7, December 14, and December 21, 1949, February 8, December 6, December 13, and December 20, 1950; *Sporting News Baseball Guide* for 1949, 92; *New York Times*, September 4, 1949; Montgomery, "Georgia's 1948 Phenoms," 73; *Sporting News Baseball Guide* for 1950, 91; Taylor, "Paul Pettit"; Klopsis, "1950," 339; *Sporting News Baseball Guide* for 1951, 102; Taylor, "Jay Porter." See also Kelley, *Baseball's Biggest Blunder*, 1–12; and *Sporting News Baseball Guide* for 1951, 151–52.
14. Marshall, *Baseball's Pivotal Era*, 165–66; *Sporting News*, December 13, December 13 and 20, 1945, January 17, February 21, February 28, and March 14, 1946, October 22 and November 5, 1947, February 11, 1948; *Chicago Tribune*, March 14, 2001; Seymour, *The People's Game*, 131–87; "School Enrollment, by Age, Race, and Sex," 370–72, 385–86; Patterson, *Grand Expectations*, 68; Des Jardins,

Walter Camp, 43; Light, *Cultural Encyclopedia of Baseball*, 172; Eig, *Luckiest Man*, 31; Marazzi and Fiorito, *Baseball Players of the 1950s*, 40; Urban, "Boudreau Stood Out."

15. *Sporting News*, September 20 and December 6, 1934, February 7, and February 28, 1946, July 2, November 12, December 3, December 10, and December 17, 1947.
16. *Sporting News Baseball Guide* for 1951, 102; Klopsis, "1950," 339; *New York Times*, December 8, 1950; *Sporting News Baseball Guide* for 1952, 109–10; S. Bryant, "1951," 345; *Sporting News Baseball Guide* for 1953, 96.
17. *Sporting News*, August 2, August 16, and December 13, 1950; American Civil Liberties Union, *Security and Freedom*, quoted in Gietschier, "Limited War," 1; *New York Times*, December 7 and 8, 1950; Patterson, *Grand Expectations*, 210–22.
18. Flynn, *The Draft, 1940–1973*, 89, 95–96, 100, 103–4, 108–9, 112, 113, 116–17, 122, 124, 168–69; *Sporting News*, August 9, 16, and 23, 1950; Roberts and Rogers, *The Whiz Kids*, 243–44, 286–87, 307, 335, 337, 339; Patterson, *Grand Expectations*, 207; Gietschier, "Limited War," 57; *Sporting News*, January 3, November 7, November 28, and December 19, 1951, January 9, February 20, March 9, and July 9, 1952, July 1, 1953; M. Miller, "Harvey Haddix"; Sarnoff, "Monty Stratton."
19. *Sporting News*, January 24, 1951; Bedingfield, "Baseball's Greatest Sacrifice: George Sulliman"; Nowlin, "Bob Neighbors"; Huber, "Bobby Brown"; Cola, "Bob Kennedy"; Corbett, "Lloyd Merriman"; Bedingfield, "Baseball's Greatest Sacrifice: Jerry Coleman"; Coleman, "More Than a Yankee," 85.
20. L. Johnson and Wolff, *Encyclopedia of Minor League Baseball*, 2nd ed., 347; Bokser, "1945," 306–7.
21. Zingg and Medeiros, *Runs, Hits, and an Era*, 107–10; White, *Creating the National Pastime*, 298; Beireis, "Divided They Fall," 12; N. J. Sullivan, *The Minors*, 217; *Sporting News*, December 13 and 20, 1945.
22. Treder, "Open Classification," 94–95; Lomax, "Not Quite Ready for Prime Time," 17–18, 24; N. J. Sullivan, *The Dodgers Move West*, 90; O'Neal, *The Pacific Coast League*, 224; Beireis, "Divided They Fall," 12–14; Nechal, "1946," 311; *Sporting News*, December 11, 1946; Marshall, *Baseball's Pivotal Era*, 261.
23. Sumner, "William G. Bramham," 121–22; Klopsis, "1943," 295–96; *Sporting News*, December 9, 1943, December 11, 1946, July 16, 1947; Nechal, "1946," 310; *New York Times*, June 25, 1963.
24. Nechal, "1946," 310; *Sporting News*, December 4 and 11, 1946.
25. House Judiciary Committee, *Study of Monopoly Power*, 1621, 1625.
26. *Baltimore Sun*, February 10, 1949; *Sporting News*, March 2, March 9, March 16, and November 23, 1949, January 4, 1950.
27. Heitz, "Rules and Scoring," 2230, 2233–38; *Sporting News*, February 1 and March 15, 1950, November 11, 1953, November 28, 1956; "Rule 2.63," *Official Baseball Rules* (completely revised for 1950); "Rule 28," *Official Baseball Rules* (revised for 1949); "Playing Rules Completely Recodified," *Sporting News Base-*

ball Guide for 1950, 93; "Rule 8.04" and "Rule 9.01(d)," *Official Baseball Rules* (completely revised for 1957); "Rule 8.04," *Official Baseball Rules* (1956).

28. *Sporting News*, March 5, 1947, April 7 and May 26, 1948, June 10, June 24, July 15, July 22, and November 11, 1953, June 30, 1954; Heitz, "Rules and Scoring," 2233, 2235–36.
29. *Sporting News*, August 3, 1949, January 18 and June 7, 1950, January 17, 1951, June 16 and October 13, 1954; *Official Baseball Rules* (revised for 1949); *Official Baseball Rules* (completely revised for 1950); Heitz, "Rules and Scoring," 2250–57.
30. *Official Baseball Rules* (revised for 1949); *Official Baseball Rules* (completely revised for 1950); Heitz, "Rules and Scoring," 2218–2237; *Sporting News*, March 9, March 23, and April 6, 1949, April 12 and May 3, 1950, March 12 and October 15, 1952, November 11, 1953.
31. Veeck with Linn, *Veeck*, 250–51; Kelley, *Baseball's Biggest Blunder*, 1–20 (emphasis in original in Kelley quote); G. H. Wolf, "1952," 349–50; *Sporting News*, July 16, July 30, August 6, and November 12, 1952.
32. Kelley, *Baseball's Biggest Blunder*, 21–49, 59–62, 64, 75–76, 94–97, 107–13; Wancho, "Harmon Killebrew"; Felber, "1954," 363.
33. Kelley, *Baseball's Biggest Blunder*, 115–27, 154, 158–61, 169–74, 195–97; *Sporting News*, October 9, October 16, November 20 (with King quote), December 11, and December 18, 1957; *Sporting News Baseball Guide* for 1958, 110.
34. *Sporting News*, February 5, July 23, July 30, November 5, and December 10, 1958, February 3 and June 1, 1960; Kelley, *Baseball's Biggest Blunder*, 175–77; *Sporting News Baseball Guide* for 1959, 118; *Sporting News Baseball Guide* for 1960, 118; Mike Lynch, "1958," 5; Kritzler and Henry, "1959," 12.
35. Marshall, *Baseball's Pivotal Era*, 185–209; Dewey and Acocella, *The Ball Clubs*, 44–245; Dewey and Acocella, *Biographical History of Baseball*, 47–48; Rosengren, *Hank Greenberg*, 297–98, 300–301 (with Daniel story).
36. Stout, *The Cubs*, 159, 165, 173–75; Stout and Johnson, *Red Sox Century*, 373–74; Faber, "Powel Crosley Jr." See also *Sporting News*, March 29, 1945, May 8, 1957, August 2, September 27, October 4, and October 11, 1961; Paul Galloway, "The Modest Millionaire," *Chicago Sun-Times*, November 26, 1972; "Ohio Un-American Activities Committee," Ohio History Central, https://ohiohistorycentral.org/w/Ohio_Un-American_Activities_Committee, accessed August 2021.
37. Marshall, *Baseball's Pivotal Era*, 186–89; Skipper, "Connie Mack"; Kuklick, *To Every Thing a Season*, 112–17; Mack, *My 66 Years in the Big Leagues*, 5; R. F. Lewis, "Oakland Athletics," 758, 766, 775–76; Dewey and Acocella, *The Ball Clubs*, 447–48, Macht, *The Grand Old Man of Baseball*, 112–13, 128, 333–34, 436, 461, 469–71; Lindberg, *White Sox Encyclopedia*, 312–16; Cardullo, "Harry Grabiner."
38. Anderson and Kimball, "Minnesota Twins," 676–77, 681–82; Hennessy, "Calvin Griffith," 63; Marshall, *Baseball's Pivotal Era*, 189–90; Hynd, *The Giants of the Polo Grounds*, 210; B. Lamb, "Harry Hempstead"; B. Lamb, "Charles A. Stone-

ham"; B. Lamb, "New York Giants Team Ownership History." See also Treder, *Forty Years a Giant*, 16–19, 37–40, 67–68, 121–28.

39. Marshall, *Baseball's Pivotal Era*, 194–96; Koppett, *Koppett's Concise History of Major League Baseball*, 212–13; Rossi, "Philadelphia Phillies," 263–64; Westcott, "Philadelphia Phillies Team Ownership History"; Dewey and Acocella, *The Ball Clubs*, 42, 429; *Sporting News*, January 27, 1944; Costello, "Bob Quinn"; Stevens, "Atlanta Braves," 22–23.
40. Marshall, *Baseball's Pivotal Era*, 199–202; Mead, *Even the Browns*, 70; Pajot and Erion, "St. Louis Browns Team Ownership History"; Borst, "Baltimore Orioles," 475–76; Dewey and Acocella, *The Ball Clubs*, 520–21; Cash, "St. Louis Cardinals," 421.
41. Marshall, *Baseball's Pivotal Era*, 194–95, 203, 204–7; R. F. Peterson, "Pittsburgh Pirates," 314–16; Dewey and Acocella, *The Ball Clubs*, 464–65; Warfield, *The Roaring Redhead*, 146–47, 155–63, 220; McCue, "Los Angeles/Brooklyn Dodgers Team Ownership History"; Lowenfish, *Branch Rickey*, 309, 318, 344–46; Levitt and Armour, "New York Yankees Team Ownership History." See also Appel, *Pinstripe Empire*, 200–204, 236–39.
42. Tiemann and Palmer, "Major League Attendance," 107–8; Odenkirk, *Of Tribes and Tribulations*, 236, 242–44; Dickson, *Bill Veeck*, 168–79; Corbett, "Bill Veeck"; Dewey and Acocella, *The Ball Clubs*, 222; Suchma, "Cleveland Indians," 585.

11. "IL A GAGNÉ SES ÉPAULETTES"

1. J. R. Walker and Bellamy, *Center Field Shot*, 68–70; *Sporting News*, August 27, September 3 (with Daniel quote), September 10, and October 8, 1947; C. Smith, *Voices of the Game*, 108; Barber, 1947, 301.
2. J. R. Walker and Bellamy, *Center Field Shot*, 4–14, 82, 89–91; Warfield, *The Roaring Redhead*, 82, 89–91; Barber, *The Broadcasters*, 127–35.
3. J. R. Walker and Bellamy, *Center Field Shot*, 15–21.
4. Corbett, "Red Barber"; C. Smith, *Voices of Summer*, 38–41; Barber, 1947, xi, 10–11; C. Smith, *Voices of the Game*, 108–9.
5. Corbett, "Mel Allen"; C. Smith, *Voices of Summer*, 96–98; C. Smith, *The Voice*, 15–33.
6. Barber, 1947, 297, 302, 303, 316–18; *Sporting News*, October 15, 1947.
7. *Sporting News*, September 3, October 8, October 15, October 22, and November 5, 1947; Leavy, *The Big Fella*, 445.
8. Greenberg, *Hank Greenberg*, 179–87; Rosengren, *Hank Greenberg*, 301–7; Benson, *Ballparks of North America*, 314–15; *Sporting News*, February 21, 1946, and February 12, 1947; Cramer, *Joe DiMaggio*, 258; Montville, *Ted Williams*, 134; Giglio, *Musial*, 181; C. P. Rogers, "Bob Feller."
9. Rosengren, *Hank Greenberg*, 305; Veeck with Linn, *Veeck*, 80–82; Light, *Cultural Encyclopedia of Baseball*, 687. See also "History of the Cactus League," *Spring Training Yearbook*, https://springtrainingmagazine.com/history4.html, accessed April 2020; and R. Johnson, "The Cactus League."

10. Light, *Cultural Encyclopedia of Baseball*, 7–8; *Sporting News*, May 23, July 17, August 7, and August 14, 1946, March 31, 1954, August 29, 1956, November 13 and December 11, 1957, April 16, 1958; *New York Times*, October 4, 1929; *New York Herald Tribune*, May 14, 1946.
11. R. Kahn, *The Boys of Summer*; R. Kahn, *The Era, 1947–1957*, 1, 3–4; Tiemann and Palmer, "Major League Attendance," 107–8.
12. Marshall, *Baseball's Pivotal Era*, 39–42; Gerlach, *The Men in Blue*, 123–25; Bohn, "Happy Chandler."
13. Lowenfish, *Branch Rickey*, 405, 421; Appel, *Pinstripe Empire*, 252–53; *Sporting News*, November 13 (with Dressen quote), December 11, and December 18, 1946, January 22, 1947; Stewart, "Chuck Dressen"; C. P. Rogers, "Red Corriden."
14. Marlett, "Leo Durocher"; Durocher with Linn, *Nice Guys Finish Last*, 22; Pietrusza, *Judge and Jury*, 323; Marshall, *Baseball's Pivotal Era*, 101–5; Lowenfish, *Branch Rickey*, 405–11; Dickson, *Leo Durocher*, 147–49.
15. Marshall, *Baseball's Pivotal Era*, 105–11; Lowenfish, *Branch Rickey*, 410–22; Dickson, *Leo Durocher*, 149–59. See also Marlett, "1947 Dodgers."
16. Marshall, *Baseball's Pivotal Era*, 111–14; Lowenfish, *Branch Rickey*, 422–25; Dickson, *Leo Durocher*, 164–69. See also Marlett, "1947 Yankees."
17. Tygiel, *Extra Bases*, 35 (with Riess quote); Tygiel, *Baseball's Great Experiment*, 64–67, 71–80.
18. Tygiel, *Baseball's Great Experiment*, 120–43; Rampersad, *Jackie Robinson*, 148–57 (with Maltin quote). "Il a gagné ses épaulettes" is apparently a lyric from "Le Nouveau Mirliton," a French folk song that Montrealers learn as children. My thanks to Michel Vigneault for this information.
19. Hogan, *Shades of Glory*, 22–26, 69–114, 127–39, 160–78; Brunson, *Black Baseball*, 1:21, 2:705; Heaphy, *The Negro Leagues*, 15, 40–41, 226–27; Odzer, "Rube Foster"; Lanctot, *Negro League Baseball*, 5; Heaphy, "The Creation of the Negro National League," 25–32.
20. Lester, *Black Baseball's National Showcase*, 1–3, 21–25; Hogan, *Shades of Glory*, 284–88.
21. Lowenfish, *Branch Rickey*, 404, 418–19; Gietschier, "Slugging and Snubbing," 11–13; Rampersad, *Jackie Robinson*, 159–67; Chandler with Trimble, *Heroes, Plain Folks, and Skunks*, 223–29.
22. Jaffe, "Jackie Robinson and the Integration Advantage"; Rampersad, *Jackie Robinson*, 169; Deane, "Awards and Honors," 260; Swaine, *The Black Stars Who Made Baseball Whole*, 45–59, 125–30.
23. Lowenfish, *Branch Rickey*, 382–83; Dickson, *Bill Veeck*, 122–31, 158; McMurray, "Larry Doby"; Tygiel, *Baseball's Great Experiment*, 219–22; *New York Times*, May 5, 1944; Swaine, "Hank Thompson"; Swaine, *The Black Stars Who Made Baseball Whole*, 26–31, 34–43, 60–64, 252–54. On the desegregation of Sportsman's Park, see *St. Louis Post-Dispatch*, May 5, 1944.
24. Light, *Cultural Encyclopedia of Baseball*, 378–79; Swaine, "Hank Thompson"; Nowlin, "Sam Jethroe"; Faber, "Carlos Bernier"; Rapoport, *Let's Play Two*,

92–93; *New York Times*, July 29 and August 21, 1942; Swaine, *The Black Stars Who Made Baseball Whole*, 66–74, 93–99, 137–52, 242–48.

25. Light, *Cultural Encyclopedia of Baseball*, 378–79; Stewart, "Minnie Minoso"; J. Morris, "Bob Trice"; Tan, "Elston Howard"; Swaine, *The Black Stars Who Made Baseball Whole*, 101–13, 173–82, 245–46, 248–50, 256–57.
26. Essington, *The Integration of the Pacific Coast League*, 1, 3, 22–24, 42–43, 47–66; Rampersad, *Jackie Robinson*, 148–49; *Sporting News*, April 7 and 14, 1948, April 19, 1950; "John Ritchey," Baseball Reference, https://www.baseball-reference.com/bullpen/John_Ritchey, accessed September 2020; Lanctot, *Campy*, 162–63; Swaine, "Roy Campanella"; Adelson, *Brushing Back Jim Crow*, 53–56; Watkins, "Dave Hoskins"; Fenster, "Earl Mann, Nat Peeples," 73. See also A. Cohen, "San Diego Breaks Pacific Coast League Color Barrier"; Sarnoff, "The San Diego Padre Who Batted for Ted Williams"; and W. J. Weiss, "The First Negro in 20th Century O.B."
27. *Sporting News*, July 7, 14, and 21, 1948, April 5, April 19, and May 24, 1950; Watkins, "Dave Hoskins"; Wright, *The South Atlantic League*, 268; Aaron with Wheeler, *I Had a Hammer*, 61; Adelson, *Brushing Back Jim Crow*, 83–86, 107–20, 135–36.
28. Burgos, *Playing America's Game*, 179–226, 270–71, 273.
29. Heaphy, *The Negro Leagues*, 198, 211–24; *Sporting News*, October 20, 1948; Hogan, *Shades of Glory*, 335, 370–71; A. R. Davis, "No League of Their Own."
30. Bohn, "Happy Chandler"; *Sporting News*, December 21, 1949; Marshall, *Baseball's Pivotal Era*, 241–44, 249, 375–84. See also Odenkirk, *Frank J. Lausche*, 155.
31. *New York Times*, January 16, 1981; Celler, *You Never Leave Brooklyn*, 59–62, 135–38; Lowe, *The Kid on the Sandlot*, 15; House Judiciary Committee, *Study of Monopoly Power*, ii.
32. Celler, *You Never Leave Brooklyn*, 152, 154, 155, 159, 162–64, 165–67.
33. Dexter, "Congress Threatens Baseball Upheaval," 94; *New York Times*, May 5, 1951; *Sporting News*, May 16 and 23, 1951 (with Wolff's interview of Celler); "Let's Make Baseball Legal," 96.
34. Dan Daniel to Emanuel Celler, June 21, 1951, and Celler to Daniel (telegram), June 22, 1951, Emanuel Celler Papers, Part I: Subject File I, 1936–1955, Box 1, Baseball, Correspondence, Folder 1951–1952; *Sporting News*, June 6 and July 4, 1951; House Judiciary Committee, *Hearings*; House Judiciary Committee, *Organized Baseball*.
35. House Judiciary Committee, *Study of Monopoly Power*, 1–4, 9–10, 15, 17–18, 23–31. Cobb's testimony can be found on pp. 4–23, Frick's on pp. 23–123, Simmons's on pp. 125–57, and Trautman's on pp. 157–250.
36. "Statement by Representative Emanuel Celler," August 3, 1951, Emanuel Celler Papers, Part I: Subject File I, 1936–1955, Box 1, Baseball, Correspondence, Folder 1951–1952; House Judiciary Committee, *Study of Monopoly Power*, 251–345, esp. 253, 254, 256, 258–59, 260, 261–62, 281, 286–90, 296–97, and 307; *Sporting News*, August 15, 1951.

37. House Judiciary Committee, *Study of Monopoly Power*, 443–70, esp. 444, 452, 458, 459, 460, 465, and 468.

38. *Sporting News Baseball Guide* for 1952, 119–20 (with Baumgartner quote); Robinson, *The Home Run Heard 'Round the World*, 151–206.

39. *Sporting News*, October 12, December 7, and December 21, 1949; Green, "1949," 333; Robinson, *The Home Run Heard 'Round the World*, 207–28 (with Smith quote); Prager, *The Echoing Green*, esp. 60–61; *New York Times*, October 8, 2006.

40. *Sporting News*, October 24 and 31, 1951; *New York Times*, October 18, 1951; House Judiciary Committee, *Study of Monopoly Power*, 471–1090, esp. 530, 734, 840, 852, 1059, and 1074.

41. House Judiciary Committee, *Study of Monopoly Power*, 1089; *Sporting News*, October 31, 1951, and June 4, 1952; House Judiciary, *Organized Baseball*, 228–32; Frick to Celler, May 28, 1952, Emanuel Celler Papers, Part I: Subject File I, 1936–1955, Box 1, Baseball, Correspondence, Folder 1951–1952.

42. J. R. Walker and Bellamy, *Center Field Shot*, 71–73; *Sporting News*, October 13, 1948; Barber and Creamer, *Rhubarb in the Catbird Seat*, 259–63; Corbett, "Red Barber"; McCue, "Los Angeles/Brooklyn Dodgers Team Ownership History."

12. "A SOUND IF NOT SPECTACULAR CHOICE"

1. Carvalho, *Frick**, 26, 38–41 (with Parker story and Holmes and Lieb quotes); *New York Times*, May 21, 1967; Holtzman, *No Cheering in the Press Box*, 27, 199 (with Hunt and Frick quotes); Boyle, "Perfect Man for the Job," 38.

2. Frick, *Games, Asterisks, and People*, 1, 3–5; Carvalho, *Frick**, 5; Einstein, *The Fireside Book of Baseball*, xvi.

3. Carvalho, *Frick**, 25–29; Corbett, "Ford Frick"; Boyle, "Perfect Man for the Job," 36.

4. Carvalho, *Frick**, 29–37; Holtzman, *No Cheering in the Press Box*, 199–200.

5. Carvalho, *Frick**, 40, 42–52; Leavy, *The Big Fella*, 62–72, 80, 222; *New York Times*, October 9, 1930; Frick, *Games, Asterisks, and People*, 108–9.

6. Carvalho, *Frick**, 52–55, 57; *Miami News*, November 27, 1958; Rice, "John Heydler."

7. Carvalho, *Frick**, 57–61, 74–75; Frick, *Games, Asterisks, and People*, 195–203. See also Vlasich, *A Legend for the Legendary*.

8. Dewey and Acocella, *The Ball Clubs*, 41; LeMoine, "Boston Braves Team Ownership History"; LeMoine, "Judge Emil Fuchs"; Fuchs and Soini, *Judge Fuchs*, 102–17; Carvalho, *Frick**, 61–65.

9. Carvalho, *Frick**, 66–73; *Sporting News*, May 9, 1935.

10. Carvalho, *Frick**, 78–84, 88–94, 97–99, 100–107.

11. Carvalho, *Frick**, 140, 143–45 (with Flaherty quote); *Sporting News*, December 27, 1950, and July 4, 1951; McCue, *Mover and Shaker*, 95–97; House Judiciary Committee, *Study of Monopoly Power*, 33–123, 1049–57.

12. *Sporting News*, January 10, February 21, March 21, July 4, August 15, August 29, and September 26, 1951; Carvalho, *Frick**, 142–43, 146–49; Marshall, *Baseball's Pivotal Era*, 385–91; *New York World-Telegram and Sun*, September 22, 1951.

13. *Sporting News*, September 26, October 3, October 31, and December 19, 1951.

14. Mead and Dickson, *Baseball*, 83–106; *Sporting News*, September 13, 1945, April 15 and 22, 1953, April 27, 1960; *New York Times*, June 20, 1945.
15. James, *New Bill James Historical Baseball Abstract*, 220–22; Condon, *The Go-Go Chicago White Sox*, 142–47.
16. Pietrusza, Silverman, and Gershman, *Baseball*, 731–33; Saccoman, "Willie Mays."
17. Pietrusza, Silverman, and Gershman, *Baseball*, 703–5; Ray, "Mickey Mantle."
18. James, *New Bill James Historical Baseball Abstract*, 220; Theodore Turocy to RetroList mailing list, July 4, 2006; *Sporting News*, December 2, 1909, August 10, 1949 (with Daniel and Frick quotes), May 24 (with Greenberg quote) and 31, 1950, January 18 and November 28, 1956, March 27 and April 24, 1957; Voiss, "1955," 372; Heitz, "Rules and Scoring," 2237.
19. *Sporting News*, August 28, 1946, June 25, July 23, August 20, and September 10, 1947, May 26, 1948, June 30, 1954, November 30, 1955, August 8, 1956.
20. *Sporting News*, June 12, 1946, August 5, 1947, March 17 and 24, 1948, May 25 and December 14, 1949, September 8, 1954, March 23, April 27, August 3, and August 10, 1955, August 6, 1958; Light, *Cultural Encyclopedia of Baseball*, 85–86; P. Morris, *A Game of Inches: The Game on the Field*, 442–45.
21. Marshall, *Baseball's Pivotal Era*, 233–34, 239; Virtue, *South of the Color Barrier*, 188–89; Briley, "Danny Gardella," 66–69; Edmonds and Houdek, *Baseball Meets the Law*, 71–72, 90. See also Federal Baseball Club of Baltimore v. National League of Professional Baseball Clubs, 259 U.S. 200 (1922); F. A. Johnson, "Baseball Law"; Gardella v. Chandler, 79 F. Supp. 260, S.D.N.Y. 1948, rev'd and remanded, 172 F.2d 402, 2nd Cir. 1949, aff'd 174 F.2d 919, 2nd Cir. 1949.
22. Marshall, *Baseball's Pivotal Era*, 239–49; Briley, "Danny Gardella," 69–73.
23. McKenna, "Global League"; *Sporting News*, April 4, April 25, and May 9, 1951; Marshall, *Baseball's Pivotal Era*, 238.
24. *Sporting News*, May 2 and 9, 1951; Harkins, "Jim Prendergast."
25. *Sporting News*, May 9, 1951; Edmonds, "Remembering Earl—Not George—Toolson."
26. Hylton, "Walter Kowalski."
27. Hylton, "Walter Kowalski"; Edmonds, "Remembering Earl—Not George—Toolson"; *Sporting News*, July 11, October 3, and December 12, 1951, March 5 and October 29, 1952, February 18, March 4, April 22, June 3, June 10, October 14, October 21, November 18, and December 23, 1953; Toolson v. New York Yankees, Inc., et al. Vol. 346 U.S., 1953.
28. J. R. Walker and Bellamy, *Center Field Shot*, 24, 27, 324, 330.
29. J. R. Walker and Bellamy, *Center Field Shot*, 24–26, 29–30.
30. J. R. Walker, *Crack of the Bat*, 180–81, 184–85, 191–93; J. R. Walker and Bellamy, *Center Field Shot*, 225; *Sporting News*, March 1, 1950; Light, *Cultural Encyclopedia of Baseball*, 604.
31. J. R. Walker and Bellamy, *Center Field Shot*, 70–73, 75–81, 83 (with Stewart quote); *Sporting News*, October 6 and 27, 1948, September 13, 1950, January 3, 1951; Marshall, *Baseball's Pivotal Era*, 384–85.

32. J. R. Walker and Bellamy, *Center Field Shot*, 82–87, 89–90 (with Parker quote).

33. J. R. Walker and Bellamy, *Center Field Shot*, 90–91, 97–107; Gregory, *Diz*, 363–90.

34. J. R. Walker and Bellamy, *Center Field Shot*, 181–82, 189 (with Carpenter and second Rickey quote); *Sporting News*, May 21 (with Meany quote) and July 2, 1947 (with McAuley quote), March 10 (with Hannegan quote), November 10, and December 15, 1948 (with first Rickey quote), June 28, 1950, May 16, 1951 (with O'Malley quote). See also House Judiciary Committee, *Study of Monopoly Power*, 1107, 1119.

35. *Sporting News*, May 19, June 2, June 9, and July 21, 1948, February 15, May 3, November 15, and December 6, 1950, January 10, 1951 (with Corum quote); G. Levy, "1948," 323–24; Green, "1949," 331; Klopsis, "1950," 339.

36. *Sporting News*, October 15, 1931, May 6, May 13, May 20, July 15, and July 22, 1953; J. R. Walker and Bellamy, *Center Field Shot*, 225–27. See also D. A. Sullivan, *Late Innings*, 42–45.

37. Carvalho, *Frick**, 157, 166–69; *Sporting News*, January 7 and December 9, 1953; G. H. Wolf, "1952," 351; Felber, "1954," 362–63.

38. J. R. Walker and Bellamy, *Center Field Shot*, 107–9; *Sporting News*, December 11 and 18, 1957, January 1, March 19, and May 28, 1958.

39. *Sporting News*, June 20, 1951, July 1, 1953, August 25, 1954, August 8, November 7, and December 12, 1956 (with Fagan quote); Felber, "1954," 363 (with Rickey remark); Voiss, "1955," 370 (with Paul quote); L. Johnson and Wolff, *Encyclopedia of Minor League Baseball*, 2nd ed., 347, 411; Mike Lynch, "1957," 379–80 (with Frick quote); Edmonds and Houdek, *Baseball Meets the Law*, 106–7; Portland Baseball Club, Inc. v. Baltimore Baseball Club, Inc., 282 F.2d 680, 9th Cir. 1960.

13. "I HAVE LONG DESIRED TO SEE CALIFORNIA"

1. Aaron with Wheeler, *I Had a Hammer*, 28–34; H. Bryant, *The Last Hero*, 38–40.

2. H. Bryant, *The Last Hero*, 19–21, 26–28, 42–44; Aaron with Wheeler, *I Had a Hammer*, 8, 13–14, 19–20, 35–39; Pollock, *Barnstorming to Heaven*, 224–32. See also B. Johnson, "Henry Aaron."

3. Aaron with Wheeler, *I Had a Hammer*, 39–41, 61, 71, 77; H. Bryant, *The Last Hero*, 44, 57; *Sporting News*, July 1, 1953.

4. *Sporting News*, November 11, 1953 (with Thisted quote); H. Bryant, *The Last Hero*, 63–69, 104–8; Aaron with Wheeler, *I Had a Hammer*, 85–88, 93–94.

5. "Age Distribution of the Population, 1950–2060 (%)," Urban Institute, https://www.urban.org/sites/default/files/2015/10/09/t2_age_distribution.pdf, accessed August 2021; Patterson, *Grand Expectations*, 61–81; "America's Great Migrations Project," Civil Rights and Labor History Consortium, University of Washington, depts.washington.edu/moving1, accessed August 2020; "Phoenix Metro Area Population, 1950–2022," Macrotrends, https://www.macrotrends.net/cities/23099/phoenix/population, accessed August 2020.

6. Patterson, *Grand Expectations*, 65–68, 70–76; Oshinsky, *Polio*, 188–203; Jackson, *Crabgrass Frontier*, 234–37, 241.

7. Jackson, *Crabgrass Frontier*, 246–61, 263–64.
8. "Television Facts and Statistics—1939–2000," Television History—the First 75 Years, www.tvhistory.tv/facts-stats.htm, accessed August 2021; "Number of TV Households in America," The American Century, https://americancentury.omeka.wlu.edu/files/original/60e94905a0e02050a5b78f10b1b02b07.jpg, accessed August 2021; J. R. Walker and Bellamy, *Center Field Shot*, 183–86, 190–92, 207 (with reference to Jordan and Drebinger quote).
9. Treder, "Open Classification," 94; *Sporting News*, August 6, August 13, and November 19, 1947; G. Levy, "1947," 315–16; *Sporting News Baseball Guide* for 1948, 90.
10. *Sporting News*, December 22, 1948; *Sporting News Baseball Guide* for 1949, 93; Lomax, "Not Quite Ready for Prime Time," 28, 31–32 (with Chandler quote); House Judiciary Committee, *Study of Monopoly Power*, 411–12; N. J. Sullivan, *The Dodgers Move West*, 93.
11. House Judiciary Committee, *Study of Monopoly Power*, 29, 86–87, 98–100, 404.
12. Lomax, "Not Quite Ready for Prime Time," 37–38; N. J. Sullivan, *The Minors*, 221–22 (with Wolf material); *Sporting News Baseball Guide* for 1952, 104–5; Treder, "Open Classification," 96–99; G. H. Wolf, "1952," 352; Beireis, "Divided They Fall," 17.
13. *Sporting News*, January 28 and August 18, 1948, April 25,1951; Kaese, *Boston Braves*, 262.
14. Daly, "Billy Southworth"; Dewey and Acocella, *The Ball Clubs*, 42–44; Light, *Cultural Encyclopedia of Baseball*, 513; Kaese, *The Boston Braves*, 263–64, 269; Finkel, "Johnny Sain" (with Hern quote); Kaplan, "Warren Spahn."
15. Dewey and Acocella, *The Ball Clubs*, 44–45, 308–9; Daly, "Billy Southworth"; Stevens, "Atlanta Braves," 24–25; Tiemann and Palmer, "Major League Attendance," 107.
16. *Sporting News*, November 2, and December 10, 1947, April 11, 1951, October 1 and December 17, 1952, March 11 and 25, 1953; *Washington Post*, October 10, 1994; Hoffmann, "County Stadium (Milwaukee, WI)"; Gershman, *Diamonds*, 164–65; Dewey and Acocella, *The Ball Clubs*, 45–308; Stevens, "Atlanta Braves," 25; *New York Times*, March 19, 1953.
17. Dennis Pajot and Greg Erion, "St. Louis Browns Team Ownership History"; L. Johnson and Wolff, *Encyclopedia of Minor League Baseball*, 2nd ed., 376, 387, 398; Dewey and Acocella, *The Ball Clubs*, 521–23; *Sporting News*, February 23, March 9, March 16, March 23, April 6, April 27, May 4, August 10, August 17, December 14, and December 28, 1949, January 18 and May 10, 1950.
18. Pajot and Erion, "St. Louis Browns Team Ownership History"; Dickson, *Bill Veeck*, 184–96; J. E. Miller, *The Baseball Business*, 26.
19. Pajot and Erion, "St. Louis Browns Team Ownership History"; Dickson, *Bill Veeck*, 188, 197–203, 207–10; Dewey and Acocella, *The Ball Clubs*, 505, 521–22; Snyder, *Cardinals Journal*, 397–98; G. H. Wolf, "1952," 348–51; *New York Times*, January 2, 2000.

20. Pajot and Erion, "St. Louis Browns Team Ownership History"; Dickson, *Bill Veeck*, 209–10 (with Daley quote); Dewey and Acocello, *The Ball Clubs*, 522–23; Miller, *The Baseball Business*, 28–31.
21. Pajot and Erion, "St. Louis Browns Team Ownership History"; Dickson, *Bill Veeck*, 210–16; Miller, *The Baseball Business*, 31–35; J. E. Peterson, *The Kansas City Athletics*, 3; Dewey and Acocella, *The Ball Clubs*, 505, 523; Borst, "Baltimore Orioles," 478–79. See also Stahl, "Gussie Busch."
22. Paxton, "The Philadelphia A's Last Stand," 133–34, 136; Skipper, "Connie Mack"; *Sporting News*, February 15, 1956, February 17, 1960, February 18, 1967; Dewey and Acocella, *The Ball Clubs*, 447–48; R. F. Lewis, "Oakland Athletics," 775–76; Macht, *The Grand Old Man of Baseball*, 113, 127–28, 333, 470–71. See also Warrington, "Departure without Dignity," 95–115.
23. Paxton, "The Philadelphia A's Last Stand," 113, 133–34, 136; Macht, *The Grand Old Man of Baseball*, 165, 470.
24. Tiemann and Palmer, "Major League Attendance," 107–8; Corbett, "Bob Dillinger"; Paxton, "The Philadelphia A's Last Stand," 113, 133–34, 136; Warrington, "Departure without Dignity," 95–96, 100–101.
25. Mehl, *The Kansas City Athletics*, 46, 57–61, 71–72, 78–81, 83–89, 92–111, 113–25; Warrington, "Departure without Dignity," 101–9; Peterson, *The Kansas City Athletics*, 12–22; Dewey and Acocella, *The Ball Clubs*, 274; Macht, *The Grand Old Man of Baseball*, 522, 530–69; *Sporting News Baseball Guide* for 1955, 95–97. See also Nathanson, *The Fall of the 1977 Phillies*, 97–102.
26. Abraham Lincoln to Charles Maltby, Superintendent of Indian Affairs for California, March 21, 1865, https://artsandculture.google.com/exhibit/a-visit-to-the-pacific-shore-california-in-the-age-of-lincoln-california-state-archives/QAKyB2KpYi2VJA?hl=en, accessed August 2021; Nelson, *The Golden Game*, 10–11, 14; Guschov, *The Red Stockings of Cincinnati*, 83–88; *Sporting News*, September 1, 1948 (with Rickey quote).
27. McCue, *Mover and Shaker*, 56–57, 111, 118–27; *Sporting News*, September 1, November 24, December 1, and December 8, 1948, January 19, 1949; Flaherty, "The Miracle Move," 7, 9, 11; Lowenfish, *Branch Rickey*, 539.
28. Nathan, *The McFarland Baseball Quotations Dictionary*, 199; Tiemann and Palmer, "Major League Attendance," 106; Hynd, *The Giants of the Polo Grounds*, 178; Alexander, *John McGraw*; Durocher with Linn, *Nice Guys Finish Last*, 237.
29. Hano, *A Day in the Bleachers*, 118, 123; Benson, *Ballparks of North America*, 257; Garratt, *Home Team*, 4–6; Tiemann and Palmer, "Major League Attendance," 107.
30. Garratt, *Home Team*, 7–10; N. J. Sullivan, *The Dodgers Move West*, 41, 44, 47–53; Dewey and Acocella, *The Ball Clubs*, 99–100; McCue, *Mover and Shaker*, 128–37. See also Treder, *Forty Years a Giant*, chapter 8.
31. Garratt, *Home Team*, 11–21; O'Neal, *The Pacific Coast League*, 113–14. See also Treder, *Forty Years a Giant*, chapter 9.
32. McCue, *Mover and Shaker*, 137–60, 191–213; N. J. Sullivan, *The Dodgers Move West*, 70–74, 75, 77–80, 83–89, 94–104.

33. Gershman, *Diamonds*, 167; Hoffmann, "County Stadium (Milwaukee, WI)"; Wild, "Remembering the Time"; Stevens, "Atlanta Braves," 25–28.
34. Gershman, *Diamonds*, 169–70, 173; Benson, *Ballparks of North America*, 25–26; Dewey and Acocella, *The Ball Clubs*, 20–22; Borst, "Baltimore Orioles," 480–81.
35. Benson, *Ballparks of North America*, 191; Peterson, *The Kansas City Athletics*, 9–12, 23–28, 104; *Sporting News Baseball Guide* for 1955, 97–98; Mehl, *The Kansas City Athletics*, 31–34, 128–33; R. F. Lewis, "Oakland Athletics," 776–77; Appel, *Pinstripe Empire*, 304–6; Tiemann and Palmer, "Major League Attendance," 108; R. F. Lewis, "Oakland Athletics," 777–80; *Sporting News*, December 14 and 28, 1960, January 25 and February 22, 1961.
36. Treder, *Forty Years a Giant*, 201; Tiemann and Palmer, "Major League Attendance," 107.

14. "HENRY, DON'T GO OUT THERE"

1. *New York Times*, November 30, 1957, and October 4, 1991 (with Pileggi quote); Buhite, *The Continental League*, 41; Shapiro, *Bottom of the Ninth*, 27.
2. *New York Times*, June 28 and August 19, 1959, October 4, 1991, February 7, 1994 (with Newfield-DuBrul quote); "Player Bio: Bill Shea (1928–1931)," Georgetown Basketball History Project, https://www.hoyabasketball.com/players/w_shea.htm, accessed August 2021; Terrell, "3rd League Cities Pin Hopes on This Man," 30–31; Pietrusza, *Major Leagues*, 280; Shapiro, *Bottom of the Ninth*, 27. See also Buhite, *The Continental League*, 40–41; and Lowenfish, *Branch Rickey*, 545–46.
3. Shapiro, *Bottom of the Ninth*, 23–29; Lowenfish, *Branch Rickey*, 497–98, 500, 531; *New York Times*, December 29, 1957, January 15, February 1, and April 29, 1958, April 16, 1959; Koppett, *The New York Mets*, 19–20; Buhite, *The Continental League*, 39–42; Rhodes and Snyder, *Redleg Journal*, 387–88.
4. *New York Times*, May 20, July 7, July 8, November 14, and November 15, 1958, May 22, June 19, July 8, and July 28, 1959; *Sporting News*, May 21, 1958; Buhite, *The Continental League*, 43–44; Shapiro, *Bottom of the Ninth*, 29–30; Carvalho, *Frick**, 210–11, 215.
5. Buhite, *The Continental League*, 49–54; Lowenfish, *Branch Rickey*, 548–52.
6. *Sporting News*, February 11, May 27, and July 8, 1959; *New York Times*, August 16, August 19, and October 5, 1959; Shapiro, *Bottom of the Ninth*, 31, 51–56; Buhite, *The Continental League*, 60–62, 81–83; Lowenfish, *Branch Rickey*, 554–56.
7. *Sporting News*, January 6, 13, and 20, 1960.
8. *New York Times*, August 20, September 9, September 18, October 15, November 14, December 11, and December 23, 1959, January 13, January 23, and April 28, 1960; *Sporting News*, January 13, January 20, and February 3, 1960.
9. *Sporting News*, January 13 and 20, 1960; Buhite, *The Continental League*, 106–14. See also Buhite, "The Continental League and Its Western Carolina League Affiliate."
10. *Sporting News*, January 20, February 3, February 17, and February 24, 1960.

11. Buhite, *The Continental League*, 113–16; *New York Times*, August 20, 1959; *Sporting News*, March 30 and April 27, 1960.
12. *Sporting News Baseball Guide* for 1961, 103; Keene, 1960, 2–4; Giglio, *Musial*, 243; Montville, *Ted Williams*, 221; *Sporting News*, January 13, January 20, January 27, February 3, February 10, February 17, March 2, March 16, March 23, March 30, April 20, and April 27, 1960; Brosnan, "You Can Consider It Came from Me," 62–64, 67–70.
13. *Sporting News*, February 3 (with Burnes quote) and April 6, 1960 (with Lieb quote).
14. *Sporting News*, April 13, 1960.
15. Hogan, *Shades of Glory*, 373; Armour, "The Effects of Integration."
16. Vincent, Spatz, and Smith, *The Midsummer Classic*, 105–89; Roberts with Rogers, *Throwing Hard Easy*, 144–45; *Sporting News Baseball Guide* for 1960, 147; *Sporting News*, May 6, May 13, May 20, May 27, June 17, and June 24, 1959.
17. Sharp, "Washington Senators I Team Ownership History"; Olson, "Minnesota Twins Team Ownership History"; Lowenfish, *Branch Rickey*, 552; Buhite, *The Continental League*, 69–70; *New York Times*, October 16, 1959; Armour, *Joe Cronin*, 266.
18. *Sporting News*, January 29, 1948, October 24, 1951, March 5, 1952, December 16, 1953, May 5, 1954; Dickson, *Bill Veeck*, 218.
19. Greenberg, *Hank Greenberg*, 215; *Sporting News*, February 2 and 16, 1955, May 22, 1957, July 16, 1958, June 3 and July 29, 1959.
20. Lowenfish, *Branch Rickey*, 561–62, 568–74; Armour, *Joe Cronin*, 266; *New York Times*, October 23, October 27, and November 17, 1959, June 30, July 18, July 19, July 20, July 21, and August 3, 1960; *Sporting News*, December 16, 1959, May 18, May 25, June 1, June 15, June 22, and July 6, 1960; Buhite, *The Continental League*, 97–103.
21. *Sporting News*, August 17, 1960.
22. Lowenfish, *Branch Rickey*, 573–74; Kritzler and Henry, "1960," 18; *Sporting News*, August 10, 1960.
23. Buhite, *The Continental League*, 168; McCue, *Mover and Shaker*, 289–93; Shapiro, *Bottom of the Ninth*, 240–41; Kritzler and Henry, "1960," 18–22.
24. *Sporting News*, November 2 (with Greenberg quote), 9, 16, and 23, 1960; McCue, *Mover and Shaker*, 290–93; *Sporting News Baseball Guide* for 1961, 110.
25. Dewey and Acocella, *The Ball Clubs*, 257–59; Buhite, *The Continental League*, 169; Koppett, *The New York Mets*, 25–27.
26. "Byron Bancroft 'Ban' Johnson," Marietta College Hall of Fame, https://pioneers.marietta.edu/honors/hall-of-fame/byron-bancroft-ban-johnson/1, accessed December 2020; Ban Johnson Amateur Baseball League website, http://www.bjbaseball.com/?nomobile=true&org=bjbaseball, accessed December 2020; Fleitz, "The Honor Rolls of Baseball," 53–59; Armour, "Will Harridge"; Armour, "Joe Cronin."
27. Macht, *The Grand Old Man of Baseball*, 471, 544, 571–74, 580; *Sporting News*, January 25, February 15, and February 22, 1961.

28. Lowenfish, *Branch Rickey*, 1–5, 575–76, 578–79, 582–93, 597.
29. Holtzman, *The Commissioners*, 15; B. Walker, "MLB Stars Say It's Time to Pull Landis Name off MVP Plaques"; B. Walker, "Landis' Name Pulled off Baseball MVP Plaques after 75 Years."
30. Appel, *Pinstripe Empire*, 238–41 (with MacPhail quote); *Sporting News*, January 6, 1960; Levitt, *Ed Barrow*, 366–69, 371–76, 378.
31. House Judiciary Committee, *Study of Monopoly Power*, viii; *New York Times*, October 7, 1947; Warfield, *The Roaring Redhead*, 218–66; McKelvey, *The MacPhails*, 90–96.
32. Greenberg, *Hank Greenberg*, 196–99, 201–2, 206, 213–15, 225, 242, 244–45, 247–48, 257, 278–79; Rosengren, *Hank Greenberg*, 314–19, 327, 331–32, 334–36, 338–40, 348, 353, 356–57; Ferkovich, "Hank Greenberg."
33. *Sporting News*, August 4, 1962; *New York Times*, July 21, 1962.
34. D. Williams, "Yogi Berra." See also Barra, *Yogi Berra*; Pessah, *Yogi*; Berra, *The Yogi Book*; Berra with Kaplan, *When You Come to a Fork in the Road*; Berra with Kaplan, *What Time Is It?*
35. Armour and Levitt, "Boston Red Sox Team Ownership History"; "Boston Changes 'Yawkey Way' to 'Jersey Street' after Concerns over Racist Legacy," NPR, April 26, 2018, https://www.npr.org/2018/04/26/605851052/boston-red-sox-want-to-strike-former-owners-name-off-street-sign.
36. Corbett, "Bill Veeck."
37. McCue, *Mover and Shaker*, 83, 106–7; Barber and Creamer, *Rhubarb in the Catbird Seat*, 284–89; Corbett, "Red Barber"; Corbett, "Mel Allen"; Barber, *The Broadcasters*, 218; Appel, *Pinstripe Empire*, 303, 355–56, 364–65; "Ford C. Frick Award," National Baseball Hall of Fame, https://baseballhall.org/discover-more/awards/887, accessed August 2021.
38. Corbett, "Ford Frick"; L. Johnson and Wolff, *Encyclopedia of Minor League Baseball*, 3rd ed., 411; Carvalho, *Frick**, 12–13.
39. *New York Times*, January 22, 2021; B. Johnson, "Henry Aaron."
40. Koppett, *The New York Mets*, 25–31, 34–25; "Mets Franchise Timeline: 1960s," Mets.com, https://www.mlb.com/mets/history/timeline-1960s, accessed December 2020; Heaphy, "New York Mets Team Ownership History"; "Mets Hall of Fame," Mets.com, https://www.mlb.com/mets/history/mets-hall-of-fame, accessed December 2020; *New York Times*, October 4, 1991, February 7, 1994.

Bibliography

ARCHIVES AND MANUSCRIPT MATERIALS

Clipping Files. *Sporting News* Research Center, St. Louis MO.

Emanuel Celler Papers. Manuscript Division, Library of Congress, Washington DC.

Harold and Dorothy Seymour Papers, 1830–2016. Collection Number 4809, Division of Rare and Manuscript Collections, Carl A. Kroch Library, Cornell University, Ithaca NY.

Turocy, Theodore, to RetroList emailing list, July 4, 2006.

Wendell Smith Papers. National Baseball Hall of Fame Library, Cooperstown NY.

World War II Selective Service Records. Records of the Selective Service System, 1926–1975, National Archives, St. Louis MO.

PUBLISHED WORKS

Aaron, Henry, with Lonnie Wheeler. *I Had a Hammer: The Hank Aaron Story*. New York: HarperCollins, 1991.

Abrams, Roger I. *The First World Series and the Baseball Fanatics of 1903*. Boston: Northeastern University Press, 2003.

———. *Legal Bases: Baseball and the Law*. Philadelphia: Temple University Press, 1998.

Achorn, Edward. *Fifty-Nine in '84: Old Hoss Radbourn, Barehanded Baseball, and the Greatest Season a Pitcher Ever Had*. New York: Smithsonian Books, 2010.

Addington, L. H. "'We Shall Not See His Like Again.'" *Baseball Magazine*, October 1947.

Adelson, Bruce. *Brushing Back Jim Crow: The Integration of Minor-League Baseball in the American South*. Charlottesville: University of Virginia Press, 2007.

Alexander, Charles C. *Breaking the Slump: Baseball in the Depression Era*. New York: Columbia University Press, 2002.

———. *John McGraw*. New York: Viking, 1988.

———. *Our Game: An American Baseball History*. New York: Henry Holt, 1992.

———. *Rogers Hornsby: A Biography*. New York: Henry Holt, 1995.

Allen, Frederick Lewis. *Since Yesterday: The 1930s in America, September 3, 1929–September 3, 1939*. New York: Harper & Row, 1986. First published 1939.

Allen, Lee. *The American League Story*. New York: Hill & Wang, 1962.

———. *The Cincinnati Reds*. New York: G. P. Putnam's Sons, 1948.

———. *The Hot Stove League: Raking the Embers of Baseball's Golden Age*. Kingston NY: Total/SPORTS ILLUSTRATED, 2000. First published 1955.

———. *The World Series: The Story of Baseball's Annual Championship*. New York: G. P. Putnam's Sons, 1969.

Alpert, Rebecca T. *Out of Left Field: Jews and Black Baseball*. New York: Oxford University Press, 2011.

American Civil Liberties Union. *Security and Freedom: The Great Challenge*. Thirtieth Annual Report. New York: American Civil Liberties Union, 1951.

Anderson, Kristin, and Christopher W. Kimball. "Minnesota Twins." In Riess, *Encyclopedia of Major League Baseball Clubs*, vol. 2, *The American League*.

Angle, Paul M. *Philip K. Wrigley: A Memoir of a Modest Man*. Chicago: Rand McNally, 1975.

Anton, Todd, and Bill Nowlin, eds. *When Baseball Went to War*. Chicago: Triumph Books, 2008.

Appel, Marty. *Pinstripe Empire: The New York Yankees from before the Babe to after the Boss*. New York: Bloomsbury, 2014.

Appel, Marty, and Burt Goldblatt. *Baseball's Best: The Hall of Fame Gallery*. New York: McGraw-Hill, 1977.

Armour, Mark L. "The Effects of Integration, 1947–86." https://sabr.org/bioproj/topic/baseball-integration-1947-1986/; accessed August 2021.

———. "Joe Cronin." https://sabr.org/bioproj/person/joe-cronin/; accessed December 2020.

———. *Joe Cronin: A Life in Baseball*. Lincoln: University of Nebraska Press, 2010.

———. "Tom Yawkey." https://sabr.org/bioproj/person/tom-yawkey/; accessed July 2021.

———. "Vern Stephens." https://sabr.org/bioproj/person/vern-stephens/; accessed July 2021.

———. "Will Harridge." https://sabr.org/bioproj/person/will-harridge/; accessed December 2020.

Armour, Mark L., and Daniel R. Levitt. "Boston Red Sox Team Ownership History." https://sabr.org/bioproj/topic/boston-red-sox-team-ownership-history/; accessed December 2020.

———. *Paths to Glory: How Great Baseball Teams Got That Way*. Washington DC: Brassey's, 2003.

Auker, Elden, with Tom Keegan. *Sleeper Cars and Flannel Uniforms: A Lifetime of Memories from Striking Out the Babe to Teeing It Up with the President*. Chicago: Triumph Books, 2001.

Bailey, Bob. "Barney Dreyfuss Buys Pittsburgh." *Baseball Research Journal* 48 (Spring 2019): 86–91.

Bak, Richard. "The Dark Days of the Black Legion." *Hour Detroit*, February 23, 2009. http://www.hourdetroit.com/Hour-Detroit/March-2009/The-Dark-Days-of-the-Black-Legion/.

Baldassaro, Lawrence. "Before Joe D: Italian Americans in the Major Leagues." In Baldassaro and Johnson, *The American Game*.

Baldassaro, Lawrence, and Richard A. Johnson, eds. *The American Game: Baseball and Ethnicity*. Carbondale and Edwardsville: Southern Illinois University Press, 2002.

Barber, Red. *The Broadcasters*. New York: Dial Press, 1970.

———. *1947: When All Hell Broke Loose in Baseball*. New York: Da Capo, 1984. First published 1982.

Barber, Red, and Robert Creamer. *Rhubarb in the Catbird Seat*. Lincoln: University of Nebraska Press, 1997. First published 1968.

Barney, Robert K., and David E. Barney. "Boston Red Sox." In Riess, *Encyclopedia of Major League Baseball Clubs*, vol. 2, *The American League*.

Barra, Allen. *Yogi Berra: Eternal Yankee*. New York: W. W. Norton, 2009.

Barrow, Edward Grant, with James M. Kahn. *My Fifty Years in Baseball*. New York: Coward-McCann, 1951.

Barthel, Thomas. *The Fierce Fun of Ducky Medwick*. Lanham MD: Scarecrow Press, 2003.

———. *Pepper Martin: A Baseball Biography*. Jefferson NC: McFarland, 2003.

Bartlett, Arthur. *Baseball and Mr. Spalding: The History and Romance of Baseball*. New York: Farrar, Straus and Young, 1951.

Baseball Blue Book. Fort Wayne IN / St. Petersburg FL, 1908–60.

Bazer, Gerald, and Steven Culbertson. "Baseball during World War II: The Reaction and Encouragement of Franklin Delano Roosevelt and Others." NINE: *A Journal of Baseball History and Culture* 10 (Fall 2001): 114–29.

Bedingfield, Gary. "George Sulliman." Baseball's Greatest Sacrifice. http://www.baseballsgreatestsacrifice.com/biographies/sulliman_george.html; accessed August 2021.

———. "Jerry Coleman." Baseball's Greatest Sacrifice. http://www.baseballsgreatestsacrifice.com/decorated/coleman-jerry.html; accessed August 2021.

———. "The 1943 All-Pro Game in England." In Anton and Nowlin, *When Baseball Went to War*.

———. "The 1945 GI World Series." In Anton and Nowlin, *When Baseball Went to War*.

———. "When Baseball Went to War." In Anton and Nowlin, *When Baseball Went to War*.

Beireis, Sean. "Divided They Fall: The Pacific Coast League's Failed Attempt to Turn Major." Senior thesis, University of Washington–Tacoma, 2014. https://digitalcommons.tacoma.uw.edu/history_theses/9/.

Bennett, John. "Jimmie Foxx." https://sabr.org/bioproj/person/jimmie-foxx/; accessed June 2021.

Benson, Michael. *Ballparks of North America: A Comprehensive Historical Reference to Baseball Grounds, Yards and Stadiums, 1845 to Present*. Jefferson NC: McFarland, 1989.

Benswanger, William. "Professional Baseball in Pittsburgh." In *The Pirates Reader*, edited by Richard Peterson, 27–32. Pittsburgh: University of Pittsburgh Press, 2003.

Berg, A. Scott. *Lindbergh*. New York: G. P. Putnam's Sons, 1998.

Berger, Ralph. "Earle Combs." https://sabr.org/bioproj/person/earle-combs/; accessed July 2021.

———. "Larry MacPhail." https://sabr.org/bioproj/person/larry-macphail/; accessed June 2021.
———. "Morrie Arnovich." https://sabr.org/bioproj/person/morrie-arnovich/; accessed August 2021.
———. "Paul Derringer." https://sabr.org/bioproj/person/paul-derringer/; accessed July 2021.
Bernstein, Sam. "Barney Dreyfuss." sabr.org/bioproj/person/barney-dreyfuss/; accessed January 2021.
Berra, Yogi. *The Yogi Book—I Really Didn't Say Everything I Said!* New York: Workman, 1998.
Berra, Yogi, and Ed Fitzgerald. *Yogi: The Autobiography of a Professional Baseball Player.* Garden City NY: Doubleday, 1961.
Berra, Yogi, with Dave Kaplan. *What Time Is It? You Mean Now? Advice for Life from the Zennest Master of Them All.* New York: Simon and Schuster, 2002.
———. *When You Come to a Fork in the Road, Take It! Inspiration and Wisdom from One of Baseball's Greatest Heroes.* New York: Hyperion, 2001.
Berra, Yogi, with Tom Horton. *Yogi: It Ain't Over.* New York: McGraw-Hill, 1989.
Betsworth, Jennifer. "Reviving and Restoring Southern Ruins: Reshaping Plantation Architecture and Landscapes in Georgetown County, South Carolina." In *Leisure, Plantations, and the Making of a New South: The Sporting Plantations of the South Carolina Lowcountry and Red Hills Region, 1900–1940*, edited by Julia Brock and Daniel Vivian, 57–82. Lanham MD: Lexington Books, 2015.
Beverage, Richard. "Farm Systems and the PCL." *Pacific Coast Potpourri*, August 2005.
Bevis, Charlie. "How the Shaughnessy Plan Redefined Success in Sports." *NINE: A Journal of Baseball History and Culture* 20 (Fall 2011): 27–39.
———. "Mickey Cochrane." https://sabr.org/bioproj/person/mickey-cochrane/; accessed June 2021.
———. *Mickey Cochrane: The Life of a Baseball Hall of Fame Catcher.* Jefferson NC: McFarland, 1998.
———. *Sunday Baseball: The Major Leagues' Struggle to Play Baseball on the Lord's Day, 1876–1934*. Jefferson NC: McFarland, 2003.
———. "Tony Lupien." https://sabr.org/bioproj/person/tony-lupien/; accessed July 2021.
Bjarkman, Peter C. *Diamonds around the Globe: The Encyclopedia of International Baseball.* Westport CT: Greenwood Press, 2005.
Blau, Clifford. "The Major League Draft." http://cliffordblau.000webhostapp.com/ml_draft.htm; accessed June 2021.
———. "Optional Assignments." http://cliffordblau.000webhostapp.com/options.htm; accessed June 2021.
Blight, David W. *Frederick Douglass: Prophet of Freedom.* New York: Simon and Schuster, 2018.
Block, David. *Baseball before We Knew It: A Search for the Roots of the Game.* Lincoln: University of Nebraska Press, 2005.

Bloodgood, Clifford. "'Pepper' Martin, the Cardinals' New Spark Plug." *Baseball Digest*, October 1931.

———. "The Tigers—In Seven Games." *Baseball Magazine*, December 1945.

Bohn, Terry. "Happy Chandler." https://sabr.org/bioproj/person/happy-chandler/; accessed August 2021.

Bokser, Andy. "1945: Resuming Peacetime Baseball." In Weingarden and Nowlin, *Baseball's Business*, vol. 1, 1901–1957.

Borst, William A. "Baltimore Orioles." In Riess, *Encyclopedia of Major League Baseball Clubs*, vol. 2, *The American League*.

Boxerman, Burton A., and Benita W. Boxerman. *Ebbets to Veeck to Busch: Eight Owners Who Shaped Baseball*. Jefferson NC: McFarland, 2003.

———. *George Weiss: Architect of the Golden Age Yankees*. Jefferson NC: McFarland, 2016.

———. *Jews and Baseball*. Vol. 1, *Entering the American Mainstream, 1871–1948*. Jefferson NC: McFarland, 2007.

Boyle, Robert. "Perfect Man for the Job." *Sports Illustrated*, April 9, 1962.

Briley, Ron. "Danny Gardella and Baseball's Reserve Clause." In Regalado and Fields, *Sport and the Law*.

Broeg, Bob, and William J. Miller Jr. *Baseball from a Different Angle*. South Bend IN: Diamond Communications, 1988.

Brosnan, Jim. "You Can Consider It Came from Me." *Sports Illustrated*, March 7, 1960.

Brunson, James E., III. *Black Baseball, 1858–1900: A Comprehensive Record of the Teams, Players, Managers, Owners, and Umpires*. 3 vols. Jefferson NC: McFarland, 2019.

Bryant, Howard. *The Last Hero: A Life of Henry Aaron*. New York: Pantheon Books, 2010.

———. *Shut Out: A Story of Race and Baseball in Boston*. New York: Routledge, 2002.

Bryant, Steven. "1951: Open Classification." In Weingarden and Nowlin, *Baseball's Business*, vol. 1, 1901–1957.

Bryson, Bill, and Leighton Housh, eds. *Through the Years with the Western League*. Des Moines IA: Privately printed, 1951.

Buege, Bob. "The Birth of the American League." In *Baseball in the Badger State*, edited by Bob Buege, 6–9. Cleveland: Society for American Baseball Research, 2001.

Buhite, Russell D. "The Continental League and Its Western Carolina League Affiliate: Branch Rickey's Second Finest Hour." *North Carolina Historical Review* 81 (October 2004): 426–60.

———. *The Continental League: A Personal History*. Lincoln: University of Nebraska Press, 2014.

Bullock, Steven R. *Playing for Their Nation: Baseball and the American Military during World War II*. Lincoln: University of Nebraska Press, 2004.

Burgos, Adrian, Jr. *Playing America's Game: Baseball, Latinos, and the Color Line*. Berkeley: University of California Press, 2007.

Burk, Robert F. *Much More Than a Game: Players, Owners, and American Baseball since 1921*. Chapel Hill: University of North Carolina Press, 2001.

———. *Never Just a Game: Players, Owners, and American Baseball to 1920*. Chapel Hill: University of North Carolina Press, 1994.

Burner, David. *Herbert Hoover: A Public Life*. New York: Alfred A. Knopf, 1979.

Burns, George. *The Third Time Around*. New York: G. P. Putnam's Sons, 1980.

Bush, Frederick C. "1929: Let's All Play by the Same Rules." In Weingarden and Nowlin, *Baseball's Business*, vol. 1, 1901–1957.

———. "1942: Green Light—Matters of Manpower and the Military." In Weingarden and Nowlin, *Baseball's Business*, vol. 1, 1901–1957.

Candaele, Kerry. "The History of Women's Baseball." In *Baseball and American Culture: A History*, by John P. Rossi, 161–64. Lanham MD: Rowman & Littlefield, 2018.

Cardullo, Steve. "Harry Grabiner." https://sabr.org/bioproj/person/harry-grabiner/; accessed August 2021.

Carney, Gene. *Burying the Black Sox: How Baseball's Cover-Up of the 1919 World Series Fix Almost Succeeded*. Dulles VA: Potomac Books, 2006.

Carvalho, John P. *Frick*: Baseball's Third Commissioner*. Jefferson NC: McFarland, 2016.

Cash, Jon David. *Before They Were Cardinals: Major League Baseball in Nineteenth-Century St. Louis*. Columbia: University of Missouri Press, 2002.

———. "St. Louis Cardinals." In Riess, *Encyclopedia of Major League Baseball Clubs*, vol. 1, *The National League*.

Cavanaugh, Jack. *Season of '42: Joe D, Teddy Ballgame, and Baseball's Fight to Survive a Turbulent First Year of War*. New York: Skyhorse Publishing, 2012.

Celler, Emanuel. *You Never Leave Brooklyn*. New York: John Day, 1953.

"Champion Dollar Guy." *Baseball Digest*, October 1951.

Chandler, Albert B., with Vance H. Trimble. *Heroes, Plain Folks, and Skunks: The Life and Times of Happy Chandler*. Chicago: Bonus Books, 1989.

Chernow, Ron. *Titan: The Life of John D. Rockefeller Sr.* 2nd ed. New York: Vintage Books, 2004. First published 1998.

Clifford, Garry, and Samuel R. Spencer Jr. *The First Peacetime Draft*. Lawrence: University Press of Kansas, 1986.

Cobbledick, Gordon. "The Cleveland Indians." In *The Book of Major League Baseball Clubs: The American League*, edited by Ed Fitzgerald, 213–41. New York: A. S. Barnes, 1952.

Cochrane, Gordon S. (Mickey). *Baseball: The Fans' Game*. With an introduction by Mark Alvarez. Cleveland: Society for American Baseball Research, 1992. First published 1939.

Cohen, Alan. "San Diego Breaks Pacific Coast League Color Barrier." *National Pastime: Pacific Ghosts*, 2019, 46–50.

Cohen, Richard M., and David S. Neft. *The World Series: Complete Play-by-Play of Every Game, 1903–1985*. New York: Collier Books, 1986.

Cola, Phil. "Bob Kennedy." https://sabr.org/bioproj/person/bob-kennedy/; accessed August 2021.

Cole, Robert. "Ersatz Octobers: Baseball Barnstorming." *Baseball History* 4 (1991): 75–103.

Coleman, Jerry, as told to Todd Anton. "More Than a Yankee: Marine Col. Jerry Coleman." In Anton and Nowlin, *When Baseball Went to War.*

Condon, Dave. *The Go-Go Chicago White Sox.* New York: Coward-McCann, 1960.

Constitution and Playing Rules of the National League of Professional Base Ball Clubs. Philadelphia: Reach & Johnston, 1876.

Constitution of the National League of Professional Base Ball Clubs. In *Spalding's Official Base Ball Guide for 1878.* Chicago: A. G. Spalding & Bro., 1878.

Contois, John. "Dom DiMaggio." https://sabr.org/bioproj/person/dom-dimaggio/; accessed July 2021.

Cook, William A. *August "Garry" Herrmann: A Baseball Biography.* Jefferson NC: McFarland, 2008.

Corbett, Warren. "Bill Veeck." https://sabr.org/bioproj/person/bill-veeck/; accessed August 2021.

———. "Bob Dillinger." https://sabr.org/bioproj/person/bob-dillinger/; accessed August 2021.

———. "Dick Wakefield." https://sabr.org/bioproj/person/dick-wakefield/; accessed August 2021.

———. "Ford Frick." https://sabr.org/bioproj/person/ford-frick/; accessed August 2021.

———. "Lloyd Merriman." https://sabr.org/bioproj/person/lloyd-merriman/; accessed August 2021.

———. "Marty Marion." https://sabr.org/bioproj/person/marty-marion/; accessed July 2021.

———. "Mel Allen." https://sabr.org/bioproj/person/mel-allen/; accessed August 2021.

———. "Red Barber." https://sabr.org/bioproj/person/red-barber/; accessed August 2021.

Costello, Rory. "Bob Quinn." https://sabr.org/bioproj/person/bob-quinn/; accessed August 2021.

Craig, Peter S. "Organized Baseball: An Industry Study of a $100 Million Spectator Sport." Senior thesis, Department of Economics, Oberlin College, 1950.

Cramer, Richard Ben. *Joe DiMaggio: The Hero's Life.* New York: Simon and Schuster, 2000.

Creamer, Robert W. *Babe: The Legend Comes to Life.* New York: Simon and Schuster, 1974.

———. *Baseball and Other Matters in 1941: A Celebration of the Best Baseball Season Ever—in the Year America Went to War.* Lincoln: University of Nebraska Press, 2000. First published 1991.

Crepeau, Richard C. *Baseball: America's Diamond Mind, 1919–1941.* Orlando: University Presses of Florida, 1980.

Cresap, Dick. "1911 Ball Liveliest of 'Em All." *Baseball Digest,* July 1949.

Dallek, Robert. *Franklin D. Roosevelt: A Political Life.* New York: Viking, 2017.

Daly, Jon. "Billy Southworth." https://sabr.org/bioproj/person/billy-southworth/; accessed August 2021.

Daniel, Daniel M. "DiMaggio, Lazzeri, Moore Deals Stand Out in Barrow's Recollections." *Baseball Magazine*, May 1950.

———. "Dreyfuss, Last of the Baseball Squires." *Baseball Magazine*, September 1931.

———. "Major Leagues Have Proud Record in War and Relief Enterprises." *Baseball Magazine*, September 1943.

Daniel, W. Harrison. *Jimmie Foxx: The Life and Times of a Baseball Hall of Famer, 1907–1967*. Jefferson NC: McFarland, 1996.

Davis, Amira Rose. "No League of Their Own: Baseball, Black Women, and the Politics of Representation." *Radical History Review* 2016 (May 2016): 74–96.

Davis, Kenneth S. *FDR: The New Deal Years, 1933–1937*. New York: Random House, 1986.

Dawidoff, Nicholas, ed. *Baseball: A Literary Anthology*. New York: Library of America, 2002.

———. *The Catcher Was a Spy: The Mysterious Life of Moe Berg*. New York: Vintage Books, 1995.

Day, Frederick J. *Clubhouse Lawyer: The Sports Fan's Guide to Life and the Law*. New York: Writer's Showcase, 2002.

Deane, Bill. "Awards and Honors." In Thorn, Palmer, Gershman, and Pietrusza, *Total Baseball*, 6th ed.

Des Jardins, Julie. *Walter Camp: Football and the Modern Man*. New York: Oxford University Press, 2015.

DeValeria, Dennis, and Jeanne Burke DeValeria. *Honus Wagner: A Biography*. New York: Henry Holt, 1995.

DeVito, Carlo. *Yogi: The Life and Times of an American Original*. Chicago: Triumph Books, 2008.

Dewey, Donald, and Nicholas Acocella. *The Ball Clubs*. New York: HarperPerennial, 1996. First published 1993.

———. *The Biographical History of Baseball*. New York: Carroll & Graf, 1995.

Dexter, Charles. "Congress Threatens Baseball Upheaval." *Sport*, August 1951.

Dickson, Paul, comp. *Baseball's Greatest Quotations*. New York: Edward Burlingame Books, 1991.

———. *Bill Veeck: Baseball's Greatest Maverick*. New York: Walker, 2012.

———. *Leo Durocher: Baseball's Prodigal Son*. New York: Bloomsbury, 2017.

Dobbins, Dick. *The Grand Minor League: An Oral History of the Old Pacific Coast League*. Emeryville CA: Woodford Press, 1999.

Dorward, Jane Finnan. "Ed Barrow's Toronto Years." In *Dominionball: Baseball above the 49th*, edited by Jane Finnan Dorward, 101–8. Cleveland: Society for American Baseball Research, 2005.

Douglas, George H. *The Early Days of Radio Broadcasting*. Jefferson NC: McFarland, 2001.

Durocher, Leo, with Ed Linn. *Nice Guys Finish Last*. New York: Simon and Schuster, 1975.

Echevarría, Roberto Gonzalez. *The Pride of Havana: A History of Cuban Baseball*. New York: Oxford University Press, 1999.

Eckhouse, Morris. *Legends of the Tribe: An Illustrated History of the Cleveland Indians*. Dallas: Taylor, 2000.

Eddleton, Oscar. "Under the Lights." *Baseball Research Journal* 9 (1980): 37–42.

Edelman, Rob, and Audrey Kupferberg. *Matthau: A Life*. Lanham MD: Taylor Trade, 2002.

Edmonds, Ed. "Remembering Earl—Not George—Toolson: The Plaintiff Who Took the New York Yankees to the US Supreme Court." https://sabr.org/research/remembering-earl-not-george-toolson-plaintiff-who-took-new-york-yankees-us-supreme-court; accessed August 2021.

Edmonds, Ed, and Frank G. Houdek. *Baseball Meets the Law: A Chronology of Decisions, Statutes and Other Legal Events*. Jefferson NC: McFarland, 2017.

Egan, James M., Jr. *Base Ball on the Western Reserve: The Early Game in Cleveland and Northeast Ohio, Year by Year and Town by Town, 1865–1900*. Jefferson NC: McFarland, 2008.

Eig, Jonathan. *Luckiest Man: The Life and Death of Lou Gehrig*. New York: Simon and Schuster, 2005.

———. *Opening Day: The Story of Jackie Robinson's First Season*. New York: Simon and Schuster, 2007.

Einstein, Charles, ed. *The Fireside Book of Baseball*. New York: Simon and Schuster, 1956.

Eisenbath, Mike. *The Cardinals Encyclopedia*. Philadelphia: Temple University Press, 1999.

Enders, Eric. *100 Years of the World Series*. N.p.: Barnes & Noble Books, 2003.

Essington, Amy. *The Integration of the Pacific Coast League: Race and Baseball on the West Coast*. Lincoln: University of Nebraska Press, 2018.

Faber, Charles F. "Carlos Bernier." https://sabr.org/bioproj/person/carlos-bernier; accessed September 2022.

———. "Powel Crosley Jr." https://sabr.org/bioproj/person/powel-crosley-jr/; accessed August 2021.

Federal Works Agency. *Final Report on the WPA Program, 1935–43*. Westport CT: Greenwood Press, 1976. First published 1943.

Felber, Bill. "1954: Looking West." In Weingarden and Nowlin, *Baseball's Business*, vol. 1, 1901–1957.

Fenster, Kenneth R. "Earl Mann, Nat Peeples, and the Failed Attempt of Integration in the Southern Association." *NINE: A Journal of Baseball History and Culture* 12 (Spring 2004): 73–101.

Ferkovich, Scott. "Hank Greenberg." https://sabr.org/bioproj/person/hank-greenberg/; accessed August 2021.

Fetter, Henry D. *Taking on the Yankees: Winning and Losing in the Business of Baseball*. New York: W. W. Norton, 2005. First published 2003.

Fidler, Merrie A. *The Origins and History of the All-American Girls Professional Baseball League*. Jefferson NC: McFarland, 2006.

Figueredo, Jorge S. *Cuban Baseball: A Statistical History, 1878–1961*. Jefferson NC: McFarland, 2003.

Finch, Robert L., L. D. Addington, and Ben M. Morgan, eds. *The Story of Minor League Baseball: A History of the Game of Professional Baseball in the United States with Particular Reference to Its Growth and Development in the Smaller Cities and Towns of the Nation—The Minor Leagues*. Columbus OH: Stoneman Press, 1952.

Findling, John E. "Chicago Cubs." In Riess, *Encyclopedia of Major League Baseball Clubs*, vol. 1, *The National League*.

Finkel, Jan. "Johnny Sain." https://sabr.org/bioproj/person/johnny-sain/; accessed August 2021.

Finoli, David. *For the Good of the Country: World War II Baseball in the Major and Minor Leagues*. Jefferson NC: McFarland, 2002.

Fitts, Robert K. *Banzai Babe Ruth: Baseball, Espionage, and Assassination during the 1934 Tour of Japan*. Lincoln: University of Nebraska Press, 2012.

Fitzgerald, Ed. "Hank Greenberg: A Study in Success." *Sport*, March 1951.

Flaherty, Vincent X. "The Miracle Move of the Dodgers from Flatbush to Fantasia." *Baseball Register*, [1960].

Fleitz, David L. "The Honor Rolls of Baseball." *Baseball Research Journal* 34 (2005): 53–59.

Fleming, G. H. *The Dizziest Season: The Gashouse Gang Chases the Pennant*. New York: William Morrow, 1984.

Flynn, George Q. *The Draft, 1940–1973*. Lawrence: University Press of Kansas, 1993.

Frick, Ford C. *Games, Asterisks, and People: Memoirs of a Lucky Fan*. New York: Crown, 1973.

Fuchs, Robert S., and Wayne Soini. *Judge Fuchs and the Boston Braves*. Jefferson NC: McFarland, 1998.

Galbraith, John Kenneth. *The Great Crash, 1929*. Boston: Houghton Mifflin, 1961.

Gallagher, Mark, and Walter LeConte. *The Yankee Encyclopedia*. 4th ed. Champaign IL: Sports Publishing, 2000.

Garratt, Robert F. *Home Team: The Turbulent History of the San Francisco Giants*. Lincoln: University of Nebraska Press, 2017.

Gerlach, Larry R. "German Americans in Major League Baseball: Sport and Acculturation." In Baldassaro and Johnson, *The American Game*.

———. *The Men in Blue: Conversations with Umpires*. New York: Viking, 1980.

Gershman, Michael. *Diamonds: The Evolution of the Ballpark*. Boston: Houghton Mifflin, 1993.

Gietschier, Steven P. "Limited War and the Home Front: Ohio during the Korean War." PhD diss., Ohio State University, 1977.

———. "Slugging and Snubbing: Hugh Casey, Ernest Hemingway, and Jackie Robinson—A Baseball Mystery." NINE: *A Journal of Baseball History and Culture* 21 (Fall 2012): 12–46.

———. "'Uncle Sam Needs Only to Call': Baseball and the United States' Peacetime Military Draft, 1940–42." NINE: *A Journal of Baseball History and Culture* 24 (Fall–Spring 2015–16): 29–56.

Giglio, James N. *Musial: From Stash to Stan the Man*. Columbia: University of Missouri Press, 2001.

Gilbert, Bill. *They Also Served: Baseball and the Home Front, 1941–1945*. New York: Crown, 1992.

Ginsburg, Dan. "John Kinley Tener." In Simon, *Deadball Stars of the National League*.

Gluekstein, Fred. "Tony Lazzeri." https://sabr.org/bioproj/person/tony-lazzeri/; accessed July 2021.

Goldblatt, Andrew. "San Francisco Giants." In Riess, *Encyclopedia of Major League Baseball Clubs*, vol. 1, *The National League*.

Goldstein, Richard. *Spartan Seasons: How Baseball Survived the Second World War*. New York: Macmillan, 1980.

Golenbock, Peter. *The Spirit of St. Louis: A History of the St. Louis Cardinals and Browns*. New York: Avon Books, 2000.

Graham, Frank. *The New York Yankees: An Informal History*. 3rd ed. New York: G. P. Putnam's Sons, 1948.

Grahek, Mike. "Clark Griffith." In Jones, *Deadball Stars of the American League*.

Green, Jeremy. "1901: Firsts, Foibles, and Failures." In Weingarden and Nowlin, *Baseball's Business*, vol. 1, *1901–1957*.

———. "1941: War and Uncertainty." In Weingarden and Nowlin, *Baseball's Business*, vol. 1, *1901–1957*.

———. "1949: Bonuses, Bargains, and Broadcasts." In Weingarden and Nowlin, *Baseball's Business*, vol. 1, *1901–1957*.

Greenberg, Hank. *Hank Greenberg: The Story of My Life*. Edited and with an introduction by Ira Berkow. New York: Times Books, 1989.

Gregory, Robert. *Diz: Dizzy Dean and Baseball during the Great Depression*. New York: Viking, 1992.

Guschov, Stephen D. *The Red Stockings of Cincinnati: Base Ball's First All-Professional Team*. Jefferson NC: McFarland, 1998.

Hailey, Gary. "Anatomy of a Murder: The Federal League and the Courts." *National Pastime: A Review of Baseball History*, Spring 1985, 62–73.

Ham, Eldon L. *Broadcasting Baseball: A History of the National Pastime on Radio and Television*. Jefferson NC: McFarland, 2011.

Hano, Arnold. *A Day in the Bleachers*. Boston: Da Capo Press, 1995. First published 1955.

Harkins, Tom. "Jim Prendergast." https://sabr.org/bioproj/person/jim-prendergast/; accessed August 2021.

Heaphy, Leslie. "The Creation of the Negro National League." In *Replays, Rivalries, and Rumbles: The Most Iconic Moments in American Sports*, edited by Steven Gietschier, 25–32. Urbana and Chicago: University of Illinois Press, 2017.

———. *The Negro Leagues, 1869–1960*. Jefferson NC: McFarland, 2003.

———. "New York Mets Team Ownership History." https://sabr.org/bioproj/topic/new-york-mets-team-ownership-history/; accessed December 2020.

Heaphy, Leslie, and Mel Anthony May, eds. *Encyclopedia of Women and Baseball*. Jefferson NC: McFarland, 2006.

Heitz, Thomas R. "Rules and Scoring." In Thorn and Palmer with Reuther, *Total Baseball*.

Helyar, John. *Lords of the Realm: The Real History of Baseball*. New York: Villard Books, 1994.

Hemphill, Paul. "Whatever Happened to What's-His-Name?" In *Lost in the Lights: Sports, Dreams, and Life*, by Paul Hemphill, 149–60. Tuscaloosa: University of Alabama Press, 2003.

Hennessy, Kevin. "Calvin Griffith: The Ups and Downs of the Last Family-Owned Baseball Team." In *Short but Wondrous Summers: Baseball in the North Star State*, edited by Daniel R. Levitt, 63–69. Phoenix: Society for American Baseball Research, 2012.

Hetrick, J. Thomas. *Misfits! The Cleveland Spiders in 1899*. Jefferson NC: McFarland, 1991.

Hittner, Arthur D. *Honus Wagner: The Life of Baseball's "Flying Dutchman."* Jefferson NC: McFarland, 1996.

Hoffmann, Gregg. "County Stadium (Milwaukee, WI)." https://sabr.org/bioproj/park/county-stadium-milwaukee-wi/; accessed August 2021.

Hogan, Lawrence D. *Shades of Glory: The Negro Leagues and the Story of African-American Baseball*. Washington DC: National Geographic, 2006.

Hoie, Bob. "The Minor Leagues." In Thorn, Palmer, Gershman, and Pietrusza, *Total Baseball*, 6th ed.

Holaday, J. Chris. *Professional Baseball in North Carolina: An Illustrated City-by-City History, 1901–1996*. Jefferson NC: McFarland, 1998.

Holland, Gerald. "The Great MacPhail: Feuds, Finale, and a Fairy Tale." *Sports Illustrated*, August 31, 1959.

Holtzman, Jerome. *The Commissioners: Baseball's Midlife Crisis*. New York: Total Sports, 1998.

———, ed. *No Cheering in the Press Box*. New York: Henry Holt, 1995. First published 1973.

Holtzman, Jerome, and George Vass. *The Chicago Cubs Encyclopedia*. Philadelphia: Temple University Press, 1997.

Honig, Donald. *Baseball America: The Heroes of the Game and Times of Their Glory*. New York: Macmillan, 1985.

Hoover, Herbert. *The Memoirs of Herbert Hoover*. Vol. 1, *Years of Adventure, 1874–1920*. New York: Macmillan, 1951.

House Judiciary Committee. *Organized Baseball: Report of the Subcommittee on Study of Monopoly Power of the Committee on the Judiciary*. 82nd Cong., 2nd sess. (1952), H. Report 2002.

———. *Study of Monopoly Power: Hearings before the Subcommittee on Study of Monopoly Power*. Serial No. 1, Part 6, "Organized Baseball," 82nd Cong., 1st sess. (1951).

Howard, Donald S. *The WPA and Federal Relief Policy*. New York: Russell Sage Foundation, 1943.

Huber, Mike. "Bobby Brown." https://sabr.org/bioproj/person/bobby-brown/; accessed August 2021.

Hubler, David E., and Joshua H. Drazen. *The Nats and the Grays: How Baseball in the Nation's Capital Survived WWII and Changed the Game Forever*. Lanham MD: Rowman and Littlefield, 2015.

Huhn, Rick. *Eddie Collins: A Baseball Biography*. Jefferson NC: McFarland, 2008.

———. *The Sizzler: George Sisler, Baseball's Forgotten Great*. Columbia: University of Missouri Press, 2004.

Hylton, J. Gordon. "Walter Kowalski: A Forgotten Man in the Legal History of Sport." Marquette University Law School Faculty Blog, May 29, 2011. https://law.marquette.edu/facultyblog/2011/05/walter-kowalski-a-forgotten-man-in-the-legal-history-of-sport/.

Hynd, Noel. *The Giants of the Polo Grounds: The Glorious Times of Baseball's New York Giants*. New York: Doubleday, 1988.

Iber, Jorge. "Mexico: Baseball's Humble Beginnings to Budding Competitor." In *Baseball Beyond Our Borders: An International Pastime*, edited by George Gmelch and Daniel A. Nathan, 75–84. Lincoln: University of Nebraska Press, 2017.

Irey, Elmer L. *The Tax Dodgers: The Inside Story of the T-Men's War with America's Political and Underworld Hoodlums*. As told to William J. Slocum. New York: Greenberg, 1948.

Isaacs, Stan. "Babe Ruth's Called Shot: A Matter of Semantics?" In *Baseball and the "Sultan of Swat": Babe Ruth at 100*, edited by Robert N. Keane, 221–29. New York: AMS Press, 2008.

Ivor-Campbell, Frederick, ed. *Baseball's First Stars*. Cleveland: Society for American Baseball Research, 1996.

———. "The Many Fathers of Baseball: Anglo-Americans and the Early Game." In Baldassaro and Johnson, *The American Game*.

Jackson, Kenneth T. *Crabgrass Frontier: The Suburbanization of the United States*. New York: Oxford University Press, 1987. First published 1985.

Jacobson, Sidney. *Pete Reiser: The Rough-and-Tumble Career of the Perfect Ballplayer*. Jefferson NC: McFarland, 2004.

Jaffe, Jay. "Jackie Robinson and the Integration Advantage." FanGraphs, April 17, 2018. https://www.fangraphs.com/blogs/jackie-robinson-and-the-integration-advantage/.

James, Bill. *The New Bill James Historical Baseball Abstract*. Rev. ed. New York: Free Press, 2001.

James, Bill, and Rob Neyer. *The Neyer/James Guide to Pitchers: An Historical Compendium of Pitching, Pitchers, and Pitches*. New York: Fireside Books, 2004.

Johnson, Bill. "Henry Aaron." https://sabr.org/bioproj/person/hank-aaron/; accessed August 2021.

Johnson, Frederic A. "Baseball Law." *United States Law Review* 73 (1939): 252–70.

Johnson, Lloyd, and Miles Wolff, eds. *The Encyclopedia of Minor League Baseball*. 2nd ed. Durham NC: Baseball America, 1997.

———, eds. *The Encyclopedia of Minor League Baseball*. 3rd ed. Durham NC: Baseball America, 2007.

Johnson, Rodney. "The Cactus League: A Brief History." https://sabraz.org/the-cactus-league-a-brief-history/; accessed April 2020.

Jones, David, ed. *Deadball Stars of the American League*. Dulles VA: Potomac Books, 2006.

Jordan, David M. *The Athletics of Philadelphia: Connie Mack's White Elephants, 1901–1954*. Jefferson NC: McFarland, 1999.

Jordan, David M., Larry R. Gerlach, and John P. Rossi. "A Baseball Myth Exploded: The Truth about Bill Veeck and the '43 Phillies." *National Pastime: A Review of Baseball History* 18 (1998): 3–13.

Joyner, Charles. *Down by the Riverside: A South Carolina Slave Community*. Urbana and Chicago: University of Illinois Press, 1984.

Kaese, Harold. *The Boston Braves*. New York: G. P. Putnam's Sons, 1948.

Kahn, E. J. *The Big Drink: The Story of Coca-Cola*. New York: Random House, 1960.

Kahn, Roger. *The Boys of Summer*. New York: Harper & Row, 1972.

———. *The Era, 1947–1957: When the Yankees, the Giants, and the Dodgers Ruled the World*. New York: Ticknor & Fields, 1993.

Kaplan, Jim. "Lefty Grove." https://sabr.org/bioproj/person/lefty-grove/; accessed June 2021.

———. *Lefty Grove: American Original*. Cleveland: Society for American Baseball Research, 2000.

———. "Warren Spahn." https://sabr.org/bioproj/person/warren-spahn/; accessed August 2021.

Kashatus, William C. *Connie Mack's '29 Triumph: The Rise and Fall of the Philadelphia Athletics Dynasty*. Jefferson NC: McFarland, 1999.

———. *One-Armed Wonder: Pete Gray, Wartime Baseball, and the American Dream*. Jefferson NC: McFarland, 1995.

Keene, Kerry. *1960: The Last Pure Season*. New York: Sports Publishing, 2013.

Keeney, Stephen R. "1936: Home Plate and Hurlers." In Weingarden and Nowlin, *Baseball's Business*, vol. 1, 1901–1957.

Kelley, Brent. *Baseball's Biggest Blunder: The Bonus Rule of 1953–1957*. Lanham MD: Scarecrow Press, 1997.

Kempner, Aviva, dir. *The Life and Times of Hank Greenberg*. 1999.

Kennedy, David M. *Freedom from Fear: The American People in Depression and War, 1929–1945*. New York: Oxford University Press, 1999.

Klein, Maury. *A Call to Arms: Mobilizing America for World War II*. New York: Bloomsbury Press, 2013.

Klier, Thomas, and James M. Rubenstein. *Who Really Made Your Car? Restructuring and Geographic Change in the Auto Industry*. Kalamazoo MI: W. E. Upjohn Institute for Employment Research, 2008.

Klopsis, Nick. "1943: War on the Home Front." In Weingarden and Nowlin, *Baseball's Business*, vol. 1, 1901–1957.

———. "1950: The Happy Dagger." In Weingarden and Nowlin, *Baseball's Business*, vol. 1, 1901–1957.

Koppett, Leonard. *Koppett's Concise History of Major League Baseball*. Philadelphia: Temple University Press, 1998.

———. *The Man in the Dugout: Baseball's Top Managers and How They Got That Way*. New York: Crown, 1993.

———. *The New York Mets: The Whole Story*. New York: Macmillan, 1970.

Korr, Charles P. *The End of Baseball as We Knew It: The Players Union, 1960–81*. Urbana and Chicago: University of Illinois Press, 2002.

Kossuth, Robert. "Boondoggling, Baseball, and the WPA: Cooperstown's Doubleday Field." NINE: *A Journal of Baseball History and Culture* 9 (Fall 2000): 56–71.

Koszarek, Ed. *The Players League: History, Clubs, Ballplayers and Statistics*. Jefferson NC: McFarland, 2006.

Krabbenhoft, Herm. "Hank Greenberg's American League RBI Record." *Baseball Research Journal* 41 (Spring 2012): 20–27.

———. "Lou Gehrig's RBI Record: 1923–39." *Baseball Research Journal* 41 (Fall 2012): 10–13.

———. "Lou Gehrig's RBI Record: Striving to Get It Right Thanks to 40 Years of Research by SABR Members." *Baseball Research Journal* 40 (Fall 2011): 12–22.

Kritzler, David M., and Alan P. Henry. "1959: Winds of Change." In Weingarden and Nowlin, *Baseball's Business*, vol. 2, 1958–2016.

———. "1960: The Missouri Compromise." In Weingarden and Nowlin, *Baseball's Business*, vol. 2, 1958–2016.

Kuklick, Bruce. *To Every Thing a Season: Shibe Park and Urban Philadelphia, 1909–1976*. Princeton NJ: Princeton University Press, 1991.

Lamb, Bill. "Charles A. Stoneham." https://sabr.org/bioproj/person/charles-a-stoneham/; accessed August 2021.

———. "Gene Paulette." https://sabr.org/bioproj/person/gene-paulette/; accessed June 2021.

———. "Harry Hempstead." https://sabr.org/bioproj/person/harry-hempstead/; accessed August 2021.

———. "John T. Powers." https://sabr.org/bioproj/person/john-t-powers/; accessed March 2021.

———. "New York Giants Team Ownership History." https://sabr.org/bioproj/topic/new-york-giants-team-ownership-history/; accessed August 2021.

Lamb, William F. "The Black Sox Scandal." In Nowlin, SABR *50 at 50*.

Lamberty, Bill. "Harry Clay Pulliam." In Simon, *Deadball Stars of the National League*.

Lanctot, Neil. *Campy: The Two Lives of Roy Campanella*. New York: Simon and Schuster, 2011.

———. *Negro League Baseball: The Rise and Ruin of a Black Institution*. Philadelphia: University of Pennsylvania Press, 2004.

Lane, F. C. "Brooklyn's New Business Manager." *Baseball Magazine*, December 1933.
———. "The Man Who Put the Punch in the World's Champions." *Baseball Magazine*, April 1927.
———. "The New President of the American League." *Baseball Magazine*, January 1928.
Langer, William L., and S. Everett Gleason. *The Challenge to Isolation, 1937–1940*. New York: Harper, 1952.
Lansche, Jerry. *The Forgotten Championships: Postseason Baseball, 1882–1981*. Jefferson NC: McFarland, 1989.
Lardner, Ring. *The Lost Journalism of Ring Lardner*. Edited by Ron Rapoport. Lincoln: University of Nebraska Press, 2017.
Leavengood, Ted. *Clark Griffith: The Old Fox of Washington Baseball*. Jefferson NC: McFarland, 2011.
Leavy, Jane. *The Big Fella: Babe Ruth and the World He Created*. New York: Harper, 2018.
LeMoine, Bob. "Boston Braves Team Ownership History." https://sabr.org/bioproj/topic/boston-braves-team-ownership-history/; accessed August 2021.
———. "Judge Emil Fuchs." https://sabr.org/bioproj/person/judge-emil-fuchs/; accessed August 2021.
———. "1934: The Reds Go under the Lights While the Braves Go to the Dogs." In Weingarden and Nowlin, *Baseball's Business*, vol. 1, *1901–1957*.
Lester, Larry. *Black Baseball's National Showcase: The East-West All-Star Game, 1933–1953*. Lincoln: University of Nebraska Press, 2001.
"Let's Make Baseball Legal." *Sport*, August 1951.
Leuchtenburg, William E. *Franklin D. Roosevelt and the New Deal, 1932–1945*. New York: Harper & Row, 1963.
———. *The Perils of Prosperity, 1914–32*. Chicago: University of Chicago Press, 1958.
Levine, Peter. *Ellis Island to Ebbets Field: Sport and the American Jewish Experience*. New York: Oxford University Press, 1992.
Levitt, Daniel R. *The Battle That Forged Modern Baseball: The Federal League Challenge and Its Legacy*. Lanham MD: Ivan R. Dee, 2012.
———. *Ed Barrow: The Bulldog Who Built the Yankees' First Dynasty*. Lincoln: University of Nebraska Press, 2008.
Levitt, Daniel R., and Mark Armour. "New York Yankees Team Ownership History." https://sabr.org/research/new-york-yankees-team-ownership-history; accessed August 2021.
Levy, Alan H. *Joe McCarthy: Architect of the Yankee Dynasty*. Jefferson NC: McFarland, 2005.
Levy, Gary. "1947: Latin America, Leo the Lip, and High School Hijinks." In Weingarden and Nowlin, *Baseball's Business*, vol. 1, *1901–1957*.
———. "1948: Concerns and Conflicts Regarding Televised Ball Grow Stronger." In Weingarden and Nowlin, *Baseball's Business*, vol. 1, *1901–1957*.
Lewis, Franklin A. *The Cleveland Indians*. New York: G. P. Putnam's Sons, 1949.
Lewis, Robert F., II. "Oakland Athletics." In Riess, *Encyclopedia of Major League Baseball Clubs*, vol. 2, *The American League*.

Lieb, Frederick G. *Baseball As I Have Known It*. Lincoln: University of Nebraska Press, 1996. First published 1977.

———. *The Boston Red Sox*. Carbondale and Edwardsville: Southern Illinois University Press, 2001. First published 1947.

———. *Connie Mack: Grand Old Man of Baseball*. New York: G. P. Putnam's Sons, 1945.

———. *The Detroit Tigers*. Kent OH: Kent State University Press, 2008. First published 1946.

———. *The Pittsburgh Pirates*. Carbondale and Edwardsville: Southern Illinois University Press, 2003. First published 1948.

———. *The St. Louis Cardinals: The Story of a Great Baseball Club*. Carbondale and Edwardsville: Southern Illinois University Press, 2001. First published 1944.

Light, Jonathan Fraser. *The Cultural Encyclopedia of Baseball*. Jefferson NC: McFarland, 1997.

Lindberg, Richard C. "Chicago White Sox." In Riess, *Encyclopedia of Major League Baseball Clubs*, vol. 2, *The American League*.

———. *The White Sox Encyclopedia*. Philadelphia: Temple University Press, 1997.

Littlewood, Thomas B. *Arch: A Promoter, Not a Poet: The Story of Arch Ward*. Ames: Iowa State University Press, 1990.

Lomax, Michael. "Not Quite Ready for Prime Time: The Pacific Coast League's Attempt to Become a Third Major League in Organized Baseball." Unpublished paper in possession of author. Later published as "Not Quite Ready for Prime Time: The Pacific Coast League's Attempt to Become a Third Major League in Baseball," *Journal of the West* 47 (Fall 2008): 14–25.

Long, Jason C. "1938: Out of the Hat." In Weingarden and Nowlin, *Baseball's Business*, vol. 1, 1901–1957.

———. "1939: The Tie Goes to the Commissioner." In Weingarden and Nowlin, *Baseball's Business*, vol. 1, 1901–1957.

Longert, Scott. *Addie Joss: King of the Pitchers*. Cleveland: Society for American Baseball Research, 1998.

Lowe, Stephen R. *The Kid on the Sandlot: Congress and Professional Sports*. Bowling Green OH: Bowling Green State University Popular Press, 1995.

Lowenfish, Lee. *Branch Rickey: Baseball's Ferocious Gentleman*. Lincoln: University of Nebraska Press, 2007.

Lowenfish, Lee, and Tony Lupien. *The Imperfect Diamond: The Story of Baseball's Reserve System and the Men Who Fought to Change It*. New York: Stein and Day, 1980.

Lynch, Michael T., Jr. *Harry Frazee, Ban Johnson and the Feud That Nearly Destroyed the American League*. Jefferson NC: McFarland, 2008.

Lynch, Mike. "1957: Sunday Night Fight." In Weingarden and Nowlin, *Baseball's Business*, vol. 1, 1901–1957.

———. "1958: The Last Word in Utter Futility." In Weingarden and Nowlin, *Baseball's Business*, vol. 2, 1958–2016.

Macht, Norman L. *Connie Mack and the Early Years of Baseball*. Lincoln: University of Nebraska Press, 2007.

———. *Connie Mack: The Turbulent and Triumphant Years, 1915–1931*. Lincoln: University of Nebraska Press, 2012.

———. *The Grand Old Man of Baseball: Connie Mack in His Final Years, 1932–1956*. Lincoln: University of Nebraska Press, 2015.

Macht, Norman L., and Robert D. Warrington. "The Veracity of Veeck." *Baseball Research Journal* 42 (Fall 2013): 17–20.

Mack, Connie. *My 66 Years in the Big Leagues: The Great Story of America's National Game*. Philadelphia: John C. Winston, 1950.

Mackey, R. Scott. *Barbary Baseball: The Pacific Coast League of the 1920s*. Jefferson NC: McFarland, 1999.

MacPhail, Lee. *My Nine Innings*. Westport CT: Meckler, 1989.

Madden, W. C., and Patrick J. Stewart. *The Western League: A Baseball History, 1885 through 1999*. Jefferson NC: McFarland, 2002.

Mann, Arthur. *Branch Rickey: American in Action*. Jefferson NC: McFarland, 1957. Republished 2004.

———. "The Larry MacPhail Story—Part 1." *Sport*, April 1955.

Marazzi, Rich, and Len Fiorito. *Baseball Players of the 1950s*. Jefferson NC: McFarland, 2004.

Markusen, Bruce. "Tiebreakers: One-Game and Three-Game Playoffs." In Thorn et al., *Total Baseball*, 7th ed.

Marlett, Jeffrey. "Leo Durocher." https://sabr.org/bioproj/person/leo-durocher/; accessed August 2021.

———. "1947 Dodgers: The Suspension of Leo Durocher." https://sabr.org/research/1947-dodgers-suspension-leo-durocher; accessed August 2021.

———. "1947 Yankees: The Yankees' Involvement with Leo Durocher's Suspension." https://sabr.org/research/1947-yankees-yankees-involvement-leo-durochers-suspension; accessed August 2021.

Marren, Joe. "1921: First with Landis." In Weingarden and Nowlin, *Baseball's Business*, vol. 1, 1901–1957.

———. "1944: A New Era without Landis." In Weingarden and Nowlin, *Baseball's Business*, vol. 1, 1901–1957.

Marshall, William. *Baseball's Pivotal Era, 1945–1951*. Lexington: University Press of Kentucky, 1999.

McCue, Andy. "Los Angeles/Brooklyn Dodgers Team Ownership History." https://sabr.org/research/los-angeles-brooklyn-dodgers-team-ownership-history; accessed August 2021.

———. *Mover and Shaker: Walter O'Malley, the Dodgers, and Baseball's Westward Expansion*. Lincoln: University of Nebraska Press, 2014.

McElvaine, Robert S. *The Great Depression: America, 1929–1941*. New York: Times Books, 1984.

McKelvey, G. Richard. *The MacPhails: Baseball's First Family of the Front Office*. Jefferson NC: McFarland, 2000.

———. *Mexican Raiders in the Major Leagues: The Pasquel Brothers vs. Organized Baseball, 1946*. Jefferson NC: McFarland, 2006.

McKenna, Brian. "Bud Fowler." https://sabr.org/bioproj/person/bud-fowler/; accessed August 2021.

———. "Global League." https://sabr.org/bioproj/topic/global-league; accessed August 2021.

McMurray, John. "Larry Doby." https://sabr.org/bioproj/person/larry-doby/; accessed September 2020.

Mead, William B. *Even the Browns: Baseball during World War II*. Mineola NY: Dover Publications, 2010. First published 1978.

———. *Two Spectacular Seasons: 1930: The Year the Hitters Ran Wild, and 1968: The Year the Pitchers Took Revenge*. New York: Macmillan, 1990.

Mead, William B., and Paul Dickson. *Baseball: The Presidents' Game*. Washington DC: Farragut, 1993.

Mehl, Ernest. *The Kansas City Athletics*. New York: Henry Holt, 1956.

Melville, Tom. *Early Baseball and the Rise of the National League*. Jefferson NC: McFarland, 2001.

Metcalf, Mark. "Organized Baseball's Night Birth." *Baseball Research Journal* 45 (Fall 2016): 47–49.

Metro, Charlie, with Tom Altherr. *Safe by a Mile*. Lincoln: University of Nebraska Press, 2002.

Miller, James Edward. *The Baseball Business: Pursuing Pennants and Profits in Baltimore*. Chapel Hill: University of North Carolina Press, 1990.

Miller, Mark. "Harvey Haddix." https://sabr.org/bioproj/person/harvey-haddix/; accessed August 2021.

Miskowiec, Abigail. "1902: A Peace Accord." In Weingarden and Nowlin, *Baseball's Business*, vol. 1, 1901–1957.

———. "1926: Changing of the Guard." In Weingarden and Nowlin, *Baseball's Business*, vol. 1, 1901–1957.

Montgomery, Wynn. "Georgia's 1948 Phenoms and the Bonus Rule." *Baseball Research Journal* 39 (Summer 2010): 72–82.

Montville, Leigh. *The Big Bam: The Life and Times of Babe Ruth*. New York: Doubleday, 2006.

———. *Ted Williams: The Biography of an American Hero*. New York: Doubleday, 2004.

Mormino, Gary. *Immigrants on the Hill: Italian-Americans in St. Louis, 1882–1982*. Urbana and Chicago: University of Illinois Press, 1986.

Morris, J. "Bob Trice." https://sabr.org/bioproj/person/bob-trice/; accessed September 2020.

Morris, Peter. *A Game of Inches: The Game behind the Scenes: The Stories behind the Innovations That Shaped Baseball*. Chicago: Ivan R. Dee, 2006.

———. *A Game of Inches: The Game on the Field: The Stories Behind the Innovations that Shaped Baseball*. Chicago: Ivan R. Dee, 2006.

Murdock, Eugene C. *Ban Johnson: Czar of Baseball*. Westport CT: Greenwood Press, 1982.

———. *Baseball between the Wars: Memories of the Game by the Men Who Played It*. Westport CT: Meckler, 1992.

Narrative of the Life of Frederick Douglass, an American Slave. New York: Cosimo Classics, 2008. First published 1845.

Nash, George H. *The Life of Herbert Hoover*. Vol. 1, *The Engineer, 1874–1914*. New York: W. W. Norton, 1983.

Nathan, David H., ed. *The McFarland Baseball Quotations Dictionary*. Jefferson NC: McFarland, 2000.

Nathanson, Mitchell. *The Fall of the 1977 Phillies: How a Baseball Team's Collapse Sank a City's Spirit*. Jefferson NC: McFarland, 2008.

Nechal, Jerry. "1946: Tranquility and Turbulence." In Weingarden and Nowlin, *Baseball's Business*, vol. 1, 1901–1957.

Neft, David S., Richard M. Cohen, and Michael L. Neft. *The Sports Encyclopedia: Baseball 2007*. New York: St. Martin's Press, 2007.

Nelson, Kevin. *The Golden Game: The Story of California Baseball*. San Francisco: California Historical Society Press, 2004.

Nemec, David. *The Beer and Whiskey League: The Illustrated History of the American Association—Baseball's Renegade Major League*. Guilford CT: Lyons Press, 2004.

———. *The Great Encyclopedia of 19th-Century Major League Baseball*. New York: Donald I. Fine, 1997.

———. *The Rules of Baseball: An Anecdotal Look at the Rules of Baseball and How They Came to Be*. New York: Lyons & Burford, 1994.

Neyer, Rob. *Rob Neyer's Big Book of Baseball Legends: The Truth, the Lies, and Everything Else*. New York: Fireside Books, 2008.

Noguchi, Takuro. "'The Residue of Design': How Branch Rickey Organized the St. Louis Cardinals, 1881–1946." Senior thesis, Brown University, 2005.

Norwood, Stephen H., and Harold Brackman. "Going to Bat for Jackie Robinson: The Jewish Role in Breaking Baseball's Color Line." *Journal of Sport History* 26 (Spring 1999): 115–41.

Nowlin, Bill. "Al Benton." https://sabr.org/bioproj/person/al-benton/; accessed July 2021.

———. "Al Niemiec." https://sabr.org/bioproj/person/al-niemiec/; accessed July 2021.

———. "Bobby Doerr." https://sabr.org/bioproj/person/bobby-doerr/; accessed July 2021.

———. "Bob Neighbors." https://sabr.org/bioproj/person/bob-neighbors/; accessed August 2021.

———. "Dave Ferriss." https://sabr.org/bioproj/person/dave-ferriss/; accessed July 2021.

———. "Lou Brissie's Amazing Comeback." In Anton and Nowlin, *When Baseball Went to War*.

———. "1907: The New Cooperation—'The Manifest Desire to Elevate the Game.'" In Weingarden and Nowlin, *Baseball's Business*, vol. 1, 1901–1957.

———. "The 1945 All-Star Game—Baseball Navy World Series." In Anton and Nowlin, *When Baseball Went to War*.

———, ed. *SABR 50 at 50: The Society for American Baseball Research's Fifty Most Essential Contributions to the Game*. Lincoln: University of Nebraska Press, 2020.

———. "Sam Jethroe." https://sabr.org/bioproj/person/sam-jethroe/; accessed August 2021.

———. *Tom Yawkey: Patriarch of the Boston Red Sox*. Lincoln: University of Nebraska Press, 2018.

———. "Yogi Berra and the D-Day Invasion." In Anton and Nowlin, *When Baseball Went to War*.

Obermeyer, Jeff. "Disposable Heroes: Returning World War II Veteran Al Niemiec Takes on Organized Baseball." https://sabr.org/journal/article/disposable-heroes-returning-world-war-ii-veteran-al-niemiec-takes-on-organized-baseball/; accessed July 2021.

O'Connor, Leslie. *Baseball/Official Baseball*. New York: Office of the Commissioner of Baseball/A. S. Barnes, 1943, 1945–46.

Odenkirk, James E. *Frank J. Lausche: Ohio's Great Political Maverick*. Wilmington OH: Orange Frazer Press, 2005.

———. *Of Tribes and Tribulations: The Early Decades of the Cleveland Indians*. Jefferson NC: McFarland, 2015.

Odzer, Tim. "Rube Foster." https://sabr.org/bioproj/person/andrew-rube-foster/; accessed August 2021.

Official Baseball Rules. Published as detachable booklets in the Spalding, Reach, Spalding-Reach, and *Sporting News* Guides.

Okkonen, Marc. *Baseball Uniforms of the 20th Century: The Official Major League Baseball Guide*. New York: Sterling, 1991.

Okkonen, Marc, and David Jones. "Francis J. Navin." In Jones, *Deadball Stars of the American League*.

Olson, Gary. "Minnesota Twins Team Ownership History." https://sabr.org/bioproj/topic/minnesota-twins-team-ownership-history/; accessed August 2021.

O'Neal, Bill. *The American Association: A Baseball History, 1902–1991*. Austin TX: Eakin Press, 1991.

———. *The International League: A Baseball History, 1884–1991*. Austin TX: Eakin Press, 1992.

———. *The Pacific Coast League, 1903–1988*. Austin TX: Eakin Press, 1990.

———. *The Southern League: Baseball in Dixie, 1885–1994*. Austin TX: Eakin Press, 1994.

Oshinsky, David M. *Polio: An American Story*. New York: Oxford University Press, 2006.

Pajot, Dennis. "1908: Major Issues in the Minors, Bribery Charges and World Series Ticket Scandal." In Weingarden and Nowlin, *Baseball's Business*, vol. 1, 1901–1957.

Pajot, Dennis, and Greg Erion. "St. Louis Browns Team Ownership History." https://sabr.org/bioproj/topic/st-louis-browns-team-ownership-history/; accessed August 2021.

Palmer, Pete, and Gary Gillette, eds. *The Baseball Encyclopedia*. New York: Barnes & Noble Books, 2004.

Pappas, Doug. "The MacPhail Report of 1946." *Outside the Lines*, Summer 1996.

Parker, Dan. "The World of Sports." In *While You Were Gone: A Report on Wartime Life in the United States*, edited by Jack Goodman, 290–310. New York: Simon and Schuster, 1946.

Parker, William Howard, Jr. *We Called Ourselves Rocketboatmen: The Untold Story of the Top-Secret LCS(S) Rocket Boat Missions of World War II at Sicily, Normandy (Omaha and Utah Beaches), and Southern France*. Pittsburgh: Dorrance Publishing, 2008.

Patterson, James T. *Grand Expectations: The United States, 1945–1974*. New York: Oxford University Press, 1996.

Paxton, Harry T. "The Philadelphia A's Last Stand." *Saturday Evening Post*, June 12, 1954.

Perrett, Geoffrey. *Days of Sadness, Years of Triumph: The American People, 1939–1945*. New York: Coward, McCann & Geoghegan, 1973.

Pessah, Jon. *Yogi: A Life behind the Mask*. New York: Little, Brown, 2020.

Peterson, John E. *The Kansas City Athletics: A Baseball History, 1955–1967*. Jefferson NC: McFarland, 2003.

Peterson, Richard F. "Pittsburgh Pirates." In Riess, *Encyclopedia of Major League Baseball Clubs*, vol. 1, *The National League*.

———. "'Slide, Kelly, Slide': The Irish in American Baseball." In Baldassaro and Johnson, *The American Game*.

Pierman, Carol J. "The All-American Girls Professional Baseball League: Accomplishing Great Things in a Dangerous World." In *Baseball and American Culture: Across the Diamond*, edited by Edward J. Rielly, 97–108. New York: Haworth Press, 2003.

Pietrusza, David. *Judge and Jury: The Life and Times of Judge Kenesaw Mountain Landis*. South Bend IN: Diamond Communications, 1998.

———. *Lights On! The Wild Century-Long Saga of Night Baseball*. Lanham MD: Scarecrow Press, 1997.

———. *Major Leagues: The Formation, Sometimes Absorption, and Mostly Inevitable Demise of Eighteen Professional Baseball Leagues*. Jefferson NC: McFarland, 1991.

Pietrusza, David, Matthew Silverman, and Michael Gershman, eds. *Baseball: The Biographical Encyclopedia*. Kingston NY: Total Sports Illustrated, 2000.

Polenberg, Richard. *War and Society: The United States, 1941–1945*. Philadelphia: J. B. Lippincott, 1972.

Pollock, Alan J. *Barnstorming to Heaven: Syd Pollock and His Great Black Teams*. Edited by James A. Riley. Tuscaloosa: University of Alabama Press, 2006.

Polner, Murray. *Branch Rickey: A Biography*. New York: Atheneum, 1982.

Pomrenke, Jacob. "1918: Baseball Returns from the Great War." In Weingarden and Nowlin, *Baseball's Business*, vol. 1, *1901–1957*.

———, ed. *Scandal on the South Side: The 1919 Chicago White Sox*. Phoenix: Society for American Baseball Research, 2015.
Prager, Joshua. *The Echoing Green: The Untold Story of Bobby Thomson, Ralph Branca, and the Shot Heard Round the World*. New York: Pantheon, 2006.
Rabinowitz, Bill. "Baseball and the Great Depression." *Baseball History* 1 (1989): 49–59.
Rader, Benjamin. *Baseball: A History of America's Game*. 3rd ed. Urbana and Chicago: University of Illinois Press, 1994.
Radford, Rich. "Navy World Series: In World War II, Norfolk Hosted Baseball's Best." *Virginian-Pilot*, July 23, 2011. https://www.pilotonline.com/sports/article_2add0ead-8422-5467-bfc7-cbafc2fdbc12.html.
Rampersad, Arnold. *Jackie Robinson: A Biography*. New York: Alfred A. Knopf, 1997.
Rapoport, Ron. *Let's Play Two: The Legend of Mr. Cub, The Life of Ernie Banks*. New York: Hachette, 2020.
Ray, James Lincoln. "Mickey Mantle." https://sabr.org/bioproj/person/mickey-mantle/; accessed August 2021.
The Reach Official American League Baseball Guide/Reach's Official American League Baseball Guide. Philadelphia: A. J. Reach, 1900–27; Philadelphia: A. J. Reach, Wright and Ditson, 1928–34; New York: American Sports Publishing, 1935–39.
Reaves, Joseph A. *Taking in a Game: A History of Baseball in Asia*. Lincoln: University of Nebraska Press, 2002.
Regalado, Samuel O., and Sarah K. Fields, eds. *Sport and the Law: Historical and Cultural Intersections*. Fayetteville: University of Arkansas Press, 2014.
Reisler, Jim, ed. *Guys, Dolls, and Curveballs: Damon Runyon on Baseball*. New York: Carroll & Graf, 2005.
Rhodes, Greg, and John Snyder. *Redleg Journal: Year by Year and Day by Day with the Cincinnati Reds since 1866*. Cincinnati: Road West, 2000.
Rice, Stephen V. "John Heydler." https://sabr.org/bioproj/person/john-heydler/; accessed August 2021.
Riess, Steven A. "Detroit Tigers." In Riess, *Encyclopedia of Major League Baseball Clubs*, vol. 2, *The American League*.
———, ed. *Encyclopedia of Major League Baseball Clubs*. 2 vols. Westport CT: Greenwood Press, 2006.
———. "From Pike to Green with Greenberg in Between: Jewish Americans and the National Pastime." In Baldassaro and Johnson, *The American Game*.
———. "Professional Sunday Baseball: A Study in Social Reform, 1892–1934." *Maryland Historian* 4 (1973): 95–108.
Ritter, Lawrence S. *The Glory of Their Times: The Story of the Early Days of Baseball Told by the Men Who Played It*. New enl. ed. New York: William Morrow, 1984.
Roberts, Robin, and C. Paul Rogers III. *The Whiz Kids and the 1950 Pennant*. Philadelphia: Temple University Press, 1996.
Roberts, Robin, with C. Paul Rogers III. *Throwing Hard Easy: Reflections on a Life in Baseball*. Lincoln: University of Nebraska Press, 2014.
Robinson, Ray. *The Home Run Heard 'Round the World*. New York: HarperCollins, 1991.

Robinson, Ray, and Christopher Jennison. *Yankee Stadium: 75 Years of Drama, Glamor, and Glory*. New York: Penguin Studio, 1998.

Rogers, C. Paul, III. "Bob Feller." https://sabr.org/bioproj/person/bob-feller/; accessed August 2021.

———. "Hugh Mulcahy." https://sabr.org/bioproj/person/hugh-mulcahy/; accessed August 2021.

———. "Red Corriden." https://sabr.org/bioproj/person/red-corriden/; accessed August 2021.

Rogers, George C., Jr. *The History of Georgetown County, South Carolina*. Columbia: University of South Carolina Press, 1970.

Roosevelt, Franklin D. "Letter on Baseball, Sports, and Sportsmanship." January 23, 1937. Online by Gerhard Peters and John T. Woolley, The American Presidency Project, https://www.presidency.ucsb.edu/documents/letter-baseball-sports-and-sportsmanship; accessed July 2021.

———. "State of the Union Address." Online by Gerhard Peters and John T. Woolley, The American Presidency Project, https://www.presidency.ucsb.edu/documents/state-of-the-union-address; accessed July 2018.

Rosengren, John. *Hank Greenberg: The Hero of Heroes*. New York: New American Library, 2013.

Rossi, John P. "Philadelphia Phillies." In Riess, *Encyclopedia of Major League Baseball Clubs*, vol. 1, *The National League*.

Roy, Louis E. *History of East Brookfield, Massachusetts, 1686–1970*. Worcester MA: Heffernan Press, 1970.

Rucker, Mark, and Peter C. Bjarkman. *Smoke: The Romance and Lore of Cuban Baseball*. Kingston NY: Total Sports Illustrated, 1999.

Saccoman, John. "Willie Mays." https://sabr.org/bioproj/person/willie-mays/; accessed August 2021.

Sarnoff, Gary. "Monty Stratton." https://sabr.org/bioproj/person/monty-stratton/; accessed August 2021.

———. "The San Diego Padre Who Batted for Ted Williams and Integrated the PCL." *National Pastime: Pacific Ghosts*, 2019, 40–43.

Schaefer, Robert H. "Lip Pike." https://sabr.org/bioproj/person/lip-pike/; accessed July 2021.

Schneider, Russell. *The Cleveland Indians Encyclopedia*. Philadelphia: Temple University Press, 1996.

"School Enrollment, by Age, Race, and Sex, 1953 to 1970, and by Age and Sex, 1940 to 1972," Series H 442–76, and "Institutions of Higher Learning, Degrees Conferred, by Ex, 1870 to 1970," Series H 751–65. In *Historical Statistics of the United States, Colonial Times to 1970*, Bicentennial edition, part 1, by U.S. Department of Commerce, Bureau of the Census. Washington DC: Government Printing Office, 1975.

Schuld, Fred. "Charles W. Somers." In Jones, *Deadball Stars of the American League*.

Seidel, Michael. *Ted Williams: A Baseball Life*. Chicago: Contemporary Books, 1991.

Selko, Jamie. *Minor League All-Star Teams, 1922–1962*. Jefferson NC: McFarland, 2007.

Seymour, Harold [and Dorothy Seymour Mills]. *The Early Years*. Vol. 1 of *Baseball*. New York: Oxford University Press, 1989. First published 1960.

———. *The Golden Age*. Vol. 2 of *Baseball*. New York: Oxford University Press, 1989. First published 1971.

———. *The People's Game*. Vol. 3 of *Baseball*. New York: Oxford University Press, 1991. First published 1990.

Shapiro, Michael. *Bottom of the Ninth: Branch Rickey, Casey Stengel, and the Daring Scheme to Save Baseball from Itself*. New York: Holt, 2010.

Sharp, Andrew. "Washington Senators I Team Ownership History." https://sabr.org/bioproj/topic/washington-senators-i-team-ownership-history/; accessed August 2021.

Shea, Stuart, with George Castle, *Wrigley Field: The Unauthorized Biography*. Washington DC: Brassey's, 2006.

Shepard, Bert, as told to Todd Anton. "Lt. Bert Shepard: From Terrorflieger to Major League Pitcher." In Anton and Nowlin, *When Baseball Went to War*.

Sher, Jack. "Larry MacPhail, the Man and the Mouth." *Sport*, July 1947.

Sherman, Ed. *Babe Ruth's Called Shot: The Myth and Mystery of Baseball's Greatest Home Run*. Guilford CT: Lyons Press, 2014.

Sickels, John. *Bob Feller: Ace of the Greatest Generation*. Dulles VA: Brassey's, 2004.

Simon, Tom, ed. *Deadball Stars of the National League*. Washington DC: Brassey's, 2004.

———, ed. *Green Mountain Boys of Summer: Vermonters in the Major Leagues, 1882–1993*. Shelburne VT: New England Press, 2000.

Simons, Herbert. "Twenty-Four Years with the Judge." *Baseball Magazine*, March 1945.

Skipper, Doug. "Connie Mack." https://sabr.org/bioproj/person/connie-mack/; accessed August 2021.

Smelser, Marshall. *The Life That Ruth Built: A Biography*. New York: Quadrangle, 1975.

Smith, Curt. *The Voice: Mel Allen's Untold Story*. Guilford CT: Lyons Press, 2007.

———. *Voices of Summer: Ranking Baseball's 101 All-Time Best Announcers*. New York: Carroll & Graf, 2005.

———. *Voices of the Game: The Acclaimed Chronicle of Baseball Radio and Television Broadcasting—From 1921 to the Present*. Updated ed. New York: Simon and Schuster, 1992. First published 1987.

Smith, Richard Norton. *An Uncommon Man: The Triumph of Herbert Hoover*. New York: Simon and Schuster, 1984.

Snyder, John. *Cardinals Journal: Year by Year and Day by Day with the St. Louis Cardinals since 1882*. Cincinnati: Emmis Books, 2006.

Solomon, Burt. *The Baseball Timeline*. New York: DK Publishing, 2001.

Spalding-Reach Official Baseball Guide. New York: American Sports Publishing, 1940–41.

Spalding's Official Baseball Guide. New York: A. G. Spalding & Bros., 1877–1906; New York: American Sports Publishing, 1907–39.
Spink, Alfred H. *The National Game*. 2nd ed. Carbondale and Edwardsville: Southern Illinois University Press, 2000. First published 1911.
Spink, J. G. Taylor. *Judge Landis and Twenty-Five Years of Baseball*. New York: Crowell, 1947.
Sporting News Baseball Guide. St. Louis: Charles C. Spink & Son, 1942–66; St. Louis: *Sporting News*, 1967–2006.
Stahl, John. "Gussie Busch." https://sabr.org/bioproj/person/gussie-busch/; accessed August 2021.
Steele, Andrew. "Philip Wrigley." https://sabr.org/bioproj/person/philip-wrigley/; accessed July 2021.
Stein, Fred. "Al Simmons." https://sabr.org/bioproj/person/al-simmons/; accessed June 2021.
Stevens, David. "Atlanta Braves." In Riess, *Encyclopedia of Major League Baseball Clubs*, vol. 1, *The National League*.
Stewart, Mark. "Chuck Dressen." https://sabr.org/bioproj/person/chuck-dressen/; accessed August 2021.
———. "Minnie Miñoso." https://sabr.org/bioproj/person/minnie-minoso/; accessed September 2020.
St. John, Adela Rogers. *Final Verdict*. Garden City NY: Doubleday, 1962.
Stockton, J. Roy. *The Gashouse Gang and a Couple of Other Guys*. New York: A. S. Barnes, 1945.
———. "Singing Sam, the Cut-Rate Man." *Saturday Evening Post*, February 22, 1947.
Stout, Glenn. *The Cubs: The Complete Story of Chicago Cubs Baseball*. Boston: Houghton Mifflin, 2007.
———. "Tryout and Fallout: Race, Jackie Robinson, and the Red Sox." *Massachusetts Historical Review* 6 (2004): 11–37.
———. *Yankees Century: 100 Years of New York Yankees Baseball*. Boston: Houghton Mifflin, 2002.
Stout, Glenn, and Richard Johnson. *Red Sox Century: The Definitive History*. Rev. and exp. ed. Boston: Houghton Mifflin, 2005. First published 2000.
Strunk, Mildred. "The Quarter's Polls." *Public Opinion Quarterly* 13 (Fall 1949): 548–49.
Suchma, Philip C. "Cleveland Indians." In Riess, *Encyclopedia of Major League Baseball Clubs*, vol. 2, *The American League*.
Sullivan, Dean A., comp. and ed. *Early Innings: A Documentary History of Baseball, 1825–1908*. Lincoln: University of Nebraska Press, 1997. First published 1995.
———, comp. and ed. *Late Innings: A Documentary History of Baseball, 1945–1972*. Lincoln: University of Nebraska Press, 2002.
Sullivan, Neil J. *The Dodgers Move West*. New York: Oxford University Press, 1989.
———. *The Minors: The Struggles and the Triumph of Baseball's Poor Relation from 1876 to the Present*. New York: St. Martin's Press, 1990.

Sumner, Jim L. "William G. Bramham: The Czar of Minor League Baseball." *Carolina Comments* 37 (1989): 116–22.

Surdam, David George. *Wins, Losses, and Empty Seats: How Baseball Outlasted the Great Depression*. Lincoln: University of Nebraska Press, 2011.

Sussman, Ely. "1932: Wealth of Changes Revitalizes Baseball in Poor Times." In Weingarden and Nowlin, *Baseball's Business*, vol. 1, 1901–1957.

———. "1935: Inspirational Delegates Churn Cream into Butter." In Weingarden and Nowlin, *Baseball's Business*, vol. 1, 1901–1957.

Swaine, Rick. *The Black Stars Who Made Baseball Whole: The Jackie Robinson Generation in the Major Leagues, 1947–1959*. Jefferson NC: McFarland, 2006.

———. "Hank Thompson." https://sabr.org/bioproj/person/hank-thompson/; accessed September 2020.

———. "Roy Campanella." https://sabr.org/bioproj/person/roy-campanella/; accessed September 2020.

Swanson, Ryan. *When Baseball Went White: Reconstruction, Reconciliation, and Dreams of a National Pastime*. Lincoln: University of Nebraska Press, 2014.

Tan, Cecilia. "Elston Howard." https://sabr.org/bioproj/person/elston-howard/; accessed September 2020.

Taylor, Dan. "Jay Porter." https://sabr.org/bioproj/person/jay-porter/; accessed August 2021.

———. "Paul Pettit." https://sabr.org/bioproj/person/paul-pettit/; accessed August 2021.

Terkel, Studs. *"The Good War": An Oral History of World War Two*. New York: Pantheon Books, 1984.

Terrell, Roy. "3rd League Cities Pin Hopes on This Man." *Sports Illustrated*, July 20, 1959.

Thomas, Joan M. "Frank DeHass Robison and Matthew Stanley Robison." In Ivor-Campbell, *Baseball's First Stars*.

Thorn, John. *Baseball in the Garden of Eden: The Secret History of the Early Game*. New York: Simon and Schuster, 2011.

Thorn, John, and Pete Palmer, with David Reuther. *Total Baseball*. New York: Warner Books, 1989.

Thorn, John, Pete Palmer, Michael Gershman, and David Pietrusza. *Total Baseball*. 6th ed. New York: Total Sports, 1999.

Thorn, John, Pete Palmer, and Michael Gershman, with Matthew Silverman, Sean Lahman, and Greg Spira. *Total Baseball*. 7th ed. New York: Total Sports, 2001.

Thornley, Stew. *Baseball in Minnesota: The Definitive History*. St. Paul: Minnesota Historical Society Press, 2006.

Tiemann, Robert L., and Pete Palmer. "Major League Attendance." In Thorn, Palmer, Gershman, and Pietrusza, *Total Baseball*, 6th ed.

Treder, Steven. "Cash in the Cradle: The Bonus Babies." *Hardball Times*, November 1, 2004.

———. *Forty Years a Giant: The Life of Horace Stoneham*. Lincoln: University of Nebraska Press, 2021.

———. "Open Classification: The Pacific Coast League's Drive to Turn Major." NINE: *A Journal of Baseball History and Culture* 15 (Fall 2006): 88–109.

Trimble, Joe. *Yogi Berra*. Rev. ed. New York: Grosset & Dunlap, 1965. First published 1952.

Turner, Frederick. *When the Boys Came Back: Baseball and 1946*. New York: Henry Holt, 1996.

Tygiel, Jules. *Baseball's Great Experiment: Jackie Robinson and His Legacy*. New York: Oxford University Press, 1983.

———. *Extra Bases: Reflections on Jackie Robinson, Race, and Baseball History*. Lincoln: University of Nebraska Press, 2002.

———. "Revisiting Bill Veeck and the 1943 Phillies." *Baseball Research Journal* 35 (2007): 109–14.

Ulrey, Adam. "Jack Graney." https://sabr.org/bioproj/person/jack-graney/; accessed July 2021.

Urban, Richard. "Boudreau Stood Out as a Player and Manager." ESPN, August 20, 2001. http://www.espn.com/classic/obit/s/2001/0810/1237896.html.

Vaughn, Gerald F. "Jorge Pasquel and the Evolution of the Mexican League." *National Pastime: A Review of Baseball History* 12 (1992): 9–13.

Veeck, Bill, with Ed Linn. *Veeck as in Wreck: The Autobiography of Bill Veeck*. Chicago: University of Chicago Press, 2001. First published 1962.

Vincent, David, Lyle Spatz, and David W. Smith. *The Midsummer Classic: The Complete History of Baseball's All-Star Game*. Lincoln: University of Nebraska Press, 2001.

Virtue, John. *South of the Color Barrier: How Jorge Pasquel and the Mexican League Pushed Baseball toward Racial Integration*. Jefferson NC: McFarland, 2008.

Vlasich, James A. *A Legend for the Legendary: The Origin of the Baseball Hall of Fame*. Bowling Green OH: Bowling Green State University Popular Press, 1990.

Voigt, David Quentin. *American Baseball*. Vol. 2, *From the Commissioners to Continental Expansion*. University Park: Pennsylvania State University Press, 1983. First published 1970.

Voiss, Dale. "1955: Majors and Minors Clash over Money." In Weingarden and Nowlin, *Baseball's Business*, vol. 1, 1901–1957.

Waddell, Nick, and Bill Nowlin. "1940: Landis' Final Reign." In Weingarden and Nowlin, *Baseball's Business*, vol. 1, 1901–1957.

Walker, Ben. "Landis' Name Pulled off Baseball MVP Plaques after 75 Years." AP News, October 3, 2020. https://apnews.com/article/race-and-ethnicity-mlb-baseball-archive-4da2c519ad279e817c0a2518f705be45.

———. "MLB Stars Say It's Time to Pull Landis Name off MVP Plaques." AP News, June 30, 2020. https://apnews.com/article/57b022c3497967230fa768819fd0e153.

Walker, James R. "The Baseball-Radio War, 1931–1935." NINE: *A Journal of Baseball History and Culture* 19 (Spring 2011): 53–60.

———. *Crack of the Bat: A History of Baseball on the Radio*. Lincoln: University of Nebraska Press, 2015.

Walker, James R., and Robert V. Bellamy Jr. *Center Field Shot: A History of Baseball on Television*. Lincoln: University of Nebraska Press, 2008.

Walsh, John Evangelist. "Babe Ruth and the Legend of the Called Shot." *Wisconsin Magazine of History* 77 (Spring 1994): 242–63.

Wancho, Joseph. "Harmon Killebrew." https://sabr.org/bioproj/person/harmon-killebrew/; accessed August 2021.

Warfield, Don. *The Roaring Redhead: Larry MacPhail—Baseball's Great Innovator*. South Bend IN: Diamond Communications, 1987.

Warrington, Robert D. "Departure without Dignity." *Baseball Research Journal* 39 (Fall 2010): 95–115.

Watkins, John J. "Dave Hoskins." https://sabr.org/bioproj/person/dave-hoskins/; accessed September 2020.

Weatherby, Charlie. "Danny Gardella." https://sabr.org/bioproj/person/danny-gardella/; accessed July 2021.

Weingarden, Steve, and Bill Nowlin, eds. *Baseball's Business: The Winter Meetings*. 2 vols. Phoenix: Society for American Baseball Research, 2016, 2017.

Weintraub, Robert. *The Victory Season: The End of World War II and the Birth of Baseball's Golden Age*. New York: Little, Brown, 2013.

Weisberger, Bernard A. *When Chicago Ruled Baseball: The Cubs–White Sox World Series of 1906*. New York: William Morrow, 2006.

Weiss, Bill, and Marshall Wright. *The 100 Greatest Minor League Baseball Teams of the 20th Century*. Parker CO: Outskirts Press, 2006.

Weiss, George M., with Robert Shaplen. "The Man of Silence Speaks," part 2, "The Best Decision I Ever Made." *Sports Illustrated*, March 13, 1961.

Weiss, William J. "The First Negro in 20th Century O.B." *Baseball Research Journal* 8 (1979): 31–35.

Wells, Donald R. *Baseball's Western Front: The Pacific Coast League during World War II*. Jefferson NC: McFarland, 2004.

Westcott, Rich. "Philadelphia Phillies Team Ownership History." https://sabr.org/research/philadelphia-phillies-team-ownership-history; accessed August 2021.

White, G. Edward. *Creating the National Pastime: Baseball Transforms Itself, 1903–1953*. Princeton NJ: Princeton University Press, 1996.

Wilbert, Warren N., and William C. Hageman. *The 1917 White Sox: Their Championship Season*. Jefferson NC: McFarland, 2004.

Wild, Matt. "Remembering the Time County Stadium Banned Carry-Ins and Everybody Got Pissed." *Milwaukee Record*, March 8, 2017. https://milwaukeerecord.com/sports/remembering-milwaukee-county-stadium-banned-carry-ins-everyone-got-pissed/.

Williams, Dave. "Yogi Berra." https://sabr.org/bioproj/person/yogi-berra/; accessed August 2021.

Williams, T. Harry. *Huey Long*. New York: Alfred A. Knopf, 1969.

Wolf, Gregory H. "1952: Changing Demographics and Broadcast Challenges." In Weingarden and Nowlin, *Baseball's Business*, vol. 1, 1901–1957.

Wolf, Thomas. *The Called Shot: Babe Ruth, the Chicago Cubs, and the Unforgettable Major League Baseball Season of 1932*. Lincoln: University of Nebraska Press, 2020.

Wolfe, Thomas. *The Web and the Rock*. New York: Harper & Brothers, 1939.

Wong, John. "FDR and the New Deal on Sport and Recreation." *Sport History Review* 29 (November 1998): 173–91.

Wright, Marshall D. *The American Association: Year-by-Year Statistics for the Baseball Minor League, 1902–1952*. Jefferson NC: McFarland, 1997.

———. *The International League: Year-by-Year Statistics, 1884–1953*. Jefferson NC: McFarland, 1998.

———. *The South Atlantic League, 1904–1963*. Jefferson NC: McFarland, 2009.

———. *The Southern Association in Baseball, 1885–1961*. Jefferson NC: McFarland, 2002.

———. *The Texas League in Baseball, 1888–1958*. Jefferson NC: McFarland, 2004.

Wrigley, William, Jr., as told to Forrest Crissey. "Owning a Big-League Ball Team." *Saturday Evening Post*, September 13, 1930.

Yardley, Jonathan. *Ring: A Biography of Ring Lardner*. New York: Atheneum, 1984. First published 1977.

Zingg, Paul J. *Harry Hooper: An American Baseball Life*. Urbana: University of Illinois Press, 1993.

Zingg, Paul J., and Mark D. Medeiros. *Runs, Hits, and an Era: The Pacific Coast League, 1903–58*. Urbana and Chicago: University of Illinois Press, 1994.

Index

Aaron, Henry: early life of, 407–8; as Major League player, 363, 409–10, 431, 443, 450, 464; as Minor League player, 364, 408–9; as Negro League player, 407–8; racism and, 364, 407–9; retirement and death of, 464
ABC (American Broadcasting Company), 397, 400, 404–5
Adams, Charles, 341, 381–82
advertising sponsors: Atlantic Refining, 49; Bulova Watch Company, 346; Coca-Cola, 49, 174, 434; Ford Motor Company, 214, 345; General Mills, 49, 176, 215, 216, 246, 348; Gillette Safety Razor Company, 214, 251, 305, 345, 347, 375, 398–400, 463; Goodrich, 49; Ivory Soap, 49–50, 346, 348; Kellogg's, 49; Liebmann Breweries, 345; Mobil Oil, 217, 346; Prima, 49, 213; Procter & Gamble, 49, 216; Socony-Vacuum, 49, 216; Wheaties, 49, 176, 346
African American players, 103, 199–200, 288–91, 297, 298, 317, 357–64. *See also* Black baseball players
airplane travel, 186, 308–9, 351, 416, 426
Alexander, Charles, 182, 427
All-American Girls' Baseball League (AAGBBL), 270–72
Allen, Lee, 15, 29, 75, 198
Allen, Mel, 345, 347–49, 375, 462–63
All-Star Game: (1933), 210–11; (1934), 211–12; (1935), 212; (1936), 212; (1937), 88, 164, 190, 207–8, 212; (1940), 212; (1941), 229; (1942), 232, 238–39, 267; (1943), 264–65; (1944), 250–51; (1945), 250–51, 261, 265; (1946), 304, 309, 310; (1948), 399; (1952), 403; (1953), 306; (1958), 448; American League success and, 212, 602; Hank Aaron in, 431; origins of, 208–11; radio and, 213–15; second, 234, 446; selection of players for, 209, 210, 212, 445; Ted Williams in, 310; television and, 399, 401, 445; World War II and, 232–34, 267
Almada Quirós, Baldomero "Mel," 297–98, 364
American Association (Major League): demise of, 6, 11, 196; National Agreement and, 5–6; night baseball and, 165; in "World Championship Series," 96
American Association (Minor League): classification of, 13–14, 16, 126–27, 180, 328; expansion and, 441–42; farm systems and, 108, 139, 433; George Trautman as president of, 330; Great Depression and, 171, 174; Great War and, 127; as an independent league, 9; integration and, 363; Minor League draft and, 99, 101, 102, 413; night baseball and, 169; playoffs and, 74–75, 170, 281, 357, 402–3; postwar attendance in, 331; salary limits and, 113; television and, 402; World War II and, 234–35, 257
American Baseball Guild, 294–96, 301, 303, 305, 353, 371

American League: baseball used by, 37, 51, 52, 56, 247; becomes a Major League, 7–8; expansion and, 447–49, 452–54; farm systems and, 108–9, 184; Federal League and, 16–17, 93–95; franchise relocations in, 8, 10, 12, 221, 421, 422, 431; integration and, 361–63; night baseball and, 165, 236–37, 307; owners divide over actions of Ban Johnson, 21–25; radio and, 48–49; settles dispute with National League, 12, 15; Sunday baseball and, 196–97; television and, 421; Western League transformed into, 7, 12, 37, 195. *See also* Barnard, Ernest Sargent; Cronin, Joe; Harridge, Will; Johnson, Ban
Anglo American players. *See* English American players
annual meetings. *See* winter meetings
antitrust regulation, baseball and: Congress and, 368–69, 371–75, 438, 446–47, 449; Federal League and, 367; Mexican League and, 391–93, 396; television and, 400, 403, 404
Appel, Marty, 458
Armour, Mark L., 282, 445
Arnovich, Morrie, 228, 308
Atlanta Braves, 464. *See also* Boston Braves; Milwaukee Braves
attendance, Major League, 8, 32, 50, 53, 450; Great Depression and, 42, 57, 58, 77, 83; Great War and, 18, 19, 110; postwar seasons and, 317–18, 343, 351, 352, 385, 412; radio and, 48, 49; television and, 349, 385, 396, 401, 412; World War II and, 232, 239, 276, 305. *See also specific clubs*
attendance, Minor League, 79, 110, 159, 160, 174, 316, 432; Great Depression and, 111, 116, 170, 181; Great War and, 17; night baseball and, 166–68; postwar seasons and, 328, 329, 331, 405, 406, 415–16; radio and, 372; World War II and, 247, 248
Auker, Elden, 85, 86, 223–24
Autry, Gene, 454
Averill, Earl, 55, 210, 212
awards. *See specific awards*

Baker, William, 26, 33
Baker Bowl, 33
Baldassaro, Lawrence, 199
balk rule, 332, 334–35, 382
ball, manufacture of, 41–42, 50–53, 56, 71, 246–47, 333, 389
Ball, Phil, 26, 29, 48, 64, 68, 95, 182, 222, 342
ballparks. *See specific ballparks*
Baltimore Orioles (1901–2), 8, 12, 221, 431. *See also* New York Yankees
Baltimore Orioles (1954–), 351, 352, 371, 404, 407, 422, 426, 432, 439, 444, 446. *See also* St. Louis Browns
Banks, Ernie, 362, 363, 450
Barber, Walter Lanier "Red": Brooklyn Dodgers and, 49, 216, 236, 258, 347, 375; Cincinnati Reds and, 186–87; early career of, 347; New York Yankees and, 462–63; retirement and death of, 463; television and, 346, 375; World Series and, 215, 217, 345–49, 375
Barnard, Ernest Sargent: as characterized by others, 1–2, 29, 455; as Cleveland Indians executive, 11, 19–21, 27–28, 68, 157; death and funeral of, 1–2, 28–29; early life of, 2–4; as journalist, 9, 11; as Minor League executive, 3–4, 8–9; as president of American League, 1–2, 27–28, 48, 52, 102, 114, 223
Barnes, Donald Lee (Don), 221–23, 234, 237, 242, 252, 261, 342, 460
barnstorming, 102–6, 110, 147, 152, 358
Barrow, Edward Grant (Ed): family and

early life of, 122–23; farm system and, 145–46; Jacob Ruppert's death and, 153; Joe McCarthy and, 148–49; as manager of Boston Red Sox, 127, 130–31, 133, 134; as manager of Detroit Tigers, 125–26; in Minor League baseball, 123–25; as New York Yankees executive, 134–36, 138–42, 144–45, 151, 259, 343; night baseball and, 235, 238; as president of Eastern League, 126–27; retirement and death of, 458; World War II and, 227, 232, 234, 241
Baseball Hall of Fame. *See* Hall of Fame
Bat and Ball Fund: Great War and, 18; World War II and, 232, 234, 239, 250, 265, 266–67, 309
batting helmets, 382, 390
BBWAA (Baseball Writers' Association of America): annual dinners of, 234, 266, 289, 441; awards and, 43, 71, 251, 360, 458; Black Sox scandal and, 24–25; Hall of Fame and, 381, 456, 459; preseason predictions of, 229, 444; radio and, 47
Bellamy, Robert V., Jr., 396–97, 400, 412–13
Benswanger, Bill, 289, 295–96
Berg, Moe, 202–4
Berra, Lawrence Peter "Yogi": family and early life of, 162, 254–56, 311; as Major League player, 451; as Minor League player, 256, 280–81; in the navy, 253, 256–57, 275; retirement and death of, 460–61
Black baseball clubs: Chicago American Giants, 358; Chicago Union Giants, 358; Cleveland Buckeyes, 391; Cuban Giants, 357–58; Homestead (PA) Grays, 358; Indianapolis Clowns, 366, 407; Kansas City Monarchs, 268, 361; Leland Giants, 358; Leland's Union Giants, 358; Newark Eagles, 361; Pittsburgh Crawfords, 358; Pythian Base Ball Club of Philadelphia, 199; Washington Elite Giants, 164
Black baseball entrepreneurs: Cum Posey, 358; Effa Manley, 361, 365; Frank Leland, 358; Gus Greenlee, 358, 365; Rube Foster, 28, 358; Sy Pollock, 366, 408
Black baseball players: Chet Brewer, 298; Connie Morgan, 366; Cool Papa Bell, 298; Cristóbal Torriente, 365; Dave Barnhill, 289; George Stovey, 200; José Méndez, 365; Josh Gibson, 298; Leon Day, 269; Mamie Johnson, 366; Martin Dihigo, 297, 365; Marvin Williams, 290; Moses Fleetwood Walker, 103, 200; Nat Peeples, 363; Showboat Thomas, 290; Terris McDuffie, 290; Theolic Smith, 298; Tom Alston, 362; Toni Stone, 366; Welday Walker, 103, 200; Willard Brown, 269, 361. *See also* Aaron, Henry; Banks, Ernie; Campanella, Roy; Clemente Walker, Roberto; Doby, Larry; Irvin, Monte; Jethroe, Sam; Mays, Willie; Miñoso Arrieta, Orestes "Minnie"; Newcombe, Don; Paige, Satchel; Robinson, Jackie
Black Sox scandal, 20, 21, 25, 27, 97–98, 193, 294, 457
bonuses, signing: after second bonus rule, 337–38, 356, 388, 439; before and during World War II, 43, 80, 120, 140, 255, 256, 319–21, 394; and first bonus rule, 321–23, 325, 335, 417, 428; Mexican League and, 299–301; and second bonus rule, 335–37. *See also* high school baseball
Boston Braves: attendance of, 58, 317, 352; farm system of, 342; finances of, 381; integration and, 290, 362; night baseball and, 264; ownership

Boston Braves (*cont*)
of, 341, 416; pennant races and, 311, 417, 418; player transactions involving, 22, 151, 337, 393, 407, 428; radio and, 215; relocation of, 352, 408, 418–19, 426, 428; Sunday baseball and, 288; television and, 372, 400, 401; World Series and, 417; World War II and, 226. *See also* Atlanta Braves; Milwaukee Braves
Boston Red Sox: attendance of, 285, 317, 418; bonus players and, 320, 325; farm system of, 173, 284, 433; finances of, 282; integration and, 288–91, 360, 362, 363; night baseball and, 166, 264; ownership of, 131, 282–86, 288, 339, 461; pennant races and, 131, 134, 153, 251, 284–85, 309–10, 313, 417; player transactions involving, 20, 59, 129–30, 133, 176, 282–83, 284, 285; Sunday baseball and, 138, 288; television and, 401, 421; World Series and, 104, 130–31, 312–13; World War II and, 240–41
Bottomley, Jim, 69–71, 73, 75, 77
Boudreau, Lou, 310, 324, 344
Boxerman, Benita W., 147, 201
Boxerman, Burton A., 147, 201
Bradley, Alva, 27, 120, 243, 249–50, 261, 317, 356
Bramham, William: as attorney and politician, 113–15; as chair of National Association's executive committee, 114–15; compared to Kenesaw Landis, 113, 117–18; night baseball and, 168; as president of National Association, 115–17, 118, 120, 170, 180, 184, 231–32, 247–48, 250, 279–80, 321; as president of various Minor Leagues, 114; retirement and death of, 330
Braves Field, 342, 381, 417
Breadon, Sam: All-Star Game and, 209, 212; Branch Rickey and, 67–68, 88; early life of, 66–67; farm system and, 69–70, 183; Larry MacPhail and, 158, 160, 303; managers and, 67, 72; as owner of St. Louis Cardinals, 67, 88, 261, 300, 312; radio and, 48; Rogers Hornsby and, 71–72; and sale of St. Louis Cardinals, 342, 419; World War II and, 246, 261
Brecheen, Harry, 311, 312–13, 420
Bridges, Tommy, 85, 86, 177, 277
Briggs, Walter, Jr., 217
Briggs, Walter, Sr., 195, 207, 217–18, 338–39
Briggs Stadium, 207, 218. *See also* Navin Field
broadcasters (selected): Al Helfer, 236, 275; Arch McDonald, 348; Bill Slater, 275, 345; Bob Stanton, 345; Buddy Blattner, 400, 404; Gordon McLendon, 397–98; Harold Arlin, 45–46; Harry Hartman, 186; Jack Graney, 217; Russ Hodges, 373; Ty Tyson, 214, 216–17; Vin Scully, 375. *See also* Allen, Mel; Barber, Walter Lanier "Red"; Husing, Ted; McNamee, Graham
Brooklyn Dodgers: attendance of, 236, 427; farm system of, 107, 112–13, 145, 328, 395, 426; finances of, 216, 319; integration and, 281, 289, 356–57, 359–60; night baseball and, 235–36, 237, 239, 257, 264; ownership of, 26, 216, 227, 256, 343, 353, 375, 383, 462; pennant races and, 216, 229, 311–12, 372–73; player transactions involving, 71, 249, 417; radio and, 49–50, 216, 258, 375, 379; relocation of, 426–27, 429–30, 434; Sunday baseball and, 137–38; television and, 345–46, 349, 372, 397, 399, 401; World Series and, 21,

130, 230–31, 345–46, 348–49, 361. *See also* Los Angeles Dodgers
Brooklyn Robins. *See* Brooklyn Dodgers
Buhite, Russell, 442
Bullock, Steven, 265, 266
Burdette, Lew, 418, 431, 450
Burgos, Adrian, Jr., 364–65
Burk, Robert, 108, 182, 276
Busch, August, 337, 456–57

Campanella, Roy, 289, 359, 360, 363, 365
Candlestick Park, 433
Cannon, Robert, 307
Carpenter, Bob, Jr., 250, 341, 401, 421
Carpenter, Bob, Sr., 341
CBS (Columbia Broadcasting System): All-Star Game broadcasts and, 213, 399; Father Charles Coughlin and, 206; Red Barber and, 375; and television broadcasts of baseball, 347, 397, 399, 400, 404–5; World Series broadcasts and, 46, 214, 345
Celler, Emanuel, 367–70, 372–75, 383, 384, 438, 458
Central League, 70; farm systems and, 146; Great Depression and, 111, 112, 116; integration and, 363–64
Chandler, Albert "Happy": American Baseball Guild and, 295, 353; Celler subcommittee and, 371; as commissioner, 279–80, 305, 307, 321, 323, 324, 326, 331, 345, 347, 349, 353, 366, 392, 399, 414; early life of, 262–63; elected commissioner, 262–63, 265, 330, 352; Jackie Robinson and, 356–57, 359, 360; Leo Durocher and, 354–56, 359; Mexican League and, 302, 353, 384, 392–93; removed as commissioner, 367, 375, 384, 434; as U.S. senator, 261
Chicago Cubs: attendance of, 314, 352; farm system of, 108, 172–73, 221; finances of, 144; integration and, 35, 200, 362; night baseball and, 165, 264; ownership of, 28, 95, 96, 339; pennant races and, 84–85, 88, 273, 311, 314; player transactions involving, 72, 77; radio and, 47–48, 49, 213; television and, 346–47, 400, 401; World Series and, 33–34, 40, 96, 130–31, 148–50, 153, 206–7, 217, 272, 275
Chicago White Sox: bonus players and, 323, 335; integration and, 362; night baseball and, 237; ownership of, 7, 96, 340, 453, 460, 462; pennant races and, 29, 96–97, 133, 134, 444, 449; player transactions involving, 22, 58–59, 62, 100, 125, 203, 424; radio and, 48, 213; World Series and, 97–98, 104, 193, 433; World War II and, 226–27, 228, 257. *See also* Black Sox scandal
Chicago White Stockings (American League). *See* Chicago White Sox
Chicago White Stockings (National League). *See* Chicago Cubs
Cincinnati Reds: attendance of, 188, 317; farm system of, 7, 68, 157, 186; finances of, 53; integration and, 362; night baseball and, 165, 187, 188–89, 235, 264, 382; ownership of, 15, 157, 185, 189, 339; pennant races and, 97, 185, 229, 273, 339; player transactions involving, 7, 62, 70, 75, 77, 82, 129, 249, 337; radio and, 48, 49, 186–87, 215, 216, 347; relocation of, 435–36; television and, 346, 404; World Series and, 24, 97–98, 154, 219, 254
Clemente Walker, Roberto, 365, 444, 449, 451
Cleveland Blues. *See* Cleveland Indians
Cleveland Indians: attendance of, 237, 285, 318–19, 343, 352; farm system

Cleveland Indians (*cont*)
of, 68, 107, 119, 157, 363; finances of, 10–11; integration and, 356, 361, 365; night baseball and, 237; ownership of, 10–11, 12, 20, 27, 37, 261, 317, 344, 351–52, 419–20, 459; pennant races and, 20–21, 97, 130, 133, 134, 284–85, 309, 313, 318, 417, 459; player transactions involving, 21, 119–20, 133, 324, 442; radio and, 215, 217; relocation of, 452; Sunday baseball and, 9; television and, 398–99, 401, 404, 421; World Series and, 20, 318, 350, 387, 398–99, 428
Cleveland Naps. *See* Cleveland Indians
Cobb, Bob, 173, 413, 426
Cobb, Ty, 40, 66, 139, 147, 152, 282, 286, 370, 381
Cochrane, Mickey: Detroit Tigers and, 59, 85–87, 151, 203, 205, 217–18, 338; family and early life of, 43; Mickey Mantle named for, 388; in the navy, 240, 267–68; Philadelphia Athletics and, 39, 40, 42–44, 55, 59, 75–76, 456
college baseball, 22, 38, 43, 61, 97, 130, 140, 147, 227, 276, 279, 323–25, 336, 394
Collins, Eddie: as coach, 282–83; as general manager, 175–76, 282–85, 290–91; as player, 38, 40, 97, 323, 456
Collins, Ripper, 75, 77, 85
Columbus OH, baseball in: early, 3–4, 9, 14; under Larry MacPhail, 157–60, 181, 185–86, 330; St. Louis Cardinals farm team and, 169, 171, 173, 176
Comiskey, Charles: Ban Johnson and, 6–7, 27; Black Sox scandal and, 25, 141; death of, 29, 340; Jack Quinn dispute and, 22, 27; as manager of Cincinnati Reds, 6–7; as owner of Chicago White Sox, 7, 96–97
Comiskey, Charley (Chuck), 340, 462
Comiskey, Dorothy, 228, 340, 462
Comiskey, Grace, 340
Comiskey, Lou, 340
Comiskey Park, 110, 210, 213, 221, 358
Connie Mack Stadium, 456. *See also* Shibe Park
Continental League, 438–42, 447–49, 452, 454, 456
Cooke, Jack Kent, 437, 442, 452
County Stadium, 418, 430–31
Cox, William, 341
Crepeau, Richard, 161, 210, 231
Cronin, Joe: as American League president, 443, 447–48, 452–53, 455; as manager, 212, 283, 290, 309–10; as player, 190, 210, 211, 283, 284, 291
Crosley, Powel, Jr., 185–89, 339, 436
Crosley Field, 185–86, 189, 262, 436. *See also* Palace of the Fans; Redland Field
Cubs Park, 314. *See also* Weeghman Park; Wrigley Field (Chicago)
Cullinan, Craig, Jr., 437, 452, 454
Cy Young Memorial Award, 360, 449

Daniel, Dan: on All-Star Game, 210; on bonuses, 319–21; on Charlie Dressen, 353–54; on duration of games, 388; on Emanuel Celler, 369; on expansion, 439; on Ford Frick, 333, 376, 380, 383; on Hank Greenberg, 338–39; on Jim Brosnan, 443; on knuckleball, 390; on Larry MacPhail, 345; on new baseball (1931), 52; on New Deal, 162; on New York Yankees, 121; on player salaries, 392, 439; preseason predictions of, 250–51, 307–8; World War II and, 229, 276
Dean, Dizzy: as broadcaster, 258, 400, 404, 420; early life of, 77–78; as Major League player, 79, 83–85, 86, 88, 191, 212, 242, 268, 382; as Minor League player, 78–80

Dean, Paul, 77, 83, 84, 86, 88
Derringer, Paul, 75, 76, 82, 83, 241–42
Detroit Tigers: attendance of, 196, 218, 285; farm system of, 173, 184, 338, 419; finances of, 439; integration and, 362; night baseball and, 235, 237, 264; ownership of, 23, 108, 125, 195–96, 208, 282, 286, 338, 453, 462; pennant races and, 23, 59, 85, 150, 195–96, 204, 205–8, 217, 250, 251, 273–74, 309, 338; player transactions involving, 59, 70, 85, 132, 133, 193, 319–20, 336, 442; radio and, 214, 215; Sunday baseball and, 196–97; television and, 396; World Series and, 85–87, 96, 191, 214–15, 219, 227, 272, 275
DeWitt, Bill, 182, 221–22, 242, 252, 322, 342, 361, 405, 418, 419–20, 423, 439
Dickey, Bill, 144, 153, 190, 211, 217, 223, 230, 281
Dickson, Paul, 316, 317
DiMaggio, Joe: early life of, 151; New York Yankees and, 152–53, 175, 190, 230, 239, 241, 242, 300, 348, 350, 388, 439; San Francisco Seals and, 151–52, 175, 176; World War II and, 226, 241, 246, 267
Doby, Larry, 361, 362–63, 365, 445, 446
Douthit, Taylor, 73, 75, 82, 182
Dressen, Charlie, 187, 353–54, 356, 373, 426, 443
Dreyfuss, Barney, 11–12, 14, 22, 27, 28, 29, 95, 108, 120, 295, 342
DuMont Television Network, 347, 397, 399, 400
Dunn, Jack, 127, 129, 146, 147, 431
Dunn, Jack, III, 421, 431, 432
Dunn, James, 20–21, 23, 27
Durocher, Leo: as broadcaster, 400; as manager, 312, 341, 353–56, 359, 366, 382, 387, 427; as player, 82, 83, 84, 86, 144, 382
Dyer, Eddie, 300, 312–13
Dykes, Jimmy, 210, 310, 423

Eastern League (1883–86), 5
Eastern League (1892–1911): classification of, 13–14, 16; Ed Barrow and, 125–26; National Association and, 8; teams in, 13, 14. *See also* International League
Eastern League (1916–32): classification of, 180–81; farm systems and, 145–47; Great Depression and, 112, 179
Eastern League (1938–62): bonuses and, 320; integration and, 357, 364; World War II and, 257
East-West All-Star Game, 358–59, 366
Ebbets, Charles, 26, 216, 343, 375
Ebbets Field: All-Star Game at, 238; condition of, 426, 428; demolition of, 442; National League playoff games at, 312, 373; night baseball at, 238; renovation of, 216, 235, 436; sale of, 430; Sunday baseball at, 138; televised games at, 346, 399, 463; World Series and, 230, 348; World War II and, 229
economic conditions, U.S., 17, 34, 40–41, 57–58, 81–82, 109–10, 291–93, 326, 410–12. *See also* Great Depression
Eisenhower, Dwight, 257, 385–86, 412
Elliott, Bob, 296, 417, 418
English American players, 197
expansion, Major League: American League and, 447, 452, 453; debate over, 371, 385, 415, 416, 429, 436, 438, 441, 447, 448, 449, 452, 459, 463; National League and, 452–54. *See also* Continental League
Exposition Park, 123

Farley, James, 261, 262, 384, 434
farm systems: Baltimore Orioles and, 432; Ban Johnson and, 50; bonus

farm systems (*cont*)
rule and, 319, 320, 325, 337; Boston Braves and, 342, 416, 417; Boston Red Sox and, 173, 176, 284; Chicago Cubs and, 173–73, 221, 308; Chicago White Sox and, 340; Cincinnati Reds and, 186, 393; Cleveland Indians and, 20, 119, 120, 459; Detroit Tigers and, 338, 419; Dick Burnett and, 335; Ernest Barnard and, 20; expansion teams and, 453, 454; John Brush and, 7, 107; Kenesaw Landis and, 87–88, 107–9, 118–21, 154, 182–85, 229, 338, 457; New York teams and, 112–13, 145–46, 230, 246, 256, 328; Pacific Coast League and, 171–73; Philadelphia Athletics and, 424; rules governing, 107–9, 368, 370, 371, 374; St. Louis Browns and, 242, 342, 419, 424; St. Louis Cardinals and, 68–70, 72–73, 75, 77, 82, 142, 154, 158, 169, 173, 181–85, 246, 311; William Bramham and, 118. *See also* working agreements
Federal Baseball Club of Baltimore v. National League of Professional Baseball Clubs, 95, 396
Federal League, 16–17, 22, 64, 93–95, 96, 127, 129, 133, 141, 367, 431
Feller, Bob, 119–20, 226, 277, 300, 350, 389
Fenway Park: African American players trying out at, 290–91; All-Star Game at, 265, 309–10; Boston Braves at, 381, 417; configuration of, 131, 135; renovation of, 283
Fetter, Henry D., 132, 135
Finley, Charlie, 433, 454, 456
Flushing Meadows Park. *See* Shea Stadium (William A. Shea Municipal Stadium)
Forbes Field: All-Star Game at, 265; configuration of, 350; night baseball at, 237; radio broadcast from, 45; World Series and, 450–51, 455
Ford, Whitey, 444, 451
Ford C. Frick Award, 463
Foster, John B., 52, 54, 56, 102
Foxx, Jimmie: Boston Red Sox and, 59, 190, 208, 211, 284; early life of, 39, 44; Philadelphia Athletics and, 34, 40, 42, 55, 58–59, 73, 456; World War II and, 273
Frazee, Harry, 21, 127, 131, 133–34
Frick, Ford: on bonus rule, 335, 337; as candidate for commissioner, 262, 383–85; Celler subcommittee and, 370, 375, 383–84, 414–15; as commissioner, 383–85, 463–64; Cy Young Award and, 360; death of, 464; on duration of games, 388; on expansion, 436, 441, 442, 448, 452, 453; family and early life of, 377–78; on farm systems, 184, 335; on franchise relocation, 414–15, 463; as head of National League Service Bureau, 380–81; integration and, 317, 356; Minor Leagues and, 404, 415, 463; official scoring and, 334; as president of National League, 189, 259, 303, 341, 381–83, 390; as sportswriter, 376, 379–80; television and, 403–4; umpires and, 333; World War II and, 227, 232, 243, 260, 261, 265, 266
Friend, Bob, 444, 449, 450
Frisch, Frank: as manager, 83, 84, 86, 87, 295; as player, 72, 75, 76, 77, 82, 83, 85, 210
Fuchs, Emil, 1, 210, 381

Galbreath, John, 342, 350, 351, 435, 438, 448
gambling, 25, 98, 114, 171, 174, 354, 381. *See also* Black Sox scandal
"game of the week," 404–5

Garagiola, Joe, 162, 254, 255, 256, 311, 312
Gardella, Danny, 299–300, 366, 391–93, 395
Gehrig, Lou: All-Star Game and, 164, 190, 207–8, 211; consecutive games streak of, 140–41; contract negotiations of, 55; early life of, 139–40, 198; illness and death of, 153–54; as Major League player, 42, 140–41, 143, 151, 153, 194, 203, 207; as Minor League player, 140, 324; World Series and, 73, 142, 143
Gehringer, Charlie, 85, 86, 190, 206, 210, 211, 216
German American players, 197–98
GI Bill of Rights, 277, 320, 323
Giles, Warren: as Minor League executive, 114, 182; as president of Cincinnati Reds, 226, 236, 246, 322, 385; as president of National League, 413, 435, 443, 448, 452–53
Gillespie, Ray, 299, 300
Gold Glove Award, 387, 464
Goldstein, Richard, 260, 268, 269
Gomez, Lefty, 144, 207–8, 210, 211, 212
Gordon, Joe, 151, 153, 230
Goslin, Goose, 85, 166, 206
Great Depression: baseball and, 42, 45, 55, 57, 59, 77, 85, 88, 161, 214, 380; East-West All-Star Game and, 358; Herbert Hoover and, 40–41; Minor Leagues and, 102, 109, 111, 117, 158, 160, 170–71, 173, 181, 247, 328; onset of, 41, 156; recovery from, 118, 190, 211, 276, 291; worsening of, 55, 57, 59, 102, 161, 170
Great War: baseball's reaction to, 17–18, 22, 50, 127, 224; baseball's recovery from, 19, 110, 114, 120, 171; Kenesaw Landis's court cases and, 92; Larry MacPhail during, 155–56. *See also* Bat and Ball Fund; Selective Service Act of 1917
Greenberg, Henry Benjamin (Hank): All-Star Game and, 190, 212; antisemitism and, 205, 206, 217; death of, 460; description of, 190–91; early life of, 191–93; as general manager, 363, 389, 447, 453–54, 459–60; home runs in 1938 by, 218–19; as Major League player, 85, 204–5, 206–8, 219, 274–75, 277, 300, 338–39, 350–51, 459; as Minor League player, 193–94; World War II and, 219–20, 226, 227–28
"Green Light" letter, 233–34, 238, 325, 326
Gregory, Robert, 78, 79
Griffith, Calvin, 340, 446–47, 452–53
Griffith, Clark: death of, 446; expansion and, 374, 447; farm system and, 184; Great War and, 18, 224; as manager, 29, 62; night baseball and, 235, 237–38, 264; as owner of Washington Senators, 1, 29, 164, 259, 283, 295, 301–2, 339, 340, 421, 452; reserve clause and, 295; television and, 421; World War II and, 224, 227, 228–29, 232, 233, 260, 261, 266. *See also* Bat and Ball Fund
Griffith Stadium: All-Star Game at, 190; neighborhood surrounding, 446; night baseball at, 237, 264; pitching mound at, 332; World War II and, 267
Grimes, Burleigh, 34, 42, 44, 73, 77, 180, 390
Grimm, Charlie, 316, 409, 410, 418, 431
Groat, Dick, 444, 449, 451
Grove, Lefty: All-Star Game and, 211; Boston Red Sox and, 59, 283; contracts of, 55; as Minor League player, 39, 44, 101; Philadelphia Athletics

Grove, Lefty (cont)
and, 31, 34, 39, 40, 42, 56, 58, 59, 203, 456; World Series and, 45, 76

Hafey, Chick, 56, 73, 75, 77, 82, 211
Haines, Jesse, 69–70, 143
Hallahan, "Wild Bill," 73, 75, 76, 210
Hall of Fame: African American players in, 298, 360, 445, 456; Cuban players in, 365; executives elected to, 455, 457, 458, 459, 461, 462, 464; Ford C. Frick Award and, 463; Old-Timers Committee of, 251, 458; origins of, 163, 380–81; players elected to, 3, 39–40, 52, 71, 85, 88, 123, 134, 175, 190, 211, 298, 360, 456, 459–60, 464; Rolls of Honor of Baseball and, 455
Haney, Fred, 222, 242, 431
Hank Aaron Award, 464
Hannegan, Robert, 262, 342, 401, 419
Harridge, Will: All-Star Game and, 209; integration and, 356; night baseball and, 236; as president of American League, 223, 259, 282, 333, 351, 353, 366, 389, 420, 422, 425; retirement of, 443, 455; as secretary of American League, 27, 223; St. Louis Browns and, 221, 223; World War II and, 234, 246–47, 249, 261, 303
Harris, Bucky, 32, 204, 283, 341, 353
Hedges, Robert, 62, 63–64, 68, 222
Hemphill, Paul, 320
Henrich, Tommy, 120, 151, 153, 230
Herman, Babe, 42, 55–56, 273
Herrmann, Garry: death of, 29; early life of, 15; as member of National Commission, 15, 21, 22, 24, 25, 106; as owner of Cincinnati Reds, 15, 26, 62, 157, 165
Heydler, John: early life of, 36; Hall of Fame and, 330; as member of National Commission, 24, 25; as president of National League, 2, 15, 33, 52, 57, 209, 380, 382
high school baseball, 102, 118–19, 320, 323, 324, 325, 335, 336
Hoie, Bob, 100, 111
Hollywood CA, baseball in, 110, 279, 285, 330; clubs moving and, 162, 172–73; D-Day and, 257; expansion and, 329, 413, 414, 416, 426; television and, 346; Tony Lupien and, 278
Hoover, Herbert: as candidate for commissioner, 262; Great Depression and, 40–41, 57, 110, 206; at Opening Day (1931), 31, 33; as presidential candidate (1928), 33; as presidential candidate (1932), 81–82; as student at Stanford, 43, 146; at World Series (1929), 34; at World Series (1931), 34, 57, 76
Hornsby, Rogers: as coach and manager, 72, 143, 176, 298, 420; New York Giants and, 72; St. Louis Cardinals and, 64–65, 66, 71–72, 73, 82, 139
Houston, baseball in: Continental League and, 436, 437, 441; Dizzy Dean and, 78–79; expansion and, 371, 416, 442, 447, 452–53, 454; franchise relocation and, 421, 448; Jim Bottomley and, 70–71; Joe Medwick and, 79–81; Pepper Martin and, 74–75; Phil Todt and, 106; St. Louis Cardinals farm team and, 69, 70, 74–75, 78–81, 106. *See also* Houston Astros; Houston Colt .45s
Houston Astros, 461. *See also* Houston Colt .45s
Houston Colt .45s, 452–54. *See also* Houston Astros
Huggins, Miller: death of, 82, 144–45; as manager of New York Yankees, 82, 133, 134, 135, 136, 138, 140–41,

142, 143; as manager of St. Louis Cardinals, 65
Husing, Ted, 46–47, 214, 348, 379
Huston, Til, 23–24, 105, 132–34, 136–37. *See also* Ruppert, Jacob

integration. *See* African American players; Negro Leagues; *specific clubs and leagues*
International League: attendance in, 331, 432; challenged by Federal League, 16–17, 127; classification of, 180, 328; Eastern League renamed, 14, 126; expansion and, 413, 437, 442; farm systems and, 69, 146, 186; finances of, 19, 110; franchise relocation and, 421, 422; Great Depression and, 171; Great War and, 18; integration and, 356–57, 361, 363; Minor League draft and, 99–102; night baseball and, 168–69; playoffs and, 169–71; salary limits and, 112; television and, 402; World War II and, 224, 225, 234, 257
Irish American players, 197–98
Irvin, Monte, 359, 362, 373
Italian American players, 198–99
Ivor-Campbell, Frederick, 197

James, Bill, 42, 98, 171, 386–88
Japan, baseball in, 203–4, 231
Jethroe, Sam, 290, 291, 362
Jewish American players, 200–205. *See also* Greenberg, Henry Benjamin (Hank)
Johnson, Arnold, 425, 432–33, 452, 456
Johnson, Ban: barnstorming and, 103; builds American League, 7, 10–11, 12; Carl Mays controversy and, 21, 23; challenged as president of American League, 23–26; Ed Barrow and, 126–27; Great War and, 17–18; illness, death, and funeral of, 27–29, 50; as journalist, 6–7; legacy of, 455; National Commission and, 14–15; New York Yankees and, 132–33; as president of American League, 20, 22, 37, 64, 223; as president of Western League, 7–8, 37, 68; radio and, 48; resigns as president of American League, 27, 114, 141, 223; Sunday baseball and, 196; transforms Western League into American League, 7–8, 14, 27, 195, 440
Johnson, Frederic, 391, 392, 394

Kahn, Roger, 352
Kansas City Athletics, 425, 443. *See also* Philadelphia Athletics
Kefauver, Estes, 438, 446, 449
Kiner, Ralph, 306, 350, 453
Kirksey, George, 437, 452, 454
Klein, Chuck, 31, 42, 56, 210
Koenig, Mark, 141, 146, 149
Korean War, 325–27, 385, 405
Korr, Charles P., 306
Kowalski, Walter, 394–96
Kuenn, Harvey, 307, 439, 442

labor relations. *See* American Baseball Guild; Cannon, Robert; Major League Baseball Players Association; Murphy, Robert; player representatives; reserve clause; Scott, Frank
Landis, Kenesaw Mountain: All-Star Game and, 211; at the ballpark, 33, 89, 96, 160; barnstorming and, 102–6; Black Sox scandal and, 98; Boston Braves and, 381; broadcasting and, 213–15, 217, 349; Dizzy Dean and, 84; elected commissioner, 26, 96, 98–99; on Ernest Barnard, 2; family and early life of, 89–90; farm systems and, 87–88, 106–7, 108–9, 118–21, 154, 182–84, 229, 338, 457; as federal judge, 91–92, 258; Federal

Landis, Kenesaw Mountain (*cont*)
League case and, 93–95; illness and death of, 251, 258–59, 263; Larry MacPhail and, 169; legacy of, 457–58; Minor League draft and, 99–100, 108; Most Valuable Player Award and, 457; politics and, 90; racial segregation and, 317; re-elected commissioner, 117–18, 141, 366; salary limits and, 112; William Bramham and, 117–18; World Series (1934) and, 86–87; World War II and, 227, 233–34, 244, 246–47, 250, 259
Lane, Bill, 162, 172, 173, 175–76
Lane, F. C., 9, 210
Lane, Frank, 186, 306, 335, 336, 413, 443, 447
Lasker, Albert, 23–24, 141
Lasker Plan, 23–25
Lausche, Frank, 262, 367, 384
Lavagetto, Cookie, 311, 348, 382
Law, Vernon, 444, 449, 450–51
Lazzeri, Tony, 72, 142–43, 199
League Park, 237, 318
Lester, Larry, 359
Levitt, Daniel R., 134, 282
Lewis, J. Norman, 306
Liberty Broadcasting System, 398
Lieb, Fred: on Bob Quinn, 3; on Connie Mack, 34, 36, 38, 56, 59; on Ford Frick, 376; on Frank Navin, 195; on Hank Greenberg, 274–75; on Kenesaw Landis, 91; on Mickey Cochrane, 267; on National League schedule, 443; on Philadelphia Athletics, 37; on Yankee Stadium, 137
litigation. *See Federal Baseball Club of Baltimore v. National League of Professional Baseball Clubs*; *Toolson v. New York Yankees*
Litwhiler, Danny, 245, 261, 303
Los Angeles, baseball in: and being the best Minor League team, 171, 172–73; Brooklyn Dodgers and, 426, 429–30; Chicago Cubs farm team and, 108, 110; expansion and, 329, 371, 374, 413, 416, 418; franchise relocation and, 221, 329, 342, 414, 418, 422, 426, 429–30; integration and, 363; prosperity of, 172–73; St. Louis Browns and, 221, 342, 414, 418, 422, 426; television and, 345. *See also* Los Angeles Angels (Major League); Los Angeles Dodgers
Los Angeles Angels (Major League), 453–54
Los Angeles Coliseum, 433, 444
Los Angeles Dodgers: attendance of, 433; Dodger Stadium and, 442; pennant races and, 431, 433, 444, 449; relocation and, 426–27, 429, 434; World Series and, 462. *See also* Brooklyn Dodgers
Louisville, baseball in, 3, 4, 11, 14; George Toolson and, 394; Junior World Series and, 74, 281, 357
Lowenfish, Lee, 296, 353
Lupien, Tony, 278–79, 296

Mack, Connie (Cornelius McGillicuddy): All-Star Game and, 210, 212; broadcasting and, 49, 345; death of, 456; demeanor of, 38; family and early life of, 29, 34–35; integration and, 356; as Major League player, 35–36; as manager of Milwaukee Creams, 37; as manager of Philadelphia Athletics, 37, 38–40, 42–45, 56–59, 144; as manager of Pittsburgh Pirates, 36–37; as Minor League player, 35; night baseball and, 236–37; as part-owner of Philadelphia Athletics, 22, 31, 37–40, 53, 144, 261, 339, 423–25, 455; and sale of Philadelphia Athletics, 455–56; as scout of young players, 38, 323; World War II and, 250

Mack, Connie, Jr., 423
Mack, Earle, 423, 424, 425, 455, 456
Mack, Roy, 423, 424, 425, 455, 456
MacPhail, Leland Stanford (Larry): broadcasting and, 187, 216, 347, 349; Celler subcommittee and, 374, 458; expansion and, 374, 448; family and early life of, 156–57; Great War and, 155–56; Happy Chandler and, 262–63; Leo Durocher and, 353–56; as Minor League club executive, 157–60, 169–70, 181, 182; night baseball and, 169, 187–89, 235–38; as part-owner of Brooklyn Dodgers, 216, 227, 229, 235, 427; as part-owner of Cincinnati Reds, 185–89, 242; as part-owner of New York Yankees, 263, 280–81, 302–4, 343, 345, 348, 458–59; retirement and death of, 459; World War II and, 227–29, 234
Major League attendance. *See* attendance, Major League
Major League Baseball Players Association, 305–7
Major League clubs. *See specific clubs*
Major League financial data, 42, 53, 58, 132, 144, 252, 276, 319; of individual clubs, 28, 58, 88, 132, 136, 141, 144, 145, 189, 242, 422, 424, 426. *See also* Minor League financial data
Major–Minor League Agreement, 12, 13, 305, 320, 330–31, 398, 402
managers. *See specific managers*
Mantle, Mickey, 386, 387–88, 439, 444, 450, 451
Marion, Marty, 88, 299, 303–5, 311, 399, 420, 441
Maris, Roger, 443, 444, 450, 464
Marshall, William, 295, 303, 338–42, 355
Martin, Pepper, 73–77, 83, 85–87, 210, 273
Mays, Carl, 21–24, 133–34
Mays, Willie, 363, 387–88, 428, 443
Mazeroski, Bill, 450, 451, 455
McCormick, Frank, 187, 278
McGillicuddy, Cornelius. *See* Mack, Connie (Cornelius McGillicuddy)
McGraw, John: All-Star Game and, 210; barnstorming and, 103, 104; Ford Frick and, 380; as manager of New York Giants, 14, 15, 96, 135, 136, 137, 140, 193, 202, 427; on new baseball (1931), 57; as player with Baltimore Orioles, 198
McKechnie, Bill, 72, 74, 151, 212
McNamee, Graham, 46, 47, 213, 214, 379
Medwick, Joe, 79–81, 83, 85–87
Memorial Stadium, 407, 432, 444. *See also* Municipal Stadium (Baltimore)
Mexican League, 296–301, 304, 353, 366, 371, 384, 391, 393
Middle Atlantic League, 80, 179, 394, 395; farm systems and, 146, 186; Great Depression and, 159, 174
military draft. *See* Military Selective Service Act of 1948; Selective Service Act of 1917; Selective Training and Service Act of 1940
Military Selective Service Act of 1948, 326
Milwaukee Braves: attendance of, 430–31; bonus players and, 337; pennant races and, 409, 431, 433, 444, 449; player transactions involving, 409; relocation of, 464; World Series and, 431. *See also* Atlanta Braves; Boston Braves
Minneapolis, baseball in: in American Association, 14, 159, 169, 171, 176; Continental League and, 436–37, 442, 447; expansion and, 448, 452; franchise relocation and, 428–29, 433, 446, 448, 453; Ted Williams and, 176; Western League and, 7–8; Willie Mays and, 387. *See also* Minnesota Twins; San Francisco Giants

Minnesota Twins, 446–47, 448, 453. *See also* Washington Senators (1901–60)
Minor League attendance. *See* attendance, Minor League
Minor League cities and towns (selected): Asheville, 177, 392, 395; Atlanta, 22, 174, 257, 321, 363, 392; Baltimore, 14, 17, 39, 44, 100, 101, 127, 129, 148, 176, 177, 281, 402, 431; Beaumont TX, 177, 194, 394; Binghamton NY, 13, 146, 177, 394; Birmingham, 79; Bridgeport CT, 13, 113, 145; Buffalo, 14, 177, 178; Cedar Rapids IA, 183–84; Chattanooga, 194, 303; Dallas, 62, 162, 194, 363; Danville IL, 80, 183; Dayton OH, 4, 9, 70; Denver, 14, 364, 437; Des Moines, 13, 14, 119, 120, 166–68; Durham NC, 113, 114, 177; El Paso, 112, 177; Erie PA, 111, 146; Evansville IN, 177, 194, 245; Ft. Smith AR, 69, 74; Grand Rapids MI, 3–4, 7, 10, 180, 364; Greenville SC, 142, 395; Guthrie OK, 73–74, 111; Hartford CT, 35, 112–13, 140, 145, 177, 194, 324; Hutchinson KS, 70, 112, 174; Independence MO, 112, 167; Indianapolis, 3, 7, 14, 68, 126, 234, 316; Jacksonville, 363, 364, 408; Jersey City, 13, 14, 162, 168, 357, 361, 402; Johnstown PA, 173–74, 395; Kansas City, 7, 8, 14, 63, 68, 70, 388, 394, 402, 432; Macon GA, 145, 177–78, 179; Milwaukee, 7, 14, 39, 120, 316–17, 393, 416, 418–19; New Orleans, 119, 120, 157, 175, 234; Norfolk VA, 177, 253, 256; Oakland, 14, 110, 144, 172, 173, 329, 394; Portland, 19, 39, 43, 173, 257, 279, 329, 371, 406, 447; Portsmouth VA, 177, 404; Providence, 14, 176, 279; Reading PA, 124, 171, 203; Richmond, 124, 127; Rochester, 14, 74, 75, 83, 114, 125, 146, 171, 173, 182, 183, 402; Sacramento, 173, 179, 183, 329; Salisbury MD, 177, 180; Salt Lake City, 39, 142, 162, 172, 173; San Diego, 162, 173, 175, 279, 285, 363, 393; Sioux City IA, 7, 14, 69, 70; Springfield MO, 173, 177; St. Joseph MO, 14, 78, 79, 182; St. Paul, 7, 14, 96, 139, 141, 146, 363, 402; Syracuse, 69–70, 74, 182, 234, 281, 357, 393–94; Terre Haute IN, 13, 61, 114; Toledo, 7, 14; Topeka KS, 70, 186; Toronto, 14, 125–26, 168, 186; Vernon CA, 22, 110, 172; Wilkes-Barre PA, 177, 364; Worcester MA, 14, 174. *See also* Columbus OH, baseball in; Hollywood CA, baseball in; Houston, baseball in; Los Angeles, baseball in; Louisville, baseball in; Minneapolis, baseball in; Montreal, baseball in; Newark, baseball in; San Francisco, baseball in; Seattle, baseball in
Minor League club and league officials (selected): Al Haraway, 364, 403; Bud Herlong Jr., 371–72; Dick Burnett, 335, 363; Edwin Johnson, 403, 437; Harry Williams, 110, 232; Jack Corbett, 390, 392–96; J. Alvin Gardner, 114, 243; John Farrell, 8, 115; Lee Keyser, 119, 166–67; Michael Sexton, 114, 115, 167; Patrick Powers, 8, 126; Paul Fagan, 405, 414, 416; Tommy Richardson, 320, 357; William H. McCarthy, 101, 172. *See also* Bramham, William; Shaughnessy, Frank; Trautman, George
Minor League clubs. *See* Minor League cities and towns (selected)
Minor League draft: Bill Veeck and, 335, 421; bonus rules and, 321, 323, 338; complaints and protests about, 7, 9, 17, 18, 50, 98, 99, 100, 129; debate over exemption from, 16, 19, 99, 100,

101, 108; Francis Richter and, 19, 100; Pacific Coast League and, 14, 329, 413–15; proposal for universal or unrestricted, 101, 102, 109, 171, 336–38; rules and prices of, 6, 13, 16, 99, 100, 102, 146, 183
Minor League financial data, 110, 116, 331, 371, 406. *See also* Great Depression; Major League financial data
Minor League managers (selected): Ben Geraghty, 409; George Selkirk, 280–81; Ike Caveney, 152; Jake Atz, 158; Jim Gleeson, 275, 280; Joe Mathes, 74
Minor League players (selected): Bill Embick, 227–28, 308; Bob Ezell, 327; Dave Hoskins, 363–64; Elbert Israel, 364; Fleming Ready, 364; Fred Thomas, 364; George Sulliman, 327; Gordon Houston, 239; Horace Garner, 364; Jackie Cohan, 326; Jim Tugerson, 364; John Ritchey, 363; Leander Tugerson, 364; Pablo Bernard, 364; Tony Freitas, 172, 179
Minor League postseason play: American Association, 170; Dixie Series, 79, 80, 117, 194; International Border Series, 117; International League, 169–70; Junior World Series, 74–75, 117, 281, 357, 402; Little Dixie Series, 117; Midwest Series, 117; Mississippi-Louisiana Series, 117; New England Championship, 117; Northern Championship, 117; Pacific Coast League, 171
Minor Leagues (selected): Appalachian League, 174, 257; Arizona-Texas League, 112, 177, 393; Arkansas-Missouri League, 116, 183, 247; Atlantic League, 123, 124, 125; Blue Ridge League, 111–12, 145; California League, 327, 364; Canadian-American League, 174, 363, 395; Cotton States League, 13, 174, 364, 403; Eastern Shore League, 43, 44, 177, 180; East Texas League, 74, 112; Evangeline League, 177, 328; Florida State League, 111, 371; Interstate League, 3, 123, 257, 308, 387; Mountain State League, 175; Mountain States League, 364, 405; Nebraska State League, 174, 179, 183; New York–Pennsylvania League, 111, 146, 173, 181; New York State League, 13; North Atlantic League, 395; North Carolina State League, 114, 392; Northern League, 119, 408; Northwestern League, 5; Oklahoma State League, 73, 111; Pacific National League, 13–14; Palmetto League, 112, 159; Pennsylvania State Association, 180, 186; PONY League, 257, 394; Rio Grande Valley League, 112, 159; South Atlantic Association, 111, 142, 158, 168, 178, 179; Southeastern League, 111, 112, 246, 247; Tri-State League, 69, 111, 395; Virginia League, 17, 114; Western Carolina League, 440–42. *See also* American Association (Minor League); Central League; Eastern League (1883–86); Eastern League (1892–1911); Eastern League (1916–32); Eastern League (1938–62); International League; Middle Atlantic League; New England League; Pacific Coast League (PCL); Piedmont League; South Atlantic League; Southern Association; Texas League; Three-I League; Western Association (1901); Western Association (1905–11, 1914–17, 1920–32, 1934–42, 1946–54); Western League (1894–99); Western League (1900–1937, 1947–58)
Minor League salary limits, 9, 111–16, 169–70, 180–81, 183, 415

Minor League split seasons, 158–59, 169, 171
Miñoso Arrieta, Orestes "Minnie," 362, 365, 445, 446
Montreal, baseball in, 14, 125–26, 170, 224; Jackie Robinson and, 281, 356–57, 359–60, 365
Moore, Terry, 88, 162, 268, 300, 311
Moses, Robert, 429, 430
Moss, John, 440–41
Most Valuable Player (MVP) Award (Major League): (1923), 151; (1924), 199; (1926), 72; (1927), 151; (1928), 43; (1929), 43; (1931), 77; (1932), 59; (1933), 59; (1935), 207; (1936), 153; (1938), 284; (1940), 219; (1942), 241; (1944), 299, 300, 303; (1945), 300; (1946), 312; (1954), 387; (1956), 388; (1957), 388; (1960), 449, 450; African American players and, 445; Hank Greenberg and, 207, 219; Henry Aaron and, 431; Kenesaw Landis and, 251, 457; National League establishes, 71; Roy Campanella and, 360; Yogi Berra and, 460
Muchnick, Isadore, 288–90
Muckerman, Richard, 242, 252, 342, 418, 419
Mulcahy, Hugh, 226, 228, 277, 308
Municipal Stadium (Baltimore), 432. *See also* Memorial Stadium
Municipal Stadium (Cleveland), 237, 318
Murdock, Eugene C., 8, 11, 136
Murphy, Robert, 293–96, 301, 303, 304, 305, 353, 371
Musial, Stan, 239, 276, 300, 311, 312, 350, 382, 442–43, 445–46
Mutual Broadcasting System, 213–15, 345, 349, 398–99

National Agreement, 5–6, 7, 8, 9, 12, 13, 14, 16, 18, 19, 98–99, 101, 105, 107, 259, 261, 263, 331
National Anthem, 31, 225, 239
National Association of Professional Base Ball Leagues (Minor Leagues): American Association and, 9; bonus rule and, 321–23; classification of leagues within, 16, 328; finances of, 117–18, 181; first meeting of, 8–9; Korean War and, 325; Mexican League and, 393; official ball of, 9; relationship of, with Major Leagues, 12–13, 18–19, 98–99, 100, 184–85; salary limits and, 112; second meeting of, 4; split seasons and, 158–59; World War II and, 231–32. *See also* Bramham, William
National Association of Professional Base Ball Players (1871–75), 10, 95, 197, 200
National Baseball Hall of Fame. *See* Hall of Fame
National Commission: barnstorming and, 104; Federal League and, 93–94, 95; Lasker Plan and, 23, 141; Minor Leagues and, 16, 106, 129; replacement of, 19, 21, 24, 96, 141; structure of, 14–15, 21–22, 25
National League: baseball used by, 33, 51–52, 57, 247; early franchise relocations in, 11–12; establishment of, 4–5, 95; expansion and, 434, 436, 448–49, 452–53, 454–55; farm systems and, 108–9, 184; Federal League and, 16–17, 93–95; integration and, 361–62; National Agreement and, 5–6; night baseball and, 187–89, 237–38, 307; radio and, 48–49; settles dispute with American League, 12–13, 15; Sunday baseball and, 196–97; umpires and, 333. *See also* Frick, Ford; Giles, Warren; Herrmann, Garry; Heydler, John; Tener, John
National League Park, 212

Navin, Frank: death of, 217; dispute of, with New York Yankees, 23–24; on Ernest Barnard, 2; farm systems and, 108, 120; Hank Greenberg and, 194, 204–5, 207; night baseball and, 235; as part-owner of Detroit Tigers, 195–97; personality of, 125, 195; Sunday baseball and, 196–97
Navin Field, 196, 207. *See also* Briggs Stadium
NBC (National Broadcasting Company): All-Star Game and, 213–14, 399; night baseball and, 167; television broadcasts of baseball and, 345–47, 397, 400, 404; World Series and, 46, 214–15, 217, 345, 347, 379
Negro Leagues: Negro American League, 358, 365, 366, 387, 407; Negro National League (1920–31), 28, 358; Negro National League (1933–48), 365–66; Negro Southern League, 164, 365, 366; Negro World Series, 358; United States League, 365; World War II and, 268, 269. *See also* East-West All-Star Game
Newark, baseball in, 13, 14, 127, 171, 357, 402; Joe Medwick and, 80; New York Yankees and, 146, 154, 280, 394; Tommy Henrich and, 120; Yogi Berra and, 280–81
Newcombe, Don, 359, 360, 373
New Deal agencies, 161–64
New England League: integration and, 363; night baseball and, 166; playoffs and, 117, 158; television and, 402
New York Giants: attendance of, 427, 428; farm system of, 107, 113, 145, 433; finances of, 137, 144, 319; integration and, 361–62; night baseball and, 188, 237–39, 264; ownership of, 339–40; pennant races and, 15, 75, 83, 84, 102, 135–36, 372–73, 387, 409–10, 427, 428; player transactions involving, 66, 72, 409, 418; radio and, 45, 46, 48–49, 215–16, 348; relocation of, 427, 428–30, 434, 435, 437; Sunday baseball and, 136–38; television and, 346, 347, 396, 397, 399, 402; World Series and, 45, 46, 97, 102, 104, 135–37, 150, 153, 372, 427, 428; World War II and, 228, 249, 266, 308. *See also* San Francisco Giants
New York Highlanders. *See* New York Yankees
New York Mets, 453, 454–55, 464–65
New York Yankees: attendance of, 134, 136, 153, 317, 343; bonus players and, 120, 319, 320; farm system of, 101, 121, 145–46, 173, 280, 388, 458; finances of, 121, 136, 141, 144, 145, 319, 439; integration and, 362, 365; night baseball and, 237–38, 264; ownership of, 136, 153, 285, 302, 343, 458; pennant races and, 23–24, 28, 39–40, 43, 45, 57, 58, 106, 133–34, 135, 138, 142, 143, 148, 153, 206, 217, 219, 222, 230, 242, 246, 251, 284–85, 309, 313, 420, 424, 439, 444, 449–50; player transactions involving, 21, 22, 62, 104, 129, 131–34, 142, 144, 151, 152, 175, 283, 418, 432; radio and, 45–46, 49, 215–16, 348; Sunday baseball and, 137–38; television and, 347, 349, 421; World Series and, 45–46, 47, 72, 73, 102, 135, 136, 142–43, 148–50, 153, 199, 219, 230–31, 246, 256, 265, 335, 345–47, 348–49, 372, 427, 431, 450–51, 458, 460, 463, 465; World War II and, 227, 229, 248, 257, 266. *See also* Baltimore Orioles (1901–2)
Niemiec, Al, 279–80
night baseball: Ban Johnson and, 50; early experiments with, 124, 164–66;

night baseball (*cont*)
General Electric and, 165–66, 168, 188, 235; on holidays, 444; Major Leagues and, 187–89, 216, 223, 235–39, 305, 307, 339, 382, 417; Minor Leagues and, 166–69, 179; television and, 397, 398, 402, 405; World War II and, 232–33, 235, 238–39, 248, 257, 264–65, 267, 270
Nugent, Gerry, 236, 341

O'Connor, Leslie, 106, 108, 183, 258–59, 263, 302
O'Doul, Lefty, 42, 152, 203
offensive explosion (1920s, 1930), 41–42, 50–51
official scoring, 331, 334; and sacrifice flies, 53–54, 57, 332–33
O'Malley, Walter: All-Star Game and, 446; as chief counsel for Brooklyn Dodgers, 343, 355; expansion and, 441, 452–54; franchise relocation and, 426–30, 436, 441; Los Angeles and, 426–30, 433; as owner of Brooklyn Dodgers, 375, 383, 384, 426–30, 435, 436, 462–63; television and, 401
Opening Day (Major League): (1912), 196; (1914), 129; (1924), 186; (1931), 31–33, 55, 75; (1933), 161; (1934), 284; (1937), 164; (1941), 386; (1942), 234, 239; (1943), 244; (1944), 250; (1945), 273, 274, 290; (1946), 302, 309, 417; (1947), 356; (1953), 421–22, 430–31; (1955), 455; (1974), 464; Dwight Eisenhower and, 386; Washington Senators and, 443
optioning players, 69, 99–100, 101–2, 109, 323
Owen, Mickey, 230, 300, 302, 366, 392

Pacific Coast League (PCL): campaign of, to become third Major League, 328–30, 374, 384, 385, 413–14, 426, 429, 447; classification of, 14, 16, 99, 126–27, 180, 328; expansion and, 384, 416; farm systems and, 39, 108, 172–73, 183, 221, 433; finances of, 19, 331; Great Depression and, 171–72; Great War and, 22; integration and, 363; Minor League draft and, 101, 102; night baseball and, 169; playoffs and, 158–59; salary limits and, 113; television and, 345, 402, 406; World War II and, 232, 248, 257, 267–68
Paige, Satchel, 268, 298, 361, 365
Palace of the Fans, 165. *See also* Crosley Field; Redland Field
Pasquel, Jorge, 296–302, 304, 353, 384, 391, 393
Paul, Gabe, 333, 339, 389, 405
Payson, Joan, 435–36, 437, 454–55
pension plan, 303–7, 399, 415, 440, 443, 445, 446
Perini, Lou: American Baseball Guild and, 296, 303; expansion and, 416, 447, 448; franchise relocation and, 418–19, 421, 426; as owner of Boston Braves, 341, 384, 416–18; television and, 431
Philadelphia Athletics: attendance of, 38, 58, 318; finances of, 58, 144, 319, 423–25, 455; integration and, 362; night baseball and, 236–37, 264; ownership of, 31, 37, 38, 423; pennant races and, 40, 44–45, 56–57, 58–59, 142–43; player transactions involving, 22, 39, 43, 44, 101, 127, 132, 136, 283, 284, 424; radio and, 49, 215; relocation of, 352, 425, 455–56; Sunday baseball and, 138; television and, 345; World Series and, 33–34, 58, 73, 75–76, 85, 148. *See also* Kansas City Athletics
Philadelphia Phillies: attendance of,

317; finances of, 423; integration and, 289, 298, 306, 362; night baseball and, 187–88, 236, 237, 264; ownership of, 26, 250, 306, 341; pennant races and, 317, 372; radio and, 45, 215, 403, 423; relocation of, 436; Sunday baseball and, 138; television and, 346, 401, 404, 423
Piedmont League: Great Depression and, 112, 114; night baseball and, 168; playoffs and, 159; television and, 404; World War II and, 257
Pierman, Carol J., 272
Pietrusza, David, 90–91, 98, 164, 183, 264
Pittsburgh Pirates: attendance of, 58, 372; integration and, 289, 362; night baseball and, 237, 265; ownership of, 11–12, 95, 289, 295, 342; pennant races and, 12, 37, 73, 273, 444, 449–50; player transactions involving, 11, 22, 36, 65, 182, 332, 336, 339, 350, 409, 424; radio and, 45, 46, 215; relocation of, 435; television and, 396, 400; World Series and, 46, 47, 143, 450–51, 455
Player Development and Promotion program, 405, 463
Player Development plan, 463
Player of the Decade Award, 450
player representatives, 296, 302, 303, 305, 306, 307, 374, 399, 446
Players League, 10, 36, 294
playoffs, Major League: (1946), 311, 312, 347; (1948), 313, 417; (1951), 373, 399–400, 427; (1959), 431
Polo Grounds: All-Star Game at, 211, 238–39; Babe Ruth and, 105, 131; eviction of New York Yankees from, 137; "Miracle of Coogan's Bluff" at, 373, 427; National League playoff games at, 373, 400, 427; New York Mets and, 465; night baseball and, 237–38; radio and, 45, 47, 214; Sunday baseball and, 138; Willie Mays's World Series catch at, 428; World War II and, 257, 268
postwar baseball, style of, 386–90
Prager, Joshua, 373
Prendergast, Jim, 393–94, 395, 396
Pulliam, Harry, 14–15

Quesada, Pete, 453
Quinn, Bob: Boston Braves and, 226, 290, 341, 381–82; Boston Red Sox and, 282; and Ernest Barnard, 3–4; as Minor League executive, 4, 157

racial segregation. *See* African American players; Negro Leagues
radio: advent of baseball on, 45; All-Star Game and, 213, 264; apprehension about, 47–49, 215–16, 348, 368, 369, 372, 385, 391, 397–98, 402–3, 405; Major League games and, 186–87, 215–17, 247, 257, 286, 317, 347, 373; night baseball and, 167, 169, 236; rights fees and, 49–50, 246, 251, 304, 305, 346, 349, 392, 396, 399, 424, 440; Westinghouse and, 45, 238; World Series and, 45–47, 102, 150, 191, 213–15, 251, 275, 345, 375, 462–63
radio stations: KDKA, 45; KUP, 47; KYW, 47; WABC, 379; WBBM, 49; WBZ, 45; WEAF, 46, 379; WFBE, 186; WGN, 47, 49; WGY, 45; WJAZ, 47; WJR, 206; WJZ, 45; WKRC, 187; WLW, 186, 215, 347; WMAQ, 47; WOR, 216, 379; WRH, 47; WSAI, 187; WTAM, 215; WWJ, 216–17
RCA (Radio Corporation of America), 46, 346, 349, 397
Redland Field, 185, 186. *See also* Crosley Field; Palace of the Fans
Reese, Pee Wee, 229, 311, 360, 374

Reiser, Pete, 229, 268, 311
relocation. *See* Boston Braves; Brooklyn Dodgers; Milwaukee Braves; New York Giants; Philadelphia Athletics; St. Louis Browns; Washington Senators (1901–60)
reserve clause: abolition of, 462; Celler subcommittee and, 368–72, 373–75; Continental League and, 440; as control on player movement, 54, 56, 68, 95, 102, 296, 301–2; Federal League and, 17, 93–95; legal uncertainty about, 107, 294–95, 296, 301–4, 385, 391–95, 449; Minor Leagues and, 5–6, 9, 13, 99, 101, 102, 109; origins of, 5; Pacific Coast League and, 415, 438; player resentment of, 24, 293, 296, 303; World War II and, 248
Reynolds, Bob, 454
Richter, Francis, 6, 12, 18–19, 100–101, 201
Rickey, Wesley Branch: as Brooklyn Dodgers executive, 256, 259, 262, 289, 313, 335, 343, 353–56, 375, 383, 426, 427; Cincinnati Reds and, 82–83; as college student, 61–63; Continental League and, 435–42, 448–49, 452, 454, 456; expansion and, 426; family and early years of, 60–62; farm systems and, 68–69, 70–71, 73, 75, 83, 108–9, 118, 120–21, 142, 145, 146, 154, 173, 181, 182–84, 311; George Sisler and, 22, 63–64; Great War and, 66; illness and death of, 457; Jackie Robinson and, 356–57, 359–60, 361, 456; Kenesaw Landis and, 87, 118–21, 154; Knothole Gang and, 64, 160, 255; Larry MacPhail and, 157–58, 169, 181, 182, 185, 353–56; as Major League player, 82–83; as Minor League player, 62; Phil Todt and, 106–7; as Pittsburgh Pirates executive, 351, 390; politics of, 81, 289, 391–92; race and, 61–62, 289, 356–57; as St. Louis Browns executive, 22, 63–64, 221; as St. Louis Browns manager, 63–64; as St. Louis Cardinals executive, 60, 64–68, 72, 77, 78, 79, 83, 84, 88, 182, 221–22, 232, 324; as St. Louis Cardinals manager, 66, 72; television and, 401
Riess, Steven A., 205, 356
Rigney, Dorothy Comiskey. *See* Comiskey, Dorothy
Rigney, Johnny, 228, 308
Roberts, Robin, 306–7, 446
Robinson, Jackie: Branch Rickey and, 356–57, 359–60, 361, 456; as Major League player, 357, 360, 365, 366, 373, 408–9, 445; as Minor League player, 281, 357, 359–60, 363, 365; as Negro League player, 290–91, 361
Rolls of Honor of Baseball. *See* Hall of Fame
Rookie of the Year Award, 360, 362, 387, 419, 445
Roosevelt, Franklin: attending baseball games, 149, 160–61, 164, 212, 386; death of, 290, 386; elected president, 81, 251; "Green Light" letter and, 233–35; military draft and, 219, 240, 259; New Deal of, 161–64; night baseball and, 188–89; World War II and, 221, 229, 233–35, 240, 250, 257, 261
Roosevelt, Theodore, 8, 90–91, 92
Root, Charlie, 31, 32, 149–50
Rowe, Schoolboy, 85, 86, 216–17
Rowland, Clarence "Pants," 97, 279, 328–29, 402, 413–14
rule book, changes in: (1920), 41; (1931), 53–54; (1950), 331–34; (1956), 389. *See also* balk rule; official scoring

Ruppert, Jacob: Ban Johnson and, 21, 23, 24; death of, 153, 343; farm systems and, 101, 144–48, 154; George Weiss and, 146, 148; influence of, 141; Kenesaw Landis and, 26; night baseball and, 237; as owner of New York Yankees, 132–33, 134, 136–37, 141, 144, 285; radio and, 49, 215–16; wealth of, 141. *See also* Huston, Til
Ruth, Babe: All-Star Game and, 210–11; barnstorming and, 102–6; Boston Braves and, 151, 381; Boston Red Sox and, 41, 73, 104, 128, 130–31, 147, 310; "called shot" and, 149–50; as coach, 216; early life of, 128–29, 198; Ford Frick and, 379, 463–64; Hall of Fame and, 381; Hank Greenberg and, 218–19; Henry Aaron and, 464; Japan and, 203; as Minor League player, 129–30, 431; New York Yankees and, 31, 33, 41–42, 44, 52, 55, 58, 73, 82, 83, 102–3, 104–6, 131–32, 134, 135, 137, 140, 142–43, 145, 150–51, 202, 464; retirement of, 212, 222, 302, 349, 458; sale of, to New York Yankees, 131, 132–33
Ryan, Ellis, 344, 367, 384, 459

Saigh, Fred, 326, 342, 401, 403, 419–20, 421
salaries: American Baseball Guild and, 294, 296; bonus rule and, 322; Great Depression and, 55–56, 83; Great War and, 18; Mexican League and, 300, 302; Minor Leagues and, 171–72, 174, 178, 180, 329, 404, 416, 463; owners' power to control, 52, 54–55, 59, 303, 306, 350; postwar, 439; proposal for minimum, 304–5; scouts and, 443; umpires and, 352, 382; World War II and, 226, 234, 239, 276. *See also* Minor League salary limits; reserve clause
salary limits, Minor League. *See* Minor League salary limits
San Francisco, baseball in: D-Day and, 257; expansion and, 371, 413, 414, 416, 447; franchise relocation and, 429; Joe DiMaggio and, 151–52, 176, 226, 241; Mission club and, 110, 173; Pacific Coast League and, 14, 100, 110, 152, 171–73, 285, 329, 394, 415; television and, 405. *See also* San Francisco Giants
San Francisco Giants, 433, 439, 443. *See also* New York Giants
Schoendienst, Red, 311, 431, 445
Scott, Frank, 306–7
scouts: Bob Connery, 65, 139, 141, 146; Bob Gilks, 139, 142; Charley Barrett, 70, 73; Hugh Duffy, 290–91; Jack Fournier, 70–71, 178, 301; Jean Dubuc, 193–94; Joe Kelley, 62, 139, 198; Paul Krichell, 134, 139, 140, 141, 192–94, 280
Seals Stadium, 152, 329, 433
Seattle, baseball in, 19, 177, 257, 279–80, 329, 346, 371, 462
Selective Service Act of 1917, 18
Selective Training and Service Act of 1940: amended in 1941, 219; baseball's reaction to, 226–29, 243, 383; enacted into law, 224–26; players registered and drafted under, 226, 227–28, 239, 247–49, 253, 259, 260–61, 276; protecting jobs of returning veterans, 277–78, 279–80; replaced by new legislation, 326. *See also* Military Selective Service Act of 1948; Selective Service Act of 1917; Universal Military Training and Service Act
Sewell, Rip, 295, 296, 304, 310
Seymour, Harold, 5, 17, 91, 161–62, 198
Shantz, Bobby, 59, 424, 451
Shaughnessy, Frank: challenge to William Bramham by, 248; Continental

Shaughnessy, Frank (*cont*)
League and, 442; National Anthem and, 225; Pacific Coast League and, 413; playoff plan and, 169–70; and signing college players, 324; television and, 401–2, 403–4, 405
Shea, William Alfred (Bill): as chair of mayor's committee, 434, 435–37; Continental League and, 436–38, 439–40, 442, 447–49, 452, 454; death of, 465; early life and career of, 434–35; expansion and, 436; Shea Stadium and, 464–65
Shea Stadium (William A. Shea Municipal Stadium), 465
Shibe, Ben, 37–39
Shibe, Jack, 39, 43, 49, 58, 423
Shibe, Tom, 27, 39, 43, 51, 58, 423
Shibe Park: All-Star Games and, 264, 446; night baseball and, 236–38; Philadelphia Phillies and, 341, 424; renovation of, 39. *See also* Connie Mack Stadium
Shotton, Burt, 66, 389, 441
Simmons, Al: batting style of, 43, 81; Chicago White Sox and, 58, 207, 210, 217; Detroit Tigers and, 217; Philadelphia Athletics and, 39, 40, 42, 55, 58, 273, 456
Sisler, George, 22, 27, 43, 63, 81, 230
Slaughter, Enos, 88, 162, 300, 311, 313
Somers, Charles, 10–11, 12, 20, 37
South Atlantic League: classification of, 328; Great Depression and, 17, 145; integration and, 364, 395, 409; playoffs and, 158; William Bramham as president of, 114
Southern Association: classification of, 16, 180, 181, 328; farm systems and, 119, 157; Great Depression and, 174–75; integration and, 363; playoffs and, 79, 194; World War II and, 234, 257
Southworth, Billy, 72, 142, 264, 269, 311, 417–18
Spahn, Warren, 387, 417, 431, 450
Spink, Taylor, 108, 118, 210, 233, 250, 261, 273, 309, 324
Sportsman's Park: All-Star Game and, 212; integration of, 361; night baseball and, 165, 223, 237; sale of, 342, 422; St. Louis Cardinals' rental of, 68, 237, 419; World War II and, 265
sportswriters: Arch Ward, 208–10; Arnold Hano, 428; Bill Corum, 275, 402; Bill Mardo, 289; Bob Broeg, 313; Bob Burnes, 68, 443; Clif Keane, 290–91; Damon Runyon, 72, 376; Dan Parker, 376, 399; Dave Egan, 278, 290; Edgar G. Brands, 50, 118, 184, 226, 384, 414; Frank Graham, 300, 376; Frank Hough, 37, 38; Frank Slocum, 376, 379; Grantland Rice, 46, 76, 143, 376; Harold Kaese, 310; Harry T. Brundidge, 70; Heywood Broun, 91, 289, 376; H. G. Salsinger, 54–55, 235; Howard Bryant, 289, 407, 409; Hugh Fullerton, 24, 205; James C. Isaminger, 27, 54, 76, 224; James Crusinberry, 24; Jerome Holtzman, 378, 457; Joe Bostic, 289–90; Joe Trimble, 253; John Drebinger, 149, 262, 326, 383, 413; John Kieran, 76, 376; Lester Rodney, 289; Nat Low, 289; Red Smith, 305, 373; Ring Lardner, 39, 47, 199, 376; Robert Boyle, 376, 378; Robert Creamer, 127, 129, 130, 229; Sam Crane, 163; Sam Jones, 37; Sam Lacy, 289; Shirley Povich, 204, 266, 267, 392; Stan Baumgartner, 278–79, 372; Stan Isaacs, 150; Tom Meany, 84, 401; Vincent X. Flaherty, 384, 426; Warren Brown, 272, 275; Wendell Smith, 289; W. O. McGeehan, 46,

376. *See also* Daniel, Dan; Gillespie, Ray; Lane, F. C.; Lieb, Fred; Richter, Francis; Spink, Taylor
spring training: in Arizona, 350–51, 459; Branch Rickey and, 63, 441; players paid during, 294, 303, 305; during postwar years, 295, 307–9; World War II and, 233, 239, 244–45, 256, 289
"Star-Spangled Banner." *See* National Anthem
Stengel, Casey: as manager, 326, 387, 388, 443, 444, 451, 460–61, 465; as player, 198, 203
Stephens, Vern, 242, 246, 251, 301
St. Louis Browns: attendance of, 32, 58, 222, 251–52, 318, 352; farm system of, 68; finances of, 53, 221–22, 242, 251–52, 419; integration and, 361; night baseball and, 223, 237, 264, 307; ownership of, 64, 95, 221–22, 342, 419–21, 460, 462; pennant races and, 63, 222–23, 242, 246, 250–51, 273–74, 419, 420, 432; player transactions involving, 22, 62, 106, 223–24, 283, 417, 424; radio and, 48, 215; relocation of, 221, 329, 352, 414, 418–21, 422, 426, 432, 442, 446; television and, 396, 420–21; World Series and, 301; World War II and, 249. *See also* Baltimore Orioles (1954–)
St. Louis Cardinals: attendance of, 48, 58, 75, 77, 160; bonus players and, 320, 324, 336, 337; farm system of, 69, 88, 101–2, 120, 145, 154, 157–58, 169, 173, 181–84; finances of, 66–68, 77; integration and, 362; night baseball and, 165, 189, 223, 237, 264; ownership of, 10, 64, 66–68, 95, 342; pennant races and, 60, 65, 72, 73, 75, 77, 83, 84–85, 88, 173, 187, 246, 251, 273, 311–12, 449; radio and, 48, 215; relocation of, 419, 420, 421, 436; television and, 347, 396, 401; World Series and, 34, 42, 43, 45, 46, 58, 72–73, 75–76, 85–87, 142–43, 150, 191, 242–43, 246, 251, 265, 312–13, 457; World War II and, 221, 246
Stoneham, Charles, 33, 56, 137, 188, 215–16, 237, 238, 339–41
Stoneham, Horace, 238, 259, 339–41, 405, 427, 428–30, 433, 435, 446
Stout, Glenn, 145, 284, 285, 339
Street, Gabby, 72, 75, 77, 79, 81, 83
Subcommittee on Study of Monopoly Power. *See* Celler, Emanuel
Sullivan, Neil, 12
Sunday baseball, 9, 18, 137–38, 147, 196–97, 288
Surdam, David George, 236

Taft, William Howard, 63
television: advent of baseball on, 345–47; All-Star Game and, 399; apprehension about, 349, 368, 369, 374, 385, 391, 397–98, 401–6, 412–13, 463; and broadcasting in color, 372; and "game of the week," 404–5; Major League games and, 396–97, 399–401, 421, 423–24; pay-per-view, 429; rights fees and, 349, 392, 421, 440; World Series and, 345, 349, 375, 398–99
television stations: KSD-TV, 399; WBKB, 346–47; WCBS, 397; WNBT, 346, 347, 397; WOR-TV, 399; WPIX, 397, 399; W2XBS, 346
Tener, John, 15, 18, 94
Terrell, Roy, 435
Terry, Bill: as manager, 212, 238, 427; as player, 42, 56, 75
Texas League: classification of, 181, 328; farm systems and, 69, 74, 78, 106, 335; integration and, 363, 364; night

Texas League (*cont*)
baseball and, 168; playoffs and, 158, 169; salary limits and, 112; World War II and, 243
Thomson, Bobby, 373, 409, 428
Three-I League: farm systems and, 183; Minor League draft and, 18, 99–100, 101; playoffs and, 80, 159; salary limits and, 112
Todt, Phil, 106–7
Toolson, George, 394–95
Toolson v. New York Yankees, 395–96
Topping, Dan, 302, 343, 432, 453, 458, 459
Trautman, George: as candidate to succeed Happy Chandler, 384; Columbus Red Birds and, 181–82; Detroit Tigers and, 324; as president of National Association, 330, 370, 393, 403, 421; School of Instruction and, 116
Treder, Steve, 320
Tripartite Pact. *See* National Agreement
Triple Crown, 59, 151, 241, 388
Trucks, Virgil, 177, 245, 268, 269, 277
Truman, Harry, 261, 293, 367, 384, 385, 386, 433
Tygiel, Jules, 356

umpires: Ban Johnson and, 7, 8, 133; Earl Rogers and, 178; Ernest Barnard and, 27; Ford Frick and, 382–83; Happy Chandler and, 352–53; integration and, 455; rule book and, 53, 332–33, 335, 382, 390; William Bramham and, 114; World Series and, 86–87, 215, 348; World War II and, 234, 243
Universal Military Training and Service Act, 326

Veeck, Bill, Jr.: Chicago Cubs and, 314–16, 462; death of, 462; early life of, 314; expansion and, 447, 459; Larry Doby and, 361; as owner of Chicago White Sox, 454, 459, 462; as owner of Cleveland Indians, 317–19, 335, 343–44, 350–51, 459; as owner of Milwaukee Brewers, 316–17; as owner of St. Louis Browns, 419–22, 423, 432; Philadelphia Phillies and, 317; World War II and, 316–17
Veeck, Bill, Sr., 24, 26, 47–48, 52, 96, 141, 148, 209
Voigt, David Quentin, 91

Wagner, Robert, 429, 430, 434, 437, 465
Wakefield, Dick, 319–20
Walker, James R., 45, 47, 215, 396–97, 398, 400–401, 412
Walker, Roberto Clemente. *See* Clemente Walker, Roberto
Washington Nationals. *See* Washington Senators (1901–60)
Washington Senators (1901–60): integration and, 362; night baseball and, 166, 238; ownership of, 1, 28, 340; pennant races and, 59, 138, 246, 251; radio and, 348; relocation of, 446–47, 448, 453; television and, 421; World Series and, 85. *See also* Minnesota Twins
Washington Senators (1961–), 453, 454
Webb, Del, 302, 343, 384, 422, 432, 452–53, 458, 459
Weeghman Park, 96, 110. *See also* Cubs Park; Wrigley Field (Chicago)
Weil, Sidney, 55, 82, 157–58, 185, 186
Weintraub, Robert, 312
Weiss, George, 146–48, 256, 365, 439, 441–42, 459, 465
Western Association (1901), 3, 4, 9
Western Association (1905–11, 1914–17, 1920–32, 1934–42, 1946–54): farm systems and, 69, 106; Great

Depression and, 112, 173, 174; night baseball and, 167
Western League (1894–99), 3, 6, 7, 9, 195, 196
Western League (1900–1937, 1947–58): classification of, 13–14, 16, 180; farm systems and, 119, 183, 186; Great Depression and, 180; integration and, 364; Minor League draft and, 99–100, 101; night baseball and, 166–68; playoffs and, 159; salary limits and, 170
West Side Grounds, 96
White, G. Edward, 91, 182
Whitney, Wheelock, Jr., 437–38, 452, 456
Williams, Joe, 34, 149, 385
Williams, Ted: Boston Red Sox and, 176, 230, 285, 300, 310, 312–13, 350, 388, 443, 450; early life of, 175; Hall of Fame and, 464; Korean War and, 327; Minneapolis Millers and, 176; San Diego Padres and, 175–76; World War II and, 240–41, 242, 310
Wilson, Jimmie, 188, 245
Wilson, Woodrow, 17
winter meetings: (1902), 12; (1913), 15; (1915), 95; (1918), 18; (1919), 19, 23; (1921), 100; (1922), 100; (1923), 101, 147; (1926), 141; (1928), 108; (1929), 48, 108; (1931), 109, 114, 148, 154; (1932), 48, 109, 113, 115, 118; (1933), 116, 118; (1934), 48, 324; (1935), 116–17, 181; (1936), 118, 119; (1937), 116, 118; (1939), 118, 184; (1940), 154, 185; (1941), 221, 232; (1942), 264; (1943), 330; (1944), 251, 259, 275; (1945), 307, 321, 328; (1946), 305, 322, 329, 330, 354; (1947), 322, 324, 413; (1948), 322, 402; (1949), 323, 366; (1950), 323, 326, 366–67, 402; (1951), 325, 385; (1952), 335, 403, 420; (1953), 336, 404; (1954), 336, 404; (1955), 389; (1957), 337, 351; (1958), 306, 337; (1959), 338, 441, 448; (1960) 453
Wolfe, Thomas, 178, 392
working agreements: Brooklyn Dodgers and, 426; Cincinnati Reds and, 186; Cleveland Indians and, 119; finances of, 112; growth of, 171; rules governing, 107, 109, 118, 154, 180, 184–85; St. Louis Cardinals and, 69, 182, 183; Western Carolina League and, 441, 442. *See also* farm systems
World Series: (1885), 96; (1903), 12; (1904), 15; (1905), 135; (1906), 97; (1907), 96; (1908), 96; (1910), 51; (1913), 210; (1915), 95, 130; (1916), 104, 130, 147; (1917), 97, 104; (1918), 104, 130–31, 150, 313; (1919), 20, 23, 24, 25, 97–98, 133, 141, 193, 205, 294; (1920), 21, 230, 318; (1921), 45, 102–3, 105, 135, 150; (1922), 45, 135, 136, 150; (1923), 46, 135, 136–37, 138; (1924), 46; (1925), 46; (1926), 46, 72, 73, 142–43, 150; (1927), 46, 47, 143, 145; (1928), 46, 72, 143, 145; (1929), 33–34, 40, 46, 85, 144, 148; (1930), 31, 34, 42, 43, 44, 45, 72, 73, 148, 379; (1931), 47, 57, 58, 75–77, 79, 102, 213, 402; (1932), 58, 148–50, 214; (1933), 83, 85, 136, 214, 427; (1934), 85–87, 189, 191, 205, 206–7, 213; (1935), 207, 214–15, 217, 349; (1936), 153, 214, 217, 427; (1937), 153, 314, 427; (1938), 153; (1939), 154, 214; (1940), 219, 226, 227, 348; (1941), 214, 226, 230–31, 354; (1942), 150, 240, 241–43, 256, 265, 303, 348; (1943), 246, 250; (1944), 251–52, 259, 301, 303; (1945), 261, 265, 272, 275, 277, 330, 339; (1946), 305, 311, 312–13, 456; (1947), 345–46, 348–49, 398, 458, 459; (1948), 318, 319, 350, 361, 375,

World Series (*cont*)
392, 398–99, 417; (1951), 372–73, 375, 388, 400; (1952), 335, 427; (1953), 463; (1954), 387, 428; (1955), 361; (1956), 199, 386, 446; (1957), 431; (1958), 431; (1959), 433, 447, 462; (1960), 450–51, 452, 455, 459–60, 465; (1961), 339; (1964), 456, 463; (1967), 313; All-Star Game and, 208, 212; Garry Herrmann and, 15; origins of, 12; radio and, 45–48, 102, 213–15, 217, 275, 304, 345–49, 375, 379, 392, 462–63; television and, 345–49, 375, 398–401; umpires and, 353. *See also* barnstorming; Black Sox scandal
World Series shares, 23, 77, 83, 104, 105, 133, 149, 205, 252, 259, 265, 305, 349, 418
World War I. *See* Great War
World War II: and baseball on D-Day, 257–58; continuation of baseball during, 224, 231–34, 243–44, 248–49, 259–60, 261; contributions of baseball to war effort during, 234–35, 244–45, 246–47, 259, 265–68; players dying in, 269–70; players in military during, 239–41, 260–61, 268–70, 272–73; players returning from, 274–75, 276–81; start of, 219, 221, 231
Wrigley, Phil: AAGBBL and, 270–72; antitrust regulation and, 374; Bill Veeck and, 314, expansion and, 416, 418, 447; as owner of Chicago Cubs, 261, 303, 339, 384; St. Louis Browns and, 221, 329; television and, 401; World War II and, 270; Wrigley Field and, 314–15
Wrigley, William, Jr., 47, 96, 108, 110, 148, 172
Wrigley Field (Chicago): construction of, 96; night baseball and, 270; renovation of, 314–16; World War II and, 270. *See also* Cubs Park; Weeghman Park

Yankee Stadium: construction of, 137, 145, 160; Continental League and, 441–42; East-West All-Star Game and, 366; sale of, 432; television and, 345; World War II and, 232, 257, 265
Yawkey, Thomas A.: death of, 461; family and early life of, 282, 285–86; integration and, 288, 291; as owner of Boston Red Sox, 176, 282–85, 309–10, 341, 353, 381, 417, 456, 461; paternalism of, 313, 339; philanthropy of, 287–88; World War II and, 226
Yawkey, William C., 195
Yawkey, William H., 125, 195, 282, 286, 287